ADVISING THE SMALL BUSINESS

FORMS AND ADVICE FOR THE LEGAL PRACTITIONER

SECOND EDITION

JEAN L. BATMAN

AMERICAN BAR ASSOCIATION
**General Practice,
Solo & Small Firm
Division**

Cover design by ABA Publishing.

Printed in the United States of America.

15 14 13   5 4 3 2

Library of Congress Cataloging-in-Publication Data

Batman, Jean L.
  Advising the small business: forms and advice for the small business advisor / Jean Batman. — 2nd ed.
    p. cm.
  Includes bibliographical references and index.
  ISBN 978-1-61438-077-1
  1. Small business—Law and legislation—United States. I. Title.
KF1659.B38 2011
346.73'0652—dc23

2011029416

Discounts are available for books ordered in bulk. Special consideration is given to state bars, CLE programs, and other bar-related organizations. Inquire at Book Publishing, ABA Publishing, American Bar Association, 321 North Clark Street, Chicago, Illinois 60654-7598.

www.ShopABA.org

CONTENTS

Chapter 4 Contracts for Small Businesses 65

Chapter 5 Legal Structures for Small Businesses 101

Chapter 6 Organizing or Cleaning Up a Corporation 117

Chapter 7 Organizing or Cleaning Up an LLC   205

Chapter 14 Providing Equity Incentives to Employees   729

Chapter 15 Liquidity Events   761

ACKNOWLEDGMENTS

Many thanks to the American Bar Association for publishing this second edition of *Advising the Small Business* and to those who opened doors for me at the American Bar Association and made it possible for me to become active as a meeting attendee, a speaker, and a leader. Special thanks to Gerald Niesar and Corinne Cooper, mentors and role models in the ABA and in my practice; Robert Keatinge, with whom I have served (often at his invitation) as program co-panelist and member of the Business Law Section's Publications Board; and Harry Henning and Richard Leisner, former Chairs of the Business Law Section's Middle Market and Small Business Committee, who welcomed me into the committee and provided unwavering support during my term as Chair of the Middle Market and Small Business Committee. Thank you to my partner in life and law, Alexander V. Choulos, and to our beautiful children, James, William, and Lauren, whose love, strength, good humor, and encouragement keep me going. Finally, thanks to my parents, Ruth and Jim Batman, who raised two young women to believe they could be whatever they wanted to be most in this world and ended up with a doctor and a lawyer.

ABOUT THE AUTHOR

Jean L. Batman founded Legal Venture Counsel, Inc. in 2004 to provide outside general counsel services to investors, entrepreneurs, and small businesses. Prior to forming Legal Venture Counsel, Ms. Batman was a Partner in the San Francisco offices of Duane Morris LLP, one of the country's 100 largest law firms. As outside general counsel to a variety of companies and individuals, Ms. Batman provides business and financial legal services to privately held entities operating in a broad range of industries including real estate development, financial and professional services, manufacturing, software, retail, biotechnology/specialty pharmaceutical, and high technology. She has written and spoken on a number of topics of interest to the business community, such as choice of entity, venture financing, and finding practical solutions to common legal problems.

Ms. Batman Chaired the ABA Business Law Section's Middle Market and Small Business Committee from 2001 to 2005, served as a Board Member of the ABA Business Law Section's Publications Board from 2001 to 2005, Co-Founded and Co-Chaired the ABA's Private Placement Broker-Dealer Task Force in 1999, and is designated closing counsel for the Small Business Administration's 504 loan program.

Prior to becoming an attorney, Ms. Batman had an active career in the Securities Industry, culminating with her position in 1989 as President of Smith-Thomas Investment Services, Inc. (a registered Broker-Dealer). During her tenure in the Securities Industry, Ms. Batman held a total of seven licenses from the National Association of Securities Dealers (now FINRA) ranging from General Sales to Finance and Operations Principal (Series 7, 6, 63, 39, 22, 24, and 27).

Ms. Batman earned an American Jurisprudence Award for excellent achievement in the study of Commercial Transactions in 1989 and served as a Judicial Extern in the California Court of Appeal for the late Hon. Justice J. Perley, 1st District in San Francisco in 1990.

Ms. Batman is a 1990 graduate of the University of California's Hastings College of Law (J.D.), and a 1985 graduate of The Paul Merage School of Business at UC Irvine (M.B.A.). She also completed her undergraduate studies at the UC Irvine (B.A.).

PREFACE

Advising the Small Business is a guide for general practitioners, small firm attorneys, and young lawyers engaged in providing legal counsel to small, privately held businesses. This second edition includes many updates and additional forms, in addition to all of the general guidance, forms, checklists, and resources from the original edition on issues that small businesses commonly face. This guidance can be invaluable to attorneys who do not have access to enough other lawyers or deal flow, or who haven't had enough experience, to know what is "standard" in this area of practice. Although there are many guides available for entrepreneurs, this book speaks to the advisor, not the entrepreneur. *Advising the Small Business* is designed to help counsel provide more effective legal and strategic guidance to small business clients, produce relevant documents, and spot issues that require further research or a specialist. Finally, *Advising the Small Business* is unique in its discussion of both how to approach an issue from scratch (e.g., drafting a contract or forming a corporation) and how to clean up an existing situation (e.g., amending agreements and corporate clean-up). A companion book, *Letters for Small Business Lawyers,* by the same author, is also now available through the ABA to provide examples of the types of letters used by lawyers providing legal counsel to small, privately held businesses.

CHAPTER 1

Representing Small Businesses

1.1 What Should You Know About Representing Small Businesses?

Small businesses comprise the majority of this country's economy, employing the majority of the total workforce in the United States. In fact, according to the Office of Advocacy of the U.S. Small Business Administration, small businesses account for half of this country's nonfarm real gross domestic product, and small firms lead when the economy is gaining jobs.[1] However, the failure rate among new businesses is estimated to be around 80 percent, which can translate into a high turnover rate among small business clients. Moreover, small business clients often have a difficult time meeting their financial obligations, including paying their legal counsel.

Your most successful small business clients probably won't stay small and may "outgrow" you if you are a sole practitioner or a member of a small firm. Moreover, the most common liquidity event or exit strategy for emerging companies is a merger or acquisition in which the emerging company merges out of existence, or is acquired, and counsel for the surviving or acquiring company takes over as your former client's legal counsel.

By now you may be wondering why anyone would choose to specialize in the representation of small businesses; but more likely, you're already working with one or more small businesses and you understand both the pains and the pleasures of a small business practice firsthand. One of the most important reasons many of us enjoy small business practice is that we get to work with entrepreneurs who have the spark of invention and inspiration in their spirits and the eternal optimism to pursue their dreams. We enjoy seeing cutting-edge technologies, learning about new products and new markets, and participating in the same at a strategic level.

---

1. See the 2010 report of the Office of Advocacy of the U.S. Small Business Administration on *The Small Business Economy, at* http://www.sba.gov/sites/default/files/sb_econ2010.pdf (last visited Mar. 27, 2011).

When engaging a new small business client, it is important to get a retainer. If you consistently demand retainers at the beginning of an engagement, you'll set the right tone for the relationship and discover that some prospective clients have an aversion to writing checks (better to learn this before you've done any work, as they likely won't be any better at writing checks down the line). Set the retainer amount higher or lower depending on the estimated cost of the initial services to be performed, what you feel comfortable with for security on payment in full, and what the market will bear. The reasons for getting a retainer are many, such as establishing yourself as a professional whose time is valuable, testing whether this is a client that will have trouble paying your invoices, and getting at least a portion of your work paid for if the client turns out to be unreliable or the project is terminated.

Giving prospective clients the option of paying retainers and ongoing legal bills by credit card can result in more new business and more timely payment of invoices. You shouldn't be expected to finance your client's organizational costs; let the banks do it.

As your clients grow, you should encourage them to consider you as their outside general counsel and to use you as their first stop when seeking any kind of legal assistance. Encourage clients to allow you to help them determine what legal services are required, and either do the work yourself or place it with appropriate counsel. You may also want to be in a position to supervise other counsel, reviewing their work product and invoices, to help your client manage its consumption of legal services and to help ensure quality and consistency.

Small business lawyers should be prepared to deal with the entire life cycle of the business, from inception to exit (or demise). This guide, while not exhaustive, will assist you in advising small businesses throughout their life cycles.

1.2 Who Is Your Client, and How Can You Avoid Conflicts of Interest?

Typically, when you are working for a small business, the company is the client. This should be clear from the very beginning and should be specifically spelled out in your written engagement letter. Your client may ask you to prepare documentation or provide counsel along the way that does not appear to relate strictly to the business of the company. In these instances it is wise to decline the request; or, if it is not against the company's interests, comply—but with a written disclaimer to the client and any other parties involved that the counsel is provided at the company's request by counsel for the company and that any individual parties should seek the advice of their own counsel. The American Bar Association, in conjunction with the Bureau of National Affairs, Inc., publishes an extensive treatise on professional conduct that is a vital resource for the determination of questions in this area.[2]

---

2. See THE BUREAU OF NATIONAL AFFAIRS, INC., ABA/BNA LAWYERS' MANUAL ON PROFESSIONAL CONDUCT now an online service at http://www.bna.com/products/lit/mopc.htm (last visited Mar. 27, 2011).

1.3   How Can You Provide Value to Your Clients?

1. Be Responsive.

One problem that many small businesses encounter when using larger law firms is slow response times (perhaps because small businesses are not a significant source of fees). In the rapidly changing environment in which so many small businesses operate, responsive legal counsel can be vital to the company's success.

2. Spot the Issues.

One of the pleasures and challenges of working for a small business is the opportunity to deal with a wide range of legal issues. Many of these issues will be ones you can handle yourself; but some will require the expertise of another lawyer specializing in a specific area such as federal taxation, patent law, international trade, litigation, and so forth. It is important to be able to identify those issues requiring another lawyer's expertise and help make sure they are handled appropriately. Helping clients identify counsel with the desired expertise, and helping them efficiently use such counsel, can be of great value to them.

3. Stay Current.

Staying current on the law in your area of practice is expected; but staying current on trends in financing terms, licensing arrangements, commercial real estate leasing rates, and other matters that your clients will deal with at one time or another will help make you an invaluable advisor at strategic times in the client's development. Some of this information will come from your experience with other clients, but it is also wise to cultivate this knowledge from other sources such as business and financial periodicals and participation in conferences, seminars, and networking groups.

4. Help Clients Avoid Common Mistakes.

When you improve your client's chances of success, you improve your own chances of having a long-standing, mutually beneficial relationship with your clients by making them financially stronger and by gaining their loyalty and trust. One way to do this is to help clients avoid common mistakes that can cost them dearly in lost time, money, or key personnel. As lawyers, we are privy to the trials and tribulations of our own clients and of many others, through the shared experiences of our colleagues. We also have access to countless case summaries read in law school, case law reporters, and annotated codes. Being able to identify situations in which a client may be headed for trouble, helping them avoid it by relaying the experience of another company (that need not be named if the attorney-client privilege is an issue), and suggesting a way to avert the problem are invaluable services. For example, when reviewing "boilerplate" with clients, relaying a war story or two is often the best way to get them to focus on a provision and choose language that works best for their circumstances.

Another way to help clients avoid common mistakes is to give them an idea of what they should expect in the way of deal terms and what should be negotiated when they embark on a new venture or relationship.

As discussed in more detail in Chapter 4, one common mistake you can help your clients avoid is the tendency of many clients to ignore the general provisions in an agreement as "boilerplate," which they somehow equate with "unimportant" or so standard as not to warrant their time and consideration. Help your clients develop a set of standard agreements for their business with a set of boilerplate provisions that actually reflect their preferences and best suit their circumstances.

5. Encourage Clients to Plan.

Many companies fail to adequately understand their current problems and capabilities before jumping into aggressive organizational changes, particularly in a difficult economy. In their zeal to move quickly, some clients forget—or learn the hard way—that diagnosis and understanding should precede change if it is to be deliberate and effective.

Encourage your clients to gain an understanding of how their organization operates, what works and doesn't work, what their organization's strengths and weaknesses are, how the pieces fit together, and how to bring these elements into alignment with their strategy. Clients should periodically evaluate products, services, and core competencies; establish measures for success and set short-term and long-term goals; and revisit their business plan regularly. This process can be built into regular meetings of boards of directors or managers, where counsel often plays a role in determining the agenda and facilitating the discussions; but clients should also include input from those in marketing, sales, product development, customer service, and so on. Companies that stay on top of their game are more likely to succeed and remain good clients for the long run.

6. Provide Templates and Samples.

Many small business owners are intent on preparing legal documents themselves to save money. And, with the availability of forms and examples on the Internet, more and more of them believe they are equipped to do so. However, many of these business owners don't understand or appreciate the significance of the language in these documents. Because they don't identify what is missing, they often end up with inapplicable, inappropriate, or disadvantageous language in their documents, while significant terms remain missing. So, it may be advisable to approach such clients with an offer to provide appropriate templates for the types of agreements and documentation they will use repeatedly in their business, examples are a Nondisclosure Agreement or form offer letter and a Confidentiality and Invention Assignment Agreement for new employees. Chapter 4, Contracts for Small Businesses, discusses these documents in more detail.

1.4 How Can You Attract and Retain Small Business Clients?

Important factors to a small business seeking legal counsel are experience, personal service and responsiveness, cost, and ability to provide networking experience, among others. Providing value to clients once you have them, as discussed above, will help you retain them. Finding new clients in the first place can be a greater challenge.

1. Let People Know What You Do.

Among your greatest sources of business referrals are your friends and colleagues. But before they can recognize a business opportunity they could refer to you, they need to have at least a general understanding of the type of work you do. There are many ways to go about doing this, some more obnoxious than others, but it is important to do something. For example, when you send e-mails to colleagues seeking a resource or referral for a client, take the opportunity to briefly describe the work you do for the client:

> Dear partners and associates,
>
> I am providing outside general counsel for a small biotech company in the San Francisco Bay Area that is in need of an international tax lawyer to assist with the structuring of an asset sale to a company in Switzerland. Please let me know if you have any recommendations.

The foregoing example does a lot more to help its recipients understand what you do than does the type of correspondence we usually see: "Hey—Does anybody know a good international tax lawyer?"

Firm announcements, newsletters, and other publications can also help establish among your friends and colleagues an understanding of what you do. But, as in the e-mail example above, the opportunity can be missed if certain details or proper attribution are missing (i.e., in client alerts and other educational materials). The use of sites such as YouTube (www.youtube.com), LinkedIn (www.LinkedIn.com), and Twitter (www.twitter.com) should be incorporated into every modern business plan, whether it's yours or your client's.

2. Go Where Entrepreneurs Go.

As lawyers, we often spend our client development time going to events with other lawyers. It's important to separate your professional development time from client development time and recognize that, although there are crossovers in each category, you have to approach each of them differently. For example, you are more likely to generate immediate business for your small business practice with speaking engagements in which your audience is comprised of entrepreneurs and business owners than with those in which your audience is comprised of other lawyers (i.e., your competitors). Speaking engagements for chambers of commerce, industry associations, business networking events, and other business-oriented organizations are a good choice for client development. Presentations and panel discussions at bar association meetings are great for establishing expertise (i.e., professional development), but are typically only an indirect route to new business (e.g., through referrals from other attorneys).

3. Remind People You're Out There.

When the opportunity comes up for someone to refer your business, or when someone needs your services, you want to be at the forefront of their mind. Besides letting people know what you do, as discussed above, correspondence, announcements, newsletters, and other publications remind people that you're there. There is a saying that there is no such thing as bad publicity, which means that the important thing is to be known. Of course, how you're known is also important, so care should be taken to ensure that the messages people receive about you convey the desired information and image. The ABA publishes an excellent guide in this regard.[3] Being more social, both in person and on Internet sites like Facebook (www.facebook.com), can be great for business; just remember to present yourself the way you want to be seen.

4. Get the Deal Done.

Businesspeople often view lawyers as naysayers and deal-killers. This is because lawyers are often more focused on why their clients can't or shouldn't do something than on helping them figure out how to achieve their objectives in an appropriate and advantageous manner.

   If you are successful in gaining your clients' trust, and they perceive that you are providing value (by saving them money, helping them avoid crucial mistakes, and helping close them the deal), they are likely to consider you a vital part of their team.

5.   Alternative Fee Arrangements; Invest in Clients.

Start-ups are often stuck in a chicken and egg dilemma in that they need to put certain legal structures in place in order to raise funds to build a company, but they don't have sufficient resources available for legal services. Taking on a

---

3. CORINNE COOPER, HOW TO BUILD A LAW FIRM BRAND (ABA 2005).

client under these circumstances should be approached from the perspective of an investor. Specifically, if you undertake legal work without a sufficient retainer, knowing the client needs to raise funds, you may end up investing a lot of time and perhaps even advancing costs that you will never recover if your client is unsuccessful. But when a prospective client is honest about their financial circumstances (although, unfortunately, they sometimes are not), and the entrepreneur and business idea are especially promising, a small business lawyer can win new business and client loyalty with flexible and alternative fee arrangements, or even investing in clients.

Much has been written lately about flat fee arrangements, and there are a lot of firms pursuing new business by offering low flat rates on services, such as incorporation (which many online services now offer, all but eliminating a former staple of the business lawyer's practice) and entity conversions, just to get the client in the door. Other approaches include agreements that give companies more predictability for legal expenses, such as monthly retainer arrangements with a floor and a ceiling, where the attorney is assured a minimum monthly retainer, and hours billed in excess of the ceiling carry over into the next month.

Even more aggressive approaches are complete fee deferrals, where payment is dependent upon the client raising funds, and/or taking equity in a client. When investing in a client, counsel should be mindful of applicable rules of professional conduct for taking an interest adverse to a client, in addition to treating the decision as whether or not the investment is worth the risk, including whether the attorney can afford to lose the time and money. Rules of Conduct applicable to an attorney taking an interest adverse to a client, such as taking equity in a client, typically require that (1) the transaction is fair and reasonable and the terms are fully disclosed to the client in writing; (2) the client is advised in writing to seek independent counsel in connection with the proposed transaction; and (3) the client consents in writing. See, for example, California Rules of Professional Conduct Rule 3-300.

1.5 Sample Documents and Checklists.

This section includes the following forms:

- Terms and Conditions for Fee Agreements (Form 1 A)
- Credit Card Acceptance Language (Form 1 B)
- Letter to Client Considering Other Counsel (Form 1 C)
- Sample Fee Deferral and Investment Provision for Fee Agreement (Form 1 D)

Form 1 A: Terms and Conditions for Fee Agreements

Note: For a friendly presentation of your fee agreement, you may wish to use a cover letter with terms and conditions in an attachment. This can be referred to as a "Fee Agreement," "Contract for Legal Services," or "Engagement Letter" (my favorite). The cover letter can be fairly brief, with space at the bottom for the client to acknowledge and agree to the terms of the engagement, as described in the attachment.

Terms and Conditions

Purpose of the Engagement. This will confirm that _____ (the "Company") has asked that the firm assist it in connection with _____ _____ [initial purpose of the engagement, e.g. the formation of a new entity (the "Company") for the conduct of your business]. We will be happy to assist the Company with these matters and such other matters as we may agree. The firm will perform the services described herein with reasonable professional skill and reasonable dispatch, subject in all material respects to the Company's direction.

Company as Client. [Once formed,] [T]he Company is the client. To the extent any officers, directors, shareholders, [or managers or members,] or employees, of the Company desire legal advice regarding their individual interests with respect to any transactions of the Company, they understand they must seek independent counsel.

Fees. Our fees will be determined by the number of hours worked, the reasonable value of legal services provided, and the billing rate of the individual performing services. At present, our hourly rates for attorneys range from $_____ to $_____. Legal assistant rates are $_____ per hour. We reserve the right to modify our hourly rates from time to time. Our minimum incremental billing is 1/10 of an hour (6 minutes). Our fees are not contingent upon the completion or success of the proposed matter.

Costs. Costs in excess of _____ Dollars ($_____) may be passed on to the Company for direct payment or may be required to be advanced by the Company in the firm's discretion.

Invoices and Payment. You will receive periodic invoices for services rendered and costs incurred on your behalf. Invoices are generally sent in the beginning of the month following the month in which services are rendered and costs are incurred and are payable upon receipt. A late charge of one percent (1%) per month on all balances outstanding for more than thirty (30) days will be added to the balance due. Timely payment in full is a condition of our continuing legal representation. This policy is conscientiously followed.

Retainer. A retainer in the amount of _____ Dollars ($_____), payable to the firm, is requested. The retainer will be deposited in our client trust account, and we will draw against those funds to satisfy our invoices in this matter. Once the retainer has been exhausted, payments will be required as set forth below.

Estimates and Outcomes. You understand that any estimate of fees and costs associated with our engagement is only an estimate, not a fixed fee or an agreed limit. The actual fees and costs incurred will depend on a variety of factors, some of which are beyond our control. At the same time, we understand that you may wish to establish a budget for your legal expenses and will work with you to establish such budgets on request. We will also work with you to help make the most efficient use of our time as practicable. You understand that, although we will perform our professional services to the best of our ability, we cannot guarantee and we have not guaranteed any outcome.

Board Membership. In the event a member of the firm joins the Company's Board of Directors, it is understood that such member's participation on the board is as an individual, not on behalf of the firm, and shall not constitute legal services.

Conflicts. The Company agrees that we may continue to represent or may undertake in the future to represent existing or new clients in any matter that is not substantially related to our work for the Company even if the interests of such clients in those other matters are directly adverse to the Company. We agree, however, that the Company's prospective consent to conflicting representation shall not apply in any instance where, as a result of our representation of the Company, we have obtained proprietary or other confidential information of a non-public nature, that, if known to such other client, could be used in any such other matter by such client to your material disadvantage.

Confidentiality. The terms of this agreement shall be kept confidential.

Identification of Client. The Company agrees that the firm may identify the Company as a client of the firm for marketing or other purposes.

Termination. The Company may terminate this Agreement at any time for any reason. Similarly, we reserve the right to terminate our representation of the Company for any reason upon reasonable notice. Following termination, we will submit a final invoice for services rendered and costs incurred, which will be due and payable upon receipt.

Prior Representation of ****. Please be advised that this firm [or one or more members of this firm through previous employment] have provided legal services to Mr. **** , a _____ [e.g. shareholder] of the Company in connection with _____ [e.g. various business and personal matters unrelated to the business of the Company]. While we do not anticipate that such prior representation will influence our judgment in providing legal counsel to the Company, we believe it is important to advise each significant shareholder of the Company of this prior relationship. Therefore, we request that a copy of this letter be given to each shareholder of the Company who holds more than five percent (5%) of its equity securities. The firm anticipates it will continue to represent Mr. ***** in various business and personal matters unrelated to the business of the Company.

Client Files and Attorney Work Product. Upon our retention as counsel, a client file will be established regarding matters related to our representation of the Company. This file may become the repository for important legal documents as well as documents prepared by attorneys reflecting the attorneys' thoughts, conclusions and impressions. The law recognizes a privilege with respect to attorney notes, known as the attorney work-product privilege. Should the Company request the removal of the files from our offices, we reserve the right to retain all attorney work-product documents generated by our professional staff. Absent written instructions regarding disposition of client files, we reserve the right to store or destroy such files upon expiration of six (6) months following the conclusion of the representation.

Entire Agreement. The terms set forth in this letter constitute our entire agreement. Any modification of the agreement must be made in writing. This agreement is binding on the Company, the firm, and the respective legal representatives and successors of each.

Alternative Dispute Resolution Provisions. [Note: alternative dispute resolutions may be added, if desired and the choices are the same as those you may provide in client contracts, except to the extent state or local laws may impose different rules to disputes between attorney and client, such as in California where the client has the right to have fee disputes determined by arbitration under California Business and Professions Code sections 6200-6206.]

Form 1 B: Credit Card Acceptance Language

For an Engagement Letter

"If you accept the terms set forth in this letter, please sign and return it to me with a check for $_____ for your retainer. Alternatively, you can return the signed engagement and retainer via fax using a credit card for payment."

For an Invoice Cover Letter

"If you would like to make your payment by credit card, please complete the information below and fax a copy to (###) ###-####."

For Engagement Letter Terms and Conditions and/or Invoice Cover Letter

TO MAKE YOUR PAYMENT BY CREDIT CARD, PLEASE COMPLETE THE FOLLOWING INFORMATION AND FAX TO (###) ###-####:

Type of Card (circle one): VISA / MasterCard / American Express / Discover

Name on Card: _____

Card Number: _____

CID: _____ [Last 3 digits on back of card, or 4 digits above card number for Am Ex]

Expiration Date (MMYY): _____

Amount of Payment: $_____

Billing Address and Zip Code: _____

Form 1 C: Letter to Client Considering Other Counsel

Sometimes a small business lawyer loses a client to success, such as when they are acquired by a large company with an in-house legal department, and sometimes clients attract investors who only trust counsel they already know and condition investment on a change of counsel. The following is some suggested language that may influence your client's decision, or at least help ensure they give the move careful consideration and feel welcome to come back to you in the future. For more sample letters, see *Letters for Small Business Lawyers,* ABA 2011, by this author.

[Attorney Letterhead]

Dear _____,

Thank you for your call this morning. As I said on the phone, I'd really like to keep your business. I understand your desire to give your prospective investors what they want, but I think it makes sense for them to at least consider letting you continue using us as the company's counsel. Specifically:

1. If there is any corporate clean-up to be done in connection with the transaction, it will be more efficient if we do it, as we are already familiar with the corporate history, and the company's documents and templates are already on our system.

2. Your prospective investors may take comfort in the fact that [give highlights of counsel's qualifications, e.g., [a]s former partners at an Am Law 100 Firm, we have big firm training and experience, but since forming a smaller firm, we are able to keep our hourly rates much lower].

3. You should also assure them that [give highlights of counsel's experience, e.g., [w]e are very experienced in angel and venture capital financing transactions, and have many Delaware corporation clients with VC backing].

4. Please share the enclosed list of our recent articles, publications, and presentations on topics relevant to our representation of the company.

5. We would be willing to do the proposed transaction on a fixed fee basis or with a cap on fees. Assuming your investors have done a few similar deals, they should have an idea of what they expect the company to spend, and I'm sure we could come up with an arrangement they would feel good about.

6. Last but not least, we have worked together off and on for more than _____ years and we have a level of trust and understanding that comes with time. I understand that is probably why your prospective investors want you to use their counsel (i.e., counsel with whom they have established a level of trust and understanding), but perhaps they should use counsel they trust as their own counsel and let the company use counsel it trusts as its counsel.

If there are other considerations of which I may not be aware, please let me know what they are so I can address them, if possible. As I said, I would really like to keep your business. In any case, I wish you and the company every success. If the company does engage new counsel, I will help make the transition a smooth one, and would welcome you and/or the company back anytime should there be occasion for us to work together again in the future.

Thank you for your consideration.

Best,

[Counsel]

Form 1 D: Sample Fee Deferral and Investment Provision for Fee Agreement

Appendix A

Deferral Fee

This Appendix supplements the foregoing Terms and Conditions for the engagement of the Firm by ****, Inc., a _____ [state] corporation to be formed (the "Company") by setting forth the terms and conditions for the Firm's waiver of its usual retainer requirement and deferral of up to $_____ in legal fees until the Company has received seed financing, in exchange for equity participation in the Company in addition to payment of accrued legal fees upon funding of the Company.

The Firm hereby agrees to waive its normal requirement of a retainer and to defer payment on up to _____ Dollars ($_____) of legal fees in exchange for a convertible note in an amount equal to the maximum fee deferral (the "**Deferral Fee**"). The convertible note for the Deferral Fee shall be convertible into equity on the same terms as the convertible notes in the Company's Seed Round of Financing, except that the Firm's conversion price shall be set at a twenty-five percent (25%) discount to the Seed Round investors' conversion price. No late fees shall be charged on the deferred legal fees during the term of the deferral.

For purposes of this agreement, the Company's "**Seed Round of Financing**" shall mean the first funds raised by the Company following the issuance of stock to the Company's founders. It is currently anticipated that stock will be issued to founders upon filing of the Company's Articles of Incorporation and that the Seed Round of Financing will consist of _____ Dollars ($_____) in the form of convertible notes issued by the Company. Variations between the actual terms and the anticipated terms of the Seed Round of Financing shall not void this agreement.

Upon closing the Seed Round of Financing, the Company shall promptly issue securities to the Firm in satisfaction of the Deferral Fee and remit payment for all fees for legal services rendered by the Firm to the date of closing. Thereafter, fees shall be invoiced and paid in accordance with the Firm's general Terms and Conditions set forth above.

CHAPTER 2

Protecting Intellectual Property

2.1 Should Your Client Be Using a Nondisclosure Agreement?

When a client is embarking on a new venture, a good nondisclosure agreement, or NDA, can be indispensable. It will help the client protect the idea, business plan, marketing plan, and other proprietary information it may need to disclose during the course of identifying and engaging suppliers, distributors, employees, and other key relationships for a successful launch.

A good NDA will prohibit both disclosure and use of the proprietary information and will provide for equitable relief in the form of an injunction, preferably without the necessity of a bond, in the event of a breach. Nondisclosure agreements may be called NDAs, Nondisclosure Agreements, Nondisclosure and Non-Circumvention Agreements, Confidentiality Agreements, Proprietary Information Agreements, and so forth, and they may be either one-way or mutual.

2.2 Does Your Client Have an Idea That May Be Patentable?

Actually, an "idea" is not patentable. To be patentable, an invention must be useful, new, and nonobvious to a person having ordinary skill in the area of technology related to the invention; and a complete description of the working invention must be provided.[1]

A patent is the grant of a property right to the inventor of a patentable invention, issued by the U.S. Patent and Trademark Office (USPTO) in the United States, or comparable authority in another country or region. The term of a new U.S. patent is twenty years from the date an application for the patent is filed with the USPTO; or in certain cases, from the date an earlier related application

---

1. See the U.S. Patent and Trademark Office guide on How to Get a Patent online at http://www.uspto.gov/web/patents/howtopat.htm.

was filed, subject to the payment of maintenance fees. U.S. patents are effective only within the United States, U.S. territories, and U.S. possessions. Under certain circumstances, patent term extensions or adjustments may be available.

A patent confers the right to the patent holder to exclude others from making, using, offering for sale, or selling any product that embodies the patented invention in the United States or importing such products into the United States. The USPTO does not assist patent holders with the enforcement of patent rights.

As described by the USPTO, there are three types of patents:[2]

1. Utility patents may be granted to anyone who invents or discovers any new and useful process, machine, article of manufacture, or composition of matter, or any new and useful improvement thereof;
2. Design patents may be granted to anyone who invents a new, original, and ornamental design for an article of manufacture; and
3. Plant patents may be granted to anyone who invents or discovers and asexually reproduces any distinct and new variety of plant.

Inventors may prepare and file their own patent applications in the USPTO and represent themselves in the proceedings. However, unless a client is already experienced in patent prosecution, it would be well advised to seek an experienced patent lawyer or agent, since even if the client were able to obtain a patent without adequate representation, the patent obtained may not adequately protect its invention. Only lawyers and agents registered to practice before the USPTO are permitted to represent inventors before the USPTO.[3]

If your client potentially has a patentable invention, it should consult a qualified patent lawyer or agent while the invention is still "new," or it will lose the right to protect the invention. Under U.S. patent law, an invention cannot be patented if, among other things, the invention was in public use or for sale in the United States for more than one year before the patent application was filed. For this reason, and because resources are often quite limited in a small business, it may be a good idea for an inventor to file a provisional patent application before testing the market for an invention that may be patentable.

2.3 What Is a Provisional Patent?

Provisional patent applications are an alternative to full-blown patent applications and were designed to provide a lower-cost first patent filing alternative to inventors in the United States for all patent types except for design inventions. Provisional patent applications are simplified by the absence of certain require-

---

2. *Id.*

3. See the General Information Concerning Patents guide at http://www.uspto.gov/web/offices/pac/doc/general/index.html (last visited Mar. 27, 2011).

ments, such as claims and oath or declaration. They also allow the inventor to establish an early filing date, after which the "Patent Pending" term may be applied in connection with the invention. However, provisional applications are not examined on their merits and must be replaced by a non-provisional patent application within 12 months of filing because the provisional application is valid for only 12 months from its filing date.[4] See the discussion in Section 2.2 for information regarding non-provisional patent applications.

2.4 In What Other Ways Can a Small Business Protect Its IP?

1. Identify Trade Secrets and Take Steps to Protect Them.

Trade secrets are protected under common law and, in most states, by the Uniform Trade Secrets Act, which was drafted by the National Conference of Commissioners on Uniform State Laws in 1970 and amended in 1985. Misappropriation of trade secrets is a form of unfair competition. The Uniform Trade Secrets Act defines a trade secret as:

> [I]nformation, including a formula, pattern, compilation, program, device, method, technique, or process, that:
>
> (1) Derives independent economic value, actual or potential, from not being generally known to the public or to other persons who can obtain economic value from its disclosure or use; and
>
> (2) Is the subject of efforts that are reasonable under the circumstances to maintain its secrecy.[5]

Therefore, it is important for a company to identify information that is valuable as a trade secret and make at least reasonable efforts to protect the secrecy of such information. Companies should preserve a record of their efforts to protect trade secret information for use in case they ever have to bring an action for misappropriation of trade secrets. One of the best ways a company can make a record of its efforts to maintain the secrecy of trade secret information is through the use of written agreements with employees and independent contractors who will have access to or help create such information during their employment with the company. It is also important to limit access to such information to those who need it to perform their duties, and to keep paper and electronic copies of such information reasonably secure.

---

4. See the USPTO guide *Provisional Application for Patent*, available online at http://www.uspto.gov/web/offices/pac/ProvApp.pdf (last visited Mar. 27, 2011).

5. See Cal. Civ. Code § 3426.1(d).

2. Make Use of Noncompetition Agreements.

Noncompetition agreements, or covenants not to compete, are often included in employment contracts and contracts for the sale of a business. In these agreements, one party agrees or covenants not to compete with the other party for a specific period of time and, typically, within a particular area. For example, it is common for salespeople to sign noncompetition agreements that prevent them from using the contacts they gain through their employment with one employer to benefit another employer. Please note that in some states, such as California, noncompetition agreements are generally viewed as being against public policy and have very limited enforceability; in other states, courts routinely uphold such agreements. However, even in the absence of a noncompetition agreement, whether for lack of agreement or unenforceability, a company still has the right to prevent the misappropriation of its trade secrets—which, in some instances, may justify an injunction preventing a former employee from working for a competitor.

3. Identify and Protect Creative Works.

Copyright law gives the creator of a literary work or work of expression the right to keep others from using their work without their permission. In general, copyright law protects all forms of expression fixed in a tangible medium, but not the underlying ideas (which may be protected through another form of intellectual property).

For works publicly distributed after March 1, 1989, copyright protection is automatically available to the creator of any work of expression that is fixed in a tangible format.[6] Putting a copyright notice on the work and registering it with the U.S. Copyright Office gives the copyright owner additional protection, but is not required. A typical copyright claim is stated as follows: "Copyright 2011. ****, Inc. All rights reserved." Or, simply, "© 2011 ****, Inc."

Copyright protection is available for "literary works" (among other things), such as books, poems, plays, newspapers, magazines, websites, software documentation, and so on, as well as "works of expression"—that is, graphic and physical representations of objects and ideas, such as paintings and photographs.

A copyright consists of the following rights initially held by the author or developer of an original work (which can be assigned or sold):

- The right to reproduce (copy) the work;
- The right to prepare derivative works;
- The right to distribute copies of the work;
- The right to perform the work; and
- The right to display the work.[7]

---

6. See the U.S. Copyright Office website at www.copyright.gov/circs/circ1.html.
7. *Id.*

For example, if your client has developed proprietary software, it could obtain a registered copyright for its computer software product. Copyright protection extends to all of the copyrightable expressions embodied in the computer program. It is best that your client register the copyright within three months of first publication (and before any infringement) so it will be entitled to statutory damages in the case of infringement.

Copyright protection is not available for ideas, program logic, algorithms, systems, methods, concepts, or layouts. Therefore, you may also want to advise your client to consider obtaining one or more patents to fully protect the intellectual property reflected in the program. Please note that if a patent application is not filed within one year of publication of the software, it will be statutorily barred.[8]

To complete an application for copyright registration of software, your client will need to provide the year of creation and the exact date of first publication of the program. The filing fee is nominal, so most of the cost is in preparing the application and materials to be submitted for registration. Copies of all or a portion of the program source code must be submitted with the application for registration. To determine how much of the program source code has to be submitted and the appropriate format for the same, your client will need to determine whether the program contains any trade secrets.

If the program does not contain trade secrets, a copy of the identifying portions of the program (i.e., the first 25 and last 25 pages of source code) is sent in human-readable form, together with the page or equivalent unit containing the copyright notice, if any. If a published user's manual or other printed documentation accompanies the computer program, a copy of the user's manual will be included along with the identifying portions of the program. In addition, if the program is embodied in a CD-ROM, ordinarily the entire CD-ROM package must be deposited, including a complete copy of any accompanying operating software and instructional manual.[9]

If the computer program does contain trade secrets, the requirements are similar but the registrant may block out the portions of the code that contain trade secrets. There are some limitations here, so if this pertains to your client's product, review the requirements in detail.

If your client is also seeking to protect screen displays (i.e., the visual component of the program), you will want to reference the screen displays in the application and submit identifying material for the screens.[10]

---

8. See the U.S. Patent and Trademark Office website guide to the Patent Process *at* http://www .uspto.gov/patents/process/index.jsp (last visited Mar. 2011).

9. See U.S. Copyright publication, Copyright Registration for Computer Programs *at* http:// www.copyright.gov/circs/circ61.pdf (last visited Mar, 27, 2011).

10. *Id.*

2.5 How Should Your Client Work with Designers and Developers?

When your clients are working with designers and developers, it is important to consider whether it makes more sense to hire an employee or an independent contractor. There are a number of factors to consider in making this decision:

1. Hiring employees usually costs employers more (in taxes, benefits, office space, equipment, training, etc.) than hiring independent contractors.
2. Working with independent contractors provides an employer more flexibility for increasing or decreasing the size of its staff.
3. Exposure to employment-related litigation is reduced when hiring an independent contractor instead of an employee.
4. Employers typically have more control over employees than over independent contractors.
5. Using a succession of different independent contractors can be disruptive, and the quality of their work may be inconsistent.
6. Copyright works created by an employee belong to the employer, but copyright works created by an independent contractor must be transferred by written agreement.

See Chapter 13 for a discussion of when an independent contractor is really an employee.

Whether a designer or developer is hired as an employee or as an independent contractor, it is important to have a written agreement that protects both the client's existing intellectual property as well as the intellectual property to be developed.

2.6 How Can Your Client Protect Its Trademarks and Domain Names?

Domain names and trademarks (or service marks) should be registered. A trademark is a distinctive word, phrase, logo, graphic symbol, or other device that is used to identify the source of a product or service and to distinguish a manufacturer's or merchant's products from anyone else's. Trademark law deals with the overlapping and conflicting uses of trademarks by different businesses, for example, if a business adopts a logo or product name that is the same or similar to one already in use.

The trademark application process is now available online as a completely electronic process through the Trademark Electronic Application System (TEAS) online filing system at http://www.uspto.gov/teas/isndex.html. TEAS is a great improvement over the old days, when everything had to be assembled in paper format and exchanged via snail mail. Although the new system is quite streamlined, registering a trademark in the United States is still a lengthy process. A recent application sent using TEAS, without any office actions or objections, took about 9 months to go from application submission date to trademark Certificate of Registration in hand.

From a clean-up perspective, it may become necessary to assign a trademark from its original owner to the entity that uses the mark on its products, for example, when an entrepreneur applies for and obtains registration of a mark before forming the entity that will ultimately pursue the business for which the mark was secured. There is an Electronic Trademark Assignment System on the USPTO website at http://etas.uspto.gov/, but you will need your own form of assignment to be uploaded in connection with the online filing. A sample form of assignment wherein all rights, title, and ownership of a trademark are assignment for nominal consideration appears at the end of this chapter.

Domain names are the the text names corresponding to the numeric IP address (or "website address") of a computer on the Internet. The domain name must be unique. Websites are accessed using domain names and are used to describe the name that follows the @ sign in an e-mail address. Compared to trademark registrations, domain name registrations are cheap, fast, and easy. However, finding an available domain name can be a challenge. There are a number of online services that can be used to search for and obtain a domain name. One of the original full-service sources for domain names and related services is Network Solutions at http://www.networksolutions.com. One with more competitive pricing is Go Daddy at http://www.godaddy.com/.

Companies should consider available domain names at the time they formulate new product names and other trademarks or service marks. New businesses often take into consideration the availability of a good domain name when choosing a name for the company. Because domain names can be acquired so easily, when your client finds a desirable domain name is available, it is probably wise to register the name right away. Domain names can be useful for a variety of purposes, including the registration of a trademark, as page screen prints from websites can be used as evidence of use of a mark when registering it with the USPTO.

2.7 What Can Your Client Do If a Desired Domain Name or Trademark Is Not Available?

Many domain names are purchased by parties that never intend to develop a website at the domain. So, if a desired domain name is taken but there is no website at the domain, chances are good the owner will sell it for the right price. However, if your client has already been using the name for some time, or has registered the name as a trademark, and the registrant holding the domain name has no intent to launch a business or any site using the domain, the Anticybersquatting Consumer Protection Act of 1999 may help make things right. This act is intended to protect the public from acts of Internet "cybersquatting," a term used to describe the bad faith, abusive registration of Internet domain names. This legislation establishes a cause of action for trademark infringement against anyone who registers a domain name that is (i) identical or confusingly similar to the owner's distinctive trademark or—in the case of a famous mark—identical, confusingly similar to, or dilutive of the owner's trademark; and (ii) registered or used by that person with a bad faith intent to profit from the owner's trademark. The act also can subject so-called cyber-squatters to criminal penalties.

Where a domain registrant claims a non-extortionate, legitimate use for the domain and for registering it, a complaining business still may be able to stop such use by establishing in court that it infringes a registered trademark. At the same time, domain name holders have been forced to go to the courts to prevent the domain registries from revoking or putting their domain names on adminis-trative hold at the request of another party that claims superior rights but has not necessarily proven infringement of a registered trademark.

If a mark similar to the mark your client wishes to register is already regis-tered, your client may still be able to register the mark with the USPTO and pro-tect the mark in its own class of goods or services. The general rule is that if an average, reasonably prudent customer would likely be confused by the use of the same or similar marks on different products or services, trademark infringement may be found to exist. However, common terms—like "sparrow," for example—have a number of seemingly identical trademark registrations, except that they apply to different classes of products or services. For example, there is a regis-tered "sparrow" trademark owned by one company for use in connection with the sale of perfume, as well as a registered "sparrow" mark owned by another company for use in connection with the sale of electric automobiles. The possi-bility of confusion and the existence or nonexistence of infringement is deter-mined on a case-by-case basis.

2.8 Will Domain Registries Block Use of a Conflicting Domain Name?

If a company has a registered trademark and someone else has registered the same word or phrase as a domain name, the owner of the trademark may be able to have the domain name registries block the use of the domain without going to court. Disputes between domain name holders and trademark owners were once subject to the sometimes controversial dispute resolution policies of Network Solu-tions, Inc., once the sole entity serving as registrant of domain names ending with the top-level domains: ".com" ".org" and ".net." Network Solutions has since joined other companies that now register .com, .org, and .net domain names in announcing it would use the Uniform Domain Name Dispute Resolution Policy adopted by the Internet Corporation for Assigned Names and Numbers (ICANN), which became effective on December 1, 1999.

The ICANN policy provides that most types of trademark-based domain-name disputes must be resolved by contract, in court, or in arbitration before a reg-istrar may cancel, suspend, or transfer a domain name. But a trademark owner seeking to fight perceived cybersquatting may initiate expedited administrative proceedings by filing a complaint with an approved dispute-resolution service provider such as the World Intellectual Property Organization, the National Arbitration Forum, or disputes.org. ICANN will cancel, transfer, or make appropriate changes to domain name registrations following a determination by one of these organizations, in a proceeding that observes ICANN-approved rules of procedure, that the alleged cybersquatter registered a domain primarily to sell or transfer it to the trademark owner; to prevent the trademark owner from using the domain; to disrupt the business of a competitor; or to attract Internet users to a site by confusing them about the source, sponsorship, or affiliation of the site. (See the ICANN policy and rules at http://www.ICANN.org.)

2.9 Sample Documents and Checklists.

This section includes the following forms:

- One-Way Nondisclosure Agreement (Form 2 A)
- Mutual Confidentiality Agreement (Form 2 B)
- Trade Secrets Agreement (Form 2 C)
- Technical Consulting Agreement (Form 2 D)
- Trademark Assignment (Form 2 E)

Form 2 A: One-Way Nondisclosure Agreement (NDA)

****, INC.

NONDISCLOSURE AND NON-CIRCUMVENTION AGREEMENT

This Nondisclosure and Non-Circumvention Agreement entered into as of this _____ day of _____, 20___ (the "Agreement"), is made by and between ****, Inc., a California corporation ("Disclosing Party"), and _____ ("Recipient").

WHEREAS, the Disclosing Party possesses certain confidential and proprietary information relating to _____ [describe the nature of the Disclosing Party's business, such as: a development stage specialty foods company] (the "Business Opportunity"); and

WHEREAS, it is the desire of the parties to explore the possibility of working together in some capacity to advance the business of the Disclosing Party;

WHEREAS, it is necessary for the Disclosing Party to furnish certain information to Recipient which is non-public, confidential and/or proprietary in nature to enable the parties to explore the possibility of working together (the "Potential Transaction");

Now, therefore, Recipient hereby confirms its desire to examine Disclosing Party's confidential and proprietary information for the purpose of evaluating the Business Opportunity (the "Evaluation") and, in consideration of being furnished with such information, agrees as follows:

1. Non-Disclosure and Restrictions on Use of Information.

(a) Information. For purposes of this Agreement, "Information" shall mean, without limitation, the identity of the Business Opportunity, all intellectual property, strategic information, financial statements or projections, business plans, prototypes, drawings, data, trade secrets, business records, customer lists, supplier agreements, partnership or joint venture agreements, license agreements, marketing plans, employee lists, policies and procedures, information relating to processes, technologies or theory and any or all other information which may be disclosed by the Disclosing Party to the Recipient in accordance with this Agreement.

(b) Non-Disclosure of Information. The Recipient acknowledges the competitive value and confidential nature of the Information and the damages that would result to the Disclosing Party if any such information were disclosed, therefore the Information will be kept confidential and shall not be disclosed by the Recipient in any manner whatsoever, in whole or in part, except that:

(i) the Recipient may disclose the Information to its directors, officers, employees, agents, and legal and financial advisers (collectively, its "Agents") solely for the purposes of the Evaluation; provided the Recipient shall transmit the Information only to Agents who need to know the Information in connection with the Evaluation; and provided, further, Recipient shall notify each of the Agents that the Information is to be held by them in confidence and not disclosed to others, or permit others to use for their benefit or to the detriment of the Disclosing Party, any of the Information; and

(ii) the Recipient shall have no non-disclosure obligation hereunder with respect to any Information which (A) has been legally made public, other than by acts of the Recipient or its Agents in violation of this Agreement or (B) was or becomes independently known or available to the Recipient, on a non-confidential basis, from a source other than the Disclosing Party and which is not subject to any restrictions or disclosure.

Recipient shall use the same degree of care to avoid disclosure of the Information as it employs with respect to its own information which it does not desire to disclose, but at all times shall use at least reasonable care.

(c) <u>Restrictions on Use/Non-Circumvention</u>. Recipient shall not use the Information, directly or indirectly, for any purpose other than Recipient's Evaluation of the Business Opportunity, and such permitted use shall absolutely cease if and when the Disclosing Party has notified the Recipient that it no longer considers the Recipient a candidate for the Potential Transaction. Without limiting the generality of the foregoing: (i) except as provided in paragraph 2, the Recipient shall not use the Information in any judicial or administrative proceeding, and (ii) the Recipient shall not use any of the Information to perform, manufacture, distribute, deliver, use or sell products or services embodying any such information, or otherwise compete with, circumvent, or act to the detriment of the Disclosing Party.

(d) <u>Loss or Misuse of the Information</u>. The Recipient shall keep a record of the location of the Information and shall notify the Disclosing Party promptly of any loss, misuse or misappropriation of the Information. The Recipient hereby agrees to indemnify Disclosing Party against all losses, damages, claims or expenses (including attorneys' fees) incurred or suffered by Disclosing Party as a result of Recipient's breach of this Agreement.

(e) <u>Title to and Return of the Information</u>. Recipient agrees that no license, either expressed or implied, is hereby created or granted to Recipient by Disclosing Party to use any of the Information other than solely for the purpose of the Evaluation of the Business Opportunity. Title to the Information shall remain in the Disclosing Party, and in the event a Potential Transaction is not consummated, the Information (and all copies, summaries, and notes of the contents thereof) shall be returned to the Disclosing Party by the Recipient in accordance with the Disclosing Party's instructions.

2. <u>Response to Legal Process</u>. In the event Recipient (or anyone to whom it transmits the Information, whether or not in compliance with this Agreement) is requested, pursuant to subpoena or other legal process, to disclose any of the Information, Recipient shall provide Disclosing Party with immediate notice so that Disclosing Party may seek a protective order or other appropriate remedy and/or waive compliance with the provisions of this Agreement. In the event that such protective order or other remedy is not obtained, or Disclosing Party waives compliance with the provisions of this Agreement, Recipient (or such other person) shall furnish only that portion of the Information which is legally required and shall exercise its best efforts to obtain a protective order or other assurance satisfactory in form and substance to Disclosing Party that confidential treatment will be accorded the Information in accordance with this Agreement.

3. <u>Disclaimer of Accuracy of Information</u>. Although the Disclosing Party has endeavored to include in the Information such information known to it which it believes to be relevant for the purpose of the Evaluation, the Recipient understands that neither the Disclosing Party nor any of its representatives or advisors has made or herein makes any representation or warranty as to the accuracy or completeness of the Information.

4. <u>Remedies</u>. The parties agree that the disclosure of the Information by Recipient in violation of this Agreement may cause irreparable harm, the amount of which

would be impossible to ascertain, and that there is no adequate remedy at law for any breach by Recipient of this Agreement. Therefore, in addition to any other rights and remedies it may have, Disclosing Party shall have available, in addition to any other available right or remedy, the right to obtain an injunction from a court of competent jurisdiction restraining such breach or threatened breach and to specific performance of any provision of this Agreement. Recipient further agrees that no bond or other security shall be required in obtaining such equitable relief and consents to the issuance of such injunction and to the ordering of specific performance.

5. <u>Assignment</u>. Recipient shall not have the right to assign its rights under this Agreement, expressly or by operation of law. This Agreement shall be binding upon and inure to the benefit of the permitted successors and assigns of the parties hereto.

6. <u>Governing Law</u>. This Agreement shall be governed by and construed in accordance with the laws of the State of _____.

7. <u>Severability</u>. The invalidity or unenforceability of any provision hereof shall in no way affect the validity or enforceability of the remainder of this Agreement or any other provision hereof.

8. <u>Modification; Waiver</u>. No oral modifications shall be effective, and no delay or failure on the part of either party to insist on compliance with any provision hereof shall constitute a waiver of such party's right to enforce such provision.

9. <u>Integration</u>. This Agreement may be executed in two (2) or more counterparts each of which shall be deemed an original, but all of such taken together shall constitute only one Agreement, superseding all prior understandings, oral or written; and it is expressly understood and that this Agreement does not obligate either party to enter into any other or further agreements.

10. <u>Attorneys' Fees</u>. In the event litigation shall be instituted to enforce any provision of this Agreement, the prevailing party in such litigation shall be entitled to recover reasonable attorneys' fees and expenses incurred in such litigation in addition to any other recovery to which such party may be legally entitled.

IN WITNESS WHEREOF, the parties have executed this agreement as of the date first above written.

DISCLOSING PARTY

****, Inc.

By: _____
       Name:
       Title:
       Address:

RECIPIENT

_____

By: _____
       Name:
       Title:
       Address:

Form 2 B: Mutual Confidentiality Agreement

CONFIDENTIALITY AGREEMENT

This Confidentiality Agreement (the "Agreement") dated as of this _____ day of _____, 20___, is by and between ****, Inc., a California corporation, and **** Corporation, a Delaware corporation.

Recitals

WHEREAS, the parties hereto each possess certain confidential and proprietary information; and

WHEREAS, in connection with the desire of the parties to explore the possibility of entering into a prospective business transaction (the "Potential Transaction"), each party (each a "Disclosing Party") is furnishing certain information to the other party (each a "Recipient") which is non-public, confidential and/or proprietary in nature. Each party confirms its desire to examine the other's confidential and proprietary information for the purpose of evaluating the Potential Transaction (the "Evaluation") and, in consideration of being furnished with such information, agrees that:

Agreement

1. <u>Non-Disclosure and Restrictions on Use of Information</u>.

(a) <u>Information</u>. For purposes of this Agreement, "Information" shall mean, without limitation, all strategic information, financial statements or projections, business plans, data, business records, customers lists, supplier agreements, partnership or joint venture agreements, marketing plans, employee lists, policies and procedures, information relating to processes, technologies or theory and any or all other information which may be disclosed by the Disclosing Party to the Recipient in accordance with this Agreement.

(b) <u>Non-Disclosure of Information</u>. The Recipient acknowledges the competitive value and confidential nature of the Information and the damages that would result to the Disclosing Party if any such information were disclosed or misused, therefore, except as otherwise expressly permitted herein, the Information will be kept confidential and shall not be disclosed by the Recipient in any manner whatsoever, in whole or in part. Notwithstanding the foregoing:

(i) the Recipient may disclose the Information to its directors, officers, employees, agents, and legal and financial advisers (collectively, its "Agents") solely for the purposes of the Evaluation; *provided* the Recipient shall transmit the Information only to Agents who need to know the Information in connection with the Evaluation; and *provided*, *further*, that such Agents agree to maintain the Information in confidence and not to disclose the Information to others, and that they will not permit others to use for their benefit or to the detriment of the Disclosing Party, any of the Information and Recipient shall be responsible for its Agents' compliance with the same; and

(ii) the Recipient shall have no non-disclosure obligation hereunder with respect to any Information which (A) has been legally made public, other than by acts of the Recipient or its Agents in violation of this Agreement or (B) was or becomes independently known or available to the Recipient, on a non-confidential basis, from a source other than the Disclosing Party and which is not subject to any restrictions or disclosure.

(c) <u>Non-Disclosure of Potential Transaction</u>. Neither the Recipient nor any of its Agents shall disclose to any third person (including, without limitation, employees and agents of the Disclosing Party):

(i) the fact that it has received any of the Information;

(ii) that discussions or negotiations are taking place concerning a Potential Transaction; or

(iii) any of the terms, conditions or other facts with respect to any such Potential Transaction, including the status thereof;

unless such disclosure is required by law and then only with prior written notice as promptly as possible to the Disclosing Party.

(d) <u>Restrictions on Use</u>. Recipient shall not use the Information, directly or indirectly, for any purpose other than Recipient's Evaluation of a Potential Transaction, and such permitted use shall absolutely cease if and when the Disclosing Party has notified the Recipient that it no longer considers the Recipient a candidate for a Potential Transaction. Without limiting the generality of the foregoing: (i) except as provided in paragraph 2, the Recipient shall not use the Information in any judicial or administrative proceeding, and (ii) the Recipient shall not use any of the Information to the detriment of the Disclosing Party.

(e) <u>Loss or Misuse of the Information</u>. The Recipient shall keep a record of the location of the Information and shall notify the Disclosing Party promptly of any loss, misuse or misappropriation of the Information. The Recipient hereby agrees to indemnify Disclosing Party against all losses, damages, claims or expenses (including attorneys' fees) incurred or suffered by Disclosing Party as a result of Recipient's breach of this Agreement.

(f) <u>Title to and Return of the Information</u>. Recipient agrees that no license, either expressed or implied, is hereby created or granted to Recipient by Disclosing Party to use any of the Information other than solely for the purpose of the Evaluation of the Potential Transaction. Title to the Information shall remain in the Disclosing Party, and in the event a Potential Transaction is not consummated, the Information (and all copies, summaries, and notes of the contents thereof) shall be returned to the Disclosing Party by the Recipient in accordance with the Disclosing Party's instructions.

2. <u>Response to Legal Process</u>. In the event that the Recipient (or anyone to whom it transmits the Information whether or not in compliance with this Agreement) is requested, pursuant to subpoena or other legal process, to disclose any of the Information, the Recipient shall provide the Disclosing Party with immediate notice so that the Disclosing Party may seek a protective order or other appropriate remedy and/or waive compliance with the provisions of this Agreement. In the event that such protective order or other remedy is not obtained, or that the Disclosing Party waives compliance with the provisions of this Agreement, the Recipient (or such other person) shall furnish only that portion of the Information which is legally required and shall exercise its best efforts to obtain a protective order or other assurance satisfactory in form and substance to the Disclosing Party that the Information will receive confidential treatment in accordance with this Agreement.

3. Disclaimer of Accuracy of Information. Although the Disclosing Party has endeavored to include in the Information such information known to it which it believes to be relevant for the purpose of the Evaluation, the Recipient understands that neither the Disclosing Party nor any of its representatives or advisors has made or herein makes any representation or warranty as to the accuracy or completeness of the Information.

4. Remedies. The parties agree that the disclosure or misuse of the Information by the Recipient in violation of this Agreement may cause irreparable harm to the Disclosing Party, the amount of which would be impossible to ascertain, and that there is no adequate remedy at law for any breach by Recipient of this Agreement. Therefore, in addition to any other rights and remedies it may have, Disclosing Party shall be entitled to obtain from a court of competent jurisdiction an order restraining any such disclosure or other breach of this Agreement and for such other relief as may be appropriate, without the necessity of posting a bond. Such remedy shall be in addition to any other remedies otherwise available to the Disclosing Party at law or in equity.

5. Assignment. Recipient shall not have the right to assign its rights under this Agreement, expressly or by operation of law. This Agreement shall be binding upon and inure to the benefit of the permitted successors and assigns of the parties hereto.

6. Governing Law. This Agreement shall be governed by and construed in accordance with the laws of the State of _____.

7. Severability. The invalidity or unenforceability of any provision hereof shall in no way affect the validity or enforceability of the remainder of this Agreement or any other provision hereof.

8. Modification; Waiver. No oral modifications shall be effective, and no delay or failure on the part of either party to insist on compliance with any provision hereof shall constitute a waiver of such party's right to enforce such provision.

9. Integration. This Agreement may be executed in two (2) or more counterparts each of which shall be deemed an original, but all of such taken together shall constitute only one Agreement, superseding all prior understandings, oral or written; and it is expressly understood and that this Agreement does not obligate either party to enter into any other or further agreements.

IN WITNESS WHEREOF, the parties to this Agreement have duly authorized and executed this Agreement as of the date first written above.

****, Inc.

By: _____

      Name:

      Title:

      Address:

**** Corporation

By: _____

      Name:

      Title:

      Address:

Form 2 C: Trade Secrets Agreement

TRADE SECRETS AGREEMENT

This Agreement is made as of this ___ day of _____, 20___, between ****, Inc. ("Company") and _____, an individual residing in the State of _____ ("Employee").

WHEREAS, Employee will be engaged by Company in a position of trust and confidence in which Employee will learn of, have access to, and develop confidential trade secret and other proprietary Information of Company; and

WHEREAS, Company desires to protect its rights in such confidential, trade secret, and other proprietary Information and to obtain the ownership of certain inventions, programs, and other creations made or developed by Employee;

NOW THEREFORE, Company and Employee, in consideration for Company's offer of employment to Employee, intending to be legally bound, agree as follows:

1. <u>Nondisclosure of Information.</u>

(a) Employee acknowledges that Company has invested and will continue to invest considerable resources in the research, development and advancement of its business and certain technology, which investment has and will continue to result in the generation of proprietary, confidential and/or trade secret Information (including data, techniques and materials, tangible and intangible), which properly belong to Company or in respect of which Company owes an obligation of confidentiality to a third party. Employee acknowledges and agrees that it would be unlawful for Employee to appropriate, to attempt to appropriate, or to disclose to anyone or use for his own benefit or for a third party's benefit such data, information, techniques or materials relating to the business of Company as conducted by Company.

(b) For purposes of this Agreement all confidential, proprietary or trade secret Information enumerated or mentioned in Section 1(a) is hereinafter referred to as "Information." Any restrictions on disclosure and use of the Information will apply to all copies of the Information, whether in whole or in part and irrespective of the media by or in which the Information is recorded or evidenced.

(c) During the term of Employee's service with Company and thereafter termination of such employment, unless authorized in writing by Company, Employee will not:

(i) use for Employee's benefit or advantage the Information; or

(ii) use the Information for the benefit or advantage of any third party; or

(iii) improperly disclose or cause to be disclosed the Information or authorize or permit such disclosure of the Information to any third party; or

(iv) deliberately or with gross negligence, use the Information in any manner which may injure or cause loss to Company directly or indirectly.

(d) Employee will not be liable for the disclosure of Information which:

(i) is in the public domain; or

37

(ii) is received rightfully by Employee from a third party having a lawful right to possess; or

(iii) is ordered by a court of law or other governmental entity and Employee takes such reasonable steps available to Employee to protect the confidentiality of the Information while complying with such order; provided however, that Employee shall maintain a detailed written record, available for Company's inspection, of all disclosures pursuant to this provision; or

(iv) was known to Employee prior to entering into this Agreement.

(e) Employee will surrender to Company at any time upon request, and upon termination of Employee's service with Company for any reason, all written or otherwise tangible documentation representing or embodying the Information, in whatever form, whether or not copyrighted, patented, or protected as a mask work or otherwise protectable, and any copies or imitations of the Information, whether or not made by the Employee.

(f) Employee agrees to provide additional services upon reasonable request for consultation for a period of up to six (6) months after termination of employment to provide Information and details with respect to any work or activity performed or materials created by Employee alone or with others during service with Company. Employee will be reimbursed for these services.

(g) Employee agrees to comply with all security regulations established by the U.S. government and by Company, its customers, employees, and other third parties for the purpose of protecting the Developments or Information as those terms are herein defined. Employee further agrees to comply with U.S. laws and regulations governing the export and re-export of commodities and technical data.

(h) Employee agrees not to disclose Information to any person affiliated with any third party who has not executed a nondisclosure agreement with Company and to disclose Information only in the course of performing her or his duties for Company.

(i) Employee agrees to refrain from making any copies of written material or tangible objects embodying Information, except as such copies are required in the performance of his duties for Company.

(j) Upon termination of employment with Company for any reason whatsoever (including by retirement, by resignation, or for cause), Employee agrees to deliver to Company all written and/or tangible materials, including all copies thereof, all magnetic and other types of Information storage media and all models, machines, mechanisms, prototypes and the like embodying any Information which he or she obtained in the course of service with Company, whether or not he or she is the author, maker, or inventor of same. Employee recognizes that this obligation requires him or her to deliver to Company upon termination of service all such written and tangible materials, including but not limited to letters, memoranda, reports, notes, notebooks, books of accounts, data, disks, drawings, prints, plans, specifications, tapes, and other data storage media and the like which he or she has in his or her possession or control.

2. Ownership of Programs and Inventions.

(a) Any and all creations, developments, discoveries, inventions, works of authorship, enhancements, modifications, and improvements, including, without limitation, computer programs, data bases, data files and the like, (hereinafter collectively referred to as "Development" or "Developments"), whether or not the Developments are copyrightable, patentable, protectable as mask works or otherwise protectable (such as by employment, contract, or implied duty), and whether published or unpublished, conceived, invented, developed, created, or produced by Employee alone or with others during the term of his or her employment with Company, will be the sole and exclusive property of Company if the Development is:

   (i) within the scope of Employee's duties assigned with his position; or

   (ii) in whole or in part, the result of Employee's use of Company's resources, including without limitation personnel, computers, data bases, communications facilities, laboratory facilities, word processing systems, programs, or office facilities.

   (b) Employee hereby acknowledges that Company will have principal supervisions and control of the development of all products or services, such that all Developments subject to Copyright will become "works made for hire" under Section 101 of the Copyright Act of 1976, as amended. Employee will disclose promptly to Company any and all Developments and will reduce such disclosures to a detailed writing upon request by Company.

   (c) During the term of Employee's service with Company, Employee agrees to assign and does hereby assign to Company all rights in the Developments created by Employee alone or with others as part of his or her duties of employment at Company, and all rights in any trademarks, copyrights, mask works, patents, trade secrets, and intellectual property rights and any applications for registration for same, in the United States and such foreign countries as Company may designate, which are related to the Developments, including without limitation all accompanying misappropriations and to receive all proceeds as related to any judgment or settlement of same. Employee agrees to execute and deliver to Company all instruments and papers Company reasonably deems necessary to vest in Company sole title to and all exclusive rights in the Developments created by Employee alone or with others as part of his or her duties of employment with Company and in all related trademarks, copyrights, mask work protection rights, and/or patent rights so created during the term of service if related to and/or dependent upon Information and/or work done by or Information learned by Employee during his or her service with Company. Employee agrees to execute and deliver to Company all instruments and papers that Company reasonably deems necessary for use in applying for trademarks, copyrights, mask work protections, patents, or such other legal protections as Company may reasonably desire. While employed by Company Employee further agrees to assist fully Company or its nominees as is reasonably required in the preparation and prosecution of any trademark, copyright, mask work protection, patent, or trade secret arbitration or litigation.

   3. Government Contracts. If performance of Employee's services involves work under government contracts, grants, or Cooperative Research and Development Agreements (CRADAS), Employee agrees to be bound by the obligations, terms, and conditions associated with such contracts, grants, or CRADAS, all of which are incorporated herein by reference as if fully set forth. If services performed include receiving, handling or developing any government classified material, Employee shall comply with all applicable security regulations and requirements, and immediately submit a confidential report to Company if Employee has any cause to believe there is any danger of espionage, improper disclosure, or misuse of funds affecting work under a government contract.

4. <u>Prior Obligations of Employee</u>. Employee warrants and represents that Employee's performance of his duties will not violate any other obligations of Employee including any other agreements to which Employee is a party. Employee will not bring any materials which are proprietary to a third party to Company without the prior written consent of such third party.

5. <u>Miscellaneous</u>.

(a) The failure of Company to object to any conduct or violation of any of the covenants made by Employee under this Agreement will not be deemed a waiver by Company of any rights or remedies Company may have under this Agreement.

(b) This Agreement is binding upon the parties hereto. Employee agrees that the obligations of this Agreement will survive the termination of Employee's employment with Company.

(c) No alterations, amendments, changes, or additions to this Agreement will be binding upon either Company or Employee unless reduced to writing and signed by both parties.

(d) No waiver of any right arising under this Agreement made by either party will be valid unless given in an appropriate writing signed by that party.

(e) Employee is fully aware of Employee's right to discuss any and all aspects of this Agreement with an attorney chosen by Employee, and Employee further acknowledges that he has carefully read and fully understands all of the provisions of this Agreement and that Employee, in all consideration for Company's offer of employment, is voluntarily entering into this Agreement.

(f) This Agreement may be executed in counterparts, each of which shall be deemed an original, but which together shall constitute one and the same instrument.

(g) The headings used in this Agreement are for convenience only and are not to be considered in construing or interpreting this Agreement.

(h) This Agreement shall be interpreted and enforced pursuant to the laws of the State of _____.

WITNESS the execution hereof as of the date first above written.

_____
Employee Signature
Name:

Form 2 D: Technical Consulting Agreement

TECHNICAL CONSULTING AGREEMENT

This Agreement is made as of this ____ day of _____, 20___ ("Effective Date"), by and between ****, Inc. (the "Company"), a _____ corporation located at _____ _____, and ****, LLC, a _____ limited liability company located at _____, for itself and its employees and agents (collectively, "Consultant").

In consideration of the mutual promises and for other valuable consideration, the receipt and sufficiency of which Consultant acknowledges, the parties agree as follows:

1. **Services and Compensation.**

(a) <u>Services Performed</u>. Consultant agrees to perform the services described in the proposal, statement of work or similar document that is incorporated into this Agreement or described on the front side of any applicable purchase order (such documents collectively referred to as the "Statement of Work" and such services referred to as the "Services"). If a specific schedule for the Services is set forth in the Statement of Work, then time is of the essence for such Services. In all other events, Consultant shall make all reasonable efforts to complete the Services as quickly as reasonably possible. This Agreement is made in conjunction with a purchase order issued by the Company to Consultant, and in addition will apply to any subsequent purchase orders and all work or services subsequently performed by Consultant, unless otherwise agreed upon between the Company and Consultant in writing. This Agreement does not authorize any work or service to be performed. The Company will only be obligated to pay for work or services when a purchase order is issued by an authorized purchasing agent of the Company.

(b) <u>Compensation & Pricing</u>. The parties agree to utilize a two-tier approach to pricing services. For Services to be billed out to the Company's end-user customer, the Company and the Consultant will share the revenue stream on a 30/70 basis (e.g. If the end-user agrees to pay $100/hour, Consultant will bill the Company $70/hour and the Company will retain $30/hour as its share of the revenue). Consultant will be responsible for defining the scope of services and pricing the work to be performed at a reasonable rate given the complexity of the work to be performed, technical certifications required and the marketplace. Should the end-user customer desire to negotiate the pricing quoted by Consultant, the Company will provide the Consultant with an opportunity to directly participate in those pricing discussions with the Company and its customer. For non-billable Services (e.g. the Company is absorbing the cost of the Services as opposed to billing out the expense to the end-user), Consultant will receive compensation at an hourly rate of $90.00 per hour. Both billable and non-billable Services will be authorized and funded via a purchase order. The Company will pay Consultant the compensation set forth in the applicable purchase order as the sole compensation for Services satisfactorily performed hereunder, up to the maximum fee stated therein. Unless otherwise set forth in the Statement of Work, any expenses incurred by Consultant in performing the Services or associated with its sales activities to secure a specific Services project will be the sole responsibility of Consultant.

2. **Relationship of Parties.**

(a) Independent Contractor. Consultant is an independent contractor and is not an agent or employee of the Company. Consultant has no authority to bind the Company by contract or otherwise without the Company's prior written authorization. Consultant will perform the Services under the general direction of the Company, but Consultant will determine, in Consultant's sole discretion, the manner and means by which the Services are accomplished, subject to the requirement that Consultant shall at all times comply with applicable law. The Company has no right or authority to control the manner or means by which the Services are accomplished. Consultant agrees to furnish all tools and materials necessary to accomplish the Services.

(b) Taxes and Benefits. Consultant agrees to pay all taxes on the compensation provided to Consultant or its employees and other individuals and entities performing Services on behalf of Consultant (collectively "Consultant's Agents"). Consultant agrees that Consultant and its Agents will not be eligible to participate in, or receive benefits under, any employee benefit plans, arrangements or policies of the Company including, but not limited to, any plan, arrangement or policy providing bonus, vacation, stock options, stock purchase, sick leave, disability, health or life insurance, 401(k), retirement, profit sharing or similar benefits for the Company's employees (collectively, "Benefit Plans"). Consultant will defend, indemnify and hold the Company harmless from and against all claims, damages, losses and expenses, including reasonable fees and expenses of attorneys and other professionals ("Costs"), relating to any obligation imposed upon the Company to pay any withholding taxes, social security, unemployment insurance, or similar items or to provide coverage or benefits under any of its Benefit Plans, in each case in connection with compensation received by Consultant or its Agents. If any of Consultant's Agents are later determined to have been common-law employees or employees of the Company for any purpose, such individual(s) nevertheless will not be entitled to participate or receive benefits under any Benefit Plan. Consultant acknowledges that no insurance whatsoever, including Worker's Compensation insurance, has been or will be obtained by the Company on Consultant's behalf.

3. **Company Property.**

(a) Definitions. "Consultant's Preexisting Works" shall mean all designs, ideas, discoveries, inventions, products, computer programs, source code, procedures, improvements, documents, information and materials developed by Consultant prior to the Effective Date of this Agreement and independent of the Company's personnel, resources and Confidential Information.

"Designs and Materials" shall mean all designs, ideas, discoveries, inventions, products, computer programs, source code, procedures, improvements, documents, information and materials made, conceived or developed by Consultant alone or with others, which result from or relate to the Services.

(b) Assignment of Ownership. Consultant hereby irrevocably transfers and assigns to the Company without further compensation, any and all of Consultant's right, title and interest in and to Designs and Materials, including, but not limited to, all copyrightable works and copyrights, patent rights, trade secrets and trademarks. Notwithstanding this assignment and transfer, if Designs and Materials incorporate or rely upon Consultant's Preexisting Works, Consultant shall continue to retain ownership of Consultant's Preexisting Works, but Consultant hereby licenses the Company to use, or have third parties use on the Company's behalf, or the Company's customer use such Preexisting Works as is reasonably required to fully exploit the Services performed by Consultant hereunder. Consultant agrees, during and for one year following the term of the Agreement to: (i) disclose promptly in writing to the Company all Designs and Materials; (ii) assist the Company to sign and provide any and all documents and render any assistance that is reasonably necessary to obtain any patent, copyright, trademark or other protection for Designs and Materials. In case any invention is described in a patent application or is disclosed to third parties by Consultant within one (1) year after the Services have been completed, it shall be presumed that the invention was conceived or made during the period in which the Services were rendered, and the invention will be assigned to the Company as set forth in this Agreement, provided that the invention results from or relates to Consultant's work with the Company. If the invention was made by Consultant prior to any association by Consultant with the Company or was made without the Confidential Information or resources of the Company, then Consultant need not assign the invention to the Company as set forth herein.

(c) <u>Moral Rights Waiver</u>. "Moral Rights" means any right to claim authorship of a work, any right to object to any distortion or other modification of a work, and any similar right, existing under the law of any country in the world, or under any treaty. Consultant hereby irrevocably transfers and assigns to the Company any and all Moral Rights that Consultant may have in any Services and Designs and Materials. Consultant also hereby forever waives and agrees never to assert against the Company, its successors or licensees, any and all Moral Rights Consultant may have in any Services or Designs and Materials.

(d) <u>Return of Company Property</u>. Consultant will return to the Company any Company property that comes into Consultant's possession in the course of this Agreement, when requested by the Company, and in all events, at the termination or expiration of this Agreement. Consultant shall not remove any Company property from the Company's premises without written authorization from the Company. Such property shall include, but not be limited to, product demonstration units, all memoranda, notebooks, drawings, blueprints and any other documents containing Confidential Information, as defined below.

4. **Confidential Information.**

(a) <u>Definition and Duty</u>. The Company may provide and Consultant may acquire information and materials from the Company and knowledge about the Company's business including, but not limited to, products, processes, programming techniques, research, customers, employees and suppliers of the Company and confidential information or trade secret information of third parties in the possession of the Company (including but not limited to the Company's customers and OEM partners, and results of Services by Consultant). All such knowledge, information and materials, and the existence of Designs and Materials, are and will be the trade secrets and confidential and proprietary information of the Company or the third party in the case of customer or OEM partner information (collectively "Confidential Information"). Confidential Information will not include, however, any information which: (i) becomes a matter of public knowledge through no fault of Consultant; (ii) is rightfully received by Consultant from a third party without restriction on disclosure; (iii) is independently developed by Consultant without the use of the Company's Confidential Information; or (iv) is rightfully in the possession of Consultant prior to its disclosure by the Company. Consultant agrees to hold all Confidential Information in strict confidence, not to disclose it to others or use it in any way, commercially or otherwise, except in performing the Services, and to disclose it to those individuals performing Services on behalf of Consultant only on a need-to-know basis. Consultant shall promptly notify the Company if it receives a subpoena or other order of a court or government agency that requires the disclosure of the Company's Confidential Information, and will give the Company an opportunity to defend, limit or protect such disclosure.

(b) Employees' Confidentiality Agreement. Consultant will ensure that each of its employees and agents who will have access to the Designs and Materials or Confidential Information of the Company executes an agreement: a) assuring the Company of its exclusive ownership and control of the Designs and Materials, obligating the individual to keep all Confidential Information confidential and not to disclose or use the Designs and Materials or Confidential Information in any way, commercially or otherwise, except in performing the Services and; b) assigning to the Company and waiving any and all Moral Rights in the Designs and Materials. Upon request, Consultant will provide the Company with copies of such agreements.

5. **Indemnification by Consultant.** Consultant will defend, indemnify and hold the Company harmless from and against all Costs arising out of or resulting from the following: (i) any action by a third party against the Company that is based upon any claim that any Services performed under this Agreement, or the results thereof, infringe a patent, copyright or other proprietary right or violate a trade secret; and (ii) any action by a third party that is based upon any negligent act or omission or willful misconduct of Consultant; and (iii) any action based upon any act or omission arising out of Consultant being on the Company's or its customer's premises.

6. **Termination and Expiration.** This Agreement will commence on the Effective Date and will continue until final completion of the Services or until terminated as provided in this Section. This Agreement may be terminated by the Company for any or no reason by giving Consultant thirty (30) days written or oral notice of such termination. Should either party default in the performance of this Agreement, or materially breach any of its material terms, the non-breaching party, at its option, may terminate this Agreement by giving written notice to the breaching party and ten days for the breaching party to cure such breach, except in the event of a material breach of Section 4 of this Agreement by Consultant, in which case the Company may terminate this Agreement immediately upon providing written notice to Consultant. Upon termination and/or expiration of this Agreement, the Company shall be obligated to pay only the amounts owing to Consultant for satisfactory Services performed up to the point of termination. Termination or expiration of this Agreement will not relieve Consultant of its obligations under Sections 2(b), 3(b)–(d), 4(a), 5, 7, 8, and 9(a), nor will expiration or termination relieve Consultant from any liability arising from any breach of this Agreement.

7. **Limitation of Liability.** IN NO EVENT SHALL THE COMPANY BE LIABLE FOR ANY SPECIAL, INCIDENTAL, IN the Company DIRECT OR CONSEQUENTIAL DAMAGES OF ANY KIND IN CONNECTION WITH THIS AGREEMENT, EVEN IF INFORMED IN ADVANCE OF THE POSSIBILITY OF SUCH DAMAGES.

8. **Warranties and Representations.**

(a) Warranty. With respect to all subject matter, including Designs and Materials and Consultant's Preexisting Works, Consultant warrants it has the right to make disclosure and use thereof without liability to others. In addition, Consultant warrants that the Services provided hereunder will be performed in a workmanlike manner, with professional diligence and skill, and in accordance with reasonable commercial standards.

(b) <u>Conflict of Interest</u>. During the term of this Agreement, no individual assigned by Consultant to perform or assist in performing Services, or who has access to Confidential Information, shall consult with or perform services for a competitor of the Company, or participate in the ownership or control of, or in any other manner be connected with, any competitor of the Company, without written agreement from the Company. For the purposes of clarification, a competitor of the Company is defined as a third party providing _____ services or _____ products to customers in the greater _____ metropolitan area. Further, if during or within one (1) year from the date an individual covered by this Section last performs work or services for the Company, such individual is engaged to consult with or performs service for a competitor or customer of the Company, Consultant shall notify the Company in writing of such engagement.

9. **General Provisions.**

(a) <u>Governing Law; Severability</u>. This Agreement will be governed by and construed in accordance with the laws of the State of _____ excluding that body of law pertaining to conflict of laws. Any suit arising out of this Agreement shall be brought in the appropriate federal or state court located in _____ County, in the State of _____, provided that such court has jurisdiction over the subject matter of the action. Each party agrees that such court shall have personal jurisdiction over it. If any provision of this Agreement is for any reason found to be unenforceable, the remainder of this Agreement will continue in full force and effect.

(b) <u>Notices</u>. Any notice, consent or approval required or permitted under this Agreement shall be in writing and shall be deemed given when delivered (1) personally; (2) by facsimile; (3) by postage mail; or (4) by email with confirmation of delivery. Notices shall be given as follows:

****, LLC

****, Inc.

_____

_____

_____

_____

Phone: _____

Phone: _____

Email: _____

Email: _____

(c) <u>Certifications, Training, and Partner Meetings</u>. Consultant may, from time-to-time, be requested to participate in OEM partner sponsored or conducted training or other business related meetings on behalf of the Company. Unless agreed in advance in writing, Consultant shall participate in such training events or meetings at its own expense. In the event that the Company desires Consultant to obtain OEM product specific certifications for the exclusive benefit of the Company, the parties will mutually determine in advance the compensation Consultant will receive in exchange for obtaining such certifications.

(d) <u>Insurance</u>. Consultant will maintain the following insurance coverage insuring against all liability of Consultant and Consultant's Agents arising out of, and in connection with, Consultant's performance of Services: (i) comprehensive general liability insurance, covering bodily injury, property damage, contractual liability and completed operation; (ii) Workers' Compensation and employer's liability insurance, if applicable; and (iii) automobile liability, products liability, professional liability, errors and omissions, and other coverage mutually agreed upon, if any of these are applicable. Consultant will maintain at least minimum coverage in amounts sufficient to insure Consultant's continuing operations. Upon request, Consultant will furnish the Company certificates evidencing such insurance coverage.

(e) Force Majeure. If performance of any obligation under this Agreement is prevented, restricted, or interfered with by causes beyond either party's reasonable control ("Force Majeure"), and if the party unable to carry out its obligations gives the other party prompt written notice of such event, then the obligations of the party invoking this provision shall be suspended to the extent necessary by such event. The term "Force Majeure" shall include, without limitation, acts of nature, fire, explosion, vandalism, storm, or other similar occurrence; orders or acts of military or civil authority; national emergencies, insurrections, riots, wars, strikes, lock-outs, work stoppages, or other labor disputes, supplier failures, shortages, breach, or delays. The excused party shall use reasonable efforts under the circumstances to avoid or remove such causes of non-performance and shall proceed to perform with reasonable dispatch whenever such causes are removed or ceased. An act or omission shall be deemed within the reasonable control of a party if committed, omitted or caused by such party, or its employees, officers, agents or affiliates.

(f) Compliance with Laws. Consultant shall comply with all laws, rules or ordinances of the United States and any applicable state or other governmental agency while supplying the Services.

(g) Complete Understanding; Modification. This Agreement, the applicable purchase order(s), and the Statement of Work, if any, constitute the complete and exclusive understanding and agreement of the parties and supersede all prior understandings and agreements, whether written or oral, with respect to the subject matter hereof. Any waiver, modification or amendment of any provision of this Agreement will be effective only if in writing and signed by the parties hereto. In the event of any conflict between any term of the purchase order(s), the Agreement or the Statement of Work, the specific conflicting term of this Agreement shall supersede the purchase order(s), which shall supersede the Statement of Work.

IN WITNESS WHEREOF, the parties have signed this Agreement as of the Effective Date.

****, INC.   ****, LLC
(****)   (CONSULTANT)

By: _____   By: _____

Name: _____   Name: _____

Title: _____   Title: _____

Date: _____   Date: _____

ADDENDUM A

STATEMENT OF WORK

The scope of services and associated compensation will be determined on a project by project basis.

Form 2 E: Trademark Assignment

TRADEMARK ASSIGNMENT

This Trademark Assignment ("***Assignment***") is made effective as of _____, 20__, from ******, **LLC** ("***ASSIGNOR***"), to ******, Inc., a California corporation ("***ASSIGNEE***").

WHEREAS, ASSIGNOR is the owner of the registered trademark ******, USPTO Registration Number _____ (the "***Mark***") together with the goodwill of the business symbolized thereby in connection with the goods on which the Mark is used (the "***Products***"); and

WHEREAS, ASSIGNOR desires to convey, transfer, assign, deliver, and contribute to ASSIGNEE all of its right, title, and interest in and to the Mark and the Products;

NOW, THEREFORE, in consideration of the payment of one dollar ($1.00) and other good and valuable consideration, the receipt and sufficiency of which is hereby acknowledged, ASSIGNOR hereby conveys, transfers, assigns, delivers, and contributes to ASSIGNEE all of ASSIGNOR'S right, title, and interest of whatever kind in and to the Mark together with: (1) the goodwill of the business relating to the Products in respect upon which the Marks are used and for which they are registered; (2) all income, royalties, and damages hereafter due or payable to ASSIGNOR with respect to the Mark, including without limitation, damages and payments for past or future infringements and misappropriations of the Mark; and (3) all rights to sue for past, present and future infringements or misappropriations of the Mark.

ASSIGNOR further covenants that it will execute all documents, papers, forms, and authorizations and take all other actions that may be reasonably necessary for securing, completing, or vesting in ASSIGNEE full right, title, and interest in the Mark and the Products.

IN WITNESS WHEREOF, ASSIGNOR has duly executed under seal and delivered this Assignment, as of the day and year first above written.

ASSIGNOR:

******, LLC

By: _____

******, Principal

49

CHAPTER 3

Business Plans

3.1 Does Your Client Need a Business Plan and/or Executive Summary?

Every business should have a plan, and committing the plan to writing forces business owners to establish goals and confront weaknesses. A complete business plan will address each of the following areas and perhaps others (such as competition and ownership structure), depending on how the plan will be used:

1. Business strategy
2. Management plan
3. Business plan milestones
4. Marketing and sales plan
5. Research and development plan
6. Operations plan
7. Financial projections
8. Funding plan

Clients should be encouraged to engage in the planning process (financial, technical, marketing, staffing, etc.) as often as possible. Too many times, small businesses lack the kinds of strategies, projections, budgets, contingency plans, and competitive analyses that business plans and executive summaries would force them to make and that might make the difference between ultimate success and failure. Whether the results of a company's planning need to be committed to a formal business plan and/or executive summary depends on the circumstances. However, written business plans and executive summaries are critical when a client is trying to raise money.

3.2 What Should Be in a Business Plan or Executive Summary?

The primary differences between a business plan and an executive summary are the length (i.e., level of detail) and the intended use.

1. Business Plans.

Business plans should be much more detailed than executive summaries and can serve both internal and external purposes for any business. Business plans should typically be treated as containing confidential and proprietary information. A nondisclosure and noncircumvention agreement (NDA) should typically be used in connection with the distribution of a business plan.

2. Executive Summaries.

Executive summaries should be very brief and easy to read. Executive summaries can be incorporated into a business plan as an introductory section, or they can be used alone as an overview for prospective investors, the press, prospective employees, and others. If the executive summary is to be made available to the press and others without an NDA, your client should be careful not to include any confidential or proprietary information in the document. However, some business concepts are too unique and proprietary to be disclosed (unless protected by a patent), even in a summary fashion, without an NDA; thus, a signed NDA should be obtained before disclosing the executive summary to anyone outside the company and counsel.

3. The Objectives of a Business Plan to Be Presented to Investors.

A detailed business plan meets these objectives:

- Describes a unique solution to a huge problem, or a product or service that can create a new market or industry (i.e., a **large market opportunity**);
- Describes a solution that is **best of class**, defensible, and customers will buy it;
- Presents a **management team** with the requisite talent and expertise to launch the company, with a hiring plan that addresses any gaps;
- Describes product development and launch milestones;
- Presents a credible **marketing and sales strategy** that demonstrates an understanding of industry dynamics and customer needs; and
- Presents a financial plan that details specific costs associated with each milestone achievement as well as phased costs of the subsequent growth leading to an exit.

4. Large Market Opportunity.

A successful large market opportunity presentation describes

- A big problem existing in the market for the product or service that causes significant customer pain;

- How the product or service will change the way people think or do things;
- Evidence that the target market can and will adopt the solution; and
- High probability that the company can become the market leader.

5. Best-of-Class Solution.

A best-of-class solution presentation demonstrates these strengths:

- The solution fits well with the unique operational and industry characteristics of the customer;
- Critical supply chain is in place, and partner dynamics are favorable;
- Integration is relatively painless, and costs are in line with value;
- There is a short-term, bottom-line benefit to the customer; and
- The solution is unique and defensible.

6. Winning Team.

A winning management team presentation will demonstrate that the team is

- Trustworthy and tenacious (track record helps);
- Balanced, but has a strong leader possessing customer empathy;
- Very knowledgeable about industry characteristics;
- Willing to partner with investors and the board of directors; and
- Flexible about changing roles as the company grows.

7. Credible Marketing and Sales Strategies.

A credible marketing and sales strategy presentation will demonstrate

- A plan for moving through the Alpha—Beta—Launch—Customer Acquisition process;
- Alignment of costs and milestones;
- Credible cost estimations for each stage of the process;
- A plan that reflects industry characteristics; and
- Potential for long-term growth.

8. Guy Kawasaki Sums It All Up.

Guy Kawasaki, one of the original Apple Computer employees turned venture capitalist, put all of the foregoing very succinctly in one of his blogs. He listed the following as the ten topics that a venture capitalist cares about:

1. The problem your company has identified in the market;
2. Your company's solution to that problem;
3. The business model;

4. The underlying magic or technology that drives the solution;
5. Marketing and sales plan;
6. Competition;
7. The team (the company's key management and advisors);
8. Projections and milestones;
9. Status and timeline; and
10. Summary and call to action.[1]

A good business plan for use in raising capital from venture capitalists will certainly highlight each of these ten factors and provide details to support them.

3.3 What Turns Investors Off in a Business Plan?

The top ten biggest business plan turnoffs, from an investor's perspective, seem to be the following:

1. The space is saturated; too much money already in play.
2. The solution requires a lot of funding to reach validation milestones.
3. The team is impossible to work with and unrealistic.
4. The solution is indefensible; no real barrier to entry.
5. There are too many alternate solutions; the solution is not compelling.
6. Naive expectations of customer adoption rate.
7. Success is achievable only by beating an industry giant.
8. The management team is geographically dispersed.
9. The board of directors is filled with inexperienced investors and managers.
10. A management team that suffers from one or more of the foregoing, but doesn't know it (and therefore hasn't addressed it).

3.4 Sample Documents and Checklists.

This section includes the following forms:

- Template for an Executive Summary (Form 3 A)
- Business Plan Outline for Retail Business (Form 3 B)
- Business Plan Outline for Technology Business (Form 3 C)

---

1. Guy Kawasaki, *The 10/20/30 Rule of PowerPoint,* at http://blog.guykawasaki.com/2005/12/the_102030_rule.html#axzz1HqJPxwA8 (Dec. 30, 2005) (last visited Mar. 27, 2011).

Form 3 A: Template for an Executive Summary

[Cover Page]

[Company Logo]

**** CORPORATION

Executive Summary

[DATE]

[Footer for cover page:]

The information contained herein, and in any attached materials, is provided for informational purposes only and does not constitute an offer to sell or a solicitation or recommendation to purchase any security. This review is for the sole use of the intended recipient(s) and may contain confidential information. If the reader of this review is not the intended recipient, you are hereby notified that you have received this document, and any attachments, in error and that any review, dissemination, distribution, or copying of this material is prohibited. The information contained herein, and in any attachments, has been obtained from sources believed to be reliable, but the author does not guarantee its accuracy or completeness.

[Header for each page following the cover page:]

Executive Summary [Date]   [Company Name]

[Bullets and summary information are to be provided in the left-hand column of the summary and more detailed information is to be provided in the text in the right-hand column:]

Headquarters:	**Business Description**
[Address 1] [Address 2] [City], [State] [Postal Code] www.[url].com **Founded:** [Month, Year] **Domicile:** [State] **Employees:** [No. of Employees] **Status:** [See Definitions] **Stage:** [See Definitions]	[Describe the business concept for the business the company is in or will be in. Be sure the description of the concept explains how the product or service will fundamentally change the way customers currently do things. Identify when the Company was formed, what it will do, what is special or proprietary about its product, service, or technology, and so forth. Include summary information about any proprietary technology, trade secrets, or unique capabilities that give the company an edge in the marketplace. If the company has existed for a few years, a brief summary of its size and progress is in order. Try to make the description 25 words or less, and mention the specific product or service.]

Key Industry Statistics:	Opportunity and Strategy
Market Data (mm/dd/yy): Symbol: Share Price: Shares Outstanding: Fully Diluted Shares: Market Capitalization: **Recent Events:** MM-YY: [Event 1] MM-YY: [Event 2] MM-YY: [Event 3] . . .	[Summarize what the opportunity is, why it is compelling, and the entry strategy planned to exploit it. This information may be presented as an outline of the key facts, conditions, competitors' vulnerabilities ("sleepiness," sluggishness, poor service, etc.), industry trends, and other evidence and logic that define the opportunity. Note plans for growth and expansion beyond the entry products or services and into other market segments (such as international markets) as appropriate.]
Strategic Partners: - [Strategic Partner 1] - [Strategic Partner 2] - [Strategic Partner 3] . . . **Distribution Channels:** - [Channel 1] - [Channel 2] - [Channel 3] . . . Date Title Status MM-YY MM-YY MM-YY **Representative Customers:** - [Customer 1] - [Customer 2] - [Customer 3] . . . **Primary Competitors:** - [Competitor 1] - [Competitor 2] - [Competitor 3] . . .	**Target Market and Projections** [Identify and briefly explain the industry and market, who the primary customer groups are, how the product(s) or service(s) will be positioned, and how the company plans to reach and service these groups. Include information about the structure of the market, the size and growth rate for the market segments or niches the company is targeting, unit and dollar sales estimates, anticipated market share, the payback period for customers, and the pricing strategy (including price versus performance/value/benefits considerations).]
Patents:	**Competitive Advantages** [Indicate the significant competitive edges the company enjoys or can create as a result of its innovative product, service, and strategy; advantages in lead time; competitors' weaknesses and vulnerabilities; and other industry conditions.]

Board of Directors: [Chairman] [Board Member 2], [Committee] [Board Member 3], [Committee] **Investors:** Participating Investment Firm Round #(s) **Advisors:**	**Management and Ownership** [Summarize the relevant knowledge, experience, know-how, and skills of the lead entrepreneur and any team members, noting previous accomplishments, especially those involving profit and loss responsibility and general management and people management experience. Include significant information, such as the size of a division, project, or prior business with which the lead entrepreneur or a team member was the driving force.] **Directors' Biographies** [Include biographies of all directors and emphasize how each will contribute to the Company's success.]
Management Compensation: [Management Compensation Table] **Employee Breakdown** Senior Management Sales & Marketing Research & Development Marketing Support Staff Administrative Support Staff	**Executive Management Biographies** [For each key person, describe in detail career highlights, particularly relevant know-how, skills, and track record of accomplishments, which demonstrate his or her ability to perform the assigned role. Include sales and profitability achievements (budget size, numbers of subordinates, new product introductions, etc.) and other prior entrepreneurial or general management results. Describe the exact duties and responsibilities of each of the key members of the management team.]
Financing History: Post Amount Money Round Raised Valuation Date Type ($MM) ($MM) MM-YY MM-YY MM-YY MM-YY **Capitalization ($MM)** Long-term Debt Convertible Debt Series [x] Preferred Common Stock	**Economics, Profitability and Harvest Potential** [Summarize the nature of the "forgiving and rewarding" economics of the venture (e.g. gross and operating margins, expected profitability and durability of those profits); the relevant time frames to attain break-even and positive cash flow; key financial projections; the expected return on investment; and so on. Be sure to include a brief description of the contribution analysis and the underlying operating and cash conversion cycle. Use key numbers whenever possible.]

Financial Performance ($MM): Year Sales COS R&D EBITDA [provide historical and projected]	
Financing Status: Currently seeking $[xx.x] million of [round #] round financing.	**The Offering** [Briefly indicate the dollar amount of equity and/or debt financing needed, how much of the company the company is prepared to offer for that financing, what principal use will be made of the capital.]
	Products and Services
[Product 1]	Describe in some detail each product or service. • Discuss the application of the product or service and describe the primary end use as well as any significant secondary applications. • Emphasize any unique features of the product and how these will create or add significant value; also, highlight any differences between what is currently on the market and what the company will offer that will account for market penetration. Be sure to describe how value will be added and the payback period to the customer—that is, discuss how many months it will take for the customer to cover the initial purchase price of the product or service as a result of its time, cost, or productivity improvements. • Include a description of any possible drawbacks (including problems with obsolescence) of the product or service. • Define the present state of development of the product or service and how much time and money will be required to fully develop, test, and introduce the product or service. Provide a summary of the functional specifications and photographs, if available, of the product.

	• Describe any of the features of the product or service that give it an "unfair" advantage over the competition. Describe any patents, trade secrets, or other proprietary features of the product or service. • Discuss any opportunities for the expansion of the product line or the development of related products or services. (Emphasize opportunities and explain how the company will take advantage of them.]
[Product 2]	
[Product 3] . . .	
Contact for More Information:	

[Footer to be included at the end of the Executive Summary:]

This Executive Summary may contain "forward-looking statements" within the meaning of the Private Securities Litigation Reform Act of 1995. These statements can be identified by introductory words such as "expects," "plans," "intends," "believes," "will," "estimates," "forecasts," "projects," or words of similar meaning, and by the fact that they do not relate strictly to historical or current facts. Forward-looking statements frequently are used in discussing potential product applications, potential collaborations, product development activities, clinical studies, regulatory submissions and approvals, and similar operating matters. Many factors may cause actual results to differ from forward-looking statements, including inaccurate assumptions and a broad variety of risks and uncertainties, some of which are known and others of which are not. No forward-looking statement is a guarantee of future results or events, and one should avoid placing undue reliance on such statements. The author claims the protection of the safe harbor for forward-looking statements that is contained in the Private Securities Litigation Reform Act.

Form 3 B: Business Plan Outline for Retail Business

CONTENTS
[RETAIL BUSINESS]

I. STATEMENT OF PURPOSE

II. SUMMARY

III. THE BUSINESS

    A. Description of the business

        1. Target market/demographic

        2. Ambiance/atmosphere

        3. Form of business entity

        4. When founded and other history

        5. Days and hours of operation

    B. Products and services to be offered

    C. Marketing information

        1. Customers/general demographics

        2. Product benefits

        3. Sales and distribution

        4. Positioning, publicity, and promotion

        5. Pricing

        6. Goals

        7. Marketing budget

        8. Marketing strategy

    D. Location of business

        1. Description of facilities

        2. Address(es)

        3. Demographics by location

    E. Competition

    F. Management

        1. Biographical information

        2. Ownership interest in the business

3. Responsibilities

4. Compensation

G. Other Personnel

H. Description of funding needs, use of proceeds, and expected return on investment

IV. FINANCIAL DATA

A. Sources and applications of funding

B. Capital equipment list

C. Balance sheet

D. Break-even analysis

E. Income projections

1. Three-year summary

2. Detail by month, first year

3. Detail by quarter, second and third years

4. Notes of explanation

F. Cash flow projections

1. Detail by month, first year

2. Detail by quarter, second and third years

3. Notes of explanation

V. SUPPORTING DOCUMENTS

Form 3 C: Business Plan Outline for Technology Business

CONTENTS
[TECHNOLOGY BUSINESS]

I. EXECUTIVE SUMMARY

II. BUSINESS DESCRIPTION

    A. The company

    B. The technology

    C. Benefits to users

    D. Benefits to customers

    E. Benefits to suppliers

    F. Company vision

III. MANAGEMENT TEAM

    A. Officer biographical information

    B. Director biographical information

    C. Advisory board biographical information

IV. COMPETITIVE ANALYSIS

    A. Identification and description of competitors

    B. Comparison of company technology to existing state of the art

V. MARKETING STRATEGY

    A. Commercialization strategy

    B. Additional marketing and business opportunities for expansion

VI. PRODUCT DESIGN AND DEVELOPMENT

    A. Introduction

    B. Technology compatibility & security

VII. FINANCIAL INFORMATION AND ANALYSIS

    A. Balance sheet

    B. Profit and loss report

    C. Pro forma financial statements

VIII. TABLE OF ATTACHMENTS

    A. Organizational documents

    B. Market statistics

    C. Patent registrations and patents pending

    D. Results of beta testing

    E. Letters of intent from prospective customers

    F. Financial plan detail

    G. Regional suppliers

    H. Software architecture

CHAPTER 4

Contracts for Small Businesses

4.1 How Can You Help Your Client Make Good Contracts?

First you have to convince clients that it's important to have certain agreements committed to writing. You may be shocked to learn how many clients fail to have written agreements for some of their most critical relationships (e.g., with key customers and suppliers). Next, take inventory of your client's existing contracts (or contract categories), the types of contracts your client will need or should have in place for the type of business being undertaken, and note any inconsistencies in the company's basic contractual terms—or, as clients are so fond of referring to it, the "boilerplate." When clients refer to certain portions of their contracts as boilerplate, they often mean those portions of the agreement they haven't given much thought to, having simply accepted whatever provisions were in the form agreement they started with. Then spend some time with your client to outline the areas where their written agreements are inconsistent, disadvantageous, or missing; and help them come up with their own set of standard terms and conditions—custom boilerplate.

One area in which your client's custom boilerplate should reflect its carefully considered preferences is dispute resolution. Of course, any party entering into a written agreement hopes, even expects, the agreement will not end up in controversy. But, after about five minutes in a law school contracts class, or a few hard knocks in the world of business, one quickly becomes convinced that disputes will arise. And, unfortunately, it doesn't matter if your client is in the right—if it can't afford to prove it is right.

Spend some time discussing dispute resolution with your clients, helping them come up with their own ideal dispute resolution process, whether it be resorting to the courts or otherwise. Then help them make sure they include the same provisions for dispute resolution in each of their contracts. Of course, there may be instances where it makes sense to vary from the client's "standard" provisions, and sometimes another party won't agree to your client's provisions; but all too often, companies simply fail to spend any time considering dispute resolutions and other boilerplate provisions that could ultimately have a significant impact on their chances for success. To the greatest extent possible, alternative dispute resolution provisions for each client should be consistent, at least within categories of contracts (e.g., employment agreements) if not in all contracts entered into. Such provisions should be the result of your client's careful consideration, with good counsel, taking into account its preferences, the type of contract, and other unique circumstances.

If your client prefers arbitration as its ultimate method of dispute resolution, it should consider an exception to allow for court issuance of injunctions against a breach or threatened breach of confidentiality provisions or unauthorized use of intellectual property and give an arbitrator specific authority to issue such an injunction. However, it often takes longer to get an arbitrator in place to make such a decision than it does to get into court for one.

The American Arbitration Association provides rules and procedures for a variety of circumstances, as well as samples and forms for use in contracts (http://www.adr.org). The more specific your client's agreements are about how arbitration should be managed and decided, the better. For agreements involving parties in more than one country, the International Chamber of Commerce provides international dispute resolution services (and has a helpful website at www.iccwbo.org). Get a copy of the rules of the forum being invoked for arbitration under the agreement, and help your client determine whether it wishes to provide additional guidelines or override any of the rules in its agreement. This may be painful the first time through; but once your client has established its preferred alternative dispute resolutions procedures, it can use them again and again with confidence.

Another, less dramatic example of boilerplate that is often inconsistent in client contracts is the notice provision. Notice provisions should be consistent to allow the client to develop standard contract procedures that help avoid rather than create problems. Your client should determine the method and timing it desires for giving and receiving notice under its contracts and make sure that its boilerplate provision is included in every one of its contracts.

In the numerous sample agreements included in this book, there are a variety of provisions for alternative dispute resolution and notice, as well as a laundry list of others you can use to help your client compile a most excellent set of boilerplate provisions for its contracts. See Section 4.4, What Should Be in Your Client's Boilerplate?

4.2 When Is It Important for a Small Business to Have a Written Agreement?

Start with the assumption that it's better to have something in writing. Clients won't always sit still long enough to put together, or pay the cost of putting together, an agreement documented to the level of perfection we lawyers would like. One advantage of establishing a client's standard terms and conditions is that it can streamline the drafting of its contracts in the future. The specific terms of an agreement are much more likely to be lost to one or more of the three "M's", if they are not in writing.

1. Avoid the Three "M's"!

Any agreement that is not committed to writing is vulnerable to the three "M's":

- **Memory.** Memories are faulty. Two honest, well-meaning people can remember something two very different ways and be adamant that they are correct.
- **Misinterpretation.** Reducing an agreement to writing will often reveal that the parties did not accurately understand each other in prior discussions and will help them have a true meeting of the minds.
- **Mood.** It's not fair or right, but people often change their minds. In so doing, they may attempt to unilaterally change the terms of an agreement.

2. Owners' Agreements.

Owners' agreements—Shareholder Agreements, LLC Agreements, Joint Venture Agreements, and so forth—although not required, are extremely important to have in writing. In a closely held business, shareholder disputes are often the beginning of the end. Privately owned corporations with a small number of shareholders should seriously consider adopting a shareholder agreement to provide buy-sell, decision-making, deadlock, and other dispute resolution (and avoidance) procedures in writing before a problem arises and they suddenly find they can't agree on anything. Unfortunately, when agreements are not reduced to writing, they often fall prey to faulty memories, misinterpretation, and mood. This is why oral agreements are so difficult to enforce and why so many types of agreements are required to be in writing. For a detailed discussion of owner agreements, please see Chapter 9.

3. Document All Other Major Relationships.

All of the relationships critical to your client's success should be documented (key suppliers, manufacturers, distributors, etc.).

4. Agreements Protecting Intellectual Property.

Agreements with independent contractors, employees, and anyone else your client deals with who will have access to, or help develop, the company's confidential and proprietary information should be subject to a written agreement protecting the company's rights in such information.

5. Standard Terms and Conditions of Sale.

Have your client take the opportunity to establish standard terms and conditions of sale and include them in estimates, purchase orders, supply agreements, and so on.

6. Website Terms of Use.

Terms of use on a client's website are the equivalent of an agreement with each and every visitor to its site. The terms should include all of the provisions one might include in a written agreement between two parties. In other words, it should include the deal terms as well as the company's own boilerplate, formulated after carefully considering the potential implications of each term and the best alternative in light of the company's circumstances. Make sure your clients are mindful of current privacy requirements in determining what kinds of information they collect through their website and how they use it. The Federal Trade Commission website at http://ftc.gov/ is a good resource for helping your clients determine best practices.

4.3 What If Your Client Has Contracts That Don't Work?

If your client has contracts that don't work, it should prepare form agreements with the assistance of counsel, using the process discussed above, and implement the new forms of agreement systematically, until all dysfunctional agreements have expired or been amended or superseded. Contracts with automatic renewal provisions should be terminated and the new form of agreement should be offered in place of renewal of the old form of agreement. Agreements without imminent renewals may be amended or superseded by agreement, if the other party is willing. However, convincing the other party to amend an agreement may be difficult if the new agreement does not benefit both parties.

4.4 What Should Be in Your Client's Boilerplate?

The following is a partial list of the types of provisions your client may want to include in its standard agreements:

1. Parties;
2. Subject of the agreement;
3. Definitions (with placement in a separate section or scattered throughout with consistent formatting to call attention to them);
4. Term;
5. Compensation or consideration;
6. Relationship of the parties (e.g., independent contractor, employer, partner, shareholder, etc.);

7. Termination; effect of termination;
8. Confidentiality;
9. Intellectual property;
10. Title and risk of loss;
11. Limitations on liability;
12. Limitations on warranty;
13. Indemnification;
14. Alternative dispute resolution;
15. Choice of law and jurisdiction;
16. Survival of certain provisions;
17. Breach, right to cure;
18. Lawyer's fees;
19. Notices;
20. Entire agreement; amendment;
21. Severability;
22. Waiver;
23. Force majeure;
24. Further assurances;
25. Authority; and
26. Counterparts.

4.5 Sample Documents and Checklists.

This section includes the following forms:

- Discussion Points for a Joint Venture or Strategic Partnership (Form 4 A)
- Mediation Followed by Arbitration (Form 4 B)
- AAA Arbitration with Ceiling for Specific Type of Dispute (Form 4 C)
- Arbitration of a Specific Issue Only (Form 4 D)
- International Arbitration (Form 4 E)
- Exception to Arbitration (Form 4 F)
- Jury Trial Waiver with Judicial Reference Alternative (Form 4 G)
- Choice of Law and Jurisdiction Based on Defendant (Form 4 H)
- Terms and Conditions of Sale (Form 4 I)
- Website Terms of Use (Form 4 J)

Form 4 A: Discussion Points for a Joint Venture or Strategic Partnership

Note: In any new relationship, it is important to explore and define the relative benefits and obligations of the parties at the outset and put them in writing. It is much easier to get this done at the outset, while energy and attention are on the nature of the new relationship and before there is an opportunity for misunderstandings to arise.

1. Identification of parties to the agreement, including names, addresses, and other information as appropriate, such as state of incorporation and authorization to conduct business in California;

2. Designation of relationship being created, e.g. partnership, or other relationship or form of organization;

3. Nature of the enterprise to be undertaken, its scope, extent and duration;

4. Name under which venture is to be carried out;

5. Contributions of each party, whether in money, property, time and skill, or other;

6. Time at which each contribution must be made and effect of failure of any party to make its contribution at the required time and in the required amount;

7. Requirements if any for additional or ongoing contributions and the effect of the failure of a party to make such contributions;

8. Right of each party to manage and control the enterprise;

9. Duties of each party other than the obligation to make contributions;

10. Designation of one party as manager, including specific duties, or the designation of a management committee;

11. Division of profits, including definition of profits, and obligations that must be satisfied before division and distribution of profits;

12. Apportionment of losses, liability, and indemnification;

13. Designation of who shall hold legal title to the joint venture property;

14. Surety bonds for party in control of the assets;

15. Percentage interest or claim of each party in property purchased or created with joint venture funds, profits, or operations;

16. Rights of or restrictions on parties to assign or transfer interest in the joint venture including, where appropriate, rights of first refusal;

17. Insurance required to protect the parties and the joint venture property (public liability, Internet, personal injury, property damage, fire, theft, workers' compensation for any employees, etc.);

18. Effect of death, insolvency, or bankruptcy of a party;

19. Records and accounting;

20. Arbitration or other dispute resolution provisions for matters not specifically fixed by the contract terms or for disputes arising under or relating to the contract;

21. Termination of or withdrawal of a party from the joint venture;

22. Rights and duties of parties on termination and winding up, including any compensation to be paid to the party charged with the duty to wind up and distribute assets;

23. Any representations and warranties to be given by each party to the other;

24. Effective date of agreement; and

25. Anything else that comes to mind in the process.

Form 4 B: Mediation Followed by Arbitration

Except as otherwise stated herein, on the written notice of either party requesting application of this Section *, all claims and disputes arising out of or relating to this Agreement shall be resolved according to the following procedure:

<u>Mediation</u>. First, all such disputes shall be mediated by a mediator to be selected by mutual agreement of the parties. In the event the parties cannot agree on a mediator within fifteen (15) days of the receipt by either of written notice of the other requesting application of this Section *, then each party shall designate a party within fifteen (15) days thereof by written notice to the other. Within fifteen (15) days thereof, the two parties selected then shall mutually designate a mediator for mediation of the dispute. The mediation shall continue from time to time until the dispute is resolved or the mediator has made a determination in writing that the dispute cannot be resolved through mediation and arbitration is recommended, provided that mediation may be terminated by either party upon fifteen (15) days notice given at any time on or after the sixty-first (61st) day after notice requesting application of this Section *. The mediator shall recommend one or more arbitrators to the parties.

<u>Arbitration</u>. Second, upon (i) a written determination by the mediator that arbitration is recommended, and (ii) written request within ten (10) days thereafter by either party, the dispute shall be submitted to arbitration under the Commercial Arbitration Rules of the American Arbitration Association (the "AAA"), before an arbitrator to be selected by the parties. If the parties cannot agree on an arbitrator within ten (10) days of one party's notice to the other party invoking the right to arbitrate, then the AAA shall appoint an arbitrator who has significant experience in arbitrating matters similar to the subject matter disputed under this Agreement. The arbitration shall commence not less than ten (10) nor more than thirty (30) days after the arbitrator has been designated. The arbitration shall be concluded as soon as reasonably possible, and the arbitrator shall make a written determination of the dispute within fifteen (15) days of the completion of the arbitration hearing. The prevailing party in any such arbitration shall be awarded reasonable attorneys' fees, expert and non-expert witness costs and expenses and other costs and expenses incurred in connection with such arbitration, unless the arbitrator, for good cause, determines otherwise. Costs and fees of the arbitrator shall be borne by the non-prevailing party, unless the arbitrator determines otherwise. The arbitrator's adjudication shall be final and fully binding upon the parties and enforceable in any court having jurisdiction thereof.

Form 4 C: AAA Arbitration with Ceiling for Specific Type of Dispute

Any disputes arising under this Agreement relating to payment of ****'s compensation or authorized costs under this Agreement shall be settled by binding arbitration between the parties hereto in accordance with the commercial arbitration rules of the American Arbitration Association. The arbitrator shall not be empowered to award as compensation more than twenty percent (20%) of the revenue received by **** with respect to this Agreement nor more than twenty thousand dollars ($20,000) for reimbursable expenses in any calendar year.

Form 4 D: Arbitration of a Specific Issue Only

LLC Agreement—Arbitration of Deadlock. If a member vote is required on any matter arising under this Agreement and there are neither sufficient votes to approve nor disapprove the matter, any member may require that the matter be submitted to arbitration in accordance with the rules of the American Arbitration Association, or such other arbitration service or arbitrator as the members may agree. The arbitration shall be held in the city in which the company's principal executive office is then situated. Each member desiring to participate in such arbitration shall be under a duty to ensure that the arbitration process proceeds expeditiously. The finding or ruling resulting from the arbitration shall be binding upon the company and each of its members.

Form 4 E: International Arbitration

Scope and Rules of Arbitration; Selection of Arbitrator. Any controversy or claim arising out of or relating to this Agreement, or to any purported breach hereof, shall be settled by arbitration in accordance with the Rules of Conciliation and Arbitration of the International Chamber of Commerce by a single arbitrator appointed in accordance with those rules. Such arbitration shall be held in San Francisco, California and shall be in English; the arbitrator selected shall, to the extent possible, be experienced in the electronics and communications fields.

Binding Award. The parties shall abide by any award rendered in such arbitration proceedings. Any such award may be entered as the basis for judgment in any court having jurisdiction over the party or the property of the party against which such award is rendered.

No Default. No party shall be considered in default under this Agreement while arbitration proceedings are pending. In case of any dispute as to the amount of payment owing to Licensor, the amount of such payment not in dispute, if any, shall be promptly paid.

Costs. Unless otherwise awarded, the costs of arbitration shall be shared equally by the parties.

Form 4 F: Exception to Arbitration

<u>Exception</u>. Notwithstanding the foregoing provisions, disputes concerning proprietary rights in the Licensed Technology, including, but not limited to, patent, trade secret, copyright and trademark rights of Licensor or Licensee, shall not be subject to arbitration, and to the extent provided by law, either party shall have the right by injunction or otherwise to enforce its rights in the Licensed Technology, the Product, or any other proprietary information to prohibit the other party or any other person or entity from using any part of the Licensed Technology, the Product, or any other proprietary information in violation of this Agreement.

Form 4 G: Jury Trial Waiver
with Judicial Reference Alternative

The parties hereby irrevocably and knowingly waive to the fullest extent permitted by law any right to a trial by jury in any action or proceeding arising out of this Agreement. The parties agree that any such action or proceeding shall be tried before a court and not a jury. In the event the parties' waiver of a trial by jury is deemed invalid, the parties hereby agree that any action or claim arising out of any dispute in connection with this Agreement, any rights, remedies, obligations, or duties hereunder, or the performance or enforcement hereof or thereof shall be determined by judicial reference.

Form 4 H: Choice of Law
and Jurisdiction Based on Defendant

Note: Agreeing to submit all disputes to the other party's jurisdiction may encourage the other party to initiate litigation against your client, instead of working to resolve any dispute without resorting to the courts, and put your client at a disadvantage regardless of who initiated the litigation. One way to approach the issue of jurisdiction and venue that does not encourage litigation is to include language along the lines of the following sample provision in contracts where your client is unable to specify its own state and local venue for jurisdiction and venue. This choice of law, jurisdiction, and venue provision is designed to discourage litigation.

In the event that any suit or action is instituted to enforce any provision in this Letter Agreement, this Letter Agreement shall be governed by and construed under the laws of the State of residence of the party not initiating such suit or action without giving effect to the principles of conflicts of laws, and the parties hereby irrevocably and unconditionally submit to the jurisdiction of the State and federal courts for or in the city or county of the principal office of the party not initiating the suit or action and agree that any legal action or proceeding relating to this Letter Agreement may be brought in such courts. The parties hereby waive to the fullest extent permitted by law in connection with any such action or proceeding any objections they may now or hereafter have to the venue of any such action or proceeding in any such court or that such action or proceeding was brought in an inconvenient court and agrees not to plead or claim the same.

Form 4 I: Terms and Conditions of Sale

****, INC.

STANDARD TERMS AND CONDITIONS OF SALE

[TO BE PRINTED ON FRONT OF THE QUOTATION]

THESE TERMS AND CONDITIONS OF SALE (THIS "AGREEMENT") APPLY TO ALL QUOTATIONS, PURCHASE ORDERS, ACKNOWLEDGMENTS AND OFFERS FOR PRODUCTS ISSUED OR RECEIVED BY ****, INC. (the "COMPANY") TO OR FROM CUSTOMER ("CUSTOMER"). COMPANY'S ACCEPTANCE OF ANY CUSTOMER PURCHASE ORDER IS EXPRESSLY CONDITIONED ON CUSTOMER'S ASSENT TO THIS AGREEMENT. NO TERMS OR CONDITIONS SET FORTH IN CUSTOMER'S PURCHASE ORDER, TO WHICH NOTICE OF OBJECTION IS HEREBY GIVEN, OR IN ANY FUTURE CORRESPONDENCE BETWEEN CUSTOMER AND COMPANY, SHALL ALTER OR SUPPLEMENT THIS AGREEMENT UNLESS BOTH PARTIES HAVE AGREED IN WRITING TO MODIFY THIS AGREEMENT. NEITHER COMPANY'S COMMENCEMENT OF PERFORMANCE NOR DELIVERY OF ANY PRODUCTS SHALL BE DEEMED OR CONSTRUED AS ACCEPTANCE OF CUSTOMER'S ADDITIONAL OR DIFFERENT TERMS AND CONDITIONS. COMPANY RESERVES THE RIGHT TO REJECT ANY ORDER OR TO CANCEL ANY ORDER PREVIOUSLY ACCEPTED IF COMPANY DETERMINES THAT CUSTOMER IS IN BREACH OF ANY TERM OR CONDITION HEREIN. NOTWITHSTANDING THE FOREGOING, IN THE EVENT CUSTOMER AND COMPANY HAVE A WRITTEN SUPPLY AGREEMENT, THE TERMS OF THE SUPPLY AGREEMENT SHALL GOVERN.

[TO BE PRINTED ON THE BACK OF THE SALES QUOTATION FORM]

1. PRICES. All quotations shall constitute offers subject to this Agreement. Unless otherwise stated in writing by Company, all prices quoted: (i) expire thirty (30) days after the date they are provided to Customer; and (ii) are exclusive of transportation, insurance, federal, state, local, excise, value-added, use, sales, property (ad valorem) and similar taxes or duties now in force or hereafter in effect. In addition to the prices quoted or invoiced, Customer agrees to pay all taxes, fees, or charges of any nature whatsoever imposed by any governmental authority on, or measured by, the transaction between Customer and Company. In the event that Company is required to collect such taxes, fees, or charges, such amounts will appear as separate items on Company's invoice and will be paid by Customer.

2. TERMS OF PAYMENT. Unless otherwise set forth on the face hereof, all invoices shall be paid in full in U.S. dollars within thirty (30) days of the invoice date. Customer shall pay a late fee of 1.5% per month. Company reserves the right at any time and for any reason to require payment in advance or COD, or to otherwise modify, suspend, or terminate any credit terms previously extended to Customer. If Company believes in good faith that Customer's ability to make any payment required hereunder is or may be impaired, Company may cancel this Agreement (or any remaining balance thereof), and Customer shall remain liable to pay for any products previously shipped. When partial shipments are made, payments shall become due in

87

accordance with the designated terms upon submission of an invoice covering any such partial shipment.

3.   DELIVERY AND TITLE. Title to the products and risk of loss or damage to the products shall pass to Customer at the products' manufacturing location, immediately upon delivery to a suitable carrier, subject to Company's security interest in such products as described below. Notwithstanding title to the products passing to Customer, title shall not pass to Customer as to any Company intellectual property rights or Company software.

4.   SHIPMENTS. In the absence of specific shipping instructions, Company shall select a carrier who shall be deemed to act as Customer's agent. Company shall be under no obligation to ship via any carrier selected by Customer if such carrier does not comply with applicable laws. Transportation charges will be collected on delivery or, if prepaid, will be subsequently invoiced to Customer. Unless otherwise indicated, Customer is obligated to obtain insurance against damage to products being shipped, and all products will be shipped in standard commercial packaging. When special or export packaging is requested or, in the opinion of Company, required under the circumstances, the cost of the same, if not set forth on the invoice, will be separately invoiced. All shipping dates are approximate and Company may change the delivery date without penalty provided Company provides Customer with reasonable notice of such change. Company shall not be responsible for any failure to perform or delay in performing under this Agreement which is directly or indirectly due to circumstances beyond its reasonable control, including, without limitation, earthquakes, governmental regulation, fire, flood, labor difficulties, civil disorder, and acts of God.

5.   ACCEPTANCE. Customer shall accept or reject products within thirty (30) days of receipt of each shipment. Failure to notify Company in writing of nonconforming products within such period shall be deemed an unqualified acceptance.

6.   DEFAULT, CANCELLATION, AND RESCHEDULING. In the event of Customer's default in payment for the products purchased hereunder, Customer shall be responsible for all reasonable costs and expenses incurred by Company in collection of any sums owing by Customer (including reasonable lawyers' fees), and Company may decline to make further shipments to Customer without in any way affecting its rights under this Agreement. If, despite any such breach by Customer, Company elects to continue to make shipments, such shipments shall not constitute a waiver of any breach by Customer or in any way affect Company's legal remedies arising from such breach. Company may ship products in quantities that vary by up to five percent (5%) of the quantity ordered by Customer and such variance shall be deemed agreed to and accepted by Customer.

7.   SECURITY INTEREST. Company hereby reserves for itself a purchase money security interest in all products sold hereunder and the proceeds thereof, in the amount of the purchase price. In the event of default by Customer in any of its obligations to Company, Company will have the right to repossess the products sold hereunder without liability to Customer. Such security interest will be satisfied by payment in full. A copy of the invoice may be filed with appropriate authorities at any time as a financing statement and/or chattel mortgage to perfect Company's security interest. Upon request, Customer will execute such financing statements and other instruments as Company may request to perfect Company's security interest herein.

8. LIMITED WARRANTY. (a) Company warrants for a period of one (1) year from the date of delivery (the "Warranty Period") that products (except any excluded software) purchased and sold hereunder will substantially conform to Company's published specifications. Repaired or replacement products provided under warranty are warranted for a period of one (1) year from the date of delivery. Notwithstanding the foregoing, Company products are not designed, and no warranty is made with respect to products used in devices intended for use in applications where failure to perform when properly used can reasonably be expected to result in significant injury (including, without limitation, military or space applications, navigation, aviation, nuclear equipment, fire fighting or rescue equipment, or for surgical implant or to support or sustain life). Customer hereby represents and warrants to Company that it will not use or sell any products for any of the foregoing purposes and Customer agrees to indemnify, defend, and hold Company harmless from all claims, damages and liabilities arising out of any such uses. This limited warranty is contingent upon proper use of the products in the applications for which they were intended and does not apply to any products that are subjected to unusual physical or electrical stress, misuse, neglect, accident or which have been altered or soldered such that they are not capable of being tested under normal test conditions, improper testing or storage, unauthorized repair, or problems that arise from any use of Company products with other products not approved by Company. This limited warranty does not include expendable components. This limited warranty is non-transferable and shall extend only to Customer, and not to any third parties (including, without limitation, Customer's suppliers, customers, or any end users).

(b) In the event of a breach of this limited warranty, Customer shall notify Company in writing by describing the nature of the non-conformity, and return such products to Company in accordance with Company's then-current returned material authorization ("RMA") policies, within the Warranty Period. Customer shall ship such products back to Company at Customer's expense. Company shall, at its option, promptly repair or replace non-conforming products, or issue a credit for the purchase price of the non-conforming products, and shall pay the costs of any such repair or replacement, including transportation costs incurred in returning repaired or replaced products to Customer unless (i) the products are not defective, in which case Customer shall pay Company reasonable costs of inspection and all transportation charges, or (ii) the products are defective due to Customer's or any third party's improper installation, repair, damage, misuse, abuse, or failure to use replacement parts and materials equivalent to Company's parts and materials, in which case Customer shall pay all costs of repair or replacement and transportation. The remedy stated in this Section 8 shall be Customer's sole remedy in case of any breach of limited warranty by Company.

(c) Customer must mark each package it returns to Company under this Section 8 with a RMA number, which Company shall furnish to Customer on request. Customer shall include with any returned products: (i) the RMA number; and (ii) a written statement specifying the reasons why Customer rejected those products.

(d) EXCEPT AS EXPRESSLY STATED IN THIS AGREEMENT, COMPANY MAKES NO WARRANTIES. ALL PRODUCTS ARE PROVIDED AS IS, AS AVAILABLE AND WITH ALL FAULTS, AND COMPANY EXPRESSLY DISCLAIMS ALL OTHER WARRANTIES, EXPRESS, STATUTORY, OR IMPLIED, INCLUDING WITHOUT LIMITATION THE IMPLIED WARRANTIES OF NON-INFRINGEMENT, MERCHANTABILITY,

FITNESS FOR A PARTICULAR PURPOSE, OR ARISING OUT OF A COURSE OF DEALING, TO THE MAXIMUM EXTENT PERMITTED BY LAW.

9.   INDEMNITY. (a) CUSTOMER INDEMNITY. Customer shall indemnify, defend and hold Company harmless from and against any and all claims brought by any third party against Company arising out of or related to Customer's use or distribution of the products purchased hereunder, including (i) any claim arising out of or related to any warranty made by or on behalf of Customer to its customers that expands any warranties provided herein or fails to limit any liability as provided herein or (ii) any breach of this Agreement by Customer; provided, Company: (a) gives prompt written notice to Customer of the institution of the suit or proceedings; and (b) permits Customer through its counsel to defend the same and gives Customer all needed information, assistance and authority to enable Customer to do so.

(b) COMPANY INDEMNITY. Subject to the limitations herein, Company shall defend any suit or proceeding brought against Customer if it is based on a claim that any product furnished hereunder constitutes an infringement of any third party copyright, trade secret or United States patent issued as of the date hereof, provided Company is promptly notified in writing by Customer and is given full and complete authority, information and assistance (at Company's expense) for defense of same. Company shall pay damages and costs therein finally awarded against Customer but shall not be responsible for any compromise or settlement made without its written consent. In providing such defense, or in the event that such product is held to infringe or the use of such product is enjoined, Company shall have the right in its sole discretion to obtain the right to continue using such product, modify such product so that it becomes noninfringing, or require the return of such product and refund to Customer the purchase price paid by Customer to Company for such product. Company's indemnity does not extend to claims of infringement arising from Company's compliance with Customer's design, specifications or instructions or the modification of the product by parties other than Company, or arising from the use of the product in combination with other products or in connection with a manufacturing or other process not supplied by Company. THE FOREGOING REMEDY IS EXCLUSIVE AND CONSTITUTES COMPANY'S SOLE OBLIGATION FOR ANY CLAIMS OF INTELLECTUAL PROPERTY INFRINGEMENT.

10. LIMITATION OF LIABILITY. IN NO EVENT SHALL COMPANY BE LIABLE TO CUSTOMER OR ANY THIRD PARTY FOR COSTS OF PROCUREMENT OF SUBSTITUTE GOODS, OR FOR ANY LOSS OF PROFITS OR LOSS OF USE, INCLUDING LOSS OR DAMAGE TO ANY NETWORKS, SYSTEMS, DATA OR FILES, COMPUTER FAILURE OR MALFUNCTION, OR FOR ANY INCIDENTAL, CONSEQUENTIAL, SPECIAL, PUNITIVE, EXEMPLARY, INDIRECT OR OTHER DAMAGES HOWEVER CAUSED AND ON ANY THEORY OF LIABILITY, ARISING OUT OF THIS AGREEMENT, WHETHER OR NOT COMPANY HAS BEEN ADVISED OF THE POSSIBILITY OF SUCH LOSS OR DAMAGE. THIS EXCLUSION ALSO INCLUDES ANY LIABILITY THAT MAY ARISE OUT OF THIRD PARTY CLAIMS AGAINST CUSTOMER. EXCEPT AS SET FORTH IN SECTION 9(b), COMPANY ASSUMES NO OBLIGATIONS OR LIABILITY OF ANY KIND WITH RESPECT TO INFRINGEMENTS OR ALLEGED INFRINGEMENTS OF UNITED STATES OR FOREIGN PATENTS, COPYRIGHTS, TRADEMARKS, OR OTHER PROPRIETARY RIGHTS ARISING OUT OF CUSTOMER'S PURCHASE, USE, OR POSSESSION OF COMPANY'S PRODUCTS AND CUSTOMER ASSUMES ALL SUCH RISK. IN NO EVENT SHALL COMPANY'S LIA-

BILITY ARISING OUT OF THIS AGREEMENT EXCEED THE PURCHASE PRICE OF THE PRODUCTS PAID BY CUSTOMER TO COMPANY AND SUBJECT TO THIS AGREEMENT. THE ESSENTIAL PURPOSE OF THIS PROVISION IS TO LIMIT THE POTENTIAL LIABILITY OF COMPANY ARISING OUT OF THIS AGREEMENT AND/OR THE SALE OF PRODUCTS TO CUSTOMER, AND THE PARTIES EXPRESSLY AGREE WITH THE RESULTING ALLOCATION OF RISK.

11. SUBSTITUTIONS AND MODIFICATIONS. Company reserves the right to (i) make substitutions and modifications in the specifications of products sold by Company, provided that such substitutions or modifications do not materially affect overall product performance, and (ii) discontinue or otherwise end-of-life any product sold hereunder.

12. PROPRIETARY RIGHTS. Customer acknowledges that the products sold by Company hereunder contain and embody trade secrets belonging to Company and Customer shall not reverse engineer any products purchased hereunder. In addition to the foregoing, Company owns all rights, title and interest in and to all other intellectual property rights, including patent and copyrights, embodied by or reflected in the products. A license solely for the use of the software contained in the product is granted hereunder and Company retains for itself all proprietary rights in and to all designs, engineering details, and other data pertaining to the products.

13. NOTICES. Any notice contemplated by or made pursuant to this Agreement shall be in writing and shall be deemed delivered on the date of delivery if delivered personally, or three (3) days after mailing if placed in the U.S. mail, postage prepaid, registered or certified mail, return receipt requested, addressed to Customer or Company (as the case may be) at the designated address, or such other address as shall be designated by at least ten (10) days prior written notice. A notice given by any means other than as specified herein will be deemed duly given when actually received by the addressee.

14. IMPORT AND EXPORT REQUIREMENTS. Customer shall, at its own expense, pay all import and export licenses and permits, pay all value-added and other VATs, customs charges and duty fees, and take all other actions required to accomplish the export and import of the products purchased by Customer. Customer understands that Company may be subject to regulation by agencies of the U.S. government, including the U.S. Department of Commerce, which prohibits export or diversion of certain technical products to certain countries. Customer warrants that it will comply in all respects with the export and re-export restrictions set forth in the export license for every product shipped to Customer.

15. APPLICABLE LAW, JURY TRIAL WAIVER, JURISDICTION, AND LIMITATION ON ACTIONS. This Agreement shall be governed by and construed under the laws of the State of _____, without regard to choice of law provisions, as applied to agreements among _____ residents entered into and to be performed entirely within _____. The United Nations Convention on the International Sale of Goods shall not apply to this Agreement or to any of the transactions contemplated hereby. THE PARTIES HEREBY IRREVOCABLY AND KNOWINGLY WAIVE TO THE FULLEST EXTENT PERMITTED BY LAW ANY RIGHT TO A TRIAL BY JURY IN ANY ACTION OR PROCEEDING ARISING OUT OF THIS AGREEMENT. The parties agree that any such action or proceeding shall be tried before a court and not a jury. The parties hereby irrevocably and unconditionally submit to the jurisdiction of the Courts of the State of _____ and of the United States of America for the

_____ District of _____ and agree that any legal action or proceeding relating to this Agreement may be brought in such courts. In the event the parties' waiver of a trial by jury is deemed invalid, the parties hereby agree that any action or claim arising out of any dispute in connection with this Agreement, any rights, remedies, obligations, or duties hereunder, or the performance or enforcement hereof or thereof shall be determined by judicial reference. Customer shall not bring any action relating to any dispute Customer may have after one (1) year of the accrual of such dispute.

16. ATTORNEYS FEES. In the event litigation shall be instituted to enforce any provision of this Agreement, the prevailing party in such litigation shall be entitled to recover reasonable attorneys' fees and expenses incurred in such litigation, including on appeal, in addition to any other recovery to which such party may be legally entitled.

17. ASSIGNMENT. This Agreement shall bind and inure to the benefit of Company's successors and assigns, including, without limitation, any entity into which Company shall merge or consolidate. Customer may not assign, directly or indirectly, by operation of law or otherwise, any of Customer's rights or obligations under this Agreement without Company's prior written consent. Any attempted assignment, delegation, or transfer by Customer without such consent of Company shall be void.

18. U.S. GOVERNMENT CONTRACTS. If the products to be sold hereunder are to be used in the performance of a U.S. Government contract or sub-contract and a U.S. Government contract number appears on Customer's purchase order, those clauses of the applicable U.S. Government procurement regulation, which are mandated by Federal Statute to be included in U.S. Government subcontracts, shall be incorporated herein by reference.

19. CONFIDENTIALITY. Customer acknowledges that all technical or business and other documentation, information and materials delivered to or learned by Customer hereunder shall be considered Company's confidential information (the "Confidential Information"). Customer hereby agrees: (i) to hold and maintain in strict confidence all Confidential Information of Company; and (ii) not to use any Confidential Information of Company except as permitted hereunder. Customer will use at least the same degree of care to protect the Company's Confidential Information as it uses to protect its own confidential information of like importance, and in no event shall such degree of care be less than reasonable care. Customer agrees that it will only provide Confidential Information to those employees who have a need to know for the purposes hereunder. Customer agrees that it shall not disclose the Company Confidential Information to any third party, including third party contractors, without written authorization from Company.

20. ERRORS AND VALIDITY OF AGREEMENT. Stenographic and clerical errors in sales made under this Agreement are subject to correction. In the event any provision of this Agreement is held to be invalid or unenforceable, then such provision shall be deemed automatically adjusted to the minimum extent necessary to conform to the requirements for validity as declared at such time and, as so adjusted, shall be deemed a provision of this Agreement as though originally included herein. In the event that the provision invalidated is of such a nature that it cannot be so adjusted, the provision shall be deemed deleted from this Agreement as though such provision had never been included herein. In either case, the remaining provisions of this Agreement will remain in full force and effect.

21. ENTIRE AGREEMENT. The terms and conditions set forth herein constitute the entire Agreement between Customer and Company and supersede any other agreements or offers, including any purchase order of Customer, prior or contemporaneous oral or written understandings, or communications relating to the subject matter hereof. Notwithstanding the foregoing, in the event Customer and Company have a written Supply Agreement, the terms of the Supply Agreement shall govern.

Form 4 J: Website Terms of Use

TERMS OF USE

ACCEPTANCE OF TERMS

, Inc., a _____ corporation (""), makes this website (the "Site"), including all information, documents, communications, files, text, graphics, software, and products available through the site (collectively, the "Materials") and all services operated by *** and third parties through the site (collectively, the "Services"), available for your use subject to the terms and conditions set forth in this document and any changes to this document that *** may publish from time to time (collectively, the "Terms of Use").

By accessing or using this Site in any way, including, without limitation, use of any of the Services, downloading of any Materials, or merely browsing the Site, you agree to and are bound by the Terms of Use.

*** reserves the right to change the Terms of Use and other guidelines or rules posted on the Site from time to time at its sole discretion. Your continued use of the Site, or any Materials or Services accessible through it, after such notice has been posted constitutes your acceptance of the changes. Your use of the Site will be subject to the most current version of the Terms of Use, rules and guidelines posted on the Site at the time of such use. You should periodically check these Terms of Use to view the then current terms. If you breach any of the Terms of Use, your authorization to use this Site automatically terminates, and any Materials downloaded or printed from the Site in violation of the Terms of Use must be immediately destroyed.

DEFINED TERMS

One of the Services offered through this Site is a collaboration service known as the *** Program. Information, materials, files, communications, and documents that are posted by users in conjunction with this service are referred to collectively as "Project Content." The group of persons among which the collaboration takes place is referred to herein as the "Work Group." All other user-supplied information, materials, files, communications, and documents, excluding the Project Content, are referred to collectively as "User Content." "*** Content" means all Materials provided by ***. Project Content, User Content, and *** Content may have different restrictions and conditions associated with them.

TYPES OF USERS

Please be aware that certain activities on this Site, such as the *** Program, are available only to persons invited by *** to participate in such activities.

INTELLECTUAL PROPERTY; LIMITED LICENSE TO USERS

The Materials and Services on this Site, as well as their selection and arrangement, are protected by copyright, trademark, patent, and/or other intellectual property laws, and any unauthorized use of the Materials or Services at this Site may violate such laws and these Terms of Use. Except as expressly provided herein, *** and its suppliers do not grant any express or implied rights to use the Materials and Services. You agree not to copy, republish, frame, download, transmit, modify, rent, lease, loan, sell, assign, distribute, license, sublicense, reverse engineer, or create derivative works based on the Site, its Materials, or its Services or their selection and arrangement, except as expressly authorized herein. In addition, you agree not to use any data mining, robots, or similar data gathering and extraction methods in connection with the Site.

In addition to the Materials and Services offered by ***, this Site may also make available materials, information, and services provided by third parties (collectively, the "Third Party Services"). The Third Party Services may be governed by separate license agreements that accompany such services. *** offers no guarantees and assumes no responsibility or liability of any type with respect to the Third Party Services, including any liability resulting from incompatibility between the Third Party Services and the Materials and Services offered by ***. You agree that you will not hold *** responsible or liable with respect to the Third Party Services or seek to do so.

Except as expressly indicated to the contrary elsewhere on this Site, you may view, download, and print the *** Content and User Content available on this Site subject to the following conditions:

1.   The *** Content and User Content may be used solely for personal, informational, and internal purposes.

2.   The *** Content and User Content may not be modified or altered in any way.

3.   The *** Content and User Content on the Site may not be distributed or sold, rented, leased, or licensed to others.

4. You may not remove any copyright or other proprietary notices contained in the *** Content and User Content.

5.   *** reserves the right to revoke the authorization to view, download, and print the *** Content and User Content available on this Site at any time, and any such use shall be discontinued immediately upon notice from ***.

6.   The rights granted to you constitute a license and not a transfer of title.

The rights specified above to view, download, and print the *** Content and User Content available on this Site are not applicable to the design or layout of this Site. Elements of this Site are protected by trade dress and other laws and may not be copied or imitated in whole or in part.

TRADEMARK INFORMATION

The trademarks, logos, and service marks ("Marks") displayed on this Site are the property of *** or other third parties. You are not permitted to use the Marks without the prior written consent of *** or such third party that may own the Marks.

LICENSE TO *** FOR USER CONTENT

Certain Services offered through this Site accommodate or require User Content. Depending upon the nature of the Service, by submitting User Content to this Site you grant *** one of the following types of licenses:

1.   For User Content that is the result of your creative efforts and which is intended to be displayed on the Site, you grant *** a worldwide, royalty-free, non-exclusive license to modify (for purposes of formatting, maintenance, or Site administration

only) and reproduce such User Content. You also grant *** the right to distribute and publicly display and perform such User Content for the purpose for which such User Content was submitted to the Site. This license will be in effect until such User Content is removed from the Site.

2. For User Content such as comments to *** on user forms, reports or suggestion forms, you grant *** and the users of this Site an unrestricted, worldwide, irrevocable license to use, reproduce, display, perform, modify, transmit, and distribute such User Content, and you also agree that *** is free to use any ideas, concepts, know-how, or techniques that you send us for any purpose without any compensation to you. However, we will not release your name or otherwise publicize the fact that you submitted such User Content to us unless: (a) you grant us permission to do so; (b) we first notify you that the User Content you submit to a particular part of the Site will be published or otherwise used with your name on it; (c) we have a good faith belief that we are required to do so by law and/or in response to a subpoena or court order; or (d) we believe it necessary in order to protect the rights of *** or others.

LICENSE TO *** FOR PROJECT CONTENT

For Project Content that is intended to be accessible only to members of your Work Group, you grant *** the right to copy, display, distribute, and otherwise use such Project Content in connection with operation of the *** Program. You agree that *** may access and/or disclose such Project Content if *** has a good faith belief that it must do so to (a) perform system administration, such as diagnosing and correcting problems, or testing any aspect of the *** Program; (b) respond to a valid court order or subpoena; (c) comply with legislation or regulations, including, without limitation, the Digital Millennium Copyright Act; (d) investigate complaints; or (e) protect *** or others from liability or damages. *** has no obligation to retain Project Content and you agree that *** shall not be liable for any failure to store Project Content.

PROHIBITED COMMUNICATIONS

You may submit only User Content or Project Content to the Site that is (a) owned by you, (b) submitted with the express permission of the owner or within the scope of the license to such content, or (c) in the public domain. You are prohibited from posting or transmitting to or from this Site any unlawful, threatening, harassing, libelous, offensive, defamatory, obscene, or pornographic materials, or other materials that would violate any law or the rights of others, including, without limitation, laws against copyright infringement, and rights of privacy and publicity. Violation of these restrictions may result in denial of or limitations on access by you to this Site.

USER CONDUCT

In using the Site, including all Services and Materials available through it, you agree: not to disrupt or interfere with any other user's enjoyment of the Site or affiliated or linked sites; not to upload, post, or otherwise transmit through the Site any viruses or other harmful, disruptive, or destructive files; not to create a false identity; not to use or attempt to use another's account, password, service, or system without authorization from ***; not to access or attempt to access any Project Content which you are not authorized to access; not to disrupt or interfere with the security of, or otherwise cause harm to, the Site, or any Services, Materials, system resources, accounts, passwords, servers, or networks connected to or accessible through the Site or any affiliated or linked sites.

MANAGING CONTENT AND COMMUNICATIONS

*** reserves the right, in its sole discretion, to delete or remove User Content from the Site and to restrict, suspend, or terminate your access to all or part of this Site, at any time without prior notice or liability. *** may, but is not obligated to, monitor or review any areas on the Site where users transmit or post User Content, including but not limited to areas where Services are available, and the substance of any User Content. To the maximum extent permitted by law, *** will have no liability related to User Content or Project Content. *** disclaims all liability with respect to the misuse, loss, modification, or unavailability of any User Content or Project Content.

WARRANTIES AND DISCLAIMERS

Except as expressly provided otherwise in a written agreement between you and *** or you and a third party with respect to such party's materials or services, this Site, and all Materials and Services accessible through this Site are provided "as is" without warranty of any kind, either express or implied, including, but not limited to, the implied warranties of merchantability or fitness for a particular purpose, or the warranty of non-infringement. Without limiting the foregoing, *** makes no warranty that (i) the Services and Materials will meet your requirements; (ii) the Services and Materials will be uninterrupted, timely, secure, or error-free; (iii) the results that may be obtained from the use of the Services or Materials will be effective, accurate, or reliable; (iv) the quality of any Products, Services, or Materials obtained or accessible by you through the Site will meet your expectations; and (v) any errors in the Services or Materials obtained through the Site, or any defects in the Site, its Services or Materials, will be corrected.

This Site could include technical or other mistakes, inaccuracies, or typographical errors. *** may make changes to the Materials and Services at this Site at any time without notice. The Materials or Services at this Site may be out of date, and *** makes no commitment to update such Materials or Services.

You understand and acknowledge that (i) *** does not control, endorse, or accept responsibility for any content, products, or services offered by third parties through the Site, including, without limitation, third party vendors and third parties accessible through links on the Site; (ii) *** makes no representation or warranties whatsoever about any such third parties, their content, products, or services; (iii) any dealings you may have with such third parties are at your own risk; and (iv) *** shall not be liable or responsible for any content, products, or services offered by third parties.

The use of the Services or the downloading or other use of any Materials through the Site is done at your own discretion and risk and with your agreement that you will be solely responsible for any damage to your computer system, loss of data, or other harm that results from such activities. *** assumes no liability for any computer virus or other similar software code that is downloaded to your computer from the Site or in connection with any Services or Materials offered through the Site. No advice or information, whether oral or written, obtained by you from *** or through or from the Site shall create any warranty not expressly stated in these Terms of Use.

PERSONAL INFORMATION AND PRIVACY

Except as otherwise expressly set forth herein, your personal information will be deemed to be confidential. With the exception of Project Content and certain types of User Content, any non-personal information or material sent to *** will generally be deemed to NOT be confidential. In any case, you understand and agree that we may disclose information about you if we have a good faith belief that we are required to do so by law or legal process, to respond to claims, or to protect the rights, property, or safety of *** or others.

LIMITATION OF LIABILITY

In no event, including, without limitation, negligence, shall ***, its subsidiaries, affiliates, agents, officers, directors, employees, partners, or suppliers be liable to you or any third party for any special, punitive, incidental, indirect, or consequential damages of any kind, or any damages whatsoever, including, without limitation, those resulting from loss of use, data, or profits, whether or not *** has been advised of the possibility of such damages, and on any theory of liability, arising out of or in connection with the use of or the inability to use this Site, its Services, or Materials, the statements or actions of any third party on or through the Site, any dealings with vendors or other third parties, any unauthorized access to or alteration of your transmissions or data, any information that is sent or received or not sent or received, any failure to store or loss of data, files, or other content, any Services available through the Site that are delayed or interrupted, or any website referenced or linked to or from this Site.

INDEMNITY AND LIABILITY

You agree to indemnify and hold ***, and its subsidiaries, affiliates, officers, directors, agents, partners and employees, harmless from any claim or demand, including reasonable attorneys' fees, made by any third party due to or arising out of content you submit, post to, or transmit through the Site (including, without limitation, any User Content, Project Content or computer viruses), your use of the Site, your connection to the Site, your violation of these Terms of Use, the actions of any member of your Work Group, or your violation of any rights of another person or entity.

GOVERNING LAW AND JURISDICTION

This Site (excluding linked sites) is controlled by *** from its offices within the state of _____, United States of America. By accessing this Site, you and *** agree that all matters relating to your access to, or use of, this Site shall be governed by the statutes and laws of the State of _____, without regard to the conflicts of laws principles thereof. You and *** also agree and hereby submit to the exclusive personal jurisdiction and venue of the Courts within the State of _____ with respect to such matters.

GENERAL

The Terms of Use and the other rules, guidelines, licenses and disclaimers posted on the Site constitute the entire agreement between *** and you with respect to your use of the Site. If for any reason a court of competent jurisdiction finds any provision of these Terms of Use, or portion thereof, to be unenforceable, that provision shall be enforced to the maximum extent permissible so as to effect the intent of the parties as reflected by that provision, and the remainder of the Terms of Use shall continue in full force and effect. Any failure by *** to enforce or exercise any provision of these Terms of Use or related right shall not constitute a waiver of that right or provision.

CHAPTER 5

Legal Structures
for Small Businesses

5.1 When Should Your Client Form a Separate Legal Entity for Its Business?

Perhaps the most fundamental benefit of forming a separate legal entity for a business is liability protection: the so-called corporate shield. Shareholders, limited partners, and limited liability company members, among others, are generally not liable for the liabilities of the company in which they have an ownership interest. However, until a company is formed, the entrepreneur is acting in a personal capacity and is personally liable.

1. Before Taking on Significant Obligations or Risks.

Before taking on any significant obligations, and before exposing themselves to any significant risks, an entity should be formed.

2. Before Creating Certain Rights.

Certain rights and relationships are intended for the business and not the individual. It often makes sense to establish an entity before such rights or relationships are established, to avoid the necessity of transferring or assigning them later, which can give rise to otherwise unnecessary expenses and potential complications. For example, an individual founder is not likely to want to personally engage the services of an employee or independent contractor, and the work product of such employee or independent contractor should belong to the business and not the individual. Nondisclosure agreements (NDAs) raise a similar issue. Founders are often in contact with potential strategic partners, advisors, employees, and others at the very earliest stages. While the individual founders could, and often do, enter into these types of agreements with third parties before forming an entity, this arrangement is not ideal; it raises issues regarding enforceability and personal liability for the

101

founders. If the company anticipates it will want to raise money at some point, it should form an entity early in the process and ensure that all significant rights and relationships belonging to the company are appropriately documented.

3. Before Raising Money.

If reasons 1 and 2 above haven't triggered entity formation before fund-raising, an entity certainly should be formed before a business raises money from investors—even from friends and family. In the absence of an entity, investors would likely be considered partners, and the whole arrangement would be subject to the three "M's" discussed in Chapter 4: memory, misinterpretation, and mood.

5.2 What Form of Entity Should Your Client Choose?

Most entrepreneurs appreciate the many benefits of forming a legal entity for the operation of their new business venture, such as shielding themselves from the liabilities of the business, raising start-up capital, and providing framework for working with co-founders. The most common entity choices for profit-seeking ventures are discussed here, although there are many others.

1. Sole Proprietorship.

A sole proprietorship is a business owned by one person. If your client opens a business, but doesn't choose an entity, the client will be a sole proprietor by default. A fictitious business name filing may be required.

2. General Partnership (GP).

A general partnership is a business enterprise, entered into for profit, that is owned by more than one person. Each person in this entity is a "partner." A general partnership may be created by a formal written agreement but also may be based on an oral agreement or just a handshake. A general partnership is also a default category that may govern a business where no entity is chosen. A written agreement can prove critical in partnership relationships, and a fictitious business name filing may be required.

3. Limited Partnership (LP).

A limited partnership is a partnership that limits the liability of certain (passive) partners for debts beyond the amount of their investment in the partnership. The investing "limited partners" enjoy limited liability but cannot participate in management and are limited to specific percentages of profit. A limited partnership requires a written agreement between the business management, consisting of the general partner or partners, and all of the limited partners. Limited partnerships generally must make a filing with the secretary of state in their state of formation. For example, in California a Form LP-1 Certificate of Limited Partnership must be filed; the form is available online at http://www.ss.ca.gov/business/lp/forms/lp-1.pdf.

4. Limited Liability Company (LLC).

A limited liability company is a very flexible form of doing business, which offers limited liability to its owners, can be taxed as a corporation or as a partnership, can be member-managed or manager-managed, and can have multiple classes of ownership. Each state in the United States now has adopted a limited liability company act (an "LLC Act"). For example, The Beverly-Killea Limited Liability Company Act of 1994 authorized the formation of limited liability companies in California and was one of the last states to adopt an LLC Act. Subsequent legislation in California permitted the formation of single-member LLCs in California. LLCs combine traditional corporate and partnership characteristics. This is a very versatile form of entity. However, certain types of businesses may not be permitted to operate as LLCs, as determined by state law. For example, in California, if the business is required to have a license under the California Business and Professions Code, it is not permitted to operate as an LLC, unless specifically authorized to do so under the Business and Professions Code. Businesses requiring licensure under the California Business and Professions (B&P) Code include general contractors, health care providers, pharmacies, veterinarians, lawyers, accountants, architects, locksmiths, funeral directors, real estate appraisers, and others. Formation documents are typically available on secretary of state websites, such as the California LLC-1 Articles of Organization, available online at http://www.ss.ca.gov/business/llc/forms/llc-1.pdf.

Forming an LLC typically involves filing a simple form, such as the California Articles of Organization, prescribed by the secretary of state's office and paying the required filing fee.

A written operating agreement or LLC agreement is also highly recommended for LLCs with more than one member.

Fewer formalities may be required in managing an LLC as compared with a corporation, but start-up costs can be higher because LLC agreements are frequently cumbersome and complicated.

The LLC is a very flexible entity with few restrictions on ownership (as contrasted with S corporations, for example). LLCs have the capacity for nearly limitless variations on management and ownership structure (e.g., different classes of ownership, preferred returns, etc.)—but note the tendency for higher start-up costs as a result.

Check your local secretary of state's website for applicable information and forms.

Be aware that some states impose additional fees on LLCs. For example, in California, in addition to the $800 Annual Minimum Franchise Tax, LLCs classified as partnerships or disregarded entities are also subject to an annual fee ranging from approximately $1,000 to $12,000 based on their total income. The California LLC fee is calculated on an apportioned basis based on total income from all sources derived or attributable to California (R&TC Section 17942(b)(1)(B)). The LLC fee is due by the 15th day of the 6th month of the current tax year, or if the LLC's tax year is less than 6 months, on the original due date of the company's tax return. Because of the Annual LLC Fee in California, the S corporation can be a more attractive alternative for companies formed or doing business in California where LLC flexibility is not required.

5. Limited Liability Partnership (LLP).

Limited liability partnerships vary by state. In California, LLPs can be used only for the practice of law, architecture, public accountancy, engineering, land surveying, or a related business. Formation documents are typically available on secretary of state websites, such as California Form LLP-1 for Registered Limited Liability Partnership Registration, available online at http://www.ss.ca.gov/business/llp/forms/llp-1.pdf.

6. S Corporation.

An S corporation (S Corp) is a small corporation whose owners have elected to be treated as a partnership for tax purposes by the Internal Revenue Service under "Subchapter S." There are quite a few restrictions on the number and type of owners and classes of stock permissible in the S Corp. However, in most ways, the S Corp is just like the C corporation ("C Corp"; see below). Limitations on S Corps include the following:

- There can be no more than 100 shareholders;
- Shareholders must be individuals, estates, tax exempt organizations, or certain trusts;
- There can be no nonresident alien shareholders;
- There can be only one class of stock (although voting and nonvoting classes are permitted);
- Banks, thrifts, insurance companies, possessions corporations, and domestic international sales corporations cannot be S Corps; and
- S Corps must have a permissible tax year—generally a December 31 year-end.

To make an S corporation election, use IRS Form 2553, available online at http://www.irs.gov/pub/irs-pdf/i2553.pdf.

7. C Corporation.

The C corporation (C Corp) is an organization formed with state government approval to act as an artificial person to carry on business. C Corps can sue or be sued, and they can issue shares of stock to raise funds. One benefit of a C Corp is that its liability for damages or debts is generally limited to its assets, so that shareholders and officers are protected from personal claims.

Corporate organizational documents for C Corps and S Corps include the following:

- Articles of Incorporation (or a Certificate of Incorporation) are filed with the Secretary of State to establish the number of authorized shares, classes of stock, par value, agent for service of process, and so forth;
- Incorporator Action (Statement of Incorporator) adopts articles and bylaws and appoints initial directors;
- Bylaws—provisions dictated largely by the applicable Corporations Code or General Corporation Law—are established to set forth corporate governance provisions within the state of formation;
- Board Resolutions (by meeting or written consent)—appointing officers, authorizing the issuance of stock, and so on—are approved; and
- Shareholders elect members of the board of directors.

For information about the minimum statutory requirements and filing instructions for the Certificate or Articles of Incorporation to be filed in the state of formation, check the website of the applicable secretary of state, such as the California secretary of state at http://www.ss.ca.gov/business/corp/pdf/articles/corp_artsgen.pdf.

8. Fictitious Business Names.

A fictitious business name filing is required if the business is conducted in any name other than the individual's or entity's legal name, for example, Jean L. Batman dba Southern California Fruit. Fictitious business name filings, or "dba" (doing business as) registrations are typically recorded at the county recorder's office in the county where the business is located, have a publication requirement (e.g., in a local newspaper), and must be periodically renewed. Other forms of doing business in which the business operates under a name other than its legal name must also comply with fictitious business name requirements.

9. How to Choose.

Here are the preliminary questions to ask your client:

- Do the parties need limited liability?

	Liability limited?	
	Yes	No
Sole Proprietor (dba)		X
General Partnership (GP)		X
Limited Partnership (LP)	X	X
Limited Liability Company (LLC)	X	
Limited Liability Partnership (LLP)	X	
S Corporation	X	
C Corporation	X	

- Do the parties want profits and losses to pass through to their personal income tax returns?

	Pass-through tax treatment?	
	Yes	No
Sole Proprietor (dba)	X	
General Partnership (GP)	X	
Limited Partnership (LP)	X	
Limited Liability Company (LLC)	X	X
Limited Liability Partnership (LLP)	X	X
S Corporation	X	
C Corporation		X

LLCs and LLPs are shown in both the "Yes" and "No" columns above because the owners can elect either tax treatment in those entities. One reason a client may *not* want profits to pass through to the personal income tax return is if he or she is using the profits of the business to fund its growth or expansion. The reasoning is that the owners of an entity taxed as a partnership (i.e., one in which profits and losses are passed through to the owners' personal income tax returns, usually by means of IRS Form K-1), will be taxed on their share of the profits, regardless of whether the profits have actually been distributed to them. This phenomenon is referred to as "phantom income," because it's income your client can be taxed on even though they never received it. One way to avoid this problem in an entity that receives pass-through tax treatment is to include a provision in the entity's operating agreement, partnership agreement, or other owners' agreement that requires minimum annual distributions designed to cover the amount of tax that will be due from each owner as a result of the entity's profits. An example form for making such a provision is included at the end of this chapter.

- Will all of the parties be actively involved in management?

	All owners active?	
	Yes	No
Sole Proprietor (dba)	X	
General Partnership (GP)	X	
Limited Partnership (LP)		X
Limited Liability Company (LLC)	X	X
Limited Liability Partnership (LLP)	X	X
S Corporation	X	X
C Corporation	X	X

10. The Bias Toward Corporations.

The corporation is an old, familiar form of entity. Technology, biotechnology, web-related start-ups, and others hoping to proceed immediately to institutional or venture financing and looking toward the public markets for liquidity should organize as corporations. The corporate form allows founders to immediately set up a capital structure that is conducive to raising capital from angels and other outside investors. In the corporate format, the owners can sell shares of stock to investors, and they can structure classes of preferred stock with certain rights and preferences that outside investors may require. If the new business will grow quickly and its owners intend to go to the public markets, it will need to be a corporation because of investor preferences and legal limitations.

The C corporation may be the best choice for your client if the owners envision any of the following:

- Raising money from venture capitals;
- Making an initial public offering (IPO) of stock;
- Forming relationships with other entities that prefer dealing with corporations;
- Building up value in the entity, rather than distributing profits;
- Benefiting from IRC Section 1202—the exclusion of up to 50 percent of the gain on sales of stock in certain types of C corporations held for more than five years; and
- Offering equity incentives to key employees.

However, a client may benefit from initially forming as an S Corp (if eligible), for the tax benefits of receiving pass-through tax treatment, and revoking the S Corp election (thereby becoming a C Corp) when it is ready to issue preferred stock, start using profits to fund growth, and so on.

11. Why Some Clients Love the LLC.

The LLC, or limited liability company, is an increasingly popular choice of entity for a new business because it combines the liability limitation of a corporation with the potential tax advantages of a pass-through entity, such as a partnership. This means there will be no taxation of the business at the entity level; instead, the business's income is "passed through" the entity and taxed to its owners. Where the owners' tax rates are lower than the corporate income tax rate, there are tax savings. And because there is no entity-level tax, the owners avoid the problem of double taxation on monies distributed to owners that occurs in the C Corp. If the new business expects to incur losses during its first year or more of operations, its owners will be able to claim those losses on their personal tax returns, creating a personal tax benefit. The organization and management structure of an LLC can be less formal and is generally more flexible than that of a corporation.

On the other hand, forming as an LLC will not avoid taxes completely. The LLC usually will be subject to fees on its organization, and annually thereafter, that are comparable to the fees charged a corporation. Some states impose additional fees on LLCs. California, for example, imposes a gross receipts tax on the revenues of the LLC, which may require the company to pay an additional several thousand dollars each year to the state. This fee has been challenged in California as an unconstitutional "tax"; but for now, the fees remain. Some states also have restrictions on the types of businesses that may use the LLC format. You will need to check the LLC Act in your state to determine whether this type of entity is available to a particular client.

5.3 Where Should Your Client's Company Be Organized?

The following questions may be helpful in helping your client select its state of formation.

1. Will Your Client Benefit from the Laws of a Particular State (i.e., Is Choice of Law an Issue)?

While some states have well-developed corporate law, others have focused on particular areas of local concern—for example, water rights, oil and gas leases, and so on. Some states may have more favorable default rules for the type of entity chosen (i.e., its LLC Act may have more favorable provisions that apply in the absence of a written agreement to the contrary). Please note that the state of formation for corporations may be freely chosen, but the state of formation for other entities, such as limited partnerships, may be required to bear at least a reasonable relation to the business of the entity.

2. What About Delaware?

For companies pursuing venture capital (VC) financing or preparing to go public, Delaware is the most common choice because:

- VCs are comfortable with Delaware corporations regardless of where they are based;
- The corporate law of the State of Delaware is generally considered to be more sophisticated, comprehensive, and well defined than that of other jurisdictions; and
- Delaware has developed a business-friendly environment—of which there are numerous legal and administrative examples (it is the most common choice among Fortune 500 companies, regardless of their primary office location).

3. Avoid Unnecessary Taxes and Regulations!

Avoiding unnecessary taxes and regulations should be part of every business strategy; in fancy business schools, this is also known as the KISS method ("keep it simple, stupid"). Many entrepreneurs believe it is less expensive to form their new business in a particular state, other than the one in which they operate, or that there may be legal advantages to organizing their new corporation or LLC in another state. However, in most cases, the differences in state laws will not significantly affect the business. So, if a company incorporates in another state, its owners are merely doubling their tax and regulatory obligations. They will also have to register to do business in the state where they operate, and comply with the fees, taxes, and filing requirements of both states. Moreover, the company will likely be required to pay a corporate agent to represent it as its agent of service of process in its state of formation, if it does not have operations there, thus adding one more annual expense to its business.

5.4 What If Your Client Does Business in More than One State?

States universally require a "foreign corporation" (i.e., one not incorporated in that state) to "qualify" before "doing business" in the state. Qualification usually consists of filing documents, paying a fee, and appointing a resident agent for service of process. "Doing business" is more often defined by the exceptions than by an enumeration of specific acts that are covered by the term. However, if the corporation elects to do business (e.g., open an office) in another state, it will be required to qualify in that state. Failure to qualify may result in financial penalties as well as the inability to bring suit in the courts of the state with respect to acts and transactions in the state during the period of noncompliance.

5.5 What If Your Client Is Operating in an Inappropriate Legal Structure?

If your client's legal structure is inappropriate in light of the tax implications of its structure, exposure to liability, risks of loss, or other circumstances, there are several alternatives to consider.

1. If your client is a sole proprietor or general partnership, or an LLC taxed as a partnership, it is a fairly simple matter to form the appropriate entity and have the owners contribute the business assets to the new entity in exchange for their ownership in the new entity.
2. If your client is a C Corp, but wants to change its tax status, it may be eligible to simply make an S Corp election, even after years of operating as a C Corp.
3. An S Corp client can easily convert to C Corp status by revoking its S Corp election or making itself ineligible for S Corp status.

4. Entity conversions are often fairly simple to accomplish, but they vary by state.
5. Mergers can also be used to change a form of entity, and many states streamline the process through "short form" merger rules.

Dissolution of an entity taxed as a corporation and formation of a new entity is probably the least attractive option for correcting an inappropriate legal structure because it will result in a taxable event. However, if the assets in the entity to be dissolved are worth less than the owners' basis in the company, this approach (the dissolve-and-start-over approach) may be successfully used to generate a tax write-off for the owners. This might be a good time to consult a federal tax expert.

5.6 What Legal Requirements Apply to All Businesses?

Some of the legal requirements that apply to all (or at least most) businesses include:

- Annual Statement of Information (officers, directors, and agent for service of process) and filing fee to secretary of state (except sole proprietor and general partnership);
- Taxes—annual franchise tax fee (except sole proprietor and general partnership), state and federal tax returns, employment taxes, sales and use taxes, personal property taxes;
- Local business license, professional licensing;
- Federal Employer Identification Number (FEIN);
- Insurance—unemployment and workers' compensation, liability, and so on; and
- Qualification to do business in other states.

5.7 How Can Your Client's Owners Avoid Personal Liability?

1. Form an Entity.

The first and most important step a client can take to avoid personal liability for the financial obligations of its business is to form an entity that provides such protection (e.g., a corporation, limited liability company, or similar entity). If your client is planning to form an entity and is in the process of designing business cards, letterhead, brochures, and other materials, it should plan to include the entity name on its collateral materials so they won't have to be reprinted to make sure it is clear to third parties that they are dealing with an entity, not an individual.

2. Avoid Personal Guarantees.

Sometimes clients are faced with a decision: provide a personal guarantee or lose a business opportunity. This frequently arises in the small business arena, where companies don't have established credit or sufficient assets to obtain a loan, commercial lease, or other business obligation without using the credit and/or assets of the individuals in the company. However, personal guarantees should be avoided if possible because they subject the guarantor to individual liability for an obligation they would not otherwise be liable for after the time, money, and effort spent on creating a corporate shield.

3. Observe Appropriate Formalities for the Entity.

For shareholders of a corporation to enjoy the benefit of the corporate shield, certain corporate formalities must be adhered to, including the maintenance of separate corporate records and accounts, the holding of annual meetings of the stockholders and directors, and the execution of documents in the company's name. So long as the corporation observes proper corporate formalities—that is, so long as the directors and officers take the corporation seriously and play by the rules—the shareholders will not be held personally liable for the corporation's obligations and liabilities.

Whenever officers are signing documents or correspondence on behalf of a corporation (or managers are signing on behalf of an LLC, LP, or LLP), they should take care to include the corporation's (or LLC's, LP's, or LLP's) name in the signature block and the title of the officer (or manager, etc.) who is signing. An example of an appropriate signature block is as follows:

**** Inc.

By:_____
[name of signatory], President

Failure to observe this formality may lead, in the context of litigation involving a signed document, to including the person who signed in an individual capacity in the lawsuit.

4. Remit All Taxes Withheld or Collected.

Certain tax obligations, for example, employment taxes withheld and sales taxes collected, can give rise to personal liability if not remitted to the government.

5. Carry Insurance.

Clients can be protected from certain obligations for which the corporate shield does not provide protection through insurance. For example, the corporate shield (used in the generic sense to include the shield provided by LLCs and other entities) will not protect an owner from liability based upon the owner's personal tortious behavior; but in many cases insurance can—such as automobile liability insurance, malpractice insurance, and directors and officers liability insurance.

5.8 Should My Client Get D&O Insurance?

Directors and officers insurance ("D&O" coverage) is great to have, if available and the company can afford it. The directors and officers of a small company are vulnerable to being personally named in lawsuits initiated by investors, employees, and others because they are typically involved in the day-to-day operations of the company and may be perceived to have a greater net worth than the company.

More and more small companies are being told by prospective board members that they will not serve on the board without insurance coverage.

D&O coverage provides protection against claims of certain types of "wrongful acts" alleged against the directors, officers, and employees of the company. D&O coverage is likened to malpractice insurance coverage for doctors or lawyers, except that it provides protection for the directors and officers of an organization against "management" liability claims.

D&O policies typically address three categories of coverage:

1. **Directors & Officers Personal Coverage/Non-Indemnifiable Loss.** This coverage applies when the company is either not permitted by law, or unable due to insolvency, to indemnify the personal liabilities of its directors and officers.
2. **Corporate Reimbursement Coverage/Indemnifiable Loss.** This coverage applies where the company does indemnify its directors and officers as permitted and/or required by law.
3. **Entity Coverage.** This coverage is provided for the entity, for losses arising from all claims made against the company, as a result of a wrongful act.

A D&O policy covers defense and settlement expenses as well as damages (but typically not punitive damages or civil fines) for claims alleging "wrongful acts"—defined as actual or alleged negligent acts, errors, misleading statements or omissions, or neglect or breach of duty by the directors or officers, individually or collectively.

Typical D&O policy exclusions can be numerous and include:

* Antitrust claims;
* Bodily injury, property damage, advertising injury, libel, slander, and so on;
* Collusive insured versus insured claims;
* Contractual liability;
* Criminal, dishonest, or illegal acts;
* ERISA violations and obligations, etc.;
* Failure to maintain insurance;
* Intellectual property claims against the company;
* Nuclear and radioactive damages;

- Personal profit and excess remuneration;
- Pollution liability;
- Prior and pending litigation;
- Public offerings;
- Rendering of professional services; and
- Wrongful acts committed before the retroactive date (if applicable).

One of the biggest mistakes companies make when obtaining D&O coverage is failing to negotiate their coverage. When shopping for D&O insurance, companies would be well advised to work with an experienced insurance broker who can help them obtain favorable coverage and pricing.

5.9 What If My Client Wants to Form a Subsidiary?

One alternative might be the establishment of a division or a separate organization within the company. A division is essentially a branch of the company's organizational chart representing a particular product, brand, or line of business; it is not a separate company. A division typically keeps separate books (i.e., is treated as a separate profit center, with its own budget), has its own clearly defined chain of command, and operates under a different name than the rest of the company, such name being a dba, pursuant to a fictitious business name registration, and registered trademark of the company. Some reasons to choose to operate a line of business as a division, rather than as a subsidiary, are the ease of formation, efficiencies of operating within one organization, the flexibility to move employees in and out of the division and to promote from other divisions of the company, and the ease of reorganizing or discontinuing a division (organizational lines can simply be redrawn).

The formation of a subsidiary may be preferable when a line of business or product is highly regulated or carries particular risks from which the rest of the company should be insulated, or where a line of business or product is being groomed for a merger or acquisition independent of the rest of the company, which can help streamline a transaction by simplifying the due diligence and approval processes. In the case of a highly regulated business, a subsidiary structure permits review by regulators of just the regulated business, excludes review of other lines of business, and isolates the regulated business from potentially conflicting or impermissible activities. For businesses involving a higher degree of risk, the subsidiary structure can insulate the rest of the company from losses and/or failure in the event of a catastrophic loss (in the absence of corporate guarantees or joint liability). Another potential advantage of the subsidiary is that it can be used as a vehicle for joint venture, in which the company shares ownership with a strategic partner. A subsidiary can be wholly or majority-owned by the company and does not have to be formed in the same venue as its parent.

Licensing and/or franchising can also be used as revenue/growth models in combination with either the division or the subsidiary approaches discussed above. For example, a subsidiary or division can be formed for the purpose of pursuing and managing the licensing of the company's intellectual property for joint ventures, third party development, etc. Licensing arrangements are not subject to any particular regulation based solely on the existence of a license relationship. Franchising, on the other hand, is a highly regulated form of doing business (by the Federal Trade Commission and at the state level), which applies to all relationships that satisfy the elements of the definition of a franchise:

- Trademark/marketing element;
- Control/assistance element with regard to the franchisee's method of operation; and
- Required payment element, which may be based on the payment of fees, payment for services, and/or the purchase of materials, inventory, and equipment.

Similar to license arrangements, the terms of franchise agreements can also vary widely in terms of use, fees, royalties, exclusivity, territory, etc. However, parties can inadvertently find themselves subject to franchise law, regardless of what their relationship is called (e.g., dealership, license, distributorship, etc), if their relationship involves all of the elements of a franchise. It is important to avoid such "hidden" or "accidental" franchises because of the protections afforded to franchisees, including the requirement of a disclosure document, called a prospectus or offering circular, covering specified information in connection with the sale of a franchise, and because failure to comply with franchise regulations can result in liability for damages, rescission, criminal penalties, civil fines, and the award of attorneys' fees. Since franchising is based on a successful product or business, it may make sense for a company to form a subsidiary to produce the product or conduct the business that it later intends to franchise in order to establish its success separate from the company's other activities.

5.10 Sample Documents and Checklists.

This section includes the following form:

- Discussion Items for Determining Form of Entity (Form 5 A)

Form 5 A: Discussion Items
for Determining Form of Entity

Considerations for Determining Capital Structure:

1. Do the parties need limited liability?

2. Do the parties want profits and losses to pass through to their personal income tax returns?

3. Will all of the parties be actively involved in management?

4. How much capital is needed?

5. How much will be raised from third parties? Debt or equity? Likely sources?

6. What would the parties providing capital expect in return?

7. Is there a form of entity that the funding source prefers or, alternatively, would avoid?

8. What level of corporate formality is possible or desired?

9. Is the business ineligible for certain forms of entity?

10. How much flexibility is required for structuring ownership and management?

11. What is the expected length of the investment/venture and what is the exit strategy?

CHAPTER 6

Organizing or Cleaning Up
a Corporation

6.1 What Is the Basic Structure of a Corporation?

Corporations are owned by their shareholders, who elect directors to manage the corporation. The management duties of the board of directors include making decisions regarding key policies and transactions and establishing the broad guidelines within which the business of the corporation will be conducted. The directors, in turn, appoint officers who carry out the day-to-day business of the corporation, such as the hiring of additional employees.

6.2 What Is Authorized Stock?

Authorized stock is the total number of shares of capital stock, whether common or preferred, that the company is authorized to issue at any given time. This number is set forth in the company's articles or certificate of incorporation.

6.3 How Many Shares Should Be Authorized?

The total number of authorized shares, and the total number of issued and outstanding shares, at the time of the company's formation is largely arbitrary and, in the end, not of high importance. However, clients should be encouraged to authorize more shares than they initially anticipate issuing, so there is authorized stock available for future transactions (making it possible, in most cases, for the board of directors to enter into such transactions without the necessity of shareholder approval to change the company's articles or certificate of incorporation). The desire for lots of authorized stock may have to be balanced against the company's desire to avoid unnecessary fees in states like Delaware, where the number of authorized shares and the stated par value of such shares may be used to determine the company's annual franchise tax fee in the state.

6.4 What Is Issued and Outstanding Stock?

Issued and outstanding stock is the total number of shares of capital stock that have been actually issued or sold to shareholders pursuant to financings, stock options, or otherwise, and that are still owned based on the corporate records of the company at any time.

6.5 What Is Issued and Outstanding Stock on an "As If Converted Basis"?

Issued and outstanding stock on an "as if converted basis" is the total number of shares of stock that are issued and outstanding at any time, plus the number of shares of stock that the issued and outstanding preferred stock could be converted into at that time. Issued and outstanding stock on an "as if converted, fully diluted basis" is the total number of shares of issued and outstanding stock on an as if converted basis, plus the total number of additional shares that would be issued and outstanding if all holders of convertible securities (e.g., options, warrants, and convertible debt) converted into stock.

6.6 What Is the Role of a Shareholder?

As an initial matter, it is important to note that even though shareholders, directors, and officers play different roles in the corporation and have different rights and responsibilities, the same individuals (or one individual) can serve as the shareholders, directors, and officers. The shareholders own the corporation and generally provide the capital and/or assets with which it commences operations. Shareholders, per se, do not take an active role in running the business. Beyond electing the directors and voting on certain key events in the corporation's life, the shareholders entrust management of the corporation to the directors and officers of the corporation.

6.7 What Are the Roles of the Officers?

Officers are appointed by the board of directors and serve at the pleasure of the board of directors, subject to any contracts of employment they may have with the corporation. The officers perform the bulk of the day-to-day operations of the corporation. Most states require that the corporation have a president, a chief financial officer (or "treasurer"), and a corporate secretary. More than one or all of these offices may be held by the same individual. A corporation may have an unlimited number of additional officer designations. These additional officers are appointed either by the board of directors or by the president or another officer, if the board has delegated the authority to make such appointments.

Standard duties of the president, the chief financial officer, and the secretary are briefly summarized below.

1. President.

The president is the chief executive officer and general manager of the corporation unless the corporation has a chairman of the board and has designated the chairman as chief executive officer. The president has general supervision, direction, and control over the corporation's business and its officers.

2. Chief Financial Officer.

The chief financial officer keeps the books and records of account of the properties and business transactions of the corporation. These duties include depositing corporate funds and other valuables in the name of the corporation and disbursing funds as directed by the board of directors.

3. Secretary.

A corporation must keep written minutes of the proceedings of its shareholders, board, and committees of the board; and it must keep a record of the shareholders, their addresses, and their holdings. The secretary usually has the duty of carrying out these functions and for giving notices of shareholders' and directors' meetings.

6.8 What Are the Duties of the Directors?

The board of directors manages the business and affairs of the corporation and exercises its corporate powers. The board may either perform these duties itself or, as is the more normal case, these duties can be performed by the officers under the direction of the board of directors. The board also has the power to delegate some of its duties to committees authorized by the board to perform these duties. In carrying out these duties, directors have a "duty of loyalty" and a "duty of care" that run both to the corporation and to the shareholders as the ultimate owners of the corporation. These duties are often referred to as "fiduciary duties." Failure to abide by these duties can result in personal liability of the directors.

The duty of loyalty dictates that a director must act in good faith and must not allow personal interests to prevail over interests of the corporation and its shareholders. Concerns as to whether a director is violating the duty of loyalty arise whenever it is proposed that the corporation enters into a transaction that benefits a director or where there may be a conflict of interest between the director and the corporation or its shareholders. Such "self-dealing" transactions are not prohibited but must be approached with great care to assure that proper corporate approval is obtained and that the transactions are fair to the corporation.

The duty of care requires a director to be diligent and prudent in managing the corporation's affairs. This concept is sometimes referred to as the duty to exercise good business judgment. Directors may be liable for actions that injure the corporation, whether the action results from the directors' negligence or from participating in or approving of a wrongful act; however, directors are not held liable merely because a carefully made decision turns out badly for the corporation. This idea, referred to as the "business judgment rule," is sometimes expressed as recognition that so long as directors exercise their judgment without fraud or conflict of interest, they will not be second-guessed by courts based on how the decisions happen to work out.

6.9 What Corporate Formalities Must Be Observed?

The regular observance of corporate formalities is an important aspect of maintaining the protections and advantages that the corporate form offers, not the least of which is to protect shareholders against imposition of personal liability for obligations incurred by the corporation. Three of the most important areas of corporate formalities are shareholder decision making, director decision making, and separation of corporate assets from personal assets. In that regard, it may be appropriate to observe the following formalities in connection with the ongoing operations of your corporation.

The shareholders should take action to elect the board of directors of the corporation annually. The election can occur at an annual meeting of the shareholders. The action also may be taken by written consent of the shareholders without a meeting, in accordance with your corporation's bylaws and the laws in your state. In addition, certain specified fundamental changes in the form of operations of the corporation require the consent or approval of the shareholders. The consent or approval can be obtained either through a formal shareholders' meeting or by written consent. These fundamental changes include amendments of the articles of incorporation, sale of all—or substantially all—of the corporation's assets, a merger or consolidation of the corporation with or into any other corporation, and a winding up and dissolution of the corporation.

Matters of more general operating policy should be considered and authorized by the board of directors of the corporation. Although there is no statutory requirement with respect to how frequently the board of directors should act, it is typical that the board of directors meets at least quarterly. In addition, a specially convened meeting of the board, as authorized by the corporation's bylaws, may be called if action is required before the next regular meeting of the board. Action by the board may also be taken by the unanimous written consent of the directors in accordance with your corporation's bylaws and the laws in your state. Board meetings can be held either in person or by conference telephone so long as all of the directors in attendance can hear each other simultaneously.

Matters appropriate for director action—which can either be immediately approved by written consent or be accumulated as they arise, pending approval by the directors—include the appointment of officers, the setting of salaries and declaration of bonuses, the appointment of board committees, the opening of corporate bank accounts, and the designation and change of corporate officers authorized as signatories. Additional matters include corporate borrowing, entering into certain kinds of contracts, adopting pension and employee benefit plans, declaring dividends or redeeming shares, amending the bylaws, action that requires a shareholder vote, and issuing and selling additional company shares or granting options to purchase additional shares.

Failure to observe appropriate formalities in conducting the business of the corporation may lead to the imposition of personal liability where the financial affairs and accounts of the corporation and those of the individuals who control it are confused to the prejudice of creditors, or where there has been an undue diversion of corporate funds or other assets to individual use. In other words, the owners of a corporation may be held personally liable when they treat the assets of the corporation as their own and add or withdraw capital from the corporation at will.

Whether the company is small or large, it is important to scrupulously keep the corporation's money separate from the personal funds of shareholders, directors, or employees. Failure to keep these accounts separate is a common problem with closely held or newly formed corporations. Such a commingling of funds is often seized upon by persons suing a corporation as a reason to disregard the corporate entity, thus enabling the litigants to sue the shareholders for the corporation's debts.

Legal requirements, such as annual state filings and payment of annual fees—as well as the filing of tax returns and the payment of state and federal taxes—are also required to maintain corporate status and remain in good standing.

6.10 What Should Be in My Client's Corporate Minutes?

You will be well served to limit the minutes of board of directors and board committee meetings to a brief narrative description of the course of the meeting. Clearly highlight decisions and actions taken by the board or committee in the form of resolutions, and include a record of how each director voted (or that the vote was unanimous) as well as the names of any directors who abstained from voting.

As set forth in *Nonprofit Governance and Management,* edited by V. Futter, J. Cion, and G. Overton and published by the American Bar Association and the American Society of Corporate Secretaries in 2002:

> The contrast between minutes and a mere mechanical record of a meeting or a transcript—full of irrelevant comment and unclear communication—is dramatic. Minutes record selectively, providing information essential to governance and management of the organization. Minutes may be used to resolve controversial matters and must be precise, clear, accurate, and consistent with the understanding of the meeting's participants. *Nonessential details may confuse the record and, in the worst case, create legal difficulties.* (Emphasis added.)

You may wish to have clients require that a resolution be passed to attach a report to the minutes, and/or to adhere to firm rules permitting only reports of great import to be bound to the minutes.

See section 6.12 for a checklist of things to include in corporate minutes and forms for the same.

6.11 What Are the Tax and Regulatory Obligations of a Corporation?

Legal requirements, such as annual state filings and payment of annual fees—as well as the filing of tax returns and the payment of state and federal taxes—are required to maintain corporate status and remain in good standing. These formalities must be carefully observed by corporations because of the swift and direct consequences of failing to do so (e.g., suspension of the corporate status and/or financial penalties).

1. Taxes.

The corporation will be required to pay estimated federal income tax in installments. Federal income tax returns must be filed on or before the fifteenth day of the third month following the close of the taxable year, unless a timely extension to file is obtained. It is usually wise for the corporation to hire an accountant to keep the corporation current with this and other tax-related requirements.

In addition, the corporation will likely be required to pay annual franchise taxes in each state where it is doing business for the privilege of exercising the corporate franchise in those states. Estimated tax for subsequent years may be payable to your state in installments.

The corporation will be required to withhold federal income tax and social security tax from taxable wages paid to its employees and deposited periodically with the appropriate Federal Tax Deposit Form. An Employer's Quarterly Federal Tax Return (IRS Form 941) must then be filed before the end of the month following each calendar quarter. The corporation may also be required to withhold state income tax from its employees' taxable wages.

2. Renewals.

Annual state filings, with the payment of annual fees, are required in the corporation's state of formation and in each state where it is qualified to do business.

3. Employer ID.

Every new employer must obtain a federal employer identification number (FEIN), which will be used on federal tax returns and certain other documents. A FEIN can be obtained by application to the Internal Revenue Service on Form SS-4.

4. More Taxes.

If the corporation owns significant personal property, it may be required to file a property statement with the county assessor and may be subject to a personal property tax. Information and forms may be obtained from your county assessor, where applicable.

If the nature of the corporation's business includes the sale at retail of tangible personal property (goods), then the corporation may be subject to sales and use taxes and would need to obtain a sellers' permit from its state and local authorities.

5. Business Licenses.

Most municipalities also require that businesses within their jurisdictions obtain a local business license.

6. Industry Regulations.

Numerous regulated businesses cannot lawfully be conducted without special licensing or permits (e.g., general contractors, insurance sales, and cosmetologists). Make sure you know what regulatory requirements are unique to your business.

6.12 Sample Documents and Checklists.

This section includes the following forms:

- First Correspondence to Newly Formed Corporation (Form 6 A)
- Second Correspondence to Newly Formed Corporation (Form 6 B)
- Articles of Incorporation—California (Form 6 C)
- Certificate of Incorporation—Delaware (Form 6 D)
- Statement of Incorporator (Form 6 E)
- Bylaws—California (Form 6 F)
- Bylaws—Delaware (Form 6 G)
- Initial Written Consent of Board of Directors (Form 6 H)
- Rules for Shareholders' Meetings (Form 6 I)
- Time and Responsibility Schedule for Annual Shareholder Meeting (Form 6 J)
- Directors' Written Consent (Form 6 K)
- Shareholders' Written Consent (Form 6 L)
- Stock Assignment Separate from Certificate (Form 6 M)
- Lost Securities Indemnity Agreement (Form 6 N)
- Foreign Corporation Certificate—Delaware (Form 6 O)
- Certificate of Amendment—Delaware (Form 6 P)

- Resignation of Officer/Director (Form 6 Q)
- Agreement for Inspector of Election (Form 6 R)
- Report of Inspector of Election (Form 6 S)
- Agreement to Terminate Voting Trust (Form 6 T)

Form 6 A: First Correspondence to Newly Formed Corporation

[Client Name]
[Client Address]

Dear [Client],

Congratulations on the formation of ****, Inc.!

Attached please find a copy of your Articles [or Certificate] of Incorporation which were filed with the California Secretary of State on _____, 20__. ****, Inc. was assigned California corporation number _____.

Also attached please find a Statement of Incorporator and a set of Bylaws for [****], Inc. for your review and consideration. For the next set of draft documents, it would be helpful for me to know your final decisions with regard to:

1. Which of you will hold the offices of:
   a. President,
   b. CFO/Treasurer, and
   c. Secretary;
2. The ownership percentage ownership each of you will hold initially; and
3. The amount each of you will be contributing to the corporation to fund start-up expenses in exchange for the issuance of your founders' stock.

You will need to obtain a Federal Employer Identification Number (FEIN) for the new entity, which you can do online by completing and submitting a Form SS-4 application. The start page is at http://www.irs.gov/businesses/small/article/0,,id=102767,00.html. Click on the "Apply Online Now" link on that page and follow the instructions. If you get stuck, give me a call. Once obtained, please send me a copy of your completed Form SS-4 and the assigned FEIN for my files. Tip: Don't use any punctuation on the application.

With the attached endorsed filed Articles of Incorporation and a FEIN, your bank should allow you to open a bank account for the new entity.

I will forward additional information to you shortly.

The balance of this correspondence is information I typically provide to newly formed U.S. corporations. It is an outline of corporate governance and operations requirements, including the roles of officers, directors, and shareholders in a U.S. corporation.

* *

I. BASIC STRUCTURE OF A CORPORATION

Corporations are just one of a number of forms in which one or more persons can come together to conduct a business in the United States. Corporations are owned by the shareholders who elect directors to manage the corporation. The management duties of the board of directors include making decisions regarding key policies and transactions and establishing the broad guidelines within which the business of the corporation will be conducted. The directors, in turn, appoint officers who carry out the day-to-day business of the corporation. Additional employees may be hired as well.

Perhaps the main distinguishing feature of a corporation is the provision of a limitation on the liability which the owners of the business, the shareholders in the case of a corporation, can incur as a result of the corporation's business affairs. So long as the corporation observes proper corporate formalities, the shareholders will not be personally liable for the corporation's obligations and liabilities. In other words, if the corporation's debts exceed the value of its assets, the corporation's creditors normally are not entitled to seek repayment from the shareholders' personal assets. Of course, a personal guarantee of an obligation would give rise to individual liability, as well as certain tax obligations, e.g. withholding taxes not remitted, and obligations based upon the personal tortious behavior of an officer or director. But, generally, the corporate shield protects individuals from corporate obligations.

The following is a brief description of the roles of the major players in a corporation, i.e., the shareholders, the directors, and the officers.

A. Shareholders

The shareholders own the corporation and provide the capital with which it commences its business. Shareholders, per se, do not take an active role in running the business. Beyond electing the directors and voting on certain key events in the corporation's life, the shareholders entrust management of the corporation to the directors and officers. The areas where shareholders need to vote and get involved in the corporate decision-making process are set forth in greater detail in the section below entitled "Observance of Corporate Formalities."

B. Directors

The board of directors manages the business and affairs of the corporation and exercises its corporate powers. The board may either perform these duties itself or, as is the more normal case, these duties can be performed by the officers under the direction of the board of directors. The board also has the power to delegate some of its duties to committees authorized by the board to perform these duties, although it is unlikely in your case that there will be much need for board committees in the near future.

In carrying out these duties directors have a "duty of loyalty" and a "duty of care" which run both to the corporation and to the shareholders as the ultimate owners of the corporation. These duties are often referred to as "fiduciary duties" in favor of the corporation and the shareholders. Failure to abide by these duties can result in personal liability of the directors.

The duty of loyalty dictates that a director must act in good faith and must not allow personal interests to prevail over interests of the corporation and its shareholders. Concerns as to whether a director is violating the duty of loyalty arise whenever it is proposed that the corporation enter into a transaction which benefits a director or where there may be a conflict of interest between the director and the corporation or its shareholders. Such "self-dealing" transactions are not prohibited but must be approached with great care to assure that proper corporate approval is obtained and that the transactions are fair to the corporation.

The duty of care requires a director to be diligent and prudent in managing the corporation's affairs. This concept is sometimes referred to as the duty to exercise good business judgment. While directors may be liable for actions which injure the corporation, whether the action results from the directors' negligence or from participation in or approval of a wrongful act, directors are not held liable merely because a carefully made decision turns out badly for the corporation. This idea, referred to as the "business judgment rule," is sometimes expressed as a recognition that so long as directors exercise their judgment without fraud or conflict of interest, they will not be second-guessed by courts based on how the decisions happen to work out.

C. Officers

Officers are appointed by the board of directors and serve at the pleasure of the board of directors subject to any contracts of employment with the corporation they may have. The officers perform the bulk of the day-to-day running of the corporation's business. Every corporation must have a president, a chief financial officer (also referred to as the "treasurer"), and a secretary. More than one of these offices can be held by the same individual. A corporation may have additional officers as well. These additional officers are either appointed by the board of directors or by the president or another officer if the board has delegated authority to make such appointments.

The following is a brief summary of the standard duties of the president, chief financial officer, and the secretary. All of these could be modified by the board of directors.

1. President. The President is the chief executive officer and general manager of the corporation unless the corporation has a Chairman of the Board and has designated the Chairman as chief executive officer. The President has general supervision, direction, and control over the corporation's business and its officers.
2. Chief Financial Officer. The Chief Financial Officer (or Treasurer) keeps the books and records of account of the properties and business transactions of the corporation. These duties include depositing corporate funds and other valuables in the name of the corporation and disbursing funds as directed by the Board of Directors.
3. Secretary. A corporation must keep written minutes of the proceedings of its shareholders, board, and committees of the board, and must keep a record of the shareholders, their addresses and their holdings. The Secretary usually has the duty of carrying out these functions and for giving notices of shareholders' and directors' meetings. In your context, where the shareholders and directors are unlikely to have separate meetings, these duties will be simplified.

II. OBSERVANCE OF CORPORATE FORMALITIES

The regular observance of corporate formalities is an important aspect of maintaining the protections and advantages which the corporate form offers, not the least of which, is the protection of shareholders against imposition of personal liability for obligations incurred by the Corporation. Three of the most important areas of corporate formalities are shareholder decision-making, director decision-making, and separation of corporate assets from personal assets. In general, it is appropriate to observe the following formalities in connection with the ongoing operations of a corporation:

A. Shareholder Action. The shareholders should take action to elect the board of directors of the Corporation annually. The election can occur at an annual meeting of the shareholders or by written consent if all of the shareholders consent to it in writing. In addition, certain specified fundamental changes in the form of operations of the Corporation require the consent or approval of the shareholders. The consent or approval can either be obtained through a formal shareholders' meeting or by written consent. These fundamental changes include the following:

1. Amendment of the Articles of Incorporation.
2. Sale of all or substantially all of the assets of the Corporation.
3. Merger or consolidation of the Corporation with or into any other corporation.
4. Winding up and dissolution of the Corporation.

B. Director Action. Matters of more general operating policy should be considered and authorized by the board of directors of the Corporation. Although there is no statutory requirement with respect to how frequently the board of directors should act, it is typical that the board of directors meets at least quarterly. In addition, a specially convened meeting of the board, as authorized by the Bylaws, may be called if action is required before the next regular meeting of the board. Action by the board may also be taken by the unanimous written consent of the directors. Although board actions may be taken by written consent without a meeting, it may prove useful to you to schedule the recordation of decisions on significant matters which have arisen on a quarterly or, at least, annual basis. Board meetings can generally be held either in person or by conference telephone so long as all of the directors in attendance can hear each other simultaneously.

Matters appropriate for director action, which can be immediately approved by written consent or which might arise and be accumulated, pending approval by the directors, include the following:

1. Appointment of officers, setting of salaries, and declaration of bonuses (at least annually, typically at a meeting of the board of directors immediately following the annual meeting of shareholders).
2. Appointment of board committees, if any.
3. Opening of corporate bank accounts and the designation and change of corporate officers authorized as signatories (any bank's corporate account form invariably includes a corporate resolution which the party executing the form represents to have been adopted by the board).
4. Corporate borrowing and the giving of security in connection therewith.
5. Consummation of material contracts for the acquisition or lease of significant assets or services or the disposition of assets or for the rendition of services outside the ordinary course of the business of the Corporation.
6. Policy decisions with respect to the construction of material assets or the investment of material amounts in research and development projects.
7. The adoption of pension, profit-sharing, bonus and other employee benefit plans.
8. The declaration of dividends or the redemption of shares.
9. Amendment of the Bylaws.
10. Review of financial statements of the Corporation.
11. Appointment of auditors, if any.
12. Any action which requires a shareholder vote.
13. The issuance and sale by the Corporation of additional shares or the grant of options to purchase additional shares.

In the case of any such actions, the secretary of the Corporation should prepare minutes of the meeting at which such actions were approved or prepare the form of written consent evidencing any such director or shareholder actions.

C. Separation of Corporate and Personal Assets. With respect to the small and/or closely-held company, owners are often careless in observing the requirements and formalities of doing business in a corporate form. This informality may lead to imposition of personal liability where the extent to which the financial affairs and accounts of a corporation and those who control it are confused to the prejudice of creditors, or where there has been an undue diversion of corporate funds or other assets to individual use. In other words, the owners of a corporation may be held personally liable when they treat the assets of the corporation as their own and add or withdraw capital from the corporation at will.

III. POST-INCORPORATION MATTERS

Although it is not intended to be exhaustive, the following checklist summarizes some of the legal requirements of a new corporation. Some of the requirements arise as a consequence of incorporation; others apply to all new businesses regardless of the form of entity. Certain requirements are highly formal and technical; many must be satisfied within a specified time period. Care must be taken to comply with these matters as they arise because in many cases there are serious penalties which can be assessed for failure to comply.

A. Qualification to Do Business in Other States. If a corporation is doing business in a state other than its state of incorporation, it must qualify to do business in each such state, typically by appointing an agent for service of process, filing qualification documentation with, and paying a fee to, such state's Secretary of State.

B. Local Business License. A corporation is typically required to obtain a business license from the city or cities in which it intends to operate.

C. Employer Identification Number (EIN). Every employer must obtain an employer identification number which will be used on federal tax returns and certain other documents.

D. Annual List of Officers, Directors, and Agent. Each year, or biannually in some states, a corporation must submit a list of officers, directors, and agent for service of process in each state in which it is qualified to do business, which informs each state as to the identity of the directors, officers, and agent for service of process of the corporation. These forms are typically filed with the state's Secretary of State.

E. Estimated Federal Income Tax. A corporation may be required to pay estimated federal income tax in installments. Your accountant should keep you current with this requirement.

F. State Tax. State franchise taxes are imposed on corporations for the privilege of exercising the corporate franchise in each state where the corporation is qualified to do business. Your accountant should also be able to keep you current with the tax requirements in each of the relevant states.

G. Tax Returns. Both federal and state income tax returns must be filed on or before the fifteenth day of the third month following the close of the taxable year, unless a timely extension to file is obtained.

H. Personal Property Taxes. If the corporation owns significant personal property it may be required to file a property statement with its local County Assessor and may be subject to a personal property tax. Forms may be obtained from the relevant County Assessor.

I. Sales and Use Taxes. If the nature of the corporation's business includes the sale at retail of tangible personal property (goods), then the corporation may be subject to sales and use taxes and would need to obtain a sellers' permit or retail license. In California, the issuing authority for this type of license is the State Board of Equalization.

J. Payroll Withholding. The corporation will be required to comply with state and federal withholding requirements with respect to wages paid to its employees. Funds withheld must be deposited in certain depositories accompanied by deposit forms. Employer's returns must also be filed quarterly. Any officer or other person charged with the withholding of taxes may become personally liable for a 100% penalty if he or she fails to file the appropriate forms or fails to pay the withheld funds to the Internal Revenue Service or state authority.

K. Federal Unemployment Tax. The "Unemployment Tax Return" (IRS Form 940) must be filed and any balance due paid annually on or before January 31. Details may be found in IRS Circular E, the "Employer's Tax Guide."

L. Unemployment Compensation Insurance. Registration with a state administered unemployment compensation insurance program may be required in any state where the Corporation has employees. Ask for the appropriate forms when setting up your payroll service.

M. Workers' Compensation. Check for state requirements regarding workers' compensation liability in each state where the corporation has employees. The required insurance may be obtained through a State Compensation Insurance Fund, or equivalent, or it may be placed with a licensed workers' compensation private carrier.

IV. GENERAL

A. Signing on Behalf of the Corporation

Whenever the officers are signing documents or correspondence on behalf of the corporation, care should be taken to include the corporation's name in the signature block and to indicate the title of the officer signing. An example of an appropriate signature block is included below:

[corporation name]

By: _____
[name of signatory], its President

Failure to do so may lead, in the context of litigation involving a signed document, to including in the lawsuit the person who signed in his or her individual capacity.

B. Bylaws

The Bylaws of a corporation are an important source of advice on corporate governance matters. While the Bylaws are not exhaustive, they contain a summary of many of the laws pertaining to corporations. Other rules exist in the general corporation law of the state in which the corporation was incorporated and of each state in which the corporation is qualified to do business.

C. Official Documents

It may be useful to designate one of the officers, such as the corporate secretary, to be the recipient of all "official" correspondence concerning the corporation and its relationships with the various agencies with which it deals. This should help avoid forgetting to submit regularly filed forms, such as the annual list of officers, directors, and agent, which though simple to complete, can lead to problems if they are not timely submitted.

D. Finances

An important feature of observing corporate formalities is to scrupulously keep the corporation's money separate from the personal funds of shareholders, directors, officers, and employees. Failure to keep funds separate is a common problem with closely held or newly formed corporations. Such a co-mingling of funds is often seized upon by persons suing a corporation as a reason why the corporate entity should be disregarded, thus enabling them to sue the shareholders for the corporation's debts, as discussed above under "Separation of Corporate and Personal Assets."

* *

Please don't hesitate to call me with any questions regarding the above, or any other matter.

Very truly yours,

_____

[Counsel]

Form 6 B: Second Correspondence to Newly Formed Corporation

[Client Name]
[Client Address]

Dear _____,

To follow-up on my prior correspondence dated [date of First Correspondence to Newly Formed Corporation], attached please find the following additional organizational documents for [****], Inc.: a draft Initial Written Consent of the Sole Director and a form of stock certificate for your review and consideration.

Don't hesitate to call with any questions or changes with regard to the attached or the Statement of Incorporator and Bylaws forwarded previously. When finalized, please send me copies of the signed Bylaws and Written Consent for my files.

Please note that there are a couple of blanks in the Director Written Consent where we need to designate the value of the consideration (cash and/or other) that is being contributed to the corporation in exchange for the shares being issued. Let me know if you need help deciding what that amount should be.

Several other items will require your attention in connection with the organization of [****], Inc.:

1. In case you have not yet obtained a Federal Employer Identification Number (FEIN) for the new entity, here is the link to the online application http://www.irs.gov/businesses/small/article/0,,id=102767,00.html. Click on the "Apply Online Now" link on that page and follow the instructions. If you have already obtained your FEIN, please send me a copy of your completed Form SS-4 and the assigned FEIN for my files.

2. You need to complete an IRS Form 2553 to elect to be treated as an S Corp. The form can be completed online and submitted via fax. Form 2553 is available online at http://www.irs.gov/pub/irs-pdf/f2553.pdf. The instructions are available at http://www.irs.gov/pub/irs-pdf/iss4.pdf. This will allow the profits and losses of the corporation to flow-through to the owners without incurring corporate level taxation. Please note that the election must be made in a timely fashion to be effective for this tax year—check with your accountant if you have any questions in that regard.

3. [Other requirements, such as: You need to complete a Statement of Information for the [California] Secretary of State and pay the $25 filing fee by _____,20__, to maintain the company's good standing. This can be done online at the following link: https://businessfilings.ss.ca.gov/ (just drop in the corporation's name or corporation number to get the correct form).]

4. Finally, please don't forget to go through the list of "Post-Incorporation Matters" in prior correspondence for some of the other things you may need to put in place for the new entity (e.g. a business license, unemployment and worker's compensation insurance, etc.).

Very truly yours,

_____

[Counsel]

Form 6 C: Articles of Incorporation—California

Note: Articles of incorporation, or certificates of incorporation as they are called in the State of Delaware, are filed with the secretary of state to form the corporation. They may be amended or amended and restated in their entirety by subsequent filing. The requirements for approval of amendments to articles or certificates of incorporation depend in part on whether shares have been issued, state law, and applicable provisions in the document being amended and the company's bylaws. The rules governing mandatory and permissible contents for articles and certificates of incorporation are governed by state law and vary from state to state. The following Articles of Incorporation form meets statutory requirements in the State of California.

ARTICLES OF
INCORPORATION OF
[****], INC.

FIRST: The name of this corporation is [****], Inc.

SECOND: The purpose of this corporation is to engage in any lawful act or activity for which a corporation may be organized under the General Corporation Law of California other than the banking business, the trust company business or the practice of a profession permitted to be incorporated by the California Corporations Code.

THIRD: The total number of shares which the Corporation is authorized to issue is [one million (1,000,000)] shares, all of which shall be Common Stock having no par value.

FOURTH: The name and address of the initial agent for service of process in the State of California is:

> [Counsel], Esq.
> [Firm]
> [Address]

FIFTH: (a) The personal liability of the directors of this corporation for monetary damages shall be eliminated to the fullest extent permissible under California law.

(b) This corporation is authorized to provide indemnification of its agents (as defined in Section 317 of the California General Corporation Law) through bylaw provisions, agreements with the agents, votes of shareholders or disinterested directors or otherwise, in excess of the indemnification otherwise permitted by such Section 317, subject only to the applicable limits set forth in Section 204 of the California General Corporation Law with respect to actions for breach of duty to the corporation and its shareholders.

(c) Any repeal or modification of the foregoing provisions of this Article shall be prospective only, and shall not adversely affect any limitation on the personal liability of a director of this corporation with respect to any act or omission occurring prior to the time of such repeal or modification.

By: _____

[Counsel], Incorporator

Form 6 D: Certificate of Incorporation—Delaware

STATE *OF* DELAWARE

CERIFICATE *OF* INCORPORATION

A STOCK CORPORATION

First: The name of this Corporation is ****, INC.

Second: The name and address of its registered office in the State of Delaware is:

_____

_____

_____

_____, Delaware _____

County of _____

Third: The purpose of the corporation is to engage in any lawful act or activity for which corporations may be organized under the General Corporation Law of Delaware.

Fourth: (a) The corporation is authorized to issue two (2) classes of stock to be designated common and preferred. The corporation is authorized to issue _____ shares of common stock and _____ shares of preferred stock, each with a par value of $_____ per share, amounting in the aggregate to _____ Dollars ($_____).

(b) The preferred shares may be issued in any number of series, as determined by the board of directors. The board may by resolution fix the designation and the number of shares of any such series and may determine, alter, or revoke the rights, preferences, privileges, and restrictions pertaining to any wholly unissued series. The board may thereafter in the same manner increase or decrease the number of share of any such series (but not below the number of share of that series then outstanding).

Fifth: The name and mailing address of the incorporator is as follows:

_____

_____

_____

Sixth: The corporation is to have perpetual existence.

Seventh: To the fullest extent permitted by the General Corporation Law of Delaware, a director of this corporation shall not be liable to the corporation or its stockholders for monetary damages for breach of fiduciary duty as a director.

Eighth: In furtherance and not in limitation of the powers conferred by statute, the board of directors is expressly authorized to make, alter, or repeal the bylaws of the corporation.

137

Ninth: Elections of directors need not be by written ballot unless the bylaws of the corporation shall so provide.

Tenth: Meetings of the stockholders may be held within or without the State of Delaware, as the bylaws may provide. Except as otherwise required under Delaware General Corporation Law, the books of the corporation may be kept outside the State of Delaware at such place or places as may be designated from time to time by the board of directors or in the bylaws of the corporation.

Eleventh: The corporation reserves the right to amend, alter, change or repeal any provision contained in this Certificate of Incorporation, in the manner now or hereafter prescribed by law, and all rights conferred upon stockholders herein are granted subject to this reservation.

I, the undersigned incorporator, for the purpose of forming a corporation under the laws of the State of Delaware, do make, file and record this Certificate, and do certify that the facts herein stated are true, and I have accordingly hereunto set my hand this ___ day of _____, 20___.

By: _____

_____, Incorporator

Form 6 E: Statement of Incorporator

Note: Articles of incorporation, or certificates of incorporation as they are called in the State of Delaware, are filed with the secretary of state to form the corporation. They may be amended or amended and restated in their entirety by subsequent filing. Rules governing mandatory and permissible contents for articles and certificates of incorporation are governed by state law and vary from state to state. The following Articles of Incorporation form meets statutory requirements in the State of California.

STATEMENT OF INCORPORATOR

OF

[****] INC.

The Articles of Incorporation of [****], INC. having been filed in the office of the Secretary of State of [California] on ____, 20__, the undersigned, being the Incorporator named in said Articles of Incorporation, does hereby state that the following actions were taken on this day for the purpose of organizing this corporation:

1. Bylaws for the regulation of the affairs of this corporation were adopted by the undersigned Incorporator as and for the Bylaws of this corporation, and the Secretary of this corporation was authorized, directed and empowered to execute a certificate of the adoption of such Bylaws and to insert such Bylaws, similarly certified, into the minute book which shall be kept at the principal executive office of this corporation in accordance with [state law, such as: Section 213 of the California Corporations Code].

2. The initial Board of Directors was determined to be comprised of one individual in accordance with Section 3.2 of the Bylaws of this corporation. [Name] was appointed to serve as the initial director of this corporation and to hold office until the first annual meeting of the shareholders or until her successor is elected and qualified.

DATED: [Date of filing of Articles/Certificate of Incorporation], 20__

_____

[Counsel], Incorporator

Form 6 F: Bylaws—California

Note: Bylaws are not filed with any public agency during the organizational process. They may generally be amended or amended and restated in their entirety upon approval by the board of directors and shareholders. However, the requirements for approval of amendments to the bylaws depend in part on whether shares have been issued, state law, and applicable provisions in the document being amended and the company's articles or certificate of incorporation. Many of the corporate governance rules and provisions contained in bylaws are dictated by state law and vary from state to state. The following Articles of Incorporation form meets statutory requirements in the State of California.

BYLAWS

OF

[****], INC.

A California Corporation

ARTICLE I Offices

Section 1.1   Principal Executive Office.

The principal executive office of the corporation shall be located at such place as the Board of Directors may from time to time authorize. If the principal executive office is located outside this state, and the corporation has one or more business offices in this state, the Board of Directors shall fix and designate a principal business office in the State of California.

Section 1.2   Other Offices.

Other business offices may at any time be established at any place or places specified by the Board of Directors.

ARTICLE II Meetings of Shareholders

Section 2.1   Place of Meetings.

All meetings of shareholders shall be held at the principal executive office of the corporation, or at any other place, within or without the State of California, specified by the Board of Directors.

Section 2.2   Annual Meeting.

The annual meeting of the shareholders shall be held at the time and date in each year fixed by the Board of Directors. At the annual meeting, directors shall be elected, reports of the affairs of the corporation shall be considered, and any other business may be transacted that is within the power of the shareholders.

Section 2.3   Notice of Annual Meeting.

Written notice of each annual meeting shall be given to each shareholder entitled to vote, either personally or by first-class mail, or, if the corporation has outstanding shares held of record by 500 or more persons (determined in accordance
with Section 605 of the General Corporation Law) on the record date for the meeting,
by third-class mail, or by other means of written communication, charges prepaid,
addressed to such shareholder at the shareholder's address appearing on the books
of the corporation or given by such shareholder to the corporation for the purpose of
notice. If any notice or report addressed to the shareholder at the address of such
shareholder appearing on the books of the corporation is returned to the corporation
by the United States Postal Service marked to indicate that the United States Postal
Service is unable to deliver the notice or report to the shareholder at such address,
all future notices or reports shall be deemed to have been duly given without further
mailing if the same shall be available for the shareholder upon written demand of the
shareholder at the principal executive office of the corporation for a period of one
year from the date of the giving of the notice or report to all other shareholders. If a
shareholder gives no address, notice shall be deemed to have been given to such
shareholder if addressed to the shareholder at the place where the principal executive office of the corporation is situated, or if published at least once in some newspaper of general circulation in the county in which said principal executive office is
located.

All such notices shall be given to each shareholder entitled thereto not less than
ten (10) days (or, if sent by third-class mail, thirty (30) days) nor more than sixty (60)
days before each annual meeting. Any such notice shall be deemed to have been
given at the time when delivered personally or deposited in the mail or sent by other
means of written communication. An affidavit of mailing of any such notice in accordance with the foregoing provisions, executed by the Secretary, Assistant Secretary
or any transfer agent of the corporation shall be prima facie evidence of the giving of
the notice.

Such notice shall specify:

(a)   the place, the date, and the hour of such meeting;

(b)   those matters that the Board of Directors, at the time of the mailing of
the notice, intends to present for action by the shareholders (but, subject to the provisions of subsection (d) below, any proper matter may be presented at the meeting
for such action);

(c)   if directors are to be elected, the names of nominees intended at the
time of the notice to be presented by the Board of Directors for election;

(d)   the general nature of a proposal, if any, to take action with respect to
approval of (i) a contract or other transaction with an interested director, (ii) amendment of the Articles of Incorporation, (iii) a reorganization of the corporation as
defined in Section 181 of the General Corporation Law, (iv) voluntary dissolution of
the corporation, or (v) a distribution in dissolution other than in accordance with the
rights of outstanding preferred shares, if any; and

(e)   such other matters, if any, as may be expressly required by statute.

Section 2.4   Special Meetings.

Special meetings of the shareholders for any purpose or purposes whatsoever
may be called at any time by the Chairman of the Board (if there be such an officer
appointed), by the President, by the Board of Directors, or by one or more shareholders entitled to cast not less than ten percent (10%) of the votes at the meeting.

Section 2.5   Notice of Special Meetings.

Upon request in writing that a special meeting of shareholders be called for any proper purpose, directed to the Chairman of the Board (if there be such an officer appointed), President, Vice President or Secretary by any person (other than the Board of Directors) entitled to call a special meeting of shareholders, the officer forthwith shall cause notice to be given to the shareholders entitled to vote that a meeting will be held at a time requested by the person or persons calling the meeting, not less than thirty-five (35) nor more than sixty (60) days after the receipt of the request. Except in special cases where other express provision is made by statute, notice of any special meeting of shareholders shall be given in the same manner as for annual meetings of shareholders. In addition to the matters required by Section 2.3(a) and, if applicable, Section 2.3(c) of these Bylaws, notice of any special meeting shall specify the general nature of the business to be transacted, and no other business may be transacted at such meeting.

Section 2.6   Quorum.

The presence in person or by proxy of persons entitled to vote a majority of the voting shares at any meeting shall constitute a quorum for the transaction of business. If a quorum is present, the affirmative vote of a majority of the shares represented and voting at the meeting (which shares voting affirmatively also constitute at least a majority of the required quorum) shall be the act of the shareholders, unless the vote of a greater number or voting by classes is required by the General Corporation Law or the Articles of Incorporation. Any meeting of shareholders, whether or not a quorum is present, may be adjourned from time to time by the vote of the holders of a majority of the shares present in person or represented by proxy thereat and entitled to vote, but in the absence of a quorum no other business may be transacted at such meeting, except that the shareholders present or represented by proxy at a duly called or held meeting, at which a quorum is present, may continue to transact business until adjournment, notwithstanding the withdrawal of enough shareholders to leave less than a quorum, if any action taken (other than adjournment) is approved by at least a majority of the shares required to constitute a quorum.

Section 2.7   Adjourned Meeting and Notice.

When any shareholders' meeting, either annual or special, is adjourned for more than forty-five (45) days, or if after adjournment a new record date is fixed for the adjourned meeting, notice of the adjourned meeting shall be given as in the case of an original meeting. Except as provided above, it shall not be necessary to give any notice of the time and place of the adjourned meeting or of the business to be transacted thereat, other than by announcement of the time and place thereof at the meeting at which such adjournment is taken.

Section 2.8   Record Date.

(a) The Board of Directors may fix a time in the future as a record date for the determination of the shareholders entitled to notice of and to vote at any meeting of shareholders or entitled to give consent to corporate action in writing without a meeting, to receive any report, to receive any dividend or other distribution, or allotment of any rights, or to exercise rights in respect of any other lawful action. The record date so fixed shall be not more than sixty (60) days nor less than ten (10) days prior to the date of such meeting, nor more than sixty (60) days prior to any other action. A determination of shareholders of record entitled to notice of or to vote at a meeting of shareholders shall apply to any adjournment of the meeting unless the Board of Directors fixes a new record date for the adjourned meeting, but the Board of Directors shall fix a new record date if the meeting is adjourned for more than forty-five (45) days from the date set for the original meeting. When a record date is so fixed, only shareholders of record at the close of business on that date are entitled to notice of and to vote at any such meeting, to give consent without a meeting, to receive any report, to receive the dividend, distribution, or allotment of rights, or to exercise the rights, as the case may be, notwithstanding any transfer of any shares on the books of the corporation after the record date, except as otherwise provided in the Articles of Incorporation or these Bylaws.

(b) If no record date is fixed:

(1) The record date for determining shareholders entitled to notice of or to vote at a meeting of shareholders shall be at the close of business on the business day next preceding the day on which notice is given or, if notice is waived, at the close of business on the business day preceding the day on which the meeting is held.

(2) The record date for determining shareholders entitled to give consent to corporate action in writing without a meeting, when no prior action by the Board of Directors has been taken, shall be the day on which the first written consent is given.

(3) The record date for determining shareholders for any other purpose shall be at the close of business on the day on which the Board of Directors adopts the resolution relating thereto, or the sixtieth (60th) day prior to the date of such other action, whichever is later.

Section 2.9   Voting.

(a) Except as provided below with respect to cumulative voting and except as may be otherwise provided in the Articles of Incorporation, each outstanding share, regardless of class, shall be entitled to one vote on each matter submitted to a vote of shareholders. Any holders of shares entitled to vote on any matter may vote part of the shares in favor of the proposal and refrain from voting the remaining shares or vote them against the proposal, other than elections to office, but, if the shareholder fails to specify the number of shares such shareholder is voting affirmatively, it will be conclusively presumed that the shareholder's approving vote is with respect to all shares such shareholder is entitled to vote.

(b) Subject to the provisions of Sections 702 through 704 of the General Corporation Law (relating to voting of shares held by a fiduciary, receiver, pledgee, or minor, in the name of a corporation, or in joint ownership), persons in whose names shares entitled to vote stand on the stock records of the corporation at the close of business on the record date shall be entitled to vote at the meeting of shareholders. Such vote may be viva voce or by ballot; provided, however, that all elections for directors must be by ballot upon demand made by a shareholder at any election and before the voting begins. Shares of this corporation owned by a corporation more than twenty-five percent (25%) of the voting power of which is owned directly by this corporation, or indirectly through one or more majority-owned subsidiaries of this corporation, shall not be entitled to vote on any matter.

(c) Subject to the requirements of the next sentence, every shareholder entitled to vote at any election for directors shall have the right to cumulate such shareholder's votes and give one candidate a number of votes equal to the number of directors to be elected multiplied by the number of votes to which such shareholder's shares are normally entitled, or to distribute votes on the same principle among as many candidates as such shareholder thinks fit. No shareholder shall be entitled to cumulate votes unless such candidate's name or candidates' names have been placed in nomination prior to the voting and the shareholder has given notice at the meeting, prior to the voting, of the shareholder's intention to cumulate such shareholder's votes. If any one shareholder has given such notice, all shareholders may cumulate their votes for candidates in nomination. The candidates receiving the highest number of affirmative votes of shares entitled to be voted for them, up to the number of directors to be elected by such shares, shall be elected. Votes against a director and votes withheld shall have no legal effect.

Section 2.10   Proxies.

(a) Every person entitled to vote shares (including voting by written consent) may authorize another person or other persons to act by proxy with respect to such shares. "Proxy" means a written authorization signed by a shareholder or the shareholder's attorney-in-fact giving another person or persons power to vote with respect to the shares of such shareholder. "Signed" for the purpose of this Section means the placing of the shareholder's name on the proxy (whether by manual signature, typewriting, telegraphic transmission, or otherwise) by the shareholder or the shareholder's attorney-in-fact. Any proxy duly executed is not revoked and continues in full force and effect until (i) a written instrument revoking it is filed with the Secretary of the corporation prior to the vote pursuant thereto, (ii) a subsequent proxy executed by the person executing the prior proxy is presented to the meeting, (iii) the person executing the proxy attends the meeting and votes in person, or (iv) written notice of the death or incapacity of the maker of such proxy is received by the corporation before the vote pursuant thereto is counted; provided that no such proxy shall be valid after the expiration of eleven (11) months from the date of its execution, unless otherwise provided in the proxy. Notwithstanding the foregoing sentence, a proxy that states that it is irrevocable, is irrevocable for the period specified therein to the extent permitted by Section 705(e) and (f) of the General Corporation Law. The dates contained on the forms of proxy presumptively determine the order of execution, regardless of the postmark dates on the envelopes in which they are mailed.

(b) As long as no outstanding class of securities of the corporation is registered under Section 12 of the Securities Exchange Act of 1934, or is not exempted from such registration by Section 12(g)(2) of such Act, any form of proxy or written consent distributed to ten (10) or more shareholders of the corporation when outstanding shares of the corporation are held of record by 100 or more persons shall afford an opportunity on the proxy or form of written consent to specify a choice between approval and disapproval of each matter or group of related matters intended to be acted upon at the meeting for which the proxy is solicited or by such written consent, other than elections to office, and shall provide, subject to reasonable specified conditions, that where the person solicited specifies a choice with respect to any such matter the shares will be voted in accordance therewith. In any election of directors, any form of proxy in which the directors to be voted upon are named therein as candidates and which is marked by a shareholder "withhold" or otherwise marked in a manner indicating that the authority to vote for the election of directors is withheld shall not be voted for the election of a director.

Section 2.11   Validation of Defectively Called or Noticed Meetings.

The transactions of any meeting of shareholders, however called and noticed, and wherever held, are as valid as though had at a meeting duly held after regular call and notice, if a quorum is present either in person or by proxy, and if, either before or after the meeting, each of the persons entitled to vote, not present in person or by proxy, signs a written waiver of notice or a consent to the holding of the meeting or an approval of the minutes thereof. All such waivers, consents, and approvals shall be filed with the corporate records or made a part of the minutes of the meeting. Attendance of a person at a meeting shall constitute a waiver of notice of and presence at such meeting, except when the person objects, at the beginning of the meeting, to the transaction of any business because the meeting is not lawfully called or convened and except that attendance at a meeting is not a waiver of any right to object to the consideration of matters required by these Bylaws or by the General Corporation Law to be included in the notice if such objection is expressly made at the meeting. Neither the business to be transacted at nor the purpose of any regular or special meeting of shareholders need be specified in any written waiver of notice, consent to the holding of the meeting or approval of the minutes thereof, unless otherwise provided in the Articles of Incorporation or these Bylaws, or unless the meeting involves one or more matters specified in Section 2.3(d) of these Bylaws.

Section 2.12   Action Without Meeting.

(a) Directors may be elected without a meeting by a consent in writing, setting forth the action so taken, signed by all of the persons who would be entitled to vote for the election of directors, provided that, without notice except as hereinafter set forth, a director may be elected at any time to fill a vacancy not filled by the directors (other than a vacancy created by removal of a director) by the written consent of persons holding a majority of the outstanding shares entitled to vote for the election of directors.

Any other action that may be taken at a meeting of the shareholders, may be taken without a meeting, and without prior notice except as hereinafter set forth, if a consent in writing, setting forth the action so taken, is signed by the holders of outstanding shares having not less than the minimum number of votes that would be necessary to authorize or take such action at a meeting at which all shares entitled to vote thereon were present and voted.

(b) Unless the consents of all shareholders entitled to vote have been solicited in writing:

(1) notice of any proposed shareholder approval of (i) a contract or other transaction with an interested director, (ii) indemnification of an agent of the corporation, (iii) a reorganization of the corporation as defined in Section 181 of the General Corporation Law, or (iv) a distribution in dissolution other than in accordance with the rights of outstanding preferred shares, if any, without a meeting by less than unanimous written consent, shall be given at least ten (10) days before the consummation of the action authorized by such approval; and

(2) prompt notice shall be given of the taking of any other corporate action approved by shareholders without a meeting by less than unanimous written consent to those shareholders entitled to vote who have not consented in writing. Such notices shall be given in the manner provided in Section 2.3 of these Bylaws.

(c) Any shareholder giving a written consent, or the shareholder's proxyholders, or a transferee of the shares or a personal representative of the shareholder or their respective proxyholders, may revoke the consent by a writing received by the corporation prior to the time that written consents of the number of shares required to authorize the proposed action have been filed with the Secretary of the corporation, but may not do so thereafter. Such revocation is effective upon its receipt by the Secretary of the corporation.

Section 2.13 Inspectors of Election.

(a) In advance of any meeting of shareholders, the Board of Directors may appoint inspectors of election to act at the meeting and any adjournment thereof. If inspectors of election are not so appointed, or if any persons so appointed fail to appear or refuse to act, the chairman of any such meeting may, and on the request of any shareholder or the holder of such shareholder's proxy shall, appoint inspectors of election (or persons to replace those who so fail or refuse) at the meeting. The number of inspectors shall be either one or three. If inspectors are appointed at a meeting on the request of one or more shareholders or holders of proxies, the majority of shares represented in person or by proxy shall determine whether one inspector or three inspectors are to be appointed.

(b) The inspectors of election shall determine the number of shares outstanding and the voting power of each, the shares represented at the meeting, the existence of a quorum and the authenticity, validity and effect of proxies; receive votes, ballots or consents; hear and determine all challenges and questions in any way arising in connection with the right to vote; count and tabulate all votes or consents; determine when the polls shall close; determine the result; and do such acts as may be proper to conduct the election or vote with fairness to all shareholders.

(c) The inspectors of election shall perform their duties impartially, in good faith, to the best of their ability and as expeditiously as is practical. If there are three inspectors of election, the decision, act or certificate of a majority is effective in all respects as the decision, act or certificate of all. Any report or certificate made by the inspectors of election is prima facie evidence of the facts stated therein.

ARTICLE III Board of Directors

Section 3.1 Powers; Approval of Loans to Officers.

(a) Subject to the provisions of the General Corporation Law and any limitations in the Articles of Incorporation relating to action required to be approved by the shareholders or by the outstanding shares, the business and affairs of the corporation shall be managed and all corporate powers shall be exercised by or under the direction of the Board of Directors. The Board of Directors may delegate the management of the day-to-day operation of the business of the corporation to a management company or other person provided that the business and affairs of the corporation shall be managed and all corporate powers shall be exercised under the ultimate direction of the Board of Directors.

(b) The corporation may, upon approval of the Board of Directors alone, make loans of money or property to, or guarantee the obligations of, any officer (whether or not a director) of the corporation or of its parent, or adopt an employee benefit plan authorizing such loans or guaranties provided that:

(1) the Board of Directors determines that such a loan, guaranty, or plan may reasonably be expected to benefit the corporation;

(2) the corporation has outstanding shares held of record by 100 or more persons (determined as provided in Section 605 of the General Corporation Law) on the date of approval by the Board of Directors;

(3) the approval by the Board of Directors is by a vote sufficient without counting the vote of any interested director(s); and

(4) the loan is otherwise made in compliance with Section 315 of the General Corporation Law.

Section 3.2   Number and Qualification of Directors.

The authorized number of directors shall be not less than three (3), nor more than five (5), except that so long as the corporation has only one (1) shareholder, the number of directors may be one (1) and so long as the corporation has only two (2) shareholders, the number of directors may be two (2). The number of directors shall always be within the authorized limits specified above, and as determined by resolution adopted by the Board of Directors. The authorized number of directors may be changed only by an amendment of the Articles of Incorporation or of these Bylaws, such amendment being duly adopted by a vote or written consent of holders of a majority of the outstanding shares, provided that any proposal to reduce the authorized number of directors to a number less than three (3) cannot be adopted if the votes cast against its adoption at a meeting, or the shares not consenting in the case of action by written consent, are equal to more than sixteen and two-thirds percent (16-2/3%) of the outstanding shares entitled to vote.

Section 3.3   Election and Term of Office.

The directors shall be elected at each annual meeting of shareholders, but, if any such annual meeting is not held or the directors are not elected thereat, the directors may be elected at any special meeting of shareholders held for that purpose. Each director, including a director elected to fill a vacancy, shall hold office until the expiration of the term for which elected and until a successor has been elected and qualified.

Section 3.4   Vacancies.

A vacancy in the Board of Directors shall be deemed to exist in case of the death, resignation or removal of any director, if a director has been declared of unsound mind by order of court or convicted of a felony, if the authorized number of directors is increased, if the incorporator or incorporators have failed to appoint the authorized number of directors in any resolution for appointment of directors upon the initial organization of the corporation, or if the shareholders fail, at any annual or special meeting of shareholders at which any director or directors are elected, to elect the full authorized number of directors to be voted for at that meeting.

Vacancies in the Board of Directors, except for a vacancy created by the removal of a director, may be filled by a majority of the directors present at a meeting at which a quorum is present, or if the number of directors then in office is less than a quorum, (a) by the unanimous written consent of the directors then in office, (b) by the vote of a majority of the directors then in office at a meeting held pursuant to notice or waivers of notice in compliance with these Bylaws, or (c) by a sole remaining director. Each director so elected shall hold office until his or her successor is elected at an annual or a special meeting of the shareholders. A vacancy in the Board of Directors created by the removal of a director may be filled only by the vote of a majority of the shares entitled to vote represented at a duly held meeting at which a quorum is present, or by the written consent of all of the holders of the outstanding shares entitled to vote.

The shareholders entitled to vote may elect a director or directors at any time to fill any vacancy or vacancies not filled by the directors. Any such election by written consent other than to fill a vacancy created by removal shall require the consent of holders of a majority of the outstanding shares entitled to vote. Any such election by written consent to fill a vacancy created by removal shall require the unanimous written consent of all shares entitled to vote for the election of such directors.

Any director may resign effective upon giving written notice to the Chairman of the Board (if there be such an officer appointed), the President, the Secretary or the Board of Directors of the corporation, unless the notice specifies a later time for the effectiveness of such resignation. If the resignation is effective at a future time, a successor may be elected to take office when the resignation becomes effective.

No reduction of the authorized number of directors shall have the effect of removing any director prior to the expiration of the director's term of office.

Section 3.5   Time and Place of Meetings.

The Board of Directors shall hold a regular meeting immediately after the meeting of shareholders at which it is elected and at the place where such meeting is held, or at such other place as shall be fixed by the Board of Directors, for the purpose of organization, election of officers of the corporation and the transaction of other business. Notice of such meeting is hereby dispensed with. Other regular meetings of the Board of Directors shall be held without notice at such times and places as are fixed by the Board of Directors. Special meetings of the Board of Directors may be held at any time whenever called by the Chairman of the Board (if there be such an officer appointed), the President, any Vice-President, the Secretary or any two (2) directors.

Except as hereinabove provided in this Section 3.5, all meetings of the Board of Directors may be held at any place within or without the State of California that has been designated by resolution of the Board of Directors as the place for the holding of regular meetings, or by written consent of all directors. In the absence of such designation, meetings of the Board of Directors shall be held at the principal executive office of the corporation. Special meetings of the Board of Directors may be held either at a place so designated or at the principal executive office of the corporation.

Section 3.6   Notice of Special Meetings.

Notice of the time and place of special meetings shall be delivered personally to each director or communicated to each director by telephone, telegraph or mail, charges prepaid, addressed to the director at the director's address as it is shown upon the records of the corporation or, if it is not so shown on such records or is not readily ascertainable, at the place at which the meetings of the directors are regularly held. In case such notice is mailed, it shall be deposited in the United States mail at least four (4) days prior to the time of the holding of the meeting. In case such notice is delivered personally or by telephone or telegraph, as above provided, it shall be so delivered at least forty-eight (48) hours prior to the time of the holding of the meeting. Such mailing, telegraphing or delivery, personally or by telephone, as above provided, shall be due legal and personal notice to such director.

Notice of a meeting need not be given to any director who signs a waiver of notice or a consent to holding the meeting or an approval of the minutes thereof, whether before or after the meeting, or who attends the meeting without protesting, prior thereto or at its commencement, the lack of notice to such director. All such waivers, consents and approvals shall be filed with the corporate records or made a part of the minutes of the meetings.

Section 3.7   Action at a Meeting: Quorum and Required Vote.

Presence of a majority of the authorized number of directors at a meeting of the Board of Directors constitutes a quorum for the transaction of business, except as hereinafter provided. Members of the Board of Directors may participate in a meeting through use of conference telephone or similar communications equipment, so long as all members participating in such meeting can hear one another. Participation in a meeting as permitted in the preceding sentence constitutes presence in person at such meeting. Every act or decision done or made by a majority of the directors present at a meeting duly held at which a quorum is present is the act of the Board of Directors, unless a greater number, or the same number after disqualifying one or more directors from voting, is required by law, by the Articles of Incorporation, or by these Bylaws. A meeting at which a quorum is initially present may continue to transact business notwithstanding the withdrawal of directors, if any action taken is approved by at least a majority of the required quorum for such meeting.

Section 3.8   Action Without a Meeting.

Any action required or permitted to be taken by the Board of Directors may be taken without a meeting, if all members of the Board of Directors shall individually or collectively consent in writing to such action. Such written consent or consents shall be filed with the minutes of the proceedings of the Board of Directors. Such action by written consent shall have the same force and effect as a unanimous vote of such directors.

Section 3.9   Adjourned Meeting and Notice.

A majority of the directors present, whether or not a quorum is present, may adjourn any meeting to another time and place. If the meeting is adjourned for more than twenty-four (24) hours, notice of any adjournment to another time or place shall be given prior to the time of the adjourned meeting to the directors who were not present at the time of the adjournment.

Section 3.10   Telephonic Meetings.

Unless specifically prohibited by the Articles of Incorporation of this corporation or these bylaws, members of the Board of Directors or of any committee of the Board of Directors may participate in and act at any meeting of such board or committee through the use of a telephone conference or other communication equipment by means of which all persons participating in the meeting can hear one another. Participation in such meetings shall constitute attendance and presence in person at the meeting of the person or persons so participating.

Section 3.11   Fees and Compensation.

Directors and members of committees may receive such compensation, if any, for their services, and such reimbursement for expenses, as may be fixed or determined by resolution of the Board of Directors.

Section 3.12   Appointment of Executive and Other Committees.

The Board of Directors may, by resolution adopted by a majority of the authorized number of directors, designate one or more committees, each consisting of two or more directors, to serve at the pleasure of the Board of Directors. The Board of Directors may designate one or more directors as alternate members of any committee, who may replace any absent member at any meeting of the committee. The appointment of members or alternate members of a committee requires the vote of a majority of the authorized number of directors. Any such committee, to the extent provided in the resolution of the Board of Directors or in these Bylaws, shall have all the authority of the Board of Directors, except with respect to:

(a) The approval of any action for which the General Corporation Law also requires shareholders' approval or approval of the outstanding shares.

(b) The filling of vacancies on the Board of Directors or in any committee.

(c) The fixing of compensation of the directors for serving on the Board of Directors or on any committee.

(d) The amendment or repeal of these Bylaws or the adoption of new Bylaws.

(e) The amendment or repeal of any resolution of the Board of Directors that by its express terms is not so amendable or repealable.

(f) A distribution to the shareholders of the corporation, except at a rate, in a periodic amount or within a price range determined by the Board of Directors.

(g) The appointment of other committees of the Board of Directors or the members thereof.

The provisions of Sections 3.5 through 3.9 of these Bylaws apply also to committees of the Board of Directors and action by such committees, mutatis mutandis (with the necessary changes having been made in the language thereof).

ARTICLE IV Officers

Section 4.1   Officers.

The officers of the corporation shall consist of the President, the Secretary, and the Treasurer, and each of them shall be appointed by the Board of Directors. The corporation may also have a Chairman of the Board, one or more Vice-Presidents, a Controller, one or more Assistant Secretaries and Assistant Treasurers, and such other officers as may be appointed by the Board of Directors, or with authorization from the Board of Directors by the President. The order of the seniority of the Vice-Presidents shall be in the order of their nomination, unless otherwise determined by the Board of Directors. Any two or more of such offices may be held by the same person. The Board of Directors shall designate one officer as the chief financial officer of the corporation. In the absence of such designation, the Treasurer shall be the chief financial officer. The Board of Directors may appoint, and may empower the President to appoint, such other officers as the business of the corporation may require, each of whom shall have such authority and perform such duties as are provided in these Bylaws or as the Board of Directors may from time to time determine.

All officers of the corporation shall hold office from the date appointed to the date of the next succeeding regular meeting of the Board of Directors following the meeting of shareholders at which the Board of Directors is elected, and until their successors are elected; provided that all officers, as well as any other employee or agent of the corporation, may be removed at any time at the pleasure of the Board of Directors, or, except in the case of an officer chosen by the Board of Directors, by any officer upon whom such power of removal may be conferred by the Board of Directors, and upon the removal, resignation, death, or incapacity of any officer, the

Board of Directors or the President, in cases where he or she has been vested by the Board of Directors with power to appoint, may declare such office vacant and fill such vacancy. Nothing in these Bylaws shall be construed as creating any kind of contractual right to employment with the corporation.

Any officer may resign at any time by giving written notice to the Board of Directors, the President, or the Secretary of the corporation, without prejudice, however, to the rights, if any, of the corporation under any contract to which such officer is a party. Any such resignation shall take effect at the date of the receipt of such notice or at any later time specified therein; and, unless otherwise specified therein, the acceptance of such resignation shall not be necessary to make it effective.

The salary and other compensation of the officers shall be fixed from time to time by resolution of or in the manner determined by the Board of Directors.

Section 4.2   The Chairman of the Board.

The Chairman of the Board (if there be such an officer appointed) shall, when present, preside at all meetings of the Board of Directors and shall perform all the duties commonly incident to that office. The Chairman of the Board shall have authority to execute in the name of the corporation bonds, contracts, deeds, leases and other written instruments to be executed by the corporation (except where by law the signature of the President is required), and shall perform such other duties as the Board of Directors may from time to time determine.

Section 4.3   The President.

Subject to such supervisory powers, if any, as may be given by the Board of Directors to the Chairman of the Board, the President shall be the chief executive officer of the corporation and shall perform all the duties commonly incident to that office. The President shall have authority to execute in the name of the corporation bonds, contracts, deeds, leases and other written instruments to be executed by the corporation. The President shall preside at all meetings of the shareholders and, in the absence of the Chairman of the Board or if there is none, at all meetings of the Board of Directors, and shall perform such other duties as the Board of Directors may from time to time determine.

Section 4.4   Vice-Presidents.

The Vice-Presidents (if there be such officers appointed), in the order of their seniority (unless otherwise established by the Board of Directors), may assume and perform the duties of the President in the absence or disability of the President or whenever the offices of the Chairman of the Board and President are vacant. The Vice-Presidents shall have such titles, perform such other duties, and have such other powers as the Board of Directors, the President, or these Bylaws may designate from time to time.

Section 4.5   The Secretary.

The Secretary shall record or cause to be recorded, and shall keep or cause to be kept, at the principal executive office and such other place as the Board of Directors may order, a book of minutes of actions taken at all meetings of directors and committees thereof and of shareholders, with the time and place of holding, whether regular or special, and, if special, how authorized, the notice thereof given, the names of those present at directors' meetings, the number of shares present or represented at shareholders' meetings, and the proceedings thereof.

The Secretary shall keep, or cause to be kept, at the principal executive office or at the office of the corporation's transfer agent, a share register or a duplicate share register in a form capable of being converted into written form, showing the names of the shareholders and their addresses, the number and classes of shares held by each, the number and date of certificates issued for the same, and the number and date of cancellation of every certificate surrendered for cancellation.

The Secretary shall give, or cause to be given, notice of all the meetings of the shareholders and of the Board of Directors and committees thereof required by these Bylaws or by law to be given, and shall have such other powers and perform such other duties as may be prescribed by the Board of Directors or by these Bylaws.

The President may direct any Assistant Secretary to assume and perform the duties of the Secretary in the absence or disability of the Secretary, and each Assistant Secretary shall perform such other duties and have such other powers as the Board of Directors or the President may designate from time to time.

Section 4.6   The Treasurer.

The Treasurer shall keep and maintain, or cause to be kept and maintained, adequate and correct accounts of the properties and business transactions of the corporation. The books of account shall at all reasonable times be open to inspection by any director.

The Treasurer shall deposit all moneys and other valuables in the name and to the credit of the corporation with such depositaries as may be designated by the Board of Directors. The Treasurer shall disburse the funds of the corporation as may be ordered by the Board of Directors, shall render to the President and directors, whenever they request it, an account of all of the Treasurer's transactions as Treasurer and of the financial condition of the corporation, and shall have such other powers and perform such other duties as may be prescribed by the Board of Directors or these Bylaws.

The President may direct any Assistant Treasurer to assume and perform the duties of the Treasurer in the absence or disability of the Treasurer, and each Assistant Treasurer shall perform such other duties and have such other powers as the Board of Directors or the President may designate from time to time.

Section 4.7   The Controller.

The Controller (if there be such an officer appointed) shall be responsible for the establishment and maintenance of accounting and other systems required to control and account for the assets of the corporation and provide safeguards therefor, and to collect information required for management purposes, and shall perform such other duties and have such other powers as the Board of Directors or the President may designate from time to time. The President may direct any Assistant Controller to assume and perform the duties of the Controller, in the absence or disability of the Controller, and each Assistant Controller shall perform such other duties and have such other powers as the Board of Directors, the Chairman of the Board (if there be such an officer appointed) or the President may designate from time to time.

ARTICLE V Execution of Corporate Instruments, Ratification, and Voting of Stocks Owned by the Corporation

Section 5.1   Execution of Corporate Instruments.

In its discretion, the Board of Directors may determine the method and designate the signatory officer or officers or other person or persons, to execute any corporate instrument or document, or to sign the corporate name without limitation, except where otherwise provided by law, and such execution or signature shall be binding upon the corporation.

All checks and drafts drawn on banks or other depositaries on funds to the credit of the corporation, or in special accounts of the corporation, shall be signed by such person or persons as the Board of Directors shall authorize to do so.

The Board of Directors shall designate an officer who personally, or through his representative, shall vote shares of other corporations standing in the name of this corporation. The authority to vote shares shall include the authority to execute a proxy in the name of the corporation for purposes of voting the shares.

Section 5.2   Ratification by Shareholders.

In its discretion, the Board of Directors may submit any contract or act for approval or ratification of the shareholders at any annual meeting of shareholders, or at any special meeting of shareholders called for that purpose; and any contract or act that shall be approved or ratified by the holders of a majority of the voting power of the corporation shall be as valid and binding upon the corporation and upon the shareholders thereof as though approved or ratified by each and every shareholder of the corporation, unless a greater vote is required by law for such purpose.

Section 5.3   Voting of Stocks Owned by the Corporation.

All stock of other corporations owned or held by the corporation for itself, or for other parties in any capacity, shall be voted, and all proxies with respect thereto shall be executed, by the person authorized to do so by resolution of the Board of Directors, or in the absence of such authorization, by the Chairman of the Board (if there be such an officer appointed), the President or any Vice-President, or by any other person authorized to do so by the Chairman of the Board, the President or any Vice-President.

ARTICLE VI Annual and Other Reports

Section 6.1   Reports to Shareholders.

The Board of Directors of the corporation shall cause an annual report to be sent to the shareholders not later than 120 days after the close of the fiscal year, and at least fifteen (15) days (or, if sent by third-class mail, thirty-five (35) days) prior to the annual meeting of shareholders to be held during the next fiscal year. This report shall contain a balance sheet as of the end of that fiscal year and an income statement and statement of changes in financial position for that fiscal year, accompanied by any report thereon of independent accountants or, if there is no such report, the certificate of an authorized officer of the corporation that the statements were prepared without audit from the books and records of the corporation. This report shall also contain such other matters as required by Section 1501(b) of the General Corporation Law, unless the corporation is subject to the reporting requirements of Section 13 of the Securities Exchange Act of 1934, and is not exempted therefrom under Section 12(g)(2) thereof. As long as the corporation has less than 100 holders of record of its shares (determined as provided in Section 605 of the General Corporation Law), the foregoing requirement of an annual report is hereby waived.

If no annual report for the last fiscal year has been sent to shareholders, the corporation shall, upon the written request of any shareholder made more than 120 days after the close of such fiscal year, deliver or mail to the person making the request within thirty (30) days thereafter the financial statements for such year as required by Section 1501(a) of the General Corporation Law. A shareholder or shareholders holding at least five percent (5%) of the outstanding shares of any class of the corporation may make a written request to the corporation for an income statement of the corporation for the three-month, six-month, or nine-month period of the current fiscal year ended more than thirty (30) days prior to the date of the request and a balance sheet of the corporation as of the end of such period and, in addition, if no annual report for the last fiscal year has been sent to shareholders, the annual report for the last fiscal year, unless such report has been waived under these Bylaws. The statements shall be delivered or mailed to the person making the request within thirty (30) days thereafter. A copy of any such statements shall be kept on file in the principal executive office of the corporation for twelve (12) months, and they shall be exhibited at all reasonable times to any shareholder demanding an examination of the statements, or a copy shall be mailed to the shareholder.

The quarterly income statements and balance sheets referred to in this Section shall be accompanied by the report thereon, if any, of any independent accountants engaged by the corporation or the certificate of an authorized officer of the corporation that the financial statements were prepared without audit from the books and records of the corporation.

Section 6.2   Report of Shareholder Vote.

For a period of sixty (60) days following the conclusion of an annual, regular, or special meeting of shareholders, the corporation shall, upon written request from a shareholder, forthwith inform the shareholder of the result of any particular vote of shareholders taken at the meeting, including the number of shares voting for, the number of shares voting against, and the number of shares abstaining or withheld from voting. If the matter voted on was the election of directors, the corporation shall report the number of shares (or votes if voted cumulatively) cast for each nominee for director. If more than one class or series of shares voted, the report shall state the appropriate numbers by class and series of shares.

Section 6.3   Reports to the Secretary of State.

(a) Every year, during the calendar month in which the original articles of incorporation were filed with the California Secretary of State, or during the preceding five calendar months, the corporation shall file a statement with the Secretary of State on the prescribed form, setting forth the authorized number of directors; the names and complete business and residence addresses of all incumbent directors; the names and complete business or resident addresses of the chief executive officer, the secretary, and the chief financial officer; the street address of the corporation's principal executive office or principal business office in this state; a statement of the general type of business constituting the principal business activity of the corporation; and a designation of the agent of the corporation for the purpose of service of process, all in compliance with Section 1502 of the Corporations Code of California.

(b) Notwithstanding the provisions of paragraph (a) of this section, if there has been no change in the information contained in the corporation's last annual statement on file in the Secretary of State's office, the corporation may, in lieu of filing the annual statement described in paragraph (a) of this section, advise the Secretary of State, on the appropriate form, that no changes in the required information have occurred during the applicable period.

ARTICLE VII Shares of Stock

Every holder of shares in the corporation shall be entitled to have a certificate signed in the name of the corporation by the Chairman or Vice Chairman of the Board (if there be such officers appointed) or the President or a Vice-President and by the Chief Financial Officer or Any Assistant Chief Financial Officer or the Secretary or any Assistant Secretary, certifying the number of shares and the class or series of shares owned by the shareholder. Any of the signatures on the certificate may be a facsimile. In case any officer, transfer agent or registrar who has signed or whose facsimile signature has been placed upon a certificate has ceased to be such officer, transfer agent or registrar before such certificate is issued, it may be issued by the corporation with the same effect as if such person were an officer, transfer agent or registrar at the date of issue.

Any such certificate shall also contain such legends or other statements as may be required by Sections 417 and 418 of the General Corporation Law, the Corporate Securities Law of 1968, federal or other state securities laws, and any agreement between the corporation and the issue of the certificate.

Certificates for shares may be issued prior to full payment, under such restrictions and for such purposes as the Board of Directors or these Bylaws may provide; provided, however, that the certificate issued to represent any such partly paid shares shall state on the face thereof the total amount of the consideration to be paid therefor, the amount remaining unpaid and the terms of payment.

No new certificate for shares shall be issued in lieu of an old certificate unless the latter is surrendered and cancelled at the same time; provided, however, that a new certificate will be issued without the surrender and cancellation of the old certificate if (1) the old certificate is lost, apparently destroyed or wrongfully taken; (2) the request for the issuance of the new certificate is made within a reasonable time after the owner of the old certificate has notice of its loss, destruction, or theft; (3) the request for the issuance of a new certificate is made prior to the receipt of notice by the corporation that the old certificate has been acquired by a bona fide purchaser; (4) the owner of the old certificate files a sufficient indemnity bond with or provides other adequate security to the corporation; and (5) the owner satisfies any other reasonable requirement imposed by the corporation. In the event of the issuance of a new certificate, the rights and liabilities of the corporation, and of the holders of the old and new certificates, shall be governed by the provisions of Sections 8104 and 8405 of the California Commercial Code.

ARTICLE VIII Inspection of Corporate Records

Section 8.1   General Records.

The accounting books and records and the minutes of proceedings of the shareholders, the Board of Directors and committees thereof of the corporation and any subsidiary of the corporation shall be open to inspection upon the written demand on the corporation of any shareholder or holder of a voting trust certificate at any reasonable time during usual business hours, for a purpose reasonably related to such holder's interests as a shareholder or as the holder of such voting trust certificate. Such inspection by a shareholder or holder of a voting trust certificate may be made in person or by agent or attorney, and the right of inspection includes the right to copy and make extracts. Minutes of proceedings of the shareholders, Board, and committees thereof shall be kept in written form. Other books and records shall be kept either in written form or in any other form capable of being converted into written form.

A shareholder or shareholders holding at least five percent (5%) in the aggregate of the outstanding voting shares of the corporation or who hold at least one percent (1%) of such voting shares and have filed a Schedule 14B with the United States Securities and Exchange Commission relating to the election of directors of the corporation shall have (in person, or by agent or attorney) the right to inspect and copy the record of shareholders' names and addresses and shareholdings during usual business hours upon five (5) business days' prior written demand upon the corporation or to obtain from the transfer agent for the corporation, upon written demand and upon the tender of its usual charges for such list, a list of the shareholders' names and addresses, who are entitled to vote for the election of directors, and their shareholdings, as of the most recent record date for which it has been compiled or as of a date specified by the shareholder subsequent to the date of demand. The list shall be made available on or before the later of five (5) business days after the demand is received or the date specified therein as the date as of which the list is to be compiled.

Every director shall have the absolute right at any reasonable time to inspect and copy all books, records and documents of every kind and to inspect the physical properties of the corporation and its subsidiaries. Such inspection by a director may be made in person or by agent or attorney, and the right of inspection includes the right to copy and make extracts.

Section 8.2   Inspection of Bylaws.

The corporation shall keep at its principal executive office in California, or if its principal executive office is not in California, then at its principal business office in California (or shall otherwise provide upon written request of any shareholder if it has no such office in California) the original or a copy of these Bylaws as amended to date, which shall be open to inspection by the shareholders at all reasonable times during office hours.

ARTICLE IX Indemnification of Officers, Directors, Employees, and Agents

Section 9.1   Right to Indemnification.

Each person who was or is a party or is threatened to be made a party to or is involved (as a party, witness, or otherwise), in any threatened, pending, or completed action, suit, or proceeding, whether civil, criminal, administrative, or investigative (hereafter a "Proceeding"), by reason of the fact that he, or a person of whom he is the legal representative, is or was a director, officer, employee, or agent of the corporation or is or was serving at the request of the corporation as a director, officer, employee, or agent of another foreign or domestic corporation, partnership, joint venture, trust, or other enterprise, or was a director, officer, employee, or agent of a foreign or domestic corporation that was a predecessor corporation of the corporation or of another enterprise at the request of such predecessor corporation, including service with respect to employee benefit plans, whether the basis of the Proceeding is alleged action in an official capacity as a director, officer, employee, or agent or in any other capacity while serving as a director, officer, employee, or agent (hereafter an "Agent"), shall be indemnified and held harmless by the corporation to the fullest extent authorized by statutory and decisional law, as the same exists or may hereafter be interpreted or amended (but, in the case of any such amendment or interpretation, only to the extent that such amendment or interpretation permits the corporation to provide broader indemnification rights than were permitted prior thereto) against all expenses, liability, and loss (including attorneys' fees, judgments, fines, ERISA excise taxes and penalties, amounts paid or to be paid in settlement, any interest, assessments, or other charges imposed thereon, and any federal, state, local, or foreign taxes imposed on any Agent as a result of the actual or deemed receipt of any payments under this Article) [reasonably] incurred or suffered by such person in connection with investigating, defending, being a witness in, or participating in (including on appeal), or preparing for any of the foregoing in, any Proceeding (hereafter "Expenses"); provided, however, that except as to actions to enforce indemnification rights pursuant to Section 9.3 of these Bylaws, the corporation shall indemnify any Agent seeking indemnification in connection with a Proceeding (or part thereof) initiated by such person only if the Proceeding (or part thereof) was authorized by the Board of Directors of the corporation. The right to indemnification conferred in this Article shall be a contract right. It is the corporation's intention that these Bylaws provide indemnification in excess of that expressly permitted by Section 317 of the California General Corporation Law, as authorized by the corporation's Articles of Incorporation.

Section 9.2   Authority to Advance Expenses.

Expenses incurred by an officer or director (acting in his capacity as such) in defending a Proceeding shall be paid by the corporation in advance of the final disposition of such Proceeding, provided, however, that if required by the California General Corporation Law, as amended, such Expenses shall be advanced only upon delivery to the corporation of an undertaking by or on behalf of such director or officer to repay such amount if it shall ultimately be determined that he is not entitled to be indemnified by the corporation as authorized in this Article or otherwise. Expenses incurred by other Agents of the corporation (or by the directors or officers not acting in their capacity as such, including service with respect to employee benefit plans) may be advanced upon the receipt of a similar undertaking, if required by law, and upon such other terms and conditions as the Board of Directors deems appropriate. Any obligation to reimburse the corporation for Expense advances shall be unsecured and no interest shall be charged thereon.

Section 9.3   Right of Claimant to Bring Suit.

If a claim under Section 9.1 or 9.2 of these Bylaws is not paid in full by the corporation within thirty (30) days after a written claim has been received by the corporation, the claimant may at any time thereafter bring suit against the corporation to recover the unpaid amount of the claim and, if successful in whole or in part, the claimant shall be entitled to be paid also the expense (including attorneys' fees) of prosecuting such claim. It shall be a defense to any such action (other than an action brought to enforce a claim for expenses incurred in defending a Proceeding in advance of its final disposition where the required undertaking has been tendered to the corporation) that the claimant has not met the standards of conduct that make it permissible under the California General Corporation Law for the corporation to indemnify the claimant for the amount claimed. The burden of proving such a defense shall be on the corporation. Neither the failure of the corporation (including its Board of Directors, independent legal counsel, or its stockholders) to have made a determination prior to the commencement of such action that indemnification of the claimant is proper under the circumstances because he has met the applicable standard of conduct set forth in the California General Corporation Law, nor an actual determination by the corporation (including its Board of Directors, independent legal counsel, or its stockholders) that the claimant had not met such applicable standard of conduct, shall be a defense to the action or create a presumption that claimant has not met the applicable standard of conduct.

Section 9.4   Provisions Nonexclusive.

The rights conferred on any person by this Article shall not be exclusive of any other rights that such person may have or hereafter acquire under any statute, provision of the Articles of Incorporation, agreement, vote of stockholders or disinterested directors, or otherwise, both as to action in an official capacity and as to action in another capacity while holding such office. To the extent that any provision of the Articles, agreement, or vote of the stockholders or disinterested directors is inconsistent with these Bylaws, the provision, agreement, or vote shall take precedence.

Section 9.5   Authority to Insure.

The corporation may purchase and maintain insurance to protect itself and any Agent against any Expense asserted against or incurred by such person, whether or not the corporation would have the power to indemnify the Agent against such Expense under applicable law or the provisions of this Article, provided that, in cases where the corporation owns all or a portion of the shares of the company issuing the insurance policy, the company and/or the policy must meet one of the two sets of conditions set forth in Section 317 of the California General Corporation Law, as amended.

Section 9.6   Survival of Rights.

The rights provided by this Article shall continue as to a person who has ceased to be an Agent and shall inure to the benefit of the heirs, executors, and administrators of such person.

Section 9.7   Settlement of Claims.

The corporation shall not be liable to indemnify any Agent under this Article (a) for any amounts paid in settlement of any action or claim effected without the corporation's written consent, which consent shall not be unreasonably withheld; or (b) for any judicial award, if the corporation was not given a reasonable and timely opportunity, at its expense, to participate in the defense of such action.

Section 9.8   Effect of Amendment.

Any amendment, repeal, or modification of this Article shall not adversely affect any right or protection of any Agent existing at the time of such amendment, repeal, or modification.

Section 9.9   Subrogation.

In the event of payment under this Article, the corporation shall be subrogated to the extent of such payment to all of the rights of recovery of the Agent, who shall execute all papers required and shall do everything that may be necessary to secure such rights, including the execution of such documents necessary to enable the corporation effectively to bring suit to enforce such rights.

Section 9.10   No Duplication of Payments.

The corporation shall not be liable under this Article to make any payment in connection with any claim made against the Agent to the extent the Agent has otherwise actually received payment (under any insurance policy, agreement, vote, or otherwise) of the amounts otherwise indemnifiable hereunder.

ARTICLE X Amendments

Section 10.1   Power of Shareholders.

New bylaws may be adopted or these Bylaws may be amended or repealed by the affirmative vote of a majority of the outstanding shares entitled to vote, or by the written assent of such shareholders entitled to vote such shares, except as otherwise provided by law or by the Articles of Incorporation.

Section 10.2   Power of Directors.

Subject to the right of shareholders as provided in Section 10.1 of this Article to adopt, amend or repeal these Bylaws, these Bylaws (other than a bylaw or amendment thereof changing the authorized number of directors, or providing for the approval by the Board, acting alone, of a loan or guarantee to any officer or an employee benefit plan providing for the same) may be adopted, amended, or repealed by the Board of Directors.

ARTICLE XI Definitions

Unless the context otherwise requires, the general provisions, rules of construction and definitions contained in the General Corporation Law as amended from time to time shall govern the construction of these Bylaws. Without limiting the generality of the foregoing, the masculine gender includes the feminine and neuter, the singular number includes the plural and the plural number includes the singular, and the term "person" includes a corporation as well as a natural person.

CERTIFICATE OF SECRETARY

The undersigned, Secretary of [****], Inc., a _____ corporation, hereby certifies that the foregoing is a full, true, and correct copy of the Bylaws of the corporation with all amendments to date of this Certificate.

WITNESS the signature of the undersigned this _____ day of _____, 20__.

_____

_____, Secretary

Form 6 G: Bylaws—Delaware

BYLAWS

OF

****, INC.

A Delaware Corporation

TABLE OF CONTENTS

BYLAWS

OF

****, INC.

ARTICLE I - MEETINGS OF STOCKHOLDERS

1.1 Place of Meetings.

Meetings of the stockholders shall be held at such place within or without the State of Delaware as designated by the Board of Directors or the person or persons calling the meeting.

1.2 Annual Meetings.

The annual meeting of the stockholders for the election of directors and the transaction of such other business as may properly come before the meeting shall be held after the close of the Corporation's fiscal year on such date and at such time as shall be designated by the Board of Directors.

1.3   Special Meetings.

Special meetings may be called at any time by the President or by a majority of the Board of Directors.

1.4   Notice of Meetings.

A written notice stating the place, date, and hour of each meeting and, in the case of a special meeting, the purpose or purposes for which the meeting is called shall be given by, or at the direction of, the Secretary or the person or persons authorized to call the meeting to each stockholder of record entitled to vote at such meeting, not less than ten (10) days nor more than sixty (60) days before the date of the meeting, unless a greater period of time is required by law in a particular case.

1.5   Quorum.

The holders of a majority of the stock issued and outstanding and entitled to vote thereat, present in person or represented by proxy, shall constitute a quorum at all meetings of the stockholders for the transaction of business except as otherwise provided by statute or by the Certificate of Incorporation. If, however, such quorum shall not be present or represented at any meeting of the stockholders, the stockholders entitled to vote thereat, present in person or represented by proxy, shall have power to adjourn the meeting from time to time, without notice other than announcement at the meeting, until a quorum shall be present or represented. At such adjourned meeting at which a quorum shall be present or represented any business may be transacted which might have been transacted at the meeting as originally notified. If the adjournment is for more than thirty (30) days, or if after the adjournment a new record date is fixed for the adjourned meeting, a notice of the adjourned meeting shall be given to each stockholder of record entitled to vote at the meeting.

When a quorum is present at any meeting, the vote of the holders of a majority of the stock having voting power present in person or represented by proxy shall decide any question brought before such meeting, unless the question is one upon which by express provision of the statutes or of the certificate of incorporation, a different vote is required in which case such express provision shall govern and control the decision of such question.

1.6   Voting.

Unless otherwise provided in the certificate of incorporation each stockholder shall at every meeting of the stockholders be entitled to one vote in person or by proxy for each share of the capital stock having voting power held by such stockholder, but no proxy shall be voted on after three years from its date, unless the proxy provides for a longer period.

ARTICLE II - DIRECTORS

2.1   Number, Election, and Term of Office.

The Board of Directors shall consist of not less than two nor more than nine members as fixed from time to time by the Board of Directors. The directors shall be elected at the annual meeting of the stockholders, except as provided in Section 2.2 of this Article, and each director elected shall hold office until his successor is elected and qualified. Directors need not be stockholders.

2.2 Vacancies.

Vacancies and newly created directorships resulting from any increase in the authorized number of directors may be filled by a majority vote of the directors then in office, although less than a quorum, or by a sole remaining director. The occurrence of a vacancy which is not filled by action of the Board of Directors shall constitute a determination by the Board of Directors that the number of directors is reduced so as to eliminate such vacancy, unless the Board of Directors shall specify otherwise. When one or more directors shall resign from the Board, effective at a future date, a majority of the directors then in office, including those who have so resigned, shall have power to fill such vacancy or vacancies, the vote thereon to take effect when such resignation or resignations shall become effective.

2.3 Meetings of Directors.

Meetings of the Board of Directors shall be held at such times and at such places within or without the State of Delaware as the Board of Directors shall determine from time to time; and no notice shall be required to be given of any such regular meeting. The Chairman or any director may call a special meeting of the Board of Directors by giving one (1) day's notice to each director by letter, telegram, electronic mail, telephone or other oral message. Attendance at any meeting without protest shall constitute a waiver of notice of such meeting.

Except as otherwise provided by these Bylaws, a total number of one director shall constitute a quorum for the transaction of business, and the vote of a majority of the directors present at any meeting at which a quorum is present shall be the act of the Board of Directors. Attendance by a director at any meeting shall constitute consent to all actions taken at such meeting unless such director enters his dissent in the minutes of the meeting, or files such dissent with the secretary of the meeting prior to the adjournment of the meeting, or with the Secretary of the Corporation immediately following adjournment of the meeting.

2.4 Action Without a Meeting.

Any action required or permitted to be taken by the Board of Directors or any committee of the Board of Directors may be taken without a meeting, if all members of the Board of Directors, or such committee, shall individually or collectively consent in writing to such action. Such written consent or consents shall be filed with the minutes of the proceedings of the Board of Directors or committee of the Board of Directors, as appropriate. Such action by written consent shall have the same force and effect as a unanimous vote of such directors.

2.5 Power of Directors.

The Board of Directors shall have all the powers normally conferred on a board of directors of a Delaware corporation, including, without limitation, (a) to charge, mortgage, hypothecate or pledge all or any of the assets of the Corporation, real or personal, movable or immovable, including book debts, rights, powers, franchises and undertakings, to secure the debt obligations or any money borrowed or other debt or liability of the Corporation and (b) to delegate to such one or more of the directors and officers of the Corporation, as allowed by law, the powers conferred on a board of directors to such extent and in such manner as the Board of Directors shall determine at the time of such delegation.

2.6   Committees of Directors.

(a) The board of directors may, by resolution passed by a majority of the whole board, designate one or more committees, each committee to consist of one or more of the directors of the corporation. The board may designate one or more directors as alternate members of any committee, who may replace any absent or disqualified member at any meeting of the committee.

(b) In the absence or disqualification of a member of a committee, the member or members thereof present at any meeting and not disqualified from voting, whether or not he or they constitute a quorum, may unanimously appoint another member of the board of directors to act at the meeting in the place of any such absent or disqualified member.

(c) Any such committee, to the extent provided in the resolution of the board of directors, shall have and may exercise all the powers and authority of the board of directors in the management of the business and affairs of the corporation, and may authorize the seal of the corporation to be affixed to all papers which may require it; but no such committee shall have the power or authority in reference to amending the certificate of incorporation, (except that a committee may, to the extent authorized in the resolution or resolutions providing for the issuance of shares of stock adopted by the board of directors as provided in Section 151(a) of the General Corporation Law of Delaware fix any of the preferences or rights of such shares relating to dividends, redemption, dissolution, any distribution of assets of the corporation or the conversion into, or the exchange of such shares for, shares of any other class or classes or any other series of the same or any other class or classes of stock of the corporation) adopting an agreement of merger or consolidation, recommending to the stockholders the sale, lease or exchange of all or substantially all of the corporation's property and assets, recommending to the stockholders a dissolution of the corporation or a revocation of a dissolution, or amending the bylaws of the corporation; and, unless the resolution or the certificate of incorporation expressly so provides, no such committee shall have the power or authority to declare a dividend or to authorize the issuance of stock or to adopt a certificate of ownership and merger. Such committee or committees shall have such name or names as may be determined from time to time by resolution adopted by the board of directors.

(d) Each committee shall keep regular minutes of its meetings and report the same to the board of directors when required.

2.7   Compensation of Directors.

Unless otherwise restricted by the certificate of incorporation or these Bylaws, the board of directors shall have the authority to fix the compensation of directors. The directors may be paid their expenses, if any, of attendance at each meeting of the board of directors and may be paid a fixed sum for attendance at each meeting of the board of directors or a stated salary as director. No such payment shall preclude any director from serving the corporation in any other capacity and receiving compensation therefor. Members of special or standing committees may be allowed like compensation for attending committee meetings.

2.8 Removal of Directors.

Unless otherwise restricted by the certificate of incorporation or bylaw, any director or the entire board of directors may be removed, with or without cause, by the holders of a majority of shares entitled to vote at an election of directors.

ARTICLE III - OFFICERS

3.1 Enumeration.

The Board of Directors from time to time shall elect officers, to serve at the pleasure of the Board. Each officer shall hold office until his or her successor is elected and qualified, or until his or her earlier resignation or removal. Any officer may resign at any time upon written notice to the Corporation. The compensation of all officers shall be fixed by, or pursuant to authority delegated by, the Board of Directors from time to time.

The officers of the Corporation shall be elected by the Board of Directors and shall consist of a Chairman of the Board, a Chief Executive Officer, a Chief Operating Officer, a President, such number of Vice Presidents (if any) and Assistant Vice-Presidents (if any) as the Board shall from time to time elect, a Secretary, such number of Assistant Secretaries (if any) as the Board shall from time to time elect, a Treasurer, such number of Assistant Treasurers (if any) as the Board shall from time to time elect, a Chief Financial Officer and such other officers (if any) as the Board shall from time to time elect. The Chairman of the Board shall be a member of the Board of Directors. The same person may hold any two or more offices.

3.2 Chairman of the Board.

The Chairman of the Board shall preside at meetings of the Board of Directors. The Chairman of the Board shall have such powers and perform such duties as shall from time to time be specified by the Board of Directors.

3.3 Chief Executive Officer.

Subject to such supervisory powers, if any, as may be given by the Board of Directors to the Chairman of the Board, if there be such an officer, the Chief Executive Officer of the Corporation shall, subject to the control of the Board of Directors, have general supervision, direction and control of the business and the officers of the Corporation. The Chief Executive Officer shall preside at all meetings of the stockholders and, in the absence or nonexistence of a Chairman of the Board, at all meetings of the Board of Directors. The Chief Executive Officer shall have the general powers and duties of management usually vested in the Chief Executive Officer of a corporation and shall have such other powers and duties as may be prescribed by the Board of Directors or these Bylaws.

3.4 President and Chief Operating Officer.

The President shall be the Chief Operating Officer and shall have such powers and perform such duties as shall from time to time be specified by the Board of Directors or delegated to the President by the Board of Directors. The President shall sign all certificates for shares of the capital stock of the Corporation and may, together with the Secretary, execute on behalf of the Corporation any contract that has been approved by the Board of Directors.

3.5 Vice President.

The Vice President or, if there shall be more than one, the Vice Presidents, in the order of their seniority unless otherwise specified by the Board of Directors, shall have all of the powers and perform all of the duties of the President during the absence or inability to act of the President. Each Vice President shall also have such other powers and perform such other duties as shall from time to time be prescribed by the Board of Directors or the President.

3.6 Secretary.

The Secretary shall record the proceedings of the meetings of the stockholders and directors in a book to be kept for that purpose, and shall give notice as required by statute or these Bylaws of all such meetings. The Secretary shall have custody of the seal of the Corporation and of all books, records, and papers of the Corporation, except such as shall be in the charge of the Treasurer or of some other person authorized to have custody and possession thereof by resolution of the Board of Directors. The Secretary may, together with the President, execute on behalf of the Corporation any contract that has been approved by the Board of Directors. The Secretary shall also have such other powers and perform such other duties as are incident to the office of the secretary of a corporation or as shall from time to time be prescribed by, or pursuant to authority delegated by, the Board of Directors.

3.7 Treasurer and Chief Financial Officer.

The Treasurer shall be the Chief Financial Officer and shall keep full and accurate accounts of the receipts and disbursements of the Corporation in books belonging to the Corporation, shall deposit all moneys and other valuable effects of the Corporation in the name and to the credit of the Corporation in such depositories as may be designated by the Board of Directors, may execute, or witness the execution of, on behalf of the Corporation any contract that has been approved by the Board of Directors, and shall also have such other powers and perform such other duties as are incident to the office of the treasurer of a corporation or as shall from time to time be prescribed by, or pursuant to authority delegated by, the Board of Directors.

3.8 Other Officers.

The powers and duties of each other officer who may from time to time be chosen by the Board of Directors shall be as specified by, or pursuant to authority delegated by, the Board of Directors at the time of the appointment of such other officer or from time to time thereafter. In addition, each officer designated as an assistant officer shall assist in the performance of the duties of the officer to which he or she is assistant, and shall have the powers and perform the duties of such officer during the absence or inability to act of such officer.

3.9 Additional Powers and Duties.

The Board of Directors may from time to time by resolution increase or add to the powers and duties of any of the officers of the Corporation. Except in cases in which the signing and execution shall have been expressly delegated by the Board of Directors to some other officer, employee or agent of the Corporation, the Chairman of the Board of Directors or the President or a Vice-President may sign and execute in the name of the Corporation all authorized deeds, mortgages, bonds, contracts or other instruments; provided, however, that a Vice-President may delegate to any other officer or manager reporting to such officer authority to sign and execute in the name of the Corporation all authorized contracts and similar instruments pursuant to a policy approved by the Board of Directors.

ARTICLE IV - INDEMNIFICATION

4.1 Directors and Officers.

The Corporation shall indemnify, to the fullest extent now or hereafter permitted by law, each director or officer (including each former director or officer) of the Corporation who was, is or becomes a party to, or a witness in, or is threatened to be made a party to, or otherwise becomes involved in as a witness or otherwise in any threatened, pending or completed action, suit or proceeding, whether civil, criminal, administrative or investigative, by reason of the fact that he or she is or was an authorized representative of the Corporation (as defined in Section 4.8 herein), against all expenses (including attorneys' fees and disbursements), judgments, fines (including excise taxes, interest and penalties) and amounts paid in settlement actually and reasonably incurred by him or her in connection with such action, suit or proceeding.

4.2 Timing of Indemnification.

The Corporation shall pay expenses (including attorneys' fees and disbursements) incurred by a director or officer of the Corporation referred to in Section 4.1 hereof in defending, prosecuting where the action was brought with the consent of the Board of Directors, or appearing as a witness in any civil or criminal action, suit or proceeding described in Section 4.1 hereof in advance of the final disposition of such action, suit or proceeding. The expenses incurred by such director or officer in his or her capacity as a director or officer of the Corporation shall be paid by the Corporation in advance of the final disposition of such action, suit or proceeding only upon receipt of an undertaking by or on behalf of such director or officer to repay all amounts advanced if it shall ultimately be determined that he or she is not entitled to be indemnified by the Corporation because he or she has not met the standard of conduct set forth in Section 4.5 hereof.

4.3 Authorized Representatives.

The Corporation may, as determined by the Board of Directors from time to time, indemnify to the fullest extent now or hereafter permitted by law, any person who was or is a party to or a witness in or is threatened to be made a party to or a witness in, or is otherwise involved in, any threatened, pending or completed action, suit or proceeding, whether civil, criminal, administrative, or investigative, by reason of the fact that he or she is or was an authorized representative of the Corporation (as defined in Section 4.8 herein), against all expenses (including attorneys' fees and disbursements), judgments, fines (including excise taxes, interest and penalties), and amounts paid in settlement actually and reasonably incurred by him or her in connection with such action, suit, or proceeding. Subject to Section 4.2 hereof, the Corporation may, as determined by the Board of Directors from time to time, pay expenses, including attorneys fees, incurred by any such person by reason of his or her participation in an action, suit or proceeding referred to in this Section 4.3 in advance of the final disposition of such action, suit or proceeding.

4.4 Nonexclusivity.

Each director and officer of the Corporation shall be deemed to act in such capacity in reliance upon such rights of indemnification and advancement of expenses as are provided in this Article. The rights of indemnification and advancement of expenses provided by this Article shall not be deemed exclusive of any other rights to which any person seeking indemnification or advancement of expenses may be entitled under any agreement, vote of stockholders or disinterested directors, decision of independent counsel, statute or otherwise, both as to action in such person's official capacity and as to action in another capacity while holding such office or position, and shall continue as to a person who has ceased to be an authorized representative of the Corporation and shall inure to the benefit of the heirs, executors, assigns and administrators of such person.

4.5 Standard for Indemnification.

Any indemnification under this Article shall be made by the Corporation only as authorized in the specific case upon a determination that indemnification of the authorized representative is proper in the circumstances because such person has acted in good faith and in a manner he or she reasonably believed to be in or not opposed to the best interests of the Corporation, and, with respect to any criminal action or proceeding had no reasonable cause to believe his or her conduct was unlawful. Such determination shall be made (1) by the Board of Directors by a majority vote of a quorum consisting of Directors who were not parties to such action, suit or proceeding, or (2) if such quorum is not obtainable, or, even if obtainable, a quorum of disinterested Directors so directs, by independent legal counsel in a written opinion, or (3) by the stockholders. The termination of any action, suit or proceeding by judgment, order, settlement, conviction, or upon a plea of nolo contendere or its equivalent, shall not, of itself, create a presumption that the officer or director did not act in good faith and in a manner which such officer or director reasonably believed to be in or not opposed to the best interests of the Corporation, and, with respect to any criminal action or proceeding, had reasonable cause to believe that such person's conduct was unlawful.

4.6 Insurance.

The Corporation shall purchase and maintain insurance on behalf of each director and officer against any liability asserted against or incurred by such director or officer in any capacity, or arising out of such director's or officer's status as such, whether or not the Corporation would have the power to indemnify such director or officer against such liability under the provisions of this Article. The Corporation shall not be required to maintain such insurance if it is not available on terms satisfactory to the Board of Directors or if, in the business judgment of the Board of Directors, either (i) the premium cost for such insurance is substantially disproportionate to the amount of coverage, or (ii) the coverage provided by such insurance is so limited by exclusions that there is insufficient benefit from such insurance. The Corporation may purchase and maintain insurance on behalf of any person referred to in Section 4.3 hereof against any liability asserted against or incurred by such person in any capacity, whether or not the Corporation would have the power to indemnify such person against such liability under the provisions of this Article.

4.7 Constituent Corporations.

For purposes of this Article, references to "the Corporation" shall include, in addition to the resulting corporation, any constituent corporation (including any constituent of a constituent) absorbed in a consolidation or merger which, if its separate existence had continued, would have had power and authority to indemnify its authorized representatives so that any person who is or was an authorized representative of such constituent corporation shall stand in the same position under this Article with respect to the resulting or surviving corporation as he or she would have with respect to such constituent corporation if its separate existence had continued.

4.8 Eligibility.

For the purposes of this Article, the term "authorized representative" shall mean a director, officer, employee or agent of the Corporation or of any subsidiary of the Corporation, or a trustee, custodian, administrator, or fiduciary of any employee benefit plan established and maintained by the Corporation or by any subsidiary of the Corporation, or a person serving another corporation, partnership, joint venture, trust or other enterprise in any of the foregoing capacities at the request of the Corporation.

ARTICLE V - SHARES OF CAPITAL STOCK

5.1 Issuance of Stock.

Shares of capital stock of any class now or hereafter authorized, securities convertible into or exchangeable for such stock, or options or other rights to purchase such stock or securities may be issued or granted in accordance with authority granted by resolution of the Board of Directors.

5.2 Stock Certificates.

Certificates for shares of the capital stock of the Corporation shall be in the form adopted by the Board of Directors, may be signed by the Chairman of the Board of Directors, or the President or Vice President and the Treasurer or the Assistant Treasurer or the Secretary or the Assistant Secretary of the Corporation, and may be sealed with the seal of the Corporation. All such certificates shall be numbered consecutively, and the name of the person owning the shares represented thereby, with the number of such shares and the date of issue, shall be entered on the books of the Corporation.

5.3 Transfer of Stock.

Shares of capital stock of the Corporation shall be transferred only on the books of the Corporation, by the holder of record in person or by the holder's duly authorized representative, upon surrender to the Corporation of the certificate for such shares duly endorsed for transfer, together with such other documents (if any) as may be required to effect such transfer.

5.4 Lost, Stolen, Destroyed, or Mutilated Certificates.

New stock certificates may be issued to replace certificates alleged to have been lost, stolen, destroyed, or mutilated, upon such terms and conditions, including proof of loss or destruction, and the giving of a satisfactory bond of indemnity, as the Board of Directors from time to time may determine.

5.5 Regulations.

The Board of Directors shall have power and authority to make all such rules and regulations not inconsistent with these Bylaws as it may deem expedient concerning the issue, transfer, and registration of shares of capital stock of the Corporation.

5.6 Record Date for Stock.

In order that the Corporation may determine the stockholders entitled to notice of or to vote at any meeting of stockholders or any adjournment thereof, or to express consent to corporate action in writing without a meeting, or entitled to receive payment of any dividend or other distribution or allotment of any rights, or entitled to exercise any rights in respect of any change, conversion or exchange of stock or for the purpose of any other lawful action, the board of directors may fix, in advance, a record date, which shall not be more than sixty (60) nor less than ten (10) days before the date of such meeting, nor more than sixty (60) days prior to any other action. A determination of stockholders of record entitled to notice of or to vote at a meeting of stockholders shall apply to any adjournment of the meeting: provided, however, that the board of directors may fix a new record date for the adjourned meeting.

ARTICLE VI - GENERAL PROVISIONS

6.1 Corporate Seal.

The Corporation may adopt a seal in such form as the Board of Directors shall from time to time determine.

6.2 Fiscal Year.

The fiscal year of the Corporation shall be as designated by the Board of Directors from time to time.

6.3 Authorization.

All checks, notes, vouchers, warrants, drafts, acceptances, and other orders for the payment of moneys of the Corporation shall be signed by such officer or officers or such other person or persons as the Board of Directors may from time to time designate.

6.4 Financial Reports.

Financial statements or reports shall not be required to be sent to the stockholders of the Corporation, but may be so sent in the discretion of the Board of Directors, in which event the scope of such statements or reports shall be within the discretion of the Board of Directors, and such statements or reports shall not be required to have been examined by or to be accompanied by an opinion of an accountant or firm of accountants.

6.5 <u>Effect of Bylaws</u>.

No provision in these Bylaws shall vest any property right in any stockholder.

ARTICLE VII - AMENDMENTS

The authority to adopt, amend, or repeal Bylaws of the Corporation is expressly conferred upon the Board of Directors, which may take such action by the affirmative vote of a majority of the whole Board of Directors at any regular or special meeting duly convened after notice of that purpose, subject always to the power of the stockholders to adopt, amend, or repeal Bylaws.

I, _____, do hereby certify:

1.   That I am the duly elected Secretary of ****, Inc., a Delaware Corporation.

2.   That the foregoing Bylaws, comprising fifteen (15) pages, including this page, constitute the Bylaws of the Corporation as of the _____ day of _____, 20___.

IN WITNESS WHEREOF, I have executed this certificate as of the _____ day of _____, 20___.

_____

_____, Secretary

Form 6 H: Initial Written Consent of Board of Directors

Note: The following is an example of an initial Directors' Written Consent form, used to complete the organizational process. The statutory and bylaws section references should be changed as necessary to reflect the applicable law in the state where the corporation was formed and the provisions in the bylaws adopted on behalf of the corporation.

WRITTEN CONSENT OF

THE SOLE DIRECTOR OF

****, INC.

_____, 20__

The undersigned director of ****, INC., a corporation organized under the [state law, such as: General Corporation Law of the State of California] does by this writing consent to the following actions and adopt the following resolutions:

By execution of this written consent, the undersigned hereby accepts her appointment as the sole director of this corporation.

WHEREAS, the original Articles of Incorporation of the corporation were filed in the office of the [California] Secretary of State on _____, 20___;

WHEREAS, the Statement of Incorporator dated as of _____, 20___ [date of formation], appoints the undersigned as the initial director of the corporation, and adopts Bylaws for the regulation of the affairs of the corporation; and

WHEREAS, it is necessary for the Board of Directors to authorize certain actions to be taken to complete the organization of the corporation;

Action of Incorporator

NOW, THEREFORE, BE IT RESOLVED, that the Statement of Incorporator and a certified copy of the Articles of Incorporation and Bylaws be inserted in the minute book of the corporation.

Principal Executive Office

RESOLVED FURTHER, that, as soon as practicable, premises suitable to become the principal and executive office of the corporation be identified by the President of the corporation and submitted to the member of this Board of Directors for consideration and approval for designation as the principal and executive office for the transaction of business of the corporation.

Election of Officers

RESOLVED, that the following persons are hereby appointed to the office(s) indicated next to their respective names:

Name	Office
[Name]	President, Treasurer, and Secretary

Minute Book

RESOLVED FURTHER, that this corporation shall maintain as part of its corporate records, a book entitled "Minute Book" which shall include, but which shall not be limited to, a record of its Articles of Incorporation and amendments thereto, its Bylaws and amendments thereto, minutes of all meetings of its Directors, and minutes of all meetings of its shareholders with the time and place of holding, whether regular or special and, if special, how authorized, the notice thereof given, the number of shares present or represented at the shareholders meetings, and the proceedings thereof; and

Form of Share Certificate

RESOLVED FURTHER, that the share certificates representing the stock of this corporation be in the form of the share certificate attached to these resolutions; and that the Secretary of the corporation is instructed to annex the form of share certificate to this unanimous written consent as Exhibit A; and

RESOLVED FURTHER, that the form of the share certificate attached to these resolutions be, and the same hereby is, approved and adopted and the Secretary of the corporation, who is instructed to insert a copy thereof in the minute book.

Bank Accounts

WHEREAS, this Board of Directors has determined that the establishment of bank accounts for the deposit and disbursement of corporate funds, and other funds which may come under the control of the corporation, is not a matter of such importance as to require that such action be taken by the Board;

WHEREAS, this Board desires to delegate the authority and responsibility for the selection of corporate bank accounts to the officers of this corporation, and to authorize such officers to establish such bank accounts without any further action being required by this Board as to any specific bank account;

NOW, THEREFORE, BE IT RESOLVED, that the President of the corporation, and such other officers as she may direct be, and each hereby is, authorized, directed, and empowered to establish such bank accounts as she or they deem appropriate and the Treasurer be, and hereby is, directed to maintain at all times an accurate and current list of all such bank accounts and to make such list immediately available to any officer or director and the corporation's auditors, upon the request of any such person or entity;

RESOLVED FURTHER, that the Secretary, or any Assistant Secretary, be and each hereby is, authorized, directed, and empowered to execute any certificate evidencing the adoption by this Board of one or more resolutions authorizing the opening of any such bank account to the extent such resolutions may be required in connection therewith; and

RESOLVED FURTHER, that the execution and delivery of any such certificate shall be deemed to constitute conclusive evidence of the due adoption by this Board of Directors of the resolutions contained therein as of the date specified in such certificate.

Fiscal Year

RESOLVED FURTHER, that the corporation hereby adopts the calendar year as its fiscal year.

Employee Tax Identification Number

RESOLVED FURTHER, that the President and such other officers as she may direct be, and each hereby is, authorized, directed, and empowered to apply for an employer's identification number on Form SS-4 on behalf of the corporation.

Section 1502 Filing

RESOLVED FURTHER, that the President and such other officers as she may designate be, and each hereby is, authorized, directed, and empowered to file with the Secretary of State of [California] a statement of the names of the directors and officers, together with a statement of the location and address of the principal office of the corporation, and designating [Jean L. Batman c/o Legal Venture Counsel, Inc., 921 Front Street, San Francisco, CA 94111,] as agent for service of process, as required by [Section 1502 of the California Corporations Code].

Incorporation Expenses

RESOLVED FURTHER, that the President and such other officers as she may direct be, and each hereby is, authorized, directed, and empowered to pay the expenses of incorporation and organization of this corporation.

Stock Issuance

WHEREAS, [Name] is the founder of the corporation; and

WHEREAS, the founder is contributing the cash and services necessary for the operation of the corporation's business;

NOW, THEREFORE, BE IT RESOLVED, that the President and such officers as she may direct be, and each hereby is, authorized, directed, and empowered to issue the specified number of shares of the corporation's Common Stock in exchange for the purchase price to be paid in the form of consideration as set forth below:

Name	Number of Shares	Purchase Price	Consideration
[Name]	**[100,000]**	$____share	$_____ in cash . . .
Total	[100,000]		$_____

RESOLVED FURTHER, that, with regard to the portion of the purchase price for the corporation's Common Stock paid in the form of consideration other than money, the Board of Directors has determined that the fair value of such consideration is equal to the portion of the purchase price to which it applies in accordance with [state law requirement, such as: Corporations Code § 409(e)];

RESOLVED FURTHER, that the President and such officers as she may direct be, and each hereby is, authorized, directed, and empowered to issue share certificates representing such shares; and

RESOLVED FURTHER, that the President, and such other officers as she may designate be, and each hereby is, directed, authorized, and empowered to make, verify and file, or cause to be filed, the necessary notices with the [California Department of Corporations] so that the shares may be offered and sold pursuant to the exemption from state securities registration requirements provided in Section [25102(f) of the California Corporations Code,] if applicable.

Omnibus

RESOLVED FURTHER, that the President and such other officers as she may designate be, and each hereby is, authorized, directed, and empowered to take such other action and to execute such additional documents as may be necessary to carry out the intent of the foregoing resolutions.

This unanimous consent is executed pursuant to [Section 307(b) of the Corporations Code of the State of California] and Section [3.8 of Article III] of the Bylaws of the corporation, which authorize the taking of action by the Board of Directors by written consent and shall be filed with the minutes of the proceedings of this Board of Directors.

Executed effective this _____ day of _____, 20___.

_____
[Name], Director

Filed with the Secretary this _____ day of _____, 20___.

_____
[Name], Secretary

Exhibit A

Form of Share Certificate

Form 6 I: Rules for Shareholders' Meetings

Note: These sample rules for the conduct of shareholders' meetings are not required, but they may prove helpful to clients who are just learning how to run a shareholders' meeting and to clients that have shareholders who are likely to cause disruptions during meetings.

RULES AND PROCEDURES FOR
SHAREHOLDERS MEETINGS OF **** CORPORATION

1. Each meeting of the Shareholders of the Company (the "Meeting") shall be conducted in accordance with these Rules and Procedures. Any matter not provided in these Rules and Procedures shall be handled in accordance with relevant laws and regulations.

2. Shareholders attending the Meeting shall submit an Admission Ticket for the purpose of signing in. The number of shares represented by shareholders attending the Meeting shall be calculated in accordance with the Admission Tickets submitted by the shareholders.

3. The Meeting shall be held at the head office of the Company or at any other appropriate place that is convenient for the shareholders to attend. The time to start the Meeting shall not be earlier than 9:00 a.m. or later than 3:00 p.m.

4. The Company may appoint designated counsel, CPA or other related persons to attend the Meeting. Persons handling affairs of the Meeting shall wear identification cards or badges.

5. The process of the Meeting shall be tape recorded or videotaped and these tapes shall be preserved for at least six (6) months.

6. The Chairman of the Board of Directors shall be the chairman presiding at the Meeting in the case that the Meeting is convened by the Board of Directors. If, for any reason, the Chairman of the Board of Directors cannot preside at the Meeting, the Vice Chairman of the Board of Directors or one of the Directors shall preside at the Meeting. If the Meeting is convened by any other person entitled to convene the Meeting, such person shall be the chairman to preside at the Meeting.

7. The Chairman shall call the Meeting to order at the time scheduled for the Meeting. If the number of shares represented by the shareholders present at the Meeting has not yet constituted the quorum at the time scheduled for the Meeting, the Chairman may postpone the starting time for the Meeting. Any postponements shall be limited to two times at the most and the Meeting shall not be postponed for longer than one hour in the aggregate. If after two postponements no quorum can yet be constituted but the shareholders present at the Meeting represent more than one-third of the total outstanding shares, tentative resolutions may be made in accordance with the agenda. If during the process of the Meeting the number of outstanding shares represented by the shareholders present becomes sufficient to constitute the quorum, the Chairman may submit the tentative resolutions to the Meeting for approval.

8. The agenda of the Meeting shall be set by the Board of Directors if the Meeting is convened by the Board of Directors. Unless otherwise resolved at the Meeting, the Meeting shall proceed in accordance with the agenda. The above provision

applies with the necessary changes to cases where the Meeting is convened by any person, other than the Board of Directors, entitled to convene such Meeting. Unless otherwise resolved at the Meeting, the Chairman cannot announce adjournment of the Meeting before all the discussion items (including special motions) listed in the agenda are resolved. The shareholders cannot designate any other person as chairman and continue the Meeting in the same or other place after the Meeting is adjourned. However, in the event that the Chairman adjourns the Meeting in violation of these Rules and Procedures, the shareholders may designate, by a majority of votes represented by shareholders attending the Meeting, one person as chairman to continue the Meeting.

9. Shareholders attending the Meeting shall have the obligation to observe Meeting rules, obey resolutions, and maintain order at Meeting place.

10. Any legal entity designated as proxy by a shareholder(s) to be present at the Meeting may appoint only one representative to attend the Meeting.

11. When a shareholder present at the Meeting wishes to address the shareholders, a Speech Note shall be filled out with a summary of the speech, the shareholder's number (or the number of Attendance Card) and the name of the shareholder. The sequence of speeches by shareholders shall be decided by the Chairman. Unless otherwise permitted by the Chairman, each shareholder shall not, for each discussion item, speak more than two times (each time not exceeding 5 minutes). In case the speech of any shareholder violates the above provision or exceeds the scope of the discussion item, the Chairman may stop the speech of such shareholder. If any shareholder present at the Meeting submits a Speech Note but does not speak, no speech should be deemed to have been made by such shareholder. In case the contents of the speech of a shareholder are inconsistent with the contents of the Speech Note, the contents of actual speech shall prevail. Unless otherwise permitted by the Chairman and the shareholder speaking, no shareholder shall interrupt the speeches of the other shareholders, otherwise the Chairman shall stop such interruption. If a corporate shareholder designates two or more representatives to attend the Meeting, only one representative can speak for each discussion item. After the speech of a shareholder, the Chairman may respond himself/herself or appoint an appropriate person to respond.

12. The Chairman may announce the end of the discussion of any resolution and go into voting when the Chairman deems it appropriate.

13. The person(s) to check and the person(s) to record the ballots during a vote by casting ballots shall be appointed by the Chairman. The result of voting shall be announced at the Meeting and placed on record.

14. Except as otherwise specified in the Certificate of Incorporation or the Bylaws of the Company, a resolution shall be adopted by a majority of the votes represented by the shareholders present at the Meeting. The resolution shall be deemed adopted and shall have the same effect as if it was voted by casting ballots if no objection is voiced after solicitation by the Chairman.

15. During the Meeting, the Chairman may, at his discretion, set time for intermission. In the case of an incident of force majeure, the Chairman may decide to temporarily adjourn the Meeting and announce, depending on the situation, when the Meeting will resume or, by resolution of the shareholders present at the Meeting, the Chairman may resume the Meeting within five days without further notice or public announcement.

16. If there is amendment to or substitute for a discussion item, the Chairman shall decide the sequence of voting for such discussion item, the amendment, and/or the substitute. If any one of them has been adopted, the others shall be deemed vetoed and no further voting shall be necessary.

17. The Chairman may utilize disciplinary officers or a security guard to assist in keeping order in the Meeting place. Such disciplinary officers or security guards shall wear marked badges for identification purpose.

18. Parliamentary procedures shall be observed in the conduct of the Meeting.

19. These Rules and Procedures shall be effective from the date they are approved by the Directors. The same applies in case of revision.

Form 6 J: Time and Responsibility Schedule for Annual Shareholder Meeting

PRELIMINARY TIME AND RESPONSIBILITY SCHEDULE

FOR

**** CORPORATION

ANNUAL SHAREHOLDER MEETING

CO Company (**** Corporation)
CC Corporate Counsel (****, LLP)
FN Financial (**** Inc.)
AU Auditors (**** CPAs LLP)

Date	Activity	Participants
February	Audit of company financial statements completed.	AU
	Determine Annual Meeting date and location, reserve site, and begin logistics for meeting and events (ongoing).	CO
	Determine possible management proposals for Annual Meeting (ongoing).	CO, CC, FN
	Prepare Board Resolutions establishing: (a) Annual Shareholder Meeting date; (b) Record Date; (c) Inspectors of election; (d) Slate of directors to be nominated; and (e) Other items to be submitted to a vote of the shareholders.	CO, CC
	Finalize contracts for meeting facilities and catering.	CO
	Meeting with management to review Annual Meeting arrangements and plans with principal officers involved and discuss: (a) Timetable; and (b) Assignment of responsibilities for tasks.	CO, CC, FN
	Contact the following re their respective roles at the Annual Meeting: (a) Inspectors of election; (b) Proxy holders; (c) Auditors; and (d) Others, if applicable.	CO, CC
	Begin preparation of shareholder mailing list.	CO

Date	Activity	Participants
March	Prepare the following forms: (a) Ballots; (b) Reports of Inspectors of Election (quorum report and report of voting results); (c) Script for presiding officer; (d) Agenda; (e) Contingency script covering emergency situations or disruptions; (f) Admission tickets; and (g) Oath of inspectors of election.	CO, CC
	Prepare company annual report.	CO, CC, FN
	Assemble Chairman's Briefing Book: all departments/lines of business/and financial units to provide status reports for chairman's reference and understanding of every aspect of the company. Copies of all Annual Meeting forms listed above and Annual Meeting rules of conduct to be included.	CO, CC, FN
	Meeting with senior management: (a) Review questions that may be raised at the Annual Meeting; (b) Update and review Chairman's Briefing Book; (c) Review Annual Meeting admissions procedures; (d) Review Annual Meeting agenda; (e) Review Annual Meeting rules of conduct and procedures; and (f) Finalize company annual report.	CO, CC, FN, AU
	Send letter to the Board of Directors with details of meetings, transportation, and schedule of events.	CO
April 1	**Record Date** Delaware requires the Record Date be no more than 60 and no less than 10 days prior to the Annual Meeting (Del. Corp. Law § 222).	
	Finalize mailing list for notice of meeting as of the Record Date.	CO
	Establish list of shareholders entitled to vote at the Annual Meeting as of Record Date—to be available for inspection during business hours and at the Annual Meeting (Del. Corp. Law § 219(a)).	CO
April 10	Mail Notice of Meeting with annual report and admission ticket procedure to all shareholders as of Record Date.	CO

Date	Activity	Participants
May 20–21	Onsite preparations: (a) Audio visual equipment; (b) Room security; (c) Vote tabulation area; (d) Final seating arrangements; (e) Catering; and (f) Rehearsal.	CO, CC, FN, AU

****

May 21	**Annual Meeting of Shareholders** 10:00 AM	CO, CC, FN, AU

****

	Board of Directors Meeting 11:00 AM Immediately following Shareholder Meeting	CO

****

Date	Activity	Participants
June	Final report from inspectors of election.	
	Prepare preliminary minutes of Annual Meeting and make available for review and revision.	CO, CC
	Prepare report of Annual Meeting to be forwarded to shareholders.	CO

Form 6 K: Directors' Written Consent

Note: The following is an example of a Directors' Written Consent form, used to evidence compliance with appropriate corporate formalities and create a record of corporate authority for actions taken on behalf of the corporation. The statutory and bylaws section references should be changed as necessary to reflect the applicable law in the state where the corporation was formed and the provisions in the bylaws adopted on behalf of the corporation.

UNANIMOUS WRITTEN CONSENT OF

THE DIRECTORS OF

****, INC.

_____, 20___

The undersigned directors of ****, INC., a corporation organized under the General Corporation Law of the State of [California,] do by this writing consent to the following actions and adopt the following resolutions:

WHEREAS certain actions are required to be taken by the Board of Directors of the corporation to establish general operating policy and the regular observance of corporate formalities;

Election of Officers

NOW, THEREFORE, BE IT RESOLVED that the following persons are hereby appointed to the office(s) indicated next to their respective names:

Name	Office
****	CEO, President, Treasurer
****	Secretary

Line of Credit

WHEREAS it has been determined to be in the best interests of the corporation to establish a line of credit with the Bank of America to help finance business operations;

NOW, THEREFORE, BE IT RESOLVED that the establishment of a line of credit with Bank of America by the President of the corporation be and hereby is ratified, adopted and approved; and

Omnibus

RESOLVED FURTHER, that the President and such other officers as he may designate be, and each hereby is, authorized, directed, and empowered to take such other action and to execute such additional documents as may be necessary to carry out the intent of the foregoing resolutions.

185

This unanimous consent is executed pursuant to [Section 307(b) of the Corporations Code of the State of California] and Section [3.8 of Article III] of the Bylaws of the corporation, which authorize the taking of action by the Board of Directors by written consent and shall be filed with the minutes of the proceedings of this Board of Directors.

Executed effective this ___ day of _____, 20___.

_____
****, Director

_____
****, Director

Filed with the Secretary this ___ day of _____, 20___.

_____
****, Secretary

Form 6 L: Shareholders' Written Consent

Note: In the following form, the references to California corporations code sections and bylaws sections should be changed to the appropriate statutory references in your state and applicable provisions in your client's bylaws.

UNANIMOUS WRITTEN CONSENT OF

THE SHAREHOLDRES OF

****, INC.

_____, 20____

The undersigned shareholders of ****, INC., a corporation organized under the General Corporation Law of the State of [California], do by this writing consent to the following actions and adopt the following resolutions in lieu of an annual or special meeting of the shareholders of the corporation:

Election of Directors

WHEREAS the shareholders of the corporation wish to elect the members of the Board of Directors by written consent in accordance with Section [2.12] of the Bylaws of the corporation; and

WHEREAS the Board of Directors has been determined to be comprised of two individuals, with one vacancy, in accordance with Section [3.2] of the Bylaws of the corporation;

NOW, THEREFORE, BE IT RESOLVED that **** and **** be and hereby are elected serve as the directors of the corporation and to hold office until their successors are elected and qualified.

This unanimous consent is executed pursuant to [Section 603 of the Corporations Code of the State of California] and Section [2.12] of Article II of the Bylaws of the corporation, which authorize the election of Directors by written consent and shall be filed with the minutes of the proceedings of the shareholders.

Executed effective this ____ day of _____, 20____.

_____
****, Shareholder

_____
****, Shareholder

Filed with the Secretary this ____ day of _____, 20____.

_____
****, Secretary

Form 6 M: Stock Assignment Separate from Certificate

STOCK ASSIGNMENT SEPARATE FROM CERTIFICATE

FOR VALUE RECEIVED, the undersigned hereby sells, assigns, and transfers unto:

PLEASE INSERT SOCIAL SECURITY OR OTHER IDENTIFYING NUMBER OF ASSIGNEE

_____
[Name]

_____(_____) Shares of the _____
[Number]

Stock of _____Corporation

represented by certificate(s) No. _____ submitted herewith and do hereby irrevocably constitute and appoint_____ attorney to transfer the said stock on the books of the within named Corporation with full power of substitution.

Dated _____   _____
[Signature]

_____
[Name]

THE SIGNATURE(S) ON THIS ASSIGNMENT MUST CORRESPOND WITH THE NAME(S) ON THE FACE OF THE CERTIFICATE IN EVERY PARTICULAR, WITHOUT ALTERATION OR ENLARGEMENT, OR ANY CHANGE.

Form 6 N: Lost Securities Indemnity Agreement

Note: In this sample agreement, the shareholder is transferring his shares back to the company, but has lost the certificate for the shares. This form can also be used in the case of a shareholder who has lost her certificate and is seeking a replacement certificate; simply delete the "assignment" references.

LOST SECURITIES INDEMNITY

AND

ASSIGNMENT AGREEMENT

This Lost Securities Indemnity and Assignment Agreement, made and entered as of this _____ day of _____, 20__, by and between _____, Inc. a [California] corporation with offices located at _____ Street, _____, [California] (the "Company"), and _____, ("Security Holder").

WHEREAS, Security Holder is a registered holder of _____ (_____) shares of the Common Stock (the "Securities") of the Company, originally issued as the Company's Common Stock Certificate No. _____ (the "Certificate");

WHEREAS, Security Holder has made, or caused to be made, a diligent search for the Certificate and has been unable to locate it and has determined that the Certificate has been lost; and

WHEREAS, in order to induce the Company to issue a replacement certificate, Security Holder will indemnify the Company from any liability, claim, demand, damages, or costs arising from the alleged loss, theft, or destruction of the Certificate or the issuance of a replacement certificate therefor;

NOW, THEREFOR, in consideration of the premises and the mutual covenants contained herein, Security Holder hereby agrees with the Company as follows:

1. Ownership. Security Holder represents that he is the legal and beneficial owner of record of the Securities represented by the Certificate, and that he has not sold, assigned, pledged, transferred, deposited under any agreement, or hypothecated any interest therein, or signed any power of attorney or other authorization that is now outstanding and in force, or otherwise disposed of the same, or any right therein.

2. Lost Securities. Security Holder represents that he has diligently searched for his Certificate, has been unable to locate it, and has determined that the Certificate has been lost.

3. Indemnification. Security Holder shall indemnify and hold the Company harmless for any liability, claim, demand, damages, or costs arising from the alleged loss of the Certificate or from the issuance of a replacement certificate therefor.

4. Found Certificate. Security Holder shall immediately surrender to the Company his original Certificate for cancellation if such Certificate comes into the possession or control of the Security Holder.

5. Assignment Separate from Certificate. For Value Received, the undersigned hereby sells, assigns and transfers unto the Company all of the Securities represented by the Certificate.

191

6. <u>Governing Law</u>. This Agreement shall be governed by and construed in accordance with the internal laws of the State of _____.

7. <u>Counterparts</u>. This Agreement may be executed in two or more counterparts, each of which shall be deemed an original but all of which, taken together, shall constitute one document.

8. <u>Successors</u>. This Agreement shall be binding on Security Holder and on the heirs, executors, administrators, successors and assigns of Security Holder.

IN WITNESS WHEREOF, the parties hereto have executed this Agreement as of the day and year first above written.

"Security Holder"

_____

_____
Name

_____
Address

_____

"The Company"
*****

By: _____

_____, President

Form 6 O: Foreign Corporation Certificate—Delaware

Note: Check with the secretary of state in the state where the company seeks to qualify to do business for the current form of Foreign Corporation Certificate, Statement and Designation by Foreign Corporation, or foreign (meaning out of state) qualification filing. These certifications typically require fairly minimal information but may have to be on a prescribed form.

STATE of DELAWARE

FOREIGN CORPORATION CERTIFICATE

The Undersigned, a corporation duly organized and existing under the laws of the State of _____, in accordance with the provisions of Section 371 of Title 8 of the Delaware Code, does hereby certify:

First: That _____ is a corporation duly organized and existing under the laws of the State of _____ and is filing herewith a certificate evidencing its corporate existence.

Second: That the name and address of its Registered Agent in said State of Delaware upon whom service of process may be had is _____

_____

_____.

Third: That the assets of said corporation are $ _____ and the liabilities thereof are $_____.

Fourth: That the business which is proposes to do in the State of Delaware is as follows: _____.

_____

Fifth: That the business which it proposes to do in the state of Delaware is the business it is authorized to do in the jurisdiction of its incorporation.

In Witness Whereof, said corporation has caused this Certificate to be signed on its behalf and its corporate seal affixed this _____day of _____, 20___.

By: _____
(Authorized Officer)

Name: _____
(Typed or Printed)

Form 6 P: Certificate of Amendment—Delaware

Note: Check with the secretary of state for the requirements of an amendment to the articles of incorporation or the certificate of incorporation. Also note that you have the option of filing an Amended and Restated Articles of Incorporation form or an Amended and Restated Certificate of Incorporation form.

STATE *of* DELAWARE
CERTIFICATE *of* AMENDMENT *of*
CERTIFICATE *of* INCORPORATION

First: That at a meeting of the Board of Directors of _____
_____
resolutions were duly adopted setting forth a proposed amendment of the Certificate of Incorporation of said corporation, declaring said amendment to be advisable and calling a meeting of the stockholders of said corporation for consideration thereof. The resolution setting forth the proposed amendment as follows:

Resolved, that the Certificate of Incorporation of this corporation be amended by changing the Article thereof numbered "_____" so that, as amended, said Article shall be and read as follows: "_____

_____
"
_____

Second: That thereafter, pursuant to resolution of its Board of Directors, a special meeting of the stockholders of said corporation was duly called and held upon notice in accordance with Section 222 of the General Corporation Law of the State of Delaware at which meeting the necessary number of shares as required by statute were voted in favor of the amendment.

Third: That said amendment was duly adopted in accordance with the provisions of Section 242 of the General Corporation Law of the State of Delaware.

Fourth: That the capital of said corporation shall not be reduced under or by reason of said amendment.

In Witness Whereof, said corporation has caused this certificate to be signed by an authorized officer, this _____ day of _____, 20___.

By: _____
(Authorized Officer)

Name: _____
(Typed or Printed)

Form 6 Q: Resignation of Officer/Director

[Personal Letterhead of Resigning Officer/Director]

[Date]

VIA PERSONAL DELIVERY

The Board of Directors
****, Inc.

_____

[Address]

_____

Re: Resignation of _____ as an Officer/Director

Dear Members of the Board of Directors of ****, Inc.:

This letter will serve as my resignation, effective immediately, from the office of _____ and from the Board of Directors of ****, Inc., a [California] corporation. It has been my pleasure to serve the company.

All property belonging to the company previously in my possession is returned herewith and itemized below.

[If applicable] Also enclosed, please find my signed Termination Certification pursuant to my Confidential Information and Invention Assignment Agreement with the company.

Very truly yours,

_____

[Name of Resigning Officer/Director]

Property Returned to ****, Inc.:
    Sony laptop computer
    Memorex back-up device containing copies of computer files
    T Mobile Blackberry device

_____

_____

Form 6 R: Agreement for Inspector of Election

AGREEMENT FOR INSPECTOR OF ELECTION

This Agreement for Inspector of Election is made as of the ___ day of _____, 20__, between ****, Inc. and ****, Inc., each a [California] corporation (together the "***Companies***"), and ****, Inc., a [California] professional corporation acting through _____, an individual licensed to practice law in the State of [California] (together the "***Inspector***").

WHEREAS, the Companies engaged ****, Inc. to provide inspector of election services in connection with their planned shareholder meetings on _____, 20__, pursuant to an engagement letter dated _____, 20__ (the "***Engagement Letter***"); and

WHEREAS, the parties wish to supplement the terms and conditions of the Engagement Letter in advance of the Companies' planned shareholder meetings;

NOW THEREFORE, in consideration of the premises and of the mutual promises and covenants herein contained, the parties agree as follows:

1. Inspector shall provide the following services in connection with the Companies' shareholder meetings on _____, 20__, including any adjournment thereof (the "***Duties***").

a. Determine the number of shares outstanding and the voting power of each, the shares represented at the meeting, the existence of a quorum, the authenticity, validity, and effect of proxies;

b. Receive votes, ballots or consents;

c. Hear and determine all challenges and questions in any way arising in connection with the right to vote;

d. Count and tabulate all votes or consents;

e. Determine when the polls shall close;

f. Determine the result; and

g. Do such acts as may be proper to conduct the election or vote with fairness to all shareholders.

2. Inspector shall perform the Duties impartially, in good faith, to the best of their ability and as expeditiously as is practical.

3. The Companies and each of them hereby represent and warrant to Inspector as follows:

a. That the board of directors of each of the Companies has authorized Inspector's appointment as inspector of election in connection with the Companies' shareholder meetings on _____, 20__;

b. That the board of directors of each of the Companies is currently comprised of the following individuals: _____;

c. That _____, is currently the President and Secretary of each of the Companies; and

d. That the documents provided to Inspector in connection with this Agreement and the Engagement Letter, including but not limited to [the Restated Articles of Incorporation, Bylaws, Share Register, and Notice of Meeting] of each of the Companies, are true, accurate, and complete copies of such documents.

4.   The Companies shall compensate Inspector in accordance with the Engagement Letter.

5.   The Companies and each of them hereby agree to indemnify, defend, and hold harmless Inspector against any and all losses, costs, expenses, and damages, including but not limited to reasonable attorneys' fees, arising out of any inaccuracy in the Companies' representations and warranties set forth in this Agreement, Inspector's performance of the Duties, or any act or failure to act by the Companies or either of them, except in the event such loss, cost, expense, or damage is due solely to Inspector's gross negligence or willful misconduct.

6.   In the event litigation shall be instituted to enforce any provision of this Agreement, the prevailing party in such litigation shall be entitled to recover reasonable attorneys' fees and expenses incurred in such litigation, including on appeal, in addition to any other recovery to which such party may be legally entitled.

IN WITNESS WHEREOF, the undersigned duly authorized representatives of the parties have executed this Agreement as of the day and year first above written

Companies:
****, Inc.   ****, Inc.

By: _____   By: _____
_____, President   _____, President

Inspector:
****, Inc.

By: _____
_____, President

Form 6 S: Report of Inspector of Election

****, Inc.:

SPECIAL SHAREHOLDERS MEETING
REPORT OF THE INSPECTOR OF ELECTIONS

A.   A special meeting of the shareholders of ****, Inc. was held on _____, 20__, at _____ [address], for the purposes of:

   1.   Approving the financial statements of each corporation.
   2.   Ratification of certain actions taken by the Board of Directors;
   3.   Ratification of the engagement of auditors; and
   4.   The election of directors.

B.   The inspector confirmed the following in advance of the meetings:

   1.   Notice of the meeting was sent to all shareholders by mail on _____, 20__, to their address of record with the corporation;
   2.   The record date for the meeting was _____, 20__; and
   3.   The undersigned was appointed inspector of election for each meeting by the governing Board of Directors of each corporation on _____, 20__.

C.   Shareholders representing _____ shares of ***, Inc., out of a total issued and outstanding of _____, or approximately _____% of the total number of shares outstanding, were present at the meeting and constituted a quorum for the conduct of business.

D.   Voting at the meeting was by written ballot. The results and the number of votes cast in person or by proxy with respect to the matters put to shareholder vote, as determined by the undersigned inspector of election are set forth below.

E.   ****, INC. Voting Results:

1.   Approval of Financial Statement:

   FOR   AGAINST   ABSTAINED
   _____   _____   _____

2.   Ratification of Board Actions Presented:

   FOR   AGAINST   ABSTAINED
   _____   _____   _____

3.   Ratification of Engagement of Auditor:

   FOR   AGAINST   ABSTAINED
   _____   _____   _____

4. Election of Directors:

_____	FOR	AGAINST	ABSTAINED
_____	_____	_____
_____	FOR	AGAINST	ABSTAINED
_____	_____	_____
_____	FOR	AGAINST	ABSTAINED
_____	_____	_____
_____	FOR	AGAINST	ABSTAINED
_____	_____	_____
_____	FOR	AGAINST	ABSTAINED
_____	_____	_____
_____	FOR	AGAINST	ABSTAINED
(Write-In)	_____	_____	_____

_____

_____, Inspector of Election

Form 6 T: Agreement to Terminate Voting Trust

AGREEMENT TO TERMINATE VOTING TRUST

This Agreement to Terminate Voting Trust (this "Agreement") dated as of _____, 20__ (the "Effective Date"), is entered into by and among the undersigned parties to that certain Voting Trust Agreement for Stock of **** Corporation dated _____, 20___ (the "Voting Trust").

WHEREAS, the beneficial owners of the stock subject to the Voting Trust have been deemed capable of safely and competently managing their own interests in such stock; and

WHEREAS, it is the desire of the parties to terminate the Voting Trust and have the shares previously subject to the trust reissued in the names of the beneficial owners thereof;

NOW THEREFOR, the parties hereto agree as follows:

1. The Voting Trust is hereby terminated pursuant to Section __ of the Voting Trust, which permits termination upon the mutual written consent of the parties thereto.
2. The certificates numbered __ and __ representing the shares of **** Corporation Common Stock previously subject to the Voting Trust shall be canceled and reissued in the names of the beneficial owners thereof without a voting trust legend.

IN WITNESS WHEREOF, the parties have executed this Agreement as of the date and year first above written.

_____
_____ [name]

_____
_____ [name]

_____
_____ [name]

CHAPTER 7

Organizing or Cleaning Up an LLC

7.1 What Is the Basic Structure of a Limited Liability Company?

The owners of the LLC are the "members" as defined in your state's Limited Liability Company Act (the "Act"). The LLC may be managed by its members, or it may be managed by one or more managers elected by the members (the "managers"). The governing agreement for the LLC is called an "Operating Agreement" or "LLC Agreement." In a member-managed LLC, each member has the power to bind the LLC. However, in a manager-managed LLC, no member has the power to bind the LLC (just as no shareholder of a corporation can bind the corporation); only a manager or authorized officer of the LLC can bind the manager-managed LLC.

The principal distinguishing feature of an LLC is the limitation of liability that the members of the LLC enjoy (like a corporation), as well as the pass-through income tax treatment enjoyed by the LLC and members (like a partnership). So long as the LLC is properly formed and in existence, and is properly operated, the members will not be personally liable for the LLC's debts, obligations, and liabilities. In other words, if the LLC's debts exceed the value of the LLC's assets, the LLC's creditors should not be entitled to seek repayment from the members' personal assets.

Of course, a personal guarantee of an LLC obligation by an LLC member would give rise to personal liability of that member to the extent specified in the guarantee (as it would for a shareholder in a corporation). Failure by a member to remit employee withholding taxes can provide another basis for personal liability of a member (as it would for a shareholder in a corporation). Liability based on the personal tortious behavior of a member would of course provide the basis for personal tort liability of that member (as it would for a shareholder in a corporation). But generally, the LLC liability shield, like the corporation's liability shield, should protect individual members from LLC debts, obligations, and liabilities.

7.2 What Are Membership Interests?

Membership interests are LLC members' entire interest in the LLC, including the members' economic interest in the company as well as their noneconomic rights, such as the right to vote or participate in the management of the company and the right to receive information concerning the company's business and affairs.

7.3 What Are Economic Interests?

An economic interest is the right to receive distributions and allocations of profits, losses, income, gain, deduction, credit, and similar items of a financial nature from an LLC. However, an economic interest does not include any other rights of members, including—without limitation—the right to vote or participate in the management of the company, except as otherwise provided in the applicable LLC Act.

7.4 Should a Specific Number of Membership Interests Be Authorized?

In a manager-managed LLC (i.e., one in which some or all of the members are not involved in management), establishing a number of authorized membership interests (or "Units," "Shares," etc.) can be used as part of a structure that permits managers to admit new members without the need for member approval, much as authorized but unissued stock can be used by the board of directors of a corporation without the necessity of shareholder approval.

7.5 What Is the Role of a Member?

The members own the LLC and provide the capital with which the LLC commences its business. In a member-managed LLC, members by definition manage the business of the LLC. In a manager-managed LLC, members as a group often do not take an active role in running the business. Normally one or two members will be intimately involved in day-to-day operations of the LLC, and other members will be passive, nonacting investors. Beyond electing the managers and voting on certain key events in the LLC's life, the members of a manager-managed LLC entrust management of the LLC to the managers (much like the shareholders of a corporation entrust management of the corporation to the directors and officers of the corporation).

The role of the members will depend on whether the LLC is member-managed or manager-managed.

Whether held by members or managers, management duties include decisions about key policies, LLC transactions, and establishment of guidelines within which the business of the LLC will be conducted. The members can hire officers and employees to perform the LLC's day-to-day business.

Whether the LLC is member-managed or manager-managed, certain matters under the Act must be submitted to the members for approval. For example, certain fundamental changes in the life of an LLC, such as a merger or liquidation of the LLC, require a vote by the members. These fundamental changes include amendment of the articles of organization, amendment of the operating agreement, merger or consolidation of the LLC, and winding up and dissolution of the LLC. The LLC's operating agreement may designate additional matters requiring member approval to ensure that the members are in agreement on designated "major decisions."

7.6 What Is the Role of a Manager?

Managers are elected by the members. At the outset managers can simply be specified in the operating agreement, which is of course approved and signed by all members. Thereafter, if the operating agreement so permits, members can hold annual or other regularly scheduled meetings to elect managers. Management duties include decisions about key policies, LLC transactions, and establishment of guidelines within which the business of the LLC will be conducted. Managers may perform these responsibilities themselves, or these responsibilities can be performed by officers and employees under the direction of the managers.

In performing these responsibilities, the LLC Act imposes on managers the same fiduciary duty with respect to the LLC and its members that a general partner owes to a general partnership and the other partners of that partnership. It is permissible to modify and otherwise refine the fiduciary duty of the manager in the operating agreement. Indeed, it is advisable to do so. Typically the operating agreement will specify fiduciary duties such as the "duty of loyalty" and the "duty of care" for LLC managers.

The duty of loyalty dictates that a manager must act in good faith and must not allow personal interests to prevail over interests of the LLC and the LLC's members. A standard example raising these issues is a proposal for the LLC to enter into a transaction that either benefits a manager or involves the manager in a conflict of interest between the manager and the LLC or its members. Such transactions are often called "self-dealing" transactions. They are not prohibited, but such transactions must be predicated upon (i) full disclosure, (ii) proper approval from disinterested managers and members, and (iii) fairness to the LLC and its members.

The duty of care requires a manager to be diligent and prudent in managing the LLC's affairs. This is sometimes referred to in corporate law as the "business judgment" rule. If a manager makes a decision, conscientiously and without fraud or conflict of interest, such manager will not be second-guessed by courts based on how that decision happens to work out for the LLC. A manager is not held liable merely because a carefully made decision turns out badly.

Like a corporation, the LLC members and managers can appoint officers for the LLC who serve at the pleasure of the managers, subject to contracts of employment (if any) such officers may have with the LLC. The officers perform the bulk of the day-to-day operation of the LLC's business. Normally an LLC will want at least a general manager (or president), a chief financial officer, and a secretary. More than one of these offices can be held by the same individual. An LLC may have additional officers. These additional officers are either appointed by the general manager or another officer if such officer has been delegated authority to make such appointments. A summary of the standard duties of LLC officers is set forth in sample Form 7 A, First Correspondence to a Newly Formed LLC, any part of which could be modified by the managers.

7.7 What Formalities Must Be Observed?

Unlike the situation for a corporation, the observance of corporate formalities is not an important part of maintaining the shield from liability and other protections and advantages offered by the LLC form of doing business. The term "corporate formalities" normally means holding annual (or other regularly scheduled) meetings of the members and managers, providing written notice in advance of such meetings, preparing detailed minutes of matters decided upon at such meetings, and so forth. The LLC Act specifically states that the failure to observe such corporate formalities "shall not be considered a factor tending to establish that the members have personal liability for any debt, obligation, or liability of" the LLC where the articles of organization or operating agreement of the LLC do not specifically require such formalities to be observed.

This does not mean that LLC members are completely free to ignore the separate legal identity of the LLC. For example, members must always keep in mind that the LLC assets and funds are in the name of and owned by the LLC, not by the LLC's members. Separating LLC assets from personal assets of the members is important.

1. Documentation of Policies and Major Decisions.

Matters of general operating policy should be considered and authorized by the general manager or the managers of the LLC. Although there is no statutory requirement with respect to how frequently the managers should act, it is advisable that the managers meet at least quarterly. In addition, a specially convened meeting of the managers may be called if action is required before the next regular meeting of the managers. Action by the managers may also be taken by the unanimous written consent of the managers. Although it is likely that most manager actions will be taken by unanimous written consent without a meeting, it may prove useful to schedule regular managers' meetings to address significant matters that have arisen on a quarterly—or, at least annual—basis. Manager meetings can be held either in person or by conference telephone so long as all managers in attendance can hear each other simultaneously.

Matters appropriate for manager action—which can be immediately approved by written consent or which might arise and be accumulated, pending approval by the managers—include the following:

1. Appointment of officers, setting of salaries, and declaration of bonuses (at least annually, typically at a meeting of the managers immediately following the annual meeting of members);
2. Appointment of manager committees, if any;
3. Opening of LLC bank accounts and the designation and change of LLC managers and officers authorized as signatories;
4. LLC borrowing and delivery of collateral in connection with such borrowing;
5. Consummation of material contracts for the purchase or lease of significant assets or services or the disposition of LLC assets or for the rendition of services outside the ordinary course of the business of the LLC;
6. Policy decisions with respect to the construction of material assets or the investment of material amounts in research and development projects;
7. The adoption of pension, profit-sharing, bonus, and other employee benefit plans;
8. The repurchase of LLC interests;
9. Amendment of LLC bylaws (if any);
10. Review of financial statements of the LLC;
11. Appointment of auditors, if any;
12. Any action that requires a member vote; and
13. The issuance and sale by the LLC of additional interests in the LLC.

In the case of any such actions, the secretary of the LLC should prepare minutes of the meeting at which such actions were approved or prepare the form of written consent evidencing any such manager or member actions.

2. Separation of Personal and Company Assets.

It is important for any company to respect the difference between the company's bank accounts, property, equipment, and other assets and personal assets owned by the company's owners. An LLC, like a corporation or other legal "person," is a separate legal entity with assets that are owned by the LLC. Any attempt by an LLC member to dispose of or use LLC property would be no more proper than an attempt by that member to dispose of or use another member's personal property. Members must respect the fact that the LLC's assets are the property of the

LLC, not the members. Similarly, an LLC member should not intermingle such member's personal assets with the company assets of the LLC.

The company's books, records, and financial statements should be maintained clearly to reflect the separation of the company's assets from the personal assets of the members. The company must conduct business in its own name (not in the individual name of any manager or member). All letterhead, business cards, bills, checks, invoices, and other company forms should show the company's full legal name (and fictitious business name, if any) and the company's current address, telephone number, and fax number.

As a statement of sound business practice, the observations made about separation of personal assets from company assets are fairly obvious. There is an additional, less obvious reason to follow those rules.

Creation of an LLC shield from liability for LLC members inevitably gives rise to attempts to pierce that shield by creditors of the LLC. This has long been the case for the liability shield of corporations. As long as there have been corporations, there have been attempts to "pierce the corporate veil": Published cases in which such attempts have been successful usually involve a recitation by the court of a dozen or so factors in support of the court's ruling that the shareholders of the corporation should be held personally liable for the debts, obligations, or other liabilities of the corporation. At the top of this list of factors are (i) failure by the shareholders to respect the corporation's separate identity (by intermingling corporate and personal assets) and (ii) some other form of misconduct by the shareholders with respect to the corporation.

Although the failure of an LLC to respect corporate formalities generally cannot be considered a factor "tending to establish that the members have personal liability" for any LLC debt, obligation, or liability (see the earlier discussion regarding observance of corporate formalities), this is not to say that LLC members can ignore the many years of corporation law developments in this area. LLC members and managers are well advised to bear in mind the foregoing observations about piercing the corporate veil.

3. Adequate Capitalization.

The company should be adequately capitalized to carry on the company's business activities. This is of course an obvious statement of sound business practice. A less obvious reason to assure that the company is and remains adequately capitalized concerns the case law, discussed above, related to piercing the corporate veil. One of the factors enunciated by some of the courts that have ruled that creditors of a corporation should be allowed to hold the shareholders personally liable for debts and obligations of the corporation is that the corporation was not adequately capitalized. Hence, adequate capitalization is an additional, important factor relating to the shield from personal liability provided by the LLC for its members.

4. Signing on Behalf of the LLC.

Whenever the LLC members, managers, or officers are signing agreements, documents, or correspondence on behalf of the LLC, care should be taken to include the LLC's name in the signature block and to indicate the title of the person signing. An example of an appropriate signature block is included below:

> [LLC name]
>
> By: _____
>
> Name: [name of individual]
>
> Title: [Member, Manager, etc.]

Failure to include the LLC's name in the signature block may lead, in the context of litigation involving a signed document, to including the person who signed the document in the lawsuit in his or her individual capacity.

5. Bylaws.

The operating agreement and articles of organization of the LLC are the authoritative source of advice as to how to do certain things that will come up from time to time. For certain types of LLCs (normally those with a larger number of members), a form of bylaws similar to those applicable to a corporation may be advisable or useful.

6. Official Documents.

A number of small LLCs have found it useful to designate one of the officers, usually the secretary, to be the recipient of all "official" correspondence concerning the LLC and its relationships with the various government agencies with which it deals. This helps to avoid forgetting to submit certain of the regularly filed forms, such as the annual statement of information and designation of agent for service of process, which are simple documents but can lead to trouble if they are not taken care of promptly.

7.8 What Are the Tax and Regulatory Obligations of an LLC?

1. Taxes.

Federal and state income tax returns must be filed on or before the fifteenth day of the third month following the close of the taxable year, unless a timely extension to file is obtained. LLC members may be required to pay estimated federal income tax in installments (like a general partner in a partnership).

The LLC will be subject to an annual minimum franchise tax in each state in which it is organized and in each state where it is qualified to do business.

The LLC may be subject to other state tax matters—such as the State Graduated Gross Receipts Fee, which is due in addition to the annual $800 franchise tax an LLC must pay in California.

The LLC will be required to withhold income tax and social security tax from taxable wages paid to its employees and deposited periodically with the appropriate Federal Tax Deposit Form. An Employer's Quarterly Federal Tax Return (IRS Form 941) must then be filed before the end of the month following each calendar quarter. Any manager, officer, or other person obliged to withhold taxes may become personally liable for a 100 percent penalty if he or she fails to pay the withheld funds to the Internal Revenue Service.

The LLC may also be required to withhold state income tax from its employees' taxable wages.

2. Renewals.

Legal requirements, such as annual state filings and payment of annual fees in each state where it is qualified to do business, are required to maintain an LLC in good standing.

3. Employer ID.

Every new employer must obtain a Federal Employer Identification Number (FEIN), which will be used on partnership information returns and certain other documents. A FEIN can be obtained by application to the Internal Revenue Service on Form SS-4.

4. More Taxes.

If the nature of the LLC's business includes the sale at retail of tangible personal property (goods), then the LLC may be subject to sales and use taxes and need to obtain a seller's permit from the appropriate authority, such as [the California State Board of Equalization]. If the LLC owns significant personal property, it may be required to file a property statement with the county assessor and may be subject to a personal property tax. Forms may be obtained from the county assessor.

5. Business Licenses.

Most municipalities require that businesses within their jurisdictions obtain a local business license.

6. Industry Regulation.

Numerous regulated businesses cannot lawfully be conducted without special licensing or permits (e.g., general contractors, insurance sales, and cosmetologists). Make sure you know what regulatory requirements are unique to your client's business.

Although it is not intended to be exhaustive, the checklist included in Form 7 A, First Correspondence to a Newly Formed LLC, summarizes some of the legal requirements applicable to a new LLC. Some of the requirements arise as a consequence of forming the LLC; others apply to all new businesses regardless of the form of organization. Certain requirements are highly formal and technical; many must be satisfied within a specified time period. Care must be taken to comply with these matters as they arise because in many cases serious penalties can be assessed for failure to comply.

7.9 Sample Documents and Checklists.

This section includes the following forms:

- First Correspondence to a Newly Formed LLC (Form 7 A)
- Limited Liability Company Certificate of Formation (Form 7 B)
- Limited Liability Company Certificate of Formation—Series (Form 7 C)
- Limited Liability Company Certificate Face (Form 7 D)
- Limited Liability Company Certificate Legend (Form 7 E)
- Managers' Written Consent for Limited Liability Company (Form 7 F)
- Written Consent of LLC Members (Form 7 G)
- Operating Agreement—California Short Form (Form 7 H)
- Operating Agreement—California Corporate Format (Form 7 I)
- Operating Agreement—Delaware Series (Form 7 J)
- Operating Agreement—Nevada Manager-Managed (Form 7 K)

Form 7 A: First Correspondence
to a Newly Formed LLC

[Client Name]
[Client Address]

Dear _____,

Congratulations on the organization of your limited liability company!

Attached please find a copy of your Articles of Organization which were filed with the [State] Secretary of State on [Date]. [****], LLC was assigned [State] LLC number _____.

Also attached please find a draft [Limited Liability Company Agreement] [Operating Agreement] for your review and consideration.

You will need to obtain a Federal Employer Identification Number (FEIN) for the new entity, which you can do online by completing and submitting a Form SS-4 application at the following link: https://sa.www4.irs.gov/sa_vign/newFormSS4.do. The instructions for completing the form can be found here: http://www.irs.gov/businesses/small/article/0,,id=102765,00.html. If you need help, please don't hesitate to call. Once obtained, I would like to have a copy of your completed Form SS-4 and the assigned FEIN for my files.

With the attached endorsed filed Articles of Organization, a FEIN, and Operating Agreement, your bank should allow you to open a bank account for the new entity.

[Other organizational matters, such as: At your convenience, but no later than _____, you need to complete a Statement of Information for submission to the California Secretary of State to maintain the company's good standing. The form is available online at the following link: http://www.ss.ca.gov/business/llc/forms/llc-12 .pdf. Enter your Secretary of State File Number to access the correct form. There is a $20.00 filing fee. If you have any questions about completing the form, please do not hesitate to call me.]

[Additional organizational matters, such as: Attached please find a copy of the Instructions for Form FTB 3522 and Limited Liability Tax Voucher for the payment of the company's annual $800 tax to the [California Franchise Tax Board].]

The remainder of this correspondence is for reference purposes and will provide you with some general information regarding the operation of a limited liability company and the roles of members, managers, and officers in a limited liability company. This email is intended to call to your attention some of the basic legal requirements to which limited liability companies are subject and which may require your attention. Please consider the matters described herein with care and keep a copy of this email with your limited liability company records for easy reference, as failure to observe some of the requirements may compromise the limited liability company or result in personal liability to its members, managers, or officers.

* *

I. BASIC STRUCTURE OF AN LLC

The owners of the LLC are the "members" as defined in the [California] Limited Liability Company Act (the "Act"). The LLC may be managed by its members, or it maybe managed by one or more managers elected by the members (the "managers"). The governing agreement for the LLC is called an "Operating Agreement". In a member-managed LLC, each member has the power to bind the LLC. However, in a manager-managed LLC, no member has the power to bind the LLC (just as no shareholder of a corporation can bind the corporation); only a manager or authorized officer of the LLC can bind the manager-managed LLC.

Management duties include decisions about key policies, LLC transactions, and establishment of guidelines within which the business of the LLC will be conducted. The managers can hire officers and employees to perform the LLC's day-to-day business.

The principal distinguishing feature of an LLC is the limitation of liability which the members of the LLC enjoy (like a corporation), as well as the pass-through income tax treatment enjoyed by the LLC and members (like a partnership). So long as the LLC is properly formed and in existence, and is properly operated, the members will not be personally liable for the LLC's debts, obligations, and liabilities. In other words, if the LLC's debts exceed the value of the LLC's assets, the LLC's creditors should not be entitled to seek repayment from the members' personal assets.

Of course, a personal guarantee of an LLC obligation by an LLC member would give rise to personal liability of that member to the extent specified in the guarantee (as it would for a shareholder in a corporation). Failure by a member to remit employee withholding taxes can provide another basis for personal liability of a member (as it would for a shareholder in a corporation). Liability based on the personal tortious behavior of a member would of course provide the basis for personal tort liability of that member (as it would for a shareholder in a corporation). But generally, the LLC liability shield, like the corporation's liability shield, should protect individual members from LLC debts, obligations, and liabilities.

The following is a brief description of the roles of the major players in an LLC—the members and the managers. Although the following is written as if members and managers are separate persons, the same individuals could serve as members and managers.

A. Members

The members own the LLC and provide the capital with which the LLC commences its business. In a member-managed LLC, members by definition manage the business of the LLC. In a manager-managed LLC, members as a group often do not take an active role in running the business. Normally one or two members will be intimately involved in day-to-day operations of the LLC, and other members will be passive, non-active investors. Beyond electing the managers and voting on certain key events in the LLC's life, the members of a manager-managed LLC entrust management of the LLC to the managers (much like the shareholders of a corporation entrust management of the corporation to the directors and officers of the corporation). Matters requiring member votes are discussed in "Member Votes" below.

B. Managers

Managers are elected by the members. At the outset managers can simply be specified in the operating agreement, which is of course approved and signed by all members. Thereafter, if the operating agreement so permits, members can hold annual or other regularly scheduled meetings to elect managers. Managers manage the business and affairs of the LLC and exercise the LLC's powers. Managers may either perform these responsibilities themselves or these responsibilities can be performed by officers and employees under the direction of the managers.

In performing these responsibilities, the Act imposes on managers the same fiduciary duty with respect to the LLC and its members that a general partner owes to a general partnership and the other partners of that partnership. It is permissible to modify and otherwise refine the fiduciary duty of the manager in the operating agreement. Indeed it is advisable to do so. Typically the operating agreement will specify fiduciary duties such as the "duty of loyalty" and the "duty of care" for LLC managers.

The duty of loyalty dictates that a manager must act in good faith and must not allow personal interests to prevail over interests of the LLC and the LLC's members. A standard example that raises these issues is a proposal that the LLC enter into a transaction which benefits a manager, or involves the manager in a conflict of interest between the manager and the LLC or its members. Such transactions are often called "self-dealing" transactions. They are not prohibited, but such transactions must be predicated upon (i) full disclosure, (ii) proper approval from disinterested managers and members, and (iii) fairness to the LLC and its members.

The duty of care requires a manager to be diligent and prudent in managing the LLC's affairs. This is sometimes referred to in corporate law as the "business judgment" rule. If a manager makes a decision, conscientiously and without fraud or conflict of interest, such manager will not be second-guessed by courts based on how that decision happens to work out for the LLC. A manager is not held liable merely because a carefully made decision turns out badly.

C. Officers

Like a corporation, the LLC members and managers can appoint officers for the LLC who serve at the pleasure of the managers, subject to contracts of employment (if any) such officers may have with the LLC. The officers perform the bulk of the day-to-day operation of the LLC's business. Normally an LLC will want at least a General Manager (or President), a Chief Financial Officer, and a Secretary. More than one of these offices can be held by the same individual. An LLC may have additional officers. These additional officers are either appointed by the General Manager or another officer if such officer has been delegated authority to make such appointments.

The following is a brief summary of the standard duties of the following officers. All of these could be modified by the managers.

1. General Manager or President. The General Manager is the Chief Executive Officer and general manager of the LLC unless the LLC has a Chairman of the Board and has designated the Chairman as Chief Executive Officer. The General Manager has general supervision, direction, and control over the LLC's business and its officers. The General Manager can also be called the President of the LLC.

2. Chief Financial Officer. The Chief Financial Officer keeps the books and records of account of the properties and business transactions of the LLC. These duties include depositing corporate funds and other valuables in the name of the LLC and disbursing funds as directed by the managers. The Chief Financial Officer also typically serves as the "tax matters partner" for the LLC as required under the Internal Revenue Code.

3. Secretary. The Secretary of an LLC keeps the LLC's Articles of Organization, Operating Agreement, record of members' addresses and holdings in the LLC, and written minutes (if any) of the proceedings of the LLC's members and managers. The Secretary usually has the duty of giving notices to members and managers of members' and managers' meetings.

II. OBSERVANCE OF "CORPORATE FORMALITIES"— NOT REQUIRED

Unlike a corporation, the observance of "corporate formalities" is not an important part of maintaining the shield from liability and other protections and advantages offered by the LLC form of doing business. The term "corporate formalities" normally means holding annual (or other regularly scheduled) meetings of the members and managers, providing written notice in advance of such meetings, preparing detailed minutes of matters decided upon at such meetings, and so forth. The Act specifically states that the failure to observe such corporate formalities "shall not be considered a factor tending to establish that the members have personal liability for any debt, obligation, or liability of the" LLC where the Articles of Organization or Operating Agreement of the LLC do not specifically require such formalities to be observed.

This does not mean that LLC members are completely free to ignore the separate legal identity of the LLC. For example, members must always keep in mind that the LLC assets and funds are in the name of and owned by the LLC, not by the LLC's members. Separation of LLC assets from personal assets of the members is very important. See "Separation of LLC and Personal Assets" below.

III. MEMBER VOTES; MANAGER ACTIONS

A. Member Votes. Certain fundamental changes in the life of an LLC, such as a merger or liquidation of the LLC, require a vote by the members. These fundamental changes include amendment of the Articles of Organization, amendment of the Operating Agreement, merger or consolidation of the LLC, and winding up and dissolution of the LLC.

B. Manager Action. Matters of general operating policy should be considered and authorized by the General Manager or managers of the LLC. Although there is no statutory requirement with respect to how frequently the managers should act, it is advisable that the managers meet at least quarterly. In addition, a specially convened meeting of the managers may be called if action is required before the next regular meeting of the managers. Action by the managers may also be taken by the unanimous written consent of the managers. Although it is likely that most manager actions will be taken by unanimous written consent without a meeting, it may prove useful to schedule regular managers' meetings to address significant matters which have arisen on a quarterly or, at least, annual basis. Manager meetings can be held either in person or by conference telephone so long as all managers in attendance can hear each other simultaneously.

Matters appropriate for manager action, which can be immediately approved by written consent or which might arise and be accumulated, pending approval by the managers, include the following:

1. Appointment of officers, setting of salaries, and declaration of bonuses (at least annually, typically at a meeting of the managers immediately following the annual meeting of members);
2. Appointment of manager committees, if any;
3. Opening of LLC bank accounts and the designation and change of LLC managers and officers authorized as signatories;
4. LLC borrowing and delivery of collateral in connection with such borrowing;
5. Consummation of material contracts for the purchase or lease of significant assets or services or the disposition of LLC assets or for the rendition of services outside the ordinary course of the business of the LLC;

6. Policy decisions with respect to the construction of material assets or the investment of material amounts in research and development projects;
7. The adoption of pension, profit-sharing, bonus and other employee benefit plans;
8. The repurchase of LLC interests;
9. Amendment of LLC bylaws (if any);
10. Review of financial statements of the LLC;
11. Appointment of auditors, if any;
12. Any action which requires a member vote; and
13. The issuance and sale by the LLC of additional interests in the LLC.

In the case of any such actions, the Secretary of the LLC should prepare minutes of the meeting at which such actions were approved or prepare the form of written consent evidencing any such manager or member actions.

IV. SEPARATION OF LLC AND PERSONAL ASSETS

It is important for any company to respect the difference between the company's bank accounts, property, equipment, and other assets and personal assets owned by the company's owners. An LLC, like a corporation or other legal "person," is a separate legal entity with assets that are owned by the LLC. Any attempt by an LLC member to dispose of or use LLC property would be no more proper than an attempt by that member to dispose of or use another member's personal property. Members must respect the fact that the LLC's assets are the property of the LLC, not the members. Similarly, an LLC member should not intermingle such member's personal assets with the company assets of the LLC.

The Company's books, records, and financial statements should be maintained clearly to reflect the separation of the Company's assets from the personal assets of the members. The Company must conduct business in its own name (not in the individual name of any manager or member). All letterhead, business card, bills, checks, invoices, and other Company forms should show the Company's full legal name (and fictitious business name, if any), and the Company's current address, telephone number, and fax number.

As a statement of sound business practice the observations made about separation of personal assets from company assets are fairly obvious. There is an additional, less obvious reason to follow those rules.

Creation of an LLC shield from liability for LLC members inevitably gives rise to attempts to pierce that shield by creditors of the LLC. This has long been the case for the liability shield of corporations. As long as there have been corporations, there have been attempts to "pierce the corporate veil." Published cases in which such attempts have been successful usually involve a recitation by the court of a dozen or so factors in support of the court's ruling that the shareholders of the corporation should be held personally liable for the debts, obligations, or other liabilities of the corporation. At the top of this list of factors are (i) failure by the shareholders to respect the corporation's separate identity (by intermingling corporate and personal assets) and (ii) some other form of misconduct by the shareholders with respect to the corporation.

Although the failure of an LLC to respect corporate formalities generally cannot be considered a factor "tending to establish that the members have personal liability" for any LLC debt, obligation, or liability (see "Observance of Corporate Formalities—Not Required" above), this is not to say that LLC members can ignore the many years of corporations law developments in this area. LLC members and managers are well advised to bear in mind the foregoing observations about piercing-the-corporate-veil.

V. ADEQUATE CAPITALIZATION

The Company should be adequately capitalized to carry on the Company's business activities. This is of course an obvious statement of sound business practice. A less obvious reason to assure that the Company is and remains adequately capitalized concerns the piercing-the-corporate-veil case law discussed above. One of the factors enunciated by some of the courts that have ruled that creditors of a corporation should be allowed to hold the shareholders personally liable for debts and obligations of the corporation is that the corporation was not adequately capitalized. Hence, adequate capitalization is an additional, very important factor relating to the shield from personal liability provided by the LLC for its members.

VI. OTHER POST-FORMATION MATTERS

Although it is not intended to be exhaustive, the following checklist summarizes some of the legal requirements applicable to a new LLC. Some of the requirements arise as a consequence of formation of the LLC; others apply to all new businesses regardless of the form of organization. Certain requirements are highly formal and technical; many must be satisfied within a specified time period. Care must be taken to comply with these matters as they arise because in many cases there are serious penalties which can be assessed for failure to comply.

A. Local Business License. The LLC may be required to obtain a business license from the city in which it intends to operate.

B. Employer Identification Number. Every employer must obtain an employer identification number which will be used on federal tax returns and certain other documents.

C. Annual LLC Statement of Information. Each year, the LLC must submit a Form LLC-12, providing a current list of names and addresses of the LLC managers (and if there are no managers, of the members), the LLC chief executive officer, and the LLC agent for service of process.

D. Estimated Federal Income Tax. The LLC members will be required to pay estimated federal income tax in installments (like a general partner in a partnership). Your accountant should keep you current with this requirement.

E. State Minimum Annual Franchise Tax. [Example: Every LLC organized, registered or doing business in the state of California is subject to an annual minimum franchise tax of $800.]

F. [Other applicable tax matters, such as: State Graduated Gross Receipts Fee. In addition to the annual $800 franchise tax, an LLC in California is subject to a graduated fee determined as follows for tax years after 2001:

(1) $900 if the LLC's total income from all sources is $250,000 or more, but less than $500,000;

(2) $2,500 if total income is $500,000 or more, but less than $1,000,000;

(3) $6,000 if total income is $1,000,000 or more, but less than $5,000,000;

(4) $11,790 if total income is $5,000,000 or more.

The fee is calculated on an apportioned basis based on total income from all sources derived or attributable to the State of California. The fee is payable with the LLC's California tax return or by the 15th day of the 6th month of the current tax year, if the LLC's tax year is less than six months. Your accountant should keep you current with the tax requirements in California.]

G. Tax Returns. Both federal and state income tax returns must be filed on or before the fifteenth (15th) day of the third month following the close of the taxable year, unless a timely extension to file is obtained.

H. Personal Property Taxes. If the LLC owns significant personal property it may be required to file a property statement with the County Assessor and may be subject to a personal property tax. Forms may be obtained from the County Assessor.

I. Sales and Use Taxes. If the nature of the LLC's business includes the sale at retail of tangible personal property (goods), then the LLC may be subject to sales and use taxes and would need to obtain a seller's permit from the [California State Board of Equalization].

J. Payroll Withholding.

1. Federal. The LLC will be required to withhold income tax and social security tax from taxable wages paid to its employees. Funds withheld must be deposited in certain depositories accompanied by a Federal Tax Deposit Form 8109. An "Employer's Quarterly Federal Tax Return" (IRS Form 941) must then be filed before the end of the month following each calendar quarter. Any manager, officer, or other person obliged to withhold taxes may become personally liable for a 100% penalty if he fails to pay the withheld funds to the Internal Revenue Service.

2. [State withholding requirements, such as California. The LLC will also be required to withhold California income tax from its employees' taxable wages. Within fifteen (15) days after becoming subject to the personal income tax withholding requirements, the employer must register with the Department of Employment Development. A booklet entitled "Employer's Tax Guide for the Withholding, Payment and Reporting of California Income Tax" may be obtained from this Department.]

K. Federal Unemployment Tax. The "Unemployment Tax Return" (IRS Form 940) must be filed and any balance due paid on or before January 31 of each year. Details may be found in IRS Circular E, the "Employer's Tax Guide."

L. [Other state requirements, such as: California Unemployment Compensation Insurance. Registration with the California Department of Employment Development (EDD) can be accomplished at the same time that the LLC applies for a seller's permit (if needed) from the Board of Equalization. Forms for returns are mailed automatically to all registered employers.]

M. [Additional state requirements, such as: Workers' Compensation. All employers must either be insured against workers' compensation liability by an authorized insurer or obtain from the Manager of Industrial Relations a certificate of consent to Self-Insure. The required insurance may be obtained through the nearest local office of the State Compensation Insurance Fund, or it may be placed with a licensed workers' compensation private carrier.]

N. Trademarks; Trade Names; Trade Secrets. Company trademarks and trade names should be registered in the Company's name with the U.S. Patent and Trademark Office. Trade secrets of the Company should be protected by obliging Company employees to sign confidentiality agreements.

O. Securities Law Matters. If all members of the Company are actively involved in the management of the Company, and have the experience and ability necessary to manage the Company, then the interests in the Company would not constitute "securities" under California or federal law. If any of the members are "passive" investors, then the offer and sale of an interest in the Company to such investor would constitute the offer and sale of a "security." Normally such offers and sales can be structured to satisfy the requirements for exemption from registration under federal and state securities laws. If no exemption is available, then the securities would require registration pursuant to federal and state securities laws. Even if an exemption from registration is available, the sale by the Company of additional interests to new investors (or additional contributions of capital by existing members) should be accompanied by the filing of a [state requirement, such as: "25102(f) Statement" with the California Department of Corporations] or, if investors are located in other states in addition to California, a Form D Notice of Sale with the Securities and Exchange Commission and the state securities law administrator in each state in which a sale is made.

P. Fictitious Business Names. If the Company intends to transact business using a name other than that specified in its Articles of Organization, the Company must file a fictitious business name statement with the clerk of the county in which it has its principal place of business. The Company must also file a fictitious business name statement in any other county in which it intends to transact business. Once a fictitious business name statement is on file with the county clerk, the statement must be published in a newspaper of general circulation in the same county once a week for four consecutive weeks. Within thirty (30) days after publication, an affidavit of publication must be filed with the county clerk's office.

Q. Qualification in Other States. States universally require a "foreign LLC" (one not incorporated in that state) to "qualify" before "doing business" in such state. Qualification usually consists of the filing of documents, payment of a fee, and appointment of a resident agent for service of process. "Doing business" is more often defined by the exceptions than by an enumeration of specific acts which are covered by that term. However, if the LLC elects to do business (e.g. open an office) in another state, it will be required to qualify in that state. Failure to qualify may result in financial penalties as well as the inability to bring suit in the courts of the state with respect to acts and transactions in the state during the period of the violation.

VII. GENERAL

A. Signing on Behalf of the LLC

Whenever the LLC members, managers or officers are signing agreements, documents, or correspondence on behalf of the LLC, care should be taken to include the LLC's name in the signature block and to indicate the title of the person signing. An example of an appropriate signature block is included below:

[LLC name]

By: _____

Name: [name of individual]

Title: [Member, Manager, etc.]

Failure to do so may lead, in the context of litigation involving a signed document, to including the person who signed the document in the lawsuit in his or her individual capacity.

B. Bylaws

The Operating Agreement and Articles of Organization of the LLC are the authoritative source of advice as to how to do certain things that will come up from time to time. For certain types of LLCs (normally those with a larger number of members), a form of bylaws similar to the type of bylaws applicable to a corporation may be advisable or useful.

C. Official Documents

A number of small LLCs have found it useful to designate one of the officers, usually the Secretary, to be the recipient of all "official" correspondence concerning the LLC and its relationships with the various government agencies with which it deals. This helps to avoid forgetting to submit certain of the regularly filed forms, such as the Annual Form LLC-12 (see item VI.C above), which are simple documents but can lead to trouble if they are not taken care of promptly.

I hope this has provided some useful guidance with respect to the process of running a business in LLC form. You may wish to keep a copy of this email with your limited liability company records for future reference. Obviously, many issues may arise which are either out of the ordinary or of special importance to the LLC. Please feel free to call me with any questions.

Very truly,

_____

[Counsel]

Form 7 B: Limited Liability Company Certificate of Formation

Note: Check with the secretary of state in your state for the current form of Certificate of Formation, Articles of Organization, or other limited liability company organizational filing. These documents typically require fairly minimal information but may have to be on a prescribed form.

STATE *of* DELAWARE
LIMITED LIABILITY COMPANY
CERTIFICATE *of* FORMATION

First: The name of the limited liability company is _____
_____

Second: The address of its registered office in the State of Delaware is _____
_____ in the City of _____,
County of _____, Delaware _____. The name of its registered agent at such address is _____.

Third: (Use this paragraph only if the company is to have a specific effective date of dissolution: "The latest date on which the limited liability company is to dissolve is _____.")

Fourth: (Insert any other matters the members determine to include herein.)
_____
_____
_____
_____
_____
_____

In Witness Whereof, the undersigned have executed this Certificate of Formation of
_____ this _____ day of _____ , 20_____.

By: _____

Authorized Person(s)

Name: _____

Typed or Printed

Form 7 C: Limited Liability Company Certificate of Formation—Series

Note: The following is an alternate form to be used for a limited liability company that will have different series of members pursuant to section 18-215 of the Delaware Limited Liability Company Act.

STATE *of* DELAWARE
LIMITED LIABILITY COMPANY
CERTIFICATE *of* FORMATION

First: The name of the limited liability company is: ****, LLC.

Second: The name and address of its registered office in the State of Delaware is:

_____

_____

_____

_____

Third: The limited liability company shall continue in existence until it is terminated by operation of law or by agreement of its member or members.

Fourth: The limited liability company may establish series of members having separate rights, powers and duties with respect to specified property and obligations of the limited liability company, each series being formed to pursue a separate business purpose or investment objective. The debts, liabilities, obligations and expenses incurred, contracted for or otherwise existing with respect to a particular series shall be enforceable against the assets of such series only, and not against the assets of the limited liability company generally, or any other series thereof, and unless otherwise provided in the limited liability company agreement, none of the debts, liabilities, obligations and expenses incurred, contracted for or otherwise existing with respect to the limited liability company generally or any other series thereof shall be enforceable against the assets of such series pursuant to Section 18-215 of the Delaware Limited Liability Company Act.

IN WITNESS WHEREOF, the undersigned being duly authorized to sign on behalf of the limited liability company has executed this Certificate on the _____ day of _____, 20___.

By: _____

Name: _____

Title: Authorized Person

227

Form 7 D: Limited Liability Company Certificate Face

Note: The following is an example of a certificate evidencing ownership of limited liability company units or shares and is to be completed by filling in the lettered blanks as follow:

A—State of organization
B—Date of organization
C—Certificate number
D—Number of units or shares issued to certificate holder
E—Company name
F—Total number of units or shares authorized for class issued to certificate holder
G—Name of certificate holder and how owned (e.g., as joint tenants with rights of survivorship)
H—Number of units or shares issued to certificate holder, written out
I—Day (e.g., 5th)
J—Month
K—Year
L & M—Names of managers or officers signing the certificate

Note:
- There should be a restrictive legend along the lines of the attached on the back of every certificate.
- The board should approve all share issuances, and a record of the approval should be kept with the LLC records.
- All share issuances give rise to the need for a consideration of securities laws and appropriate notice filings.

LLC Certificate Face

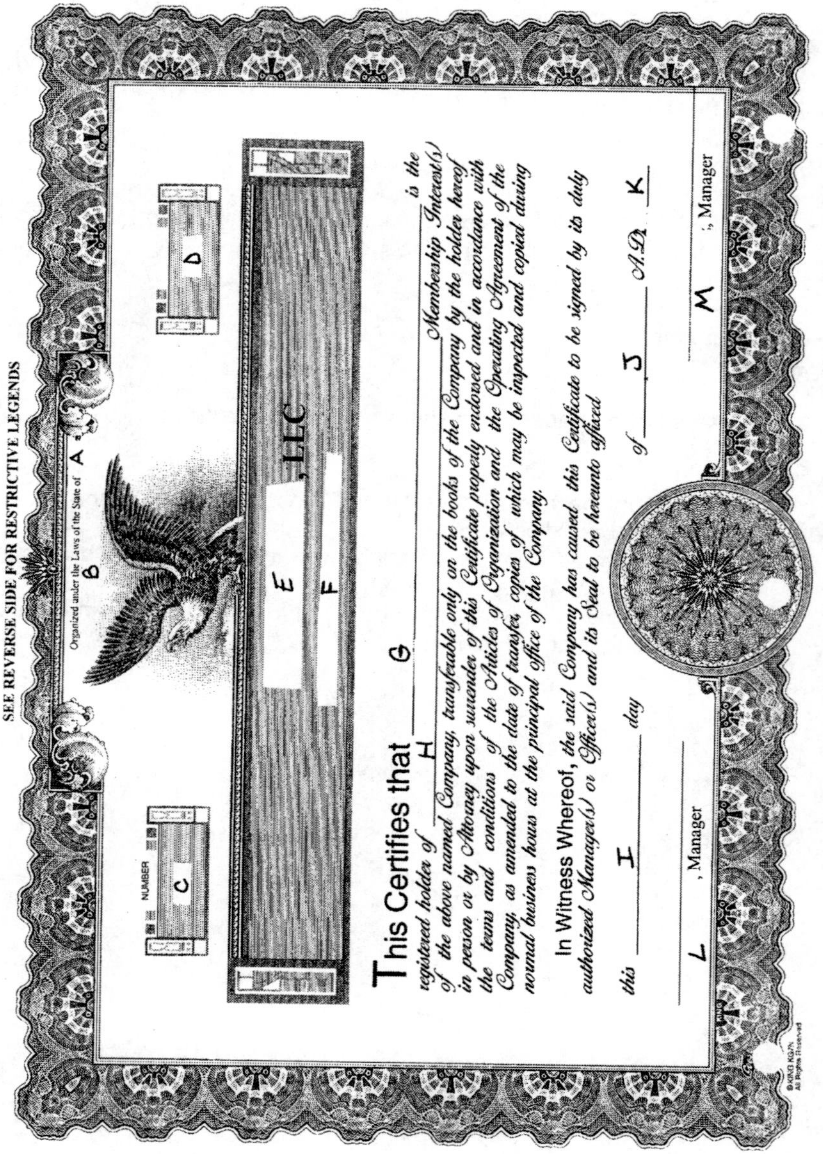
SEE REVERSE SIDE FOR RESTRICTIVE LEGENDS

NUMBER C

D

Organized under the Laws of the State of A

B

E, LLC

F

This Certifies that G is the registered holder of H *Membership Interest(s) of the above named Company, transferable only on the books of the Company by the holder hereof in person or by Attorney upon surrender of this Certificate properly endorsed and in accordance with the terms and conditions of the Articles of Organization and the Operating Agreement of the Company, as amended to the date of transfer, copies of which may be inspected and copied during normal business hours at the principal office of the Company.*

In Witness Whereof, *the said Company has caused this Certificate to be signed by its duly authorized Manager(s) or Officer(s) and its Seal to be hereunto affixed*

this I *day of* J *A.D.* K

L, Manager

M, Manager

Form 7 E: Limited Liability Company Certificate Legend

Note: The restrictive legend on the back of any certificate evidencing securities issued pursuant to an exemption from registration, and/or that are subject to an agreement that further restricts their transferability (e.g., an operating agreement with rights of first refusal) can take a variety of forms. The following is one example.

LLC Certificate Legend

THE SECURITIES REPRESENTED BY THIS CERTIFICATE HAVE NOT BEEN REGISTERED UNDER THE SECURITIES ACT OF 1933, AS AMENDED (THE "ACT"), OR UNDER ANY STATE SECURITIES LAWS, AND MAY NOT BE OFFERED, SOLD, TRANSFERRED, PLEDGED OR HYPOTHECATED IN THE ABSENCE OF AN EFFECTIVE REGISTRATION STATEMENT FOR SUCH SECURITIES UNDER THE ACT OR AN OPINION OF COUNSEL SATISFACTORY TO THE COMPANY THAT AN EXEMPTION FROM SUCH REGISTRATION IS AVAILABLE.

THE SECURITIES REPRESENTED BY THIS CERTIFICATE ARE SUBJECT TO CERTAIN RESTRICTIONS ON TRANSFER SET FORTH IN THAT CERTAIN OPERATING AGREEMENT BETWEEN THE COMPANY AND THE ORIGINAL HOLDER HEREOF.

For Value Received, _____ *hereby sell, assign and transfer unto* _____

Membership Interest(s) represented by the within Certificate, and do hereby irrevocably constitute and appoint

_____ *Attorney to transfer the said Membership Interest(s) on the books of the within named Company with full power of substitution in the premises.*

Dated _____ _____

In presence of

_____

NOTICE: THE SIGNATURE OF THIS ASSIGNMENT MUST CORRESPOND WITH THE NAME AS WRITTEN UPON THE FACE OF THE CERTIFICATE, IN EVERY PARTICULAR, WITHOUT ALTERATION OR ENLARGEMENT, OR ANY CHANGE WHATEVER.

_____

Form 7 F: Managers' Written Consent for Limited Liability Company

Note: The following is an example of a Managers' Written Consent form, used to appoint officers and create a record of authority for actions taken on behalf of the company. The statutory and operating agreement section references obviously need to reflect the law in the state where the limited liability company was formed and the operating agreement adopted by the members. This form assumes that the LLC is manager-managed and that it has adopted a corporate format for company governance, including the appointment of officers to manage the day-to-day business of the LLC. For this LLC format, most corporate forms (i.e., director and shareholder actions, bylaws, certificates evidencing ownership, etc.) are easily modified for use by the LLC. If the LLC you are working on is member-managed, the same format can be used, simply by substituting "Member" for "Manager."

**UNANIMOUS WRITTEN CONSENT OF
THE MANAGERS OF
****, LLC**
_____, 20___

The undersigned Managers of ****, LLC, a limited liability company organized under the Beverly-Killea Limited Liability Company Act, do by this writing consent to the following actions and adopt the following resolutions:

WHEREAS certain actions are permitted to be taken by the Managers of the company to establish general operating policy;

Election of Officers

NOW, THEREFORE, BE IT RESOLVED that the following persons are hereby appointed to the office(s) indicated next to their respective names:

Name	Office
****	CEO, President, Treasurer
****	Secretary

Line of Credit

WHEREAS it has been determined to be in the best interests of the company to establish a line of credit with the Bank of America to help finance business operations;

NOW, THEREFORE, BE IT RESOLVED that the establishment of a line of credit with Bank of America by the President of the company be and hereby is ratified, adopted and approved; and

Omnibus

RESOLVED FURTHER, that the President and such other officers as he may designate be, and each hereby is, authorized, directed and empowered to take such other action and to execute such additional documents as may be necessary to carry out the intent of the foregoing resolutions.

This unanimous consent is executed pursuant to Section ___ of Article ___ of the Operating Agreement of the company, which authorize the taking of action by the Managers by written consent and shall be filed with the minutes of the proceedings of the Managers of the company.

Executed effective this ____ day of _____, 20__.

_____
****, Manager

_____
****, Manager

Filed with the Secretary this ____ day of _____, 20___.

_____
****, Secretary

Form 7 G: Written Consent of LLC Members

WRITTEN CONSENT OF
THE MEMBERS OF
****, LLC
[Date]

In accordance with Section _____ of the Operating Agreement of the limited liability company and [Section 17104(i) of the California Corporations Code], the undersigned, constituting all of the Members of ****, LLC, a [California] limited liability company (the "Company"), hereby take the following actions and adopt the following resolutions by written consent:

RESOLVED: That the undersigned Members of the Company deem it advisable and to be in the best interest of the Company that [Article II, Section 2.3] of the Operating Agreement of the Company be amended to read as follows:

"2.3 **Purpose.** The Company is organized to engage in any lawful act or activity for which a limited liability company may be organized under the [California Limited Liability Company Act.]"

IN WITNESS WHEREOF, the undersigned Members of the Company have executed this Written Consent as of the date first set forth above.

_____   _____

Name: _____   Name:_____

Form 7 H: Operating Agreement—
California Short Form

This Operating Agreement is entered into as of the ___ day of _____, 20___ by the signatories to this Agreement (each a "Member," collectively the "Members"). The Members desire to form a limited liability company pursuant to the Beverly-Killea Limited Liability Company Act upon the following terms and conditions:

ARTICLE I
Name, Place of Business, and Agent

The name of the Company is ****, LLC. Its principal place of business is _____, or such other place or places as the Members may hereafter determine. Its resident agent in the State of California is _____ an individual whose address is _____, California _____.

ARTICLE II
Business, Purpose, and Term of Company

Section 2.1 *Purposes.* The purpose of the Company shall be to develop, manufacture, and sell products incorporating proprietary inventions and licensed technologies and all such things related to such business for which limited liability companies may be formed under the Act.

Section 2.2 *Term of Company.* The term of the Company shall commence on the date the Articles of Organization are filed with the California Secretary of State in accordance with the provisions of the Act and shall continue on a perpetual basis unless dissolved pursuant to Article VI of this Agreement.

ARTICLE III
Capital Contributions

Section 3.1 *Capital Contributions by Members.* Capital Contributions shall be made from time to time as the Members shall determine.

Section 3.2 *Capital Accounts.* A Capital Account shall be maintained for each Member to which shall be credited (i) the Member's Capital Contributions, and (ii) all Company revenues. The Capital Account shall be debited with (i) all costs, expenses, and losses of the Company and (ii) the amount of any distributions (including return of capital) made to each Member. No interest shall be paid on a Member's Capital Account.

ARTICLE IV
Allocation of Profits and Distributions

Section 4.1 *Allocation of Profits and Losses.* All profits and losses of the Company shall be allocated to the Members in accordance with their ownership percentages. The ownership percentages of the Members shall be as follows:

****	$33^1/_3$
****	$33^1/_3$
****	$33^1/_3$

The ownership percentages of the Members may be modified by unanimous approval of the Members.

Section 4.2 *Allocation of Distributions.* All distributions of cash or other assets of the Company shall be made to the Members when and as determined by the Members.

ARTICLE V
Management of the Company

Section 5.1 *General.* The Company shall be managed by its Members. The Members shall each have the right, power and authority to manage, direct and control all of the business and affairs of the Company, to transact business on behalf of the Company, to sign for the Company or on behalf of the Company or otherwise to bind the Company.

Section 5.2 *Powers of the Members.* The Members shall have the right, power and authority, in the management of the business and affairs of the Company, to do or cause to be done any and all acts deemed by the Members to be necessary or appropriate to effectuate the business, purposes and objectives of the Company at the expense of the Company, including but not limited to the execution of all documents or instruments in all matters necessary, desirable, convenient or incidental to the purpose of the Company or the making of investments of Company funds. The Members shall have full, exclusive, and complete discretion, power, and authority, subject in all cases to the other provisions of this Agreement and the requirements of applicable law, to delegate the management, control, administration, and operation of the business and affairs of the Company or the custody of the Company's assets for all purposes stated in this Agreement. Such delegation shall be as provided in such documentation as the Members shall determine. Any such delegation shall not cause the Members to cease to be responsible for the Company's management.

Section 5.3 *Officers.* The Members may appoint individuals with or without such titles as they may elect, including the titles of President, Vice President, Treasurer, and Secretary, to act on behalf of the Company with such power and authority as the Members may delegate in writing to any such persons.

Section 5.4 *Reserved.*

Section 5.5 *Reliance by Third Parties.* Any person or entity dealing with the Company may rely on a certificate signed by a Member as to:

(i) The identity of the Members;

(ii) The existence or non-existence of any fact or facts which constitute a condition precedent to acts by the Member or are in any matter germane to the affairs of the Company;

(iii) The persons who are authorized to execute and deliver any instrument or document of or on behalf of the Company; or

(iv) Any act or failure to act by the Company or as to any other matter whatsoever involving the Company.

Section 5.6 *Actions Requiring Member Approval.* Notwithstanding any other provision of this Agreement, the written consent of the Members shall be required to approve the following matters:

(i) The dissolution or winding up of the Company;

(ii) The merger or consolidation of the Company;

(iii) The sale, transfer, contribution, exchange, mortgage, pledge, encumbrance, lease or other disposition or transfer of all or substantially all of the assets of the Company;

(iv) The declaration of any distributions by the Company; and

(v) Amendments to this Agreement.

ARTICLE VI
Dissolution

The Company shall be dissolved, and shall terminate and wind up its affairs, upon the first to occur of the following:

(a) The determination by the Members to dissolve the Company; or

(b) The entry of a decree of judicial dissolution pursuant to Section 17351 of the Act.

ARTICLE VII
Governing Law and Jurisdiction

This Agreement, including its existence, validity, construction and operating effect, and the rights of each of the parties hereto, shall be governed by and construed in accordance with the laws of the State of California (without regard to principles of conflicts of laws).

ARTICLE VIII
Indemnification

Section 8.1 *Indemnification and Liability.* (a) To the maximum extent permitted by applicable law, the Members shall not be liable to the Company or any other third party (i) for mistakes of judgment, (ii) for any act or omission suffered or taken by such Member, or (iii) for losses due to any such mistakes, action or inaction.

(b) Except as may be restricted by applicable law, the Members shall not be liable for and the Company shall indemnify the Members against, and agrees to hold the Members harmless from, all liabilities and claims (including reasonable attorney's fees and expenses in defending against such liabilities and claims) against the Members, or any of them, arising from the Members' performance of duties in conformance with the terms of this Agreement.

(c) The Members may consult with legal counsel or accountants selected by the Members and, to the maximum extent permitted by applicable law, any action or omission suffered or taken in good faith in reliance and in accordance with the written opinion or advice of any such counsel or accountants (provided such counsel or accountants have been selected with reasonable care) shall be fully protected and justified with respect to the action or omission so suffered or taken.

ARTICLE IX
Assignment of Interests

Upon prior approval of the Members, a Member may Transfer all or part of his or her Membership Interest in the Company. Any attempt by a Member to Transfer all or part of his or her Membership Interest in the Company without the prior approval of the Members shall be void.

ARTICLE X
Winding Up and Distribution of Assets

Section 10.1 *Winding Up.* If the Company is dissolved, the Members shall wind up the affairs of the Company.

Section 10.2 *Distribution of Assets.* Upon the winding up of the Company, subject to the provisions of the Act, the Members shall pay or make reasonable provision to pay all claims and obligations of the Company, including all costs and expenses of the liquidation and all contingent, conditional or unmatured claims and obligations that are known to the Members but for which the identity of the claimant is unknown. If there are sufficient assets, such claims and obligations shall be paid in full and any such provision shall be made in full. If there are insufficient assets, such claims and obligations shall be paid or provided for according to their priority and, among claims and obligations of equal priority, ratably to the extent of assets available therefor. Any remaining assets shall be distributed to the Members.

ARTICLE XI
Definitions

As used herein, the following terms shall have the indicated definitions.

"Act" means the Beverly-Killea Limited Liability Company Act, as may be amended from time to time.

"Articles of Organization" means the Articles of Organization of the Company as filed with the California Secretary of State on _____, 20___ as the same may be amended from time to time.

"Agreement" means this Operating Agreement, as may be amended from time to time.

"Capital Account" means a separate accounting maintained with respect to each Member pursuant to Section 3.2 of this Agreement.

"Capital Contribution" means a contribution by a Member to the capital of the Company.

"Company" means ****, LLC, a California limited liability company.

"Member" means each of the signatories to this Agreement.

"Membership Interest" means the ownership interest of each Member in the Company, including any and all rights, powers, benefits, duties or obligations conferred or imposed on a Member under the Act or this Agreement.

"Transfer" means a transfer, assignment, pledge or encumbrance relative to any Membership Interest in the Company.

IN WITNESS WHEREOF, the Members have executed and delivered this Operating Agreement as of the day and year first above written.

MEMBERS:

_____
[Name]

_____
[Address]

_____
[Name]

_____
[Address]

_____
[Name]

_____
[Address]

Form 7 I: Operating Agreement— California Corporate Format

****, LLC
OPERATING AGREEMENT

TABLE OF CONTENTS

241

Article IX General Provisions
  9.1. Assurances.
  9.2. Notifications.
  9.3. Specific Performance.
  9.4. Integration.
  9.5. Applicable Law.
  9.6. Headings.
  9.7. Binding Provisions.
  9.8. Jurisdiction and Venue.
  9.9. Interpretation.
  9.10. Separability of Provisions.
  9.11. Counterparts.
  9.12. Estoppel Certificate.

SHAREHOLDERS LIST
BYLAWS

This Operating Agreement (this "Agreement") is entered into as of the _____ day of _____, 20___ by and among the signatories to this Agreement.

EXPLANATORY STATEMENT

The parties have agreed to organize a limited liability company in accordance with the terms and subject to the conditions set forth in this Agreement.

NOW, THEREFORE, the parties agree as follows:

ARTICLE I
DEFINED TERMS

The following capitalized terms shall have the respective meanings specified in this Article I. Capitalized terms not defined in this Agreement shall have the meanings specified in the Act.

"Act" means the California Limited Liability Company Act, as amended from time to time.

"Adjusted Capital Balance" means, as of any day, an Interest Holder's total Contributions less all amounts actually distributed as a return of Capital Contributions to the Interest Holder pursuant to Article IV hereof. If any Interest is transferred in accordance with the terms of this Agreement, the Transferee shall succeed to the Adjusted Capital Balance of the transferor to the extent the Adjusted Capital Balance relates to the Interest transferred.

"Affiliate" means, (a) Person directly or indirectly controlling, controlled by, or under common control with another Person; (b) a Person owning or controlling ten percent (10%) or more of the outstanding voting securities or beneficial interests of another Person; (c) an officer, director, or partner of another Person; and/or (d) any affiliate of any such Person.

"Agreement" means this Operating Agreement, as amended from time to time including each exhibit hereto.

"Assignee" means a Person who has acquired an Economic Interest in the LLC but is not a Shareholder.

"Board of Directors" means the Managers of the Company as described in the Bylaws.

"Bylaws" means the Bylaws of ****, LLC attached hereto as Exhibit B.

"Capital Account" means the account to be maintained by the Company for each Interest Holder in accordance with the following provisions:

(i) an Interest Holder's Capital Account shall be credited with the amount of money and the fair market value of any property contributed to the Company (net of liabilities secured by such property that the Company either assumes or to which such property is subject) the amount of any Company unsecured liabilities assumed by the Interest Holder, and the Interest Holder's distributive share of Profit and any item in the nature of income or gain specially associated to the Interest Holder pursuant to the provisions of Article IV; and

(ii) an Interest Holder's Capital Account shall be debited with the amount of money and the fair market value of any Company property distributed to the Interest Holder (net of liabilities secured by such distributed property that the Interest Holder either assumes or to which such property is subject), the amount of any unsecured liabilities of the Interest Holder assumed by the Company.

If any Interest is transferred pursuant to the terms of this Agreement, the transferee shall succeed to the Capital Account of the transferor to the extent the Capital Account is attributable to the transferred Interest. It is intended that the Capital Accounts of all Interest Holders shall be maintained in compliance with the provisions of Regulation Section 1.704-1(b), and all provisions of this Agreement relating to the maintenance of Capital Accounts shall be interpreted and applied in a manner consistent with that Regulation.

"Capital Proceeds" means the gross receipts received by the Company from a Capital Transaction.

"Capital Transaction" means any transaction not in the ordinary course of business which results in the Company's receipt of cash or other consideration other than Contributions, including, without limitation, proceeds of sales or exchanges or other dispositions of property not in the ordinary course of business, financings, refinancings, condemnations, recoveries of damage awards, and insurance proceeds.

"Cash Flow" means all cash derived from operations of the Company (including interest received on reserves), without reduction for any non-cash charges, but less cash used to pay current operating expenses and to pay or establish reasonable reserves for future expenses, debt payments, capital improvements, and replacements as determined by the Board of Directors.

"Code" means the Internal Revenue Code of 1986, as amended, or any corresponding provision of any succeeding revenue law.

"Company" means the limited liability company formed in accordance with this Agreement.

"Contribution" means any money, property, or services rendered, or a promissory note or other binding obligation to contribute money or property, or to render services as permitted in this title, which a Shareholder contributes to the Company as capital in that Shareholder's capacity as a Shareholder pursuant to an agreement between the Shareholders, including an agreement as to value.

"Director" means Manager.

"Economic Interest" means a person's right to share in the income, gains, losses, deductions, credit, or similar items of, and to receive distributions from, the Company, but does not include any other rights of a Shareholder including, without limitation, the right to vote or to participate in management, or any right to information concerning the business and affairs of the Company.

"Interest Holder" means any Person who holds an Economic Interest, whether as a Shareholder or as an Assignee of a Shareholder.

"Involuntary Withdrawal" has the meaning provided therefor in Section 6.2(c).

"Manager" means any Person on the Company's Board of Directors, as more specifically described in the Bylaws.

"Member" means any Person who executes a counterpart of this Agreement as a Shareholder and any Person who subsequently is admitted as a Shareholder of the Company who has not resigned, withdrawn or been expelled as a Shareholder or been dissolved (if not an individual).

"Negative Capital Account" means a Capital Account with a balance of less than zero.

"Percentage" means, with respect to any Shareholder, that percentage which such Shareholder's Shares constitutes of the aggregate of all Shares outstanding at the time the Percentage is determined.

"Person" means and includes an individual, corporation, partnership, association, limited liability company, trust, estate, or other entity.

"Positive Capital Account" means a Capital Account with a balance greater than zero.

"Profit" and "Loss" means, for each taxable year of the Company (or other period for which Profit or Loss must be computed), the Company's taxable income or loss determined in accordance with IRC Section 703(a), with the following adjustments:

(i) all items of income, gain, loss, deduction, or credit required to be stated separately pursuant to IRC Section 703(a)(1) shall be included in computing taxable income or loss; and

(ii) any tax-exempt income of the Company, not otherwise taken into account in computing Profit or Loss, shall be included in computing taxable income or loss; and

(iii) any expenditures of the Company described in IRC Section 705(a)(2)(B) (or treated as such pursuant to Regulation Section 1.704-1(b)(2)(iv)(i)) and not otherwise taken into account in computing Profit or Loss, shall be subtracted from taxable income or loss; and

(iv) gain or loss resulting from any taxable disposition of Company property shall be computed by reference to the book value as adjusted under Regulation Section 1.704-1(b) ("adjusted book value") of the property disposed of, notwithstanding the fact that the adjusted book value differs from the adjusted basis of the property for federal income tax purposes; and

(v) in lieu of the depreciation, amortization, or cost recovery deductions allowable in computing taxable income or loss, there shall be taken into account the depreciation computed based upon the adjusted book value of the asset.

"Regulation" means the income tax regulations, including any temporary regulations, from time to time promulgated under the Code.

"Secretary of State" means the Secretary of State of the State of California.

"Shareholder" means Member.

"Shareholder Interest" means a Shareholder's rights in the Company, collectively, including the Shareholder's Economic Interest, any right to vote or participate in management, and any right to information concerning the business and affairs of the Company.

"Shares" means units of equity ownership of the Company, generally carrying with them all of the rights of Shareholder Interest (defined above), as more specifically described in the Bylaws. Shares are analogous to shares of stock in a corporation.

"Transfer" means, when used as a noun, any sale, hypothecation, pledge, assignment, attachment, or other transfer, and, when used as a verb, to sell hypothecate, pledge, assign, or otherwise transfer.

"Voluntary Withdrawal" means a Shareholder's disassociation from the Company by means other than a Transfer or an Involuntary Withdrawal.

ARTICLE II
FORMATION AND NAME; OFFICE; PURPOSE; TERM

2.1 <u>Organization.</u>

The parties hereby organize a limited liability company pursuant to the Act and the provisions of this Agreement. The Company has caused Articles of Organization to be prepared, executed, and filed with the Secretary of State.

2.2. <u>Name of the Company.</u>

The name of the Company shall be "****, LLC." The Company may do business under that name and such other name or names as the Board of Directors may determine. If the Company does business under a name other than that set forth in its Articles of Organization, the Company shall file and publish a fictitious business name statement as required by law.

2.3. <u>Purpose.</u>

The Company is organized solely to engage in the business of _____ _____, and to do any and all other acts or things that may be necessary, convenient, or incidental to that purpose.

2.4. <u>Term.</u>

The Company shall continue in existence perpetually, unless sooner dissolved as provided by this Agreement or required by the Act.

2.5. <u>Principal Place of Business.</u>

The Company's principal place of business shall be located at _____ _____, or at any other place in the State of California which the Board of Directors may determine.

2.6. <u>Resident Agent.</u>

The Company's initial resident agent for service of process in the State of California shall be _____, whose address in California is _____ _____.

2.7. <u>Shareholders.</u>

The signature, name, address, and number of Shares of each Shareholder are set forth on Exhibit A.

2.8. <u>Tax Treatment as a Partnership.</u>

The Company shall initially be treated as a partnership for tax purposes under federal and state tax laws and shall continue to elect to be treated as a partnership for tax purposes until such time as the Board of Directors determines it is in the best interests of the Company to elect to be taxed as a corporation.

ARTICLE III
SHAREHOLDERS; CAPITAL; CAPITAL ACCOUNTS

3.1. <u>Shares.</u>

The Company shall be authorized to issue that number of Shares as is authorized in Section 5.1 of the Bylaws.

3.2. <u>No Additional Contributions.</u>

After the initial capital Contributions agreed to herein have been made, no Shareholder shall be required to contribute any additional capital to the Company, and no Shareholder shall have personal liability for any obligation of the Company except as expressly provided by law.

3.3. <u>No Interest on Contributions.</u>

Neither Shareholders nor Interest Holders shall be paid interest with respect to Contributions.

3.4. <u>Return of Contributions.</u>

No Interest Holder shall have the right to receive the return of any Contribution or withdraw from the Company, except as specifically set forth herein.

3.5. <u>Form of Return of Capital.</u>

If an Interest Holder is entitled to receive the return of a Contribution, the Company may distribute in lieu of money, notes, or other property having a value equal to the amount of money distributable to such Person.

3.6. <u>Capital Accounts.</u>

A separate Capital Account shall be maintained for each Interest Holder.

ARTICLE IV
PROFIT, LOSS, AND DISTRIBUTION

4.1. <u>Allocations of Profit or Loss and Distributions of Cash.</u>

Profit or Loss shall be allocated to the Interest Holders in proportion to their Percentages. Distributions of cash shall be made at the discretion of the Board of Directors to each Shareholder in proportion to such Shareholder's ownership of the Company.

4.2. <u>Liquidation and Dissolution.</u>

(a) If the Company is liquidated, the assets of the Company shall be distributed to the Interest Holders in accordance with the balances in their respective Capital Accounts, after giving effect to all Contributions, distributions, and allocations for all periods. Distributions to the Interest Holders pursuant to this Section 4.2(a) shall be made in accordance with Regulation Section 1.704-1(b)(2)(ii)(b)(2).

(b) No Interest Holder shall be obligated to restore a Negative Capital Account.

4.3. <u>General.</u>

(a) Except as otherwise provided in this Agreement, the timing and amount of all distributions shall be determined by the Board of Directors.

(b) If any assets of the Company are distributed in kind to the Interest Holders, those assets shall be valued on the basis of their fair market value, and any Interest Holder entitled to any interest in those assets shall receive that interest as a tenant-in-common with all other Interest Holders so entitled. Unless the Shareholders otherwise agree, the fair market value of the assets shall be determined by an independent appraiser who shall be selected by the Board of Directors. The Profit or Loss for each unsold asset shall be determined as if the asset had been sold at its fair market value, and the Profit or Loss shall be allocated as provided in Section 4.1 and shall be properly credited or charged to the Capital Accounts of the Interest Holders prior to the distribution of the assets in liquidation pursuant to Section 4.2.

(c) All Profit and Loss shall be allocated, and all distributions shall be made to the Persons shown on the records of the Company to have been Interest Holders as of the last day of the taxable year for which the allocation or distribution is to be made. Notwithstanding the foregoing, unless the Company's taxable year is separated into segments, if there is a Transfer or an Involuntary Withdrawal during the taxable year, the Profit and Loss shall be allocated between the original Interest Holder and the successor on the basis of the number of days each was an Interest Holder during the taxable year; provided, however, the Company's taxable year shall be segregated into two or more segments in order to account for Profit, Loss or proceeds attributable to a Capital Transaction or to any other extraordinary non-recurring items of the Company.

(d) The Board of Directors may amend this Article IV to comply with the Code and the Regulations promulgated under IRC Section 704(b) if it determines in its sole discretion such an amendment is necessary or advisable. However, any amendment to this Article IV that materially affects Distributions made to an Interest Holder must be approved in advance by the effected Interest Holder.

ARTICLE V
MANAGEMENT: RIGHTS, POWERS, AND DUTIES

5.1. <u>Management and Board of Directors.</u>

The Company shall be managed by a Board of Directors comprised of Shareholders as provided in the Bylaws of the Company which are incorporated herein and made a part of this Operating Agreement. The initial Board of Directors shall be comprised of the following founding Shareholders of the Company: _____, _____, and _____. No Director shall cause the Company to incur any financial obligation in excess of _____ Dollars ($_____) without the approval of the Board of Directors.

5.2. <u>Limited Authority of Shareholders.</u>

Except as otherwise specifically set forth herein, Shareholders who are not Directors may not act as agents of the Company and shall have no authority to bind the Company.

5.3. <u>Standard of Care.</u>

The fiduciary duties a Director owes to the Company and the other Shareholders are those of a director of a California corporation to the corporation and its shareholders.

5.4. <u>Indemnification of Each Director.</u>

(a) Each Director shall not be liable, responsible, or accountable, in damages or otherwise, to any Shareholder or to the Company for any act performed by such Director within the scope of the authority conferred on such Director by this Agreement, and within the standard of care specified in Section 5.3.

(b) The Company shall indemnify each Director for any act performed by such Director within the scope of the authority conferred on the Director by this Agreement, unless such act constitutes grossly negligent or reckless conduct, intentional misconduct, or a knowing violation of law.

ARTICLE VI
TRANSFER OF INTERESTS AND
WITHDRAWALS OF SHAREHOLDERS

6.1. <u>Transfers.</u>

Except as provided herein, no Shareholder may Transfer all, or any portion of, or any interest or rights in, the Shareholder Interest owned by the Shareholder. Each Shareholder hereby acknowledges the reasonableness of this prohibition in view of the purposes of the Company and the nature of the Company and the relationship of the Shareholders. The attempted Transfer of any portion or all of a Shareholder Interest in violation of the prohibition contained in this Section 6.1 shall be deemed invalid, null and void, and of no force or effect, except any Transfer mandated by operation of law and then only to the extent necessary to give effect to such Transfer by operation of law.

(a) A Shareholder may Transfer all or any portion of or any interest or rights in the Shareholder's Economic Interest if all of the following conditions ("Conditions of Transfer") are satisfied:

(1) the Transfer may be accomplished without registration, or similar process, under federal and state securities laws;

(2) the transferee delivers to the Company a written agreement to be bound by the terms of this Agreement;

(3) the Transfer will not result in the termination of the Company pursuant to IRC Section 708;

(4) the Transfer will not result in the Company being subject to the Investment Company Act of 1940, as amended;

(5) the transferor or the transferee delivers the following information to the Company: (i) the transferee's taxpayer identification number; and (ii) the transferee's initial tax basis in the transferred Shareholder Interest; and

(6) unless the proposed transfer is a gift to an immediate family member of the Shareholder or is being made solely for estate planning purposes, such Shareholder has first made a written offer to transfer such interest to the Company and/or the Remaining Shareholders on the same terms and has left such offer open for a period of at least thirty (30) days immediately prior to such transfer.

(b) If the Conditions of Transfer are satisfied, the Shareholder may Transfer all or any portion of the Shareholder's Economic Interest. The Transfer of an Economic Interest pursuant to this Section 6.1 shall not result in the Transfer of any of the transferor's other Shareholder rights. The transferee of the Economic Interest shall have no right to: (1) become a Shareholder; (2) exercise any Shareholder rights other than those specifically pertaining to the ownership of an Economic Interest; or (3) act as an agent of the Company.

(c) Notwithstanding the foregoing, the initial members of the Board of Directors shall have a twenty-four (24) month vesting requirement with regard to seventy-five percent (75%) of their Shares. In other words, of the Shares listed on Exhibit A for _____, _____, and _____, twenty-five percent (25%) is vested and seventy-five percent (75%) is subject to vesting. One-twenty-fourth (1/24) of the Shares subject to vesting shall vest at the end of each month following the effective date of this Agreement. Vesting shall cease upon the Voluntary or Involuntary Withdrawal of such Director and the unvested portion of the Shares previously held by such withdrawn Director shall return to the status of authorized but unissued Shares. Only the vested portion of a Director's Economic Interest shall be subject to Transfer. In any action requiring Shareholder approval, Directors may vote all of their Shares, i.e. both the vested Shares and the Shares subject to vesting under this provision.

6.2. Withdrawal of a Shareholder.

(a) If a Shareholder Transfers all of his Economic Interest in the Company, such Shareholder shall be deemed to have Voluntarily Withdrawn from the Company and his Shareholder rights shall terminate.

(b) Upon an Involuntary Withdrawal of a Shareholder, the Withdrawn Shareholder and the Company shall have the respective rights and obligations set forth in this Section and in Section 6.3.

(c) "Involuntary Withdrawal" means, with respect to the initial members of the Board of Directors, such Director's resignation from the Board of Directors or removal from the Board pursuant to the Bylaws. With respect to all Shareholders, including members of the Board of Directors, the occurrence of any of the following events shall be deemed an Involuntary Withdrawal:

(1) the Shareholder makes an assignment for the benefit of creditors;

(2) the Shareholder is bankrupt;

(3) the Shareholder files a petition seeking for the Shareholder any reorganization, arrangement, composition, readjustment, liquidation, dissolution, or similar relief under any state law;

(4) the Shareholder seeks, consents to, or acquiesces in the appointment of a trustee for, receiver for, or liquidation of the Shareholder or of all or any substantial part of the Shareholder's properties;

(5) if the Shareholder is an individual, the Shareholder's death or adjudication by a court of competent jurisdiction as incompetent to manage the Shareholder's person or property;

(6) if the Shareholder is acting as a Shareholder by virtue of being a trustee of a trust, the termination of the trust;

(7) if the Shareholder is a partnership or limited liability company, the dissolution and commencement of winding up of the partnership or limited liability company;

(8) if the Shareholder is a corporation, the dissolution of the corporation or the revocation of its charter;

(9) if the Shareholder is a partnership, limited liability company or corporation, a change in control of such entity;

(10) if the Shareholder is an estate, the distribution by the fiduciary of the estate's entire interest in the Company; or

(11) if the Shareholder is a limited liability company, the filing of an action seeking a decree of judicial dissolution of the Shareholder pursuant to Section 17351 of the Act.

(d) Involuntary Withdrawal. Immediately upon the occurrence of an Involuntary Withdrawal, the withdrawn Shareholder or his successor in interest shall thereupon become an Economic Interest Holder but shall not be a Shareholder. However, the Board of Directors may in its sole discretion grant such Economic Interest Holder Shareholder status, provided the Economic Interest Holder delivers to the Company a written agreement to be bound by the terms of this Agreement. In the event Shareholder status is granted to a withdrawn Shareholder or his successor in interest under this provision, such Shareholder's Shares shall not be subject to buy-out under Section 6.3.

(e) Notwithstanding the foregoing, a portion of the Shares held by the initial members of the Board of Director shall be subject to vesting as set forth in Section 6.1(c). Only the vested portion of a withdrawn Director's Shares shall be subject to buy-out under Section 6.3.

6.3. Optional Buy-out in Event of Involuntary Withdrawal.

(a) Upon the Involuntary Withdrawal of a Shareholder, the withdrawn Shareholder or the successor in interest to such Shareholder (the "Withdrawn Shareholder") shall be deemed to have offered for sale to the Company and/or the remaining Shareholders all of the Shares of the Withdrawn Shareholder. The date of the offer shall be deemed to be the date the Board receives notice of the withdrawal.

(b) The offer shall be and remain irrevocable for a period of sixty (60) days. At any time during the offer period, the Company may accept the offer by giving written notice to the Withdrawn Shareholder. If the Board of Directors determines the Company will not accept the offer, the Board shall notify the remaining Shareholders of such determination and they shall have the right to purchase the Withdrawn Shareholder's Shares upon written notice of their acceptance to the Withdrawn Shareholder within the offer period. If more than one of the remaining Shareholders wishes to purchase the Withdrawn Shareholder's Shares, each such Shareholder shall purchase a pro rata share based on their relative Percentages.

(c) The written notice of acceptance shall fix a closing date for the purchase which shall be not earlier than ten (10) or later than ninety (90) days after the expiration of the offer period.

(d) If the Company or one or more remaining Shareholders accepts the offer, each such purchaser shall purchase all or their pro rata share of the Withdrawn Shareholder's Shares for the price equal to the amount the Withdrawn Shareholder would receive if the Company were liquidated and the amount equal to the Agreed Value were available for distribution to the Shareholders pursuant to Section 4.4. The purchase price shall be paid in cash on the closing date.

(e) If the Company and remaining Shareholders fail to accept the offer, the Withdrawn Shareholder shall thereafter be treated as an Economic Interest Holder but shall not have the right to exercise any other rights of a Shareholder.

6.4. Agreed Value.

"Agreed Value" shall mean the dollar amount last agreed upon in writing by the Board of Directors as the value of entire Company as a going concern. The Agreed Value as of the date of this Agreement is _____ Dollars ($_____). Subsequent determinations of Agreed Value shall be made from time to time based on a review of the Company's financial condition at such times as the Board of Directors determines in its sole discretion. Each new Agreed Value determination shall be dated and kept with the records of the Company. Notwithstanding the foregoing, if the date of the most recent determination of Agreed Value is more than eighteen (18) months prior to the date of the event giving rise to the purchase and sale of a Shareholder Interest, the purchase price shall be determined by agreement between the buyer and the seller or, if no such agreement can be reached, by appraisal. To determine the appraised value, appraisals shall be performed by one appraiser selected by the person selling a Shareholder Interest and one appraiser selected by the person who is to purchase the Shareholder Interest. If the two appraisers cannot agree on a value, they shall select a third appraiser and the decision of a majority of the three appraisers shall be binding on all parties.

ARTICLE VII
DISSOLUTION, LIQUIDATION, AND
TERMINATION OF THE COMPANY

7.1. Events of Dissolution.

The Company shall be dissolved at the time specified for its dissolution, if any, in the Articles of Organization, upon approval of a majority in interest of the Shareholders, or upon the entry of a decree of judicial dissolution, as specified in Section 17350 of the Act.

7.2. No Dissolution upon Withdrawal of Shareholder.

The Company shall not automatically dissolve upon the Voluntary or Involuntary Withdrawal of any Shareholder.

7.3. Procedure for Winding Up and Dissolution.

If the Company is dissolved, the Board of Directors shall wind up or cause the wind up of its affairs. On winding up of the Company, the assets of the Company shall be distributed, first to creditors of the Company, including Interest Holders who are creditors, in satisfaction of the liabilities of the Company, and then, to the Interest Holders in accordance with Section 4.2.

7.4. Filing of Certificate of Cancellation.

Upon completion of the affairs of the Company, the Board of Directors shall promptly file, or cause to be filed, the Certificate of Cancellation of Articles of Organization with the Secretary of State. If there is no member of the Board of Directors, then the Certificate of Cancellation shall be filed by the remaining Shareholders; if there are no remaining Shareholders, the Certificate shall be filed by the last Person to be a Shareholder; if there is neither a member of the Board of Directors, a remaining Shareholder, nor a Person who last was a Shareholder, the Certificate shall be filed by the legal or personal representatives of the Person who last was a Shareholder.

ARTICLE VIII
TAX ELECTIONS

8.1. <u>Tax Matters Partner.</u>

**** shall be the initial Tax Matters Partner for purposes of IRC Section 6231(a)(7), and shall have all the authority granted by the Code to the Tax Matters Partner, provided that he shall not have the authority without first obtaining the consent of all Shareholders to do any of the following:

(a) Enter into a settlement agreement with the Internal Revenue Service that purports to bind the Shareholders.

(b) File a petition as contemplated in IRC Section 6226(a) or IRC Section 6228.

(c) Intervene in any action as contemplated in IRC Section 6226(b)(5).

(d) File any request contemplated in IRC Section 6227(b).

(e) Enter into an agreement extending the period of limitations as contemplated in IRC Section 6229(b)(1)(B).

At such time as the Board of Directors appoints a Chief Financial Officer, the Chief Financial Officer shall become the Tax Matters Partner with the authority granted herein.

8.2. <u>Tax Elections.</u>

The Tax Matters Partner shall have the authority to make all Company elections permitted under the Code, including, without limitation, elections of methods of depreciation and elections under IRC Section 754. The decision to make or not make an election shall be at the Tax Matters Partner's sole and absolute discretion.

ARTICLE IX
GENERAL PROVISIONS

9.1. <u>Assurances.</u>

Each Shareholder shall execute all certificates and other documents and shall do all such filing, recording, publishing, and other acts as the Board of Directors deems appropriate to comply with the requirements of law for the formation and operation of the Company and to comply with any laws, rules, and regulations relating to the acquisition, operation, or holding of the property of the Company.

9.2. <u>Notifications.</u>

Any notice, demand, consent, election, offer, approval, request, or other communication (collectively a "notice") required or permitted under this Agreement must be in writing and delivered personally, sent by certified or registered mail, postage prepaid, return receipt requested or sent by overnight courier. Any notice to be given hereunder by the Company shall be given by the Board of Directors. A notice must be addressed to an Interest Holder at the Interest Holder's last known address on the records of the Company. A notice to the Company must be addressed to the Company's principal office. A notice delivered personally will be deemed given only when acknowledged in writing by the Person to whom it is delivered. A notice that is sent by mail will be deemed given three (3) business days after it is mailed. A notice that is sent by courier will be deemed given one (1) business day after it is couriered.

Any party may designate, by notice to all of the others, substitute addresses or addressees for notices; and, thereafter, notices are to be directed to those substitute addresses or addressees.

9.3. Specific Performance.

The parties recognize that irreparable injury will result from a breach of any provision of this Agreement and that money damages will be inadequate fully to remedy the injury. Accordingly, in the event of a breach or threatened breach of one or more of the provisions of this Agreement, any party who may be injured (in addition to any other remedies which may be available to that party) shall be entitled to one or more preliminary or permanent orders (i) restraining and enjoining any act which would constitute a breach or (ii) compelling the performance of any obligation which, if not performed, would constitute a breach.

9.4. Integration.

This Agreement constitutes the complete and exclusive statement of the agreement among the Shareholders. It supersedes all prior written and oral statements, including any prior representation, statement, condition, or warranty. Except as expressly provided otherwise herein, this Agreement may not be amended without the written consent of all of the Shareholders.

9.5. Applicable Law.

All questions concerning the construction, validity, and interpretation of this Agreement and the performance of the obligations imposed by this Agreement shall be governed by the internal law, not the law of conflicts, of the State of _____.

9.6. Headings.

The headings herein are inserted as a matter of convenience only and do not define, limit, or describe the scope of this Agreement or the intent of the provisions hereof.

9.7. Binding Provisions.

This Agreement is binding upon, and to the limited extent specifically provided herein, inures to the benefit of, the parties hereto and their respective heirs, executors, administrators, personal and legal representatives, successors, and assigns.

9.8. Jurisdiction and Venue.

Any suit involving any dispute or matter arising under this Agreement may only be brought in the appropriate United States District Court in the State of _____ or any State Court in _____ having jurisdiction over the subject matter of the dispute or matter. All Shareholders hereby consent to the exercise of personal jurisdiction by any such court with respect to any such proceeding.

9.9. Interpretation.

Common nouns and pronouns shall be deemed to refer to the masculine, feminine, neuter, singular, and plural, as the identity of the Person may in the context require. References to articles, sections (or subdivisions of sections), exhibits, annexes, or schedules are those of this Agreement, unless otherwise indicated.

9.10. Separability of Provisions.

Each provision of this Agreement shall be considered separable; and if, for any reason, any provision or provisions herein are determined to be invalid and contrary to any existing or future law, such invalidity shall not impair the operation of or affect those portions of this Agreement which are valid.

9.11. Counterparts.

This Agreement may be executed simultaneously in two or more counterparts, each of which shall be deemed an original and all of which, when taken together, constitute one and the same document. The signature of any party to any counterpart shall be deemed a signature to, and may be appended to, any other counterpart.

9.12. <u>Estoppel Certificate.</u>

Upon request by the Board of Directors, each Shareholder shall, within ten (10) days deliver a certificate stating that, to the Shareholder's knowledge: (a) this Agreement is in full force and effect; (b) this Agreement has not been modified except by any instrument or instruments identified in the certificate; and (c) Shareholder is not in breach of this Agreement. If the certificate is not received within the 10-day period, each Shareholder hereby grants the Board of Directors the power and authority to execute and deliver the requested certificate on behalf of the Shareholder, without qualification, pursuant to this power of attorney.

[Shareholders' Signatures Are Set Forth in Exhibit A]

EXHIBIT A

IN WITNESS WHEREOF, the parties have executed, or caused this Agreement to be executed, as set forth in this Exhibit A.

SHAREHOLDERS:

Date: _____

Name: _____

Address: _____

_____

Number of Shares: _____

Date: _____

Name: _____

Address: _____

_____

Number of Shares: _____

Date: _____

Name: _____

Address: _____

_____

Number of Shares: _____

EXHIBIT B
BYLAWS of ****, LLC

TABLE OF CONTENTS

[Section references are to the California Limited Liability Company Act (Corporations Code); An * indicates there is no specific statutory authority for the subject matter addressed.]

INTRODUCTORY NOTE

These Bylaws are an integral part of the Operating Agreement of ****, LLC (the "Company").

ARTICLE I
SHAREHOLDERS

Section 1.1. Place of Meetings.

All the meetings of Shareholders shall be held at the principal executive office of the Company, or at any other place, within or without the State of California, specified by the Board of Directors. The place of any meeting of Shareholders shall be specified in the notice calling such meeting.

Section 1.2. Annual Meeting.

The annual meeting of the Shareholders shall be held at 10:00 A.M., on the second Tuesday in April of each year, if not a legal holiday, and if a legal holiday, on the next business day following. In the event the annual meeting of Shareholders shall not be held on the date above specified, the Board of Directors shall cause a meeting in lieu thereof to be held as soon thereafter as convenient, and any business transacted or election held at such meeting shall be as valid as if such business were transacted or election held at the annual meeting. At the annual meeting, reports of the affairs of the Company shall be considered, and any other business may be transacted which is within the power of the Shareholders.

Section 1.3. Special Meetings.

A special meeting of the Shareholders for any purpose or purposes whatsoever may be called at any time by any Director, or by one or more Shareholders holding Shares entitled to cast, in the aggregate, in excess of ten percent (10%) of the votes at the meeting.

Upon request in writing to any Director by any Shareholder or Shareholders entitled to call a special meeting of Shareholders, the Director to whom such request is made forthwith shall cause notice to be given to the Shareholders entitled to Vote that a meeting of the Shareholders will be held at a time, requested by the person or persons calling the meeting, which shall be not less than ten (10) nor more than sixty (60) days after the receipt of such request.

Section 1.4. Notice of Meetings.

(a) Whenever Shareholders are required or permitted to take any action at a meeting, a written notice of the meeting shall be given not less than ten (10) nor more than sixty (60) days before the date of the meeting to each Shareholder entitled to vote thereat. Such notice shall state the place, date and hour of the meeting and the general nature of the business to be transacted, and no other business may be transacted at such meeting.

(b) Notice of a Shareholders' meeting or any report shall be given either personally or by first class mail or other means of written communication, addressed to the Shareholder at the address of such Shareholder appearing on the books of the Company or given by the Shareholder to the Company for the purpose of notice; or if no such address appears or is given, at the place where the principal executive office of the Company is located or by publication at least once in a newspaper of general circulation in the county in which the principal executive office is located. The notice or report shall be deemed to have been given at the time when delivered personally or deposited in the mail or sent by other means of written communication.

If any notice or report addressed to the Shareholder at the address of such Shareholder appearing on the books of the Company is returned to the Company by the United States Postal Service marked to indicate that the United States Postal Service is unable to deliver the notice or report to the Shareholder at such address, all future notices or reports shall be deemed to have been duly given without further mailing if any such notice or report shall be available for the Shareholder at the principal executive office of the Company for a period of one year from the date of the giving of the notice or report to all other Shareholders.

(c) When a Shareholders' meeting is adjourned to another time or place, notice need not be given of the adjourned meeting if the time and place thereof are announced at the meeting at which the adjournment is taken. At the adjourned meeting, the Company may transact any business which might have been transacted at the original meeting. If the adjournment is for more than forty five (45) days or if after the adjournment a new record date is fixed for the adjourned meeting, a notice of the adjourned meeting shall be given to each Shareholder of Record entitled to Vote at the meeting.

Section 1.5. Consent to Shareholders' Meetings and Actions Without Meetings.

(a) The actions taken at any meeting of Shareholders, however called and noticed, and wherever held, have the same validity as if taken at a meeting duly held after regular call and notice, if a quorum is present either in person or by Proxy, and if, either before or after the meeting, each of the Persons entitled to vote, not present in person or by Proxy, signs a written waiver of notice or consents to the holding of the meeting or approves of the minutes thereof. All such waivers, consents, and approvals shall be filed with the corporate records or made a part of the minutes of the meeting. Attendance of a Person at a meeting shall constitute a waiver of notice of and presence at such meeting except when the Person objects at the beginning of the meeting to the transaction of any business because the meeting is not lawfully called or convened. Attendance of a Person at a meeting is not a waiver of any right to object to the consideration of matters required by law to be included in the notice but not so included, if such objection is expressly made at the beginning of the meeting. Neither the business to be transacted nor the purpose of any regular or special meeting of Shareholders need be specified in any written waiver of notice, except that any Shareholder approval at a meeting, other than unanimous approval by those entitled to vote, shall be valid only if the general nature of the proposal so approved is stated in the notice of meeting or in any written waiver of notice.

(b) Any action that may be taken at any annual or special meeting of the Shareholders may be taken without a meeting and without prior notice, if a consent in writing, setting forth the action so taken, shall be delivered to the Company within sixty (60) days of the record date for that action by Shareholders having not less than the minimum number of votes that would be necessary to authorize or take that action at a meeting at which all Shareholders entitled to vote thereon were present and voted.

Unless the consents of all Shareholders entitled to vote have been solicited in writing, (A) notice of any Shareholder approval of an amendment to the Articles of Organization or Operating Agreement (including these Bylaws), dissolution of the Company as provided in Section 17350 of the California Corporations Code, or a merger of the Company as provided in Section 17551 of the California Corporations Code, without a meeting by less than unanimous written consent shall be given at least ten (10) days before the consummation of the action authorized by such approval to those Shareholders entitled to vote who have not consented in writing; and (B) prompt notice shall be given of the taking of any other corporate action approved by Shareholders without a meeting by less than unanimous written consent to those Shareholders entitled to Vote who have not consented in writing. The provisions of Section 1.4(b) of these Bylaws shall apply to such notices.

Any Shareholder giving a written consent, or the Shareholder's proxyholder, may revoke the consent by a writing received by the Company prior to the time that written consents of Shareholders having the minimum number of votes that would be required to authorize the proposed action have been filed with the Company, but may not do so thereafter. Such revocation is effective upon its receipt by the Company at the Principal Executive Office.

Section 1.6. Quorum.

A Majority in Interest of the Shareholders, represented in person or by Proxy, shall constitute a quorum at a meeting of Shareholders. If a quorum is present at a duly held meeting, the affirmative vote of the majority of the Shares represented and Voting at the meeting on any matter shall be the act of the Shareholders unless the vote of a greater number or voting by classes is required by law, the Articles of Organization or the Operating Agreement, including these Bylaws.

The Shareholders present at a duly called or held meeting at which a quorum is present may continue to transact business until adjournment, notwithstanding the loss of a quorum, if any action taken after the loss of a quorum (other than adjournment) is approved by the requisite percentage of Shares specified by law, or in the Article of Organization or the Operating Agreement, including these Bylaws.

In the absence of a quorum, any meeting of Shareholders may be adjourned from time to time by the vote of a majority of the Shares represented either in person or by Proxy, but no other business may be transacted, except as provided above.

Section 1.7. Voting Rights.

(a) The Shareholders shall only be entitled to vote on the following matters: amendments to the Articles of Organization or Operating Agreement of the Company, the dissolution of the Company, a merger of the Company, matters set forth in Sections 4.3(d) and 8.1 of the Operating Agreement, and such other matters as may now or hereafter be required to be submitted to the Shareholders by law or are submitted to a vote of the Shareholders by the Board of Directors. Except as set forth in Section 4.3(d) of the Operating Agreement, Economic Interest Holders of the Company shall not be entitled to vote on any matter submitted to a vote of the Shareholders. Except as otherwise provided by law and except as may be otherwise provided in the Articles of Organization or the Operating Agreement, including these Bylaws, each outstanding Share shall be entitled to one vote on each matter submitted to a vote of Shareholders. Any Shareholder entitled to vote on any matter may vote part of the Shares in favor of the proposal and refrain from voting the remaining Shares or vote them against the proposal, but, if the Shareholder fails to specify the number of Shares such Shareholder is voting affirmatively, it will be conclusively presumed that the Shareholder's approving vote is with respect to all Shares such Shareholder is entitled to vote.

(b) Every person entitled to vote Shares may authorize another person or persons to act by Proxy with respect to such Shares. No Proxy shall be valid after the expiration of eleven (11) months from the date thereof unless otherwise provided in the Proxy. Subject to the foregoing, every Proxy shall continue in full force and effect until revoked by the person executing it prior to the vote pursuant thereto. Such revocation may be effected by a writing delivered to the Company stating that the Proxy is revoked or by a subsequent Proxy executed by the person executing the prior Proxy and presented to the meeting, or, as to any meeting, by attendance at the meeting and voting in person by the person executing the Proxy. A Proxy is not revoked by the death or incapacity of the maker unless, before the vote is counted, written notice of such death or incapacity is received by the Company.

If the Company has outstanding Shares held of record by one hundred (100) or more persons, and it distributes any form of Proxy or written consent to ten (10) or more Shareholders, it shall afford an opportunity on the Proxy or form of written consent to specify a choice between approval and disapproval of each matter or group of related matters intended to be acted upon at the meeting for which the Proxy is solicited or by such written consent, and shall provide, subject to reasonable specified conditions, that where the person solicited specifies a choice with respect to any such matter, the Shares will be voted in accordance therewith.

Section 1.8. Determination of Shareholders of Record.

(a) In order that the Company may determine the Shareholders entitled to notice of any meeting or to vote, or entitled to receive any distribution or to exercise any rights in respect of any other lawful action, a Director, or Shareholders representing more than ten (10) percent of the Interests of Shareholders, may fix, in advance, a record date which shall not be more than sixty (60) nor less than ten (10) days prior to the date of such meeting nor more than sixty (60) days prior to any other action.

If no record date is fixed: (i) the record date for determining Shareholders entitled to notice of or to vote at a meeting of Shareholders shall be at the close of business on the business day next preceding the day on which notice is given or, if notice is waived, at the close of business on the business day next preceding the day on which the meeting is held; (ii) the record date for determining Shareholders entitled to give consent to Company action in writing without a meeting, shall be the day on which the first written consent is given; (iii) the record date for determining Shareholders for any other purpose shall be at the close of business on the day on which the Board of Directors adopts the resolution relating thereto, or the sixtieth (60th) day prior to the date of such other action, whichever is later.

A determination of Shareholders of Record entitled to notice of or to vote at a meeting of Shareholders shall apply to any adjournment of the meeting unless the Director or Shareholders who called the meeting fix a new record date for the adjourned meeting, but the Director or Shareholders who called the meeting shall fix a new record date if the meeting is adjourned for more than forty five (45) days from the date set for the original meeting.

Shareholders at the close of business on the record date are entitled to notice and to vote or to receive the distribution, or to exercise the rights, as the case may be, notwithstanding any Transfer of any Shares on the books of the Company after the record date, except as otherwise provided by law, in the Company's Articles of Organization or by agreement.

ARTICLE II
BOARD OF DIRECTORS

Section 2.1. Number and Term of Office.

As set forth more fully in Section 2.6 below, the Company shall be managed by a Board of Directors comprised of one or more Shareholders who shall be responsible for the day-to-day operations of the Company. The authorized number of Directors on the Company's Board of Directors shall be not less than two (2), nor more than five (5), except that in the event the Company has only one (1) Shareholder, the number of Directors may be one (1). The number of Directors shall always be within the authorized limits specified above, and as determined by resolution adopted by the Board of Directors. The authorized number of Directors may be changed only by an amendment of this section of the Bylaws approved by the Shareholders.

Section 2.2. Vacancies.

Vacancies on the Board of Directors shall be filled by appointment of one or more directors by resolution adopted by the Board of Directors. A vacancy or vacancies in the Board of Directors shall be deemed to exist in the case of the death, resignation, or removal of any Director, or an increase in the authorized number of Directors.

Any or all Directors may be removed for failure to devote his full-time effort to the business of the Company, or for failure to act in the best interests in the Company, as determined by the remaining members of the Board of Directors in their sole discretion, upon written notice to the Director to be removed and the expiration of two (2) successive ten (10) day right to cure periods. Any such removal shall be without prejudice to the rights, if any, of the Director under any contract of employment.

Any Director may resign effective upon giving written notice to the Company or the Board of Directors of the Company, unless the notice specifies a later time for the effectiveness of such resignation. If the resignation is effective at a future time, a successor may be appointed to take office when the resignation becomes effective. As such, resignation shall not prejudice the rights of the Company under any contract of employment to which such resigning Director is a party.

Section 2.3. Meetings.

The Board of Directors shall hold a regular meeting immediately after the meeting of Shareholders at the place where such meeting is held. No notice of such meeting shall be required.

Meetings of the Board of Directors may be called by any two Directors.

Regular meetings of the Board of Directors may be held without notice if the time and place of such meetings are fixed by the Bylaws or the Board of Directors. Special meetings of the Board of Directors shall be held upon four (4) days' notice by mail or forty eight (48) hours' notice delivered personally or by telephone, facsimile, or telegraph. A notice, or waiver of notice, need not specify the purpose of any regular or special meeting of the Board. Notice of a meeting need not be given to any Director who signs a waiver of notice or a consent to holding the meeting or an approval of the minutes thereof, whether before or after the meeting, or who attends the meeting without protesting, prior thereto or at its commencement, the lack of notice to such Director. All such waivers, consents, and approvals shall be filed with the Company records or made a part of the minutes of the meeting.

A majority of the Directors present, whether or not a quorum is present, may adjourn any meeting to another time and place. If the meeting is adjourned for more than twenty four (24) hours, notice of any adjournment to another time or place shall be given prior to the time of the adjourned meeting to the Directors who were not present at the time of the adjournment.

Meetings of the Board of Directors may be held at any place within or without the state which has been designated in the notice of the meeting or, if not stated in the notice or if there is no notice, at the principal executive offices of the Company or any other place designated by resolution of the Board.

Members of the Board of Directors may participate in a meeting through use of conference telephone or similar communications equipment, so long as all Directors participating in such meeting can hear one another. Participation in a meeting pursuant to this paragraph constitutes presence in person at such meeting.

Section 2.4. Quorum.

A majority of the authorized number of Directors constitutes a quorum of the Board of Directors for the transaction of business.

Every act or decision done or made by a majority of the Directors present at a meeting duly held at which a quorum is present is the act of the Board of Directors, unless a greater number is required by the Company's Articles of Organization or Operating Agreement, including these Bylaws. A meeting at which a quorum is initially present may continue to transact business notwithstanding the withdrawal of Directors, if any action taken is approved by at least a majority of the required quorum for such meeting.

Section 2.5. Action Without a Meeting.

Any action required or permitted to be taken by the Board of Directors may be taken without a meeting, if all members of the Board shall individually or collectively consent in writing to such action. Such written consent or consents shall be filed with the minutes of the proceedings of the Board. Such action by written consent shall have the same force and effect as a unanimous vote of such Directors.

Section 2.6. General and Specific Powers and Duties.

Subject to any provision or limitations of the Company's Articles of Organization, the Operating Agreement, including these Bylaws, and the California Corporations Code that limit the power of Directors, the business and affairs of the Company shall be managed and all corporate powers shall be exercised by or under the direction of the Board of Directors. The Board of Directors may delegate the management of day-to-day operation of the business of the Company to officers, a management company, or other person, provided that the business and affairs of the Company shall be managed and all Company powers shall be exercised under the ultimate direction of the Board.

A Director shall perform the duties of a Director, including duties as a member of any committee of the Board of Directors upon which the Director may serve, in good faith, in a manner such Director believes to be in the best interests of the Company and with such care, including reasonable inquiry, as an ordinarily prudent person in a like position would use under similar circumstances.

No Director shall cause the Company to incur any financial obligation in excess of Five Thousand Dollars ($5,000) without the approval of the Board of Directors.

Section 2.7. Appointment of Committees.

The Board of Directors may, by resolution adopted by a majority of the authorized number of Directors, designate one (1) or more committees, each consisting of two (2) or more Directors, to serve at the pleasure of the Board.

The Board of Directors may designate one or more Directors as alternate members of any committee to replace any absent member at any meeting of the committee. The appointment of members or alternate members of a committee requires the Vote of a majority of the authorized number of Directors.

Any such committee, to the extent provided in the resolution of the Board or in these Bylaws, shall have all the authority of the Board, except with respect to: (i) approving any action for which Shareholders' approval or approval of the outstanding Shares is required by law; (ii) filling vacancies on the Board or any committee;

(iii) fixing compensation of the Directors for serving on the Board or on any committee; (iv) amending, repealing or adopting Bylaws; (v) amending or repealing any resolution of the Board, which by its express terms is not so amendable or repealable; (vi) making a distribution to the Shareholders of the Company as defined in Section 17001(j) of the California Corporations Code (or any successor provisions thereto), except at a rate or in a periodic amount or within a price range determined by the Board; or (vii) appointing other committees of the Board or the members thereof.

The Board shall designate a chairman for each committee who shall have the sole power to call any committee meeting other than a meeting set by the Board. Except as otherwise established by the Board, the provisions of these Bylaws which apply to Directors shall apply to committees of the Board and actions by such committees, with those provisions being changed that should be changed in order to apply to such committees and their actions.

Section 2.8. Fees and Compensation.

Directors and members of committees may receive such compensation, if any, for their services and such reimbursement for expenses as may be fixed or determined by resolution of the Board of Directors.

ARTICLE III
OFFICERS

Section 3.1. Designation of Officers.

The Company may have a President, a Secretary, and a Chief Financial Officer and such other officers as the Board of Directors may determine. If the Board shall name one or more persons as Vice Presidents, the order of their seniority shall be in the order of their nomination, unless otherwise determined by the Board. Any number of offices may be held by the same person. All officers of the Company shall hold office from the date appointed until their successors are appointed and take office; provided that all officers may be removed at any time at the pleasure of the Board, subject to the rights, if any, of an officer under any contract of employment. Upon the removal, resignation, death, or incapacity of any officer, the Board may declare such office vacant and fill such vacancy. Any officer may resign at any time upon written notice to the Company, without prejudice to the rights, if any, of the Company under any contract to which the officer is a party. The salary and other compensation of the officers shall be fixed from time to time by resolution of the Board.

No officer shall cause the Company to incur any financial obligation in excess of Five Thousand Dollars ($5,000) without the approval of the Board of Directors.

Section 3.2. Duties of the Chairman of the Board.

The Board of Directors may in its discretion elect a Chairman of the Board. The Chairman of the Board shall, when present, preside at all meetings of the Board. He shall have authority to execute in the name of the Company bonds, contracts, deeds, leases and other written instruments to be executed by the Company (except where by law the signature of the President is required) and shall perform such other duties prescribed by these Bylaws or as the Board may from time to time determine.

Section 3.3. Duties of the President.

Subject to the supervisory powers of the Board of Directors, the President shall be the Chief Executive Officer of the Company and shall perform all the duties commonly incident to that office. The President shall preside at all meetings of the Shareholders and, in the absence of the Chairman of the Board or, if there be none, at all meetings of the Board, and shall perform such other duties prescribed by these Bylaws or as the Board may from time to time determine.

Section 3.4. Duties of the Vice President.

If the Board of Directors shall appoint one or more Vice Presidents, the Vice Presidents, in the order of their seniority, unless otherwise established by the Board, may assume and perform the duties of the President in the absence or disability of the President or whenever the office of President is vacant. The Vice Presidents shall have such titles, perform such other duties, and have such other powers as prescribed by these Bylaws or the Board shall designate from time to time.

Section 3.5. Duties of the Secretary.

(a) The Secretary shall attend all meetings of the Shareholders, of the Board of Directors, and of any committee of the Board appointed pursuant to Section 2.7 of Article II, and shall take the minutes of the meeting. If the Secretary is unable to attend, the Secretary or the presiding officer of the meeting shall designate another person to take the minutes of the meeting.

The Secretary shall keep or cause to be kept at the principal executive office or such other place as the Board may order, a minute book of all meetings and actions of the Shareholders, the Board, and any committee of the Board. The minutes of each meeting shall contain an accurate account of the proceedings of the meeting, the time and place of the meeting whether it was regular or special, and, if special, how it was authorized, a copy of the notice given of the meeting, the names of those present at Board or committee meetings, and the percentage of Shares present or represented at Shareholders' meetings.

(b) The Secretary shall give, or cause to be given, notice, in conformity with these Bylaws, of all meetings of the Shareholders, and of all meetings of the Board or any such committee requiring notice.

(c) The Secretary shall keep or cause to be kept at the principal executive office or at the office of the Company's transfer agent or registrar, Shareholder Register, or a duplicate Shareholder Register, showing the names of the Shareholders and their addresses, the number and classes of Shares held by each, and, if certificates representing Shares are used, the number and date of certificates issued for same and the number and date of cancellation of every certificate surrendered for cancellation.

(d) The Secretary shall keep the seal, if any, of the Company in safe custody and shall perform such other duties and have such other powers prescribed by these Bylaws or as the Board shall designate from time to time.

Section 3.6. Duties of the Chief Financial Officer.

The Chief Financial Officer shall keep or cause to be kept adequate and correct books and records of accounts of the properties and business transactions of the Company and shall render statements of the financial affairs of the Company in such form and as often as required by the Board of Directors. The Chief Financial Officer, subject to the order of the Board, shall have the custody of all funds and securities of the Company. The Chief Financial Officer shall perform all other duties commonly incident to such office and shall perform such other duties and have such other powers prescribed by these Bylaws or as the Board shall designate from time to time. Unless the Board has elected a separate Treasurer, the Chief Financial Officer shall be deemed to be the Treasurer of the Company for purposes of giving any reports or executing any certificates or other documents.

ARTICLE IV
EXECUTION OF COMPANY INSTRUMENTS, RATIFICATION OF
CONTRACTS, AND VOTING OF SHARES OWNED BY THE COMPANY

Section 4.1. Execution of Company Instruments.

The Board of Directors may, in its discretion, determine the method and designate the signatory officer or officers or other person or persons to execute any Company instrument or document, or to sign the Company name without limitation,
except where otherwise provided by law, and such execution or signature shall be
binding upon the Company. No officer, agent, employee, or person purporting to act
on behalf of the Company shall have any power or authority to bind the Company in
any way, to pledge the Company's credit, or to render the Company liable for any
purpose or in any amount, unless that person was acting with the authority duly
granted by the Board as provided in these Bylaws, or unless an unauthorized act
was later ratified by the Company.

All checks and drafts drawn on banks or other depositories of funds to the credit
of the Company, or in special accounts of the Company, shall be signed by such person or persons as the Board shall authorize.

Section 4.2. Ratification by Shareholders.

The Board of Directors may, in its discretion, submit any contract or act for
approval or ratification of the Shareholders at any annual meeting of Shareholders or
at any special meeting of Shareholders called for that purpose. Any contract or act
which shall be approved or ratified by the Shareholders or by the outstanding Shares
shall be as valid and binding upon the Company and upon the Shareholders thereof
as though approved or ratified by each and every Shareholder of the Company,
unless a greater vote is required by law for such purpose.

Section 4.3. Voting of Shares Owned by the Company.

All Shares, stock or other interests owned or held by the Company for itself or
for other parties in any capacity shall be voted, and all proxies with respect thereto
shall be executed, by the person authorized to do so by resolution of the Board of
Directors, or, in the absence of such authorization, by the Chairman of the Board,
the President or by any Vice President.

ARTICLE V
SHAREHOLDER INTERESTS

Section 5.1. Form of Share Certificates.

The Company shall have the authority to issue ten million (10,000,000) Shares
of the Company which, when issued and outstanding, shall represent Shareholder
Interests in the Company.

If the Board of Directors shall determine that Share certificates shall be issued,
every holder of Shares in the Company shall be entitled to have a certificate signed
in the name of the Company by such officers and Directors as the Board of Directors
may determine in its sole discretion, certifying the Shares and the class or series of
Shares owned by the Shareholder. Any or all of the signatures on the certificate may
be facsimile. In case any officer, transfer agent, or registrar who has signed or whose
facsimile signature has been placed upon a certificate shall have ceased to be such
officer, transfer agent, or registrar before such certificate is issued, the issuance of

such certificate by the Company shall have the same effect as if such person were an officer, transfer agent, or registrar at the date of issue.

The Shares have no preferences, qualifications, limitations, restrictions, nor any special or relative rights, including convertible rights. If the Shares of the Company are classified, or if any class has two (2) or more series, there shall appear on the certificate one of the following: (i) a statement of the rights, preferences, privileges, and restrictions granted to or imposed upon each class or series authorized to be issued and upon the holders thereof; (ii) a summary of such rights, preferences, privileges, and restrictions with reference to the provisions of the Articles of Organization establishing the same; or (iii) a statement setting forth the office or agency of the Company from which Shareholders may obtain, upon request and without charge, a copy of the statement referred to in (i) above.

There shall also appear on the certificate the statements required by all of the following clauses to the extent applicable: (i) the fact that the Shares are subject to restrictions upon transfer; (ii) if the Shares are assessable or are not fully paid, a statement that they are assessable or, on partly paid Shares, the total amount of the consideration to be paid therefor and the amount paid thereon; (iii) the fact that the Shares are subject to an irrevocable Proxy or restrictions upon voting rights contractually imposed by the Company; (iv) the fact that the Shares are redeemable; and (v) the fact the Shares are convertible and the period for conversion. Any such statement or reference thereto on the face of the certificate required by this paragraph shall be conspicuous.

When the Company's Articles of Organization are amended in any way which affects the statements contained in the certificates for outstanding Shares, or when it becomes desirable for any reason, in the discretion of the Board of Directors, to cancel any outstanding certificate for Shares and issue a new certificate therefor conforming to the rights of the holder, the Board may order any holders of outstanding certificates for Shares to surrender and exchange them for new certificates within a reasonable time to be fixed by the Board. The order may provide that a holder of certificates so ordered to be surrendered is not entitled to vote or to receive distributions or exercise any of the other rights of a Shareholder until a Shareholder has complied with the order, but such order operates to suspend such rights only after notice and until compliance. The duty of surrender of any certificates may also be enforced by civil action.

Section 5.2. Transfer of Shares

Subject to any applicable restrictions on transfer imposed by the Company or by law, Shares of the Company may be Transferred in any manner permitted or provided by law. Before any Transfer of a Share is entered upon the books of the Company or any new certificate issued therefor, the old certificate properly endorsed shall be surrendered and canceled, except when a certificate has been lost or destroyed.

Section 5.3. Lost Certificates.

The Company shall issue a new Share certificate in the place of any certificate theretofore issued by it, alleged to have been lost, stolen, or destroyed, provided that, prior to the issuance of such new certificate the Company may require the owner of the lost, stolen, or destroyed certificate or the owner's legal representative to give the Company a bond (or other adequate security) sufficient to indemnify it against any claim that may be made against it (including any expense or liability) on account of the alleged loss, theft or destruction of any such certificate or the issuance of such new certificate.

ARTICLE VI
ANNUAL REPORT
(Non Waivable Provision)

In the event the Company shall have more than thirty five (35) Shareholders, an annual report shall be sent to the Shareholders not later than the one hundred and twentieth (120th) day after the close of the fiscal year of the Company or no later than fifteen (15) days (or, if sent by third class mail, thirty five (35) days) prior to the annual meeting of Shareholders for the next succeeding fiscal year, whichever shall first occur. The annual report shall contain a balance sheet as of the end of the fiscal year and an income statement and statement of changes in financial position for the fiscal year, prepared in accordance with generally accepted accounting principles applied on a consistent basis, and accompanied by any report thereon of independent accountants or, if there is no such report, the certificate of an authorized officer or Director of the Company that the statements were prepared without audit from the books and records of the Company. No such report need be sent if the number of Shareholders of Record is less than one hundred (100).

ARTICLE VII
TAX INFORMATION
(Non Waivable Provision)

The Company shall send, or cause to be sent, to each Shareholder or holder of an Economic Interest, within ninety (90) days after the end of each taxable year, such information as is necessary to complete federal and state income tax or information returns. If the Company shall have thirty five (35) or fewer Shareholders, the foregoing tax information shall be accompanied by a copy of the Company's federal, state, and local income tax or information returns for the corresponding year.

ARTICLE VIII
AMENDMENTS

These Bylaws shall be subject to amendment or repeal, and new Bylaws may be adopted, by the approval of a majority of the outstanding Shares. Subject to the right of the Shareholders to adopt, amend, or repeal these Bylaws, these Bylaws (other than a Bylaw or an amendment thereof changing the authorized number of Directors) may be adopted, amended, or repealed by the affirmative vote of a majority of the Directors.

ARTICLE IX
DEFINITIONS

As used in these Bylaws, the following terms shall have the meanings indicated unless otherwise expressly provided to the contrary or unless the context in which such terms are used indicates that a different meaning is intended:

(a) "Meeting" and "meetings" shall include all meetings of Shareholders or Directors or committees, as the case may be, whether annual, regular, or special.

(b) "Principal executive office" shall mean that place which is from time to time fixed by the Board of Directors as the principal executive office for the transaction of the business of the Company.

(c) "Approved by [approval of] the outstanding Shares" shall mean approved or ratified by the affirmative vote of a majority of the outstanding Shares entitled to vote. Such approval shall include the affirmative vote of a majority of the outstanding Shares of each class or series entitled to vote as a class or series on the matter being voted upon and shall also include the affirmative vote of such greater proportion (including all) of the outstanding Shares of any class or series if such greater proportion is required.

(d) "Approved by [approval of] the Shareholders" shall mean "approved by [approval of] the outstanding Shares."

(e) "On the certificate" means that a statement appears on the face of a Share certificate or on the reverse thereof with a reference thereto on the face or, in the case of an uncertificated security, that the applicable provisions of subdivision (b) of Section 8103, paragraph (b) or (c) of subdivision (1) of Section 8202, subdivision (b) of Section 8204, subdivision (2) of Section 8304, or Section 8408 of the Commercial Code have been complied with.

(f) "Majority in Interest of the Shareholders" means the absolute majority of the Shares outstanding on the record date of the meeting or the vote or consent as appropriate.

(g) "Operating Agreement" means the agreement by and among the Shareholders of this Company, dated as of August 4th, 2005, of which these Bylaws are a part.

(h) "Proxy" means a written authorization signed by a Shareholder or the Shareholder's attorney-in-fact giving another person or persons power to vote with respect to the Shares of such Shareholder; "signed" for the purpose of this section means the placing of the Shareholder's name on the Proxy (whether by manual signature, typewriting, telegraphic transmission, or otherwise) by the Shareholder or the Shareholder's attorney-in-fact. "Proxyholder" means the person or persons to whom a Proxy is given.

(i) "Series" of Shares means those Shares within a class which have the same rights, preferences, privileges, and restrictions but which differ in one or more rights, preferences, privileges, or restrictions from other Shares within the same class.

(j) "Shareholder" means one who is a holder of record of a Shareholder Interest.

(k) "Vacancy" when used with respect to the Board of Directors means any authorized position of Director which is not then filled by a duly appointed Director, whether caused by death, resignation, removal, change in the authorized number of Directors (by the Board or the Shareholders), or otherwise.

(l) "Written" or "in writing" includes facsimile and telegraphic communication.

Form 7 J: Operating Agreement—Delaware Series

Note: This is an example of a Delaware limited liability company agreement, set up to provide for a series of members to pursue different business objectives, as well as to provide for a class of members (the "Working Members") who are employees of the company and are receiving their membership interests as an incentive. Working members are subject to vesting and have only a profits interest.

OPERATING AGREEMENT
FOR
****, LLC,
A DELAWARE LIMITED LIABILITY COMPANY
_____, 20____

TABLE OF CONTENTS

OPERATING AGREEMENT
FOR
****, LLC
A DELAWARE LIMITED LIABILITY COMPANY

This Operating Agreement, is made as of this _____ day of _____, 20___, by and among the signatories to this Agreement and any party subsequently admitted as a Member according to the terms and conditions of this Agreement (the "Members"), with reference to the following facts:

A. Effective _____, 20___, the Certificate of Formation for ****, LLC, a limited liability company organized under the laws of the State of Delaware (the "Company"), was filed with the Delaware Secretary of State.

B. The Company will continue the business activities previously conducted by ****, a California corporation ("Systems"), including _____ (the "Business").

C. Expansion and successful continuation of the Business requires expanded ownership and the establishment of management procedures and organizational structures that the Members believe can be best accomplished through the Company.

D. The Members desire to provide for the following: (i) capitalization of the Company; (ii) relationships among the Members; (iii) admission of additional Persons as Members; (iv) rules for the orderly succession of ownership and control of the Company; (v) appropriate restrictions to prevent ownership of interests in the Company by Persons not admitted as Members; and (vi) repurchase of interests in the Company from Persons who terminate their employment with the Company, among others.

E. The Members therefore desire to adopt and approve this Operating Agreement for the Company.

NOW, THEREFORE, the Members hereby adopt this Operating Agreement for the Company under the laws of the State of Delaware upon the terms and subject to the conditions set forth herein.

SECTION 1
DEFINITIONS

When used in this Agreement, the following terms shall have the meanings set forth below (all terms used in this Agreement that are not defined in this Section 1 shall have the meanings set forth elsewhere in this Agreement):

"Act" means the Delaware Limited Liability Company Act, as codified in Del. Code Title 6, Section 18-101, et seq., as the same may be amended from time to time.

"Affiliate" means any Person directly or indirectly controlling ****, LLC (including Controlling Persons), any Controlled Entity of ****, LLC, and any Controlled Entity of a Person who is a Controlling Person of ****, LLC.

"Agreement means this Operating Agreement, as originally executed and as amended from time to time.

"Approved Budget" means a budget for each Fiscal Year of the Company adopted with Board Approval.

"Assignee" means the owner of an Economic Interest who has not been admitted as a substitute Member in accordance with Section 4.2.

"Bankruptcy" means: (a) the filing of an application by a Member for, or his or her consent to, the appointment of a trustee, receiver, or custodian of his or her assets; (b) the entry of an order for relief with respect to a Member in proceedings under the United States Bankruptcy Code, as amended or superseded from time to time; (c) the making by a Member of a general assignment for the benefit of creditors; (d) the entry of an order, judgment or decree by any court of competent jurisdiction appointing a trustee, receiver or custodian of the assets of a Member unless the proceedings and the person appointed are dismissed within ninety (90) days; or (e) the failure by a Member generally to pay his or her debts as the debts become due within the meaning of Section 303(h)(1) of the United States Bankruptcy Code, as determined by the Bankruptcy Court, or the admission in writing of his or her inability to pay his or her debts as they become due.

"Board Approval" means the approval, consent or affirmative vote either in a meeting or in writing, of at least a numerical majority of the active Directors, regardless of how many Directors are at a meeting. For example, if there are three (3) Directors, Board Approval would require the approval, consent or affirmative vote of at least two (2); if there are five (5) or four (4) Directors, Board Approval would require approval, consent or affirmative vote of three (3) Directors.

"Board of Directors" means the group of Persons appointed or elected to serve as Directors pursuant to Section 5.2 of this Agreement, which group shall, acting as a group, have authority to direct the activities of the Company, supervise and direct the Officers of the Company and exercise general management authority over the affairs of the Company pursuant to this Operating Agreement.

"Business" means the business of the Company and such other activities as may be engaged in by the Company from time to time as permitted under the Certificate of Formation and Section 2.6 of this Agreement.

"Business Assets" means all assets used in the Business whether by Systems or by the Company as of the date of this Agreement, and all assets hereafter acquired by the Company, including tangible and intangible assets.

"Buy-Out Insurance" means life insurance purchased and designated as Buy-Out Insurance pursuant to Section 4.9(a).

"Capital Account" means, with respect to any Member, the capital account that the Company establishes and maintains for such Member pursuant to Section 3.5.

"Capital Contribution" means the total amount of cash and the agreed fair market value of property contributed to the Company by the Members as required under Section 3 and as set forth in Exhibit A to this Agreement.

"Capital Event" means: (i) a sale, disposition or redemption of all or a substantial portion of the Units, Membership Interests or Business Assets of the Company, whether for cash, property or in the context of a sale, merger, or reorganization, if after the event, the Persons who were Members immediately before the event hold less than fifty percent (50%) of the entity which owns the Business Assets after the event, and (ii) with respect to a particular Member, a sale of Units pursuant to Section 8.

"Cause" means any of the following forms of conduct on the part of a Member: (i) conviction in any jurisdiction of any felony, or conviction of a misdemeanor involving fraud, an act of moral turpitude, or material loss to the Company's business, assets or reputation, (ii) a fraud, misappropriation or embezzlement of funds or assets of Company (whether or not the subject of a criminal conviction), (iii) gross misconduct or gross negligence of duties and responsibilities as an employee of, or consultant or service provider to Company or to Systems, including, without limitation, a material breach of those duties and responsibilities set forth in any agreement between Company and the Member or Systems and the Member or violation of established rules and policies of Company, (iv) repeated violation or failure to execute any reasonable written instructions or directions of the Company's Board of Directors, the Company President, Chief Executive Officer or other person having authority over the employment, consulting or service activities of the Member, and (v) a material breach of a Member's obligations under this Agreement which is not cured within thirty (30) days after written notice thereof. In determining whether Cause exists, the Board of Directors, the Company, and any Member may seek a judicial determination without being required to first comply with Section 12.7.

"Certificate" means the Certificate of Formation for the Company originally filed with the Delaware Secretary of State and as amended from time to time.

"Class" means a group of Working Units issued to Working Members pursuant to Section 3.2 of this Agreement, all of which are issued at the same Threshold Value.

Each Class of Working Units shall be designated with a capital letter associated with the Threshold Value at which the Class of Working Units is issued.

"Code" means the Internal Revenue Code of 1986, as amended from time to time.

"Common Member" means a Member holding Common Units.

"Common Unit" means the Units issued to Common Members pursuant to Section 3.2 of the Agreement.

"Company" means ****, LLC, a Delaware limited liability company and all of its Controlled Entities.

"Company Valuation" means the value of the Company as a going concern, as determined pursuant to the procedure set forth in Exhibit D to this Agreement.

"Compensation" means amounts paid to a Working Member for time and efforts on behalf of the Company either as a periodic payment under a contract between the Working Member and the Company in the nature of a base salary, wage or pay rate or as a bonus payment made pursuant to a contract or Company bonus program. Compensation shall be treated for all purposes as either deductible payroll or as a deductible "guaranteed payments" pursuant to Section 707(c) of the Code.

"Confidential Information" means all information not in the public domain regarding the Company including, without limitation: (i) information constituting Work Product, (ii) information regarding the Company's products, services, procedures, markets, customers, customer lists, clients, suppliers, contracts and financial information learned or obtained during the term of this Agreement, (iii) any confidential information regarding the Company's clients, customers and suppliers, including without limitation, any trade secrets and any information subject to a confidentiality agreement or non-disclosure agreement to which Company is a party, and (iv) all of the Company's trade secrets and proprietary information, software programs, data, data books, market surveys, techniques, product or service designs, protocols and plans, marketing plans, formulae, ideas and financial plans, business plans and internal bookkeeping and accounting records.

"Control" means, in the case of a corporation, partnership or limited liability company, the Person with a direct or indirect interest in the entity holds at least fifty one percent (51%) of voting control of the entity or sufficient authority to make decisions on behalf of the entity without being overridden, and, in the case of a trust, the Person is a trustee (or the trustee is itself a Controlled Entity) with power to vote the Units held by the trust.

"Controlled Entity" means a corporation, partnership, limited liability company or trust under the Control of a Member.

"Controlling Person" means a Person who, as the shareholder, partner, member, manager or trustee of a Member, directly or indirectly, through one or more intermediaries, is in Control of the Member.

"Covered Member" means a Member whose life is insured by Buy-Out Insurance or key Person Insurance pursuant to Section 4.9.

"Distributable Cash" means the amount of cash which the Board of Directors determine to be available for distribution to the Members, taking into account all debts, liabilities and obligations of the Company then due and working capital and other amounts which the Board of Directors deems necessary for the Business or to place into reserves for customary and usual claims with respect to the Business.

"Economic Interest" means an economic interest in the Company represented by, Capital Accounts, the Units and the Percentage Interests, including the right to receive distributions of the Company's assets and allocations of Net Profits and Net

Losses, income, gain, loss, deduction, credit and similar items from the Company pursuant to this Agreement and the Act, but shall not include any other rights of a Member, including without limitation, the right to vote or participate in the management of the Company or, except as provided in the Act, any right to information concerning the business and affairs of the Company. Economic Interest also may refer to a person who holds an Economic Interest, as a Member, former Member or Assignee.

"Excess Loss Share" means a Member's share of a Guarantee Obligation exceeding the Member's Percentage Interest of such Guarantee Obligation as provided in Section 3.10(a).

"Fiscal Year" means the Company's fiscal year, which shall be the calendar year.

"Former Member's Interest" means the Membership Interest and Economic Interest of a Person who has been subject of a Termination Event, including all Units held by the Former member and by and any of such Former Member's Permitted Transferees, as further defined in Section 8.1(b).

"Guarantee Obligation" means an obligation or liability of the Company which is: entered into pursuant to Section 3.10 and, with respect to which any Member is required to guarantee personally, collateralize with personal assets or indemnify a creditor or potential creditor of the Company.

"Guarantor Member" means any Member who is personally liable for a Guarantee Obligation or who has collateralized a Guarantee Obligation with personal assets under Section 3.10.

"Indemnifiable Loss" means a liability, cost, loss, damage or expense with respect to a Guarantee Obligation including without limitation, reasonable attorneys' fees and costs, and interest expenses incurred by any and all Members with respect to the Guarantee Obligation as defined in Section 3.10 of this Agreement.

"Key Person Insurance" means insurance either designated as key person Insurance under Section 4.9(b) or proceeds of Buy-Out Insurance exceeding the amount needed to pay the Redemption Price of a Member's Former Member Interest.

"Majority Interest" means those Members who hold a majority of the Units held by all Members, or, if Majority Interest expressly refers to a group of less than all Members (such as the Common Members or the Working Members), then Majority Interest means those Members (or the Member) included in such reference group who hold a majority of the Units held by all Members in such group.

"Member" means each Person who (a) is an initial Member or who has been admitted to the Company as a Member pursuant to Section 4.2, or is an Assignee who has become a Member pursuant to Section 7, and (b) has not become the subject of a Termination Event or ceased to be a Member for any reason. Unless otherwise specified, the term "Member" may refer to any Member, including a Common Member or Working Member, and the plural "Members" may refer to all classes of Members.

"Membership Interest" means a Member's entire interest in the Company including both the Member's Economic Interest and all non-economic rights such as the right to vote or participate in the management, and the right to receive information concerning the business and affairs of the Company.

"Net Profits" and "Net Losses" mean, for each Fiscal Year or other period, an amount equal to the Company's taxable income or loss for such year or period, determined under Code Section 703(a) (for this purpose, all items of income, gain, loss or deduction required to be stated separately pursuant to Code Section 703(a)(1) shall be included in taxable income or loss), with the following adjustments:

(a) Any income of the Company that is exempt from federal income tax and not otherwise taken into account in computing Net Profits or Net Losses shall be added to such taxable income or loss.

(b) Any expenditures of the Company described in Code Section 705(a)(2)(b) or treated as Code Section 705(a)(2)(B) expenditures pursuant to Regulations Section 1.704-1(b)(2)(iv)(i), and not otherwise taken into account in computing Net Profits or Net Losses shall be subtracted from such taxable income or loss.

(c) Compensation of all Members shall be treated either as payroll or as "guaranteed payments" pursuant to Section 707(c) of the Code and shall be deducted in calculating Net Profits and Net Losses.

(d) If Capital Accounts of Members have been adjusted pursuant to Section 3.5(b), gain or loss resulting from any disposition of Business Assets (whether for sale of a single Business Asset or all of the Company's Business Assets) shall be computed by reference to the most recent value of such Business Asset used in adjusting Capital Accounts pursuant to Section 3.5(b), rather than the adjusted tax basis of such Business Asset.

(e) Special Allocations to Members pursuant to Section 6.2 shall not be taken into account in calculating Net Profits or Net Losses.

"Officer" shall mean the Persons to whom executive responsibilities are delegated by the Board of Directors pursuant to Section 5.3 of this Agreement.

"Operating Net Profits" means all Net Profits other than Net Profits attributable to a Capital Event.

"Percentage Interest" means the percentage determined by the percentage of total number of Units (including Common Units and Working Units) outstanding for the entire Company which are held by each Member, as such percentage may be adjusted from time to time as the result of Transfers, issuance of additional Units, or repurchase or redemption of Units by the Company pursuant to this Agreement. The Percentage Interest is used to determine the Economic Interests of Members in Net Profits, Net Losses and distributions from the Company.

"Permitted Transfer" means a Transfer of Units complying with the terms of Section 7.2 of this Agreement.

"Person" means an individual, partnership, limited partnership, limited liability company, corporation, trust, estate, association or any other entity.

"Redemption Price" means the purchase price to be paid for a Former Member's Interest as determined pursuant to Section 8.2 and Exhibit D of this Agreement.

"Regulations" means the regulations in force as final or temporary issued by the U.S. Department of Treasury pursuant to its authority under the Code, and any successor regulations.

"Right of First Refusal" means the right of the Company to purchase the Units or Economic Interest of a Member pursuant to Section 7.3.

"Series" means a group of Business Assets and related economic and Business activities of the Company designated as a separate "series" as provided in Section 18-215 of the Act and with respect to which Members may have separately established rights, all as set forth in Exhibit E to this Agreement. Each Series shall be designated with a Roman numeral associated with the corresponding description of that Series set forth in Exhibit E to this Agreement.

"Service Agreement" means a written agreement entered into between the Company and a Member with respect to performance of services by the Member on behalf of the Company, including Compensation to be paid for such services.

"Special Allocation" means an allocation of Net Profits or Net Losses, or items of gross income, gain, expense or loss in any manner other than as set forth in Section

6.1 of this Agreement, adopted pursuant to Section 6.2(a) with Board Approval and the approval of each of the Members whose allocations of Net Profits or Net Losses will be affected by such allocation.

"Standard Vesting Schedule" means the schedule for conversion of Working Units from Unvested Units into Vested Units set forth in Section 3.3(c).

"Subscription Agreement" means the agreement which must be signed by a Person other than a Member who is an original signatory to this Agreement as a condition of admission as a Member pursuant to Section 4.2, which Subscription Agreement may be included in the Unit Certificate or in the form attached hereto as Exhibit C-1 (for newly issued Units) or Exhibit C-2 (for Transferees) to this Agreement.

"Target Market" means _____ and such additional geographical locations in which the Company or a Series is actively engaged in Business at the time the scope and extent of the Target Market is determined.

"Termination Event" means, with respect to any Member, one or more of the following: (i) the death, withdrawal or resignation of a Member (whether or not in compliance with this Agreement or the terms of the Service Agreement), (ii) termination of a Working Member's Service Agreement for any reason, including, without limitation, by reason of death, disability, resignation or other form of termination, whether voluntary or involuntary; provided that the expiration of the term of a Service Agreement shall not be a Termination Event if the Working Member continues to deliver services to the Company and the Service Agreement is replaced by a successor agreement within a reasonable time after its expiration; (iii) the Transfer or attempted Transfer of a Member's interest in the Company or any Units in violation of Section 7; or (iv) upon notice by the Company to the Member of a material breach of any of the provisions of this Agreement, either immediately if such breach cannot be cured, or within ten (10) days after such notice if cure of the breach is reasonably possible. In the event that a Working Member has Transferred Working Units to a Controlled Entity or Permitted Transferee, "Termination Event" shall occur with respect to such Controlled Entity or Permitted Transferee if the original holder of the Working Units experiences a Termination Event.

"Threshold Value" means an amount equal to the Unit Value of a Common Unit on the date a Working Unit is granted to a Working Member. The Threshold Value corresponds to the portion of the Company Valuation in which the Working Unit (or Class of Working Units) is not entitled to share upon the occurrence of a Capital Event or sale of the Working Unit. (For example, a Class of Working Units issued at a time when the Unit Value of Common Units is $1.00 would have a Threshold Value of $1.00, and the holder of those Working Units would not be entitled to participate in the proceeds of a Capital Event or receive payment upon a sale of the Working Units unless, and to the extent, the Unit Value of Common Units at such time exceeded the Threshold Value. Thus, a Capital Event which resulted in distribution of $2.50 with respect to each Common Unit would exceed the $1.00 Threshold Value of the Class of Working Units by $1.50 and would result in a distribution of $1.50 with respect to each Working Unit of that Class.)

"Transfer" means a disposition, whether voluntary or involuntary, of any Membership Interest.

"Transferor" and "Transferee" mean the Person attempting or making a Transfer and the Person receiving the Transfer, respectively.

"Unit" means a measure of the Economic Interest of a Common Member, Working Member or Assignee in the Net Profits, Net Losses and distributions as determined under Section 6. Units shall be designated as Common Units or Working Units.

"Unit Certificate" means a certificate representing the Units issued to a Member in the form set forth on Exhibit B to this Agreement, and, in the case of a Working Member, setting forth any Vesting Restrictions.

"Unit Value" means the amount which a particular Unit would be worth if cash equal to the Company Valuation were realized upon sale of all Company assets and distributed, net of liabilities and reasonable costs and expenses, to all Members holding Common Units and Working Units (including both Vested Units and Unvested Units), pursuant to the procedure set forth in greater detail on Exhibit D to this Agreement.

"Unvested Unit" means a Working Unit while such Unit remains subject to Vesting Restrictions.

"Valuation Increase" and "Valuation Decrease" mean the increase or decrease, respectively, if any, in the Company Valuation from one issuance of Units (including either Common Units or Working Units or rights convertible into Common Units) to a later issuance of Units, or between the Company Valuation at the time of the most recent issuance of Units and a repurchase by the Company of a material amount of Units from a Member.

"Vested Unit" means a Working Unit which was formerly an Unvested Unit and with respect to which the Vesting Restrictions have ceased to apply under Section 3.3(b) and the terms of the Unit Certificate.

"Vesting Restrictions" means the restrictions applicable to Unvested Units under Section 3.3.

"Vesting Schedule" means a schedule of times or events set forth in a Working Member's Unit Certificate specifying the time or events which will cause Unvested Units to convert into Vested Units.

"Working Member" means a Person who holds Working Units and who is subject to a Service Agreement, a Controlled Entity of the Person to whom Working Units originally were issued, or a Permitted Transferee of such Working Units.

"Working Unit" means a Unit issued to, or with respect to, a Working Member as part of a designated Class of Working Units pursuant to Section 3.2 and which is not issued in exchange for cash or property and which represents an Economic Interest in future Net Profits of the Company.

"Work Product" means those Business Assets which are intangible assets and any new concepts, plans, reports, software, know-how, trade secrets, techniques, protocols, specifications, machines, methods, processes, formulas, algorithms, routines, subroutines, codes, programs, apparatuses, peripherals, accessories, access methods, expressions, compositions of matter, local or wide area network, design, architectures, interfaces, uses, plans or configurations of any kind, discovered, conceived, developed, made or produced or any improvements of them or other property rights associated with any product or service created as a result of the performance of services by Members for the Company. Notwithstanding the foregoing, "Work Product" does not include a Member's skills, knowledge or expertise used to create the Work Product (even if such items were enhanced, refined or modified in the course of the Member's activities), and Work Product shall not include an invention which would fully qualify under Section 2870 of the California Labor Code, if the Member were a California employee of Company.

SECTION 2
ORGANIZATIONAL MATTERS

2.1 <u>Formation and Qualification</u>. The Members have formed a Delaware limited liability company under the laws of the State of Delaware by filing a Certificate of Formation with the Delaware Secretary of State and entering into this Agreement.

The rights and liabilities of the Members shall be determined pursuant to the Act and this Agreement. The Company shall also qualify and register to engage in business in any other jurisdiction in which the activities of the Company require such qualification or registration.

2.2 <u>Name</u>. The name of the Company shall be "****, LLC." The Business of the Company may be conducted under that name or, upon compliance with applicable laws, any other name that the Board of Directors deems appropriate or advisable. The Chief Executive Officer or any other Officer shall file any fictitious name certificates and similar filings, and any amendments thereto, that the Board of Directors considers appropriate or advisable.

2.3 <u>Term</u>. The term of this Agreement commenced as of the _____ day of _____, 20___, and shall continue until terminated as provided in Section 11.

2.4 <u>Office and Agent.</u> The Company shall continuously maintain a registered agent in the State of Delaware. The name and address of the registered agent in the State of Delaware is _____, _____, Delaware _____. The principal office of the Company shall be located at _____, _____, or such other location as the Members may determine.

2.5 <u>Names and Addresses of the Members and the Directors</u>. A record of the names and addresses of the Members and the Directors shall be maintained as required under Section 10.1(b). A Member who changes his or her address shall notify the Company of such change.

2.6 <u>Business of the Company</u>. The Company shall not engage in any business or activities other than the following without Board Approval and the consent of a Majority Interest of the Members:

(a) _____;

(b) any business activities designated and adopted as the business activities of a Series; and

(c) such other activities related to or expanding upon the foregoing, as may be necessary or advisable in the discretion of the Board of Directors to further the interests of the Company.

2.7 <u>Establishment and Designation of Series</u>. The Company may, with Board Approval and the approval of a Majority Interest of the Members, at any time and from time to time, authorize the division of the Business, Business Assets, Members and Membership Interests into two or more Series. Any such authorization shall be set forth in Exhibit E to this Agreement in sufficient detail to satisfy the requirements of Section 18-215 of the Act and shall (a) establish and designate, and fix and determine the relative rights, powers, privileges, preferences and duties of the Series (including, without limitation, voting rights, distribution rights, transfer restrictions, conversion rights and redemption rights) so authorized; (b) set forth the purposes, powers, policies, restrictions and limitations of the Series so authorized; (c) be effective as of the date specified therein; and (d) be incorporated into this Agreement by reference. Unless and until a separate Series is described in Exhibit E and adopted by the Company, all Business activities and Business Assets of the Company shall be treated as Business activities and Business Assets of the Company generally, and thereafter, any Business activities and Business Assets not included as part of a separate Series in Exhibit E shall constitute a single Series designated as Series I.

(a) <u>Assets and Liabilities Associated with Series</u>.

(i) The Company shall maintain separate and distinct records for each Series and shall cause the assets, debts, liabilities, obligations, expenses, profits and losses associated with each such Series to be held and accounted for separately from the other assets, debts, liabilities, obligations, expenses, profits and losses of the Company and any other Series.

(ii) All Capital Contributions received by the Company for the issue or sale of Membership Interests of a particular Series together with all Business Assets in which such Capital Contributions is invested or reinvested, all income, earnings, profits, and proceeds thereof, including any proceeds, Net Profits or net Losses received by the Company from a Capital Event involving such Business or Business Assets, shall irrevocably belong to that Series for all purposes, subject only to the rights of creditors of such Series and except as may otherwise be required by applicable tax laws. In the event that there are any Business Assets, Net Profits, Net Losses or any item of income, gain, expense or loss, funds or payments which are not readily identifiable as belonging to any particular Series, the Board of Directors shall allocate them among any one or more Series in such manner and on such basis as the Board of Directors deems fair and equitable. Each such allocation by the Board of Directors shall be conclusive and binding upon the Members and any holder of an Economic Interest of all types, Series and Classes for all purposes.

(iii) All liabilities, expenses, costs, charges and reserves of the Company which are readily associated with a particular Series shall be charged against the Business Assets associated with that Series, and any liabilities, expenses, costs, charges and reserves of the Company that are not readily associated with a particular Series shall be allocated and charged by the Board of Directors to, between or among any one or more of the Series, in such manner and on such basis as the Board of Directors deems fair and equitable. Each such allocation by the Board of Directors shall be conclusive and binding upon the Members and any holder of an Economic Interest of all types, Series and Classes for all purposes

(iv) The debts, liabilities, obligations and expenses incurred by, contracted for or otherwise existing with respect to a particular Series shall be enforceable against the assets associated with that Series only, and not against the assets associated with any other Series (or against the assets of the Company generally). The Manager shall cause notice of this limitation to be set forth in the Certificate of Formation of the Company (whether originally or by amendment) to be filed in the Office of the Delaware Secretary of State pursuant to the Act. All Persons who extend credit to (or with respect to) a particular Series, or who contract with (or with respect to) or have a claim against a particular Series, may look only to the assets associated with that Series for repayment of such credit of to enforce or satisfy any such contract or claim.

(b) Rights, Powers and Privileges of Series.

(i) Purpose. Unless otherwise limited by the authorization creating the Series, the purpose of any Series created hereunder shall be as set forth in Section 2.6 of this Agreement.

(ii) Rights of Members. Unless otherwise provided in the authorization creating the Series and except as set forth in this Section 2.7, the rights, powers, privileges, limitations, and restrictions, including voting rights, of the Members of a particular Series shall be as otherwise set forth in this Agreement.

SECTION 3
UNITS; CAPITAL STRUCTURE; CAPITAL CONTRIBUTIONS; VESTING OF WORKING UNITS; COMPANY LIABILITIES, AND GUARANTEE OBLIGATIONS

3.1 Units. Economic Interests in the Company shall be represented by Units. Units may be issued at the discretion of the Board of Directors as provided in Section 3.2 of this Agreement, or in such additional classes or Series as may be adopted with Board Approval and the consent of a Majority Interest of the Members. As of the date of this Agreement, the Company has issued to the Members the number of Units of the type and Class set forth next to each Member's name on Exhibit A to this Agreement. Exhibit A shall be updated periodically to reflect issuance of additional Units, repurchase of Units by the Company, or such other Transfers or forfeitures of Units which may occur. The Board of Directors is further authorized to enter into options, warrants or convertible debt instruments which obligate the Company to issue Units in the future to the extent issuance of Units would be permitted under Section 3.2 in the same circumstances. Any Units subject to future issuance under any outstanding warrants, options or convertible debt instruments shall be treated as reserved for issuance under Section 3.2 and those Units shall not be available for issuance while the option, warrant or convertible debt instrument remains unexercised and outstanding. Except as provided in this Agreement or in any other written agreement between the Company and any Member, no Member shall have any preemptive, preferential or other right to participate in the future issuance or sale of any Units or of any warrants, subscriptions, options, conversion rights with respect to Units.

3.2 <u>Types of Units</u>. Initially, two types of Units shall be available for issuance: Common Units and Working Units. Units may be issued at the direction of the Board of Directors in the numbers and under the terms and conditions set forth in this Section 3.2 and subject to all other applicable provisions of this Agreement. Any issuance of Units in excess of the number of Units authorized in this Section 3.2, with terms and conditions different than those terms and conditions provided in this Section 3.2 shall not be permitted unless first adopted with Board Approval and the consent of a Majority Interest of the Members. Issuance of all Units shall be reflected on Exhibit A to this Agreement, together with the name, address and contact information for the Member to whom the Units are issued and other information, such as the type of Unit issued, the Capital Contribution, if any, made in exchange for the Units, the Class and Threshold Value of any Working Units issued, and any other information needed to allow the Company and the Board of Directors to execute the terms of this Agreement.

(a) <u>Common Units</u>. Common Units are Units issued in exchange for Capital Contributions in the form of cash or property not less than the Unit Value established by the Board at the time the Common Units are issued (or at the time options, warrants or convertible debt instruments convertible into the Common Units are issued). The Company is authorized to issue an aggregate of _____ Common Units. The Board of Directors may determine to issue Common Units authorized and available for issuance at a Unit Value in exchange for Capital Contributions in an amount not less than the Unit Value of the Common Units outstanding immediately before the new Common Units are issued. Members holding Common Units shall have the right to participate in all allocations of Net Profits and Net Losses and in all distributions of capital and Net Profits of the Company immediately upon issuance of the Units.

(b) <u>Working Units</u>. Working Units are Units that may be issued to Working Members without the requirement of Capital Contributions as an equity-based incentive for their efforts on behalf of the Company. Working Units shall be issued only with Board Approval. Each Working Unit issued shall be issued as part of a Class of Working Units associated with the Threshold Value at which the Class of Working Units is issued. Each Class of Working Units shall be designated with a capital letter. The Company is authorized to issue an aggregate (including all Classes of Working Units) of _____ Working Units. Holders of Working Units issued in a

Class are not entitled to participate in any portion of the Company Valuation existing on the date that Class of Working Units is issued, which Company Valuation will correspond to the Threshold Value associated with the Class, which will be equivalent to the Unit Value of a Common Unit at that Company Valuation. Working Units of a designated Class are entitled to participate in the same manner as Common Units with respect to all allocations of Net Profits and all Company Valuation Increases occurring after the Class is issued. Economic participation of Working Units is strictly limited to participation in future Net Profits (including Company Valuation Increases) occurring after the Class of Working Units is issued. Working Units shall be evidenced by a Unit Certificate in the form of Exhibit B to this Agreement, setting forth the number and Class of Working Units issued. The Working Members and all Working Units issued to Working Members shall be subject to all applicable provisions of this Agreement, including those provisions set forth in Section 3.3 relating to restrictions upon Working Units and vesting of such Working Units. Working Units may be granted as of any day of the Company's Fiscal Year, provided that any Working Units granted as of any day other than the first day of a Fiscal Year shall not be eligible to participate in Operating Net Profits, Net Losses or distributions derived from Operating net Profits until the first day of the Fiscal Year following the date the Working Units were issued. The holder of the Working Units shall be eligible to participate in Net Profits and distributions resulting from a Capital Event immediately upon issuance of the Working Units.

 3.3 <u>Working Members; Vesting of Units</u>.

 (a) <u>Imposition of Vesting Restrictions</u>. Upon issuance of Working Units, the Board of Directors may, but shall not be required, to designate all or a portion of the Working Units as Unvested Units subject to Vesting Restrictions. The Vesting Restrictions, if any, shall be set forth in the Unit Certificate issued to the Working Member together with a Vesting Schedule. The Board of Directors may adopt any Vesting Schedule they determine to be appropriate at the time of issuance, including a Vesting Schedule under which some or all of the Working Units are Vested Units at the time issued. The Board of Directors may accelerate the Vesting Schedule for any Working Member, but once issued, the Vesting Schedule cannot be deferred, delayed or subjected to additional conditions without the agreement of the Working Member.

 (b) <u>Standard Vesting Schedule</u>. Although the Board of Directors is permitted to impose any Vesting Schedule deemed appropriate, the "Standard Vesting Schedule" is intended to occur over a period of four (4) years after Unvested Units are issued as follows: (i) upon issuance, all Units will be Unvested Units; (ii) on the date twelve (12) months after the issuance of the Units, twenty-five percent (25%) of the issued Units will be converted automatically from Unvested Units to Vested Units; and (iii) quarter-annually thereafter, on each of the succeeding twelve (12) quarter-annual anniversaries of the issuance of the Units, an additional six and one quarter percent (6.25%) of the issued Units will convert automatically from Unvested Units into Vested Units. No conversion of Unvested Units shall occur after the date of the Termination Event affecting the Working Member to whom the Unvested Units were issued.

 (c) <u>Nature of Vesting Restrictions; Forfeiture of Unvested Units</u>. Upon the occurrence of a Termination Event to a Working Member, any Unvested Units shall be immediately and automatically forfeited, without payment of consideration or repurchase price. The Unit Certificate representing such Unvested Units shall be delivered to the Company, which will promptly reissue a Unit Certificate for the number of Vested Units, if any, held by the Working Member at the time of the Termination Event and which are not repurchased pursuant to Section 8 of this Agreement.

(d) <u>Economic Participation of Unvested Units</u>. At all times prior to the occurrence of a Termination Event with respect to a Working Member, such Working Member shall be entitled to participate with respect to Unvested Units in all allocations of Net Profits and distributions on the same basis as Vested Units of the same class. Except as provided in Section 3.3(f), all rights of a Working Member with respect to Unvested Units shall terminate immediately and automatically upon the occurrence of a Termination Event and no further allocation of Net Profits or Net Losses shall be made with respect to such Unvested Units except to the extent necessary to allocate Net Profits to match distributions actually made with respect to the Unvested Units prior to the Termination Event.

(e) <u>Voting with Respect to Unvested Units</u>. Members holding Unvested Units shall be entitled to all rights of Members whose Units are Vested Units with respect to voting, access to information and participation in the affairs of the Company.

(f) <u>Unvested Units and Capital Events</u>. Upon the occurrence of a Capital Event, all outstanding Unvested Units shall automatically convert into Vested Units; provided that the Board of Directors may, in its discretion, enter into arrangements with an acquiring party under which the payment or distribution of the share of Net Profits or other proceeds from a Capital Event with respect to Unvested Units may be deferred until such Unvested Units would otherwise have converted into Vested Units, and the Board of Directors shall have full power and authority to enter into such deferral or similar arrangements on behalf of Working Members holding Unvested Units. In the event such an arrangement is entered for deferred payment to Working Members holding Unvested Units (including arrangements under which options or restricted stock of a successor to the Company are substituted for the Unvested Units), any deferred amount payable with respect to an Unvested Unit shall: (A) be at least substantially equivalent (disregarding time value) to the after-tax share of distributions the Working Member would have received as the result of the Capital Transaction if the Unvested Unit had been a Vested Unit; (B) reasonably secured through an escrow or other arrangement; and (C) payable immediately upon the earliest to occur of: (1) the date the Unvested Unit would have converted into a Vested Unit; (2) the date of termination of the Working Member's Service Agreement by action taken by the Company or the successor to the Company without the Working Member's voluntary consent or action, other than for "Cause," as defined in the Working Member's Service Agreement.

(g) <u>Vesting Restrictions on Units Other Than Working Units</u>. Generally, Common Units will not be subject to Vesting Restrictions. The Board of Directors may issue Common Units subject to Vesting Restrictions in circumstances they deem appropriate, and in such cases such Common Units shall be subject to the provisions of Sections 3.3(a) through (f) as if the Common Units were Working Units, provided, however, that upon forfeiture of Unvested Units, the Company shall pay to the Member the lesser of (i) the amount paid for the Common Unit, or (ii) the Unit Value of the Common Unit on the date the Termination Event occurs.

3.4 <u>Capital Contributions, Additional Capital Contributions; Issuance of Units</u>.

(a) No Member shall be required to make any Capital Contribution other than as required: (i) under Section 3.2; (ii) under Sections 3.9 and 3.10 with respect to Guarantee Obligations, or (iii) as a condition of admission as a Member under Section 4.2.

(b) Subject to the limits set forth in Section 3.2, the Board of Directors may raise additional Capital Contributions at any time funds are required for the Business of the Company by issuance of Common Units pursuant to Section 3.2(a). The Board of Directors may propose that additional Capital Contributions be raised by issuing additional Common Units in excess of the limits set forth in Section 3.2 at any time funds are required for the Business of the Company, or seek increases of such limits for raising Capital Contributions in the future; provided that any such action shall require the approval of a Majority Interest of the Members.

(c) Any increase in the limit on the number of Working Units which may be issued under Sections 3.2(b) or 3.2(c) shall be subject to Board Approval and the approval of a Majority Interest of the Members.

3.5 <u>Capital Accounts</u>.

(a) <u>Maintenance of Capital Accounts</u>. The Company shall establish and maintain an individual Capital Account for each Member in accordance with the applicable rules under Regulations Section 1.704-1(b)(2)(iv). In general, a Member's Capital Account shall be (i) increased by (A) the Member's Capital Contributions, and (B) the Member's allocable share of Net Profits (and any specially allocated gain or income under Section 6.2); and (ii) decreased by (A) the Member's allocable share of Net Losses (and any losses or expenses specially allocated under Section 6.2), and (B) the amount or value of any distribution made to the Member; provided, however that in the unlikely event application of these general rules otherwise conflicts with Regulations Section 1.704-1(b)(2)(iv), the applicable provisions of the Regulations shall control. In the event a Member transfers all or a part of a Membership Interest in accordance with this Agreement, the portion of the Capital Account attributable to the transferred Membership Interest shall carryover to the new owner of the Membership Interest.

(b) <u>Adjustments of Capital Accounts</u>. The Capital Accounts of all existing Members shall be subject to adjustment upon issuance of new Units if such new Units are issued at a time when the Company Valuation has changed from the Company Valuation at the time of the prior issuance, as determined by the Board of Directors. Capital Accounts shall also be subject to adjustment if a significant number of Units are repurchased by the Company. The amount of the adjustment to the Capital Accounts shall be determined by treating the amount of Valuation Increase or Valuation Decrease as Net Profits or Net Losses attributable to a Capital Event under Sections 6.1(c) and 6.1(a), respectively, and then applying the Capital Account maintenance rules under Section 3.5(a).

3.6 <u>No Interest</u>. No Member shall be entitled to receive any interest on his or her Capital Contributions.

3.7 <u>No Withdrawal Rights</u>. No Member or Economic Interest holder shall have any right to withdraw Capital Contributions or any portion of a Capital Account in advance of the time distributions of Distributable Cash would be required to be made with respect to such Member or Economic Interest under Section 6.

3.8 <u>No General Member Liability for Company Obligations</u>. Except as explicitly provided by Sections 3.9 and 3.10 of this Agreement, no Member shall, by reason of being a Member or acting in the conduct of the Business, be liable or accountable, directly or indirectly, including by way of indemnification, contribution, assessment, or otherwise, for the debts, obligations, or liabilities of the Company or another Member or Manager, whether such liability arises in tort, contract, or otherwise.

3.9 <u>Guarantee Obligations</u>. Neither the Company nor any Member shall enter into a Guarantee Obligation without prior Board Approval and the approval of a Majority Interest of the Members. In the event a Guarantee Obligation receives Board Approval, each Member (including each Member later admitted to the Company) agrees that upon request of any Guarantor Member who is personally liable with respect to a Guarantee Obligation, each other Member shall be obligated to execute such personal guarantee or indemnity or provide personal collateral in the same manner as required or requested of the Guarantor Member. The Company shall make reasonable efforts to cause any Guarantee Obligation entered into by any Guarantor Member to be several and not joint, thus limiting the obligation of each Member with respect to any Guarantee Obligation to each such Member's respective Percentage Interest.

3.10 <u>Member Cross-Indemnification for Guarantee Obligations</u>. In the event that the Company cannot pay any portion of a Guarantee Obligation when due and any one or more Guarantor Members incurs any liability, cost, loss, damage or expense with respect to a Guarantee Obligation including without limitation, reasonable attorneys fees and costs, and interest expenses incurred by any Member (an "Indemnifiable Loss"), each Member shall indemnify each other Member for his or her Excess Loss Share as set forth in this Section 3.10. This indemnity obligation shall become effective and enforceable against each Member upon written demand of any Guarantor Member without any need for further action on the part of such Guarantor Member.

(a) <u>Payment of Indemnity Obligations</u>. In the event of an Indemnifiable Loss, each Member shall be responsible for his or her Percentage Interest of such Indemnifiable Loss, and any Guarantor Member may, immediately upon written demand upon the other Members, require each Member to contribute his or her Percentage Interest of the Indemnifiable Loss toward payment of the Indemnifiable Loss. In the event the amount of the Indemnifiable Loss paid or incurred by a Member is in excess of that Member's Percentage Interest of the total Indemnifiable Loss (the "Excess Loss Share"), the other Members shall become severally indebted to the Member who has paid the Excess Loss Share in an amount equal to a sum determined by multiplying the aggregate amount of the Excess Loss Share by the respective Percentage Interests of such Members. Each Member severally agrees to pay the Member who has paid the Excess Loss Share the aforementioned amount within ten (10) business days after notice of written demand, together with interest thereon (if any) commencing on the date of delivery of such request at the rate announced in the Wall Street Journal (Western Edition) as the "prime rate" plus three percent (3%), but in no event shall such rate of interest exceed the maximum rate permissible under law.

(b) <u>Primary Liability</u>. The liability of the Members under this Section 3.10 is direct and primary and is not conditioned or contingent upon prior pursuit of any remedies by any Guarantor Member.

(c) <u>Defense of Actions</u>. In the event any action is brought by a creditor or related third party to enforce a Guarantee Obligation, the Guarantor Member shall promptly notify the Company and each Member of such action. The Company shall at its sole cost and expense defend any action involving a Guarantee Obligation; provided, however, that if the Company then has insufficient financial resources to defend such action, the Members shall bear the cost and expense thereof in proportion to their Percentage Interests. In such event, a Majority Interest of the Members shall have the right to select any and all counsel who may be retained to defend an action involving a Guarantee Obligation. Notwithstanding the foregoing, the Guarantor Member(s) shall have the right to approve any and all counsel who may be retained by Company or the Members to defend any action involving a Guarantee Obligation. A Majority Interest of the Members shall have the right to approve any settlement of the action.

(d) <u>Waiver</u>. The Members hereby jointly and severally waive their rights and agree not to settle any claim established against Company arising out of a Guarantee Obligation to any creditor without the prior written consent of the Guarantor Members unless such settlement results in a complete and unconditional release of all such Guarantor Members with respect to their obligations in connection with such Guarantee Obligation.

(e) Default. In the event of a default or failure of a Member to meet his or her obligations under this Section 3.10, the Percentage Interest of the defaulting Member shall be excluded in calculating the Percentage Interests of the remaining Members and their respective shares of the Indemnifiable Loss and indemnity obligations hereunder, provided that each non-defaulting Member shall thereafter have a right to indemnity from the defaulting Member.

(f) Indemnification Obligation of Company Not Affected. Each Member who pays an Indemnifiable Loss, whether directly as a Guarantor Member or through an indemnity payment or contribution under this Section 3.10 shall be entitled to indemnification by the Company under Section 3.11.

3.11 Indemnification of Members by the Company. The Company agrees, to the extent of Business Assets and subject to the terms of this Agreement, to indemnify and hold each Member harmless from and against, and to reimburse each Member on demand for, any damage, loss, cost, or expense (including attorney fees and costs of investigation incurred in defending against and/or settling such damage, loss, cost, or expense) reasonably incurred by the Member arising out of or in connection with the ordinary and proper conduct of the business of the Company or incurred by the Member for the preservation of the Business or Business Assets, including, without limitation, any liability with respect to a Guarantee Obligation. No Member, when acting in the ordinary and proper conduct of the business of the Company or for the preservation of the Business or Business Assets, shall have any liability to the Company or to any other Member of the Company for any loss suffered by the Company that arises out of any action or inaction of the Member.

SECTION 4
MEMBERS

4.1 Limited Liability. Except as expressly set forth in Section 3.8 and 3.9 of this Agreement or as otherwise agreed by the Members or as required by law, no Member shall be personally liable for any debt, obligation or liability of the Company, whether that liability or obligation arises in contract, tort or otherwise, and no Member shall be required to guarantee any loan or obligation of the Company.

4.2 Admission of Members. A Person may be admitted to the Company as a Member only if such Person meets the following requirements:

(a) Board of Directors approve of the admission;

(b) In the event a Person is to be admitted to the Company as a Common Member, such Person contributes to the Company the Unit Value of the Common Units as a Capital Contribution, and the Person agrees to be bound by terms of this Operating Agreement by executing a Subscription Agreement;

(c) In the event a Person is to be admitted as a Working Member, the Person (i) executes or is subject to a Services Agreement, (ii) executes a Unit Certificate setting forth the Vesting Restrictions, if any, applicable to the Working Units issued to the Person, and (iii) agrees to be bound by terms of this Operating Agreement by executing the Unit Certificate or a separate Subscription Agreement; and

(d) The admission of the Person as a Member will not terminate the Company within the meaning of Section 708(b) of the Code.

The admission as a Member shall be effective on the first date all of the applicable requirements of this Section 4.2 are met.

4.3 <u>Withdrawals or Resignations</u>. Any Member may withdraw or resign as a Member at any time upon ninety (90) days prior written notice to the Company, without prejudice to the rights, if any, of the Company or the other Members under any contract to which the withdrawing Member is a party.

4.4 <u>Termination of Working Member</u>. Upon the occurrence of a Termination Event affecting a Working Member (including a voluntary withdrawal or resignation), the Membership Interest of any Working Member shall be terminated and such Member, or his or her successor(s) in interest, shall thereafter be deemed to be an Assignee holding an Economic Interest subject to the following:

(a) <u>Unvested Units</u>. Any Unvested Units held by a Working Member at the time of a Termination Event shall be forfeited without consideration and shall not represent a continuing Economic Interest in the Company after the date of the Termination Event.

(b) <u>Vested Units</u>. Any Vested Units held by a Working Member at the time of a Termination Event may be retained after the Termination Event, provided that any such Vested Units shall be subject to the provisions of Section 8 regarding the obligations of a former Member to sell Units after a Termination Event if the Company elects to repurchase such Units. If such former Member continues to hold an Economic Interest as an Assignee with respect to the Vested Units, such Assignee shall not be entitled to any distributions of Capital Contributions or any portion of the Capital Account of such Assignee except to the extent, and at the time, Members with similar Economic Interests receive such distributions.

(c) <u>Acknowledgment</u>. Each Member acknowledges and agrees that: (i) termination of a Membership Interest upon the occurrence of a Termination Event, and (ii) the retention of the former Member's Capital Account balance upon the occurrence of a Termination Event until such time as distributions with respect to the Assignee's Units as required under this Agreement are reasonable provisions, given the closely held nature of the Company, the anticipated limitations on Distributable Cash which will be available to the Company, and other circumstances existing as of the date hereof.

4.5 <u>Remuneration to Members</u>. Except pursuant to a Service Agreement or as otherwise specifically provided in this Agreement, no Member is entitled to remuneration for acting in the Business.

4.6 <u>Members Are Not Agents</u>. Pursuant to Section 5.1, the management of the Company is vested in the Board of Directors, and, by express delegation, to the Officers. The Members shall have no power to participate in the management of the Company except as expressly authorized by this Agreement and except as expressly required by the Act. No Member, acting solely in the capacity of a Member, is an agent of the Company nor does any Member, unless expressly and duly authorized in writing to do so by the Board of Directors, have any power or authority to bind or act on behalf of the Company.

4.7 <u>Voting Rights</u>. Members shall have the voting, approval or consent rights expressly provided in this Agreement. Except as otherwise set forth in this Agreement or the Act, in all matters in which a vote, approval or consent of the Members is required, a vote, consent or approval of a Majority Interest shall be sufficient to authorize or approve such act. Except as otherwise specifically provided in this Agreement, all votes, approvals or consents of the Members may be given, withheld, conditioned or delayed as the Members may determine individually in their sole and absolute discretion.

4.8 <u>Meetings of Members</u>.

(a) <u>Meetings</u>. No regular meeting of the Members are required to be held; however, a meeting of the Members may be called by the President of the Company, by any two Directors, or by Members holding at least ten percent (10%) of the outstanding

Units for the purpose of considering any matter with respect to which the Members have rights to vote, approve or consent.

(b) <u>Notice of Meetings</u>. All meetings of Members shall be noticed, held and conducted pursuant to the Act. A written notice of any such meeting shall be given to each Member not less than ten (10) days or more than sixty (60) days before the date of the meeting. The notice shall state the place, date and hour of the meeting and the general nature of the business to be transacted. All notices shall be given in accordance with Section 12.11 of this Agreement.

(c) <u>Voting; Minutes</u>. A Majority Interest of the Units represented in person or by proxy shall constitute a quorum at any meeting of Members. In any instance in which a vote, approval or consent of Members is required under this Operating Agreement, such vote, approval or consent may be obtained in any manner permitted by the Act, including by action at a duly called meeting of the Members or by written consent of the minimum number of Members required to vote, approve or consent in such instance. All votes, approvals and consents shall be filed with the Company's records or made a part of the minutes of the Members' meeting.

4.9 <u>Life Insurance on Members</u>.

(a) <u>Funding of Redemption Price</u>. The Company intends to purchase, and, if such insurance can be purchased at a reasonable premium cost, the Company shall purchase and maintain in effect during the term of this Agreement, a policy or policies of insurance on the life of each Member, in such face amounts as are determined from time to time by the Board of Directors as appropriate to fund the Redemption Price for such Member, and such policy (or portion of a policy) shall be designated as "Buy-Out Insurance." The Company shall be the owner and beneficiary of each such policy. Each such policy is first intended to fund the Company's purchase of the Former Member's Interest of a Former Member whose life is insured thereby (the "Covered Member"). The cost of premiums of Buy-Out Insurance for each Covered Member shall be allocated among all Members in proportion to their respective Percentage Interests at the time the premiums are due and shall be paid out of the Members' respective distributable shares of Net Profits. The proceeds of any Buy-Out Insurance policy shall be allocated among the Members (excluding the Covered Member) according to their respective Percentage Interests as of the date of the Covered Member's death. The Company shall apply the proceeds of each such policy first to the Redemption Price for the deceased Covered Member's Former Member Interest, and any excess of the amount shall be treated as proceeds of Key Person Insurance subject to Section 4.9(b).

(b) <u>Key Person Insurance</u>. All benefits from Buy-Out Insurance not used for the purpose of funding the Redemption Price payable for the Covered Member's Former Member Interest shall be designated as Key Person Insurance. The Company also may purchase and maintain such other, separate policy or policies of Key Person Insurance covering the life of any Covered Member or Members as may be decided from time to time by the Board of Directors. The Company shall be the owner and beneficiary of any such policies of Key Person Insurance, and the Company shall have the right to retain the proceeds thereof. The cost of premiums attributable to Key Person Insurance shall be allocated among all Members in proportion to their respective Percentage Interests at the time the premiums are due and shall be paid out of the Members' respective distributable shares of Net Profits. The proceeds of any Key Person Insurance policy shall be allocated among the Members (excluding the Covered Member) according to their respective Percentage Interests as of the date of the Covered Member's death.

(c) <u>Member Cooperation</u>. Each Member agrees to cooperate fully with the Company in arranging for the purchase of Buy-Out insurance and/or Key Person Insurance.

SECTION 5
MANAGEMENT AND CONTROL OF THE COMPANY

5.1 <u>Management of the Company</u>.

(a) <u>Status and Conduct of the Board of Directors</u>. The Directors of the Company shall be the "managers" of the Company as provided in the Act. In the event of a vacancy in the Board of Directors, the remaining Directors, acting as a group pursuant to this Agreement, may exercise the powers of the full Board of Directors until the vacancy is filled. The Board of Directors shall make decisions and exercise authority by consensus, or if no consensus can be reached on an issue, by Board Approval, which shall require the approval, consent or vote of a numerical majority of all of the Directors, regardless of the number attending a meeting or seeking to act by written consent, or if no numerical majority is reached, with the approval of a Majority Interest of the Members.

(b) <u>Powers of the Board of Directors</u>. Subject to the provisions of this Agreement and the Act relating to actions required to be approved by the Members under Section 5.1(c), the Business, Business Assets and affairs of the Company shall be managed and all powers of the Company shall be exercised by or under the direction of the Directors, acting as a Board of Directors. All decisions respecting any matter affecting or arising out of the conduct of the Business shall be made either (i) with Board Approval, or (ii) by an Officer or Officers acting pursuant to the authority delegated by the Board of Directors and this Agreement. Specifically, but not by way of limitation, the Board of Directors shall be authorized in the name and on behalf of the Company, to cause the Company to do all things necessary or appropriate to carry on the Business of the Company on a day-to-day basis, and to otherwise exercise all powers and authority granted by the Act and by this Agreement.

(c) <u>Limitations on Power of Board of Directors</u>. The Board of Directors shall not have authority hereunder to cause the Company to engage in the following transactions without first obtaining the approval of the Members as indicated:

(i) The merger of the Company with another limited liability company, limited partnership, corporation, general partnership or other Person shall be subject to the approval of a Majority Interest of the Members.

(ii) Participation of the Company in any Capital Event shall be subject to the approval of a Majority Interest of the Members.

(iii) An alteration of the primary purpose or business of the Company as set forth in Section 2.6 shall require approval of a Majority Interest of the Members;

(iv) Any act which would make it impossible to carry on the business of the Company shall require the approval of a Majority Interest of the Members;

(v) Any other transaction described in this Agreement as requiring the vote, consent or approval of the Members shall require the action of the Members so indicated.

5.2 <u>Rules Regarding the Board of Directors</u>.

(a) <u>Election and Qualification of Directors; Initial Directors</u>. Directors shall be elected at an annual meeting of Members. Only individual Persons who are either Members or Controlling Persons shall be eligible to serve as Directors. The names of the initial Directors and any Person elected to serve as a Director shall be set forth on Exhibit A to this Agreement or in other records of the Company, and shall be updated as changes occur.

(b) <u>Number of Directors; Increase or Decrease of the Board</u>. The number of Directors is hereby fixed at _____ (__) until changed by the approval, consent or vote of a Majority Interest of the Members. The number of Directors constituting the Board of Directors shall be determined by the consent of a Majority Interest of the Members, and the number of Directors may be increased or decreased at any time and from time to time only by the consent of a Majority Interest of the Members.

(c) <u>Tenure</u>. Each Director shall hold office until the first to occur of: (i) the next annual meeting of the Members at which his successor is duly elected and qualified, or (ii) until his earlier death, resignation or removal.

(d) <u>Vacancies</u>. Unless and until filled by the Members, any vacancy in the Board of Directors, however occurring, including a vacancy resulting from an enlargement of the Board of Directors, may be filled by Board Approval. A Member elected to fill a vacancy shall be elected for the unexpired term of his predecessor in office, and a Member chosen to fill a position resulting from an increase in the number of Directors shall hold office until the first to occur of: (i) the next annual meeting of the Members at which his successor is duly elected and qualified, or (ii) until his earlier death, resignation or removal.

(e) <u>Resignation</u>. Any Director may resign by delivering his written resignation to the Company at its principal office or to the President or Secretary. Such resignation shall be effective upon receipt unless it is specified to be effective at some other time or upon the happening of some other event.

(f) <u>Regular Meeting</u>. Regular meetings of the Board of Directors may be held without notice at such time and place as shall be determined from time to time by the Board of Directors; provided that any Director who is absent when such a determination is made shall be given notice of the determination. A regular meeting of the Board of Directors may be held without notice immediately after and at the same place as the annual meeting of Members.

(g) <u>Special Meeting</u>. Special meetings of the Board of Directors may be held at any time and place designated in a call by the President, two or more Directors, or by one Director in the event that there is only a single Director.

(h) <u>Notice of Special Meeting</u>. Notice of any special meeting of the Board of Directors shall be given to each member of the Board of Directors by the Secretary or by the Officer or one of the Directors calling the meeting. Notice shall be duly given to each Director (i) by giving notice to such member in person or by telephone at least (24) hours in advance of the meeting, (ii) by delivering written notice by hand, to his last known business or home address at least (24) hours in advance of the meeting, or (iii) by mailing written notice to his last known business or home address at least (72) hours in advance of the meeting. A notice or waiver of notice of a meeting of the Board of Directors need not specify the purposes of the meeting.

(i) <u>Meetings by Telephone Conference Calls</u>. Directors or any members of any committee designated by the Board of Directors may participate in a meeting of the Board of Directors or such committee by means of conference telephone or similar communications equipment by means of which all persons participating in the meeting can hear each other, and participation by such means shall constitute presence in person at such meeting.

(j) <u>Quorum</u>. A majority of the total number of Directors shall constitute a quorum at all meetings of the Board of Directors. In the event one or more of the Directors shall be disqualified to vote at any meeting, then the required quorum shall be reduced by one for each such member so disqualified; provided, however, that in no case shall less than three (3) Directors constitute a quorum. In the absence of a quorum at any such meeting, a majority of the Directors present may adjourn the meeting from time to time without further notice other than announcement at the meeting, until a quorum shall be present.

(k) <u>Action at Meeting</u>. At any meeting of the Board of Directors at which a quorum is present, the vote of a majority of all of the Directors (including those Directors who are absent) shall be sufficient to take any action, unless a different vote is specified by law, the Certificate of Formation or this Agreement.

(l) <u>Action by Consent</u>. Any action required or permitted to be taken at any meeting of the Board of Directors or of any committee of the Board of Directors may be taken without a meeting, if a numerical majority of the Directors or members of the committee, as the case may be, consent to the action in writing.

(m) <u>Removal</u>. Except as otherwise provided by the Act, any one or more or all of the Directors may be removed, for any reason whatsoever, with or without cause, by the affirmative vote of a Majority Interest of the Members.

(n) <u>Compensation of Directors</u>. The Directors are not entitled to remuneration for services rendered other than (i) allocations of Net Profits, Net Losses and distributions in his or her capacity as a Member as set forth in Section 6, and (ii) Compensation provided under the Service Agreement, if any, of a Director. The Company shall reimburse the Directors for out of pocket costs paid or incurred on behalf of the Company in compliance with the Company's general reimbursement policy.

(o) <u>Devotion of Time by Directors</u>. Performance by the Directors of their duties is expected to require considerable time and effort, and the Directors shall contribute such time and effort as is necessary to complete such duties in a prudent manner.

5.3 <u>Officers</u>. The Board of Directors may delegate certain areas of responsibility to the Officers of the Company, which Officers shall be appointed by the Board of Directors. Day to day administration of the Company operations and business activities are delegated to and are the responsibility of the Officers. The acts, authority and responsibilities of the Officers are subject to the direction, guidance, discretion and authority of the Board of Directors and are further subject to the limitations set forth in Section 5.1(c). The Officers of the Company shall be a Chief Executive Officer, a President, an Executive Vice President, a Chief Financial Officer, a Vice President—Sales, and a Secretary. The duties and responsibilities of the Officers are set forth in Section 5.4. The Company may also have, at the discretion of the Board of Directors, such other officers as may be deemed necessary or appropriate, including one or more assistant officer positions. Any number of offices may be held by the same person.

(a) <u>Appointment of Officers</u>. The Officers of the Company shall be appointed by the Board of Directors, and each shall serve at the pleasure of the Board of Directors. The Officers shall each hold office for such period, have such authority and perform such duties as are set forth in this Agreement or as the Board of Directors may from time to time determine.

(b) <u>Removal and Resignation of Officers</u>. Subject to the rights, if any, of an Officer under any contract of service or employment, any Officer may be removed, either with or without cause, by the Board of Directors at any time. Any Officer may resign at any time by giving written notice to the Company. Any resignation shall take effect at the date of the receipt of that notice or at any later time specified in that notice; and, unless otherwise specified in that notice, the acceptance of the resignation shall not be necessary to make it effective. Any resignation is without prejudice to the rights, if any, of the Company under any contract to which the Officer is a party.

(c) <u>Vacancies in Offices</u>. A vacancy in any office because of death, resignation, removal, disqualification or any other cause shall be filled by the Board of Directors in the same manner prescribed in Section 5.3(a) for regular appointments to that office.

5.4 Duties of Officers.

(a) Chief Executive Officer. The Chief Executive Officer shall have responsibility for the general supervision, direction and control of the Business, Officers, and shall assume primary responsibility for strategic and financial planning, as well as overall marketing strategies of the Company. The Chief Executive Officer shall have the general powers and duties of management usually vested in the chief executive of a company, and shall have such other powers and duties as may be prescribed by the Board of Directors.

(b) President. The President shall assist the Chief Executive Officer in management of executive functions of the Company and shall have primary responsibility for sales and delivery of professional services by the Company. The President shall report to the Chief Executive Officer.

(c) Executive Vice President. The Executive Vice President shall be responsible for business development and market development activities of the Company. The Executive Vice President shall report to the Chief Executive Officer.

(d) Chief Financial Officer. The Chief Financial Officer shall have primary responsibility for proposing preliminary budgets for consideration and adoption by the Board of Directors of an Approved Budget. The Chief Financial Officer shall keep and maintain adequate and correct books and records of accounts of the properties and business transactions of the Company, including accounts of its assets, liabilities, receipts, disbursements, gains, losses, capital, retained earnings and Membership Interests. The Chief Financial Officer shall deposit all monies and other valuables in the name and to the credit of the Company with such depositaries as may be designated by the Board of Directors, shall disburse the funds of the Company as required by the Company's business activities or as may be ordered by the Board of Directors or the Chief Executive Officer, shall render to the Board of Directors, whenever they request it, an account of all transactions and of the financial condition of the Company, and shall have other powers and perform such other duties as may be prescribed by the Board of Directors.

(e) Vice President—Sales. The Vice President—Sales shall assist the President in supervision and direction of the Company's sales force, sales promotions and customer and client contacts. The Vice President—Sales shall report to the President.

(f) Secretary. The Secretary shall keep or cause to be kept, at the principal executive office or such other place as the Board of Directors may direct, records of all meeting of Members, including the notice given, the names of those present, and the proceedings. The Secretary shall also give, or cause to be given, notice of all meetings of the Members required by this Agreement or by law to be given, and shall have such other powers and perform such other duties as may be prescribed by the Board of Directors.

(g) Other Officer Positions. Any other Officer positions and titles created or appointed by the Board of Directors shall have such duties, responsibilities and authority as are assigned by the Board of Directors.

5.5 Transactions between the Company and its Directors, Officers, and Members. The Board of Directors may cause the Company to engage in transactions with its Directors, Officers and Members and/or their affiliates provided that (i) such transaction is not expressly prohibited by this Agreement, (ii) the terms and conditions of such transaction, on an overall basis, are fair and reasonable to the Company and are at least as favorable to the Company as those that are generally available from persons capable of similarly performing them, and (iii) the transaction is approved by a majority of the disinterested Directors (even if that majority is less than a majority of all the Directors), or if there are no disinterested Directors, then by a Majority Interest of all of the Members.

5.6 <u>Performance of Duties; Liability of Directors or Officers</u>. A Director or Officer shall not be liable to the Company or to any Member for any loss or damage sustained by the Company or any Member, unless the loss or damage shall have been the result of fraud, deceit, gross negligence, reckless or intentional misconduct, or a knowing violation of law by such Director or Officer. The Director or Officer shall not be personally liable under any judgment of a court, or in any other manner, for any debt, obligation or liability of the Company, whether that liability or obligation arises in contract, tort or otherwise, solely by reason of being a Director or Officer or both a Director and Officer of the Company.

5.7 <u>Indemnification</u>. The Company shall indemnify, defend and hold harmless any Director or Officer (the "Indemnified Party") who was or is a party or is threatened to be made a party to any threatened, pending or completed action, suit or proceeding, whether civil, criminal, administrative or investigative, against losses, damages, claims or expenses actually and reasonably incurred by it for which such Indemnified Party has not otherwise been reimbursed (including reasonable attorneys' fees, judgments, fines and amounts paid in settlement) in connection with such action, suit or proceeding, by reason of any acts, omissions or alleged acts or omissions arising out of the Indemnified Party's activities as a Director or Officer (or in the Director's statutory capacity as a manager of the Company) on behalf of the Company or in furtherance of the interests of the Company, so long as the Indemnified Party did not act in a manner constituting gross negligence, recklessness or willful misconduct. The termination of any action, suit or proceeding by judgment, order, settlement, or upon a plea of nolo contendere or its equivalent, shall not of itself create a presumption that the Indemnified Party's conduct constituted gross negligence, recklessness or willful misconduct.

SECTION 6
ALLOCATIONS OF NET PROFITS
AND NET LOSSES AND DISTRIBUTIONS

6.1 <u>Allocations of Net Profits and Net Losses</u>. Net Profits and Net Losses are calculated by treating all Compensation paid to Working Members either as deductible salary or wages or as a deductible "guaranteed payment" (or, if Compensation is paid through Systems, as a deductible reimbursement of cost of labor). Thus all amounts paid as Compensation are taken into account in determining Net Profits or Net Losses and thus, are not allocated under this Section 6. After determination of Net Profits or Net Losses for the Fiscal Year, allocations are to be made as follows:

(a) <u>Net Losses</u>. Net Losses for each Fiscal Year shall be allocated in the following order and priority:

(i) First, Net Losses shall be allocated among the Common Members and Working Members until the Capital Account balances of all Common Members and Working Members have been reduced to zero in the following manner: Net Losses shall be allocated among the Members within this group in proportion to their respective Percentage Interests, until the first Member's Capital Account balance is reduced to zero, at which point no further allocation shall be made to the Member or Members with zero Capital Account balances, and thereafter allocations of Net Losses shall continue in proportion to the Percentage Interests of those Members with positive Capital Accounts until the next Member's Capital Account balance is reduced to zero, and continuing in the same manner until the Capital Accounts of all Working Members and Common Members have been reduced to zero.

(ii) Thereafter, among the Members according to their respective Percentage Interests.

(b) <u>Operating Net Profits</u>. Operating Net Profits for each Fiscal Year shall be allocated in the following order and priority:

(i) First, to those Members who have received previous allocations of Net Losses under Section 6.1(a)(i) (to the extent not offset by prior allocations under this Section 6.1(b)(i) or Section 6.1(c)(i) or by adjustments to Capital Accounts pursuant to Section 3.5(b)) in the reverse order and in the same amount that Net Losses were allocated among the Members under Section 6.1(a)(i), until all allocations of Net Losses under Section 6.1(a)(i) have been entirely reversed and offset by allocations of Net Profits; and

(ii) Thereafter, any remaining Operating Net Profits shall be allocated among the Members according to their Percentage Interests.

(c) <u>Net Profits from Capital Events</u>. Net Profits from Capital Events shall be allocated in the following order and priority:

(i) First, to those Members who have received previous allocations of Net Losses under Section 6.1(a)(i) (to the extent not offset by prior allocations under this Section 6.1(b)(i) or Section 6.1(c)(i) or by adjustments to Capital Accounts pursuant to Section 3.5(b)) in the reverse order and in the same amount that Net Losses were allocated among the Members under Section 6.1(a)(i), until all allocations of Net Losses under Section 6.1(a)(i) have been entirely reversed and offset by allocations of Net Profits; and

(ii) Thereafter, any remaining Net Profits from a Capital Event shall be allocated among the Members according to their Percentage Interests.

6.2 <u>Special Allocation Rules</u>.

(a) <u>Special Allocations</u>. The Company may allocate Net Profits or Net Losses, or items of gross income, gain, expense or loss in any manner approved by the Board of Directors and all of the Members whose allocations of Net Profits or Net Losses would be affected by the Special Allocation, provided that such Special Allocation complies with the requirements of Section 704(b) of the Code. The terms of any Special Allocation adopted by the Company pursuant to this Section 6.2(a) shall be set forth on Exhibit F to this Agreement which shall be initialed by each Member required to approve such Special Allocation or otherwise documented in a manner which evidences the approval by all Members required. Any Special Allocation adopted with respect to any Fiscal Year shall be adopted not later than April 15 of the year following the close of such Fiscal Year.

(b) <u>Curative Allocations</u>. Although allocations different than those set forth in Section 6.1 are not anticipated, for federal tax purposes the Company will comply with all applicable rules set forth in Code Section 704(b) and the Regulations in the event of unanticipated economic circumstances, and in the event required by the Code or Regulations, the Board of Directors shall make such allocations as are required in a manner intended to preserve, to the extent possible, the economic terms of this Agreement, including allocations made in one Fiscal Year in order to comply with the Code and Regulations and which are reversed or offset in a later year.

6.3 <u>Code Section 704(c) Allocations</u>. Notwithstanding any other provision in this Section 6, and in accordance with Code Section 704(c) and the Regulations, income, gain, loss and deduction with respect to any property contributed to the capital of the Company shall, solely for tax purposes, be allocated among the Members so as to take account of any variation between the adjusted basis of such property to the Company for federal income tax purposes and its fair market value on the date of contribution. Similarly, allocations of taxable income, gain, loss and deduction with respect to Valuation Increases or Valuation Decreases which have previously been taken into account in the Capital Accounts of the Members for book purposes shall, when recognized for tax purposes, be allocated among the Members in a manner which will allocate income and gains ratably to those Members who have experienced Valuation Increases and will allocate tax losses and deductions ratably to those Members who have experienced prior Valuation Decreases; provided that all such allocations shall be made according to Section 704(c) of the Code and the Regulations. Allocations pursuant to this Section 6.3 are solely for purposes of federal, state and local taxes. As such, they shall not affect or in any way be taken into account in computing a Member's Capital Account or share of Net Profits, Net Losses or other items or distributions pursuant to any provision of this Agreement.

6.4 <u>Allocation with Respect to Transferred or Changed Interests</u>.

(a) <u>Common Units and Working Units</u>. In the event a Common Unit or Working Unit is transferred or changed during a Fiscal Year, Net Profits or Net Losses for such Fiscal Year shall be allocated by weighting the Percentage Interest for the number of days during the Fiscal Year each Person held the Percentage Interest. For example, if a Member is admitted with Common Units having a Percentage Interest of one percent (1%) at the midpoint of the year, his or her allocable share of Net Profits would be one-half percent (0.5%). Similarly, if a Member transfers Common Units with a Percentage Interest of two percent (2%) to an Assignee after one quarter of a Fiscal Year, the transferring Member would be allocated one-half percent (0.5%) and the transferee would be allocated one and one-half percent (1.5%) for the Fiscal Year.

(b) <u>Allocations With Respect to Forfeited Unvested Units</u>. Any Unvested Unit which is forfeited during a Fiscal Year under Section 4.4(a), regardless of when such forfeiture occurs, shall not be counted in calculating the Percentage Interest of the Member or Person who forfeited such Unvested Units for any portion of the Fiscal Year; provided, however, that to the extent that actual distributions of Distributable Cash have been made with respect to the forfeited Unvested Units prior to the Termination Event which caused the forfeiture, an amount of Net Profit equal to the amount distributed with respect to the Unvested Unit shall be allocated to such Unvested Unit.

6.5 <u>Distributions by the Company</u>.

(a) <u>Distributions of Operating Net Profits</u>. During each Fiscal Year, Distributable Cash shall first be distributed as follows:

(i) First, among the Members holding Common Units and Working Units, according to their respective Percentage Interests, provided that such distributions shall not exceed the cumulative amount of Net Profits which have not been previously distributed as of the time of distribution.

(ii) Thereafter, any distributions exceeding the limit set forth in Section 6.5(a)(i) shall be distributable as set forth in Section 6.5(b).

(b) <u>Distributions Following a Capital Event</u>. Following a Capital Event, Distributable Cash shall be distributed among the Members according to the balances of their respective Capital Accounts, which Capital Accounts shall reflect the Members' allocations of Net Profits or Net Losses from such Capital Event. Distributable Cash will then be distributed according to the adjusted Capital Account balances.

(c) <u>Tax Distributions</u>. For the purpose of funding tax liabilities of Common Members and Working Members, an amount equal to not less than forty-five percent (45%) of the Net Profits allocated among the Members pursuant to Section 6.1(b)(ii) shall be distributed among the Members within ninety (90) days following the end of the Fiscal

Year with respect to which the distribution is being made and shall be in proportion to the Percentage Interests of all such Members. All distributions made during the Fiscal Year under Section 6.5(a) shall count toward the requirement of this Section 6.5(c), excluding those distributions made during the first ninety (90) days of a Fiscal Year which relate to the prior Fiscal Year.

(d) <u>General Distribution Rules</u>.

(i) All distributions shall be made only to the Persons who, according to the books and records of the Company, are the holders of record of the Economic Interests in respect of which such distributions are made on the actual date of distribution.

(ii) The Board of Directors may, in their discretion, at the time a distribution would otherwise occur with respect to particular Working Units, treat any advances made to, or other amounts owed to the Company by Working Members as advance distributions of amounts distributable with respect to Working Units, and thus offset the amount of the distribution by all or a portion of the advances or other amounts owed to the Company.

(iii) Neither the Company nor any of the Directors or Officers shall incur any liability for making distributions according to this Section 6.5.

SECTION 7
TRANSFER AND ASSIGNMENT OF INTERESTS

7.1 <u>Transfer and Assignment of Interests</u>.

(a) No Member or holder of an Economic Interest shall be entitled to Transfer all or any part of his or her Membership Interest or any Units, except pursuant to a Permitted Transfer under Section 7.2, the Right of First Refusal procedure under Section 7.3, or the provisions of Section 7.6 relating to an Approved Sale of Units of the Company.

(b) Unvested Units shall not be subject to Transfer to any extent or under any circumstances.

7.2 <u>Permitted Transfers</u>.

(a) <u>Vested Units</u>. Notwithstanding the restriction set forth in Section 7.1, any Member may Transfer, from time to time, any or all of his or her Units (except for any Unvested Units) in any of the following circumstances: (i) with the prior approval of the Board of Directors, which approval may be given or withheld in the sole discretion of the Directors, (ii) by a Member to a Controlled Entity subject to the provisions of Section 7.2(c); or (iii) to any trust for the benefit of the Member and/or a member of a Member's immediate family (that is, the spouse and children of a Member), provided the trust is a Controlled Entity.

(b) <u>Unvested Units</u>. A Transfer of Unvested Units cannot be a Permitted Transfer under this Section 7.2, and any attempted Transfer of Unvested Units shall be void and shall constitute a Termination Event which will result in automatic forfeiture of the Unvested Units pursuant to Section 4.4(a) of this Agreement.

(c) <u>Controlled Entities</u>. A Member may Transfer a Membership Interest, including Common Units, and/or Working Units (other than Unvested Units), to a Controlled Entity, and a Member which is a Controlled Entity may Transfer a Membership Interest to its Controlling Person. A Member who holds an interest in a Controlled Entity which owns Units may transfer ownership interests in the Controlled Entity to any Person who is a member of the Transferor's immediate family (that is, the spouse, parents, siblings, and children of the Transferor) provided that the Transfer does not cause the entity to cease to be a Controlled Entity and further provided that the transferee is not a Person engaged in any Competitive Activity. Any Transfer or other action or event (whether or not such event would otherwise constitute a Termination Event) which causes an entity to cease to be a Controlled Entity shall be a Termination Event with respect to the Units or Membership Interest held by the former Controlled Entity. The Controlled Entity may transfer Units or a Membership Interest only to the Controlling Person controlling the Controlled Entity or to any other Person to whom such Controlling Person would be eligible to make a Permitted Transfer under this Section 7.2.

(d) <u>Section 8 Continues to Apply</u>. Any Units or Membership Interest subject to a Permitted Transfer shall remain subject to the provisions of Section 8 of this Agreement to the same extent and in the same manner as if the Units or Membership Interest continued to be held by the transferring Member.

(e) <u>Subscription of Transferee Required</u>. Notwithstanding the foregoing provisions of this Section 7.2, no Transfer shall qualify as a Permitted Transfer unless the Transferee executes a written subscription in the form attached to this Agreement as Exhibit C-2, agreeing to be bound by the terms of this Agreement, and in particular, the provisions of Section 8, as those terms apply to the original transferring Member. To illustrate this requirement, if a Working Member transfers Units to a trust for her child and to a Controlled Entity, in the event of a later termination of the Service Agreement of the Working Member and the Company or upon the occurrence of another Termination Event affecting the Working Member, all Units held by the child's trust, the Controlled Entity and any Units retained by the Working Member would be subject to purchase by Company as set forth in Section 8.

7.3 <u>Right of First Refusal</u>. If any Transferor receives a bona fide offer to purchase all or any part of the Transferor's Economic Interest or otherwise proposes to Transfer Units (other than Unvested Units which may not be transferred for any reason or purpose), or is required by operation of law or other involuntary transfer to do so, the Transferor shall first offer such Units to the Company in accordance with the following provisions:

(a) Transferor shall deliver a written notice (the "Option Notice") to the Company and the other Members stating (i) the Transferor's bona fide intention to transfer such Economic Interest, (ii) the Economic Interest to be transferred, (iii) the purchase price and terms of payment for which the Transferor proposes to transfer such Economic Interest, and (iv) the name and address of the proposed transferee.

(b) The Company shall have the right, but not the obligation, fully and freely assignable to any Person, to elect to purchase any share of such Economic Interest proposed to be transferred upon the price and terms of payment designated in the Option Notice. The Company shall exercise this right only with the approval of a Majority Interest of the Members other than the Transferor. The right shall be exercised, if at all, by written notice given by the Company to the Transferor and the other Members within twenty (20) days after receipt of the Option Notice. If the Option Notice provides for the payment of non-cash consideration, the Company may elect to pay the consideration in cash equal to the Board of Directors' good faith estimate of the present fair market value of the non-cash consideration. The failure of the Company to submit a notice within the applicable period set forth in this Section shall constitute an election by the Company not to purchase any of the Economic Interest which may be so transferred.

(c) If the Company elects to purchase or obtain any or all of the Economic Interest designated in the Option Notice, then the closing of such purchase shall occur within sixty (60) days after receipt of the Option Notice and the Transferor, the Company and the other Members shall execute such documents and instruments and make such deliveries as may be reasonably required to consummate such purchase.

(d) If the Company elects not to purchase or obtain, or defaults in its obligation to purchase or obtain, all of the Economic Interest designated in the Option Notice, then the Transferor may transfer the portion of the Economic Interest described in the Option Notice not so purchased, to the proposed transferee, providing such transfer (i) is completed within ninety (90) days after the date of the Option Notice, and (ii) is made on terms no less favorable to the Transferor than disclosed in the Option Notice. If such Economic Interest is not so transferred, the Transferor must give a new Option Notice in accordance with this Section or otherwise comply with Section 7.2 prior to any other or subsequent transfer of such Economic Interest.

7.4 Substitution of Members. A transferee of a Membership Interest or Economic Interest shall have the right to become a substitute Member only if such Person meets the requirements of Section 4.2 of this Agreement. The admission of a substitute Member shall not release the Member who assigned the Membership Interest from any liability that such Member may have to the Company.

7.5 Transfers in Violation of This Agreement. Any attempted transfer in violation of this Section 7 whether voluntary or involuntary, including, without limitation, transfers in connection with dissolution of marriage, or transfers as a consequence of Bankruptcy, shall be null and void and of no effect whatever. Notwithstanding the foregoing sentence, if a transfer in violation of this Section 7 is required to be recognized by a court of competent jurisdiction, the transferee shall hold an Economic Interest only and shall have no right to vote or participate in the management of the Company or to exercise any rights of a Member. Such transferee shall only be entitled to receive the share of the Company's Net Profits, Net Losses and distributions of the Company's assets to which, and at such time, as the transferor would otherwise have been entitled.

7.6 Approved Sale of Units; Sale of Assets.

(a) Notice of Sale of Units. In response to a bona fide offer of a third party to purchase not less than 50% of the outstanding Units of the Company, the Company or the Member receiving such offer shall promptly notify all Members. If such offer to purchase Units is approved by the Board of Directors and a Majority Interest of the Members (an "Approved Sale"), the Board of Directors shall provide written notice of the Approved Sale to all Members and holders of Economic Interests not less than fifteen (15) business days prior to such Approved Sale. This Section 7.6 shall not apply to issuance of Units by the Company to a new Member unless as a part of the same transaction more than 50% of the previously outstanding Units will be sold to a third party or redeemed or purchased by the Company.

(b) "Drag-Along" Right. The Company has the right to require all Members to participate in the Approved Sale and sell all or a portion of their Units (such portion to be determined by requiring each Member to sell his or her proportionate share, based on such Percentage Interest of the total Units to be sold in the Approved Sale) to the purchaser on the same terms applicable to all other Units subject to purchase. The decision to exercise this right shall be made by the Board of Directors, and notice of the decision and the number of Units to be sold by each Member or holder of an Economic Interest as well as the terms applicable to such sale shall be provided to the Members and holders of Economic Interests at least five (5) days in advance of the Approved Sale.

(c) "Tag-Along" Right. Upon receipt of a notice of an Approved Sale, each Member or holder of an Economic Interest shall have the right to participate in the Approved Sale and sell all or a portion of his or her Units (such portion to be determined by allowing each Member to sell his or her proportionate share, based on Percentage Interests, of the total Units to be sold in the Approved Sale) to the purchaser on the same terms applicable to all other Units subject to purchase. Any Member or holder of an Economic Interest shall notify the Company of his or her exercise of this right at least five (5) days prior to the date of the Approved Sale.

(d) <u>Arrangements for Unvested Units</u>. In the event of an Approved Sale or in the event of a sale by the Company of substantially all of the Business Assets, the Board of Directors are authorized to enter into binding arrangements with respect to Unvested Units, pursuant to which the consideration received by Members for such Unvested Units is subjected to vesting requirements, restrictions and contingencies similar to, but not of greater duration than, those imposed on the Unvested Units.

SECTION 8
PURCHASE RIGHTS, CONSEQUENCES OF TERMINATION EVENTS, DISSOLUTION OF MARRIAGE, AND TERMINATION OF MEMBERSHIP INTEREST

8.1 <u>Termination Event</u>.

(a) <u>Consequence of Termination Event</u>. Upon the occurrence of a Termination Event affecting a Member, the Company shall continue without dissolution or liquidation. The Company shall have the fully and freely assignable right to purchase, and if such right is exercised, the Member (or his or her successor(s) in interest or legal representative) whose actions, or circumstances resulted in the Termination Event shall sell, the Former Member's Interest as provided in this Section 8.

(b) <u>Former Member's Interest</u>. For purposes of this Section 8, and except as provided in Section 8.6, the Former Member's Interest shall include all Units held, at the time of the Termination Event, either (i) by the Member, or (ii) by any Person who received such Units as the result of a Permitted Transfer, but shall not include any Unvested Units which are forfeited immediately and automatically upon the occurrence of a Termination Event.

8.2 <u>Redemption Price</u>. The purchase price for the Company (or any assignee) to reacquire or redeem the Former Member's Interest (the "Redemption Price") shall be the aggregate Unit Values for all of the Working Units and Common Units which constitute the Former Member's Interest on the date of the Termination Event as determined as set forth on Exhibit D to this Agreement.

8.3 <u>Notice of Intent to Purchase</u>. Within thirty (30) days after the Redemption Price of the Former Member's Interest has been determined in accordance with Exhibit D, the Company shall notify the Former Member or the Former Member's successor in interest in writing of its desire to purchase all or any portion of the Former Member's Interest. The Company may assign its right to purchase under this Section 8 to any Person in whole or in part with the approval of the Board of Directors.

8.4 <u>Payment of Redemption Price</u>. The Company or the Company's assignees, as the case may be, shall pay the Redemption Price at the closing in the form of (i) cash; (ii) a full-recourse promissory note (the "Note") bearing interest at the applicable federal rate for mid term obligations (annual compounding) under Section 1274(a) of the Code in effect on the day of closing; or (iii) a combination of cash and a Note. Principal and interest on the Note shall be payable in a maximum of five (5) equal annual installments with payments commencing one year following Closing. In all cases, the Note shall be (i) prepayable without premium or penalty, and (ii) payable in full in the event of a Capital Transaction.

8.5 <u>Closing of Purchase of Former Member's Interest</u>. The closing of sale and purchase of a Former Member's Interest pursuant to this Section 8 shall be held at the principal office of Company no later than sixty (60) days after the determination of the Redemption Price, except that if the closing date falls on a Saturday, Sunday, or [Delaware] legal holiday, then the closing shall be held on the next succeeding business day. At the closing, the Former Member shall deliver to the Company an instrument of transfer (containing warranties of title and no encumbrances) conveying the Former Member's Interest to the Company or to the Person or Persons exercising the Company's rights under this Section 8. The Former Member and the Company shall do all things and execute and deliver all papers as may be reasonably necessary to consummate such sale and purchase in accordance with the terms and provisions of this Agreement.

8.6 <u>Insurance Funded Payment of Purchase Price</u>.

(a) In the event the Company owns Buy-Out Insurance with respect to a Former Member, in the event the Termination Event of the Former Member results from the death of the Former Member, in addition to the right to purchase the Former Member's Interest provided under Section 8.1, the Company shall have the obligation to purchase the Former Member's Interest pursuant to the terms of this Section 8 to the extent the Redemption Price can be funded with the proceeds of the Buy-Out Insurance covering the Former Member. The Company's obligation shall apply only to that portion of the Former Member's Interest which can be purchased with the proceeds of the Buy-Out Insurance, and any remaining portion of the Former Member's Interest shall be subject to purchase under the normal provisions of this Section 8 as if this Section 8.6 did not apply. If the proceeds of the Buy-Out Insurance are received by the Company before the closing of the purchase, then, notwithstanding Section 8.4, the Redemption Price shall be paid in cash to the extent of the proceeds of the Buy-Out Insurance. If the proceeds of the Buy-Out Insurance have not been received as of the date of closing, then the Redemption Price may be paid in any manner permitted under Section 8.4, provided that within ten (10) days after receipt of the proceeds of the Buy-Out Insurance, to the extent of any outstanding balance due under any Note used to pay the Repurchase Price, such insurance proceeds shall be applied to prepay the Note.

(b) In the event the Termination Event of a Former Member results from any event other than death and the Company chooses to continue the Buy-Out Insurance during the term a Note issued in payment of the Redemption Price remains outstanding, then, upon the later death of the Former Member, within ten (10) days after receipt of the proceeds of the Buy-Out Insurance, to the extent of any outstanding balance due under any Note used to pay the Repurchase Price, such insurance proceeds shall be applied to prepay such Note.

8.7 <u>Dissolution of Marriage</u>.

(a) Any Membership Interest subject to transfer, disposition or allocation in connection with a marital settlement agreement, legal separation, dissolution of marriage, annulment of marriage or similar procedure (a "Marital Dissolution"), as to assets and property, community or separate, of any Member, shall be allocated in the property division to the extent possible to the Member and not the Member's spouse (the "Former Spouse"). If, however, a Former Spouse receives, retains or is awarded any Membership Interest (which shall become an Economic Interest in the hands of the Former Spouse), the Member shall promptly give notice thereof to the Company, and the Company shall have the right to purchase, and the Former Spouse shall have the obligation to sell, such Former Spouse's Economic Interest as provided in this Section 8.7.

(b) In the event of a Marital Dissolution, the Member involved in the Marital Dissolution shall have the option, exercisable for a period of ninety (90) days following Marital Dissolution (or the transfer of the Membership Interest or Economic Interest pursuant to the Marital Dissolution, if later), to purchase any or all of the Former Spouse's Economic Interest at the price and terms provided in this Section 8.7.

(c) If, for any reason, the Member does not exercise the option to purchase all of the Former Spouse's Economic Interest within ninety (90) days after the Marital Dissolution (or the transfer of the Economic Interest pursuant to the Marital Dissolution, if later), the Member shall promptly give notice of such fact to the Company. The Company shall have the assignable option, exercisable at any time thereafter, to purchase and redeem any or all of the Former Spouse's Economic Interest at the price and on the terms provided in this Section 8.7.

(d) A purchase of the Economic Interest of a Former Spouse pursuant to this Section 8.7 shall be initiated by the Company or the Member or other Person exercising the Company's right as assignee by providing a notice of intent to purchase to the Board of Directors and the Former Spouse. Within thirty (30) days following the determination of the Redemption Price pursuant to Section 8.7(e), the Company or Person who filed the notice of intent to purchase shall, by written notice to the Former Spouse, either confirm or withdraw such notice. If the notice of intent to purchase is confirmed, the closing for the sale of the Former Spouse's Economic Interest shall be held pursuant to the procedure for closing of sale of a Former Member's Interest under Sections 8.4 and 8.5 of this Agreement.

(e) The purchase price of a Former Spouse's Economic Interest shall be determined pursuant to the method for determination of the Redemption Price set forth in Section 8.2; provided that the determination of the Redemption Price shall be initiated by a notice of intent to purchase and all deadlines shall be measured from the date of such notice rather than from the notice of a Termination Event; and, further provided that the Redemption Price shall be determined as of the Marital Dissolution, unless the notice of intent to purchase is given more than 180 days after the Marital Dissolution, in which event, the determination shall be made as of the date notice of intent to purchase is given.

(f) If the Company and the Member who has experienced the Marital Dissolution collectively do not exercise their option as to all of the Former Spouse's Economic Interest, then the Former Spouse shall continue to hold the unpurchased portions solely as an Economic Interest subject to the provisions of this Agreement, including the terms of Section 7.4 which sets forth conditions on the right of the Former Spouse to become a substitute Member.

SECTION 9
CONFIDENTIALITY, WORK PRODUCT, NONCOMPETITION

9.1 <u>Confidential Information</u>. The Members agree that all Confidential Information is the sole property of the Company and that at all times, both during and after such time as a Member continues to hold a Membership Interest or an Economic Interest, they will keep in confidence and trust all Confidential Information, and will not use or disclose any Confidential Information to any other Person without the written consent of the Company, except as may be necessary in the ordinary course of performing their duties as a Member, Director and/or Officer of the Company.

9.2 <u>Competitive Activities</u>.

(a) <u>Non-Competition</u>. Each Member hereby agrees that, while a Member of the Company, such Member (including the Member's Controlled Entities, Controlling Person, shareholders, employees, and agents) will not, without the express written consent of the Company, directly or indirectly, anywhere in the United States engage in any business (whether as owner, part-owner, shareholder, member, partner, director, officer, trustee, employee, agent, advisor or consultant, or in any other capacity), other than the Company's Business, whose business, activities, products or services are directly competitive with the Business. Each Member further agrees that, if the Company repurchases the Member's Membership Interest as provided in Section 8, the foregoing non-competition agreement shall automatically be extended with respect to activities included in the Business at the time of such repurchase as well as any line of business which the Company has actively pursued (as evidenced by written plans, management committee consideration, commitment of staff, capital investment, market research or negotiations with clients and/or prospective partners) within two (2) years prior to the date of repurchase as follows: (i) for a period of two (2) years from the date of repurchase under Section 8 with respect to all of the Company's Business in the Target Market; and (ii) for a period of one (1) year from the date of repurchase under Section 8 with respect to all of the Company's other Business activities. Notwithstanding anything herein to the contrary, a Member may make passive investments in any enterprise the shares of which are publicly traded if such investment constitutes less than one percent (1%) of the equity of such enterprise.

(b) <u>Non-Solicitation</u>. Each Member agrees that such Member (including the Member's Controlled Entities, Controlling Person, shareholders, employees, and agents) will not, while a Member of the Company and for a period of one (1) year thereafter, directly or indirectly solicit, recruit, induce, or take away any Officer, employee, supplier, customer, or client of the Company or its direct or indirect subsidiaries or affiliates, either for the Member's direct benefit or for the benefit of any other Person. This one-year period shall be tolled for any time period in which a former Member (including its Controlled Entities, Controlling Person, shareholders, employers and agents) is in violation of this provision.

(c) <u>Limitation</u>. The prohibition on competitive activity set forth in Section 9.2(a) shall not apply to a Working Member who ceases to be a Working Member by reason of his or her removal, expulsion or involuntary termination of status unless such removal, expulsion or involuntary termination is for Cause.

(d) <u>Further Limitations</u>. Except as set forth in Section 9.2(a), and subject to the requirements of any Service Agreement between the Company and a Member, Members may engage in whatever activities they choose, without having or incurring any obligation to offer any interest in such activities to the Company and without incurring any liability to any other Member or the Company for any lost opportunity.

9.3 <u>Work Product</u>.

(a) <u>Ownership of Work Product</u>. All Work Product shall be the sole property of the Company whether as "Works for Hire" or otherwise and each Member hereby assigns to Company all of such Member's right, title and interest in and to such Work Product, including patent rights, copyrights and trade secrets. Company shall have full title to and full ownership of the Work Product developed by a Working Member, either alone or with others (whether or not any such persons are employees or consultants to Company). Company may copyright, patent, license, sublicense, transfer, commercialize, exploit or otherwise dispose of the Work Product, or any aspect, version or part thereof.

(b) <u>Disclosure to Company</u>. A Member shall disclose promptly and in writing to Company all Work Product created or discovered by such Member in the course of delivering services to the Company, which such Member, alone or with others, whether or not such others are employees or consultants to the Company, conceives or makes within the scope of this Agreement, and will not disclose any such Work Product to others, except as required by the Company. Any records maintained by the Member relating to the Work Product are the product of the Company and shall be available to the inspection of the Company upon request. Upon termination of such Working Member's services with the Company or termination of such Member's Membership Interest, all such records shall be delivered to the Company, subject to the Member's right to copy such materials which are not Work Product or which the Company consents to permit in writing.

9.4 <u>Survival</u>. The provisions of this Agreement and obligations of the Members relating to Confidential Information, Competitive Activities and Work Product as set forth in this Section 9 shall survive the resignation, withdrawal or termination of a Director or Member.

SECTION 10
ACCOUNTING, RECORDS, REPORTING BY MEMBERS

10.1 <u>Books and Records</u>.

(a) <u>General</u>. The books and records of the Company shall be kept at its principal office, and the financial position and the results of its operations recorded, in accordance with the accounting methods followed for federal income tax purposes. The books and records of the Company shall reflect all the Company transactions and shall be appropriate and adequate for the Company's business.

(b) <u>Member and Director Information</u>. The names and addresses of Members and Board of Directors, and all information regarding Capital Contributions, Units, and Percentage Interests initially reflected on Exhibit A to this Agreement, and all changes or updates to such identifying and ownership information including, without limitation, admission of new Members, issues of Common Units or Working Units, Additional Capital Contributions and Transfers of Units shall be maintained and updated by the Company in an updated form of Exhibit A to this Agreement, or, at the discretion of the Board of Directors, in a form from which a report or reports can be issued setting forth the information initially presented in Exhibit A in a reasonably up-to-date form.

10.2 <u>Inspection Rights</u>.

(a) <u>Inspection Rights of Directors</u>. The Directors individually shall have the right to examine any and all of the information, books and records of the Company including all documents contemplated by or described in this Agreement, including all documents, books and records described in Section 10.1 for a purpose reasonably related to the Director's rights and duties under this Agreement.

(b) <u>Limited Inspection Rights of Members</u>. The Board of Directors and Officers shall have the rights to keep confidential from the Members, for such periods as the Board of Directors deem reasonable, any information which the Board of Directors reasonably believes to be a trade secret or in the nature of a trade secret or other information, the disclosure of which the Board of Directors in good faith believe would damage the Company, the Business, or which the Company is required by law or under contract to keep confidential.

Furthermore, the rights of Members to review the books and records of the Company and receive information regarding the Company shall be strictly limited to (i) an annual balance sheet and income statement for the Company, (ii) tax information required to be distributed to Members under Section 10.3, and (iii) such other information as the Board of Directors choose to disseminate to the Members from time to time; provided that notwithstanding the foregoing restrictions, it is the Board of Directors' intent to provide sufficient information to Members to permit the Members to make informed decisions on any matter subject to the vote, consent or approval of the particular class of Member.

(c) Subject to Section 10.2(b), upon the request of any Member, for purposes reasonably related to the interest of that Member, the Officers of the Company shall promptly deliver to the requesting Member, at the expense of the requesting Member, a copy of any of the information required to be maintained under Section 10.1.

(d) Subject to Section 10.2(b), each Member may request to inspect and copy during normal business hours (i) any of the Company records described in Section 10.1, and (ii) promptly after their becoming available, a copy of the Company's federal, state, and local income tax or information returns for each Fiscal Year. The Board of Directors shall cause the Company to respond to such request as promptly as practical (but in no event in less than five (5) business days), and, in their discretion, may, pursuant to Section 10.2(b), permit access to all or some portion of the books and records requested or deny the request.

(e) Any request for inspection by a Member under this Section 10.2 may be made by that Person or that Person's agent or attorney.

10.3 <u>Annual Statements</u>.

(a) The Chief Financial Officer, at Company expense, shall cause to be prepared at least annually, at Company expense, information necessary for the preparation of the Members' federal and state income tax returns. The Board of Directors or Officers shall send or cause to be sent to each Member within ninety (90) days after the end of each taxable year such information as is necessary to complete federal, state and international income tax or information returns.

(b) The Board of Directors, at Company expense, shall cause to be filed at least annually the information required by the Delaware Secretary of State. The Board of Directors also shall cause to be filed on a timely basis any other information required to be filed with a state in which the Company is doing business.

10.4 <u>Filings</u>. The Chief Financial Officer, at Company expense, shall cause the income tax returns for the Company to be prepared and timely filed with the appropriate authorities. The Chief Financial Officer, at Company expense, shall also cause to be prepared and timely filed, with appropriate federal and state regulatory and administrative bodies, amendments to, or restatements of, the Certificate and all reports required to be filed by the Company with those entities under the Act or other then current applicable laws, rules, and regulations. If a Director required by the Act to execute or file any document fails, after demand, to do so within a reasonable period of time or refuses to do so, any other Director or Member may prepare, execute and file that document with the Delaware Secretary of State.

10.5 <u>Bank Accounts</u>. The Chief Financial Officer shall maintain the funds of the Company in one or more separate bank accounts in the name of the Company, and, except as expressly permitted in this Agreement, shall not permit the funds of the Company to be commingled in any fashion with the funds of any other Person.

10.6 <u>Accounting Decisions and Reliance on Others</u>. All decisions as to accounting matters, except as otherwise specifically set forth herein, shall be made by the Chief Financial Officer. The Chief Financial Officer may rely upon the advice of the Company's accountants as to whether such decisions are in accordance with accounting methods followed for federal income tax purposes.

10.7 <u>Tax Matters for the Company</u>. The Chief Financial Officer shall act as the Tax Matters Partner pursuant to Section 6231 of the Code, and in such capacity shall from time to time cause the Company to make such tax elections as it deems to be in the best interests of the Company and the Members. The Tax Matters Partner shall represent the Company, at the Company's expense, in connection with all examinations of the Company's affairs by tax authorities, including resulting judicial and administrative proceedings, and shall expend the Company funds for professional services and costs associated therewith.

SECTION 11
DISSOLUTION AND WINDING UP

11.1 <u>Dissolution</u>. The Company shall be dissolved, its assets shall be disposed of, and its affairs wound up on the first to occur of the following:

(a) The entry of a decree of judicial dissolution;

(b) The vote or approval of the Board of Directors and approval of a Majority Interest of the Members;

(c) The sale of all or substantially all of the Business Assets.

11.2 <u>Winding Up</u>. Upon the occurrence of any event specified in Section 11.1, the Company shall continue solely for the purpose of winding up its affairs in an orderly manner, liquidating its assets, and satisfying the claims of its creditors. The Board of Directors (or, if none, the Members) shall be responsible for overseeing the winding up and liquidation of Company, shall take full account of the liabilities of Company and assets, shall either cause its assets to be sold or distributed, and if sold as promptly as is consistent with obtaining the fair market value thereof, shall cause the proceeds therefrom, to the extent sufficient therefor, to be applied and distributed as provided in Section 11.4. The Directors or Members winding up the affairs of the Company shall not be entitled to compensation for such services, other than Compensation provided under the Service Agreements, if any, of such Directors or Members.

11.3 <u>Distributions in Kind</u>. Any non-cash asset distributed to one or more Members shall first be valued at its fair market value to determine the Net Profits or Net Losses that would have resulted if such asset were sold for such value, such Net Profits or Net Losses shall then be allocated pursuant to Section 6, and the Members' Capital Accounts shall be adjusted to reflect such allocations. The amount distributed and charged to the Capital Account of each Member receiving an interest in such distributed asset shall be the fair market value of such interest (net of any liability secured by such asset that such Member assumes or takes subject to). The fair market value of such asset shall be determined by the Board of Directors, or if none, by a Majority Interest of the Members.

11.4 <u>Order of Payment Upon Dissolution</u>. After determining that all the known debts and liabilities of the Company, including without limitation, debts and liabilities to Members who are creditors of the Company, have been paid or adequately provided for, the remaining assets shall be distributed to the Members in proportion to the positive balances of their respective Capital Accounts.

11.5 <u>Limitations on Payments Made in Dissolution</u>. Except as otherwise specifically provided in this Agreement, each Member shall only be entitled to look solely at the assets of the Company for the return of his or her positive Capital Account balance and shall have no recourse for his or her Capital Contribution and/or share of Net Profits (upon dissolution or otherwise) against the Directors or any other Member.

11.6 <u>Certificate of Cancellation</u>. The Board of Directors, or if none, the Members, shall cause to be filed in the office of, and on a form prescribed by, the Delaware Secretary of State, a Certificate of Cancellation upon the completion of the winding up of the affairs of the Company.

11.7 <u>No Action for Dissolution</u>. Except as expressly permitted in this Agreement, a Member shall not take any voluntary action seeking dissolution of the Company. The Members acknowledge that irreparable damage would be done to the goodwill and reputation of the Company if any Member should bring an action in court to dissolve the Company under circumstances where dissolution is not required by Section

11.1. This Agreement has been drawn carefully to provide fair treatment of all parties and equitable payment in liquidation of the Economic Interests. Accordingly, except where the Board of Directors or Members have failed to liquidate the Company as required by this Section 11, each Member hereby waives and renounces his or her right to initiate legal action to seek the appointment of a receiver or trustee to liquidate the Company or to seek a decree of judicial dissolution of the Company.

SECTION 12
MISCELLANEOUS

12.1 <u>Complete Agreement</u>. This Agreement and the Certificate of Formation constitute the complete and exclusive statement of agreement among the Members with respect to the subject matter herein and replace and supersede all prior written and oral agreements or statements by and among the Members or any of them, except to the extent such terms are set forth in the Service Agreements. The Service Agreements incorporate all of the provisions of this Agreement, but constitute separate agreements establishing terms for the specific relationship between the Company and each of the individual Working Members.

12.2 <u>Binding Effect</u>. Subject to the provisions of this Agreement relating to transferability, this Agreement will be binding upon and inure to the benefit of the Members and their respective successors and assigns.

12.3 <u>Parties in Interest</u>. Except as expressly provided in the Act, nothing in this Agreement shall confer any rights or remedies under or by reason of this Agreement on any Persons other than the Members and their respective successors and assigns nor shall anything in this Agreement relieve or discharge the obligation or liability of any third person to any party to this Agreement, nor shall any provision give any third person any right of subrogation or action over or against any party to this Agreement.

12.4 <u>Pronouns; Statutory References</u>. All pronouns and all variations thereof shall be deemed to refer to the masculine, feminine, or neuter, singular or plural, as the context in which they are used may require. Any reference to the Code, the Regulations, the Act, or other statutes or laws will include all amendments, modifications, or replacements of the specific sections and provisions concerned.

12.5 <u>Headings</u>. All headings herein are inserted only for convenience and ease of reference and are not to be considered in the construction or interpretation of any provision of this Agreement.

12.6 <u>Choice of Law; Jurisdiction</u>. This Agreement shall be construed and enforced in accordance with the laws of the State of [Delaware]. Each Member hereby consents to the exclusive jurisdiction of the state and federal courts sitting in _____, [Delaware] in any action on a claim arising out of, under or in connection with this Agreement or the transactions contemplated by this Agreement, provided such claim is not required to be arbitrated pursuant to Section 12.7. Each Member further agrees that personal jurisdiction over him or her may be effected by service of process by registered or certified mail addressed as provided in Section 12.11 of this Agreement, and that when so made shall be as if served upon him or her personally.

12.7 <u>Mediation and Arbitration</u>. Except as otherwise provided in this Agreement, any controversy or claim arising out of or relating to this Agreement or the breach thereof shall be settled by mediation, or by arbitration before a single arbitrator in San Francisco, California.

(a) <u>Mediation</u>. The parties shall, before the commencement of arbitration proceedings, attempt in good faith to settle their dispute by mediation.

(b) <u>Arbitration</u>. Any matter not settled by mediation shall be submitted to the American Arbitration Association for final and binding arbitration in San Francisco, California. The costs of the arbitration, including any American Arbitration Association administration fee, the arbitrator's fee, and costs for the use of facilities during the hearings, shall be borne equally by the parties to the arbitration. Attorneys' fees shall be awarded to the prevailing or most prevailing party as determined by the arbitrator. The provisions of the Commercial Arbitration Rules of the American Arbitration Association shall apply to the arbitration. The arbitrator shall not have any power to alter, amend, modify or change any of the terms of this Agreement nor to grant any remedy which is either prohibited by the terms of this Agreement, or not available in a court of law.

12.8 <u>Exhibits</u>. All Exhibits attached to this Agreement are incorporated and shall be treated as if set forth herein.

12.9 <u>Severability</u>. If any provision of this Agreement or the application of such provision to any person or circumstance shall be held invalid, the remainder of this Agreement or the application of such provision to persons or circumstances other than those to which it is held invalid shall not be affected thereby.

12.10 <u>Additional Documents and Acts</u>. Each Member agrees to execute and deliver such additional documents and instruments and to perform such additional acts as may be necessary or appropriate to effectuate, carry out and perform all of the terms, provisions and conditions of this Agreement and the transactions contemplated hereby.

12.11 <u>Notices</u>. Any notice to be given or to be served upon the Company or any party hereto in connection with this Agreement must be in writing (which may include facsimile and email) and will be deemed to have been given and received when delivered to the address specified by the party to receive the notice. Such notices will be given to a Member at the address specified in Exhibit A hereto. Any party may, at any time by giving five (5) days' prior written notice to the other parties, designate any other address in substitution of the foregoing address to which such notice is to be given.

12.12 <u>Amendments</u>. This Agreement may not be amended except by a written instrument adopted by the Board of Directors and approved by a Majority Interest of the Members.

12.13 <u>No Interest in Company Property; Waiver of Action for Partition</u>. No Member or Assignee has any interest in specific property or Business Assets of the Company. Without limiting the foregoing, each Member and Assignee irrevocably waives during the term of the Company any right that he or she may have to maintain any action for partition with respect to the property or Business Assets of the Company.

12.14 <u>Attorney Fees</u>. In the event that any dispute between the Company and the Members or among the Members arising out of or related to this Agreement should result in litigation or arbitration, the prevailing party in such dispute shall be entitled to recover from the other party all reasonable fees, costs and expenses of enforcing any right of the prevailing party, including without limitation, reasonable attorneys' fees and expenses, all of which shall be deemed to have accrued upon the commencement of such action and shall be paid whether or not such action is prosecuted to judgment. Any judgment or order entered in such action shall contain a specific provision providing for the recovery of attorney fees and costs incurred in enforcing such judgment and an award of prejudgment interest from the date of the breach at the maximum rate of interest allowed by law.

All of the Members of ****, LLC, a Delaware limited liability company, have executed this Operating Agreement, effective as of the date written above.

MEMBERS:

_____

Name: _____

_____

Name: _____

_____

Name: _____

_____

Name: _____

EXHIBIT A

CAPITAL CONTRIBUTIONS, NAMES
AND ADDRESSES
OF MEMBERS AND DIRECTORS
_____, 20___

Member's Name and Address	Capital Units Contribution	Units Number	Units Type & Class	Units or Threshold Value When Issued
_____	$_____	_____	_____	_____
_____				
_____	$_____	_____	_____	_____
_____				
_____	$_____	_____	_____	_____
_____				
_____	$_____	_____	_____	_____
_____				
_____				

Initial Directors (Managers)   **Officers**

_____   _____
_____   _____
_____   _____
_____   _____

EXHIBIT B

UNIT CERTIFICATE
CLASS _ WORKING UNITS
CERTIFICATE NO. _____   _____ UNITS

****, LLC
A Delaware Limited Liability Company
Formed on _____, 20___

    This certifies that _____ is a Member of ****, LLC and is the registered holder of _____ (_____) Class _ Working Units of equity ownership of ****, LLC, transferable only on the books of the Company.

    The Membership Interest in the Company represented by this Certificate and the rights of the holder as a Member of the Company are determined by the terms of the Company's Certificate of Formation filed with the Delaware Secretary of State, the Operating Agreement of the Company, and the Delaware Limited Liability Company Act (Del. Code Title 6, Section 18-101, et seq.) as such instruments and acts may be amended. The Units represented hereby are transferable only as permitted in the Company's Operating Agreement. THE UNITS REPRESENTED HEREBY ARE FURTHER SUBJECT TO ANY VESTING RESTRICTIONS SET FORTH ON THE REVERSE SIDE OF THIS CERTIFICATE, AND ANY UNITS WHICH ARE "UNVESTED UNITS" UNDER THOSE VESTING RESTRICTIONS MAY BE FORFEITED UNDER CERTAIN CIRCUMSTANCES SET FORTH IN THE COMPANY'S OPERATING AGREEMENT.

    This Unit Certificate is issued as of this _____ day of _____, 20___ and is effective only if two copies are countersigned by the holder and one is returned to the Company within thirty (30) days after issuance.

SUBSCRIPTION

I wish to acquire the Membership Interest and Units in ****, LLC as set forth on this Certificate. I have read the Operating Agreement of the Company, and I know and understand the terms of the Operating Agreement including those terms relating to the Vesting Restrictions on any Unvested Shares. I hereby subscribe to the Operating Agreement and agree to abide by and be subject to all of the terms and provisions of the Operating Agreement. I agree that my Membership Interest and Units are subject to the terms of the Operating Agreement, and I further agree and acknowledge that my Units are subject to any Vesting Restrictions set forth on the reverse of this Certificate.

Signed: _____

Name: _____

VESTING RESTRICTIONS
(Standard—Subject to Board Discretion)
(WORKING MEMBERS)

_____ (_____) of the Units represented by this Certificate are Unvested Units, subject to all restrictions on Units under the Company's Operating Agreement, including, without limitation, those Vesting Restrictions imposed on Unvested Units by the Board of Directors.

Subject to the terms of the Operating Agreement, _____ (_____) Units (25% of the total Unvested Units represented by this Certificate) will convert from Unvested Units into Vested Units, automatically and without further action, on _____, 20___ and thereafter, on a quarterly basis on the, an additional _____ (_____) Units (6.25% of the total Unvested Units) will convert from Unvested Units into Vested Units. Unless earlier cancelled under the terms of the Operating Agreement, on an after _____, 20___ all Units represented by this Certificate will be Vested Units.

EXHIBIT C-1
(Member Form)

SUBSCRIPTION AGREEMENT
****, LLC

A Delaware Limited Liability Company
Formed on _____, 20____

I wish to become a Member of ****, LLC, a Delaware Limited Liability Company (the "Company"). I have read the Operating Agreement of the Company, and I know and understand its terms. I hereby subscribe to the Operating Agreement and agree to abide by and be subject to all of the terms and provisions of the Operating Agreement and agree that my Membership Interest is subject to the provisions of the Operating Agreement.

I understand that investing in the Company involves a high degree of risk, including the risk of losing all or a substantial portion of my Capital Contribution. I have such financial and business knowledge and experience that I am capable of evaluating the risks and merits of this investment, and I have had an opportunity to ask any questions and obtain any additional information desired concerning the Company prior to making a Capital Contribution. I also understand that no federal or state agency has made any determination as to the fairness of the investment or has recommended it.

Date: _____

Signed:_____

Name: _____

AGREED TO AND ACCEPTED ON BEHALF OF ****, LLC:

Date: _____

****, LLC,

By: _____

Name: _____,
Chief Executive Officer

315

EXHIBIT C-2
(Permitted Transferee Form)

SUBSCRIPTION AGREEMENT

****, LLC

A Delaware Limited Liability Company
Formed on _____, 20____

I wish to become a Member of ****, LLC, a Delaware Limited Liability Company (the "Company"). I have read the Operating Agreement of the Company, and I know and understand its terms. I hereby subscribe to the Operating Agreement and agree to abide by and be subject to all of the terms and provisions of the Operating Agreement and agree that my Membership Interest is subject to the provisions of the Operating Agreement.

I understand that as a Permitted Transferee of Working Units, the Units represented by this Certificate are subject to forfeiture or repurchase by the Company in the event of a Termination Event affecting the Transferor.

Date: _____

Signed:_____

Name: _____

AGREED TO AND ACCEPTED ON BEHALF OF ****, LLC:

Date: _____

****, LLC,

By: _____

Name: _____,
Chief Executive Officer

317

EXHIBIT D

DETERMINATION OF COMPANY
VALUATION, UNIT VALUE, AND
REDEMPTION PRICE

1. <u>Unit Values</u>. Unit Value is determined by treating the Company Valuation as of a particular date as the cash distributable upon liquidation of the Company after payment of all creditors and then determining the amount which would be distributable to each type and Class of Unit (Common Unit, Working Units). For purposes of determining Unit Values, Units subject to options or conversion or similar rights shall be treated as outstanding only if the Unit Value for the Units subject to the option or conversion right is higher than the exercise or conversion price, and the option exercise or conversion price shall be taken into account as an amount paid for the Units. Working Units will always have a lower Unit Value than either Common Units.

2. <u>Company Valuation</u>. The formula and procedure for determining the Company Valuation will differ for purposes of issuing Units as compared to the repurchase or redemption of Units under Section 8 of this Agreement.

(a) <u>Upon Issuance of Units</u>. Upon issuance of Units, the Company Valuation shall be established in the discretion of the Board of Directors, based upon its good faith determination, taking into account the full going concern value and earnings potential of the Company. Any Valuation Increase or Valuation Decrease shall be based upon determination of Company Valuation in connection with and in the same manner as in the issuance of Units, taking into account the full going concern value and future prospects of the Company.

(b) <u>Determination of Company Valuation and Redemption Price of Units Upon Repurchase or Redemption of Units</u>. The Company Valuation upon repurchase or redemption of Units under Section 8 of this Agreement entails valuation of a liquidation value for the Company in that the selling Former Member will not realize the full going concern value or value to be derived from future prospects of the Company. In the event of a repurchase under Section 8 of this Agreement, the Company Valuation and Redemption Price shall be determined within seventy-five (75) days following receipt of actual notice of the Termination Event.

EXHIBIT E

DESCRIPTION OF SERIES

EXHIBIT F

SPECIAL ALLOCATIONS

1. Any expense or deduction arising as the result of issuance of Common Units to a Common Member shall be specially Allocated to that Common Member.

2. Proceeds from Buy-Out Insurance and Key Person Insurance are allocated to Members other than the Covered Member.

Member Initials:

_____   _____   _____   _____

CONSENT OF SPOUSE

The undersigned is the spouse of a party to the Operating Agreement (the "Agreement") of ****, LLC (the "Company"). I acknowledge and agree as follows: I have read the Agreement and I understand its contents. I am aware that under terms of the Agreement, in the event my spouse terminates his or her relationship with the Company, my spouse grants the Company and/or the other Members an option to purchase all of Membership Interest, including my community property interest (if any) in the Membership Interest, or any Economic Interest that I may have received from my spouse through a Transfer. I understand that under certain circumstances, this option may subject an Economic Interest I may hold to repurchase at a formula price determined under the Agreement.

I hereby consent to the provisions of the Agreement that could potentially apply to me as a spouse or Economic Interest holder. I agree that the Membership Interest held by my spouse and my Economic Interest in it are subject to the provisions of the Agreement and that I will take no action at any time to hinder operation of the Agreement on such Membership Interest or my Economic Interest.

Date: _____

Signed: _____

Name: _____

Form 7 K: Operating Agreement— Nevada Manager-Managed

OPERATING AGREEMENT OF
****, LLC,
A NEVADA LIMITED LIABILITY COMPANY

THIS OPERATING AGREEMENT is made as of the _____ day of _____, 20___, by and among the members of ****, LLC, a Nevada limited liability company (the "Company"), all of whom have signed this operating agreement.

NOW THEREFORE, pursuant to the Act (as hereinafter defined), the following agreement, including, without limitation, Appendix 1 (Tax Accounting Procedures), and Appendix 2 (Articles of Organization) attached hereto and by reference incorporated herein shall constitute the operating agreement, as amended from time to time, for the Company.

ARTICLE 1
DEFINITIONS

1.1. <u>General Definitions</u>. The following terms used in this Operating Agreement shall have the following meanings (unless otherwise expressly provided herein). Other capitalized terms used herein have the meanings set forth in Section 1.1 (Tax Definitions) of Appendix 1 (Tax Accounting Procedures).

"Act" means the Nevada Limited Liability Company Act, Nev. Rev. Stat. §§ 86.011 to 86.590, as amended from time to time.

"Affiliate" means a Person that directly, or indirectly through one or more intermediaries, controls, is controlled by, or is under common control with, a specified Person. For the purpose of this definition, the term "control" shall mean the possession, direct or indirect, of the power to direct or cause the direction of the management and policies of a Person, whether through the ownership of voting securities, by contract or otherwise.

"Agreement" shall mean this Operating Agreement, including Appendix 1 (Tax Accounting Procedures) and Appendix 2 (Articles of Organization) hereto as originally executed and as amended from time to time.

"Business Day" shall mean a day other than a Saturday, a Sunday, or a state or federally recognized holiday on which banks in Nevada are permitted to close.

"Business Hours" shall mean 8:00 A.M. to 5:00 P.M. Standard Time or Daylight Time, as the case may be, at a location specified in this Agreement. If no location is specified, a reference to Business Hours shall refer to Business Hours as determined by Pacific Standard Time or Pacific Daylight Time, as the case may be.

"Capital Contribution" means the Initial Capital Contribution of a Member together with the amount of money and the fair market value (as determined by the Manager as of the date of contribution) of other property contributed, or services rendered or to be rendered, to the Company by a Member with respect to such Membership Interest in the Company.

"Code" shall mean the Internal Revenue Code of 1986 or corresponding provisions of subsequent superceding federal revenue laws.

"Company" shall refer to ****, LLC, a Nevada limited liability company.

"Entity" shall mean any general partnership, government entity, limited partnership, limited liability company, corporation, joint venture, trust, business trust, cooperative, association or similar organization.

"Fiscal Year" shall mean the taxable year of the Company for federal income tax purposes as determined by Code Section 706 and the Regulations thereunder.

"Initial Capital Contribution" means the Capital Contributions agreed to be made by the initial Members as described in Section 5.1.

"Manager" shall mean one or more Managers. Specifically, "Manager" shall mean the initial Manager designated by this Agreement, or any other Persons that succeed such Manager in that capacity. References to a Manager in the singular or as him, her, it, itself, or other like references shall also, where the context so requires, be deemed to include the plural or the masculine or feminine references or as the case may be.

"Managing Person" shall mean a Manager, officer, director, or their agents.

"Member" shall mean those Persons executing this Agreement and any Person who may hereafter become an additional or Substitute Member.

"Membership Interest" means a Member's Units, and the associated right to vote on or participate in management, the right to share in Profits, Losses, and distributions, and any and all benefits to which the holder of such Units may be entitled pursuant to this Agreement, together with all obligations to comply with the terms and provisions of this Agreement.

"Net Cash Flow" means the gross cash proceeds from Company operations (including all sales and dispositions of Property) less the portion thereof used to pay or establish reserves for all Company expenses, debt payments, capital improvements, replacements, and contingencies, all as determined by the Manager. Net Cash Flow shall not be reduced by depreciation, amortization, cost recovery deductions or similar allowances, but shall be increased by any reductions of reserves.

"Person" shall mean any individual or Entity, and the heirs, executors, administrators, legal representatives, successors, and assigns of such Person where the context so requires.

"Property" means all real and personal property, tangible and intangible, owned by the Company.

"Regulations" means the federal income tax regulations, including temporary (but not proposed) regulations promulgated under the Code.

"Substitute Member" means a transferee of a Membership Interest who has been admitted to all of the rights of membership pursuant to Article 11.

"Voting Units" or "Units" as to any Member shall mean and refer to Units which entitle the holder to cast one vote for each such Unit held (except pursuant to Article 11 hereof) on all matters reserved for their approval, consent or consideration. The initial number of Voting Units are as shown next to the name of such Member in Section 5.1 hereof.

ARTICLE 2
FORMATION OF COMPANY

2.1. Formation. Upon the filing of its initial Articles of Organization with the Nevada Secretary of State on _____, 20___, in the form attached hereto as Appendix 2, the Company was formed as ****, LLC., a Nevada limited liability company under and pursuant to the Act. The parties hereto shall take all actions that are necessary, consistent or appropriate in connection with such formation and continued existence of the Company, as may be requested from time to time by the Manager.

2.2. <u>Name</u>. The name of the Company is ****, LLC.

2.3. <u>Principal Place of Business</u>. The principal place of business of the Company within the State of Nevada shall first be at _____, Nevada _____. The Company may locate its places of business and registered office at any other place or places as the Members or Manager may from time to time deem advisable.

2.4. <u>Registered Office and Agent</u>. The Company's registered office shall first be at _____, Nevada _____. The name of its initial registered agent at such address shall be _____.

2.5. <u>Term</u>. Unless the Company is dissolved in accordance with the provisions of this Agreement, the Act, or other Nevada law, the existence of the Company shall be perpetual.

ARTICLE 3
BUSINESS OF COMPANY

3.1. <u>Permitted Businesses</u>. The purpose of the Company shall be to engage in the business of _____.
Upon the unanimous consent of the Members, the Company may engage in any other lawful business and to do any lawful act concerning any and all lawful business for which a limited liability company may be organized under the laws of the State of Nevada.

3.2. <u>Limits on Foreign Activity</u>. The Company shall not directly engage in business in any state, territory or country which does not recognize limited liability companies or the effectiveness of the Act in limiting the liabilities of the Members of the Company. If the Company desires to conduct business in any such state, it shall do so through an Entity which will ensure limited liability to the Members.

ARTICLE 4
CONTRIBUTIONS TO COMPANY

4.1. <u>Issuance of Units and Members' Initial Capital Contributions</u>. There are hereby authorized and issued _____ (_____) Voting Units divided as set forth in Section 5.1. hereof. Each Member shall contribute the Initial Capital Contribution as set forth in Section 5.1 below, concurrently with signing this Agreement or as otherwise determined by the Manager. The Initial Capital Contribution first shall be applied to the organizational expenses of the Company, including without limitation, legal, accounting and promotional fees and costs and thereafter retained as initial working capital for the Company.

4.2. <u>Additional Capital Contributions</u>. Except with respect to the Initial Capital Contributions and as otherwise provided for under the Act, unless all Members agree, no Member shall be obligated to make any additional Capital Contributions to the Company. If the Company needs additional capital to meet its obligations, it shall seek such capital in the following manner:

a. First, from additional Capital Contributions from the Members of the Company in proportion to their Voting Units;

b. Second, from any source from which the Company may borrow additional capital, including, without limitation, any Member, provided, however, no Member shall be obligated to make a loan to the Company;

c. Third, from an additional disproportionate Capital Contribution from one (1) or more Members of the Company. Such disproportionate Capital Contributions shall be deemed "Extraordinary Capital Contributions" and shall be entitled to a Priority Return as calculated in Section 7.2 hereof;

d. From the admission of one or more new Members in accordance with the provisions set forth herein for the admission of new Members.

4.3. <u>Withdrawal or Reduction of Members' Contributions to Capital</u>.

a. A Member shall not receive out of the Company's Property any part of such Member's contributions to capital until all liabilities of the Company, excluding liabilities to Members on account of their contributions to capital, have been paid or there remains Property of the Company sufficient to pay them.

b. Subject to the provisions of Section 4.3(a) hereof, a Member may rightfully demand distribution of its Capital Account only upon the dissolution of the Company.

c. A Member shall not resign from the Company before the dissolution and winding up of the Company pursuant to Article 12 hereof, unless Members holding a majority of the Voting Units consent. A resigning Member's vote shall be included in determining whether such majority consent has been granted.

d. A Member resigning with the consent of Members holding a majority of the Voting Units shall be entitled to receive, within a reasonable time after resignation, the fair market value of its interest as of the date of resignation as determined by the accountants regularly employed by the Company.

e. A Member, irrespective of the nature of such Member's contribution, has the right to demand and receive only cash in return for such Member's contribution to capital.

4.4. <u>Miscellaneous</u>.

a. <u>No Interest on Capital Contribution</u>. No Member shall be entitled to or shall receive interest on such Member's Capital Contribution.

b. <u>No Withdrawal of Capital Contribution</u>. No Member may demand a return of his Capital Contribution except as expressly provided herein or in the Act.

4.5. <u>No Third Party Beneficiaries</u>. The provisions of this Article 4 are not intended to be for the benefit of and shall not confer any rights on any creditor or other Person (other than a Member in such Member's capacity as a Member) to whom any debts, liabilities or obligations are owed by the Company or any of the Members.

ARTICLE 5
INITIAL CAPITAL CONTRIBUTIONS AND MEMBERSHIP INTERESTS

5.1. <u>Initial Interests</u>. The Initial Capital Contribution and the initial Membership Interest of each Member is as follows:

Member	Capital Contribution	Voting Units
_____	_____	_____
_____	_____	_____
_____	_____	_____
_____	_____	_____
Totals:	_____	_____

5.2. <u>Securities Law Qualification</u>. THE MEMBERS AGREE THAT THE MEMBERSHIP INTERESTS HAVE BEEN ACQUIRED FOR INVESTMENT AND HAVE NOT BEEN REGISTERED UNDER THE SECURITIES ACT OF 1933, AS AMENDED (THE "1933 ACT"), OR THE SECURITIES LAWS OF ANY STATE AND, THEREFORE, THE MEMBERS MUST BEAR THE ECONOMIC RISK OF INVESTMENT IN THE COMPANY FOR AN INDEFINITE PERIOD OF TIME. THERE IS NO PUBLIC

TRADING MARKET FOR THE MEMBERSHIP INTERESTS AND IT IS NOT ANTICIPATED THAT ONE WILL DEVELOP. ADDITIONALLY, THERE ARE SUBSTANTIAL RESTRICTIONS UPON THE TRANSFERABILITY OF THE MEMBERSHIP INTERESTS. SALE OR ASSIGNMENT BY A MEMBER OF ITS MEMBERSHIP INTERESTS OR SUBSTITUTION OF MEMBERS MAY BE SUBJECT TO CERTAIN CONSENTS. THE MEMBERSHIP INTERESTS CANNOT BE RESOLD OR TRANSFERRED WITHOUT (i) REGISTRATION UNDER THE 1933 ACT, OR (ii) AN EXEMPTION FROM REGISTRATION. THEREFORE, MEMBERS MAY NOT BE ABLE TO LIQUIDATE THEIR INVESTMENTS IN THE EVENT OF AN EMERGENCY. FURTHER, MEMBERSHIP INTERESTS MAY NOT BE READILY ACCEPTED AS COLLATERAL FOR A LOAN. MEMBERSHIP INTERESTS SHOULD BE CONSIDERED ONLY AS A LONG TERM INVESTMENT.

ARTICLE 6
ALLOCATIONS OF PROFITS AND LOSSES

6.1. <u>Allocation of Profits</u>. After giving effect to the special allocations set forth in Section 1.2 of Appendix 1, Profits for any Fiscal Year shall be allocated as follows:

a. First, one hundred percent (100%) in proportion to the losses reallocated to each Member pursuant to Section 6.3 hereof, in an amount equal to the excess, if any, of (i) the cumulative Losses allocated to such Members pursuant to Section 6.3 hereof for all prior Fiscal Years, over (ii) the cumulative Profits allocated to such Members pursuant to this Section 6.1(a) for all prior Fiscal Years;

b. Second, one hundred percent (100%) to the Members, in proportion to, and to the extent of the excess, if any, of (i) the cumulative Losses allocated to each Member pursuant to Section 6.2(c) hereof for all prior Fiscal Years, over (ii) the cumulative Profits allocated to each Member pursuant to this Section 6.1(b) for all prior Fiscal Years;

c. Third, one hundred percent (100%) to the Members, in proportion to, and to the extent of the excess, if any, of (i) the sum of (A) the cumulative Priority Return (as defined in Section 7.2 hereof) of each Member from the commencement of the Company to the last day of such Fiscal Year, plus (B) the cumulative Losses allocated to each Member pursuant to Section 6.2(b) hereof for all prior Fiscal Years, over (ii) the cumulative Profits allocated to such Member pursuant to this Section 6.1(c) for all prior Fiscal Years;

d. Fourth, the balance, if any, thirty percent (30%) to the Manager and seventy percent (70%) to the Members pro rata in proportion to their Units.

6.2. <u>Allocation of Losses</u>. After giving effect to the special allocations set forth in Section 1.2 of Appendix 1, Losses for any Fiscal Year shall be allocated as follows, subject to Section 6.3 hereof:

a. First, thirty percent (30%) to the Manager and seventy percent (70%) to the Members pro rata in proportion to such Member Units, to the extent of the excess, if any, of (A) the cumulative Profits allocated pursuant to Section 6.1(d) hereof for all prior Fiscal Years, over (B) the cumulative Losses allocated pursuant to this Section 6.2(a)(i) for all prior Fiscal Years;

b. Second, one hundred percent (100%) to the Members, in proportion to, and to the extent of the excess, if any, of (i) the cumulative Profits allocated to each such Member pursuant to Section 6.1(c) hereof for all prior Fiscal Years, over (ii) the cumulative Losses allocated to such Members pursuant to this Section 6.2(c) for all prior Fiscal Years; and

c. The balance, if any, to the Members pro rata in proportion to such Members' Units.

6.3. <u>Loss Limitation and Reallocation</u>. The Losses allocated pursuant to Section 6.2 hereof shall not exceed the maximum amount of Losses that can be so allocated without causing any Member to have an Adjusted Capital Account Deficit at the end of the Fiscal Year. In the event that some, but not all of the Members would have an Adjusted Capital Account Deficit as a consequence of an allocation of Losses pursuant to Section 6.2 hereof, the limitation set forth in this Section 6.3 shall be applied on a Member by Member basis and Losses not allocable to any Member as a result of such limitation shall be allocated to the other Members in accordance with the positive balances in such Members' Capital Accounts so as to allocate the maximum permissible Losses to each Member under Regulations Section 1.704-1(b)(2)(ii)(d).

ARTICLE 7
DISTRIBUTIONS

7.1. <u>Net Cash Flow</u>. Except as otherwise provided in Section 12.2 (on liquidation) hereof, and subject to the mandatory tax distribution set forth in Section 7.3 hereof, Net Cash Flow shall be distributed with respect to a Fiscal Year at times determined by the Manager in the following order and priority:

a. First, to the Members in proportion to and until each Member has received an amount equal to the excess, if any, of such Member's cumulative Priority Return (as defined in Section 7.2 below) from the inception of the Company to the end of such Fiscal Year, over the sum of all prior distributions to such Member pursuant to this Section 7.1(a);

b. Second, to the Members in proportion and to the extent of their respective Unreturned Extraordinary Capital Contributions (as defined in Section 7.2 below); and

c. The balance, if any, thirty percent (30%) to the Manager and seventy percent (70%) to the Members pro rata in proportion to such Members' Units.

7.2. <u>Unreturned Extraordinary Capital Contribution and Priority Return</u>. The "Priority Return" of any particular Member means a sum equal to twelve percent (12%) per annum, determined on the basis of a year of 365 or 366 days, as the case may be, for the actual number of days occurring in the period for which the Priority Return is being determined, cumulative (but not compounded), of the average daily balance of such Member's Unreturned Extraordinary Capital Contribution (as hereinafter defined) from time to time during the period for which the Priority Return relates, commencing on the date that such Member first makes an Extraordinary Capital Contribution pursuant to Section 4.2(c) hereof. The "Unreturned Extraordinary Capital Contribution" of any Member on any particular date shall be equal to the excess, if any, of the aggregate Extraordinary Capital Contributions then made as of such date by such Member pursuant to Section 4.2(c) hereof, over the aggregate distributions then made as of such date to such Member pursuant to Section 7.1(b) or Section 12.2 hereof.

7.3. <u>Tax Distribution</u>. Except as otherwise provided in Section 12.2 (on liquidation), and provided that no distribution shall be made which will cause or increase an Adjusted Capital Account Deficit (as defined in Appendix 1 hereto) for a Member, the Company shall distribute (to the extent that sufficient funds exist after provision for expenses and reserves) no less than the Tax Distribution Amount (as defined below) pursuant to Sections 7.1(a) and 7.1(c) no later than ninety (90) days after the close of each Fiscal Year. The "Tax Distribution Amount" shall be determined for each Fiscal Year by: (A) multiplying the Marginal Tax Rate (as defined below) for that Fiscal Year by the taxable income of the Company (as determined under Code Section 703(a)) for that Fiscal Year, and subtracting (B) the sum of all other distributions with respect to such Fiscal Year. The "Marginal Tax Rate" for any particular Fiscal Year shall be the highest tax rate that would be imposed on any Member under either Section 1 or 11 of the Code, whichever is higher, for that Fiscal Year.

7.4. <u>Suspended Distributions</u>. Notwithstanding any other provision of this Article 7, a Member may not receive a distribution from the Company to the extent that such distribution would create or increase such Member's Adjusted Capital Account Deficit as defined in Appendix 1 (a "Suspended Distribution"). However, for purposes of Section 7.1 hereof, any Suspended Distributions which would otherwise have been made pursuant to Section 7.1 hereof shall be treated as having been made. All or any portion of any Member's Suspended Distribution shall be made to such Member at the earliest possible time that such distribution can be made without violating the provisions of this Section 7.4.

ARTICLE 8
BOOKS, RECORDS, AND ACCOUNTING

8.1. <u>Books and Records</u>.

a. The Company shall maintain or cause to be maintained books of account that accurately reflect all items of income and expenditure relating to the business of the Company and that accurately and completely disclose the results of the operations of the Company. Such books of account shall be maintained on the method of accounting selected by the Company and on the basis of the Fiscal Year. Each Member, upon not less than seventy-two (72) hours advance written notice to the Manager of the Company, at such Member's own expense, shall have the right to inspect, copy, and audit the Company's books and records at any time during normal Business Hours without notice to any other Member.

b. The Company shall keep at its registered office such records as are required by the Act.

8.2. <u>Tax Returns</u>. The Company shall prepare and timely file, or cause to be prepared and timely filed, all income tax and other tax returns of the Company. The Company shall furnish to each Member a copy of all such returns together with all schedules thereto and such other information which each Member may reasonably request in connection with such Member's own tax affairs.

8.3. <u>Bank Accounts</u>. The Company shall establish and maintain one or more separate accounts in the name of the Company in one or more federally insured banking institutions of its choosing into which shall be deposited all funds of the Company and from which all Company expenditures and other disbursements shall be made. Funds may be withdrawn from such accounts on the signature of the Manager.

ARTICLE 9
MANAGEMENT

9.1. <u>General Management</u>.

a. The business and affairs of the Company shall be managed by or under the direction of one or more Managers, who need not be Members of the Company. The initial Manager shall be _____, who shall remain as Manager until such Manager's death, bankruptcy, incompetence, resignation or removal by a unanimous vote of the Members. In the event of the initial Manager's death, the Members of the Company shall immediately become the interim Managers of the Company until such time as replacement Manager(s) is appointed by Members holding a majority of the Voting Units (including the representative or successor to the initial Manager's Membership Interest). In the event of incompetence, resignation or removal, a successor

Manager or Managers shall be elected upon such event, and annually thereafter, by Members holding a majority of the Voting Units.

b. The Manager shall direct, manage and control the business of the Company and, subject to the limitations and qualifications set forth in this Article 9, shall have full and complete authority, power and discretion to make any and all decisions and to do any and all things which the Manager shall deem to be reasonably required in light of the Company's business and objectives. Without limiting the generality of the foregoing, the Manager shall have power and authority to:

i. acquire property from any Person as the Manager may determine. The fact that a Member is directly or indirectly an Affiliate of such Person shall not prohibit the Manager from dealing with that Person;

ii. establish policies for investment and invest Company funds (by way of example but not limitation, in time deposits, short term governmental obligations, commercial paper or other investments);

iii. make distributions of available cash to Members;

iv. employ accountants, legal counsel, managers, managing agents or other experts or consultants to perform services for the Company with compensation from Company funds;

v. enter into any transaction on behalf of the Company involving the incurrence of any indebtedness or the hypothecation, encumbrance, or granting of a security interest or lien upon any Company Property;

vi. purchase liability and other insurance to protect the Company's Property and business;

vii. organize Entities to serve as the Company's subsidiaries and to determine the form and structure thereof;

viii. establish a Board of Directors; delegate management decisions thereto; appoint Directors thereto and remove Directors therefrom;

ix. establish offices of President, Vice President, Secretary and Treasurer; delegate to such offices daily management and operational responsibilities; appoint Persons to act as such officers and remove Persons therefrom; and

x. establish reasonable payments or salaries to Persons appointed as officers and directors.

c. Where this Agreement specifies an act of the Manager, it means an act taken by majority vote of the Managers when more than one Manager exists.

d. Unless authorized to do so by this Agreement or by the Manager, no Managing Person, Member, agent, or employee of the Company shall have any power or authority to bind the Company in any way, to pledge its credit or to render it liable pecuniarily for any purpose. However, the Manager may act (or may cause the company to act) by a duly authorized power of attorney.

9.2. <u>Act Requiring Member Unanimous Approval and Limitation on Powers of Manager</u>. Notwithstanding anything to the contrary in this Agreement, the Manager shall not engage in any of the following transactions without the unanimous vote or consent of the Members:

a. the merger or consolidation of the Company with any other Entity;

b. a sale of all or substantially all of the Company's assets;

c. the voluntary commencement of a bankruptcy proceeding with the Company as a debtor or any assignment for the benefit of creditors of the Company.

d. any action which would result in a change in any Member's percentage interest of profits, losses, or distributions, except pursuant to compliance with Appendix 1;

e. any action which would result in a change in the Capital Contributions required from any Member;

f. any action which would result in an increase in the personal liability imposed upon any Member;

g. the issuance of any additional Membership Interests; or

h. any amendments to the Articles of Organization or this Agreement.

9.3 <u>Compensation</u>. The Manager of the Company shall receive thirty percent (30%) of the Profits of the Company pursuant to Sections 6.1(d) and 7.1(c) hereof, and reimbursement of expenses incurred as Manager, as the sole compensation for services rendered as a Manager.

9.4 <u>Mediation and Arbitration</u>.

a. If a dispute arises out of or relates to this Agreement, or the breach thereof, and if said dispute cannot be settled through direct discussions within five (5) days of first consideration, the Members and Manager agree to first endeavor to settle the dispute in an amicable manner by mediation administered by the American Arbitration Association (the "AAA") under its Commercial Mediation Rules, before resorting to arbitration administered by the American Arbitration Association in accordance with its Commercial Arbitration Rules (except otherwise provided herein) by written notice to the other Members and Managers, as applicable. The Member or Manager electing arbitration shall by such notice to other Members or Manager name an arbitrator. The second arbitrator shall be chosen by the noticed Members or Manager, as applicable, within ten (10) days after such notice. If the noticed Members or Managers do not appoint such second Arbitrator, then the AAA shall be requested to submit a list of five (5) persons to serve as the second arbitrator and the first arbitrator shall select a name from such list within five (5) days of its submission; a third arbitrator shall be selected by the first and second arbitrators within five (5) days of the selection of the first and second arbitrators, and if the arbitrators fail to so select a third arbitrator, then the third arbitrator shall be selected from the remaining members of the list of five (5) received from AAA through the process of each of the first two (2) arbitrators in turn striking names from the list until one (1) name remains.

b. The decision of any two (2) of the arbitrators shall be final and binding upon the Members and Manager. The arbitrators shall determine the rights and obligations of the Members and Manager according to this Agreement and the substantive laws of Nevada. The parties hereby agree that in any such arbitration each Member and Manager shall be entitled to discovery of the others as provided by the Nevada Revised Statutes pertaining to civil procedure; provided, however, any such discovery shall be completed within four (4) months from the date of the selection of the second arbitrator, unless such period is extended by agreement of the Members and Manager or by order of the arbitrators, and any disputes concerning discovery shall be determined by the arbitrators with any such determination being binding on the Members and Manager. The arbitrators shall be requested to render an opinion within fifteen (15) days after the date that discovery is completed. The arbitrators shall apply Nevada substantive law and Nevada evidentiary law to the proceeding. The arbitrators shall have the power to grant all legal and equitable remedies and award compensatory damages provided by Nevada law. Punitive or exemplary damages shall not be awarded for any breach or alleged breach of this Agreement and the Members and Manager waive any right to seek, claim or receive such punitive or exemplary damages. The arbitrators shall be bound by the terms of this Agreement. The arbitrators shall not be empowered or authorized to add to, subtract from, delete or in any other way modify the terms of this Agreement. The arbitrators shall prepare in writing and provide to the parties an award including factual findings and the reasons on which the decision is based. The decision of the arbitrators shall be final and binding on the Members and Manager and judgment thereon may be entered by any court having jurisdiction. The arbitrators may award the prevailing party its cost in connection with the arbitration including, without limitation, attorney fees.

c. Notwithstanding any other provision of this Section 9.4, no resort to arbitration shall be required if a third Person's participation is essential to avoid the possibility of an inconsistent or otherwise incomplete resolution of all associated issues or controversies, and such third Person declines to participate in and be bound by the results of the arbitration.

d. No Member, whether or not a party to such arbitration, and no arbitrator, shall disclose the existence, content or results of any arbitration hereunder without the prior written consent of all parties to such arbitration.

9.5. <u>No Liability for Certain Acts</u>. A Managing Person of the Company shall perform such Managing Person's duties, in good faith, in a manner such Managing Person reasonably believes to be in the best interests of the Company. A Managing Person does not, in any way, guarantee the return of the Members' Capital Contributions or a profit for the Members from the operations of the Company. A Managing Person shall not be responsible to any Members because of a loss of their investment in the Company or a loss in the operations of the Company, unless the loss shall have been the result of the Managing Person not acting in good faith as provided in this Section. A Managing Person shall incur no liability to the Company or to any of the Members as a result of engaging in any other business or venture. A Manager shall be entitled to any other protection afforded to Manager under the Act. A Managing Person who so performs such Managing Person's duties shall not have any liability by reason of being or having been a Managing Person of the Company. In performing the duties of a Managing Person, a Managing Person shall be entitled to rely on information, opinions, reports or statements, including financial statements and other financial data, in each case prepared or presented by persons and groups listed below unless such Managing Person has knowledge concerning the matter in question that would cause such reliance to be unwarranted:

a. one or more employees or other agents of the Company whom the Managing Person believes in good faith to be reliable and competent in the matters presented;

b. legal counsel, public accountants, or other Persons as to matters that the Managing Person believes in good faith to be within such Persons' professional or expert competence; or

c. a committee, upon which such Managing Person does not serve, duly designated in accordance with the provisions of this Agreement, as to matters within its designated authority, which committee the Managing Person believes in good faith to merit confidence.

9.6. <u>Managing Persons Have No Exclusive Duty to Company</u>. A Managing Person shall not be required to manage the Company as such Managing Person's sole and exclusive activity, and each Managing Person may have other business interests and may engage in other activities in addition to those relating to the Company, even if such activities may be in competition with the Business of the Company. Neither the Company nor any Member shall have any right, by virtue of this Agreement or the existence of the Company, to share or participate in such other investments or activities of any Managing Person regardless of whether such opportunities have been presented to the Company.

9.7. <u>Indemnity of Managing Persons</u>.

a. The Company agrees to indemnify, pay, protect and hold harmless Managing Persons from and against any and all liabilities, obligations, losses, damages, penalties, actions, judgments, suits, proceedings, costs, expenses and disbursements of any kind or nature whatsoever (including, without limitation, all reasonable costs and expenses of defense, appeal and settlement of any and all suits, actions or proceedings instituted against the Managing Persons or the Company and all costs of investigation in connection therewith) which may be imposed on, incurred by, or asserted against the Managing Persons or the Company in any way relating to or arising out of, or alleged to relate to or arise out of, any action or inaction on the part of the Company or on the part of a Managing Person, acting in a manner believed in good faith to be in the best interests of the Company, in connection with the formation, operation and/or management of the Company, the Company's purchase and operation of Property, and/or as a result of the Managing Person agreeing to act as a Managing Person of the Company. If any action, suit or proceeding shall be pending or threatened against the Company or a Manager relating to or arising out of, or alleged to relate to or arise out of, any such action or nonaction, a Manager shall have the right to employ, at the expense of the Company, separate counsel of such Manager's choice in such action, suit or proceeding and the Company shall advance the reasonable out-of-pocket expenses in connection therewith. The satisfaction of the obligations of the Company under this Section shall be from and limited to the assets of the Company and no Member shall have any personal liability on account thereof. The foregoing rights of indemnification are in addition to and shall not be a limitation of any rights of indemnification as provided in Sections 86.411 through 86.451 of the Act, as such may be amended from time to time.

b. This Section shall not limit the Company's power to pay or reimburse expenses incurred by a Managing Person in connection with such Managing Person's appearance as a witness in a proceeding at a time when the Managing Person has not been made a named defendant or respondent in the proceeding.

c. The Company may indemnify and advance expenses to an employee or agent of the Company who is not a Managing Person to the same or to a greater extent as the Company may indemnify and advance expenses to a Managing Person.

d. The Company may purchase and maintain insurance on behalf of any Person who is or was a Managing Person, Member, employee, fiduciary, or agent of the Company or who, while a Managing Person, Member, employee, fiduciary, or agent of the Company, is or was serving at the request of the Company as a manager, member, director, officer, partner, trustee, employee, fiduciary, or agent of any other foreign or domestic limited liability company or any corporation, partnership, joint venture, trust, other enterprise, or employee benefit plan against any liability asserted against or incurred by such Person in any such capacity or arising out of such Person's status as such, whether or not the Company would have the power to indemnify such Person against such liability under the provisions of this Section. Any such insurance may be procured from any insurance company designated by the Managers of the Company, whether such insurance company is formed under the laws of this state or any other jurisdiction of the United States or elsewhere.

e. Any indemnification of or advance of expenses to a Managing Person in accordance with this Section, if arising out of a proceeding by or on behalf of the Company, shall be reported in writing to the Members with or before the notice of the next Members' meeting.

f. Notwithstanding the termination of employment, it is recognized that disputes may arise between the Company and third parties, or between a Managing Person and third parties, the resolution of which may require the cooperation of the Managing Person or the Company, respectively, including, but not limited to, conferring with counsel and assisting in preparation work in litigation matters, providing factual information to the other party, and giving depositions and testimony in judicial and administrative proceedings. Notwithstanding the termination of a Managing Person's employment, both the Company and Managing Person shall cooperate and thereby act reasonably and in good faith to assist the other, without any charge or compensation, except the requesting party shall reimburse the other party for all reasonable out-of-pocket costs incurred in connection herewith. The Managing Person's cooperation is a continuing condition to the indemnification and hold harmless provisions under this Section.

g. Notwithstanding the provisions of the above subsections (a) through (f) of this Section 9.7, no Managing Person shall be indemnified from any liability resulting from fraud, bad faith, willful misconduct or gross negligence.

ARTICLE 10
RIGHTS AND OBLIGATIONS OF MEMBERS

10.1. Limitation of Liability.

a. Each Member's liability shall be limited as set forth herein in the Act and other applicable law. A Member will not personally be liable for any debts or losses of the Company, except as provided in the Act.

b. When a Member has received the return in whole or in part of such Member's Capital Contribution, the Member is nevertheless liable to the Company for any sum, not in excess of the return of its Capital Contribution with interest at the rate provided for judgments under the laws of the State of Nevada, necessary to discharge the Company's liability to all creditors of the Company who extended credit or whose claims arose before the return of such Member's Capital Contribution.

c. When a Member has received a distribution wrongfully conveyed by the Company, the Member shall hold such distribution as trustee for the Company.

10.2. Member Indemnity. The Company agrees to indemnify, pay, protect and hold harmless any Member (on demand and to the satisfaction of the Member) from and against any and all liabilities, obligations, losses, damages, penalties, actions, judgments, suits, proceedings, costs, expenses and disbursements of any kind or nature whatsoever in any way relating to any agreement, liability, commitment, expense or obligation of the Company which may be imposed on, incurred by, or asserted against the Member solely as a result of such Member being a Member (including, without limitation, all reasonable costs and expenses of defense, appeal and settlement of any and all suits, actions or proceedings instituted against the Member and all costs of investigation in connection therewith). The satisfaction of the obligations of the Company under this Section shall be from and limited to the assets of the Company and no Member shall have any personal liability on account thereof. The foregoing rights of indemnification are in addition to and shall not be a limitation of any rights that may be provided in the Act.

10.3. List of Members. Upon written request of any Member, the Company shall provide a list showing the names, addresses and Units of the Members in the Company.

10.4. Voting. Subject to Section 11.2 hereof, Members shall be entitled to one vote for each Voting Unit held, on all matters reserved for their approval or consent, including but not limited to Section 9.2 hereof.

10.5. Additional Members. Except as provided in Section 11.2 hereof, no Person shall be admitted to the Company as an additional Member without the unanimous consent of the Members.

ARTICLE 11
RESTRICTIONS ON TRANSFERABILITY

11.1. Right to Pledge. Every Membership Interest may be pledged to secure any borrowing of a Member or its Affiliate, provided that any Person acquiring such Membership Interest pursuant to such pledge shall not have the right to be admitted as a Member but shall be entitled only to receive such allocations and distributions as are otherwise payable with respect to such Member's Membership Interest under this Agreement.

11.2. <u>Admission of Substitute Member; Successors by Operation of Law</u>.

a. A Member may freely transfer or assign all or any portion of its Membership Interest to other Members or Affiliates of Members. If a Member transfers or assigns some or all of its Membership Interest to a Person who is not already a Member or an Affiliate, and non-transferring Members unanimously approve of such proposed transfer or assignment, the transferee or assignee of the Membership Interest shall become a Substitute Member.

b. If all Members do not unanimously approve of such transfer or assignment, the transferee or assignee of the Membership Interest shall have no right to participate in the management of the business and affairs of the Company, to vote, or to be admitted as a Member, but shall only be entitled to receive the share of profits, losses and distributions, to which the transferring or assigning Member would otherwise be entitled. As a condition to the receipt of same, the transferee or assignee may be required by the Members to pay the associated Capital Contributions to which the transferor or assignor would have been liable. With respect to all or any portion of a Membership Interest that is transferred or assigned, the Substitute Member has the rights and powers and is subject to the restrictions and liabilities that are associated with such Membership Interest which accrued prior to the date of substitution, except that the substitution of the assignee does not release the assignor from existing liability to the Company.

c. In any event, no transfer or assignment of all or any portion of a Membership Interest in the Company (including the transfer or assignment of any right to receive or share in profits, losses, or distributions) shall be effective unless and until written notice (including the name and address of the proposed transferee or assignee, the interest to be transferred or assigned, and the date of such transfer or assignment) has been provided to the Company and the nontransferring or nonassigning Member(s). Every Person before becoming a Substitute Member must assume this Agreement, as amended from time to time, in writing.

d. Notwithstanding the foregoing:

i. if a Member who is an individual dies or is adjudged by a court of competent jurisdiction to be incompetent to manage the Member's person or property, the Member's executor, administrator, guardian, conservator, or other legal representative may exercise all of the Member's rights for the purpose of settling the Member's estate or administering the Member's property, including any power the Member has under the Articles of Organization or this Agreement to act as a Member, including but not limited to voting or transferring the Member's Membership Interest; and

ii. if a Member is a corporation, trust or other entity that is dissolved or terminated, the powers and rights of that Member may be exercised by its legal representative or successor, including any power the Member has under the Articles of Organization or this Agreement to act as a Member, including but not limited to voting or transferring the Member's Membership Interest.

11.3. <u>Right of First Refusal</u>. Except for transfers to other Members, to Affiliates of the transferor, or by operation of law, no Member shall transfer all or any portion of its Membership Interest unless such Member (the "Seller") first offers to sell such Membership Interest (the "Offered Interest") pursuant to the terms of this Section 11.3.

a. <u>Limitation on Transfers</u>. No transfer may be made under this Article 11 unless the Seller has received a bona fide written offer (the "Purchase Offer") from a Person (the "Purchaser") to purchase the Offered Interest for a purchase price (the "Offer

Price") denominated and payable in United States dollars at closing or according to specified terms, with or without interest, which offer shall be in writing signed by the Purchaser and shall be irrevocable for a period ending no sooner than the day following the end of the Offer Period, as hereinafter defined.

b. <u>Offer Notice</u>. Prior to making any transfer that is subject to the terms of this Section 11.3, the Seller shall give to the Company and each Member holding Voting Units written notice (the "Offer Notice") which shall include a copy of the Purchase Offer and an offer (the "Firm Offer") to sell the Offered Interest to the Company or to the Members holding Voting Units (the "Offerees") for the Offer Price, payable according to the same terms as (or more favorable terms than) those contained in the Purchase Offer, provided that the Firm Offer shall be made without regard to the requirement of any earnest money or similar deposit required of the Purchaser prior to closing, and without regard to any security (other than the Offered Interest) to be provided by the Purchaser for any deferred portion of the Offer Price.

c. <u>Offer Period</u>. The Firm Offer shall be irrevocable for a period (the "Offer Period") ending at 11:59 P.M., local time at the Company's principal place of business, on the ninetieth (90th) day following the day of the Offer Notice.

d. <u>Acceptance of Firm Offer</u>. At any time during the first thirty (30) days of the Offer Period, the Company may accept the Firm Offer as to all but not less than all of the Offered Interest by giving written notice of such acceptance to the Seller and the members. If the Company does not accept the firm Offer within such first thirty (30) days of the Offer Period, then within the second thirty (30) days of the Offer Period, any Offeree may accept the Firm Offer as to all or any portion of the Offered Interest, by giving written notice of such acceptance to the Seller and the Company. Such acceptance notice shall indicate the maximum percentage of the Membership Interests that such Offeree (an "Accepting Offeree") is willing to purchase (the "Percentage Offer"). If Offerees do not accept the Firm Offer as to all of the Offered Interest, the Firm Offer shall be deemed to be rejected in its entirety. If Accepting Offerees in the aggregate accept the Firm Offer with respect to all of the Offered Interest, the Firm Offer shall be deemed to be accepted, and each such Accepting Offeree shall be deemed to have accepted such portion of the Offered Interest as follows:

i. if the Percentage Offer of each Accepting Offeree is equal to, or greater than, such Accepting Offeree's Voting Units divided by the total Voting Units held by all Members other than the Selling Member (the "Current Ownership Percentage"), each Accepting Offeree shall be deemed to have accepted such portion of the Offered Interest that corresponds to its Current Ownership Percentage;

ii. if one or more Accepting Offerees have offered to purchase a portion of the Offered Interest that is less than its Current Ownership Percentage, first each Accepting Offeree shall be deemed to have accepted the lesser of: (a) its Percentage Offer, or (b) its Current Ownership Percentage. Then the remainder of the Offered Interest shall be deemed accepted by each Accepting Offeree who offered to purchase a portion greater than its Current Ownership Percentage (a "Residual Accepting Offeree"), in the same proportion that such Residual Accepting Offeree's Voting Units bears to the total Voting Units held by all Residual Accepting Offerees, until: (a) the Offered Interest has been fully accepted or (b) the Percentage Offer of a Residual Accepting Offeree has been reached. If the Percentage Offer of a Residual Accepting Offeree has been reached before the Offered Interest has been fully accepted, such Residual Accepting Offeree shall thereafter no longer constitute a Residual Accepting Offeree, and the remaining Residual Accepting Offerees shall be deemed to accept the balance of the Offered Interest in a similar fashion until the Offered Interest has been fully accepted.

The foregoing is intended to prevent an unexpected and unintended dilution of interests when an Accepting Offeree has expressed its willingness to purchase a portion of an Offered Interest that is at least equal to its Current Ownership Percentage, and shall be interpreted consistently therewith.

e. <u>Closing of Purchase Pursuant to Firm Offer</u>. If the Firm Offer is accepted, the closing of the sale of the Offered Interest shall take place within thirty (30) days after the Firm Offer is accepted or, if later, the date of closing set forth in the Purchase Offer. The Seller and all Accepting Offerees shall execute such documents and instruments as may be necessary or appropriate to effect the sale of the Offered Interest pursuant to the terms of the Firm Offer and this Section 11.3.

f. <u>Sale Pursuant to Purchase Offer If Firm Offer Rejected</u>. If the Firm Offer is not accepted in the manner provided herein, the Seller may sell the Offered Interest to the Purchaser at any time within sixty (60) days after the last day of the Offer Period, provided that such sale shall be made on terms no more favorable to the Purchaser than the terms contained in the Purchase Offer and provided further that such sale complies with other terms, conditions, and restrictions of this Agreement that are applicable to sales of Membership Interests and are not expressly made inapplicable to sales occurring under this Section 11.3. If the Offered Interest is not sold in accordance with the terms of the preceding sentence, the Offered Interest shall again become subject to all of the conditions and restrictions of this Section 11.3.

ARTICLE 12
DISSOLUTION AND TERMINATION

12.1. <u>Dissolution</u>.

a. The Company shall be dissolved upon the occurrence of any of the following events (a "Dissolution Event"):

i. if the Company voluntarily enters bankruptcy chapter VII or another insolvency proceeding that contemplates its final liquidation, or does so involuntarily and such proceeding is not vacated or dismissed within one hundred twenty (120) days after commencement thereof; or

ii. at the election of the Manager in his sole discretion.

The death, withdrawal or termination of any Member for any reason shall not constitute a Dissolution Event unless such dissolution is required by Nevada law.

b. As soon as possible following the occurrence of any Dissolution Event the appropriate representative of the Company shall make all filings and do all acts necessary to dissolve the Company.

12.2. <u>Distribution of Assets Upon Dissolution</u>. In settling accounts after dissolution, the assets of the Company shall be distributed in the following order:

a. First, to pay those liabilities to creditors, in the order of priority as provided by law (except those to Members on account of their Capital Contributions);

b. The balance, if any, to the Members pro rata in accordance with the positive balances in their Capital Accounts, after giving effect to all contributions, distributions and allocations for all periods.

12.3. <u>Winding Up</u>. Except as provided by law, upon dissolution, each Member shall look solely to the assets of the Company for the return of its Capital Contribution. If the Company Property remaining after the payment or discharge of the debts and liabilities of the Company is insufficient to return the Capital Contribution of each Member, such Member shall have no recourse against any other Member. The winding up of the affairs of the Company and the distribution of its assets shall be conducted exclusively by the Manager, who is hereby authorized to take all actions necessary to accomplish such distribution, including without limitation, selling any Company assets the Manager deems necessary or appropriate to sell. In the discretion of the Manager, a pro rata portion of the amounts that otherwise would be distributed to the Members under this Article may be withheld to provide a reasonable reserve for unknown or contingent liabilities of the Company.

12.4. Notice of Dissolution. Within ninety (90) days of the happening of a Dissolution Event, the Manager shall give written notice thereof to each of the Members, to the banks and other financial institutions with which the Company normally does business, and to all other parties with whom the Company regularly conducts business, and shall publish notice of dissolution in a newspaper of general circulation in each place in which the Company generally conducts business.

ARTICLE 13
MISCELLANEOUS PROVISIONS

13.1. Notices. Any notice or communication required or permitted to be given by any provision of this Agreement, including, but not limited to, any consents, shall be in writing and shall be deemed to have been given and received by the Person to whom directed (a) when delivered personally to such Person or to an officer or partner of the Member to which directed, (b) when transmitted by facsimile transmission, with evidence of a confirmed transmission, to the facsimile number of such Person who has notified the Company and every other Member of its facsimile number and received during Business Hours on a Business Day at the destination of such facsimile transmission, (c) the following Business Day after being otherwise transmitted by facsimile, with evidence of a confirmed transmission, to the facsimile number of such Person who has notified the Company and every other Member of its facsimile number, or (d) three (3) Business Days after being posted in the United States mails if sent by registered, express or certified mail, return receipt requested, postage and charges prepaid, or one (1) Business Day after deposited with overnight courier, return receipt requested, delivery charges prepaid, in either case addressed to the Person to which directed at the address, if any, shown on the page containing their signatures, or such other address of which such Person has notified the Company and every other Member. If no address appears on the page containing a Member's signature and if the Company and the Members have not been notified of any other address at which such Person shall receive notifications, then a notice delivered to the Manager, who shall reasonably attempt to forward the notice to such Person, shall constitute sufficient notice to such Person.

13.2. Application of Nevada Law. This Agreement, and the application and interpretation hereof, shall be governed exclusively by its terms and by the laws of the State of Nevada, and specifically the Act. Clark County, Nevada shall be the exclusive venue for any action brought by any party in any way related to this Agreement.

13.3. Waiver of Action for Partition. Each Member irrevocably waives during the term of the Company any right that such Member may have to maintain any action for partition with respect to the Property of the Company.

13.4. Amendments. A proposed amendment to this Agreement shall become effective at such time as it has been unanimously approved by the Members.

13.5. Construction. Whenever the singular number is used in this Agreement and when required by the context, the same shall include the plural, and the masculine gender shall include the feminine and neuter genders and vice versa.

13.6. <u>Headings</u>. The headings in this Agreement are inserted for convenience only and are in no way intended to describe, interpret, define, or limit the scope, extent or intent of this Agreement or any provision hereof.

13.7. <u>Waivers</u>. The failure of any party to seek redress for violation of or to insist upon the strict performance of any covenant or condition of this Agreement shall not prevent a subsequent act, which would have originally constituted a violation, from having the effect of an original violation, except in the event of a written waiver to the contrary that specifically states that this Section 13.7 shall be inapplicable.

13.8. <u>Rights and Remedies Cumulative</u>. The rights and remedies provided by this Agreement are cumulative and the use of any one right or remedy by any party shall not preclude or waive the right to use any or all other remedies. Said rights and remedies are given in addition to any other rights the parties may have by law, statute, ordinance or otherwise.

13.9. <u>Severability</u>. If any provision of this Agreement or the application thereof to any Person or circumstance shall be invalid, illegal or unenforceable to any extent, the remainder of this Agreement and the applications thereof shall not be affected and shall be enforceable to the fullest extent permitted by law.

13.10. <u>Heirs, Successors and Assigns</u>. Each and all of the covenants, terms, provisions and agreements herein contained shall be binding upon and inure to the benefit of the parties hereto and, to the extent permitted by this Agreement, their respective heirs, legal representatives, successors and assigns.

13.11. <u>Creditors</u>. None of the provisions of this Agreement shall be for the benefit of or enforceable by any creditors of the Company.

13.12. <u>Counterparts</u>. This Agreement may be executed in counterparts, each of which shall be deemed an original but all of which shall constitute one and the same instrument.

13.13. <u>Further Assurances</u>. The Members and the Company agree that they and each of them will take whatever action or actions as are deemed by counsel to the Company to be reasonably necessary or desirable from time to time to effectuate the provisions or intent of this Agreement, and to that end, the Members and the Company agree that they will execute, acknowledge, seal, and deliver any further instruments or documents which may be necessary to give force and effect to this Agreement or any of the provisions hereof, or to carry out the intent of this Agreement or any of the provisions hereof.

13.14. <u>Entire Agreement</u>. This Agreement, including every Appendix attached hereto, sets forth all (and is intended by all parties hereto to be an integration of all) of the promises, agreements, conditions, understandings, warranties, and representations among the parties hereto with respect to the Company; and there are no promises, agreements, conditions, understandings, warranties, or representations, oral or written, express or implied, among them other than as set forth herein.

13.15. <u>Time of Essence</u>. Time is of the essence of this Agreement and all of the terms, provisions, covenants and conditions hereof.

13.16. <u>Conflicts of Interest</u>. The Members hereby acknowledge that (i) _____ _____ has acted as counsel for the Company in connection with the formation of the Company and the drafting of this Operating Agreement, (ii) that each of the other parties has been advised to seek independent counsel in connection with such matters, and (iii) that counsel for the Company does not represent any individual Member either directly or indirectly through the Company.

IN WITNESS WHEREOF, the Members have executed this Agreement to be effective as of the date first written above.

Signed: _____

Name: _____

Address: _____

_____

Fax: _____

Telephone: _____

Signed: _____

Name: _____

Address: _____

_____

Fax: _____

Telephone: _____

Signed: _____

Name: _____

Address: _____

_____

Fax: _____

Telephone: _____

APPENDIX 1
TAX ACCOUNTING PROCEDURES

1.0. <u>References to Sections of the Code or Regulations</u>. References within this Appendix to sections of the Code or Regulations shall be applied by substituting for the Regulations' terms of "partnership" and "partner" the terms "limited liability company" (or "company") and "member," respectively.

1.1. <u>Tax Definitions</u>. The following terms used in this Agreement and Appendix shall have the following meanings:

a. "Adjusted Capital Account Deficit" with respect to any Member means the deficit balance, if any, in such Member's Capital Account as of the end of any Fiscal Year after giving effect to the following adjustments: (i) credit to such Capital Account the sum of (A) any amount which such Member is obligated to restore to such Capital Account pursuant to any provision of this Agreement, plus (B) an amount equal to such Member's share of Company Minimum Gain (as defined in Section 1.2(a) hereof) and determined under Regulations Section 1.704-2(g), and such Member's share of Member Nonrecourse Debt Minimum Gain (as defined in Section 1.2(b) hereof) and as determined under Regulations Section 1.704-2(i)(5), plus (C) any amounts which such Member is deemed to be obligated to restore pursuant to Regulations Section 1.704-1(b)(2)(ii)(c); and (ii) debit to such Capital Account the items described in Regulations Sections 1.704-1(b)(2)(ii)(d)(4), (5) and (6).

b. "Asset Value" with respect to any Company asset means:

i. The fair market value when contributed of any asset contributed to the Company by any Member;

ii. The fair market value of any Company asset when such asset is distributed to any Member;

iii. The fair market value of all Property at the time of the happening of any of the following events: (A) the admission of a Member to, or the increase of a Membership Interest of an existing Member in, the Company in exchange for a Capital Contribution; (B) the distribution of any asset distributed by the Company to any Member as consideration for a Membership Interest in the Company; or (C) the liquidation of the Company under Regulations Section 1.704-1(b)(2)(ii)(g); or

iv. The Basis of the asset in all other circumstances.

For purposes of this definition, fair market value shall be determined by the Manager.

c. "Basis" with respect to an asset means the adjusted basis from time to time of such asset for federal income tax purposes.

d. "Capital Account" means an account maintained for each Member in accordance with Regulations Sections 1.704-1(b) and 1.704-2 and to which the following provisions apply to the extent not inconsistent with such Regulations:

i. There shall be credited to each Member's Capital Account: (1) such Member's Capital Contributions; (2) such Member's distributive share of Profits; (3) any items of income or gain specially allocated to such Member under this Agreement; and (4) the amount of any Company liabilities (determined as provided in Code Section 752(c) and the Regulations thereunder) assumed by such Member or to which Property distributed to such Member is subject;

ii. There shall be debited to each Member's Capital Account (1) the amount of money and the Asset Value of any Property distributed to such Member pursuant to this Agreement; (2) such Member's distributive share of Losses; (3) any items of expense or loss which are specially allocated to such Member under this Agreement, and (4) the amount of liabilities (determined as provided in Code Section 752(c) and the Regulations thereunder) of such Member assumed by the Company (within the meaning of Code Section 704) or to which Property contributed to the Company by such Member is subject; and

iii. The Capital Account of any transferee Member shall include the appropriate portion of the Capital Account of the Member from whom the transferee Membership Interest was obtained.

e. "Depreciation" for any Fiscal Year or other period means the cost recovery deduction with respect to an asset for such year or other period as determined for federal income tax purposes, provided that if the Asset Value of such asset differs from its Basis at the beginning of such year or other period, depreciation shall be determined as provided in Regulations Section 1.704-1(b)(2)(iv)(g)(3).

f. "Profits" and "Losses" for any Fiscal Year or other period means an amount equal to the Company's taxable income or loss for such year or period determined in accordance with Code Section 703(a) and the Regulations thereunder with the following adjustments:

i. All items of income, gain, loss and deduction of the Company required to be stated separately shall be included in taxable income or loss;

ii. Income of the Company exempt from federal income tax shall be treated as taxable income;

iii. Expenditures of the Company described in Code Section 705(a)(2)(B) or treated as such expenditures under Regulations Section 1.704-1(b)(2)(iv)(i) shall be subtracted from taxable income;

iv. In the event the Asset Value of any Company asset is adjusted pursuant to Sections 1.1(b)(ii) or (iii) of this Appendix, the amount of such adjustment shall be taken into account as gain or loss from the disposition of such asset for the purposes of computing Profits or Losses;

v. Gain or loss resulting from the disposition of Property from which gain or loss is recognized for federal income tax purposes shall be determined with reference to the Asset Value of such Property;

vi. Depreciation shall be determined based upon Asset Value as determined under Regulations Section 1.704-1(b)(2)(iv)(g)(3) instead of as determined for federal income tax purposes; and

vii. To the extent an adjustment to the adjusted tax basis of any Company asset pursuant to Code Section 734(b) or Code Section 743(b) is required pursuant to Regulations Section 1.704-1(b)(2)(iv)(m)(4) to be taken into account in determining Capital Accounts as a result of a distribution other than in complete liquidation of a Membership Interest, the amount of such adjustment shall be treated as an item of gain (if the adjustment increases the basis of the asset) or loss (if the adjustment decreases the basis of the asset) from the disposition of the asset and shall be taken into account for purposes of computing Profits and Losses.

viii. Items which are specially allocated shall not be taken into account.

1.2. Special Allocations of Profits and Losses.

a. Minimum Gain Chargeback. Notwithstanding any other provision of this Appendix, if there is a net decrease in Company Minimum Gain (as defined in Regulations Section 1.704-2(d)) during any Fiscal Year, then each Member shall be allocated such amount of income and gain for such year (and subsequent years, if necessary) determined under and in the manner required by Regulations Section 1.704-2(f) as is necessary to meet the requirements for a minimum gain chargeback as provided in that Regulation.

b. Member Nonrecourse Debt Minimum Gain Chargeback. Notwithstanding any other provision of this Appendix, if there is a net decrease in Member Nonrecourse Debt Minimum Gain (as defined in accordance with Regulations Section 1.704-2(1)(3)) attributable to a Member Nonrecourse Debt (as defined in Regulations Section 1.704-2(b)(4)) during any Fiscal Year, any Member who has a share of the Member Nonrecourse Debt Minimum Gain attributable to such Member Nonrecourse Debt determined in accordance with Regulations Section 1.704-2(1)(5) shall be allocated such amount of income and gain for such year (and subsequent years, if necessary) determined under and in the manner required by Regulations Section 1.704-2(1)(4) as is necessary to meet the requirements for a chargeback of Member Nonrecourse Debt Minimum Gain as is provided in that Regulation.

c. Qualified Income Offset. If a Member unexpectedly receives any adjustment, allocation or distribution described in Regulations Section 1.704-1(b)(2)(ii)(d)(4), (5) or (6), items of Company income and gain shall be specifically allocated to such Member in an amount and manner sufficient to eliminate, to the extent required by the Regulations, the Adjusted Capital Account Deficit of such Member as quickly as possible, provided that an allocation pursuant to this Subsection shall be made only if and to the extent that such Member would have an Adjusted Capital Account Deficit after all other allocations provided for in Sections 6.1, 6.2, and 6.3 of the Agreement and this Section 1.2 have been made without giving effect to this Subsection (c).

d. Gross Income Allocation. In the event any Member has a deficit Capital Account at the end of Fiscal Year which is in excess of the sum of (i) the amount such Member is obligated to restore pursuant to this Agreement, and (ii) the amount such Member is deemed to be obligated to restore pursuant to Regulations 1.704-2(g)(1) and 1.704-2(1)(5), each such Member shall be specially allocated items of Company income and gain in the amount of such excess as quickly as possible, provided that an allocation pursuant to this Subsection shall be made only if and to the extent that such Member would have a deficit Capital Account after all other allocations provided for in Sections 6.1, 6.2 and 6.3 of the Agreement and this Section 1.2 have been made without giving effect to Subsection 1.2(c) and this Subsection 1.2(d).

e. Nonrecourse Deductions. Nonrecourse Deductions (as defined and determined in Regulations Sections 1.704-2(b) and 1.704-2(c)) for any Fiscal Year shall be allocated among the Members in proportion to their Units.

f. Member Nonrecourse Deductions. Any Member Nonrecourse Deductions (as defined under Regulations Section 1.704-2(1)(2)) shall be allocated pursuant to Regulations Section 1.704-2(1)(1) to the Member who bears the economic risk of loss with respect to the "Member Nonrecourse Debt" to which it is attributable.

g. Code Section 754 Adjustment. To the extent that an adjustment to the Basis of any asset pursuant to Code Section 734(b) or Code Section 743(b) is required to be taken into account in determining Capital Accounts as provided in Regulations Section 1.704-1(b)(2)(iv)(m), the adjustment shall be treated (if an increase) as an item of gain or (if a decrease) as an item of loss, and such gain or loss shall be allocated to the Members consistent with the allocation of the adjustment pursuant to such Regulation.

h. Allocations Relating to Taxable Issuance of Interests. Any income, gain, loss or deduction realized by the Company as a direct or indirect result of the issuance of Units by the Company (the "Issuance Items") shall be allocated among the Members, so that, to the extent possible, the net amount of such Issuance Items, together with all other allocations under this Agreement to each Member, shall be equal to the net amount that would have been allocated to each such Member if the Issuance Items had not been realized.

i. Purpose and Application. The purpose and the intent of the special allocations provided for in Section 6.3 of the Agreement and Sections 1.2(a) through (g) of this Appendix are to comply with the provisions of Regulations Sections 1.704-1(b) and 1.704-2, and such special allocations are to be made so as to accomplish that result. However, to the extent possible, the Manager, in allocating items of income, gain, loss, or deduction among the Members, shall take into account the special allocations in such a manner that the net amount of allocations to each Member shall be the same as such Member's distributive share of Profits and Losses would have been had the events requiring the special allocations not taken place. The Manager shall apply the provisions of this Section in whatever order the Manager reasonably believes will minimize the effect of the special allocations.

1.3. General Provisions.

a. Except as otherwise provided in this Agreement, the Members' distributive shares of all items of Company income, gain, loss, and deduction are the same as their distributive shares of Profits and Losses.

b. The Company shall allocate Profits, Losses, and other items properly allocable to any period using any method permitted by Code Section 706 and the Regulations thereunder.

c. To the extent permitted by Regulations Section 1.704-2(h) and Section 1.704-2(1)(6), the Company shall endeavor to avoid treating distributions as being from the proceeds of a Nonrecourse Liability (as defined in Regulations Section 1.752-1(a)(2)) or a Member Nonrecourse Debt.

d. If there is an increase or decrease in one or more Member's Units in the Company during a Fiscal Year, each Member's distributive share of Profits or Losses or any item thereof for such Fiscal Year shall be determined by any method prescribed by Code Section 706(d) or the Regulations thereunder that takes into account the varying Members' Interests in the Company during such Fiscal Year.

e. The Members agree to report their shares of income and loss for federal income tax purposes in accordance with the provisions of this Appendix.

1.4. Code Section 704(c) Allocations. Solely for federal income tax purposes and not with respect to determining any Member's Capital Account, distributive shares of Profits, Losses, other items, or distributions, a Member's distributive share of income, gain, loss, or deduction with respect to any Property (other than money) contributed to the Company, or with respect to any Property the Asset Value of which was determined as provided in this Agreement upon the acquisition of Membership Interest in the Company by a new Member or existing Member in exchange for a Capital Contribution, shall be determined in accordance with Code Section 704(c) and the Regulations thereunder or with the principles of such provisions.

In the event the Asset Value of any Company asset is adjusted pursuant to Section 1.1(b)(iii) hereof, subsequent allocations of income, gain, loss, and deduction with respect to such asset shall take account of any variation between the adjusted basis of such asset for federal income tax purposes and its Asset Value in the same manner as under Code Section 704(c) and the Regulations thereunder.

1.5. Curative Reallocations Regarding Payments to Members. To the extent that compensation paid to any Member by the Company ultimately is not determined to be a guaranteed payment under Code Section 707(c) or a payment other than in his capacity as a Member pursuant to Code Section 707(a), the Member shall be specially allocated gross income of the Company in an amount equal to the amount of such compensation, and the Member's Capital Account shall be adjusted to reflect the payment of such compensation. If the Company's gross income for a Fiscal Year is less than the amount of such compensation paid in such year, the Member shall be specially allocated gross income of the Company in the succeeding year or years until the total amount so allocated equals the total amount of such compensation.

1.6. Special Basis Adjustment. At the request of either the transferor or transferee in connection with a transfer of a Membership Interest in the Company, the Manager may, in its sole discretion, cause the Company to make the election provided for in Code Section 754 and maintain a record of the adjustments to Basis of Property resulting from that election. Any such transferee shall pay all costs incurred by the Company in connection with such election and the maintenance of such records.

1.7. Tax Matters Member.

a. _____, is hereby designated the Tax Matters Member (as defined in Section 6231(a)(7) of the Code) on behalf of the Company.

b. Without the unanimous consent of the Members owning one hundred percent (100%) of the Voting Units, the Tax Matters Member shall have no right to extend the statute of limitations for assessing or computing any tax liability against the Company or the amount of any Company tax item.

c. If the Tax Matters Member elects to file a petition for readjustment of any Company tax item (in accordance with Code Section 6226(a)) such petition shall be filed in the United States Tax Court unless the Members owning one hundred percent (100%) of the Voting Units unanimously agree otherwise.

d. The Tax Matters Member shall, within ten (10) business days after receipt thereof, forward to each Member a photocopy of any correspondence relating to the Company received from the Internal Revenue Service. The Tax Matters Member shall, within ten (10) business days thereof, advise each Member in writing of the substance of any conversation held with any representative of the Internal Revenue Service.

e. Any reasonable costs incurred by the Tax Matters Member for retaining accountants and/or lawyers on behalf of the Company in connection with any Internal Revenue Service audit of the Company shall be expenses of the Company. Any accountants and/or lawyers retained by the Company in connection with any Internal Revenue Service audit of the Company shall be selected by the Tax Matters Member and the fees therefor shall be expenses of the Company.

1.8. Deemed Liquidation. If no Dissolution Event has occurred, but the Company is deemed liquidated for federal income tax purposes within the meaning of Regulations Section 1.704-1(b)(2)(ii)(g), the Company shall not be wound up and dissolved but its assets and liabilities shall be deemed to have been distributed to the Members and contributed to a new Company which shall operate and be governed by the terms of this Agreement.

APPENDIX 2
ARTICLES OF ORGANIZATION

[to be attached]

CHAPTER 8

Organizing or Cleaning Up
a Partnership

8.1 What Are the Basic Partnership Types and Structures?

The two primary types of partnerships are the following, although other variations have been created by statute and may vary by state:

1. General Partnerships.

General partnerships, like sole proprietorships, are often formed by default. When two or more people enter into a business venture together without forming a legal entity, they create a general partnership. General partnerships are not particularly desirable as a form of doing business, because all of the partners are vulnerable to being held personally liable for the obligations and liabilities of the business. In the absence of a partnership agreement providing for the manner in which profits and losses are to be shared, profits in a general partnership are shared equally among the partners. For the specific provisions governing general partnerships in your state, see your state's Revised Uniform Partnership Act (RUPA) and the partnership agreement, if any.

2. Limited Partnerships.

Limited partnerships are traditionally comprised of two or more persons, with at least one designated as the general partner and at least one limited partner. The general partner has unlimited liability for the obligations of the business, while the limited partners are entitled to limited liability (similar to a shareholder in a corporation or a member in an LLC). Limited partnerships are established pursuant to statutory requirements, and they are formed by the filing of a statement with the secretary of state. To maintain their limited liability status, limited partners must be passive; that is, they may not participate in the management of the company. General partners are typically entities that offer their owners limited liability, rather than individuals, so no individual is subjected to unlimited liability.

Limited partnerships are governed by their limited partnership agreements and the provisions of the Uniform Limited Partnership Act adopted in their state of formation.

8.2 What Are the Roles of Partners?

1. General Partnerships.

In the absence of an agreement to the contrary, each partner has an equal right to participate in the management and control of the business. Each partner may be held jointly and severally liable for a copartner's wrongdoing or tortious act (e.g., the misapplication of another person's money or property). In a general partnership, each partner is deemed an agent of the partnership, such that any partner apparently carrying on partnership business can bind all of the partners, making them personally liable for the resulting obligations. What's worse, each partner can be held liable for each other partner's wrongdoing or tortious act, such as their embezzlement or professional malpractice.

2. Limited Partnerships.

Under the 2001 Uniform Limited Partnership Act, limited partnership rules are stated independently of the rules for general partnerships and limited liability companies. As a stand-alone body of law, the new Limited Partnership Act incorporates many provisions from RUPA and the Uniform Limited Liability Company Act (ULLCA), making it long and complex.

The 2001 Uniform Limited Partnership Act takes into account the widespread use of LLPs and LLCs under circumstances in which limited partnerships used to be the norm. It also accommodates the more narrow circumstances in which the limited partnership remains a preferable form of entity, namely (i) sophisticated, manager-entrenched commercial deals whose participants commit for the long term, and (ii) estate planning arrangements (family limited partnerships). Therefore the Limited Liability Act was drafted to support, and defaults to, strong centralized management that is strongly entrenched and passive investors with little control over or right to exit the entity.

8.3 What Formalities Must Be Observed?

The formalities required depend on the type of partnership and the terms of the partnership agreement. They can vary widely.

8.4 What Are the Tax and Regulatory Obligations of a Partnership?

1. Taxes.

Income in partnerships is allocated among the partners and is not taxed at the entity level (i.e., partnerships are pass-through entities for tax purposes). Therefore, partnerships are required to file information returns, rather than filing income tax returns like all other forms of business. Information returns report the operation's income, deductions, gains, losses, and so on that are passed through to its partners. All partners must include their share of these items on their individual tax returns. Partners may be required to pay estimated federal income tax in installments.

The partnership will be required to withhold federal income tax and social security tax from taxable wages paid to its employees and deposited periodically with the appropriate Federal Tax Deposit Form. An Employer's Quarterly Federal Tax Return (IRS Form 941) must then be filed before the end of the month following each calendar quarter. The partnership may also be required to withhold state income tax from its employees' taxable wages.

2. Renewals.

Legal requirements, such as annual state filings and the payment of annual fees, are required of limited partnerships, but not of general partnerships.

3. Employer ID.

Every new employer must obtain a Federal Employer Identification Number (FEIN) that will be used on partnership information returns and certain other documents. A FEIN can be obtained by application to the Internal Revenue Service on Form SS-4 or using the online application at http://www.irs.gov/businesses/small/article/0,,id=102767,00.html.

4. More Taxes.

If the partnership owns significant personal property, it may be required to file a property statement with the county assessor and may be subject to a personal property tax. Information and forms may be obtained from your county assessor, where applicable. If the nature of the corporation's business includes the sale at retail of tangible personal property (goods), then the corporation may be subject to sales and use taxes and would need to obtain a sellers' permit from its state and local authorities.

5. Business Licenses.

Most municipalities require that businesses within their jurisdictions obtain a local business license.

6. Industry Regulation.

Numerous regulated businesses cannot lawfully be conducted without special licensing or permits (e.g., general contractors, insurance sales, and cosmetologists). Make sure you know what regulatory requirements are unique to your business.

8.5 Sample Documents and Checklists.

This section includes the following forms:

- Certificate of Limited Partnership—Delaware (Form 8 A)
- Limited Partnership Agreement—California (Form 8 B)
- Amendment to Limited Partnership Agreement (Form 8 C)
- One-Page General Partnership Agreement (Form 8 D)
- Partnership Agreement for LLP—California (Form 8 E)

Form 8 A: Certificate of Limited Partnership—Delaware

Note: Check with the secretary of state in your state for the requirements and prescribed forms, if any, for the formation of a limited partnership.

STATE *of* DELAWARE
CERTIFICATE *of* LIMITED PARTNERSHIP

The Undersigned, desiring to form a limited partnership pursuant to the Delaware Revised Uniform Limited Partnership Act, 6 Delaware Code, Chapter 17, do hereby certify as follows:

First: The name of the limited partnership is _____
_____

Second: The name and address of the Registered Agent is _____
_____
_____

Third: The name and mailing address of each general partner is as follows:
_____
_____
_____

In Witness Whereof, the undersigned has executed this Certificate of Limited Partnership of _____
as of _____ .

By _____
General Partner(s)

Name: _____
Typed or Printed

Form 8 B: Limited Partnership Agreement—California

**** FUND IV, L.P.
LIMITED PARTNERSHIP AGREEMENT

TABLE OF CONTENTS

357

**** FUND IV, L.P.
LIMITED PARTNERSHIP AGREEMENT

This Agreement is made and entered into as of the ___ day of _____, 20__, by and among ****, LLC, a California limited liability company (the "General Partner"), and each of the persons whose names are set forth under the heading "Limited Partners" on the Schedule of Partners attached hereto, who hereby form **** Fund IV, L.P., a California limited partnership (the "Partnership"), pursuant to the California Revised Limited Partnership Act, as follows:

Article I
Name, Purpose, and Principal Office of Partnership

1.1 <u>Partnership Name</u>. The name of the Partnership is Fund IV, L.P. The partners of the Partnership are the General Partner and the Limited Partners (collectively, the "Partners", individually a "Partner"). The affairs of the Partnership shall be conducted under the Partnership name or such other name as the General Partner may, it its discretion, determine.

1.2 <u>Partnership Purpose</u>. The primary purpose of the Partnership is to identify and recruit promising emerging growth companies and provide a variety of consulting, technical and other services as well as cash investments to those companies in exchange for stock equity in those companies. The Partnership shall engage in such other activities as are related to the foregoing that the General Partner, in its reasonable opinion, determine to be necessary or advisable to further the business of the Partnership.

1.3 <u>Principal Office; Registered Office</u>. The principal office of the Partnership shall be _____, or such other place or places within the United States as the General Partner may from time to time designate.

Article II
Term and Termination of the Partnership

2.1 <u>Term of Partnership.</u> The term of the Partnership shall commence upon the filing of the Certificate of Limited Partnership of the Partnership with the Secretary of State of the State of _____ and shall continue until the earlier of (i) _____ (which date may be extended at the discretion of the General Partner if the Limited Partners have received distributions of at least three (3) times their initial capital contributions by such date), or (ii) the bankruptcy, or dissolution and commencement of winding up, of the General Partner (the "Partnership Term").

2.2 <u>Events Affecting a Member of the General Partner</u>. The death, temporary or permanent incapacity, insanity, incompetency, bankruptcy, expulsion, retirement, withdrawal, removal, liquidation, dissolution, reorganization, sale of substantially all of the assets of or a change in the ownership or nature of any member of the General Partner or the admission of additional members to the General Partner shall not dissolve the Partnership, unless such event causes a bankruptcy, or dissolution and commencement of winding up of the General Partner.

2.3 <u>Events Affecting a Limited Partner of the Partnership</u>. The death, incapacity, insanity, incompetency, bankruptcy, liquidation, dissolution, reorganization, merger, sale of substantially all the stock or assets of, or other change in the ownership or nature of a Limited Partner shall not terminate the Partnership.

Article III
Capital Contributions

3.1 <u>Initial Capital Contributions.</u> Upon the execution of this Agreement, each Partner shall contribute to the Partnership cash or property (the "Capital Contribution" of the Partner) as follows:

3.1.1 <u>General Partner</u>. The General Partner shall contribute cash or a promissory note (in the principal amount) equal to _____ [e.g. one percent (1%) of the initial capital contributions made by the Limited Partners].

3.1.2 <u>Limited Partner.</u> Each Limited Partner shall contribute cash in an amount equal to _____ Dollars ($___) multiplied by the number of units of interest in the Partnership ("Unit"), or fractions thereof, he, she or it acquires and as set forth on Schedule 3.1 appended hereto.

3.2 <u>Placement of Funds.</u> All funds received during subscription will be placed in a separate interest-bearing escrow account (the "Escrow"). At such time as _____ [e.g. ten (10)] Units, yielding gross proceeds in the amount of _____ Dollars ($_____) have been acquired, then (a) interest earned during the term of the Escrow (net of fees and expenses of the escrow agent) will be paid to the Limited Partners, and (b) the proceeds from the sale of the Units, shall be disbursed to the Partnership. Should the minimum number of Units not be sold on or before _____, or the date of termination of the offering of such Units, if earlier, then, all funds will be refunded promptly to each subscriber, such refund to be made in full, together with any interest earned thereon.

3.3 <u>No Additional Capital Contributions; Liability</u>. No Partner shall be required to contribute any additional capital to the Partnership, and no Limited Partner shall have personal liability for any obligation of the Partnership except as expressly provided by law.

3.4 <u>No Interest on Capital Contributions</u>. Except as otherwise provided in this Agreement, no Partner shall be paid interest with respect to his, her or its contribution to Partnership capital.

3.5 <u>Return of Capital Contributions</u>. Except as otherwise provided in this Agreement, no Partner shall have the right to receive the return of any Capital Contribution or withdraw from the Partnership, except upon the dissolution of the Partnership.

3.6 <u>Form of Return of Capital Contribution.</u> If a Partner is entitled to receive the return of any Capital Contribution, the General Partner may distribute in lieu of money, notes, securities or other property having a value equal to the amount of money distributable to such Partner.

3.7 <u>General Partner Entitled To Purchase Units.</u> Subject to the provisions of Sections 3.1 and 3.2, the General Partner and/or any Affiliate of the General Partner may acquire Units from time to time on its, his or her own behalf and for its, his or her own benefit, provided that such right shall not create any preference in rights or benefits in favor of the General Partner and/or any Affiliate of the General Partner or permit the General Partner and/or any Affiliate of the General Partner to buy Units other than at the same cash price and on the same terms as are available to any other Limited Partner.

3.8 <u>Unit Certificates.</u>

3.8.1 <u>Certificate</u>. At the sole discretion of the General Partner, a Unit may be represented by a certificate (the "Certificate"). The exact contents of the Certificate may be determined by the General Partner, but any Certificate shall be issued substantially in conformity with the following requirements. The Certificates shall be respectively numbered serially, as they are issued and shall be signed by the General Partner. Each Certificate shall state the name of the Partnership, the fact that the Partnership is organized under the laws of the State of _____ as a limited partnership, the name of the person to whom the Certificate is issued and the date of issue. A statement of the designations, preferences, qualifications, limitations, restrictions, and special or relative rights of the Units, if any, shall be set forth in full or summarized on the face or back of the Certificates which the Partnership shall issue, or in lieu thereof, the Certificate may set forth that such a statement or summary will be furnished to any holder of a Unit upon request without charge. Notwithstanding the foregoing, the face of each Certificate shall contain a legend substantially in the following form:

"THE UNITS OF THE PARTNERSHIP REPRESENTED BY THIS CERTIFICATE HAVE NOT BEEN REGISTERED UNDER THE SECURITIES ACT OF 1933, AS AMENDED, OR QUALIFIED UNDER ANY STATE SECURITIES LAWS, AND MAY NOT BE SOLD, TRANSFERRED, ASSIGNED OR HYPOTHECATED UNLESS THERE IS AN EFFECTIVE REGISTRATION STATEMENT UNDER SUCH ACT OR LAWS COVERING SUCH UNITS, OR THE HOLDER RECEIVES AN OPINION OF COUNSEL FOR THE HOLDER OF THE UNITS SATISFACTORY TO THE PARTNERSHIP, STATING THAT SUCH SALE, TRANSFER, ASSIGNMENT OR HYPOTHECATION IS EXEMPT FROM THE REGISTRATION AND PROSPECTUS DELIVERY REQUIREMENTS OF SUCH ACT AND THE QUALIFICATION REQUIREMENTS UNDER APPLICABLE STATE LAW. THESE UNITS MAY ALSO BE SUBJECT TO ADDITIONAL RESTRICTIONS UNDER THE TERMS OF THE PARTNERSHIP'S AGREEMENT. "

Each Certificate shall be otherwise in such form as may be determined by the General Partner.

     3.8.2 <u>Cancellation of Certificate.</u> Except as herein provided with respect to lost, stolen, or destroyed Certificates, no new Certificates shall be issued in lieu of previously issued Certificates until former Certificates for a like number of Units shall have been surrendered and canceled. All Certificates surrendered to the Partnership for transfer shall be canceled.

     3.8.3 <u>Replacement of Lost, Stolen, or Destroyed Certificate</u>. Any Limited Partner claiming that his, her or its Certificate is lost, stolen or destroyed may make an affidavit or affirmation of that fact and request a new Certificate. A new Certificate may be issued of the same tenor and representing the same interest in the Partnership as was represented by the Certificate alleged to be lost, stolen or destroyed.

Article IV
Capital Accounts and Allocations

     4.1 <u>Capital Accounts.</u> A "Capital Account" (as described herein) shall be maintained on the Partnership's books for each Partner. In the event any interest in the Partnership is transferred in accordance with the terms of this Agreement, the transferee shall succeed to the Capital Account of the transferor to the extent it relates to the transferred interest.

     4.2 <u>Definitions</u>. Unless the context requires otherwise, the following terms have the meanings specified in this Section:

     4.2.1 <u>Adjusted Capital Contribution.</u> The amount of a Partner's Initial Capital Contribution plus the sum of any future contributions to Capital he, she or it subsequently contributes to the Partnership less the aggregate amount of all Partnership distributions made to him or her.

4.2.2 <u>Book Value</u>. The Book Value with respect to any asset shall be the asset's adjusted basis for federal income tax purposes, except as follows:

(a) The initial Book Value of any asset contributed by a Partner to the Partnership shall be the fair market value of such asset at the time of contribution, as determined by the contributing Partner and the Partnership. The preceding sentence shall not be interpreted as authorizing the General Partner to contribute to the Partnership any asset other than cash or to accept other than cash contributions from any Limited Partner.

(b) In the discretion of the General Partner, the Book Values of all Partnership assets may be adjusted to equal their respective fair market values, as determined by the General Partner, and the resulting unrecognized gain or loss allocated to the Capital Accounts of the Partners pursuant to Section 4.3 below as of the following times: (A) the acquisition of an additional interest in the Partnership by any new or existing Partner (other than a Limited Partner who is admitted (or increases his, her or its interest) within six (6) months of the effective date of this Agreement) in exchange for more than a de minimis Capital Contribution; and (B) the distribution by the Partnership to a Partner of more than a de minimis amount of Partnership assets, unless all Partners receive simultaneous distributions of either undivided interests in the distributed property or identical Partnership assets in proportion to their interests in the Partnership.

(c) The Book Values of all Partnership assets shall be adjusted to equal their respective fair market values, as determined by the General Partner, and the resulting unrecognized gain or loss allocated to the Capital Accounts of the Partners as Net Income or Loss pursuant to Section 4.3 below upon the termination of the Partnership pursuant to the provisions of this Agreement.

(d) The Book Values of Partnership assets shall be increased or decreased to the extent required under Treasury Regulation Section 1.704-1(b)(2)(iv)(m) in the event that the adjusted tax basis of Partnership assets are adjusted pursuant to Code Sections 732, 734 or 743.

(e) The Book Value of a Partnership asset shall be adjusted by the depreciation, amortization or other cost recovery deductions, if any, taken into account by the Partnership with respect to such asset in computing Net Income or Loss.

4.2.3 <u>Capital Account</u>. An account maintained by the Partnership with respect to each Partner in accordance with the following provisions: The Capital Account of each Partner shall be increased by:

(a) the amount of money contributed to the Partnership by such Partner,

(b) such Partner's share of Net Income (or other items of book income or gain) allocated to its Capital Account pursuant to this Agreement, and

(c) any other amounts required by Treasury Regulation Section 1.704-1(b), provided that the General Partner determines that such increase is consistent with the economic arrangement among the Partners as expressed in this Agreement. and shall be decreased by:

(d) the amount of money and the fair market value of any property distributed by the Partnership (determined pursuant to Section 11.2 hereof as of the Date of Distribution of such property) to such Partner pursuant to the provisions of this Agreement (net of any liabilities secured by such property that such Partner is considered to assume or hold subject to for purposes of Section 752 of the Code),

(e) such Partner's share of Capital Transaction Loss and Net Loss (or other items of book loss or expense) allocated to its Capital Account pursuant to this Agreement, and

(f) any other amounts required by Treasury Regulation Section 1.704-1(b), provided that the General Partner determines that such decrease is consistent with the economic arrangement among the Partners expressed in this Agreement.

One Capital Account shall be maintained for the General Partner in its capacity as general partner of the Partnership, and another wholly separate Capital Account shall be maintained for the General Partner in its capacity as a Limited Partner of the Partnership, if any. Any reference in this Agreement to the "General Partner's Capital Account," the "Capital Account of the General Partner" or the like shall refer to the Capital Account maintained for the General Partner in its capacity as general partner of the Partnership. In addition, for purposes of this Agreement, allocations and distributions made to the General Partner in its capacity as a Limited Partner of the Partnership shall be treated as having been made to a Limited Partner and, accordingly, shall not be treated as having been made to the General Partner.

4.2.4 <u>Fiscal Quarter.</u> The Fiscal Quarters of the Partnership shall begin on January 1, April 1, July 1, and October 1, and end on March 31, June 30, September 30, and December 31, respectively.

4.2.5 <u>Fiscal Year.</u> The Partnership's first Fiscal Year shall begin on the date hereof and end on December 31, 2000. Thereafter, the Partnership's Fiscal Year shall commence on January 1 of each year and end on December 31 of such year or, if earlier, the date the Partnership terminated during such year pursuant to Section 2.1 or otherwise. The General Partner at any time may elect a different Fiscal Year if permitted by the Code and the applicable Treasury Regulations.

4.2.6 <u>Interim Period.</u> If a Partnership interest is transferred, the number of Units of any Partner changes, a Partner withdraws or a new Partner is admitted to the Partnership other than on the first day of any Fiscal Quarter during the Partnership Term, or if the General Partner shall so elect, then the date of such event or election (the "Interim Date") shall commence an Interim Period. An Interim Period shall end on the last day of the Fiscal Quarter in which the Interim Period began or on the day immediately preceding the beginning of a new Interim Period, whichever is earlier.

4.2.7 <u>Net Income and Net Loss.</u> Net Income and Net Loss shall be the Net Book Income or Loss of the Partnership for any relevant period, determined as of the last day of such period.

4.2.8 <u>Net Book Income or Loss.</u> The Net Book Income or Loss of the Partnership shall be computed in accordance with Federal income tax principles under the method of accounting elected by the Partnership for federal income tax purposes as applied without regard to any recharacterization of transactions or relationship that might otherwise be required under such tax principles and as otherwise adjusted pursuant to the following provisions. The Net Book Income or Loss of the Partnership shall be computed, inter alia, by:

(a) including as income or deductions, as appropriate, any tax exempt income and related expenses that are neither properly included in the computation of taxable income nor capitalized for federal income tax purposes;

(b) including as a deduction when paid or incurred (depending on the Partnership's method of accounting) any amounts utilized to organize the Partnership or to promote the sale of (or to sell) an interest in the Partnership, except that amounts for which an election is properly made by the Partnership under Section 709(b) of the Code shall be accounted for as provided therein;

(c) including as a deduction any losses incurred by the Partnership in connection with the sale or exchange of property notwithstanding that such losses may be disallowed to the Partnership for federal income tax purposes under the related party rules of Code Sections 267(a)(1) or 707(b) or otherwise; and

(d) calculating the gain or loss on disposition of Partnership assets and the depreciation, amortization or other cost recovery deductions, if any, with respect to Partnership assets by reference to their Book Value rather than their adjusted tax basis.

4.2.9 <u>Sale or Exchange</u>. A sale, exchange, liquidation or similar transaction, event, or condition with respect to any assets (except realizations of purchase discounts on commercial paper, certificates of deposit, or other money-market instruments) of the Partnership of the type that would cause any realized gain or loss to be recognized for income tax purposes under the Code (as determined without giving effect to the related party rules of Code Sections 267(a)(1), 707(b) and any other provision that defers or eliminates recognition or gain or loss based upon the relationship between transferor and transferee).

4.3 <u>Allocation of Net Income or Loss.</u> Net Income or Loss shall be allocated as follows:

(a) <u>Allocation of Net Income</u>. Except as otherwise provided in Article XIV, at the end of each Fiscal Year of the Partnership, Net Income of the Partnership shall be allocated:

(i) first, solely to the Partners until such time as the amount allocated constitutes the Partner's Adjusted Capital Contribution plus a pretax internal rate of return on each Partner's Adjusted Capital Contribution of _____ [e.g. eight percent (8%) per annum (the "8% Preferred Return"), based upon annual compounding, a three hundred sixty- (360)-day year of twelve (12) thirty- (30)-day months and no compounding for periods of less than one (1) full year (collectively the "Preferred Return")], and

(ii) thereafter, _____ [e.g. thirty percent (30%)] to the General Partner and _____ [e.g. seventy percent (70%)] to the Limited Partners as a group.

(b) <u>Allocation of Net Loss</u>. Except as otherwise provided in Article XIV, at the end of each Fiscal Year of the Partnership the Net Loss (if any) of the Partnership for such Fiscal Year shall be allocated to the Partners in proportion to the respective aggregate amounts of Net Income (if any) allocated to them.

4.4 <u>Allocation Among Limited Partners</u>. Except as otherwise specifically provided in this Agreement, all Net Income and Loss (and items thereof) allocated to the Capital Accounts of the Limited Partners as a group for any period shall be allocated among the Limited Partners in proportion to their respective Units as of the end of such period.

Article V
Management Fee: Expenses

5.1 <u>Management Fee</u>. The General Partner shall be compensated for services rendered to the Partnership until the Date of Termination for each Fiscal Quarter by the payment by the Partnership in cash to the General Partner (or its designee) on the first day of such Fiscal Quarter (or portion thereof) of a management fee; provided, however, that the management fee for the Partnership's first Fiscal Quarter shall be payable on the Initial Contribution Date. The management fee for each of the Partnership's Fiscal Quarters shall be an amount equal to _____
[e.g. six hundred twenty-five thousandths of one per cent (0.625%) of the sum of the capital contributions of all of the Partners of the Partnership as of the first day of each such Fiscal Quarter; provided, however, that the management fee for the Part-

nership's first Fiscal Quarter shall be based upon the ratio the number of days in the period beginning on the first day of the Partnership Term and ending on the last day of the Partnership's first Fiscal Quarter, bears to ninety (90)].

5.2 <u>Expenses</u>. The Partnership shall bear all taxes, costs and expenses incurred in connection with the activities of the Partnership, including costs and expenses related to its organization and dissolution and winding up.

5.3 <u>Competing Activities of General Partner</u>. The General Partner and its agents, employees and Affiliates may engage or invest in, independently or with others, any business activity of any type or description, including, without limitation, those that might be the same as or similar to the Partnership's business and that might be in direct or indirect competition with the Partnership. Neither the Partnership nor any Partner shall have any right in or to such other ventures or activities or to the income or proceeds derived therefrom. Neither the General Partner nor any agent, employee or Affiliate of the General Partner shall be obligated to present any investment opportunity or prospective economic advantage to the Partnership, even if the opportunity is of the character that, if presented to the Partnership, could be taken by the Partnership. The General Partner, its agents, employees and Affiliates shall have the right to hold any investment opportunity or prospective economic advantage for its, his or her own account or to recommend such investment opportunity to persons other than the Partnership. The Partners acknowledge that the General Partner, its members and Affiliates own and/or manage, or may hereafter own and/or manage, other businesses, including businesses that may compete with the Partnership and for the General Partner's time. The Partners hereby waive any and all rights and claims which they may otherwise have against the General Partner, agents, employees and Affiliates as a result of any such activities.

Article VI
Withdrawals by and Distributions to the Partners

6.1 <u>Interest</u>. No interest shall be paid to any Partner on account of his, her or its interest in the capital of, or on account of its investment in, the Partnership.

6.2 <u>Withdrawals by the Partners</u>. No Partner may withdraw any amount from his, her or its capital account unless such withdrawal is made pursuant to this Article VI.

6.3 <u>Distributions</u>. The General Partner may make distributions to the Partners during the Partnership Term as follows:

(a) The General Partner may, in its sole discretion, prior to the Date of Termination, make distributions of cash or distribute in kind property with such distributions being made as follows:

(i) first, solely to the Partners until such time as each Partner has received aggregate distributions equal to his, her or its Preferred Return; and

(ii) thereafter, _____ [e.g. thirty percent (30%)] to the General Partner and _____ [e.g. seventy percent (70%)] to the Limited Partners as a group.

(b) Immediately prior to any distribution in kind of any Partnership assets pursuant to any provision of this Agreement, the difference between the fair market value and the Book Value of any Partnership assets distributed shall be allocated to the Capital Accounts of the Partners as Net Income or Loss pursuant to Article IV or Section 10.3, as appropriate.

(c) Securities distributed in kind pursuant to this Section 6.3 shall be subject to such conditions and restrictions as the General Partner determines are legally required. Such restrictions shall apply equally to the Securities distributed to all Partners.

(d) At any time, the General Partner may distribute cash or Securities to all Partners in the proportions specified in Section 6.3(a), provided that, immediately after the proposed distribution the Capital Account Balance of the General Partner (as determined after adjusting such balance for the amount of such distribution and any Net Income or Loss deemed recognized by the Partnership pursuant to Section 6.3(b) as a result thereof) will not be negative.

(e) At any time, the General Partner may, in its sole discretion, distribute cash or Securities to the Limited Partners in proportion to their Units.

(f) Except as provided in Section 14.7 hereof or as otherwise required by law, no Partner shall be obligated at any time to repay or restore to the Partnership all or any part of any distribution made to it from the Partnership in accordance with the terms of this Section 6.3.

6.4 <u>Allocation of Distributions Among Limited Partners</u>. Except as otherwise specifically provided in this Agreement, any distribution to the Limited Partners as a group shall be allocated among the Limited Partners in proportion to their respective Units as of the date of the distribution.

Article VII
Management

7.1 <u>Management</u>. The General Partner shall have the sole and exclusive right to manage, control, and conduct the affairs of the Partnership and to do any and all acts on behalf of the Partnership (including exercise of rights to elect to adjust the tax basis of Partnership assets and to revoke such elections and to make such other tax elections as the General Partner shall deem appropriate).

7.2 <u>No Control by the Limited Partners</u>. The Limited Partners shall take no part in the control or management of the affairs of the Partnership nor shall a Limited Partner have any authority to act for or on behalf of the Partnership.

7.3 <u>Indebtedness.</u> The General Partner may borrow money or otherwise incur indebtedness on behalf of the Partnership.

7.4 <u>Admission of Additional Partners</u>. The General Partner may admit additional Limited Partners or accept additional contributions to capital from an existing Limited Partner or existing Limited Partners upon such terms as the General Partner deems advisable.

Article VIII
Investment Representations

8.1 <u>Investment Representation of the Limited Partners</u>. This Agreement is made with each Limited Partner in reliance upon such Limited Partner's representation to the Partnership, which by executing this Agreement the Limited Partner hereby con-firms, that such Limited Partner's interest in the Partnership is to be acquired for investment, and not with a view to the sale or distribution of any part thereof, and that such Limited Partner has no present intention of selling, granting participation in, or otherwise distributing the same, but subject nevertheless to any requirement of law that the disposition of such Limited Partner's property shall at all times be within such Limited Partner's control. Each Limited Partner further represents that such Limited Partner does not have any contract, undertaking, agreement, or arrangement with any person to sell or transfer to any third person such Limited Partner's interest in the Partnership. Each Limited Partner understands and acknowledges that such Limited Partner's interest in the Partnership is an illiquid investment and no public market now exists, or will hereafter exist, for any of the Partnership's interests.

8.2 <u>Accredited Investor and Investment Company Act Representations.</u> Each Limited Partner represents that such Partner has such knowledge and experience in financial and business matters as to be capable of evaluating the merits and risks of an investment in the Partnership and that such Partner is an accredited investor, as that term is defined in Regulation D promulgated by the Securities and Exchange Commission. Except as otherwise disclosed in writing to the General Partner, each Limited Partner further represents that (i) such Limited Partner is not, nor would be but for the exception provided in paragraph 3(c)(1) or 3(c)(7) of the Investment Company Act of 1940, as amended (the "1940 Act"), an investment company (as defined in the 1940 Act); (ii) such Limited Partner's Capital Commitment does not exceed forty percent (40%) of such Limited Partner's assets; (iii) such Limited Partner's shareholders, partners or other holders of equity or beneficial interests in such Limited Partner are not able to decide individually whether to participate, or the extent of their participation, in such Limited Partner's investment in the Partnership; (iv) to the best of such Limited Partner's knowledge, such Limited Partner does not control, nor is controlled by or under common control with, any other Limited Partner; (v) the Limited Partner was not formed for the specific purpose of investing in the Partnership; (vi) the Limited Partner would be considered, and the interest in the Partnership held by the Limited Partner would be considered to be beneficially owned by, "one person" for purposes of Section 3(c)(1) of the 1940 Act; and (vii) no other person or persons will have a beneficial interest in such Limited Partner's interest in the Partnership other than as a shareholder, partner or other beneficial owner of equity interests in such Limited Partner.

Article IX
Restrictions on Transfer

No Limited Partner shall sell, assign, mortgage, hypothecate, encumber or otherwise transfer his, her or its Units in the Partnership, or any interest therein, (collectively, a "Transfer") without the written consent of the General Partner which consent may be withheld in the sole discretion of the General Partner and shall not be subject to challenge by any potential transferor or transferee. In addition, in the event of a permitted Transfer, the transferee shall not be admitted as a substitute Limited Partner without the consent of the General Partner, which consent may be withheld in the sole discretion of the General Partner and shall not be subject to challenge by any transferor or transferee. A Transfer shall be effective, unless otherwise agreed by the General Partner, as of the close of business on the last day of the Fiscal Quarter in which the Transfer occurs.

Article X
Dissolution and Liquidation of the Partnership

10.1 <u>Liquidation Procedures.</u> Upon termination of the Partnership at the expiration of the Partnership Term or upon the occurrence of an event of dissolution described in Section 2.2 above:

(a) The affairs of the Partnership shall be wound up and the Partnership shall be dissolved.

(b) Distributions in dissolution may be made in cash or in kind or partly in cash and partly in kind. To the extent not inconsistent with Section 14.7 of this Agreement, each security (and each class of Securities, or portion of a class of Securities having a tax basis per share or unit different from other portions of such class) distributed in kind shall be distributed ratably in accordance with the Partners' positive Capital

Account balances unless such distribution would result (i) in a violation of a law or regulation applicable to any Partner or a tax penalty to any Partner, in which event, upon receipt by the General Partner of notice to such effect, such Partner may designate a different entity to receive the distribution, or designate, subject to the approval of the General Partner, an alternative distribution procedure or (ii) in a distribution of fractional shares. Each such security shall be valued at fair market value in accordance with Section 11.2 as of the Date of Distribution of such Security and shall be subject to reasonable conditions and restrictions necessary or advisable in order to preserve the value of the assets distributed, or for legal reasons.

(c) The General Partner shall use its reasonable best judgment as to the most advantageous time for the Partnership to sell investments or to make distributions in kind provided that any such sales shall be made as promptly as is consistent with obtaining the fair value thereof.

(d) The proceeds of dissolution shall be applied to payment of liabilities of the Partnership and distributed to the Partners in the following order:

(i) to the creditors of the Partnership, other than Partners, in the order of priority established by law;

(ii) to the Partners, in repayment of any loans made to the Partnership;

(iii) to the Partners, in respect of the positive balances in their Capital Accounts.

10.2 <u>Date of Termination.</u> The "Date of Termination" shall mean the date on which the term of the Partnership terminates pursuant to Sections 2.1 or 2.2 above.

10.3 <u>Final Allocations.</u> The closing Capital Accounts of all the Partners shall be computed as of the Date of Termination as if the Date of Termination were the last day of an Interim Period, and then adjusted in the following manner:

(a) All assets and liabilities (including contingent liabilities) of the Partnership shall be valued as of the Date of Termination pursuant to Section 11.2 below.

(b) The resulting net amount of the unrecognized gain or loss on the Partnership's assets and liabilities as of the Date of Termination shall be deemed to have been recognized (pursuant to a deemed sale or exchange of the Partnership's assets and deemed payment of the Partnership's liabilities) and shall be allocated to the Capital Accounts of the Partners in accordance with the provisions of Article IV (and corresponding adjustments shall be made to the Book Values of such assets). In addition, allocations of Net Income and Loss shall be adjusted (and corresponding adjustments made to the Capital Accounts of the Partners) to the extent necessary, if any, so that over the life of the Partnership aggregate allocations of items of Net Income and Loss shall have been effected in the manner specified in this Agreement.

(c) All allocations to the Partners of Net Income or Loss or items thereof for all periods after the Date of Termination shall be made as provided in Article IV.

ARTICLE XI
Financial Accounting

11.1 <u>Financial and Tax Accounting.</u> The books and records of the Partnership and the General Partner shall be kept in accordance with the provisions of this Agreement and otherwise in accordance with generally accepted accounting principles consistently applied.

11.2 <u>Valuation of Securities and Other Assets Owned by the Partnership.</u> The valuation of Securities and other assets and liabilities under this Agreement shall be at fair market value. The General Partner shall have the power at any time to determine the fair market value of any assets and liabilities of the Partnership pursuant to this Section 11.2.

ARTICLE XII
Other Provisions

12.1 <u>Governing Law</u>. This Agreement shall be governed by and construed under the laws of the State of California as applied to agreements among residents of that state made and to be performed entirely within the state.

12.2 <u>Notices</u>. Any notice or other communication that a Partner desires to give to another Partner shall be in writing, and shall be deemed effectively given upon personal delivery or upon deposit in any United States mailbox, by registered or certified mail, postage prepaid, or upon transmission by telegram or telecopy, addressed to the other Partner at the address shown on the Schedule of Partners or at such other address as a Partner may designate by fifteen (15) days' advance written notice to the other Partners.

12.3 <u>Power of Attorney</u>. By signing this Agreement, each of the Limited Partners designates and appoints the General Partner his, her or its true and lawful attorney, in his, her or its name, place and stead to make, execute, sign, and file such instruments, documents, or certificates that may from time to time be required of the Partnership by the laws of the United States of America, the laws of the State of California, or any other state in which the Partnership shall conduct its investment activities in order to qualify or otherwise enable the Partnership to conduct its affairs in such jurisdictions. Such attorney is not hereby granted any authority on behalf of the Limited Partners to amend this Agreement except that as attorney for each of the Limited Partners, the General Partner shall have the authority to amend this Agreement and the Certificate of Limited Partnership as may be required to affect admissions of additional partners, transfers of Limited Partnership interests, or reductions in the Limited Partnership interests of certain Partners as provided in Section 3.4.

12.4 <u>Amendment</u>. This Agreement may be amended only with the written consent of the General Partner and Limited Partners holding a majority of the Units; provided that the General Partner may amend this Agreement without the consent of the Limited Partners to clarify any ambiguities or errors in this Agreement or to effect any amendments that do not adversely affect Limited Partners. No term or condition contained in the exhibits to this Agreement may be waived, discharged, terminated, or modified without the consent of the General Partner and Limited Partners holding a majority of the Units.

12.5 <u>Exculpation</u>. Neither the General Partner nor any of its agents, employees, or Affiliates, shall be liable to a Limited Partner or the Partnership for honest mistakes of judgment, or for action or inaction, taken in good faith for a purpose that was reasonably believed to be in the best interests of the Partnership, or for losses due to such mistakes, action, or inaction, or to the negligence, dishonesty, or bad faith of any employee, broker, or other agent of the Partnership, provided that such employee, broker, or agent was selected, engaged or retained and supervised with reasonable care. The General Partner may consult with counsel and accountants in respect of Partnership affairs and be fully protected and justified in any action or inaction that is taken in accordance with the advice or opinion of such counsel or accountants, provided that they shall have been selected with reasonable care.

12.6 <u>Indemnification</u>. The Partnership agrees to indemnify, out of the assets of the Partnership only, the General Partner, its members and partners and its agents and Affiliates to the fullest extent permitted by law and to save and hold them harmless from and in respect of all (a) reasonable fees, costs, and expenses paid in connection with or resulting from any claim, action, or demand against the General Partner, its members or partners, the Partnership or their agents and Affiliates that arise out of or in any way relate to the Partnership, its properties, business, or affairs and

(b) such claims, actions, and demands and any losses or damages resulting from such claims, actions, and demands, including amounts paid in settlement or compromise (if recommended by attorneys for the Partnership) of any such claim, action or demand; provided, however, that this indemnity shall not extend to conduct not undertaken in good faith to promote the best interests of the Partnership.

12.7 <u>Limitation of Liability of the Limited Partners</u>. Except as required by law, no Limited Partner shall be bound by, nor be personally liable for, the expenses, liabilities, or obligations of the Partnership. Each Limited Partner shall be obligated and liable to the Partnership to make capital contributions to the Partnership pursuant to Article III and for any obligation or liability of such Limited Partner to the Partnership pursuant to Section 14.7.

12.8 <u>Tax Matters Partner.</u> The General Partner shall be the Partnership's Tax Matters Partner ("TMP"). The TMP shall have the right to resign by giving thirty (30) days' written notice to the Limited Partners. Upon the resignation, dissolution or bankruptcy of the TMP, a successor TMP shall be elected by Limited Partners holding at least two-thirds of the Units. The TMP shall employ experienced tax counsel to represent the Partnership in connection with any audit or investigation of the Partnership by the Internal Revenue Service ("IRS") and in connection with all subsequent administrative and judicial proceedings arising out of such audit. The fees and expenses of such, and all expenses incurred by the TMP in serving as the TMP, shall be Partnership expenses pursuant to Section 5.2 and shall be paid by the Partnership. Notwithstanding the foregoing, it shall be the responsibility of the Partners, at their expense, to employ tax counsel to represent their respective separate interests. If the TMP is required by law or regulation to incur fees and expenses in connection with tax matters not affecting each of the Partners, then the TMP may, in its sole discretion, seek reimbursement from or charge such fees and expenses to the Capital Accounts of those Partners on whose behalf such fees and expenses were incurred. The TMP shall keep the Limited Partners informed of all administrative and judicial proceedings, as required by Section 6223(g) of the Code, and shall furnish to each Limited Partner who so requests in writing, a copy of each notice or other communication received by the TMP from the IRS except such notices or communications as are sent directly to such Partner by the IRS. The relationship of the TMP to the Limited Partners is that of a fiduciary, and the TMP has a fiduciary obligation to perform its duties as TMP in such manner as will serve the best interests of the Partnership and all of the Partnership's partners. To the fullest extent permitted by law, the Partnership agrees to indemnify the TMP and its agents and save and hold them harmless, from and in respect to all (i) reasonable fees, costs and expenses in connection with or resulting from any claim, action, or demand against the TMP, the General Partner, or the Partnership that arise out of or in any way relate to the TMP's status as TMP for the Partnership, and (ii) all such claims, actions, and demands and any losses or damages therefrom, including amounts paid in settlement or compromise of any such claim, action, or demand; provided that this indemnity shall not extend to conduct by the TMP adjudged (i) not to have been undertaken reasonably and in good faith to promote the best interests of the Partnership or (ii) to have constituted gross negligence, recklessness or intentional wrongdoing by the TMP.

12.9 <u>Other Instruments and Acts</u>. The Partners agree to execute any other instruments or perform any other acts that are or may be necessary to effectuate and carry on the Partnership created by this Agreement.

12.10 <u>Binding Agreement</u>. This Agreement shall be binding upon the transferees, successors, assigns, and legal representatives of the Partners.

12.11 <u>Effective Date</u>. The Limited Partnership Agreement shall be effective on the date that the Certificate of Limited Partnership of the Partnership is filed with the office of the Secretary of State of the State of California.

12.12 <u>Entire Agreement</u>. This Agreement constitutes the entire agreement of the Partners and supersedes all prior agreements between the Partners with respect to the Partnership.

12.13 <u>Titles; Subtitles</u>. The titles and subtitles used in this Agreement are used for convenience only and shall not be considered in the interpretation of this Agreement.

12.14 <u>Partnership Name</u>. The Partnership shall have the exclusive ownership and right to use the Partnership name (and any name under which the Partnership shall elect to conduct its affairs) as long as the Partnership continues. No value shall be placed upon the name or the goodwill attached to it for the purposes of determining the value of any Partner's Capital Account or interest in the Partnership.

12.15 <u>Counsel to the Partnership</u>. The Partnership has initially selected ****, LLP ("Partnership Counsel") as legal counsel to the Partnership. Each Limited Partner acknowledges that Partnership Counsel does not represent any Limited Partner in its capacity as a Limited Partner in the absence of a clear and explicit written agreement to such effect between the Limited Partner and Partnership Counsel (and then only to the extent specifically set forth in such agreement), and that in the absence of any such agreement Partnership Counsel shall owe no duties directly to a Limited Partner. In the event of any dispute or controversy arises between any Limited Partner and the Partnership, or between any Limited Partner or the Partnership, on the one hand, and the General Partner or any affiliate of the General Partner that Partnership Counsel represents, on the other hand, then each Limited Partner agrees that Partnership Counsel may represent such General Partner or the Partnership (and in the case where the dispute is between any Limited Partner on one hand, and both the Partnership and the General Partner on the other hand, Partnership Counsel may represent both the Partnership and the General Partner) in any such dispute or controversy to the extent permitted by the Rules, and each Limited Partner hereby consents to such representation. Each Limited Partner further acknowledges that, whether or not Partnership Counsel has in the past represented or is currently representing such Limited Partner with respect to other matters, Partnership Counsel has not represented the interests of any Limited Partner in the preparation and negotiation of this Limited Partnership Agreement. Counsel to the Partnership may also be counsel to the General Partner.

Article XIII

Miscellaneous Definitions

Unless the context requires otherwise, when used in this Agreement, the following terms have the meanings set forth below:

13.1 <u>Affiliate</u>. With reference to the General Partner (a) a person directly or indirectly controlling, controlled by, or under common control with the General Partner; (b) a manager or member of the General Partner; (c) the immediate family of a manager or member of the General Partner; and/or (d) any Affiliate of any of the foregoing. With reference to a member or employee of the General Partner, any corporation, association, limited liability company, partnership, or other entity of which such person has direct or indirect control or is, directly or indirectly, a general partner, member, manager, officer, or director, and any other person controlling, controlled by, or under direct or indirect common control with such person. With reference to a Limited Partner, any person controlling, controlled by, or under direct or indirect common control with such person.

13.2 <u>Bankruptcy</u>. A person or entity shall be deemed bankrupt if.

(a) any proceeding is commenced against such person or entity as "debtor" for any relief under bankruptcy or insolvency laws, or laws relating to the relief of debtors, reorganizations, arrangements, compositions, or extensions and such proceeding is not dismissed within ninety (90) days after such proceeding has commenced, or

(b) such person or entity commences any proceeding for relief under bankruptcy or insolvency laws or laws relating to the relief of debtors, reorganizations, arrangements, compositions, or extensions.

13.3 <u>Code.</u> The Internal Revenue Code of 1986, as amended from time to time (and any corresponding provisions of succeeding law).

13.4 <u>Date of Distribution</u>. The date on which all conditions precedent to making the distribution have been satisfied.

13.5 <u>Securities</u>. Securities of every kind and nature and rights and options with respect thereto, including stock, notes, bonds, debentures, evidences of indebtedness, and other business interests of every type, including interests in partnerships, joint ventures, proprietorships, and other business entities.

13.6 <u>Securities Act.</u> The Securities Act of 1933, as amended.

13.7 <u>Treasury Regulations</u>. Treasury Regulations shall be the Income Tax Regulations promulgated under the Code, as such Regulations may be amended from time to time (including corresponding provisions of succeeding Regulations).

Article XIV
Miscellaneous Tax Compliance Provisions

14.1 <u>Substantial Economic Effect</u>. The provisions of Article IV and the other provisions of this Agreement relating to the maintenance of Capital Accounts and procedures upon liquidation of the Partnership are intended to comply generally with the provisions of Treasury Regulation Section 1.704-1, and shall be interpreted and applied in a manner consistent with such Regulation and, to the extent the subject matter thereof is otherwise not addressed by this Agreement, the provisions of Treasury Regulations Section 1.704-1 are hereby incorporated by reference unless the General Partner shall determine that such incorporation will result in economic consequences inconsistent with the economic arrangement of the Partner expressed in this Agreement. In the event the General Partner shall determine that it is prudent to modify the manner in which the Capital Accounts, or any debits or credits thereto, are computed or allocated or the manner in which distributions and contributions upon liquidation (or otherwise) of the Partnership (or any Partner's interest therein) are effected in order to comply with such Regulations and other applicable tax laws, or to assure that the Partnership is treated as a partnership for tax purposes, or to achieve the economic arrangement of the Partners as expressed in this Agreement, then notwithstanding Section 12.7 hereof, the General Partner may make such modification, provided that it is not likely to have more than an insignificant detrimental effect on the tax consequences and total amounts distributable to any Limited Partner pursuant to Articles VI and VIII as applied without giving effect to such modification. The General Partner shall also (i) make any adjustments that are necessary or appropriate to maintain equality between the Capital Accounts of the Partners and the amount of Partnership capital reflected on the Partnership's balance sheet, as computed for book purposes pursuant to this Agreement, in accordance with Regulations Section 1.704-1(b)(2)(iv)(g), and (ii) make any appropriate modifications in the event unanticipated events (such as the incurrence of nonrecourse indebtedness) might otherwise cause the allocations under this Agreement to not comply with Treasury Regulations Section 1.704-1(b) (and in the case of the incurrence of nonrecourse indebtedness, Treasury Regulation Section 1.704-2) provided in each case that the General Partner determines that such adjustments or modifications shall not result in economic consequences inconsistent with the economic arrangement among the Partners as expressed in this Agreement.

14.2 <u>Qualified Income Offset</u>. Notwithstanding the provisions of Article IV and Section 10.3(c), the allocations provided therein shall be subject to the following exceptions:

(a) In the event any Partner's Capital Account has an Unadjusted Excess Negative Balance (as defined in subsection (f) of this Section 14.2) at the end of any Fiscal Year such Partner will be reallocated items of Net Income for such Fiscal Year (and, if necessary, future Fiscal Years) in the amount necessary to eliminate such Unadjusted Excess Negative Balance as quickly as possible.

(b) In the event any Partner unexpectedly receives any adjustments, allocations or distributions described in Treasury Regulations Sections 1.704l(b)(2)(ii)(d)(4) through (d)(6), items of Net Income shall be specially allocated to such Partner's Capital Account in an amount and manner sufficient to eliminate, to the extent required by Treasury Regulations Section 1.704-1(b)(2)(ii)(d), the Excess Negative Balance (as defined in subsection (e) of this Section 14.2) in such Partner's Capital Account created by such adjustments, allocations or distributions as quickly as possible. This subsection (b) of Section 14.2 is intended to and shall in all events be interpreted so as to constitute a "qualified income offset" within the meaning of Treasury Regulations Section 1.704-1(b)(2)(ii)(d).

(c) A Partner's Capital Account shall not be allocated any item of Net Loss to the extent such allocation would cause such Capital Account to have an Excess Negative Balance (as defined in subsection (e) of this Section 14.2).

(d) Any special allocations pursuant to this Section 14.2 shall be taken into account as soon as possible in computing subsequent allocations, so that over the term of the Partnership the net amount of any items so allocated and the profit, gain, loss, income and expense and all other items allocated to each Partner shall, to the extent possible, be equal to the net amount that would have been allocated to each such Partner if such original allocations pursuant to this Section 14.2 had not occurred.

(e) For purposes of this Section 14.2, "Excess Negative Balance" shall mean the excess of the negative balance in a Partner's Capital Account (computed with any adjustments which are required for purposes of Treasury Regulations Section 1.704l(b)(2)(ii)(d)) over the amount such Partner is obligated to restore to the Partnership (computed under the principles of Treasury Regulations Section 1.704-1(b)(2)(ii)(c)) inclusive of any addition to such restoration obligation pursuant to application of the provisions of Treasury Regulations Section 1.704-2 or any successor provisions thereto.

(f) For purposes of this Section 14.2, "Unadjusted Excess Negative Balance" shall have the same meaning as Excess Negative Balance, except that the Unadjusted Excess Negative Balance of a Partner shall be computed without affecting the reductions to such Partner's Capital Account which are described in Treasury Regulations Section 1.704-1(b)(2)(ii)(d).

14.3 <u>Imputed Income</u>. To the extent the Partnership has taxable interest income or expense imputed with respect to any promissory note or other obligation between any Partner and the Partnership, as maker and holder respectively, pursuant to Section 483, Sections 1271 through 1288, or Section 7872 of the Code, such imputed interest income shall be specially allocated to the Partner to whom such promissory note or other obligation relates, and such Partner's Capital Account shall be adjusted as appropriate to reflect the recharacterization as interest of a portion of the principal amount of such promissory note or other obligation and to reflect any deemed contribution or distribution of such interest income. The foregoing provision of this Section 14.3 shall not apply to any interest or original issue discount expressly provided for in any such promissory note or other obligation.

14.4 <u>Income Tax Allocations to Correspond to Book Allocations</u>. Except as otherwise provided in Sections 14.5 and 14.6, or as otherwise required by the Code and the rules and Treasury Regulations promulgated thereunder, Partnership income, gain, loss, deduction, or credit for income tax purposes shall be allocated in the same manner the corresponding book items are allocated pursuant to this Agreement. In the event the Book Value of any Partnership asset is adjusted pursuant to the terms of this Agreement, subsequent allocations of income, gain, loss and deduction with respect to such asset shall take account of any variation between the adjusted basis of such asset for federal income tax purposes and its Book Value in the same manner as under Code Section 704(c) and the Treasury Regulations thereunder.

14.5 <u>Allocations with Respect to Contributed Property</u>. In accordance with Code Section 704(c) and the Treasury Regulations thereunder, income, gain, loss and deduction with respect to any asset contributed to the capital of the Partnership shall, solely for tax purposes, be allocated between the Partners so as to take account of any variation between the adjusted basis of such property to the Partnership for federal income tax purposes and its initial Book Value.

14.6 <u>Allocation of Deemed Gain from Distributions</u>. If a distribution to a Partner results in taxable income or gain to the Partnership, then such taxable income or gain shall be allocated, to the extent permitted pursuant to Section 704(b) of the Code and the regulations promulgated thereunder, to the Partner who received the distribution.

14.7 <u>Compliance with Timing Requirements of Regulations</u>.

(a) Notwithstanding any other provision of this Agreement or the Act, in the event the Partnership is "liquidated" within the meaning of Treasury Regulations Section 1.704-1(b)(2)(ii)(g), (i) distributions shall be made pursuant to Article X to the Partners who have positive Capital Accounts in compliance with Treasury Regulations Section 1.7041(b)(2)(10)(b)(2) and (ii) if the Capital Account of any Partner (General or Limited) has a deficit balance (after giving effect to all contributions, distributions and allocations for all taxable years, including the year during which such liquidation occurs), then the Partner shall have no obligation at any time to repay or restore to the Partnership all or any part of any distribution made to it, him or her from the Partnership in accordance with the terms of Article VI or make any contribution to the capital of the Partnership with respect to such deficit and such deficit shall not be considered a debt owed to the Partnership or to any other person for any purpose whatsoever. In the discretion of the General Partner, a pro rata portion of the distributions that would otherwise be made to the Partners pursuant to this Section 14.7 or Article X may be:

(i) distributed to a trust established for the benefit of the Partners for the purposes of liquidating Partnership assets, collecting amounts owed to the Partnership, and paying any contingent or unforeseen liabilities or obligations of the Partnership arising out of or in connection with the Partnership. The assets of any such trust shall be distributed to the Partners from time to time, in the reasonable discretion of the General Partner, in the same proportions as the amount distributed to such trust by the Partnership would otherwise have been distributed to the Partners pursuant to this Agreement; or

(ii) withheld to provide a reasonable reserve for Partnership liabilities (contingent or otherwise) and to reflect the unrealized portion of any installment obligations owed to the Partnership, provided that such withheld amounts shall be distributed to the Partners as soon as practicable.

(b) Notwithstanding the provisions of Section 14.7(a), in the event the Partnership is liquidated within the meaning of Treasury Regulations Section 1.704l(b)(2)(ii)(g) but a distribution of the Partnership's assets is not otherwise required pursuant to Article X hereof, the Partnership's assets shall not be distributed to the Partners as set forth in Section 14.7(a). Instead, the Partnership shall be deemed to have contributed all of its assets and liabilities to a new Partnership and distributed interests in the new Partnership to the Partners and thereafter such new Partnership will be treated as the Partnership. Notwithstanding any provision of this Agreement to the contrary, in no event shall such deemed contribution and distribution affect the economic arrangement among the Partners as expressed in this Agreement (including, without limitation, their Capital Account Balances or rights to receive distributions).

14.8 <u>Recharacterizations of Transactions</u>. Any income, gain, loss or deduction (collectively, the "Recharacterization Items") realized as a direct or indirect result of the issuance (the "Issuance") of a Partnership interest by the Partnership to a Partner or the recharacterization (the "Recharacterization") of a distribution as a payment for tax purposes shall be allocated among the Partners so that (after effecting appropriate adjustments to the Capital Accounts of the Partners to reflect the tax treatment of the Issuance or the Recharacterization) the aggregate amount (including any distributions recharacterized as payments for tax purposes and any amounts received upon liquidation of the Partnership) that each Partner is entitled to receive from the Partnership over the life thereof (and each accounting period thereof) is equal to the aggregate amount that each such Partner would have been entitled to receive had the Issuance resulted in no income, gain, loss or deduction to either the Partnership or any of its Partners (including the recipient of the Partnership interest) or had the Recharacterization not occurred, as the case may be. In addition, to the extent possible without contravening the preceding sentence, the Recharacterization Items shall be allocated in a manner that puts each Partner, as soon as possible, in the same after-tax position as they would have been in had the Issuance resulted in no income, gain, loss or deduction to either the Partnership or any of its Partners (including the recipient of the Partnership interest) or had the Recharacterization not occurred, as the case may be.

14.9 <u>Sharing Arrangement; Interest in Partnership Items</u>. The Partners agree that the allocation and distribution provisions contained in this Agreement represent the sharing arrangement as between the Partners and represent their interests in such allocated items and, therefore, in the event that any transaction or relationship between the parties to this Agreement is recharacterized, allocations and adjustments hereunder shall be made in a manner which maintains the Capital Account balances of the Partners and the rights of the Partners to receive distributions at the same levels they would have been had no such Recharacterization occurred.

14.10 <u>Withholding</u>. The Partnership shall at all times be entitled to make payments with respect to any Partner in amounts required to discharge any obligation of the Partnership to withhold or make payments to any governmental authority with respect to any federal, state, local or other jurisdictional tax liability of such Partner arising as a result of such Partner's interest. To the extent each such payment satisfies an obligation of the Partnership to withhold with respect to any distribution to a Partner on which the Partnership did not withhold or with respect to any Partner's allocable share of the income of the Partnership, each such payment shall be deemed to be a loan by the Partnership to such Partner (which loan shall be deemed to be immediately due and payable) and shall not be deemed a distribution to such Partner. The amount of such payments made with respect to such Partner, plus interest, on each such amount from the date of each such payment until such amount is repaid to the Partnership at an interest rate per annum equal to the prime rate, from time to time in effect, of Bank of America shall be repaid to the Partnership by (i) deduction from any distributions made to such Limited Partner pursuant to this Agreement or (ii) earlier payment by such Partner to the Partnership, in each case as determined by the General Partner in its discretion. The General Partner may, in its discretion, defer making distributions to any Partner owing amounts to the Partnership pursuant to this Section 14.10 until such amounts are paid to the Partnership and shall in addition exercise any other rights of a creditor with respect to such amounts. Each Limited Partner agrees to indemnify and hold harmless the Partnership, and the General Partner and each of its members from and against any liability for taxes, interest or penalties which may be asserted by reason of the failure to deduct and withhold tax on amounts distributable or allocable to said Limited Partner. Any amount payable as indemnity hereunder by a Limited Partner shall be paid promptly to the Partnership upon request for such payment from the General Partner and if not so paid, the General Partner and the Partnership shall be entitled to claim against and deduct from the Capital Account of, or from any distribution due to, the affected Limited Partner for all such amounts.

IN WITNESS WHEREOF, the Partners have executed this Agreement as of the date first above written.

GENERAL PARTNER:
****, LLC

By: _____

Managing Member

LIMITED PARTNERS:

By: _____

Print Name: _____

Address: _____

_____

By: _____

Print Name: _____

Address: _____

_____

SCHEDULE OF PARTNERS

Partner   Initial Contribution   Capital Commitment

Name: _____   _____   _____

Tax ID. No.: _____

Address: _____

_____

Name: _____   _____   _____

Tax ID. No.: _____

Address: _____

_____

Form 8 C: Amendment to Limited Partnership Agreement

AMENDMENT
TO
**** FUND IV, L.P.
LIMITED PARTNERSHIP AGREEMENT

This Amendment to the **** Fund IV, L.P., Limited Partnership Agreement (the "Amendment") is made and entered as of the ___ day of _____, 20__, by and among ****, L.L.C., a [California] limited liability company (the "General Partner"), and each of the persons whose names are set forth under the heading "Limited Partners" on the Schedule of Partners attached hereto. The General Partner and the Limited Partners are collectively referred to herein as the "Parties."

RECITALS

A. The General Partner and the Limited Partners formed **** Fund IV, L.P. (the "Partnership") pursuant to the terms of the Limited Partnership Agreement, dated as of _____, 2006 (the "Limited Partnership Agreement").

B. The General Partner and the Limited Partners desire to amend the terms of the Limited Partnership Agreement pursuant to Section 12.4 therein under the terms and conditions of this Amendment.

AGREEMENT

NOW THEREFORE, in consideration of the mutual terms and conditions contained herein, the Parties agree as follows:

1. Amendment of Article III. The Limited Partnership Agreement is hereby amended to delete Article III in its entirety and insert the following article in its place:

Article III
Capital Contributions

3.1 <u>Initial Capital Contributions</u>. Upon the execution of this Agreement, each Partner shall contribute to the Partnership cash or property (the "Capital Contribution" of the Partner) as follows:

3.1.1 <u>General Partner</u>. The General Partner shall contribute cash or a promissory note (in the principal amount) equal to one percent (1%) of the initial capital contributions made by the Limited Partners.

3.1.2 <u>Limited Partner</u>. Each Limited Partner shall contribute cash in an amount equal to One Hundred Thousand Dollars ($100,000) multiplied by the number of units of interest in the Partnership ("Unit"), or fractions thereof, he, she or it acquires and as set forth on Schedule 3.1 appended hereto.

3.2 <u>Placement of Funds</u>. All funds received during subscription will be placed in a separate interest-bearing escrow account (the "Escrow"). At such time as ten (10) Units, yielding gross proceeds in the amount of One Million Dollars ($1,000,000) have been acquired, then (a) interest earned during the term of the Escrow (net of fees and expenses of the escrow agent) will be paid to the Limited Partners, and

(b) the proceeds from the sale of the Units, shall be disbursed to the Partnership. Should ten (10) Units not be sold on or before December 31, 20__, or the date of termination of the offering of such Units, if earlier, then, all funds will be refunded promptly to each subscriber, such refund to be made in full, together with any interest earned thereon.

3.3 <u>No Additional Capital Contributions; Liability</u>. No Partner shall be required to contribute any additional capital to the Partnership, and no Limited Partner shall have personal liability for any obligation of the Partnership except as expressly provided by law.

3.4 <u>No Interest on Capital Contributions</u>. Except as otherwise provided in this Agreement, no Partner shall be paid interest with respect to his, her or its contribution to Partnership capital.

3.5 <u>Return of Capital Contributions</u>. Except as otherwise provided in this Agreement, no Partner shall have the right to receive the return of any Capital Contribution or withdraw from the Partnership, except upon the dissolution of the Partnership.

3.6 Form of Return of Capital Contribution. If a Partner is entitled to receive the return of any Capital Contribution, the General Partner may distribute in lieu of money, notes, securities or other property having a value equal to the amount of money distributable to such Partner.

3.7 <u>General Partner Entitled to Purchase Units</u>. Subject to the provisions of Sections 3.1 and 3.2, the General Partner and/or any Affiliate of the General Partner may acquire Units from time to time on its, his or her own behalf and for its, his or her own benefit, provided that such right shall not create any preference in rights or benefits in favor of the General Partner and/or any Affiliate of the General Partner or permit the General Partner and/or any Affiliate of the General Partner to buy Units other than at the same cash price and on the same terms as are available to any other Limited Partner.

3.8 <u>Unit Certificates</u>.

3.8.1 <u>Certificate</u>. At the sole discretion of the General Partner, a Unit may be represented by a certificate (the "Certificate"). The exact contents of the Certificate may be determined by the General Partner, but any Certificate shall be issued substantially in conformity with the following requirements. The Certificates shall be respectively numbered serially, as they are issued and shall be signed by the General Partner. Each Certificate shall state the name of the Partnership, the fact that the Partnership is organized under the laws of the State of California as a limited partnership, the name of the person to whom the Certificate is issued and the date of issue. A statement of the designations, preferences, qualifications, limitations, restrictions, and special or relative rights of the Units, if any, shall be set forth in full or summarized on the face or back of the Certificate which the Partnership shall issue, or in lieu thereof, the Certificate may set forth that such a statement or summary will be furnished to any holder of a Unit upon request without charge. Notwithstanding the foregoing, the face of each Certificate shall contain a legend substantially in the following form:

THE UNITS OF THE PARTNERSHIP REPRESENTED BY THIS CERTIFICATE HAVE NOT BEEN REGISTERED UNDER THE SECURITIES ACT OF 1933, AS AMENDED, OR QUALIFIED UNDER ANY STATE SECURITIES LAWS, AND MAY NOT BE SOLD, TRANSFERRED, ASSIGNED OR HYPOTHECATED UNLESS THERE IS AN EFFECTIVE REGISTRATION STATEMENT UNDER SUCH ACT OR

LAWS COVERING SUCH UNITS, OR THE HOLDER RECEIVES AN OPINION OF COUNSEL FOR THE HOLDER OF THE UNITS SATISFACTORY TO THE PART-NERSHIP, STATING THAT SUCH SALE, TRANSFER, ASSIGNMENT OR HYPOTH-ECATION IS EXEMPT FROM THE REGISTRATION AND PROSPECTUS DELIVERY REQUIREMENTS OF SUCH ACT AND THE QUALIFICATION REQUIREMENTS UNDER APPLICABLE STATE LAW. THESE UNITS MAY ALSO BE SUBJECT TO ADDITIONAL RESTRICTIONS UNDER THE TERMS OF THE PARTNERSHIP'S AGREEMENT.

Each Certificate shall be otherwise in such form as may be determined by the Managers.

3.8.2 <u>Cancellation of Certificate</u>. Except as herein provided with respect to lost, stolen, or destroyed Certificates, no new Certificates shall be issued in lieu of previously issued Certificates until former Certificates for a like number of Units shall have been surrendered and canceled. All Certificates surrendered to the Partnership for transfer shall be canceled.

3.8.3 <u>Replacement of Lost, Stolen, or Destroyed Certificate</u>. Any Limited Partner claiming that his, her or its Certificate is lost, stolen or destroyed may make an affidavit or affirmation of that fact and request a new Certificate. A new Certificate may be issued of the same tenor and representing the same interest in the Partnership as was represented by the Certificate alleged to be lost, stolen or destroyed."

2. <u>Other Provisions</u>.

a. <u>Governing Law</u>. The Amendment shall be governed by and construed under the laws of the State of [California] as applied to agreements among [California] residents made and to be performed entirely within California.

b. <u>Continuing Effect of Limited Partnership Agreement</u>. The Limited Partnership Agreement, as amended hereby, is hereby confirmed and ratified as the date hereof and shall otherwise remain in full force and effect.

IN WITNESS WHEREOF, the Partners have executed the Amendment as of the date first above written.

GENERAL PARTNER:

****, LLC

By: _____

Managing Member

LIMITED PARTNERS:

By: _____

Print Name: _____

Address: _____

_____

SCHEDULE OF PARTNERS

Partner	Initial Contribution	Capital Commitment
Name: _____	_____	_____
Tax ID. No.: _____		
Address: _____		
_____		
_____		

Form 8 D: One-Page General Partnership Agreement

GENERAL PARTNERSHIP AGREEMENT

The parties to this agreement are _____, referred to in this agreement as the "Partners" or individually as a "Partner." The Partners have formed a general partnership to _____ ("Partnership").

A. <u>Allocation of Profits and Losses</u>. The net profits or losses earned by the Partnership during the fiscal year will be divided equally between the Partners (i.e. fifty percent to each Partner).

B. <u>Management and Operations</u>. Each Partner will contribute his full time and skill to the operation of the Partnership business, and will share equally in the management of the Partnership business affairs. Partners may transact any business, negotiate, contract, or represent the Partnership in any manner for the benefit of the Partnership, except: 1) no Partner will enter a contract obligating the Partnership for five thousand dollars ($5,000) or more without the prior approval of the other Partner; 2) no Partner will act as guarantor, surety, or indemnitor on any obligation that could result in a liability for the Partnership without the prior written consent of the other partner.

C. <u>Fiscal Year and Books of Account</u>. The Partnership fiscal year shall be the calendar year. All books of account will be maintained at the offices of the Partnership, and will be open for inspection by either Partner at any reasonable time.

D. <u>Bank Accounts</u>. The Partnership will establish one or more general business bank accounts in which all Partnership receipts will be deposited and from which all Partnership and Partner business expenses will be paid. Each Partner, acting alone, shall have signature authority on the Partnership's bank account(s).

E. <u>Applicable Law</u>. The laws of the State of [California] and the provisions of the Uniform Partnership Act, as in effect from time to time, will apply to the interpretation of this agreement and to operation of the Partnership.

The undersigned have executed this agreement at [San Francisco, California] this _____ day of _____ , 20__.

Form 8 E: Partnership Agreement for LLP—California

****, LLP
LIMITED LIABILITY PARTNERSHIP AGREEMENT
[DATE]

TABLE OF CONTENTS

PARTNERSHIP AGREEMENT

THIS AGREEMENT, made as of this _____ day of _____, 20___, is among the individuals hereinafter signing as partners of the limited liability partnership, ****, LLP. The partners are engaged as a limited liability partnership in the general practice of law and desire to continue the partnership and to confirm their understandings among themselves as set forth in this partnership agreement. The partners hereby agree as follows:

1. Limited Liability Partnership Status; Partnership Name; Liability for Partnership Obligations; Term; Method of Accounting; Capital Accounts; Net Profits and Net Losses.

1.1 <u>LLP Status</u>. The Partnership shall be a registered limited liability partnership under the laws of the State of California. This registered limited liability partnership shall hereinafter be referred to as "the Partnership." In order to be a Partner, a person must be a "licensed person" as defined in § 16101(7) of the Corporations Code authorized to practice law (a "Licensed Person") or a person authorized to practice law in a jurisdiction or jurisdictions other than California. If a Partner ceases to be qualified as a Partner pursuant to this section, the event shall be treated as an expulsion of the Partner.

1.2 <u>Partnership Name and Principal Address</u>. The name of the Partnership shall be ****, LLP. The Partnership shall have the right to continue or discontinue to use in its name the name of a Partner who has died or retired. The principal address of the Partnership shall be _____, or a subsequent address of the Partnership's choosing.

1.3 <u>Compliance with Security Requirements</u>. The Partnership will satisfy the statutory security requirements of Corporations Code Section 16956 in the following manner: In accordance with Cal. Corp. Code § 16956(a)(2)(A), by maintaining a policy or policies of insurance against liability imposed on or against it by law for damages arising out of claims in an amount for each claim of at least one hundred thousand dollars ($100,000) multiplied by the number of licensed persons rendering professional services on behalf of the Partnership; however, the total aggregate limit of liability under the policy or policies of insurance shall not be less than five hundred thousand dollars ($500,000) and is not required to exceed seven million five hundred thousand dollars ($7,500,000) in any one designated period as defined in such Code Section.

Whenever a new Partner is added to the Partnership, the Partnership will ensure that the Partnership is still in compliance with the statutory security requirements.

Each Partner, by virtue of that Partner's status as a Partner, automatically guarantees payment of any difference between the maximum amount of security required by such Code Section and the security otherwise provide by the Partnership. The aggregate amount paid by all Partners under these guarantees may not exceed that difference. The withdrawal of a Partner does not affect the right and obligations of the Partner arising before withdrawal.

1.4 <u>Term</u>. The term of the Partnership shall begin as of the filing date of the registered limited liability partnership registration for the Partnership as filed with the California Secretary of State and continues until dissolved by mutual agreement of the parties or otherwise terminated as provided in this Agreement.

1.5 <u>Method of Accounting</u>. The Partnership books of account will be kept on a cash and calendar year basis.

1.6 <u>Capital Accounts</u>. The Partnership shall establish an individual capital account for each Partner. Capital accounts shall be maintained on a cash basis of accounting. Each Partner's capital account consists of his or her capital contributions to the Partnership capital made by that Partner pursuant to this Agreement, increased by his or her share of Net Profits, decreased by his or her share of Net Losses and distributions, and adjusted in accordance with applicable provisions of the Internal Revenue Code and Treasury Regulations.

1.7 <u>Net Profits and Net Losses</u>. "Net Profits" and "Net Losses" shall mean the income, gain, loss, deductions, and credits of the Partnership in the aggregate or separately stated, as appropriate, determined in accordance with accounting principles employed under the method of accounting, at the close of each fiscal year on the Partnership's information tax return filed for federal income tax purposes. Net Profits and Net Losses, except for Net Profits and Net Losses from Capital Events, shall be divided among the Partners each calendar year in accordance with their Percentage Interests for that year. The "Percentage Interest" of each Partner for this purpose shall be determined by dividing such Partner's income related distributions (including without limitation Base Compensation, bonuses and return on capital) (as determined in accordance with the policies of the firm) for the year in question by the total income related distributions for all Partners for such year. The intent of the Partners is that Net Profits and Net Losses for each year should be shared and borne by the Partners in the same proportions that they share total compensation.

1.8 Net Profits, Net Losses and Distributions of Cash from Capital Events.

(a) A "Capital Event" is any event outside of the normal business operation of the Partnership, such as a sale of the Partnership's assets.

(b) Net Profits and Net Losses from Capital Events for any tax year shall be divided among the Partners in accordance with the ratio of their capital accounts as of the end of the most recent tax year. For this purpose, the capital account of a Partner shall not include the portion that is represented by a capital note.

(c) Cash from a Capital Event which is available for distribution shall be distributed in the same ratio as Net Profit or Net Loss from the Capital Event was allocated among the Partners.

2. Management. In any matter requiring a vote of the Partners, each Partner shall have one vote; provided, however, that in the event of a tie vote, the Managing Partner shall have two votes so as to be able to break the tie. The Partners shall:

(a) By 75% majority vote, formulate or alter major policies of the firm and provide policy direction to the Managing Partner and to committees. Any policies so adopted shall be binding on the Partners. Attached hereto as Appendices 1 through 5 are policies and procedures existing as of the date of original execution of this Agreement that have been adopted by and are binding on the Partners as contemplated herein:

(i) Appendix 1 – Partner Compensation Policy; Distribution Policies and Procedures.

(ii) Appendix 2 – Capitalization Policies and Procedures.

(iii) Appendix 3 – Mediation and Binding Arbitration of Disputes.

(iv) Appendix 4 – Financial Interests in Clients.

(v) Appendix 5 – Benefits.

(b) By 75% majority vote, admit a new Partner or Partners.

(c) By 75% majority vote of the other Partners, expel a Partner. A Partner may be expelled on the grounds that, in the judgment of a 75% majority of the other Partners, the Partner to be expelled has:

(i) Engaged in personal misconduct, ethical misconduct or other misconduct of such a serious nature as to render the Partner's continued presence in the Partnership intolerable or detrimental to the firm;

(ii) Been expelled, suspended or otherwise significantly disciplined by the final action of any professional organization pertaining to the practice of law; or

(iii) Been convicted by any court of any offense punishable as a felony.

(d) By majority vote, elect for a two-year term of office (subject to subsection (g) below) a Managing Partner (chief executive officer) for the firm.

(e) By majority vote, hire a director of administration of the firm, after receiving the Managing Partner's recommendation.

(f) Establish by majority vote:

(i) The operating budget for each fiscal year;

(ii) The capital budget for each fiscal year;

(iii) Rates charged for attorney services;

(g) By majority vote, remove or replace the Managing Partner at any time.

(h) By majority vote, decide whether and how to merge with, acquire or be acquired by other entities.

(i) By majority vote, decide such other matters as they may determine from time to time.

3. Managing Partner.

3.1 Functions. The Managing Partner shall manage the firm and is hereby delegated all management authority except those matters described in paragraph 2 above requiring specific approval by the Partners. In carrying out these functions, the Managing Partner will act as the Partnership's principal liaison with the firm's director of administration, if any.

3.2 Selection. The Managing Partner shall be appointed by a majority vote of the Partners.

3.3 Term. The term of office of the Managing Partner shall be two (2) years, subject to removal at any time by majority vote of the Partners.

3.4 Succession. There shall be no specific constraints on the Managing Partner succeeding himself or herself.

3.5 Formal Reporting. Regular periodic meetings of the Partnership at which the Managing Partner will report on his or her activities shall be held and may be called by the Managing Partner or a majority of the Partners.

3.6 Effective Determination of Policies and Procedures. All policies, procedures and decisions within the areas delegated to the Managing Partner shall be binding on the Partnership and all Partners.

3.7 Obligations. The Managing Partner also will be empowered to obligate the Partnership in an amount not exceeding $100,000 per transaction. Any transaction obligating the Partnership in a greater amount must be approved in advance by a majority of the Partners.

3.8 Practice Guidelines and Procedures. The Managing Partner is authorized to set practice guidelines and procedures (the "Practice Guidelines and Procedures"). The Practice Guidelines and Procedures are to provide the minimum standards for process and procedure followed by Partners. The Managing Partner has sole authority to determine whether a Partner has complied with the Practice Guidelines and Procedures.

4. Records, Depositories, and Independent Accountants.

4.1 Maintenance of Records. The Managing Partner will cause the Partnership to maintain at its office financial records and accounts in accordance with methods established with the advice of the Partnership's independent certified public accountants and maintained and applied on a consistent basis.

4.2 Inspection of Records. Subject to reasonable restrictions upon disclosure or use of information otherwise than for purposes related to the Partnership, each Partner shall be entitled at all reasonable times to inspect and copy all such records and accounts reflecting the financial affairs of the Partnership.

4.3 Depositories. The Managing Partner will designate the banks or other depositories in which the funds of the Partnership are to be deposited. Counter-signature of at least one other Partner will be required for withdrawals exceeding $2,500.

4.4 Preparation and Distribution of Financial Reports and Tax Returns. The Managing Partner will cause to be prepared and distributed to all Partners such financial reports in such form as the Managing Partner shall deem appropriate to disclose periodically the current financial condition of the Partnership and results of its operations and will designate independent certified public accountants who shall audit or review the financial statements, records and accounts of the Partnership and prepare for distribution to all Partners such financial information and tax returns as may be required by law or by the Partnership.

4.5 Prohibited Acts. No Partner, without the 75% majority vote of the Partners, shall:

(a) Practice law other than through the Partnership;

(b) On behalf of the Partnership, endorse any note on behalf of, become surety for, or act as an accommodation party for, any person or entity other than the Partnership;

(c) Accept from a client any personal gift, gratuity, payment, or other law firm opportunity valued at more than $500; or

(d) Accept or continue any position on any Board of Directors of a for-profit entity. Any Partner may serve on the Board of Directors of any not-for-profit entity after receiving a written disclaimer from such entity that the Partner is serving in his personal capacity, is not serving in his capacity as a lawyer, and is not serving in his capacity as a Partner of ****, LLP.

5. Amendment of Agreement; New Partners.

(a) This agreement may be amended at any time by the vote or written agreement of three-fourths of the Partners; provided, however, that the Managing Partner shall have the authority to amend this agreement, to the extent required under the California Uniform Partnership Act of 1994, for the sole purpose of admitting a new Partner or Partners who have been approved in accordance with subparagraph 2(b) above and of removing a Partner or Partners who have dissociated from the Partnership.

(b) A new Partner shall become a Partner on such date as the Managing Partner may establish, provided that the new Partner executes this agreement prior to the date of his or her admission to the Partnership.

6.   Dissolution and Winding Up.

6.1 Dissolution. The Partnership shall be dissolved, its assets shall be disposed of, and its affairs wound up on the first to occur of the following:

(a) A vote by a majority of the Partners to dissolve the Partnership. For this purpose, a dissociation of a Partner under subsection 9.1(a) constitutes a vote of that Partner to dissolve and wind up the Partnership business.

(b) Upon an entry of a decree of dissolution pursuant to § 16801 of the Corporations Code.

(c) The sale of all or substantially all of the assets of the Partnership.

6.2 Winding Up. Upon the occurrence of any event specified in Section 6.1, the Partnership shall continue solely for the purpose of winding up its affairs in an orderly manner, liquidating its assets, and satisfying the claims of its creditors. The Partners shall be responsible for overseeing the winding up and liquidation of the Partnership, shall take full account of the liabilities and assets of the Partnership, shall either cause its assets to be sold or distributed, and if sold, shall cause the proceeds therefrom, to the extent sufficient therefor, to be applied and distributed as provided in Section 6.4.

6.3 Distributions in Kind. Any non-cash asset distributed to one or more Partners shall first be valued at its fair market value to determine the Net Profit or Net Loss that would have resulted if such asset were sold for such value. The amount distributed and charged to the capital account of each Partner receiving an interest in such distributed asset shall be the fair market value of such interest (net of any liability secured by such asset that such Partner assumes or takes subject to). The fair market value of such asset shall be determined by the Partners or, if any Partners object by an independent appraiser (any such appraiser must be recognized as an expert in valuing the type of asset involved) selected by the Partners.

6.4 Order of Payment of Liabilities Upon Dissolution. After determining that all known debts and liabilities of the Partnership in the process of winding-up, including, without limitation, debts and liabilities to Partners who are creditors of the Partnership, have been paid or adequately provided for, the remaining assets shall be distributed to the Partners in accordance with their positive capital accounts after taking into account income and loss allocations for the Partnership's taxable year during which liquidation occurs. Such liquidating distributions shall be made by the end of the Partnership's taxable year in which the Partnership is liquidated, or, if later, within 90 days after the date of such liquidation.

6.5 Compliance with Regulations. All payments to the Partners upon the winding and dissolution of the Partnership shall be strictly in accordance with the positive capital account balance limitation and other requirements of Treasury Regulations Section 1.704-1(b)(2)(ii)(d).

6.6 Limitations on Payments Made in Dissolution. Except as otherwise specifically provided in this Agreement, each Partner shall only be entitled to look solely at the assets of Partnership for the return of his or her positive capital account balance and shall have no recourse for his or her capital contributions and/or share of Net Income (upon dissolution or otherwise) against any other Partner.

7. Partner's Interest in the Partnership. Each of the undersigned hereby agrees that (a) he or she has no right, and, unless ordered to do so by a court of competent jurisdiction, will not attempt, to sell or transfer all or any portion of his or her interest in the Partnership to anyone else or to pledge, mortgage, hypothecate or otherwise dispose of all or any portion of his or her interest in the Partnership in any way; (b) after dissociation, he or she has no right to continue to participate in the Partnership; (c) he or she has no right or interest in specific property of the Partnership, including without limitation the tangible property, accounts receivable or work in progress of the firm; (d) he or she has no right or interest in the goodwill of the firm, if any, and under no circumstance shall he or she receive any payment on account of goodwill, except as may result from dissolution of the Partnership as described in Section 6 above; (e) if any claim of any kind is made against his or her interest in the firm, or against him or her because of his or her interest in the firm, he or she will immediately notify the Managing Partner, and in resisting such claim will protect the interests of the firm and of the other Partners to the best of his or her ability; (f) except as provided in subsection 7(g) below, in the event of withdrawal, bankruptcy, expulsion, death, permanent disability or retirement (as defined below) of a Partner, the payments, if any, to be made to him or her or to his or her estate (or trust or other designee specified in a notarized writing from the Partner to the Managing Partner) under policies or procedures adopted pursuant to this Agreement and in effect at the time of such withdrawal, bankruptcy, expulsion, death, permanent disability or retirement, shall be in full settlement of his or her interest in the Partnership, including without limitation any interest in the tangible property, accounts receivable and work in progress of the firm; and (g) in the event of death, permanent disability or retirement (as defined below) of a Partner, he or she (or his or her estate, or trust or other designee specified in a notarized writing from the Partner to the Managing Partner) is entitled to the same bonuses (including the Collections Bonus and the Additional Bonus, as defined in Appendix 1) that he or she would have received from the firm at the end of the year absent death, permanent disability or retirement, adjusted for that percentage of the year that he or she did not work for the firm.

8. Events Not Causing Dissolution.

(a) The admission of a new Partner shall not cause dissolution of the Partnership.

(b) The death, resignation, retirement, expulsion or other withdrawal of a Partner shall not cause dissolution of the Partnership.

9.   Dissociation of a Partner.

9.1 Events of Dissociation. A Partner is dissociated from the Partnership upon the occurrence of any of the following events:

(a) Withdrawal of a Partner from the Partnership following delivery of a notice, in writing to each other Partner of his or her intention to withdraw as a Partner on a date specified in such notice not earlier than thirty (30) days following delivery thereof.

(b) Bankruptcy of a Partner.

(c) Expulsion of a Partner pursuant to this Agreement.

(d) Retirement of a Partner upon three (3) months written notice to each of the other Partners. For the purposes of this Agreement, "retirement" (as opposed to withdrawal) shall be defined as either of (i) a withdrawal in conjunction with which the retiring Partner agrees in writing not to go into the private practice of law or associate with any other law firm for a period of at least five (5) years within any of the counties of California specified below, or (ii) a request for retirement (as opposed to withdrawal) accompanied by a majority vote of the other Partners to accept the retirement regardless of the acceptance of another position. The counties referred to above are the following counties: San Francisco, San Mateo, Alameda, Contra Costa, Marin, Santa Cruz and Santa Clara.

(e) Determination by a majority vote of the other Partners that a Partner is permanently disabled, such determination to be made only after a period of disability exceeding one hundred and twenty (120) consecutive days or an aggregate of one hundred eighty (180) days within a period of two (2) consecutive calendar years or the appointment of a guardian or general conservator for the Partner.

(f)   Death of a Partner.

(g) Determination by the Managing Partner, in his or her judgment, that a Partner has violated the Practice Guidelines and Procedures.

9.2 Purchase of Dissociated Partner's Interest.

(a) If an Event of Dissociation occurs, and the Partners do not elect to dissolve the Partnership, the Partnership shall purchase and the dissociated Partner shall sell the dissociated Partner's interest in the Partnership at a price equal to the balance in his or her capital account determined on a cash basis on the date of dissociation, and no more.

The purchase price for a Partner's interest shall be paid as follows:

The purchase price shall be paid at the election of the firm (taking into account such factors as it may in its discretion determine, including without limitation the financial health of the firm and the extent of its debts) either (i) in cash within 90 days immediately following the date of dissociation or (ii) in twenty-four (24) equal consecutive monthly installments of principal and interest commencing ninety days immediately following the date of dissociation. Unpaid principal shall bear interest from the date which is ninety days immediately following the date of dissociation at the rate of seven percent (7%) per annum.

The rights of the dissociated Partner and the Partnership in connection with the purchase of the dissociated Partner's interest in the Partnership are fully set forth in this Section 9, and no other rights or procedures set forth in the Uniform Partnership Act of 1994 or other state law which would otherwise apply shall be applicable thereto including without limitation determination of the purchase price or the terms and conditions of payment thereof.

10. Notices. All notices that are provided for herein, or in any policy or procedure adopted by the Managing Partner, to any Partner or a former Partner shall be in writing and shall be deemed given upon personal delivery or upon mailing by prepaid first class certified return receipt requested U.S. Mail directed to such Partner's or former Partner's address shown in the records of the Partnership or such other address as any Partner or former Partner may designate in writing by notice addressed and delivered or mailed to the Managing Partner.

11. Summary of Limited Liability. This Partnership has fulfilled all requirements necessary to secure its status as a registered limited liability Partnership. Subject to the exceptions set forth in California Corporations Code Section 16306(c), a Partner in this Partnership is not liable or accountable, directly or indirectly, including by way of indemnification, contribution, assessment, or otherwise, for debts, obligations, or liabilities of or chargeable to the Partnership or any other Partner, whether arising in tort, contract, or otherwise, that are incurred, created, or assumed by the Partnership while the Partnership is a registered limited liability Partnership, by reason of being a Partner or acting in the conduct of the business or activities of the Partnership. Nothing in this Agreement is intended to render the Partners liable for Partnership obligations

for which they are not personally liable under Corporation Code Section 16306(c). This Paragraph overrides any other provision in this Agreement that is or might be interpreted as inconsistent with this principle.

                                                        _____

Partner signature, name

_____

Date

_____

Partner signature, name

_____

Date

APPENDICES
TO
****, LLP
PARTNERSHIP AGREEMENT

TABLE OF CONTENTS

APPENDIX 1
PARTNER COMPENSATION POLICY;
DISTRIBUTION POLICIES AND PROCEDURES

The firm's Partner compensation system is as follows:

1. BASE COMPENSATION. Base compensation is that amount that will be distributed to each partner, according to his or her Base Compensation level, by way of monthly draws over the course of the calendar year. Base Compensation for each partner ("Base Compensation") will be determined annually by the Managing Partner, after consultation with all partners and with approval of a majority of the partners. The target Base Compensation for each partner shall be one-third (1/3) of that partner's expected income related distributions for that year. Notwithstanding the immediately preceding sentence, for 20__, the Base Compensation for each partner shall be $20,000 per month.

2. BONUS POOL. Any net income available for distribution in excess of aggregate Base Compensation will be allocated to a bonus pool which will be distributed to partners in accordance with the schedule set forth in Section 3 below. From the bonus pool, provided that his or her Capital Contribution Obligation has been met (as set forth in the firm's Capitalization Policies and Procedures (Appendix 2 to the partnership Agreement)), each partner shall be paid an amount equal to the amount by which 50% of his or her collections of his or her own billed hours for the calendar year exceed the amount of Base Compensation paid to him or her during that calendar year (the "Collections Bonus"). In the event that cash available for distribution from the bonus pool is not sufficient to pay the Collections Bonuses in full, each partner's Collections Bonus will be reduced proportionately. Provided that his or her Capital Contribution Obligation has been met, in the event that additional cash is available for distribution after payment of the Collections Bonus, it shall be distributed, subject to all appropriate deductions described in Section 3(D) below, as an Additional Bonus (the "Additional Bonus"). The percentage of the Additional Bonus pool to which each partner is entitled (prior to deductions) shall be set by the Managing Partner with approval by a majority of the partners. The initial Additional Bonus percentages shall be:

Partner A	67%
Partner B	33%

3. DISTRIBUTION POLICIES AND PROCEDURES

A. GENERAL POLICY. The timing and amounts of regular draws and distributions (collectively, "Distributions") will be determined from time to time by the Managing partner, subject to the limitations and procedures set forth herein.

B. DETERMINATION OF SCHEDULED DISTRIBUTIONS

(1) Annual Determination of Scheduled Distributions. At the beginning of each fiscal year, the Managing Partner will communicate to all partners the scheduled Distributions for such year and the methodology used in establishing scheduled Distributions. Scheduled Distributions may be based upon budgeted levels of Base Compensation (as defined in the Partner Compensation Policy) or another measure of anticipated current year income, or actual previous year income, or other appropriate

measures applied in a manner determined by the Managing Partner to be reasonable. The amount scheduled to be distributed to a partner will reflect all appropriate deductions described in paragraph D below.

(2) Interim Adjustments to Scheduled Distributions. In the event that the firm's net income budget is revised during the year, or it appears at any point that budgeted net income cannot reasonably be expected to be achieved, or if it appears that sound fiscal judgment so requires, the Managing Partner will review the scheduled Distributions for the year and may establish revised scheduled Distributions for the remainder of the fiscal year.

C. LIMITATIONS ON ACTUAL DISTRIBUTIONS. In no event will aggregate actual Distributions with respect to any period from the beginning of the fiscal year through the end of any fiscal quarter be permitted to exceed the sum of (1) the firm's actual net income available for distribution for such period and (2) 50% of the firm's actual paid-in capital (not including capital note obligations) as of the end of such period. If necessary in order to comply with the foregoing limitation, scheduled Distributions will be reduced in a manner determined by the Managing Partner to be reasonable.

D. DEDUCTIONS FROM DISTRIBUTIONS. In connection with each determination of scheduled Distributions, the Managing Partner will determine the basis on which monthly, quarterly or other Distributions will be offset by amounts properly chargeable to individual partners. Such amounts may include, without limitation, (1) required capital contributions, (2) mandatory and voluntary contributions to profit sharing and other retirement plans, and (3) personal expenses, if any.

E. RECONCILIATION OF DISTRIBUTIONS TO INCOME AVAILABLE FOR DISTRIBUTION. On or before the 15th day of each fiscal year, or as promptly thereafter as reasonably possible, any firm cash available for distribution from income that remains undistributed from the previous year will be distributed to the partners, allocated pursuant and subject to the firm's Partner Compensation Policy (Sections 1 and 2 above) and the Capitalization Policies and Procedures (Appendix 2 to the Partnership Agreement). Final adjustments, if any, for each fiscal year will be made in the first Distribution following issuance of the opinion of the firm's independent accountants on the firm's financial statements for such year. Distributions to a partner with respect to any fiscal year in excess of his or her allocated share of net income available for distribution for that year will be charged to that partner in four equal quarterly installments during the ensuing year.

APPENDIX 2
CAPITALIZATION POLICIES AND PROCEDURES

A. GENERAL POLICY. It is the policy of the firm that individual partners contribute to the firm on an ongoing basis permanent capital to help fund the operation and growth of the firm, to establish the firm's creditworthiness, and to maintain a reasonable debt-to-equity ratio.

B. TARGET CAPITAL. At the beginning of each calendar year, the partners by majority vote will set the firm's target for permanent capital, taking into consideration the factors set forth in paragraph A above. The initial target for permanent capital is $400,000. The target for permanent capital in any calendar year (after 20__) shall not exceed three times the average monthly operating expense of the previous calendar year.

C. IMPLEMENTATION. It is the goal of the capitalization policy that each partner's capital contribution should be equal. It is recognized however, that it would be difficult for newer partners to the firm to fund such a contribution immediately.

Accordingly, it is in the intent of this policy to establish procedures, through use of promissory notes payable in regular installments and regular capital augmentation contributions by all partners, to both reduce the gap between current levels of capital and the target capital and, on an ongoing basis, provide for what is anticipated to be ever-increasing levels of target capital.

(1) Capital Obligation. At the beginning of each calendar year, the capital obligation of each partner (the Partner's "Capital Obligation") shall be the amount that is arrived at by dividing the then current target capital by the then number of partners. The capital obligation of newly admitted partners shall be calculated in the same manner.

(2) Capital Notes. At the beginning of each calendar year, each partner shall sign a promissory note (a "Capital Note") in an amount that is arrived at by subtracting the total amount of capital contributed by that partner (including the amount of capital augmentation contributed by the partner from his or her bonus from the previous calendar year and any other contributions during the present calendar year, but not including the unpaid principal of any promissory note previously signed by that partner) (the Partner's "Capital Contribution") from that Partner's Capital Obligation as it exists at the beginning of the calendar year. Such note shall be non-interest bearing and shall be paid in equal quarterly installments amortized over a five-year period. Each such promissory note shall be canceled upon the execution by that partner of a new promissory note at the beginning of the following calendar year.

(3) Capital Augmentation. Each partner shall contribute each year, payable from that partner's year-end Collections Bonus and Additional Bonus, additional capital in the amount of:

(a) 5% of the firm's net income allocated to that partner;

(b) an amount greater than the amount in part (a) to make the amounts of all Partners' Capital Contribution equal (the "Capital Contribution Obligation"); or

(c) an amount less than the amount in part (a) if that lesser amount will completely satisfy that partner's total Capital Obligaton.

The amount of capital augmentation to be paid in any year by each partner who is making payment on a capital note to the firm shall be 5% of the firm's net income allocated to that partner for that year less amounts paid by that partner on the promissory note for that year.

(4) Capital Calls. Based upon the financial condition of the firm, and in particular based on the firm's debt-to-equity ratio and the anticipated need for additional capital in any period, the Managing Partner, upon approval of a majority of the partners, may make special calls for additional capital to be funded over a reasonable period as determined by the Managing Partner.

(5) Return on Capital. At the end of each calendar year, an initial allocation of the firm's income will be made to those partners who have invested monies in the capital of the firm. The allocation will be 8% of the average amount of money in each partner's capital account during the course of the year. No allocation will be made on the portion of any partner's capital account that is represented by a capital note. The allocation will occur prior to the determination of the amount of the firm's income remaining, after distribution of Base Compensation, for payment of bonuses, and will be paid along with year-end bonuses. In the event there is not sufficient income, after distribution of Base Compensation, for this allocation to be paid in full, the unpaid portion of this allocation will carry over as an additional amount to be allocated at the end of the next calendar year. The Managing Partner may at the beginning of each year, and with notice to all partners, alter the percentage allocation, upon considering such factors as the financial health of the firm and prevailing market interest rates.

(6) Return of Capital. In the event a Partner's Capital Contribution exceeds the partner's Capital Obligation, the firm may return at such partner's request some or all of the overpayment, provided that the firm's overall target for permanent capital has been met.

APPENDIX 3
MEDIATION AND BINDING ARBITRATION
OF DISPUTES

1. Any dispute, controversy, or claim (i) between any one or more partners or former partners and the firm, or (ii) between or among any one or more partners or former partners, which arises out of or relates to this Agreement or the partnership, including but not limited to any rights or duties of any one or more partners or former partners concerning the partnership, the firm or any one or more of its partners or former partners, any claims by any one or more partners or former partners against the firm and/or any one or more of its partners or former partners, and/or any one or more claims by the firm against any one or more of its partners or former partners (referred to herein collectively as the "Dispute" or the "Disputes"), shall be subject to non-binding mediation, and if not then resolved, shall be finally determined exclusively by binding arbitration, conducted as set forth below. The Disputes include, but are not limited to, tort claims (common law or statutory, state or federal, intentional or otherwise, including but not limited to claims of breaches or violations of statutory or common law protections from discrimination, harassment, hostile working environment and other such conditions), and contract claims.

2. Each partner agrees that any Dispute, and all matters concerning any Dispute, shall be considered strictly confidential and shall not be disclosed to any person outside the firm except with respect to the mediation and arbitration processes described below, or as otherwise expressly agreed to by the firm in writing through the Managing Partner or as required by law or contractual obligations of the firm. Any documents filed with a court or with any other judicial or quasi-judicial officer shall be filed under seal and shall be subject to a protective order designed to maintain the full confidentiality of the Dispute.

3. Notwithstanding the foregoing or any other provision contained in this paragraph, the parties shall have the right at any time to request one or more provisional remedies from a court of competent jurisdiction pursuant to California Code of Civil Procedure ("CCP") Section 1281.8. Any request for provisional remedies, and all related court documents, shall be filed under seal and shall be subject to a protective order consistent with Paragraph 2 above.

A. MEDIATION.

1. Any Dispute shall first be the subject of a non-binding mediation ("Mediation") conducted by a retired judge or other mediator who is a member of Judicial Arbitration & Mediation Services, Inc./Endispute ("JAMS"), in San Francisco, California, or any substantially equivalent organization if JAMS is unable or unwilling to perform such services. Any partner or former partner may initiate the Mediation by written notice to the Managing Partner of the firm and, if applicable, to all other partners involved in the Dispute. The firm may initiate the Mediation by written notice to the partner(s) or former partner(s) involved in the Dispute. The date such notice is given is called the "Mediation Initiation Date."

2. The mediator ("Mediator") shall be a retired judge or other mediator affiliated with JAMS, selected either by mutual agreement of the parties to the Dispute, or if they cannot so agree within twenty (20) calendar days after the Mediation Initiation Date, by the Chief Judicial Officer of JAMS or through such other procedures as

JAMS regularly follows. If the parties to the Dispute mutually agree, a Mediator other than a member of JAMS may be selected in place of a JAMS Mediator.

3. The Mediation shall be held within twenty (20) calendar days after the Mediator is selected, or such longer period as the parties to the Dispute and the Mediator mutually decide. The parties shall seek in good faith to resolve the Dispute in the Mediation.

B. ARBITRATION.

1. If a Dispute is not fully resolved by mutual agreement of the parties at the Mediation, the Dispute shall be finally determined by a binding arbitration ("Arbitration") conducted by a single arbitrator chosen by the parties as described below. Any partner(s) or former partner(s) may initiate the Arbitration by written notice to the Managing Partner of the firm, and to the partner(s) or former partner(s) involved in the Dispute, and to JAMS. The firm may initiate the Arbitration by written notice to the partner(s) or former partner(s) involved in the Dispute and to JAMS. The date such notice is given is called the "Arbitration Initiation Date."

2. Except as expressly modified herein, the Arbitration shall be conducted in accordance with the provisions of CCP Sections 1280 et seq. or their successor sections and shall constitute the exclusive remedy for the determination of any Dispute, including whether such Dispute is subject to Arbitration. The Arbitration shall be conducted by and before JAMS, or any substantially equivalent organization if JAMS is unable or unwilling to perform such services, under the procedures of the arbitration association, except as modified herein.

3. The arbitrator ("Arbitrator") shall be a retired judge or other arbitrator affiliated with JAMS, selected either by mutual agreement of the parties to the Dispute, or if they cannot so agree within twenty (20) calendar days after the Arbitration Initiation Date, by the Chief Judicial Officer of JAMS or through such other procedures as JAMS regularly follows. If the parties to the Dispute mutually agree, an Arbitrator other than a member of JAMS may be selected in place of a JAMS Arbitrator.

4. The provisions of CCP Section 1283.05 or its successor section(s) are incorporated in and made a part of this paragraph. Depositions may be taken and full written discovery may be obtained in any Arbitration under this Appendix in accordance with said section(s).

5. Within thirty (30) calendar days after the Arbitrator is chosen, the Arbitrator, upon application of any party, shall hold a Pre-Hearing Conference with the parties for the purposes of narrowing the issues, establishing a discovery schedule, setting procedures for any law and motion proceedings, and otherwise arranging for the most expeditious hearing possible of the Dispute.

6. The Arbitration Hearing shall be held in San Francisco, California, and shall commence as soon as reasonably possible after the Arbitration Initiation Date. The Arbitration Hearing shall be conducted according to the discretion of the Arbitrator: judicial rules relating to the order of proof, the conduct of the hearing and the presentation and admissibility of evidence need not be followed. Any relevant information, including hearsay, may be admitted by the Arbitrator regardless of its admissibility as evidence in court, but the Arbitrator also shall be authorized to exclude evidence.

7. The parties shall have the power to subpoena witnesses to attend the Arbitration hearing pursuant to CCP Section 1282.6. The Arbitrator shall have full power to give such directions and to make such orders in the conduct of the Arbitration, including setting pre-Arbitration procedures and scheduling any motions to correct or amend the Arbitration Award, as the Arbitrator deems just and appropriate.

8. The Arbitrator shall, within fifteen (15) calendar days after the conclusion of the Arbitration hearing, issue a written award and a brief written statement of decision describing the reasons for the award, including the calculation of any damages awarded (the "Arbitration Award"). The Arbitration Award shall dispose of all of the Disputes that are the subject of the Arbitration. The Arbitrator shall be empowered to award compensatory or actual damages in the amount established by the preponderance of the evidence, but shall NOT have the authority (i) to award non-economic damages, such as for emotional distress, pain and suffering or loss of consortium, (ii) to award punitive damages, or (iii) to reform, modify or materially change this Agreement. Subject to such restrictions, the Arbitrator shall be authorized to grant temporary, preliminary and permanent equitable or injunctive relief, but only with respect to the following: (i) prohibitions against any disparagement or harassment by any of the parties against any of the other parties; (ii) maintaining complete confidentiality regarding the Mediation and Arbitration proceedings and the Disputes; and (iii) protection against wrongful use of trade secrets, unlawful restraints of competition, or any form of unfair competition. The Arbitrator, and not a court, shall also be authorized to determine whether the provisions of this Appendix apply to a dispute, controversy or claim sought to be resolved in accordance with this Appendix.

9. Except as provided herein, the parties shall bear their own attorneys' fees, costs, and disbursements and shall bear equally the fees and costs of JAMS and the Mediator and the Arbitrator.

10. Absent the filing of an application to correct or vacate the Arbitration Award under CCP Sections 1285 et seq., each party shall fully perform and satisfy the terms of the Arbitration Award within fifteen (15) calendar days of the service of the Arbitration Award.

11. The Arbitration Award shall be final and binding upon the parties without appeal or review except as permitted by California law. Any party may apply to any court of competent jurisdiction for confirmation and entry of judgment based on the Arbitration Award, provided that the confidentiality provisions of paragraph 12 herein shall apply to any such proceeding. The following time periods set forth in the CCP shall be shortened as follows: Section 1288 – from four years to 90 days to file and serve a petition to confirm an award; and from 100 days to 30 days to file and serve a petition to vacate or correct an award; Section 1288.2 – from 100 days to 30 days to file and serve a response to vacate or correct an award. In connection with any application to confirm, correct or vacate the Arbitration Award, any appeal of any order rendered pursuant to any such application, or any other action required to enforce the Arbitration Award, the prevailing party shall be entitled to recover its reasonable attorneys' fees, disbursements and costs incurred in such post-Arbitration Award activities.

12. If any party who is claimed to be subject to binding arbitration under this Appendix seeks to challenge the Arbitrator's determination under CCP Section 1285 et seq., that challenge shall be determined exclusively by binding arbitration conducted by a panel of three (3) retired judges or other arbitrators affiliated with JAMS (the "Appeal Panel"). The Appeal Panel shall be chosen in the same manner as provided herein for the selection of the Arbitrator. The provisions of paragraphs "B.2." through and including "B.7." of this Appendix shall apply to such arbitration appeal. Notwithstanding paragraph "B.8." of this Appendix, if the appeal processes of this Appendix are utilized, the prevailing party or parties in such arbitration appeal

shall be awarded reimbursement for its or their reasonable attorneys' fees, costs and disbursements (including, for example, expert witness fees and expenses, photocopy charges, travel expenses, etc.) and the fees and costs of JAMS and the Mediator, the Arbitrator and the Appeal Panel incurred throughout the mediation/arbitration/arbitration appeal process herein.

13. By agreeing to the binding arbitration provisions herein, the partners and the firm understand and accept the fact that they are thereby waiving certain rights and protections which may otherwise be available if a Dispute were determined by litigation in court, including, but not limited to, a right to a jury trial, a right to appeal (other than as provided herein), and a right to invoke formal rules of procedure and evidence.

14. If any portion of this Appendix is held to be unenforceable, that portion shall be considered severable from the remainder of this Appendix, and such remainder of this Appendix shall continue in full force and effect.

APPENDIX 4
FINANCIAL INTERESTS IN CLIENTS

In the course of business, however, opportunities to invest in firm clients or other entities might arise. This Appendix addresses policies and procedures for such investments.

1. INVESTMENT DECISIONS. Decisions regarding the investment of firm funds in equity or other financial instruments shall be made by majority vote of the partners. Such investments will be made solely in furtherance of the business objectives of the firm.

2. INVESTMENT CRITERIA. It shall be the policy of the firm to decline to accept equity or other non-cash compensation for services rendered to clients. All investments in equity and other financial instruments must be made by payment of the fair market price for the equity or other instrument. Neither the firm nor any of its partners may own a controlling interest in any client and may not acquire more than 1% of the outstanding shares of any client. No investment shall be made that will result in the denial of coverage of a client by the firm's professional liability insurer.

3. INDIVIDUAL INVESTMENTS BY PARTNERS. In the event the firm decides by majority vote of the partners to decline an investment opportunity, one or more partners may make such investment individually, provided that the restrictions of Section 2 above are followed.

4. LIQUIDATION OF INVESTMENTS; DISTRIBUTION OF PROCEEDS OF INVESTMENT. The Managing Partner, upon consultation with the other partners, shall make decisions regarding the liquidation of investment assets. Proceeds from such liquidation will be distributed among the partners according to the percentages governing the Additional Bonus.

APPENDIX 5
BENEFITS

The partnership shall provide the following benefits to partners, the specifics of which shall be determined or modified from time to time by a majority vote of the partners:

1. Life insurance
2. Health insurance for each partner and immediate family, including spouse or domestic partner and children
3. Cell phone
4. Other benefits as determined from time to time by a majority vote of the partners

CHAPTER 9

Founders and Advisors

9.1 What Is a Founder?

There is much confusion over what makes someone a founder, and whether it has any legal significance. A founder is really nothing more than a designation that the original promoters of an idea bestow on one another to identify to the outside world who is credited with getting the company off the ground. Often, a key hire may come in well after the company has been formed and in the end be described as a founder.

The expression has no legal significance per se. However, venture capitalists (VCs) do distinguish founders from other employees for certain reasons. For example, VCs often require the founders to make certain representations and warranties individually at the time of the first round of investment. In addition, VCs might want to impose certain vesting restrictions on the stock of founders, but not be so concerned with the other employees on the theory that the founders really constitute the brain trust. (Nonetheless, late hires, especially late executive management hires, are often treated like founders by VCs for such purposes).

9.2 When Should Founders Have a Written Agreement?

In some cases, it will make sense for the founders of a new venture to have a written agreement even before they form the entity in which they ultimately intend to pursue the enterprise. This is because if they begin jointly pursuing the new venture for a period of time before forming an entity, they will have entered into a general partnership and will be governed by the default rules for such enterprises unless they reduce the terms of their relationship to writing. See Chapter 8, Organizing or Cleaning Up a Partnership.

9.3 What Is Founders Stock?

Founders of companies often make the mistake of waiting until they have received a strong indication of interest from an investor before they incorporate and issue their stock. Forming a company too close in time to raising capital can create a significant tax issue. Specifically, if founders issue themselves stock at the time of formation for $.01 per share (for example) and then within a short period of time, outside investors pay $1.00 or more per share (for example), it might appear upon an IRS audit that the founders issued themselves stock at significantly below the fair market value per share. The difference between what the founders paid for their stock, and the fair market value of that stock based on the sale to outside investors, may be characterized as compensation income resulting in what could be significant tax liability to the founders. If, on the other hand, founders stock is issued long before investor commitment, and certain significant milestones are achieved in the interim, this risk decreases substantially.

The earlier stock is issued, the earlier the capital gains period begins to run. Upon a liquidity event, stock that has been held for one year or more will be taxed at the capital gains rate, which is currently 20 percent. Gains on stock held for less than one year are taxable at an individual's ordinary income tax rate, which can be significantly higher than the capital gains tax rate.

9.4 How Many Shares Should Founders Receive?

As discussed in Chapter 6, the total number of authorized shares, and the total number of issued and outstanding shares, at the time of formation of the company is largely arbitrary, and in the end not of high importance. What really matters is the relative allocation of the equity among the founders. The numbers of shares authorized and outstanding can be, and often are, adjusted upward through stock splits. Notwithstanding this, there are a couple of guiding factors.

Prospective hires often focus more on the total number of shares awarded to them (either outright as restricted stock or by the grant to them of options to purchase the shares) rather than the percentage of the company that such shares represent. As a result, the company should consider putting in place an equity incentive plan that has a significant number of shares, often between 1,000,000 and 2,000,000 shares. At the high end of the range, this will allow the company to make awards in the market range in terms of both percentage and raw numbers (i.e., 2 to 3 percent for a vice president of business development, at 50,000 to 70,000 shares). In addition, this plan allows the company to establish a low issuance price (in the case of restricted stock) or exercise price (in the case of options).

Venture capitalists often have an opinion about the number of shares of common stock that should be issued and outstanding at the time of their investment. They usually run numbers around an assumed purchase price in the range of $1.00 per share for a first or "Series A" round. Some VCs are more concerned about the initial purchase price than others, and their input will dictate what the capital structure of the company looks like. For sake of discussion, if we assume that a VC firm is going to put $5 million into a company with a pre-money valuation of $5 million, and require a 20 percent employee pool, that would translate to an employee pool with 2,000,000 shares.

The issuance of stock among the founding group is a determination to be made among the founders. The decision is typically based on relative contributions to the formation of the company, including the conception of the idea, leadership in promoting the idea, assumption of risk to launch the company, sweat equity, writing of a business plan, and development of any underlying technology. In addition to preformation contributions, the potential for future impact on commercializing the idea may be a factor, including the background and experience that each person brings with them.

9.5 How Should Equity Be Apportioned Among Founders?

If three people jointly conceive of an idea that is based on a business model rather than a technology, it would not be unusual for them to split the company evenly at formation. However, if one person conceived the idea, wrote the business plan, and assembled the team, a split of 50, 25, and 25 percent might be more appropriate. In addition, it is often the case that when the business plan is based on a proprietary technology, the developer of the technology receives a significantly higher percentage of the company. However, if the technologist is fortunate to attract as a cofounder a CEO with established industry credentials and connections, that person's business experience might level the playing field and suggest a more equal split of founders equity.

If you are the lead promoter of an idea and are faced with making the initial proposal regarding the division of equity, keep in mind that nibbling around the edges of a prospective cofounder's equity position may not engender the level of trust and cohesiveness that is so essential among the members of a founding team. The objective is to reach an allocation that is perceived to be fair and that leaves all of the founders with proper incentives to do what is necessary to make the business a success.

9.6 Should Your Client Formalize Its Relationship with Its Advisors?

Every successful business is the result of input from a variety of sources and factors. Entrepreneurs typically have mentors or other influencers in their lives who contribute significantly—and sometimes regularly—to the direction of the enterprise. Often these are people who do not want a formal relationship with the company, such as in the role of an officer or director, but who are willing to lend their name and the benefit of their experience to assist the company and bolster the strength of the company's management team. This connection can be particularly helpful when the founders are relatively inexperienced. The formation and use of a board of advisors is a great way to formalize advisor relationships, acknowledge the contributions such advisors make to the success of the business, and bolster the strength of the company's management team without subjecting the advisors to the responsibilities and liabilities of being a manager, officer, or director of the company.

9.7 What Are Owners Agreements, and What Should They Cover?

Contracts among business owners often take the form of a buy-sell agreement, shareholder agreement, stock restriction agreement, operating agreement, or partnership agreement, among others. This book contains several examples of owners agreements, which present sample provisions for a variety of circumstances owners may wish to cover regardless of the form of entity in which they do business, or even the existence of an entity. The desired provisions can be selected and combined from sample agreements included in chapters dealing with different entity types. Some important uses of such an agreement include:

- Determining the relative contributions, duties, and responsibilities of the parties;
- Determining the relative rights, benefits, and returns of the parties;
- Establishing and protecting intellectual property rights;
- Addessing conflicts of interest, noncompetition, and protection of trade secrets;
- Restricting the transferability of ownership; providing rights of first refusal;
- Succession planning; buy-sell provisions;
- Employee incentives;
- Procedures for the valuation of the business;
- Preventing competitive activities or use of trade secrets;
- Deadlock and dispute resolution provisions; and
- Defining applicable law, venue, and jurisdiction.

A well-drafted buy-sell agreement will contain many additional provisions, such as the following:

- Provisions relating to maintaining the status of an S corporation so that no shareholder can terminate its status;
- Provisions allowing stock to be transferred to family members or trusts for estate planning purposes;
- Provisions that transfers by operation of law (e.g., death or divorce) should trigger the right of the company and other shareholders to purchase the stock;
- Life insurance provisions, including allowing the company to purchase life insurance on the life of a shareholder, and the right of a shareholder

to purchase the life insurance at its cash value upon termination of
employment; and

- Provisions that each shareholder's stock certificate include a legend giving notice that the stock is subject to the provisions of a buy-sell agreement and that a copy of the same can be reviewed at the offices of the
company.

A carefully drafted buy-sell agreement will promote the goal of allowing
the business to continue while fairly compensating a terminating owner.

The drafting of an owners agreement is also an excellent opportunity to
assist your client with planning for potential discord among owners before a dis-
agreement arises, potential changes in owner circumstances (such as termination
of employment, disability, retirement, and death), and sharing ownership with
employees. This should be a collaborative process, beginning with helping your
client define its objectives for the agreement and getting time estimates for certain objectives (such as a liquidity event, retirement, etc.). Next, design an agreement that addresses the stated objectives and covers contingencies, giving careful
consideration to an appropriate valuation procedure or formula. Once the agreement is finalized and signed, help your client identify appropriate times to revisit
the agreement (e.g., when circumstances have changed in a way that makes a
valuation method inappropriate or the client's objectives have changed).

Revisit the agreement periodically!

9.8 Should a Small Business Impose Vesting Requirements?

A growing company will inevitably see employees come and go, and there may
also be changes in the company's ownership. However, many ownership changes
can be avoided if vesting provisions are imposed. Typical vesting provisions
require that an individual remain with the business for at least one year before
being vested in any portion of equity ownership. This is referred to as a "one-
year cliff," typically involving 25 percent of the total, with the remainder vesting
monthly over the next three years. One way to approach vesting is through a
stock restriction agreement, which is an agreement among the shareholders of a
corporation in which they agree to certain limitations on their shareholder rights.
Stock restriction agreements are often used to ensure that stock issued to founders is properly "earned" by each founding stockholder, by imposing vesting provisions or giving the company the right to purchase shares held by a founder in
the event the founder leaves the company within a certain period of time.

9.9 What Is a Section 83(b) Election?

Stock restriction agreements can have significant tax consequences. Unless the
founder makes an election under Internal Revenue Code (IRC) Section 83(b)
within thirty days after receiving shares subject to the restriction agreement, the

founder is subject to tax. This is because the shares vest on the amount by which the value of the vested shares at the time they vest exceeds the amount paid by the founder for the vested shares. If the founder makes a Section 83(b) election upon receiving the shares, he or she is taxed, upon receiving the shares, on the amount by which the value of the shares at the time of receipt exceeds the amount paid for the shares. If it is expected that the founder's shares will appreciate significantly in value, therefore, it may be a good idea to make a Section 83(b) election.

9.10 What Are Typical Vesting Requirements?

Five basic parameters need to be established in a typical stock restriction agreement with regard to vesting: (i) duration of vesting schedule; (ii) up-front vesting; (iii) cliff vesting; (iv) acceleration upon termination; and (v) acceleration upon change of control or initial public offering (IPO). Venture capitalists have established certain acceptable ranges for these parameters, and they serve as the best guide for determining what vesting should be self-imposed by the founders. By self-imposing restrictions before VC funding, the VCs might satisfy themselves that what is in place is acceptable; as a result, the founders may end up with slightly more favorable terms than they otherwise would receive from VCs on this point. The following are some general parameters, which tend to change over time due to the labor market and can vary by industry.

Founders stock generally vests over three years. It is fairly common in VC transactions for founders to have some percentage of their stock vested up front. VCs will often agree to this if a significant amount of effort was put into the company before funding. The range of up-front vesting typically falls between 10 and 25 percent.

Vesting is said to be on a "cliff" basis when a certain minimum period of time must elapse before any additional shares of stock vest. Six- and twelve-month cliff vesting is fairly common, with the current trend toward the shorter end of that range.

Any number of circumstances could lead to termination of the founder's employment. VCs often take the position that the equity must be earned, and that if the founder leaves for any or no reason, no additional stock vests. There are four basic circumstances in which a founder might leave the company: (i) resignation (for no reason and for good reason), (ii) termination (for cause and without cause), (iii) death, and (iv) disability. In the event the employee resigns voluntarily or is terminated for cause, no additional stock vests under most agreements. However, an argument can be made that if the founder is terminated without cause, or resigns for good reason (in other words, is forced out), there should be some compensation to the founder out of fairness and as a means of keeping the board of directors honest. While VCs resist any acceleration under these circumstances, occasionally founders are able to negotiate for an acceleration of six to twelve months. In the event of a founder's death or disability, six-month acceleration is fairly common, presumably as a good will gesture in a time of hardship.

VCs will generally permit either an additional one-year vesting or 50 percent vesting upon a change of control. A founder can make certain assumptions about when the change of control for the company would be most likely to occur and determine which of these two options appears most preferable. For example, if the vesting duration is three years, and the founders anticipate a sale of the business after year one, the founder would be better off with one-year acceleration because it would always result in more acceleration than would 50 percent after the first year.

Occasionally founders are able to obtain full acceleration upon change of control, and it is not always an unreasonable starting point for negotiation. After all, if the company is sold and the founders are still with the company, they likely made significant contributions to put the company in a position to be bought. VCs, however, are very reluctant to allow for full acceleration upon change of control. Their primary argument is that the value of the company diminishes if the founders stock vests fully upon change of control because the founders have less incentive to work for the acquirer after the acquisition. This is why some companies will not make deals with companies that provide for full acceleration upon change of control. What VCs are not as quick to tell founders is that they stand to benefit significantly if the founders stock does not vest upon a change of control, because their relative percentage of ownership determined at the time of the change of control increases to the extent that the founders' percentages decrease. If the VCs do not permit for full acceleration, an alternative is to request that they agree to provide for full acceleration if the founder is let go or resigns for good reason within one year following a change of control.

9.11 How Should Ownership Be Valued for Purposes of a Buyout?

For purposes of buy-sell provisions, value can be determined by the market value (if there is a market for the company's equity), appraised value, book value, a formula, mediation, or any number of other approaches and variations.

Conflicting interests will be at play, such as the desire to provide liquidity while preserving the company's ability to continue in business. However, if the parties to an agreement are determining how value will be established for a buyout at a point when they do not know whether they will ultimately be on the buying or selling end of the bargain, the chosen approach is more likely to be fair than it would be if the parties were forced to resolve the issue after a need had arisen.

9.12 Sample Documents and Checklists.

This section includes the following forms:
- Founders Agreement (Form 9 A)
- Shareholder Agreement (Form 9 B)
- Offer Notice Pursuant to Right of First Refusal (Form 9 C)
- Provision to Deal with Phantom Income (Form 9 D)
- Insurance-Funded Buyout Provision (Form 9 E)
- Bylaws for a Board of Advisors (Form 9 F)
- Board of Advisors Agreement (Form 9 G)
- Valuation Provision for Buy-Sell Agreement (Form 9 H)
- Indemnification Agreement for Director or Advisor (Form 9 I)

Form 9 A: Founders Agreement

Note: The following is an example of a fairly simple agreement between the founders of a new business before its incorporation. A more detailed agreement may be desirable and could continue to govern the relationship after incorporation as a shareholder agreement. See the sample owners agreements in Chapter 10 for examples of more detailed provisions that could be adopted by founders. In the event the corporation is never formed and a dispute arises between the founders, the rules of partnership would likely be applied. However, an agreement such as the following can be useful in preventing the application of default rules to certain matters where the parties reached an agreement, thereby avoiding an undesirable result as well as preventing faulty memories from perpetuating the dispute.

FOUNDERS AGREEMENT

This agreement is made between _____ (Founder A) and _____ (Founder B) for the purpose of forming a [California] corporation called *******, Inc., hereafter referred to as the Corporation. Founder A agrees to contribute the assets described in Exhibit A attached hereto, collectively valued at _____ Dollars ($_____) in exchange for a fifty percent (50%) ownership of the Corporation to be formed. Founder B agrees to contribute _____ Dollars ($_____) in cash in exchange for a fifty percent (50%) ownership in the Corporation.

Founder A and Founder B further agree as follows:

1. INCOME AND EXPENSES. The income and expenses of the Corporation will be allocated between Founder A and Founder B on a fifty-fifty basis until the Corporation has achieved aggregate sales in the amount of one million dollars ($1,000,000.00). Upon the one million dollar mark, the Corporation will begin making preferred payments to Founder A in the amount of not less then two percent (2%) per year of sales until fifty thousand dollars ($50,000.00) has been paid to Founder A as compensation for his early efforts on behalf of the business of the Corporation.

2. ASSETS & LIABILITIES. All assets and liabilities of the Corporation will be allocated between Founder A and Founder B on a fifty-fifty basis unless otherwise noted in this agreement.

3. MANAGEMENT DUTIES AND RESTRICTIONS. Founder A and Founder B shall have equal rights in the management of the Corporation. Neither Founder A nor Founder B may borrow or lend money, or make, deliver, or accept any commercial paper, or execute any mortgage, security agreement, bond, or lease, or purchase or contract to purchase, or sell or contract to sell any property or assets of the Corporation or their individual interest in the Corporation without the other's consent.

4. BANKING. Founder A and Founder B shall deposit all funds of the Corporation in its name in such checking account or accounts as designated. All withdrawals therefrom are to be made upon checks or wire transfers signed or endorsed by Founder A, Founder B or an appointed agent acting on the Corporation's behalf.

5. BOOKS. The books and accounting records of the Corporation shall be maintained and kept at the principal business location of the Corporation. The accounting records shall be kept on a cash basis and the fiscal year of the Corporation will end on December 31. The accounting records shall be closed and balanced at the end of each fiscal year.

6.   SALE OF THE CORPORATION OR ASSETS. If Founder A and Founder B decide to sell the Corporation or any of the assets of the Corporation, other than furniture, fixtures and office equipment, the proceeds from the sale of the Corporation or the Corporation's assets will be distributed in the following way: all outstanding debts and liabilities of the Corporation will be paid before any other distribution is made. Once all debts and liabilities of the Corporation are paid, the Corporation will distribute to Founder A an amount equal to the difference between what has already been paid to Founder A under paragraph 1 and the fifty thousand dollars ($50,000.00) agreed upon in paragraph 1 of this Agreement. The remaining proceeds, if any, will be split equally between Founder A and Founder B.

The furniture, fixtures and office equipment of the Corporation is subject to sale only upon Founder A or Founder B's consent. In addition, Founder A or Founder B has the right to purchase all or a portion of the assets from the Corporation at a fair market price. If a fair market price can not be agreed upon, the Corporation can hire an agreed upon third party to set the price of the sale.

7.   DISOLUTION OF THE CORPORATION. If both Founder A and Founder B elect to dissolve the Corporation, Founder A and Founder B shall proceed with reasonable promptness to liquidate the assets of the Corporation. The furniture, fixtures and office equipment of the Corporation is subject to sale only upon Founder A or Founder B's consent. In addition, Founder A or Founder B has the right to purchase all or a portion of the assets from the Corporation at a fair market price. If a fair market price can not be agreed upon, the Corporation can hire an agreed upon third party to set the price of the sale.

8.   BUYOUT. Founder A or Founder B may elect to sell their shares in the Corporation to the other for an agreed upon price. If an amount can not be agreed upon, the Corporation will hire an agreed upon third party to set the price of the sale.

9.   DEATH. Upon the death of either Founder A or Founder B, the surviving owner may allow either Founder A's spouse or Founder B's spouse the right to step into the deceased shareholder's shoes and have all the rights and privileges of the deceased shareholder. If the surviving shareholder does not allow this to happen, the Corporation will be dissolved according to paragraph 7 of this Agreement. The proceeds from the liquidation of the Corporation otherwise payable to the deceased shareholder will go to whoever has been designated by either such deceased shareholder to receive the proceeds of the liquidation in the event of his or her death.

10. ARBITRATION. Any controversy or claim arising out of or relating to this Agreement, or the breach hereof, shall be settled by arbitration, in accordance with the rules of the American Arbitration Association, and judgment upon the award rendered may be entered in any court having jurisdiction thereof.

In witness whereof the parties have signed this Agreement. The laws of _____ shall govern any dispute arising under or relating to this Agreement.

Executed this _____day of _____, 20____ in [San Francisco, California].

_____
[Founder A]

_____
[Founder B]

EXHIBIT A
ASSETS CONTRIBUTED BY FOUNDER A

Form 9 B: Shareholder Agreement

SHAREHOLDER AGREEMENT

This Agreement is made and entered as of the ___ day of _____, 20___, by and among ******, Inc., a _____ corporation, and the undersigned shareholders of the corporation (the "Shareholders").

RECITALS

WHEREAS, the Shareholders currently are the owners of 100% of the issued and outstanding shares of the capital stock of the corporation and are Active in the Business (as defined below) of the corporation;

WHEREAS, there is no ready market for the purchase or sale of the capital stock of the corporation;

WHEREAS, the Shareholders wish to protect the management and control of the corporation against intrusion by persons not Active in the Business of the corporation or not acceptable to the Shareholders as co-owners of the corporation's business, and to provide a ready market for their shares of capital stock of the corporation (the "Shares") under certain circumstances;

WHEREAS, one of the Shareholders is paying a portion of the purchase price for his Shares in the form of consulting services to be performed for the corporation; and

WHEREAS, the Shareholders thus deem it to be in their best interests to provide for certain restrictions on their transfer of the Shares and to create certain options and obligations for their purchase and sale of the Shares, and the voting of the Shares, all as provided below;

NOW, THEREFORE, in consideration of the premises and the mutual covenants herein contained, it is hereby agreed as follows:

1. PURPOSES OF AGREEMENT; DEFINITIONS.

    (a) Protective Purpose. It is the purpose of this Agreement to protect the management and control of the corporation against intrusion by persons not Active in the Business of the Corporation or not acceptable to the Shareholders as co-owners or managers of the corporation's business.

    (b) Market Purpose of Agreement. It is also the purpose of this Agreement to provide for and/or limit the disposition of the Shares held by the Shareholders under certain circumstances.

    (c) "Shareholder" Defined. The term "Shareholder," as used in this Agreement, shall be deemed to mean the signatories to this Agreement and any other person who hereafter becomes a holder of Shares.

    (d) "Active in the Business" Defined. The term "Active in the Business", as used in this Agreement, shall mean involved in the day-to-day business of the corporation as an officer, independent contractor, or employee of the corporation, or involved in the policy and direction of the corporation as a member of the Board of Directors.

    (e) Shares Subject to Vesting. In consideration of the fact that %%% is paying the purchase price for his Shares in the form of consulting services to be performed for the corporation, his Shares shall be subject to vesting as follows: one-sixtieth (1/60th) of the One Hundred Eleven Thousand (111,000) Shares to be issued to him shall vest at the end of each month of service to the corporation he completes pursuant to that

certain Software Maintenance and Support Agreement between the corporation and
_____, Inc. dated of even date herewith (the "Consulting Agreement"),
beginning on the date first set forth above. The unvested portion of the Shares held
by Mr. **** may be voted by him but is not subject to transfer, sale, assignment,
hypothecation, encumbrance or alienation and will return to the status of authorized
but unissued Shares in the event of such Shareholder's resignation, death, disability,
retirement, termination from ********, Inc., or in the event of the termination of the
Consulting Agreement. In the event Company is acquired or merges with another
entity which is not majority owned by the Shareholders, Mr. ****'s shares shall
become fully vested immediately prior to the closing of such sale or merger.

    2.   ENFORCEMENT PROVISIONS.

    (a) General Restriction on Transfer. Except as hereinafter set forth, neither
the Shares nor any interest therein, including without limitation the right to vote the
Shares, shall be validly sold, exchanged, assigned, pledged or encumbered or otherwise transferred, for consideration or by way of gift, bequest, or otherwise, either voluntarily, involuntarily, or by operation of law, and no purported transferee shall be
recognized as a shareholder of the corporation for any purpose whatsoever unless
and until said Shares shall have been released from the restrictions upon transfer as
hereinafter provided; and in any such case the purported transferee shall sign a
counterpart of this Agreement.

    (b) Occurrence of Transfer. A transfer or attempt to transfer subject to the
provisions of this Agreement shall be deemed to occur whenever any interest in any
of the Shares is transferred or attempted to be transferred, irrespective of whether
any change in the record ownership thereof occurs.

    (c) Agreement Available For Inspection. An original copy of this Agreement
duly executed by the corporation and by the Shareholders shall be delivered to the
corporation's Secretary and shall be made available at the principal office of the corporation for inspection by any person requesting it.

    (d) Legend. Each certificate evidencing the Shares issued after the effective
date of this Agreement shall have conspicuously printed on it the following legend:

> THE TRANSFER, SALE, ASSIGNMENT, HYPOTHECATION, ENCUM-
> BRANCE OR ALIENATION OF THE SHARES REPRESENTED BY THIS
> CERTIFICATE IS RESTRICTED BY A SHAREHOLDER AGREEMENT
> AMONG ALL OF THE SHAREHOLDERS OF THIS CORPORATION AND
> THIS CORPORATION DATED _____, 20___. A COPY OF THE SHARE-
> HOLDER AGREEMENT IS AVAILABLE FOR INSPECTION DURING NOR-
> MAL BUSINESS HOURS AT THE PRINCIPAL OFFICE OF THE CORPORA-
> TION. ALL OF THE TERMS AND PROVISIONS OF THE SHAREHOLDER
> AGREEMENT ARE HEREBY INCORPORATED BY REFERENCE AND
> MADE A PART OF THIS CERTIFICATE.

    (e) Printing Legend on Existing Certificates. Each Shareholder shall immedi-
ately upon execution of this Agreement, present the certificate representing his or
her Shares to the Secretary and cause the Secretary to print on the certificate, in a
prominent manner, the legend set forth in paragraph 2(d) of this Agreement, if such
certificates have already been issued.

    (f) Restrictions on After-Acquired and After-Issued Shares. The terms of this
Agreement shall apply to all of the Shares in existence at the time this Agreement is
executed, to any Shares transferred in any manner by a Shareholder, and to any
additional Shares the corporation may issue to a holder of Shares as a recapitaliza-

tion, reorganization, stock dividend, stock split or reverse stock split. The corporation may require that a transferee, as a condition of transfer, execute an agreement similar to this Agreement. Any new shares issued by the corporation shall be subject to the legend condition set forth in paragraph 2(d) of this Agreement.

(g) <u>Deposit with Corporation</u>. Concurrently with the execution of this Agreement, each Shareholder shall endorse a stock assignment separate from the certificate representing his or her Shares and shall deposit the assignment and the certificate representing his or her Shares with the Secretary. Despite the endorsement and deposit, each Shareholder shall have the right to vote his or her Shares and receive dividends paid on them until his or her Shares are sold or transferred as provided in this Agreement.

(h) <u>Remedies</u>. The rights and remedies provided by this Agreement are cumulative and the use of any one right or remedy by any party shall not preclude or waive its right to use any or all other remedies. Said rights and remedies are given in addition to any other rights the parties may have at law or in equity. Without limiting the foregoing, the parties hereto agree that irreparable harm would occur in the event that any of the terms of this Agreement were not performed fully by the parties hereto or were otherwise breached, and that money damages are an inadequate remedy for breach of the Agreement because of the difficulty of ascertaining and quantifying the amount of resulting damage. Therefore, it is agreed that the parties hereto shall be entitled to an injunction or injunctions to restrain, enjoin and prevent breaches of this Agreement by the other parties and to enforce specifically the terms and provisions of this Agreement, and that no bond or other security shall be required in obtaining such equitable relief and the undersigned hereby consent to the issuance of such injunction and to the ordering of specific performance.

(i) <u>Delays</u>. Except where a time period is specified, no delay on the part of any party in the exercise of any right, power, privilege or remedy hereunder shall operate as a waiver thereof, nor shall any exercise or partial exercise of any such right, power, privilege or remedy preclude any further exercise thereof or the exercise of any right, power, privilege or remedy.

3. <u>TRANSFERS DURING LIFETIME</u>.

(a) <u>Notice of Offer</u>. In the event any Shareholder (the "Offering Shareholder") desires to sell or otherwise transfer any or all of his Shares to the other Shareholders (the "Remaining Shareholders"), subject to the limitations set forth in subparagraph 3(e) below, or to a third party or parties other than a Shareholder's individual retirement account or a trust created for estate planning purposes, then, in any such event, the Offering Shareholder shall give written notice to the Secretary of the corporation (the "Offer Notice") and shall specify in the Offer Notice the following:

(i) the name, address and occupation of the proposed transferee(s) and the number of Shares proposed to be transferred to the proposed transferee(s) (the "Offered Shares");

(ii) the price per share and terms of sale set by the Offering Shareholder for the Offered Shares or that the transfer is by way of gift or otherwise for no consideration.

The price specified pursuant to (ii) above or, if applicable, the price specified pursuant to subparagraphs 3(e) and 3(f) below, shall constitute, and shall hereinafter be referred to as, the "Offered Price." Delivery of the Offer Notice to the Secretary shall be deemed to be an offer by the Offering Shareholder to sell the Offered Shares to the corporation and the Remaining Shareholders at the Offered Price. Such offer may be accepted in the "Offer Period," which shall be the forty-five (45) day period commencing on the date the Offer Notice is delivered to the Secretary (the "Offer

Date"), and may not be withdrawn by the Offering Shareholder during the Offer Period.

(b) <u>Right of Corporation to Purchase Offered Shares</u>. If the corporation is then in a position under applicable laws of the State of [California] to acquire shares issued by it, the corporation shall have the right to acquire all or, subject to the last sentence of subparagraph 3(d), a portion of the Offered Shares at the Offered Price. Said right shall be exercised within ten (10) days after the Offer Date by notice in writing transmitted to all shareholders stating the corporation's intent to acquire the Offered Shares.

(c) <u>Right of Remaining Shareholders to Purchase Offered Shares</u>. If the corporation cannot then legally acquire the Offered Shares or if the corporation does not exercise its right to do so within the period specified in subparagraph 3(b), the Secretary shall, within five (5) days after the expiration of such period, deliver a copy of the Offer Notice to the Remaining Shareholders. Subject to the provisions of subparagraph 3(d) below, the Remaining Shareholders shall have the right, but shall be under no obligation, to acquire all or part of the Offered Shares at the Offered Price.

(d) <u>Purchase of Offered Shares by Remaining Shareholders</u>. Prior to the expiration of the Offer Period, the Remaining Shareholders, or any of them, if they desire to acquire the Offered Shares, shall deliver by mail or otherwise to the Secretary a written notice (the "Acceptance Notice") of their acceptance of the Offering Shareholder's offer, stating the number of said shares each of them desires to purchase at the Offered Price. Within five (5) days of its receipt, the Secretary shall deliver to the Offering Shareholder a copy of the Acceptance Notice(s). Delivery of a copy of the Acceptance Notice(s) to the Offering Shareholder shall create a binding contract between the Remaining Shareholders signing the Acceptance Notice and the Offering Shareholder. Notwithstanding anything herein contained to the contrary, in the event the corporation and the Remaining Shareholders have elected to purchase only a portion of the Offered Shares on or before the last day of the Offer Period, then each contract for the purchase and sale of only a portion of the Offered Shares shall become null and void at the option of the Offering Shareholder, exercised in a written notice given to the corporation and/or the Remaining Shareholders on or before the fifth (5th) business day following the end of the Offering Period. In the event more than one of the Remaining Shareholders wishes to purchase some or all of the Offered Shares, each Remaining Shareholder shall have the right to purchase a pro rata number of the Offered Shares based on such Shareholder's ownership interest in the corporation prior to the purchase of the Offered Shares.

(e) <u>Offer for Non-Cash Consideration</u>. In the event the Offered Shares are proposed to be transferred, either in whole or in part, for a consideration other than cash, then each of the Remaining Shareholders and the corporation shall have the right to acquire the Offered Shares in the manner and upon the terms and conditions herein set forth at a price per share in cash determined as set forth in paragraph 6.

(f) <u>Offer for No Consideration</u>. In the event that the Offered Shares are proposed to be transferred for no consideration, then each of the Remaining Shareholder and the corporation shall have the right to acquire the Offered Shares upon the terms and conditions herein set forth at the purchase price per share determined in the manner set forth in paragraph 6.

(g) <u>Notice of Offers to Acquire All or Portion of Offered Shares</u>. In the event the Offering Shareholder receives no offers or offers for only a portion of the Offered Shares from the corporation and the Remaining Shareholders, and the Offering Shareholder exercises his option specified in subparagraph 3(d) hereof, the Offering Shareholder may transfer the Offered Shares at any time within sixty (60) days from the expiration of the Offering Period to the proposed transferee for the Offered Price as specified in the Offer Notice; provided, however, that the prospective transferee shall receive and hold the Offered Shares subject to all of the provisions and restrictions of this Agreement.

(h) Payment of Purchase Price. In the absence of a separate agreement between the Offering Shareholder and the Remaining Shareholders and/or the corporation regarding the terms of payment for the Offered Shares, the transfer of the Offered Shares to the Remaining Shareholders and/or the corporation, shall be consummated in the following manner: the Secretary shall set a closing date which shall be within thirty (30) days of receipt by the Offering Shareholder of the notice specified in paragraph 3(b) or the Acceptance Notice specified in paragraph 3(d) (the "Closing Date"). At least ten (10) days prior to the Closing Date, the Secretary shall notify the Remaining Shareholders and/or the corporation in writing as to the number of such shares which he or it is obligated to acquire, the purchase price per share, and the Closing Date (the "Closing Notice"), and shall also send a copy of the Closing Notice to the other party or parties to the transaction. On or before the Closing Date, each purchaser of shares shall deliver to the Secretary the purchase price of the Offered Shares to be acquired by him or it in cash or by certified check made out to the Offering Shareholder. Subject to receipt of the cash or checks for the purchase price, on the Closing Date the Secretary shall transfer said shares of stock on the books of the corporation by registering such Shares in the name of the transferee or transferees who have delivered to him the purchase price for the Offered Shares; and the Secretary shall, at the same time, transmit the purchase price to the Offering Shareholder.

(i) Default. If the corporation or Remaining Shareholders fail to deliver to the Secretary on or prior to the Closing Date the aggregate purchase price of the Shares to be acquired by such transferee(s), the Secretary shall immediately notify in writing the other party or parties of such default, and shall, unless and until instructed to the contrary by said transferee(s), hold in trust for said transferee(s) the certificate or certificates representing the number of Offered Shares as to which such default has occurred. In the event of any such default, the transferor shall be entitled to pursue such remedies at law or in equity to which he may be entitled for the transferee's breach of the obligation to acquire said Shares.

4.   DEATH OF A SHAREHOLDER.

(a) Purchase by Corporation. Each Shareholder agrees that the corporation shall redeem the vested portion of any Shares standing of record in the name of a deceased Shareholder or in the name of an entity in which a deceased Shareholder is a majority owner (the "Deceased Shareholder") at the time of his death (the "Redemption"). Consummation of such Redemption shall occur in the manner specified in subparagraph 3(h) on the date set by the Secretary, which date shall be within sixty (60) days following the qualification of the executor or other representative of the Deceased Shareholder or within ninety (90) days of the death of the Deceased Shareholder, whichever is earlier. Upon Redemption, the corporation shall pay the estate of the Deceased Shareholder for such Deceased Shareholder's Shares a price determined according to paragraph 6 of this Agreement.

(b) Purchase by Surviving Shareholders. If the corporation, for any reason, cannot legally perform the provisions of subparagraph 4(a) of this Agreement, in whole or in part, the surviving Shareholders shall purchase on the terms and conditions and at the price specified in paragraph 6 from the estate of the Deceased Shareholder all of the Shares owned by the Deceased Shareholder that the corporation is unable to purchase.

(c) <u>Transfer of Deceased Owner's Shares to Shareholder Spouse.</u> Notwithstanding anything herein to the contrary, in the event the spouse of the Deceased Shareholder is a shareholder of record, either alone or jointly with the Deceased Shareholder, immediately prior to the Deceased Shareholder's death, at the option of such spouse the Shares of the Deceased Shareholder may be transferred to such spouse, either by operation of law or by purchase of such Shares at the purchase price and in the manner specified in subparagraph 4(a) hereinabove.

(d) <u>Costs.</u> The estate of the Deceased Shareholder shall bear, and hold the corporation harmless from, all costs and expenses required for securing court orders, court decrees, court approvals and tax clearances required to enable the estate of the Deceased Shareholder to transfer to the corporation and/or the surviving Shareholders full legal and equitable title to the Deceased Shareholder's Shares.

(e) <u>Estate of Deceased Shareholder Defined</u>. The term "estate of the Deceased Shareholder" as used in this Agreement shall mean and include as those terms are defined by the law of the State of California:

(i) the duly appointed and qualified executor or administrator of the Deceased Shareholder;

(ii) the surviving joint tenant of the Deceased Shareholder where Shares are owned by the Deceased Shareholder and a person who is not Active in the Business of the corporation; and,

(iii) any other person who may, because of the community property or other law of any jurisdiction, acquire without formal probate proceedings any right, title or interest in or to the Deceased Shareholder's Shares.

   5.   <u>OTHER EVENTS CONSTITUTING AN OFFER TO SELL.</u>

(a) In the event any Shareholder Active in the Business of the corporation (the "Offering Shareholder"):

(i) terminates his employment with the corporation (whether as an employee or independent contractor);

(ii) resigns from the Board of Directors;

(iii) is terminated by the corporation from employment with the corporation;

(iv) is adjudicated a bankrupt, voluntary or involuntary, or makes an assignment for the benefit of creditors;

(v) files a complaint for involuntary dissolution of the corporation pursuant to Section 1800(a) of the California Corporations Code or similar provision then in effect; or

(vi) elects to wind up and dissolve the corporation pursuant to Section 1900(a) of the California Corporations Code or similar provision then in effect;

or any other event should occur which, were it not for the provisions of this Agreement, would cause a Shareholder's Shares, or any part thereof, to be transferred, assigned, canceled, or sold to any person, voluntarily or involuntarily, under circumstances which would not bring such transfer within paragraphs 3 or 4 of this Agreement, then such event shall be deemed to constitute an offer to sell the Shares so being transferred, assigned or sold and shall give rise to the same rights to purchase as are set forth in paragraph 3 of this Agreement for an Offer Notice, on the terms set forth therein.

(b) Notwithstanding the foregoing, if the transfer described in paragraph 5(a) arises out of a decree of dissolution or separate maintenance or property settlement or separation agreement, or out of a disposition by the spouse of a Shareholder to a person other than said Shareholder, then such Shareholder shall have the exclusive right, for a period of thirty (30) days, to purchase such Shares (to be exercised by giving written notice to the Secretary and to the spouse or personal representative, heirs, or assigns of the spouse), at the purchase price per Share determined in the manner set forth in paragraph 6.

(c) Upon the occurrence of any event which shall be deemed an offer to sell under this paragraph 5, the Offering Shareholder shall immediately notify the Secretary of the occurrence of such event in the manner set forth in subparagraph 3(a).

(d) <u>Fifth Year Option</u>. Upon the fifth (5th) anniversary of this Agreement, Shareholder _____ shall be deemed to have offered to sell his Shares under this paragraph 5 and the same rights to purchase shall arise as are set forth in paragraph 3 of this Agreement for an Offer Notice, on the terms set forth therein.

6.   <u>PURCHASE PRICE</u>.

(a) <u>Appraised Value</u>. Except as otherwise specifically provided herein, the purchase price per share at which Offered Shares shall be bought and sold in any calendar year shall be determined by appraisal. Within thirty (30) days after the occurrence of the event requiring the determination of the price for the Shares under this Agreement, the corporation shall employ an appraiser to appraise the Shares and determine their value. The cost of the appraisal shall be paid by the corporation. Notwithstanding anything herein to the contrary, the corporation shall not be required to obtain an appraisal more than once in any twelve (12) month period.

(b) <u>Life Insurance</u>. The corporation may purchase and maintain life insurance policies insuring the lives of the Shareholders wherein the beneficiary of the policy shall be designated by each Shareholder so insured in an amount mutually determined by the corporation and the Shareholder. The existence of such coverage shall relieve the corporation of any obligation to purchase Offered Shares pursuant to the redemption provisions in paragraph 4 of this Agreement, and the payment of such death benefit to the Shareholder's designated beneficiary shall be deemed a full and complete satisfaction and discharge of all such deceased Shareholder's rights, claims, ownership and interests, and those of his estate, hereunder against the corporation, other than any claim or obligation based upon a debt for money lent to or borrowed from the corporation, and the Deceased Shareholder's Shares shall be canceled.

7.   <u>VOTING AND GOVERNANCE COVENANTS</u>.

(a) <u>Board Members</u>. The Shareholders shall vote their Shares as necessary to elect _____ and _____ to the Board of Directors. In the event _____ or _____ cease to serve as a member of the Board, the resulting vacancy shall be filled by the Director ceasing to serve, or if she is unable to make such designation, by the remaining member(s) of the Board. The corporation shall reimburse the reasonable expenses of Directors for costs incurred in attending meetings of the Board of Directors; and

(b) <u>Board Powers</u>. The Board of Directors shall meet periodically to conduct the regular business of the Board, including the review of the corporation's financial condition and the approval of its operating budget. Expenditures not accurately reflected in the current operating budget approved by the Board shall be approved by the Board of Directors in advance. All compensation to be paid to officers of the corporation, including the reimbursement of expenses shall be approved by the Board of Directors in advance. No additional Shares shall be issued, no options for Shares granted, and no instruments executed by the corporation which are convertible into Shares without the approval of the Board of Directors in advance.

(c) <u>Limitation on Shareholder Dilution</u>. As of the date first set forth above, the relative ownership of the Shareholders, on a fully diluted basis, is as follows:

XXXX	80.0%
$$$$$	10.0%
%%%%	10.0%

Unless the Shareholders unanimously agree otherwise in writing, the undersigned shall vote their Shares and exercise their powers as members of the Board of Directors of the corporation as required to ensure that the corporation does not issue additional Shares in any transaction that disproportionately dilutes any of the Shareholders (i.e. Shares may be issued pro rata to the Shareholders, such as in a stock split, or may be issued to third parties in such transactions as the Board of Directors may deem advisable to advance the interests of the corporation).

8. <u>NOTICES</u>. All notices required by this Agreement shall be written, and either personally delivered or sent by registered U.S. mail, postage prepaid. Notice to be given to the corporation shall be delivered or addressed to the corporation at its principal place of business. Notices to be given to the Shareholders shall be delivered or addressed to them at their respective addresses given to the Secretary for the purpose of notice or, if no such address is given, in care of the corporation at its principal place of business.

9. <u>ADDITIONAL SHARES</u>. This Agreement shall apply to any shares hereinafter issued to a party hereto and to any stock dividend, stock split, or other distribution of shares of the corporation made upon or in exchange for the Shares.

10. <u>TERMINATION OF AGREEMENT</u>. This Agreement shall terminate on:

    (a) The written agreement of all the parties;

    (b) The dissolution or bankruptcy of the corporation;

    (c) The death of all of the Shareholders within a period of sixty (60) days, such termination to be deemed to have occurred on the day preceding the date of death of the first Shareholder;

    (d) At such time as only one Shareholder remains, the Shares of the other Shareholders having been transferred or redeemed in full; or

    (e) The effectiveness of a registration of the securities of the corporation under the Securities Act of 1933 in connection with an initial public offering by the corporation.

11. <u>AGREEMENT TO PERFORM NECESSARY ACTS</u>. Each party agrees to perform any further acts and execute and deliver any documents which may be reasonably necessary to carry out the provisions of this Agreement.

12. <u>AMENDMENT OF AGREEMENT</u>. The provisions of this Agreement may be waived, altered, amended, or repealed, in whole or in part, only upon the written consent of the parties hereto.

13. <u>SUCCESSORS AND ASSIGNS</u>. This Agreement shall bind and inure to the benefit of the successors, assigns, personal representatives, heirs and legatees of the respective parties.

14. <u>VALIDITY CLAUSE</u>. It is intended that each section of this Agreement shall be viewed as separate and divisible, and in the event that any such section shall be held to be invalid, the remaining sections shall continue to be in full force and effect.

15. <u>COPY OF AGREEMENT</u>. Immediately after execution of this Agreement by the parties hereto, an original counterpart hereof shall be delivered to the Secretary and shall be shown by him to any person making inquiry concerning it.

16. <u>PRONOUNS</u>. All personal pronouns used in this Agreement, whether used in the masculine, feminine or neuter gender, shall include all other genders.

17. <u>COUNSEL FOR THE CORPORATION</u>. Each Shareholder acknowledges that counsel for the corporation, [Legal Venture Counsel, Inc.,] drafted this Shareholder Agreement on behalf of the corporation. Each Shareholder acknowledges that such Shareholder:

    (a) has been advised that his or her interests in the Agreement may conflict with those of the corporation and the other Shareholders;

(b) has been advised that this Agreement may have tax consequences; and

(c) has been advised to seek independent counsel regarding this Agreement.

18. <u>ATTORNEYS FEES</u>. In the event that any suit or action is instituted to enforce any provision in this Agreement, the prevailing party in such dispute shall be entitled to recover from the losing party all fees, costs and expenses of enforcing any right of such prevailing party under or with respect to this Agreement, including without limitation, such reasonable fees and expenses of attorneys and accountants, which shall include, without limitation, all fees, costs and expenses of appeals.

19. <u>GOVERNING LAW AND CONSENT TO PERSONAL JURISDICTION</u>. This Agreement shall be governed by and construed under the laws of the State of [California] without giving effect to the principles of conflicts of laws. The parties hereby irrevocably and unconditionally submit to the jurisdiction of the Courts of the State of California and of the United States of America for the Northern District of California and agree that any legal action or proceeding relating to this Agreement may be brought in such courts. The parties hereby waive to the fullest extent permitted by law in connection with any such action or proceeding any objections they may now or hereafter have to the venue of any such action or proceeding in any such court or that such action or proceeding was brought in an inconvenient court and agrees not to plead or claim the same.

20. <u>WAIVER OF RIGHT TO JURY TRIAL</u>. The parties hereby irrevocably and knowingly waive to the fullest extent permitted by law any right to a trial by jury in any action or proceeding, including, without limitation, any counterclaim, arising out of this Agreement, or any other agreements or transactions related hereto or thereto. The parties agree that any such action or proceeding shall be tried before a court and not a jury. In the event the parties' waiver of a trial by jury is deemed invalid, the parties hereby agree that any action or proceeding, including, without limitation, any counterclaim, arising out of this Agreement, or any other agreements or transactions related hereto or thereto, shall be determined by judicial reference.

21. <u>COUNTERPARTS</u>. This Agreement may be executed in counterparts, each of which shall be deemed an original, but all of which together shall constitute one and the same instrument.

22. <u>NO AGREEMENT REGARDING EMPLOYMENT</u>. The undersigned acknowledge and agree that nothing in this Agreement shall confer any right with respect to continuation of employment by the corporation or interfere in any way with the rights of the parties to terminate the employment of any of the undersigned at any time, with or without cause.

IN WITNESS WHEREOF, the undersigned have executed this Agreement effective as of the day and year first above written.

SHAREHOLDERS   ******, INC.**

_____   By: _____,
[name]   President

_____
[name]

_____
[name]

Form 9 C: Offer Notice Pursuant to Right of First Refusal

OFFER NOTICE

TO: Corporate Secretary of ****, Inc.

FROM: _____

RE: Proposed Stock Transfer

The undersigned shareholder (the "***Offering Shareholder***") of ****, Inc., a [California] corporation (the "***Company***"), hereby gives notice pursuant to Section ___ of that certain Shareholder Agreement between the Company and its shareholders dated _____, 20__, as amended on _____, 20__ (the "***Shareholder Agreement***"), of his intention to sell his shares in the Company as follows:

Proposed Transferee: _____ [name]

                                     _____ [address]

                                     _____

Number of Shares: _____ (the "**Offered Shares**");

Price per Share: $_____ (the "**Offered Price**")

Terms: Payable in full at the time of transfer.

Pursuant to Section ___ of the Shareholder Agreement, this Offer Notice shall be deemed to be an offer by the undersigned to sell the Offered Shares to the Company and/or the remaining shareholders at the Offered Price, which offer shall remain open for a period of _____ days.

If the Company and remaining shareholders do not timely elect to purchase all of the Offered Shares, Offering Shareholder may transfer the Offered Shares to the proposed transferee at any time within _____ days from the expiration of this offer on the terms set forth herein. Please see the Shareholder Agreement for details.

DATE: _____, 20__

OFFERING SHAREHOLDER

_____

_____[name]

Form 9 D: Provision to Deal with Phantom Income

<u>Tax Distribution</u>. Except as provided elsewhere in this Agreement for distributions to be made upon liquidation, and provided that no distribution shall be made which will cause or increase an adjusted capital account deficit for a Member, the Company shall distribute (to the extent that sufficient funds exist after provision for expenses and reserves) no less than the Tax Distribution Amount (as defined below) no later than ninety (90) days after the close of each fiscal year. The "Tax Distribution Amount" shall be determined for each fiscal year by: (A) multiplying the Marginal Tax Rate (as defined below) for that fiscal year by the taxable income of the Company (as determined under Internal Revenue Code Section 703(a)) for that fiscal year, and subtracting (B) the sum of all other distributions with respect to such fiscal year. The "Marginal Tax Rate" for any particular fiscal year shall be the highest tax rate that would be imposed on any Member under either Section 1 or 11 of the Internal Revenue Code, whichever is higher, for that fiscal year.

Form 9 E: Insurance-Funded Buyout Provision

<u>Life Insurance.</u> The Company may purchase and maintain a life insurance policy insuring the life of a Member wherein the beneficiary of the policy shall be designated by the Member and the minimum death benefit shall be _____ dollars ($_____), which shall be at least the amount of the last Agreed Value. The existence of such coverage shall relieve the Company of any obligation to make payments pursuant to this Agreement, and the payment of such death benefit to the Member's designated beneficiary shall be deemed a full and complete satisfaction and discharge of all such deceased Member's rights, claims, ownership and interests, and those of his estate, hereunder against the Company, other than any claim or obligation based upon a debt for money lent to or borrowed from the Company.

Form 9 F: Bylaws for a Board of Advisors

BOARD OF ADVISORS
BYLAWS

Article I. Purpose

Section 1. The basic purpose of the Board of Advisors will be to help ensure that the mission statement of ****, Inc. (the "Company") are fulfilled. The Board of Advisors will assist in setting and accomplishing the goals and objectives of the Company.

Section 2. The objectives of the Board of Advisors shall include the following:
   A. Provide guidance in planning and evaluating the business activities and programs of the Company,
   B. Evaluate the marketing plan of the Company and provide input as to how it could be strengthened,
   C. Serve as a resource to the members of the Board of Directors of the Company,
   D. Increase the awareness and interest of the _____ industry in the products and services of the Company,
   E. Identify subjects toward which the Company should direct research and development,
   F. Help assess the uses of existing financial resources, determine the need for additional financial support, if any; and identify financing sources when necessary,
   G. Such other matters as the Board of Directors may request.

Article II. Membership

Section 1. The Board of Advisors shall consist of approximately _____ (____) members who are representatives of the _____ industry. The Board shall at all times be reflective of the diverse segments of the _____ industry with representatives from the following areas of the industry: (1) _____, (2) _____, (3) _____, (4) _____, (5) other areas as appropriate.

Section 2. _____, _____, _____, and _____, will serve as ex-officio members.

Section 3. One membership position is reserved for a representative from _____ _____.

Section 4. One membership position is reserved for the immediate past president of the _____.

Article III. Officers

Section 1. The Board shall have a Chair, who shall be elected by the Board.

Section 2. The Chair's duties shall include:
   A. Preside at all meetings of the Board.
   B. Work with the Executive Committee in developing the agenda for Board meetings.

433

C. Appoint such ad hoc committees as are necessary to conduct the business of the Board.

D. Assume other duties as necessary for the effective functioning of the Board.

Section 3. The term of the Chair shall be for two (2) years. If elected as Chair on the third (3rd) year of the term, the appointment will automatically be extended for one (1) year.

Section 4. The Board shall have a Vice Chair, who shall be elected by the Board. The Vice Chair shall serve as Chair-Elect of the Board.

Section 5. The Vice Chair's duties shall include:

A. Preside at meetings of the Board in the absence of the Chair.

B. Assume such other duties as are necessary for the effective functioning of the Board.

Section 6. The term of the Vice Chair shall be for two (2) years. If elected as Vice Chair in the third (3rd) year of the term, the appointment will automatically be extended for one (1) year.

Section 7. The Board shall have a Second Vice Chair, who shall be elected by the Board. The term of the Second Vice Chair shall be for two (2) years. If elected as Second Vice Chair in the third (3rd) year of the term, the appointment will automatically be extended for one (1) year.

Section 8. The Second Vice Chair's duties shall include:

A. Preside at meetings of the Board in the absences of the Chair and Vice Chair.

B. Assume such other duties as are necessary for the effective functioning of the Board.

Article IV. Standing Committees

Section 1. The Board shall have an Executive Committee.

Section 2. The members of the Executive Committee shall be the Chair of the Board, the Vice Chair of the Board, and the Second Vice Chair.

Section 3. The Executive Committee's responsibilities shall include:

A. Developing the agenda for Board meetings.

B. Considering special needs of the Company.

Section 4. The Executive Committee shall meet on a quarterly basis.

Section 5. The Board shall have a Nominating Committee.

Section 6. The members of the Nominating Committee shall include the Chair of the Board, the First Vice Chair, and two members-at-large elected by the Board of Advisors.

Section 7. The Nominating Committee's responsibilities shall include:

A. Nominating the Chair of the Board.

B. Nominating the Vice Chair (Chair-Elect) of the Board.

C. Nominating the Second Vice Chair of the Board.

D. Nominating new members of the Board.

Section 8. The Nominating Committee will present its recommendations for Chair, Vice Chair, Second Vice Chair, and new members to the Board.

Article V. Selection and Term of Board Members

Section 1. New members of the Board of Advisors shall be appointed by the Board of Directors upon the recommendation of members of the Board of Advisors and will serve pursuant to the terms of these Bylaws and a Board of Advisors Agreement with the Company.

Section 2. The term of appointment of Board members shall be for three (3) years. Any member shall be eligible for reappointment. The term of service will be based on the fiscal year.

Article VI. Meetings

Section 1. The Board shall hold two (2) regular meetings each year. Special meetings may be called as they are needed.

Section 2. The Chair of the Board shall preside over the meetings.

Section 3. The agenda for each meeting shall be developed by the Executive Committee and shall be distributed to each member prior to the meeting.

Article VII. Amendments

Section 1. These Bylaws may be altered or amended at any duly held meeting of the Board. Notice of any proposed change must be on the agenda of the meeting at which the change is to be considered.

Section 2. A three-quarters (3/4) vote of the members (excluding ex-officio members) present shall be required for an amendment to be passed.

Form 9 G: Board of Advisors Agreement

BOARD OF ADVISORS AGREEMENT

This Agreement is made and entered as of the _____ day of _____, 20___, by and between **** Inc., a _____ corporation ("Company") and _____ ("Advisor").

Company is engaged in the business of _____ _____.

Advisor has expertise, contacts and other relevant skills, and can provide significant assistance to Company in _____ _____; and

The members of the Board of Directors (the "Directors") desire to have the assistance and counsel of Advisor pursuant to the provisions of the Bylaws of the Board of Advisors (the "Bylaws") of the Company;

Now therefore, in consideration of the premises and the mutual covenants and agreements contained herein, the parties hereby agree as follows:

1. Appointment of Advisor.

Advisor is hereby appointed to the Board of Advisors of Company. Advisor's term shall commence on the date of this Agreement and continue for a period of three (3) years as provided in the Bylaws, or until the date upon which Advisor shall resign or be removed as provided below.

2. Effective Date.

The effective date of this Agreement shall be _____, 20___.

3. Duties and Responsibilities of Advisor.

3.1 Advisor shall serve as a member of the Company Board of Advisors with duties and responsibilities to consist of assisting the Board of Directors within Advisor's special expertise and experience as described in the Bylaws.

3.2 Advisor shall attend each meeting of the Board of Advisors, which meetings shall not exceed one (1) per calendar quarter. In addition, Advisor shall respond, with reasonable dispatch, to requests from the Directors for advice with respect to significant management, planning, marketing and other questions which arise from time to time and which are within the areas of Advisor's expertise and experience.

3.3 Advisor agrees to introduce the Directors of Company to persons and companies which Advisor may know who may be interested in the investment opportunity represented by Company.

4. Compensation of Advisor.

4.1 As compensation for his services under this Agreement, Advisor is hereby assigned, subject to the Vesting Criteria set forth in Subsection 4.2, _____ (____) shares of Common Stock in the Company, (the "Advisor's Interest"). Advisor understands and agrees that Advisor's Interest is subject to dilution resulting from any capital transaction of Company which occurs after the date of this Agreement, such as the sale of equity securities, or grant of interests to employees, Directors, other Advisors, and others.

4.2 Advisor's Interest is subject to a vesting requirement at the rate of _____ percent (___%) of Advisor's Interest for each full calendar quarter lapsing after the date hereof; such that if Advisor shall remain a member of the Board of Advisors continuously from the date of this Agreement until the _____ (___) anniversary of such date, Advisor shall be fully vested at that time with respect to the entire Advisor's Interest.

4.3 In the event Advisor's services under this Agreement are terminated pursuant to Section 5 below, Company shall have the right to repurchase the portion of Advisor's Interest that is unvested at the date of such termination for an aggregate consideration consisting of _____ Dollars ($_____) per share, and Advisor hereby agrees to sell such portion of the Advisor's Interest to Company on such terms in such event.

5. Termination of Advisor.

5.1 Advisor shall have the right at any time to resign from the Board of Advisors by giving notice to the Board of Directors. Such resignation shall be effective upon receipt by the Board of Directors.

5.2 The Directors shall have the right to terminate Advisor (a) upon a good faith determination by the Board of Directors that Advisor is not able to render advice or other services of value to Company; or, (b) upon a good faith determination by the Directors that Advisor has failed to perform his duties as specified in Section 3 above, or has violated his agreements as specified in Section 6 below, or is otherwise in material breach of this Agreement. Such a termination for cause shall only be effective if the Directors shall have given Advisor notice in writing, not less than thirty (30) days prior to the effective date of such termination, of their intention to terminate Advisor upon such a determination, specifying therein the ground or grounds for such termination, and shall have given Advisor the opportunity to correct the problem or deficiency which constitutes the grounds for termination for cause, if such matter is capable of being fully corrected.

6. Confidentiality and Non-Circumvention.

6.1 For purposes of this Agreement, the term "Confidential Information" shall include all information disclosed by Company to Advisor that is marked or designated on the cover envelope in writing as "Confidential" or with words of similar import, and all information discussed orally that is claimed to be confidential at the time of discussion.

6.2 Advisor shall utilize his best efforts to maintain and preserve the confidentiality of the Confidential Information and shall not, without the prior written consent of Company, disclose Confidential Information to third parties, or use Confidential Information for personal or business purposes without the prior written consent of Company.

6.3 Advisor shall use the same degree of care to avoid disclosure of Confidential Information that he employs with respect to his own information which he does not desire to disclose, but at all times shall use at least reasonable care.

6.4 The confidentiality obligations imposed in this Agreement shall not apply to materials and information if (a) such materials or information is in the public domain at the time of disclosure, through no wrongful act of Advisor; or (b) such materials or information is generally known to Advisor at the time of disclosure without obligation concerning its confidentiality; or (c) such materials or information is furnished to a third party by Company under no obligation of confidentiality; or (d) as may be required by law.

6.5 The terms and conditions of this Agreement shall apply to all Confidential Information disclosed by Company to Advisor during the period beginning the effective date of this Agreement and ending two years after the effective date of termination of this Agreement. The obligations of this Agreement as to non-disclosure of Confidential Information shall remain in effect for five (5) years after the date of such disclosure to Advisor.

6.6 Advisor shall not use any Confidential Information in Advisor's own business or any affiliated business without the prior written consent of Company, and then only to the extent specified in such consent. Advisor shall not contact any of Company's Directors, officers, employees, affiliates or associates to circumvent Company or the purposes of this Agreement.

7. Relationship of the Parties.

The relationship of the parties under this Agreement shall be, and shall at all times remain one of independent contractors and not that of employer and employee or joint venturers.

8. Entire Agreement; Amendment.

This Agreement and the Bylaws contains the entire agreement between the parties hereto with respect to the subject matter hereof and there are no promises, covenants, or representations which are not contained herein. This Agreement may not be amended or modified except by a writing executed by both of the parties hereto. This Agreement shall be binding upon and shall inure to the benefit of the successors and assigns of the parties hereto.

9. Notices.

All notices under this Agreement shall be in writing and shall be served by personal service, or registered mail, return receipt requested. Notice by mail shall be addressed to the respective party at its address set forth on the signature page hereof. Either party may change its address for notice by a notice given in the manner specified herein.

10. Governing Law.

This Agreement shall be governed by, and construed under, the laws of the State of _____.

11. Headings.

The Section headings herein are intended for reference and shall not by themselves determine the construction or interpretation of this Agreement.

12. Severability.

Should a court or other body of competent jurisdiction determine that any provision in this Agreement is invalid or unenforceable, the remaining provisions in this Agreement nevertheless shall be deemed valid and enforceable, and continue in full force and effect without being impaired or invalidated in any way.

13. Counterparts.

This Agreement may be executed in two or more counterparts, all of which taken together shall constitute one and the same Agreement.

Entered into as of the date first written above:

**** Inc.

[Address]

By: _____, President

Advisor

_____

[Signature]

_____

[Name]

_____

[Address]

_____

[Social Security Number]

Form 9 H: Valuation Provision for Buy-Sell Agreement

Purchase Price and Valuation of Shares. The purchase price for the Shares in respect of which the purchase option is exercised shall be the value of such Shares as set forth in subsection (a) below, as modified pursuant to subsections (b) and (d), below.

(a) The value of each Share as of the date of this Agreement is hereby declared to be _____ Dollars ($_____) per Share.

(b) Immediately after each of Company's annual Shareholders' meetings, or at such other times as Shareholders agree, Company and Shareholders may reaffirm or revise the determination of the value of the Shares set forth in (a), above. Agreement by Shareholders owning a majority of the Shares then owned by Shareholders shall be required either to reaffirm or revise any determination of value. Any reaffirmation or revision shall be set forth in a written statement which will be attached to the original of this Agreement.

(c) For purposes of subsection (d), below, the "Declared Value" means the value established under subsection (a), as reaffirmed or revised in accordance with subsection (b). The "Valuation Date" means the date on which Shareholders last determined the value of Shares either pursuant to (a) or (b), above.

(d) The Declared Value of each Share shall be adjusted as follows: Company's undistributed net income or net loss from operations shall be determined for the period beginning on the Valuation Date and ending on the last day of the month before the date the option to purchase arose (the "Determination Date"). The value of each share shall be increased or decreased, as is appropriate, by an amount equal to the Company's net income or net loss divided by the Shares outstanding as of the Determination Date. Any adjustment shall be made by the Company's then-serving accountants in accordance with generally accepted accounting principles and with the practices customarily employed by Company, subject to the following instructions:

(i) Irrespective of the amount of depreciation on the books of Company, for purposes of this adjustment only, depreciation shall be calculated on a straight line method over the useful life of the asset as shown on the books of Company.

(ii) Even if Company has received or is entitled to receive any life insurance proceeds by reason of the death of any Shareholder, those proceeds shall not be added to the net book value, and net worth shall be exclusive of such insurance proceeds.

(iii) The income or loss shall be considered on an after tax basis.

(iv) Contingent or unliquidated liabilities shall be disregarded for the purpose of making the adjustments provided in this subsection.

(v) Any distributions to Shareholders by way of dividends or otherwise (other than payment of indebtedness to any Shareholder) since the Valuation Date shall, for purposes of adjusting the Declared Value, be treated as an expense.

(vi) The above adjustments shall be final and binding upon the parties and the amount of undistributed net income or net loss per Share shall, as the case may be, be added to or subtracted from the price per Share determined in accordance with this Section. It is understood that no allowances shall be made for goodwill, any alleged bonus value in any lease in which Company is lessor or lessee, other intangible assets, nor shall any discount be taken because of minority interest or bonus be added for control.

(e) If Company or Shareholders purchase the Shares of Offeror, and at the purchase date Company is indebted, in a liquidated amount, to Offeror for advances or loans by Offeror to Company, then, in addition to the payment of the purchase price for the Shares, Company shall repay such indebtedness or the other Offerees shall purchase such indebtedness for full value from Offeror in proportion to the number of Shares purchased by Offerees. The indebtedness shall be purchased in the same manner and upon the same terms as though such indebtedness had been added to the purchase price for the Shares, but in no event on terms less favorable to Offeror than provided in any underlying evidence of indebtedness.

Form 9 I: Indemnification Agreement for Director or Advisor

INDEMNIFICATION AGREEMENT

This Indemnification Agreement (the "**Agreement**") is made as of _____, 20___, by and between ****, Inc., a [Delaware] corporation (the "**Company**"), and the undersigned member of the Board of Directors of the Company (the "**Indemnitee**").

WHEREAS, the Company and Indemnitee recognize the substantial increase in corporate litigation in general, subjecting directors to expensive litigation risks;

WHEREAS, Indemnitee does not regard the current protection available as adequate under the present circumstances, and Indemnitee and other directors of the Company may not be willing to continue to serve as directors without additional protection; and

WHEREAS, the Company desires to attract and retain the services of highly qualified individuals, such as Indemnitee, to serve as a director of the Company and to indemnify its directors so as to provide them with the maximum protection permitted by law.

WHEREAS, in view of such considerations, the Company desires to provide, independent from the indemnification to which the Indemnitee is otherwise entitled by law and under the Company's Certificate of Incorporation and Bylaws, indemnification to the Indemnitee and advances of expenses, all as set forth in this Agreement to the maximum extent permitted by law;

NOW, THEREFORE, to induce the Indemnitee to continue to serve the Company and in consideration of these premises and the mutual agreements set forth in this Agreement, as well as other good and valuable consideration, the receipt and sufficiency of which are hereby acknowledged, the Company and the Indemnitee hereby agree as follows:

1. **Indemnification.**

(a) <u>Third Party Proceedings</u>. The Company shall indemnify Indemnitee if Indemnitee is or was a party or is threatened to be made a party to any threatened, pending or completed action or proceeding, whether civil, criminal, administrative or investigative (other than an action by or in the right of the Company) by reason of the fact that Indemnitee is or was a director, officer, employee or agent of the Company, or any subsidiary of the Company, by reason of any action or inaction on the part of Indemnitee while a director or by reason of the fact that Indemnitee is or was serving at the request of the Company as a director, officer, employee or agent of another corporation, partnership, joint venture, trust or other enterprise, against expenses (including attorneys' fees), judgments, fines and amounts paid in settlement (if such settlement is approved in advance by the Company, which approval shall not be unreasonably withheld) actually and reasonably incurred by Indemnitee in connection with such action or proceeding if Indemnitee acted in good faith and in a manner Indemnitee reasonably believed to be in or not opposed to the best interests of the Company, and, with respect to any criminal action or proceeding, had no reasonable cause to believe Indemnitee's conduct was unlawful. The termination of any action or proceeding by judgment, order, settlement, conviction, or upon a plea of nolo contendere or its equivalent, shall not, of itself, create a presumption that Indemnitee did not act in good faith and in a manner which Indemnitee reasonably believed to be in or not opposed to the best interests of the Company, or with respect to any criminal action or proceeding, that Indemnitee had reasonable cause to believe that Indemnitee's conduct was unlawful.

(b) <u>Proceedings by or in the Right of the Company</u>. The Company shall indemnify Indemnitee if Indemnitee was or is a party or is threatened to be made a party to any threatened, pending or completed action or proceeding by or in the right of the Company or any subsidiary of the Company to procure a judgment in its favor by reason of the fact that Indemnitee is or was a director, officer, employee or agent of the Company, or any subsidiary of the Company, by reason of any action or inaction on the part of Indemnitee while a director or by reason of the fact that Indemnitee is or was serving at the request of the Company as a director, officer, employee or agent of another corporation, partnership, joint venture, trust or other enterprise, against expenses (including attorneys' fees) and, to the fullest extent permitted by law, amounts paid in settlement, in each case to the extent actually and reasonably incurred by Indemnitee in connection with the defense or settlement of such action or proceeding if Indemnitee acted in good faith and in a manner Indemnitee reasonably believed to be in or not opposed to the best interests of the Company and its shareholders, except that no indemnification shall be made in respect of any claim, issue or matter as to which Indemnitee shall have been finally adjudicated by court orders or judgment to be liable to the Company in the performance of Indemnitee's duty to the Company and its shareholders unless and only to the extent that any court in which such action or proceeding is or was brought shall determine upon application that, despite the adjudication of liability but in view of all the circumstances of the case, Indemnitee is fairly and reasonably entitled to indemnity for such expenses which the court shall deem proper.

(c) <u>Mandatory Payment of Expenses</u>. To the extent that Indemnitee has been successful on the merits or otherwise in defense of any action, suit or proceeding referred to in Section 1(a) or Section 1(b) or the defense of any claim, issue or matter therein, Indemnitee shall be indemnified against expenses (including attorneys' fees) actually and reasonably incurred by Indemnitee in connection therewith. Without limiting the foregoing, if any action, suit or proceeding is disposed of, on the merits or otherwise (including a disposition without prejudice), without (i) the disposition being adverse to the Indemnitee, (ii) an adjudication that the Indemnitee was liable to the Company, (iii) a plea of guilty or nolo contendere by the Indemnitee, (iv) an adjudication that the Indemnitee did not act in good faith and in a manner he reasonably believed to be in or not opposed to the best interests of the Company, or (v) with respect to any criminal proceeding, an adjudication that the Indemnitee had reasonable cause to believe his conduct was unlawful, the Indemnitee shall be considered for the purpose hereof to have been wholly successful with respect thereto.

2. **Expenses; Indemnification Procedure.**

(a) <u>Advancement of Expenses</u>. The Company shall advance all expenses incurred by Indemnitee in connection with the investigation, defense, settlement or appeal of any civil or criminal action or proceeding referenced in Section 1(a) or (b) hereof (but not amounts actually paid in settlement of any such action or proceeding). Indemnitee hereby undertakes to repay such amounts advanced only if, and to the extent that, it shall ultimately be determined that Indemnitee is not entitled to be indemnified by the Company as authorized hereby. The advances to be made hereunder shall be paid by the Company to Indemnitee within ten (10) days following receipt of an undertaking (the "**Undertaking**"), substantially in the form attached hereto as Exhibit 1, by or on behalf of the Indemnitee to repay the amount of any such advance if and to the extent that it shall ultimately be determined that the Indemnitee is not entitled to indemnification for such amount. The Undertaking shall be unsecured and shall bear no interest.

(b) Notice/Cooperation by Indemnitee. Indemnitee shall, as a condition precedent to his or her right to be indemnified under this Agreement, give the Company notice in writing as soon as practicable of any claim made against Indemnitee for which indemnification is or will be sought under this Agreement. Notice to the Company shall be directed to the President or Chief Executive Officer of the Company at the address shown on the signature page of this Agreement (or such other address as the Company shall designate in writing to Indemnitee). Notice shall be deemed received three (3) business days after the date postmarked if sent by domestic certified or registered mail, properly addressed; otherwise notice shall be deemed received when such notice shall actually be received by the Company. In addition, Indemnitee shall give the Company such information and cooperation as it may reasonably require and as shall be within Indemnitee's power.

(c) Procedure. Any indemnification and advances provided for in Section 1 and this Section 2 shall be made promptly, and in any event within 60 days after receipt by the Company of the written request of the Indemnitee, unless with respect to such requests the Company determines, by clear and convincing evidence, within such 60-day period that the Indemnitee did not meet the applicable standard of conduct. Such determination shall be made in each instance by: (a) a majority vote of the directors of the Company who are not at that time parties to the action, suit or proceeding in question ("**disinterested directors**"), even though less than a quorum; or (b) a committee of such disinterested directors designated by majority vote of such disinterested directors, even though less than a quorum; (c) if there are no such disinterested directors, or if such disinterested directors so direct, by independent legal counsel (who may be regular legal counsel to the Company) in a written opinion, or (d) a majority vote of a quorum of the outstanding shares of stock of all classes entitled to vote for directors, voting as a single class, which quorum shall consist of stockholders who are not at that time parties to the action, suit or proceeding in question. If a claim under this Agreement, under any statute, or under any provision of the Company's Certificate of Incorporation or Bylaws providing for indemnification, is not paid in full by the Company within the time allowed, Indemnitee may, but need not, at any time thereafter bring an action against the Company to recover the unpaid amount of the claim and, subject to Section 10 of this Agreement, Indemnitee shall also be entitled to be paid for the expenses (including attorneys' fees) of bringing such action. It shall be a defense to any such action (other than an action brought to enforce a claim for expenses incurred in connection with any action or proceeding in advance of its final disposition) that Indemnitee has not met the standards of conduct which make it permissible under applicable law for the Company to indemnify Indemnitee for the amount claimed, but the burden of proving such defense shall be on the Company and Indemnitee shall be entitled to receive interim payments of expenses pursuant to Section 2(a) unless and until such defense may be finally adjudicated by court order or judgment from which no further right of appeal exists. It is the parties' intention that if the Company contests Indemnitee's right to indemnification, the question of Indemnitee's right to indemnification shall be for the court to decide, and neither the failure of the Company (including its Board of Directors, any committee or subgroup of the Board of Directors, independent legal counsel, or its shareholders) to have made a determination that indemnification of

Indemnitee is proper in the circumstances because Indemnitee has met the applicable standard of conduct required by applicable law, nor an actual determination by the Company (including its Board of Directors, any committee or subgroup of the Board of Directors, independent legal counsel, or its shareholders) that Indemnitee has not met such applicable standard of conduct, shall create a presumption that Indemnitee has or has not met the applicable standard of conduct.

(d) <u>Notice to Insurers</u>. If, at the time of the receipt of a notice of a claim pursuant to Section 2(b) hereof, the Company has director and officer liability insurance in effect, the Company shall give prompt notice of the commencement of such proceeding to the insurers in accordance with the procedures set forth in the respective policies. The Company shall thereafter take all necessary or desirable action to cause such insurers to pay, on behalf of the Indemnitee, all amounts payable as a result of such proceeding in accordance with the terms of such policies.

(e) <u>Assumption of Defense and Selection of Counsel</u>. In the event the Company shall be obligated under Section 2(a) hereof to pay the expenses of any proceeding against Indemnitee, the Company, if appropriate, shall be entitled to assume the defense of such proceeding, with counsel approved by Indemnitee, which approval shall not be unreasonably withheld, upon the delivery to Indemnitee of written notice of its election so to do. Notwithstanding the foregoing, the Company shall not be permitted to settle any action or claim on behalf of Indemnitee in any manner which would impose any unindemnified liability or penalty on the Indemnitee or require any acknowledgment of wrongdoing on the part of Indemnitee without Indemnitee's written consent, which consent shall not be unreasonably withheld. After delivery of such notice, approval of such counsel by Indemnitee and the retention of such counsel by the Company, the Company will not be liable to Indemnitee under this Agreement for any fees of counsel subsequently incurred by Indemnitee with respect to the same proceeding, provided that (i) Indemnitee shall have the right to employ his or her counsel in any such proceeding at Indemnitee's expense; and (ii) if (A) the employment of separate counsel by Indemnitee has been previously authorized by the Company, (B) Indemnitee shall have reasonably concluded that there may be a conflict of interest between the Company and Indemnitee in the conduct of any such defense, or (C) the Company shall not, in fact, have employed counsel to assume the defense of such proceeding, then the fees and expenses of Indemnitee's counsel shall be at the expense of the Company. The Company shall not be entitled, without the consent of the Indemnitee, to assume the defense of any claim brought by or in the right of the Company or as to which counsel for the Indemnitee shall have reasonably made the conclusion provided for in clause (ii)(B) above.

3. **Additional Indemnification Rights; Nonexclusivity.**

(a) <u>Scope</u>. Notwithstanding any other provision of this Agreement, the Company hereby agrees to indemnify the Indemnitee to the fullest extent permitted by law, notwithstanding that such indemnification is not specifically authorized by the other provisions of this Agreement, the Company's Certificate of Incorporation, the Company's Bylaws or by statute. In the event of any change, after the date of this Agreement, in any applicable law, statute, or rule which expands the right of a Delaware corporation to indemnify a member of its board of directors, such changes shall be, ipso facto, within the purview of Indemnitee's rights and the Company's obligations under this Agreement. In the event of any change in any applicable law, statute or rule which narrows the right of a Delaware corporation to indemnify a member of its board of directors, such changes, to the extent not otherwise required by such law, statute or rule to be applied to this Agreement shall have no effect on this Agreement or the parties' rights and obligations hereunder.

(b) <u>Nonexclusivity</u>. The indemnification provided by this Agreement shall not be deemed exclusive of any rights to which Indemnitee may be entitled under the Company's Certificate of Incorporation, its Bylaws, any agreement, any vote of stockholders or disinterested directors, the Delaware General Corporation Law, or otherwise, both as to action in Indemnitee's official capacity and as to action in another capacity while holding such office. The indemnification provided under this Agreement shall continue as to Indemnitee for any action taken or not taken while serving in an indemnified capacity even though he or she may have ceased to serve in any such capacity at the time of any action, suit or other covered proceeding.

4.   **Partial Indemnification.** If Indemnitee is entitled under any provision of this Agreement to indemnification by the Company for some or a portion of the expenses, judgments, fines or penalties actually or reasonably incurred by him in the investigation, defense, appeal or settlement of any civil or criminal action or proceeding, but not, however, for the total amount thereof, the Company shall nevertheless indemnify Indemnitee for the portion of such expenses, judgments, fines or penalties to which Indemnitee is entitled.

5.   **Officer and Director Liability Insurance.** The Company shall obtain and maintain a policy or policies of insurance with reputable insurance companies which: (i) provide the officers and directors of the Company with coverage for losses from wrongful acts, or which ensure the Company's performance of its indemnification obligations under this Agreement, and (ii) are acceptable to the Board of Directors. In all policies of director and officer liability insurance, Indemnitee shall be named as an insured in such a manner as to provide Indemnitee the same rights and benefits as are accorded to the most favorably insured of the Company's directors. Notwithstanding the foregoing, the Company shall have no obligation to obtain or maintain such insurance if the Board of Directors of the Company determines in good faith that such insurance is not available on commercially reasonable terms.

6.   **Severability.** Nothing in this Agreement is intended to require or shall be construed as requiring the Company to do or fail to do any act in violation of applicable law. The Company's inability, pursuant to court order, to perform its obligations under this Agreement shall not constitute a breach of this Agreement. The provisions of this Agreement shall be severable as provided in this Section 6. If this Agreement or any portion hereof shall be invalidated on any ground by any court of competent jurisdiction, then the Company shall nevertheless indemnify Indemnitee to the fullest extent permitted by any applicable portion of this Agreement that shall not have been invalidated, and the balance of this Agreement not so invalidated shall be enforceable in accordance with its terms.

7.   **Exceptions.** Any other provision herein to the contrary notwithstanding, the Company shall not be obligated pursuant to the terms of this Agreement:

(a)   Claims Initiated by Indemnitee. To indemnify or advance expenses to Indemnitee with respect to proceedings or claims initiated or brought voluntarily by Indemnitee and not by way of defense, except with respect to proceedings brought to establish or enforce a right to indemnification under this Agreement or any other statute or law or otherwise as required under Section 145 of the Delaware General Corporation Law, but such indemnification or advancement of expenses may be provided by the Company in specific cases if the Board of Directors has approved the initiation of such suit; or

(b)   <u>Lack of Good Faith</u>. To indemnify Indemnitee for any expenses incurred by Indemnitee with respect to any proceeding instituted by Indemnitee to enforce or interpret this Agreement, if a court of competent jurisdiction determines that each of the material assertions made by Indemnitee in such proceeding was not made in good faith or was frivolous; or

(c) <u>Insured Claims</u>. To indemnify Indemnitee for expenses or liabilities of any type whatsoever (including, but not limited to, judgments, fines, excise taxes or penalties, and amounts paid in settlement) to the extent such expenses or liabilities have been paid directly to Indemnitee by an insurance carrier under a policy of officers' and directors' liability insurance maintained by the Company; or

(d) <u>Claims under Section 16(b)</u>. To indemnify Indemnitee for expenses or the payment of profits arising from the purchase and sale by Indemnitee of securities in violation of Section 16(b) of the Securities Exchange Act of 1934, as amended, or any similar successor or foreign statute; or

(e) <u>Claims for Indemnitee's Acts or Omissions</u>. To indemnify Indemnitee for any acts or omissions, or transactions from which a director may not be relieved of liability under applicable law or pertinent public policy.

8. **Construction of Certain Phrases.**

(a) For purposes of this Agreement, references to the "Company" shall include, in addition to the resulting corporation, any constituent corporation (including any constituent of a constituent) absorbed in a consolidation or merger which, if its separate existence had continued, would have had power and authority to indemnify its directors, officers, and employees or agents, so that if Indemnitee is or was a director, officer, employee or agent of such constituent corporation, or is or was serving at the request of such constituent corporation as a director, officer, employee or agent of another corporation, partnership, joint venture, trust or other enterprise, Indemnitee shall stand in the same position under the provisions of this Agreement with respect to the resulting or surviving corporation as Indemnitee would have with respect to such constituent corporation if its separate existence had continued.

(b) For purposes of this Agreement, references to "other enterprises" shall include employee benefit plans; references to "fines" shall include any excise taxes assessed on Indemnitee with respect to an employee benefit plan; and references to "serving at the request of the company" shall include any service as a director, officer, employee or agent of the Company which imposes duties on, or involves services by, such director, officer, employee or agent with respect to an employee benefit plan, its participants, or beneficiaries.

9. **Effectiveness of Agreement.** This Agreement shall be effective as of the date set forth on the first page and may apply to acts or omissions of Indemnitee which occurred prior to such date if Indemnitee was an officer, director, employee or other agent of the Company, or was serving at the request of the Company as a director, officer, employee or agent of another corporation, partnership, joint venture, trust or other enterprise, as the time such act or omission occurred.

10. **Attorneys' Fees.** In the event that any action is instituted by Indemnitee under this Agreement to enforce or interpret any of the terms hereof, Indemnitee shall be entitled to be paid all court costs and expenses, including reasonable attorneys' fees, incurred by Indemnitee with respect to such action, unless as a part of such action, the Delaware Court of Chancery determines that each of the material assertions made by Indemnitee as a basis for such action were not made in good faith or were frivolous. In the event of an action instituted by or in the name of the Company under this Agreement or to enforce or interpret any of the terms of this Agreement, Indemnitee shall be entitled to be paid all court costs and expenses, including attorneys' fees, incurred by Indemnitee in defense of such action (including with respect to Indemnitee's counterclaims and cross-claims made in such action), unless as a part of such action the court determines that each of Indemnitee's material defenses to such action were made in bad faith or were frivolous.

11. **No Rights of Continued Service.** This Agreement shall not impose any obligation of the Company to continue Indemnitee's service to the Company beyond any period otherwise required by law or by other agreements or commitments of the parties, if any.

12. **Miscellaneous.**

(a) <u>Governing Law</u>. This Agreement and all acts and transactions pursuant hereto and the rights and obligations of the parties hereto shall be governed, construed and interpreted in accordance with the laws of the State of [Delaware], without giving effect to principles of conflict of law.

(b) <u>Consent to Jurisdiction</u>. The Company and the Indemnitee each hereby irrevocably consent to the exclusive jurisdiction of [the Court of Chancery of Delaware] for any purpose in connection with any actions or proceedings that arise out of or relate to this Agreement.

(c) <u>Entire Agreement; Enforcement of Rights</u>. This Agreement sets forth the entire agreement and understanding of the parties relating to the subject matter herein and merges all prior discussions between them. No modification of or amendment to this Agreement, nor any waiver of any rights under this Agreement, shall be effective unless in writing signed by the parties to this Agreement. The failure by either party to enforce any rights under this Agreement shall not be construed as a waiver of any rights of such party.

(d) <u>Construction</u>. This Agreement is the result of negotiations between, and has been reviewed by, each of the parties hereto and their respective counsel, if any; accordingly, this Agreement shall be deemed to be the product of all of the parties hereto, and no ambiguity shall be construed in favor of or against any one of the parties hereto.

(e) <u>Notices</u>. Unless otherwise provided in this Agreement, any notice, demand or request required or permitted to be given under this Agreement shall be in writing and shall be deemed sufficient when directed to the President or Chief Executive Officer of the Company at the address shown on the signature page of this Agreement (or such other address as the Company shall designate in writing) and when delivered personally or three business days after being postmarked, as certified or registered mail, with postage prepaid, and addressed to the party to be notified at such party's address as set forth below or as subsequently modified by written notice.

(f) <u>Counterparts</u>. This Agreement may be executed in two or more counterparts, each of which shall be deemed an original and all of which together shall constitute one instrument.

(g) <u>Successors and Assigns</u>. This Agreement shall be binding upon the Company and its successors and assigns, including any direct or indirect successor by purchase, merger, consolidation or otherwise to all, substantially all or a substantial part of the business or assets of the Company. This Agreement shall inure to the benefit of Indemnitee and Indemnitee's heirs, legal representatives, executives and administrators. The Company shall require and cause any successor (whether direct or indirect, and whether by purchase, merger, consolidation or otherwise) to all, substantially all or a substantial part of the business or assets of the Company, by written agreement in form and substance satisfactory to the Indemnitee, expressly to assume and agree to perform this Agreement in the same manner and to the same extent that the Company would be required to perform if no such succession had taken place.

(h) <u>Subrogation</u>. In the event of payment under this Agreement, the Company shall be subrogated to the extent of such payment to all of the rights of recovery of

Indemnitee, who shall execute all documents required and shall do all acts that may be necessary to secure such rights and to enable the Company to effectively bring suit to enforce such rights.

(i) <u>Mutual Acknowledgement</u>. Both the Company and Indemnitee acknowledge that in certain instances, Federal law or applicable public policy may prohibit the Company from indemnifying its directors under this Agreement or otherwise. Indemnitee understands and acknowledges that the Company has undertaken or may be required in the future to undertake with the Securities and Exchange Commission to submit the question of indemnification to a court in certain circumstances for a determination of the Company's right under public policy to indemnify Indemnitee.

IN WITNESS WHEREOF, the parties hereto have executed this Agreement as of the date first above written.

****, INC.   **DIRECTOR**

By:

Name:_____, President and CEO   Name:

Address: _____   Address: _____

_____   _____

EXHIBIT 1

UNDERTAKING

1. This Undertaking is submitted pursuant to the Indemnification Agreement, dated as of _____, 20__, between ****, Inc., a [Delaware] corporation (the "Company"), and the undersigned (the "**Agreement**"). Capitalized terms used but not defined herein shall have the respective meanings set forth in the Agreement.

2. I am requesting certain Expense Advances in connection with a Claim.

3. I hereby undertake to repay such Expense Advances if it shall ultimately be determined that I am not entitled to be indemnified by the Company therefor under the Agreement or otherwise.

4. The Expense Advances are, in general, all related to: _____

_____

Signed: _____

Name: _____

Dated: _____

CHAPTER 10

Raising Money Through Private Placements

10.1 Which Laws Should a Small Business Be Aware of When Raising Money?

Even when a client already has a group of friends and family lined up for a seed round of financing, they need to be aware of their securities law obligations because there are a number of legal issues and requirements to be concerned about. The applicable requirements will be determined in part by the number of investors, which state (or states) they are located in, and whether they are all "accredited investors," as that term is defined in Rule 501 of Regulation D under the federal securities laws.

Whenever a company raises funds by selling common stock, membership interests, limited partnerships, convertible debentures, or other securities, it must comply with applicable securities laws. This basic rule applies regardless of the consideration received—services, cash, notes, or other property such as stock in another company. Generally, whenever an "issuer" (i.e., the company selling its equity) wishes to sell securities, it must register those securities with the Securities and Exchange Commission (SEC) and appropriate state regulators, unless one of the many exemptions from registration applies to the proposed sale. For offerings that qualify for an exemption from registration, rules must be observed governing the way in which the offering is conducted, the filing of notices, payment of fees, consents to service, and in some cases submission of offering documents to regulatory authorities. Companies often rely on the so-called "private placement" exemptions from the securities registration requirements. Typically, an issuer can sell stock to any number of accredited investors and to a limited number of investors who don't meet the accredited investor standard in a private (i.e., nonpublic) offering.

Reasonable disclosure about the business must always be made to prospective investors; and if the company is selling stock to investors who are not accredited,

453

specific written information about the business must be provided. When a company relies on these exemptions, it will be required to make certain notice filings with the Securities and Exchange Commission (SEC) and with state securities regulators in states in which offers or sales are made. Failure to comply with the securities laws can subject a company or its principals to investors' claims for their money back ("rescission" claims) and other penalties.

Whenever a company is dealing with securities law issues, a lawyer should be consulted. Problems with early stage fund-raising may subject the company to rescission claims and could dissuade venture capitalists, institutional investors, and fund-raisers from working with the company later.

Rule 506 of Regulation D is a "safe harbor" for the private offering exemption, assuring issuers that they are within the Section 4(2) exemption if they satisfy the standards within the rule. The criteria for reliance upon the Rule 506 exemption from registration are that the offering be made without any means of "general solicitation"; that the offering be made to no more than thirty-five persons who are not "accredited investors"; that each nonaccredited investor be financially sophisticated (that is, has such knowledge and experience in financial and business matters that he or she is capable of evaluating the merits and risks of the investment); and that if the offering is made to any nonaccredited investors, the same detailed disclosures required in comparable public offerings be made to them.

Blue Sky compliance (meaning the securities law compliance in each state where the securities are offered or sold) for Rule 506 offerings was simplified by the National Securities Markets Improvement Act of 1996 (NSMIA), Section 18(b)(4)(D) of the Securities Act of 1933, which preempts a state's registration requirements with respect to securities being offered and sold under Rule 506 of Regulation D. States are permitted only to (i) require a notice filing from the issuer, (ii) impose a filing fee, and (iii) require the issuer to consent to service of process in the state. In accordance with NSMIA, each state generally requires an issuer that offers and sells securities in its state pursuant to Rule 506 to submit the following materials within fifteen days after the first sale of securities in that state in order to qualify for an exemption from registration: (a) an executed copy of Form D Notice of Sale of Securities, (b) an executed copy of Form U-2 Uniform Consent to Service of Process, and (c) a filing fee. A Form D must be electronically filed with the SEC.

The *Securities Lawyer's Deskbook,* a website maintained by University of Cincinnati College of Law, is a great resource for accessing the federal securities laws (at http://www.law.uc.edu/CCL/index.html). The Securities and Exchange Commission website is also a great resource at http://www.sec.gov.

10.2 What Is an Accredited Investor?

Regulation D, Rule 501, of the Securities Act of 1933 defines an "Accredited Investor" as any person who falls within any of the following categories, or who an issuer (the company selling securities) reasonably believes comes within any of the following categories, at the time of the sale of the securities to that person:

Any bank as defined in Section 3(a)(2) of the act, or any savings and loan association or other institution as defined in Section 3(a)(5)(A) of the act whether acting in its individual or fiduciary capacity; any broker or dealer registered pursuant to Section 15 of the Securities Exchange Act of 1934; any insurance company as defined in Section 2(a)(13) of the act; any investment company registered under the Investment Company Act of 1940 or a business development company as defined in Section 2(a)(48) of that act; any small business investment company licensed by the U.S. Small Business Administration under Section 301(c) or (d) of the Small Business Investment Act of 1958; any plan established and maintained by a state, its political subdivisions, or any agency or instrumentality of a state or its political subdivisions, for the benefit of its employees, if such plan has total assets in excess of $5,000,000; any employee benefit plan within the meaning of the Employee Retirement Income Security Act of 1974 if the investment decision is made by a plan fiduciary, as defined in Section 3(21) of such act, which is either a bank, savings and loan association, insurance company, or registered investment adviser, or if the employee benefit plan has total assets in excess of $5,000,000 or, if a self-directed plan, with investment decisions made solely by persons that are accredited investors;

Any private business development company as defined in Section 202(a)(22) of the Investment Advisers Act of 1940;

Any organization described in Section 501(c)(3) of the Internal Revenue Code, corporation, Massachusetts, or similar business trust, or partnership, not formed for the specific purpose of acquiring the securities offered, with total assets in excess of $5,000,000;

Any director, executive officer, or general partner of the issuer of the securities being offered or sold, or any director, executive officer, or general partner of a general partner of that issuer;

Any natural person whose individual net worth, or joint net worth with that person's spouse, at the time of his purchase exceeds $1,000,000, excluding the value of the person's primary residence;

Any natural person who had an individual income in excess of $200,000 in each of the two most recent years or joint income with that person's spouse in excess of $300,000 in each of those years and has a reasonable expectation of reaching the same income level in the current year;

Any trust, with total assets in excess of $5,000,000, not formed for the specific purpose of acquiring the securities offered, whose purchase is directed by a sophisticated person as described in Rule 506(b)(2)(ii); and

Any entity in which all of the equity owners are accredited investors.

10.3 Does It Matter Where the Investors Reside?

The state or country of residence of each investor dictates which securities laws govern the offering. For example, an offering solely to investors residing in a single state is exempt from federal regulation, whereas an offering to investors in several states is governed by federal law and by the laws of each state in which an investor resides.

As discussed more fully in the sample blue-sky memorandum (included as Form 10 D in section 10.11), in accordance with NSMIA, each state generally requires an issuer that offers and sells securities in the state pursuant to Rule 506 to file the following materials in order to qualify for an exemption from registration: (i) an executed copy of Form D; (ii) an executed copy of Form U-2, uniform consent to service of process; and (iii) pay a filing fee at the time of filing. These materials, in addition to supplemental materials required by Alabama, Connecticut, Louisiana, Massachusetts, New Hampshire, and Tennessee, generally must be filed with each state within fifteen days after the first sale of securities in that state. However, New York requires filings before an offering, Florida requires the delivery of disclosure information to an investor before a sale, and Louisiana and Oklahoma require filings before, or within a prescribed time period of, the receipt of money or a subscription agreement from an investor.

New York and Florida have different filing requirements for offerings under Rule 506. New York requires a notification filing on its own Form 99 in addition to the filing of a federal Form D. Florida requires an issuer to register as a "dealer" in addition to making a notice filing pursuant to NSMIA because the securities laws of Florida include an issuer of securities in its definition of a "dealer." Therefore, to avoid having the principals of an issuer register as dealers in the State of Florida, the issuer should conduct its offering of securities in Florida pursuant to Florida's limited offering exemption. The eligibility and disclosure requirements of this exemption are set forth in Form 10 A, Outline for Private Placement Memorandum. The issuer's private placement memorandum (or PPM), if one has been prepared, should contain the information required to be disclosed to investors in Florida under this exemption. However, please note that the private placement memorandum is required to contain the legend set forth in Form 10 A, and the purchasers in Florida must also be provided with an unaudited balance sheet and statement of profit and loss of the issuer as of a date not earlier than the end of the issuer's last fiscal year. This exemption is self-executing and, provided requirements of Florida's limited offering exemption are met, no filing is required to be made with the Florida Division of Securities. For a complete guide to state securities laws and other helpful resources, go to http://www.BlueSkyLinks.com. Useful forms can be found at http://www.nasaa.org/industry_regulatory_resources/Uniform_Forms/.

The specific requirements of each state in which your client intends to make offers and/or sales of securities should be checked prior to commencement of the offering. The Internet has made this task much less time consuming and expensive than it once was. While the information contained in the memorandum of

Blue Sky Law Requirements for Rule 506 of Regulation D (Form 10 D) at the end of this chapter is believed to be accurate, more current and complete information is typically available on each state's securities division website, and should be reviewed for updates and best practices before any offering is made.

In addition to the availability of an exemption at the state level for SEC Regulation D private placements through NSMIA, many states have limited offering exemptions that may be relied upon in a private placement offering. For example, the Colorado Securities Act contains three registration exemptions that are often used with private offerings: Section 11-51-308(1)(1), Section 11-51-308(1)(j), and Section 11-51-308(1)(p):

- Section 11-51-308(1)(1) has no Colorado filing requirement and may be used by issuers who are relying on Section 4(2) under the Securities Act of 1933, but usually not Regulation D; and commissions may not be paid to anyone other than a licensed broker-dealer.
- Section 11-51-308(1)(j) has no Colorado filing requirement and may be used by issuers who are making offers to no more than 20 persons in Colorado and selling to no more than 10 purchasers in Colorado, but commissions may not be paid to anyone other than a licensed broker-dealer and the issuer must reasonably believe that the investors are purchasing for investment only.
- Section 11-51-308(1)(p), outlined in Form 10 D (Blue Sky Law Requirements and Rule 506 of Regulation D), is a safe-harbor type of exemption and does not have offeree/investor numbers limitations. Other than Regulation A offerings, these securities are restricted from resale by federal law and are purchased for investment purposes only. Commissions may not be paid to anyone other than a licensed broker-dealer. Section 11-51-308(1)(p) requires the issuer to submit a fee of $75 made out to the "Colorado State Treasurer" along with one copy of whatever documents are submitted to the SEC (usually the Form D). A Consent to Service of Process and a cover letter with a brief description of the applicable state and federal citations and a contact person for the filing should be included. The filing should be submitted concurrently at the time of the federal filing, no later than fifteen days after the first Colorado sale. Submit this filing to Colorado Division of Securities, 1560 Broadway, Suite 900, Denver, CO 80202. See the Colorado Division of Securities website at http://www.dora.state.co.us/securities/privoff.htm.

Another example is the New Jersey exemption under N.J.S.A. 49:3-50(b)(9), which provides an exemption for sales to no more than ten New Jersey residents in any twelve-month period, provided that the investors purchase for investment purposes only, no commission is paid directly or indirectly for soliciting buyers in New Jersey, and the securities are not offered or sold by general solicitation or general advertisement. This is a self-executing exemption such that no fees, forms, or other documents need be filed with the Bureau. However, to request a waiver of any conditions of this exemption, you must file Form NJBOS-19 with the Bureau of Securities, which is available online at http://www.state.nj.us/lps/ca/bos/bosform.htm.

Under the federal regulatory regime, pursuant to Rule 506 of Regulation D, an issuer will be required to file with the Securities and Exchange Commission a federal Form D within fifteen days after the first sale of security. Form D can only be filed electronically through the SEC's Electronic Data Gathering, Analysis, and Retrieval (EDGAR) online filing system at https://www.onlineforms.edgarfiling .sec.gov/. However, prior to filing, an issuer must obtain a Central Index Key (CIK) number assigned by the SEC and obtain EDGAR access codes, which can be time consuming and should be completed in advance of an offering to ensure timely compliance with the notice filing requirement. Complete instructions for obtaining a CIK number and EDGAR access codes are available on the SEC website at http:// www.sec.gov/divisions/corpfin/formdfiling.htm. Please note that your pop-up settings must be set to "allow" to successfully navigate the EDGAR filing system, and some browsers seem to work better than others (I've had best luck with Explorer).

Copies of the forms and notices discussed in this chapter are available online at the Internet addresses listed here.

Form D	http://www.sec.gov/about/forms/formd.pdf
Form U-2	http://www.nasaa.org/Industry_Regulatory_Resources/ Uniform_Forms/
U-2A	http://www.nasaa.org/Industry_Regulatory_Resources/ Uniform_Forms/
U-4	http://www.nasaa.org/Industry_Regulatory_Resources/ Uniform_Forms/
Form 99	http://www.ag.ny.gov/bureaus/investor_protection/investors/ form99.pdf
State Notice/ Further State Notice	http://www.ag.ny.gov/bureaus/investor_protection/investors/ forms/State_Notice.pdf

10.4 What If Investors Provide Goods and Services Rather than Cash?

A fact that is sometimes hard for clients to accept is that if they issue securities in exchange for goods and services, it is a "sale"—the same as if it had received cash. In such cases, the securities laws apply.

10.5 Is It Okay to Put Fund-Raising Information on a Website?

No general solicitation is permitted in connection with a private offering of securities, thus the designation of the offering as "private." Don't let your client put fund-raising information on its website, or it will likely be deemed to have made a general solicitation in connection with its sale of securities.

A problem that often arises in meeting the criteria of the Rule 506 safe harbor is that either the company's officers and directors or the selling agent inadvertently engages in an act that is deemed to constitute a general solicitation, or at least cannot be affirmatively shown not to involve a general solicitation (the burden of proof being upon the person seeking to rely upon the exemption). Often the problem arises indirectly, and the company's management or the soliciting agent are not aware of the issue until it is too late.

A typical action that raises a general solicitation issue is a mass mailing to potential investors, even if the mailing is confined to accredited investors. To preclude these issues from arising, the company's management and the selling agent should review carefully in advance the strategies for solicitation of investors in the offering. Form letters, particularly to strangers, should be avoided, as should mailings with similar contents to a large number of persons. An appropriate procedure is to forward the offering materials or an executive summary to persons with whom management or the selling agent has an existing, established relationship (such as, for example, an existing securities customer of the selling agent) to determine if the recipient has any interest in the offering. The contact should be direct and personal, not general and to a number of persons, and particularly not to a number of strangers. A mass mailing by a selling agent in an attempt to solicit for itself, through advertising, newsletter, or otherwise, new accredited customers (especially strangers) can be deemed a general solicitation if the company's offering is then in progress—unless steps are taken to preclude any person so solicited from becoming an investor in that pending offering.

One common occurrence that creates general solicitation issues is the appearance of a company's management before a meeting of an investment forum consisting of potential investors, even if confined to accredited investors. The nature of these gatherings and how they are assembled will determine whether they are deemed to involve a general solicitation. Some of these groups have sought and obtained no-action letters from the Securities and Exchange Commission assuring that the Commission will not take any administrative action if their methods of operation are confined to certain stated circumstances. Companies that desire to appear before such groups should inquire before appearing as to whether the group has obtained such a no-action or interpretive letter and whether the circumstances recited in these letters are being observed. Otherwise, the ability to proceed with funding may be impaired or precluded.

Another common occurrence that creates general solicitation issues is media coverage at or near the time of the offering. If the company becomes the object of media reporting, even if not sought out by the company, a general solicitation may be deemed to be involved. Particularly problematic are news reports or articles that mention the company's possible financial success or the fact that it is or may be seeking financing. Unless the company is then actually engaged in product or service marketing efforts, reports by the media should generally be avoided. If product or service marketing efforts are then actually in progress, media coverage should be confined to information concerning the company's products or services, and then only to the extent that it might be of interest to potential customers.

Hopefully, it goes without saying that no solicitation of investors should be entered into directly or indirectly by any form of paid advertising, whether in newspapers or on radio or television. Such activity is usually inconsistent with the concept of a "private" offering and in any event is expressly prohibited by Regulation D.

The foregoing are examples of typical ways in which a "general solicitation" issue can arise. There are many other possibilities, of course. It is thus important for those persons involved in a private offering to be alert to the general solicitation prohibition and the ways that it may be violated, and to ask securities counsel for guidance when doubts arise before irreversible action has been taken.

10.6 What Is Restricted Stock?

Restricted stock is stock that is held outright, but subject to a right of repurchase as to unvested portions, or subject to other restrictions or limitations. The term "restricted stock" is also used to refer to shares sold in private placements and subject to securities law restrictions on resale. Restricted stock may be preferable over nonqualified stock options to the recipient because, if the recipient makes an election under Internal Revenue Code (IRC) Section 83(b) upon receiving the stock, any appreciation in the value of the stock after receipt is taxable at long-term capital gain rates when the stock is sold if the recipient has held the stock for more than one year. Thus, the tax issues generally associated with options are avoided. Restricted stock also entitles the holder to voting rights, a benefit that may make a key employee feel more involved in the ownership of the company.

10.7 What Is a Private Placement Memorandum?

The mandatory disclosures for an offering in which up to thirty-five of the investors are not "accredited" (a Reg. D Rule 506 offering) are typically organized into a private placement memorandum (or PPM).

The disclosure requirements for a PPM are essentially the same as would be required under Part II of Form 1-A for a Reg. A offering, which is available online at http://www.sec.gov/about/forms/form1-a.pdf. Part II of Form 1-A is set forth in a questionnaire/fill-in-the-blank format and can be used to help gather or identify the necessary information to be included in your PPM. This chapter includes a skeleton PPM (Part II of Form 1-A) that can be used to draft a PPM; see Form 10 A.

The financial disclosure requirements depend on the amount being raised, with the minimum level (offerings up to $2 million) being the information required under Item 310 of Reg. S-B—with the exception that only the balance sheet must be audited. The full text of Reg. S-B (and lots of other tantalizing information) is available on the SEC website (http://www.sec.gov).

It is a good idea to have each of the principals of the company complete a questionnaire to identify whether there are any other mandatory disclosure items. A standard Directors' and Officers' Questionnaire can be used for that purpose (see Form 10 B).

In early stage offerings—where the company is raising funds through the sale of its securities to a limited number of investors, all of whom are accredited investors and all of whom have some preexisting relationship with the issuer—it is impractical and inefficient to prepare a complete private placement memorandum. Instead, the company might decide to provide certain abbreviated disclosure materials to the prospective investors in the form of an executive summary, business plan, and financial information. The company would then document the investment transactions through individual stock purchase agreements or detailed subscription agreements containing extensive investor representations. These representations include acknowledgments in which subscribers represent and warrant that that they have conducted due diligence, have had the opportunity to ask questions, and have received information from the company to their satisfaction. The company usually will consult with counsel to make a final determination of the appropriate form of these documents and/or whether and to what extent the company should prepare a private placement memorandum.

Before making a final determination about the form of documentation your client's offering will require, you should consider and decide upon the structure of the proposed offering. In sum, you should begin to assemble the following information to prepare for the private placement.

1. Names, Permanent Residence Addresses, and Economic Status of All Prospective Investors.

It is important to anticipate the jurisdictions in which the securities will be offered and sold. The issuer needs to anticipate blue-sky filing requirements in all jurisdictions. Are the prospective investors accredited investors?

2. Proposed Offering Amount/Targeted Aggregate Offering Proceeds.

How much will the company seek in the private placement? Will the company pay any commissions or other fees to securities professionals, consultants, or others in connection with the private placement? What expenses, if any, are estimated to be attributed to the private placement? Is the company seeking to raise a minimum amount (before which it will use funds raised from prospective investors), or will it accept and use any and all offering proceeds as soon as they are received?

3. Proposed Statement of Use of Proceeds.

How does the company propose using the proceeds to be raised by the private placement? All private placement memoranda and similar disclosure documents contain some statement or analysis of how the company plans to use the proceeds raised in the offering.

Even if the issuer does not prepare and disseminate a complete private placement memorandum, investors should be informed about use of proceeds. This information will also be required for the notices filed with the SEC and state securities regulators.

4. Proposed Structure of the Security to Be Offered.

Will the investors receive common stock, nonvoting common stock, preferred stock, or some other form of equity? If preferred stock, what will be the liquidation rights, voting rights, and other rights, preferences, and privileges?

Most venture capital funds and organized angel groups or angel funds expect to receive preferred stock in a private placement offering, which will have a set of fairly standard rights, preferences, and privileges. In larger or later offerings, certain rights or privileges pertaining to the preferred stock placed with an institutional investor or investors may be heavily negotiated by the investors (or a lead investor) and the issuer.

If a new class of security will be created and offered in the private placement, the issuer will need to amend its charter (its articles or certificate of incorporation) to designate the new class of securities. This may require the approval of existing equity security holders.

5. Current and Projected Financial Information.

While the issuer is not required to have audited financial statements, it is generally expected that the issuer will have current, internally prepared or externally prepared—but unaudited—financial statements for prospective investors.

Financial statements will consist, at a minimum, of a current balance sheet and a statement of income or profit and loss statement. Most issuers will also provide prospective investors with either a private placement memorandum or business plan, executive summary, or other document that includes projected income and expense information.

10.8 Can My Client Pay Finder's Fees?

The idea that "finders" are exempt from the requirement of broker-dealer registration is a common misconception. Companies should be strongly discouraged from paying "finder's fees" that may be illegal and/or jeopardize their ability to rely on an exemption from registration. Unfortunately, it is rare that a company has sufficient contacts to meet its capital needs without assistance from an intermediary, such as a finder or professional placement agents. The typical compensation arrangement for such an intermediary is to pay a "transaction-based fee" (i.e., a fee based on the amount of capital they successfully identify for the company). However, federal securities law requires that a person "engaged in the business of raising capital" for others must be registered as a broker-dealer and become a member of the Financial Industry Regulatory Authority (FINRA, formerly the National Association of Securities Dealers, or NASD). If an intermediary accepts a transaction-based fee more than once, or is involved in more than just the provision of contact information, that person or agency may be deemed to be "engaged in the business" and operating illegally, if not appropriately registered. Most state securities laws have similar requirements. The American Bar Association Section of Business Law's Task Force on Private Placement Broker Dealers published its "Report and Recommendations" on this subject at 60 *Business Lawyer* 959 (May 2005), and remains one of the preeminent treatises on this subject.

Legislation adopted in California in 2005, significantly increased the risk exposure for companies and "finders" for transactions involving California residents or California issuers. Specifically, California Corporations Code section 25501.5 was enacted to give investors the right to rescind a transaction if an unregistered broker-dealer was involved, and the right to pursue damages if the investor no longer holds the securities. Investors also have the right to recover attorney's fees, costs and treble damages up to $10,000 for such cases in California. Persons engaged in unlicensed broker-dealer conduct can be subject to administrative, civil, and criminal sanctions.

10.9 Are There Any Record-Keeping Requirements?

The burden of proving the availability of an exemption from registration is on the company asserting it, and companies selling securities have an affirmative obligation to make full and fair disclosures in connection with any offering of securities. It is therefore wise to prepare and preserve a written record of the offering, during the ordinary course of the offering, to make it admissible as evidence if required.

The following records should be maintained and preserved in connection with a private placement securities offering:

- A list of investors, with addresses, telephone numbers, who they are, and how contact was developed (which cannot be by means of general solicitation);
- A list of persons who received copies of the private placement memorandum, business plan, or other offering materials, and the control number for each copy (which is typically entered on the cover page of the document for identification and tracking);
- Copies of all term sheets, business plans, private placement memoranda, and supplements used in the offering, identified by date;
- A file of source materials for factual disclosures in the offering materials;
- All original subscription agreements (with representations of investment intent and other information critical to qualification for exemption);
- The agreement engaging the selling agent, if any, and related correspondence;
- A certificate signed by the officers of the company to certify that the offering has been terminated, that the records of the offering are accurate and complete, and that there was no general solicitation in connection with the offering;
- A certificate signed by the selling agent, if any, stating that the offering has been terminated, that each investor was furnished a copy of the offering materials, and that there was no general solicitation in connection with the offering; and
- Copies of the certificates for the securities, with appropriate legends.

These records should be kept secure for at least the period of the applicable statutes of limitations. It is also a good idea for the company to maintain a D&O policy covering securities law claims for private offerings.

10.10 What If Your Client Violates Securities Laws?

If your client violates the securities laws, the company, its officers, directors and principal shareholders, and others involved in selling the securities may be held liable for the full amount raised, plus interest and lawyer's fees in one or more individual lawsuits or a class action on behalf of all investors. If applicable disclosure requirements are violated (technically "securities fraud"), the liability may not be dischargeable in personal bankruptcy.

Issues regarding securities law compliance are often raised by regulators, often at the instigation of investors or competitors. Such actions can hinder a company's ability to raise additional capital or to go public in a timely and orderly fashion. Securities law violations will likely preclude a company from obtaining an opinion that an exemption was available for a past offering when such an opinion is required in connection with a subsequent private or public offering. Underwriters may refuse to work with a company with a questionable compliance record until the applicable statutes of limitations have run (typically three years from the last closing).

Proactive measures can be taken if a company violates securities laws; for example, a carefully orchestrated rescission offer can be presented in which all appropriate disclosures are made and all other applicable rules are observed. However, a successful rescission offer is an option only for companies that are capable of returning investor funds to investors who request it.

10.11 Sample Documents and Checklists.

This section includes the following forms:

- Outline for Private Placement Memorandum (Form 10 A)
- Directors' and Officers' Questionnaire (Form 10 B)
- Subscription Agreement (Form 10 C)
- Blue-Sky Law Requirements and Rule 506 of Regulation D (Form 10 D)

Form 10 A: Outline for Private Placement Memorandum

PRIVATE PLACEMENT MEMORANDUM
[COMMON] [SERIES A PREFERRED] STOCK
[100,000] SHARES
[$1.00]/SHARE
$100,000

20____ ,

COVER PAGE

Type of Securities Offered:	[Common] [Series A Preferred] Stock
Maximum Number of Shares Offered:	[100,000] Shares
Minimum Number of Shares Offered:	N/A
Price per Share:	[$1.00]
Total Proceeds if Maximum Sold:	[$100,000]

No commissioned selling agent is selling shares and there is no finder's fee or similar payment to any person in this offering.

There is no escrow of proceeds. Once subscriptions are accepted, the funds are immediately available to the company.

Transfer of the securities offered herein is restricted.

INVESTMENT IN SMALL BUSINESSES INVOLVES A HIGH DEGREE OF RISK AND INVESTORS SHOULD NOT INVEST ANY FUNDS IN THIS OFFERING UNLESS THEY CAN AFFORD TO LOSE THEIR ENTIRE INVESTMENT. SEE THE SECTION BELOW ON RISK FACTORS FOR A DISCUSSION OF THE RISKS MANAGEMENT BELIEVES PRESENT THE MOST SUBSTANTIAL RISKS TO AN INVESTOR IN THIS OFFERING.

IN MAKING AN INVESTMENT DECISION, INVESTORS MUST RELY ON THEIR OWN EXAMINATION OF THE ISSUER AND THE TERMS OF THE OFFERING INCLUDING THE MERITS AND RISKS INVOLVED. THESE SECURITIES HAVE NOT BEEN RECOMMENDED OR APPROVED BY ANY FEDERAL OR STATE SECURITIES COMMISSION OR REGULATORY AUTHORITY. FURTHERMORE, THESE AUTHORITIES HAVE NOT PASSED UPON THE ACCURACY OR ADEQUACY OF THIS DOCUMENT. ANY REPRESENTATION TO THE CONTRARY IS A CRIMINAL OFFENSE.

THE U.S. SECURITIES AND EXCHANGE COMMISSION DOES NOT PASS UPON THE MERITS OF ANY SECURITIES OFFERED OR THE TERMS OF THE OFFERING, NOR DOES IT PASS UPON THE ACCURACY OR COMPLETENESS OF ANY OFFERING CIRCULAR OR SELLING LITERATURE. THESE SECURITIES ARE OFFERED UNDER AN EXEMPTION FROM REGISTRATION. HOWEVER, THE COMMISSION HAS NOT MADE AN INDEPENDENT DETERMINATION THAT THESE SECURITIES ARE EXEMPT FROM REGISTRATION.

This company is in the development stage.

Table of Contents

THIS PRIVATE PLACEMENT MEMORANDUM CONTAINS ALL OF THE REPRE-
SENTATIONS BY THE COMPANY CONCERNING THIS OFFERING AND NO PER-
SON SHALL MAKE DIFFERENT OR BROADER STATEMENTS THAN THOSE
CONTAINED HEREIN, INVESTORS ARE CAUTIONED NOT TO RELY UPON ANY
INFORMATION NOT EXPRESSLY SET FORTH IN THIS PRIVATE PLACEMENT
MEMORANDUM.

This Private Placement Memorandum, together with financial statements and other
attachments, consists of a total of __ pages.

The Company

Risk Factors

Risks Related to Our Business
Risks Related to Our Financial Condition
Risks Related to Our Intellectual Property
Risks Related to Our Stock

Business and Properties

What We Do
How We Do It
We Are In the Development Stage

Note
    After reviewing the nature and timing of the events and milestones listed above, potential investors should reflect upon whether the achievement of each of these events and milestones within the estimated time frame is realistic and should assess the consequences of delays or failure of achievement in making an investment decision.

Our Products and Technologies
The Industry

Note
    Please note that because this Private Placement Memorandum focuses primarily on details concerning the company, rather than the industry in which we operate, potential investors may wish to conduct their own separate investigation of the _____ industry to obtain broader insight in assessing our prospects.

Our Employees and Facilities
Intellectual Property

Offering Price Factors

Note
    After reviewing these offering price factors, potential investors should consider whether or not the offering price for the securities is appropriate at the present stage of the company's development.

Use of Proceeds

    The following table sets forth the estimated use of proceeds from this offering in general terms. Please see the detailed financial statements and projections attached as exhibits to this memorandum and incorporated herein for details.

Note
    After reviewing the portion of the offering allocated to the payment of offering expenses, and to the immediate payment to management any fees, reimbursements, past salaries or similar payments, potential investors should consider whether, in

light of other funds available to us, the remaining portion of the offering proceeds available for future development of our business and operations would be adequate.

Capitalization

The following is a summary of our current capitalization and an illustration of what our capitalization will look like if the maximum number of shares being offered in this offering is sold.

Description of Securities

Plan of Distribution

The securities being offered hereby have not been registered under the Securities Act of 1933, as amended (the "Securities Act"), or any state "blue sky" or securities laws. The shares cannot be sold, transferred, assigned or otherwise disposed of except in compliance with applicable federal and state securities laws and will not be transferred of record except in compliance with said laws. A legend to the following effect will appear upon the certificates of the securities:

THE SECURITIES REPRESENTED BY THIS INSTRUMENT HAVE NOT BEEN REGISTERED UNDER THE FEDERAL SECURITIES ACT OF 1933, AS AMENDED, OR REGISTERED OR QUALIFIED UNDER THE SECURITIES LAW OF ANY STATE AND MAY NOT BE SOLD OR OTHERWISE TRANSFERRED UNLESS (1) THERE IS AN EFFECTIVE REGISTRATION STATEMENT FOR THE SECURITIES UNDER THE ACT AND ANY APPLICABLE STATE SECURITIES LAW, (2) SUCH TRANSFER IS MADE IN COMPLIANCE WITH RULE 144 UNDER THE ACT AND PURSUANT TO REGISTRATION OR QUALIFICATION UNDER ANY APPLICABLE STATE SECURITIES LAW OR EXEMPTION THEREFROM, OR (3) THERE IS AN OPINION OF COUNSEL SATISFACTORY TO THE CORPORATION THAT SUCH REGISTRATION IS NOT REQUIRED AS TO SAID TRANSFER, SALE OR OFFER.

None of our securities have been qualified to trade on any market or exchange system and there can be no assurance that any of our securities will at any time in the future qualify to trade on any market or exchange system.

Dividends, Distributions, and Redemptions

Officers and Key Personnel of the Company

Directors of the Company

Note

After reviewing the information concerning the backgrounds of our officers, directors, and other key personnel, potential investors should consider whether or not these persons have adequate background and experience to develop and operate the company and to make it successful. In this regard, the experience and ability of management are often considered the most significant factors in the success of a business.

Principal Stockholders

The following are our principal owners, meaning those who beneficially own directly or indirectly ten percent or more of our total outstanding common and preferred stock, on an as-if-converted basis, and the average price per share paid by such shareholders, the number of shares they hold, and their percentage ownership now and if the maximum number of shares being offered in this Private Placement Memorandum is sold:

Name	Average Price/Share	No. of Shares	% of Total	% of Total If Maximum Is Sold
Totals				

Management Relationships, Transactions, and Remuneration

We have paid the following amounts of remuneration to our officers, directors, and key personnel for the last fiscal year:

Note

    After reviewing the above, potential investors should consider whether or not the compensation to management and other key personnel directly or indirectly, is reasonable in view of the present stage of the company's development.

Litigation

Federal Tax Aspects

Note

    Potential investors are encouraged to see their own personal tax consultant and/or independent legal counsel for an explanation of how these tax provisions may affect them individually and to advise them of the extent to which any tax benefits may be available or advantageous to the particular investor.

Miscellaneous Factors

    This offering involves certain material risks. See "Risk Factors" for a discussion of certain factors that should be considered by prospective investors before investing in the shares offered hereby. In making an investment decision investors must rely on their own examination of the company and the terms of the offering, including the merits and risks involved.

    This memorandum contains certain forward-looking statements within the meaning of Section 27A of the Securities Act of 1933, as amended, and Section 21E of the Securities Act of 1934, as amended. Such forward-looking statements are made pursuant to the safe harbor provisions of the Private Securities Litigation Reform Act of 1995. These forward-looking statements are not historical facts and are based on current expectations, estimates, and projections about our industry; our beliefs and assumptions; and our goals and objectives. Words such as "anticipates," "expects," "intends," "plans," "believes," "seeks," and "estimates," and variations of these words and similar expressions are intended to identify forward-looking statements. These statements are only predictions, are not guarantees of future performance, and are subject to risks, uncertainties, and other factors, some of which are beyond our control, are difficult to predict, and could cause actual results to differ materially from those expressed or forecasted in the forward-looking statements. These risks and uncertainties include those set forth in this memorandum.

This memorandum speaks only as of its date, and the information and expressions of opinion contained herein are subject to change without notice. Neither delivery of this memorandum nor any sale made hereunder shall, under any circumstances, create any implication that there has been no change in the affairs of the company since the date hereof. The summaries of and references to all documents, statutes, reports and other instruments referred to in this memorandum do not purport to be complete, comprehensive or definitive, and each such summary and reference is qualified in its entirety by reference to each document, statute, report or instrument.

No person has been authorized to give any information or to make any representations not contained in this memorandum in connection with this offering. If given or made, such information or representation must not be relied upon as having been authorized by the company.

The shares are subject to certain restrictions on transfer. There currently is no trading market for any of the securities of the company, and none is expected to develop for the company's securities following this offering. Prospective investors must be able to bear the economic risk of the investment for an indefinite period of time, because the securities cannot be sold or transferred except as permitted by the securities act of 1933, as amended, and applicable provisions of state securities laws. If, as a result of some change of circumstances arising from an event not now in contemplation, or for any other reason, an investor wishes to transfer his or her securities, such investor may find no market for those securities.

This offer can be withdrawn at any time before closing and is specifically made subject to the terms described in this memorandum. The company reserves the right to reject any subscription in whole or in part, or to issue to any subscriber shares in an aggregate amount less than that subscribed for.

The company has determined it will not accept subscriptions from any prospective investor unless it has reasonable grounds to believe, and does believe immediately prior to accepting such subscription, that such investor, either alone or together with an offeree representative, has such knowledge and experience in financial and business matters that the prospective investor is capable of evaluating the merits and risks of the investment in the company described herein and is able to bear the economic risks of such investment. Delivery of this memorandum to anyone other than the person for whom this memorandum is intended is unauthorized and any reproduction of this memorandum, in whole or in part, without the prior written consent of the company is prohibited.

Prior to the issuance of any securities, prospective investors shall be given the opportunity to ask questions and receive answers concerning any aspect of the investment, and to obtain any additional information, to the extent the company possesses such information or can acquire it without unreasonable effort or expense, necessary to verify the accuracy of the information contained in this memorandum.

Prospective investors are not to construe the contents of this memorandum as legal, tax or investment advice. Each investor should consult his own legal counsel, accountant, or business advisor as to legal, tax and related matters concerning his possible investment in the securities offered hereby.

Prospective investors are hereby invited to arrange for a meeting with the officers of the company or its duly authorized representatives to discuss the terms of this offering or any of the matters discussed herein. At any such meeting, representatives of the company will also answer any material questions raised by prospective investors. Prospective investors are invited to request from the company copies of any documents or instruments which they deem material to their investment decision.

Management Discussion and Analysis of Certain Relevant Factors

The following discussion should be read in conjunction with our financial statements and the related notes and financial information appearing elsewhere in this memorandum. In addition to historical information, the following discussion and other parts of this memorandum contain forward-looking statements relating to future events and our future financial performance, which involve risks and uncertainties. Our actual risks could differ materially from those anticipated in these forward-looking statements as a result of certain factors, including those set forth under "Risk Factors," "Description of Business," and elsewhere in this memorandum.

Attachments:

Form 10 B: Directors' and Officers' Questionnaire

[***] CORPORATION
DIRECTORS' AND OFFICERS' QUESTIONNAIRE

This Questionnaire is being furnished to all persons who are or will be directors, officers and five percent (5%) or more shareholders, of [***] Corporation (the "Company"), which intends to which intends to offer and sell its securities in a private placement. This Questionnaire relates to certain information that the Company will be required to disclose in its Private Placement Memorandum and related materials in connection with such offer and sale (the "Disclosure Documents"). Unless otherwise directed, please answer every question herein.

Please complete, sign and return this Questionnaire to the Company's counsel at _____ as soon as possible, but in no case later than [_____, 20__. You should retain a copy for your personal files.

Unless stated otherwise, answers should be given as of the date you complete this Questionnaire. Please answer each question with reference to the attached Appendix which provides definitions of those terms that are capitalized throughout the Questionnaire. If there is any situation about which you have any doubt, please give relevant facts so that the information may be reviewed by us. Additionally, any questions you may have with regard to the completion or use of this Questionnaire may be directed to the Company's counsel at _____.

I. PERSONAL INFORMATION

1. If you are or will be a director, or Executive Officer of the Company, or the Beneficial Owner of five percent (5%) or more of any class of equity securities of the Company, please furnish the following information:

A. Please set forth your full name: _____

B. Please indicate your business address: _____

C. Please indicate your birth date: _____

D. Please indicate your Social Security Number or other personal identification number: _____

E. Are you related by blood, marriage, or adoption to any director, Executive Officer of the Company, or to any Affiliate of the Company? If so, state the identity of the director, Executive Officer, or Affiliate and the nature of the relationship. Relationships more remote than first cousin need not be mentioned: _____

II. OCCUPATIONS AND DIRECTORSHIPS

1. Please indicate all positions and offices with the Company which you presently hold or have been chosen to hold: _____

2. If you are or will be a director or Executive Officer, state your term of office as such and any period(s) during which you have served as such: _____

3. Were you selected to serve in your present capacity with the Company pursuant to any arrangement or understanding between yourself and any other person (other than directors or Executive Officers of the Company acting solely in their capacities as such)? If so, describe the arrangement or understanding below (attach a rider if more space is required): _____

4. Please give a brief account of your business experience during the past five years (together with applicable dates); include your principal occupations and

473

employment during that period and the name and principal business of any corporation or other organization in which such occupations and employment were carried on. If you are an Executive Officer of the Company and have been employed by the Company for less than five years, include a brief explanation of the nature of your responsibilities in prior positions. What is required is information relating to the level of your professional competence, which may include, depending upon the circumstances, such specific information as the size of the operation supervised. You may attach your response or write in the space provided: _____

_____

5.   If you are a director, or nominated or chosen to become a director, please list each directorship which you hold in any corporation having securities registered pursuant to Section 12 of the Securities Exchange Act of 1934, as amended (the "Exchange Act"), or subject to the requirements of Section 15(d) of the Exchange Act, or any registered investment company: _____

_____

6.   Are any of the corporations which you listed in response to item 5 above competitive with the business of the Company: _____

_____

III.   BUSINESS RELATIONSHIPS

1.   During the Company's last fiscal year did you or any other director, Executive Officer, Principal Shareholder, or any of their Affiliates, to your knowledge, have any Material interest, direct or indirect, in any transaction or proposed transaction involving more than $60,000 to which the Company was a party? If your answer is "Yes," please name the interested Person, indicate the Person's relationship to the Company, identify and describe the transaction, give the amount of the transaction, explain the Person's interest in the transaction, and, where practicable, state the approximate amount of the Person's interest in the transaction: _____

_____

2.   Do you, or any other present director, Executive Officer, Principal Shareholder, or any of their Affiliates, to your knowledge, have any Material interest, direct or indirect, in any proposed transaction involving more than $60,000 to which the Company is to be a party? If your answer is "Yes," please name the interested Person, indicate the Person's relationship to the Company, identify and describe the proposed transaction, give the amount of the proposed transaction, explain the Person's interest in the proposed transaction, and where practicable, state the approximate amount of the Person's interest in the proposed transaction:_____

_____

3.   If you are a director, are you a member or employee of or counsel to a law firm which the Company has retained during the last fiscal year or which the Company proposes to retain in the current fiscal year: _____

   If the answer is "Yes," please set forth the amount of fees paid to such law firm during the last fiscal year: _____

4.   If you are a director, are you a director, partner, officer, or employee of any investment banking firm which has performed services for the Company (other than as a participating underwriter in a syndicate) during the Company's last fiscal year, or which the Company proposes to employ in the current fiscal year? Answer: _____

If the answer is "Yes," please set forth the amount of fees paid to such investment banking firm during the last fiscal year: _____

---

5.   If you are a director, are you now, or have you been during the Company's last fiscal year, an officer, director, employee of, or do you now own, or have you owned directly or indirectly, in excess of a ten percent (10%) equity interest in any firm, corporation, or other business or professional entity:

A.   Which has made payments to the Company for property or services during the Company's last fiscal year in excess of 5% of the Company's consolidated gross revenues for its last full fiscal year or the other entities consolidated gross revenues for its last full fiscal year (in calculating payments for property and services the following may be excluded: (i) payments where the rates or charges involved in the transaction are determined by competitive bids, or the transaction involves the rendering of services as a public utility at rates or charges fixed in conformity with law or governmental authority; and (ii) payments which arise solely from the ownership of securities of the Company and no extra or special benefit not shared on a pro rata basis by all holders of the class of securities is received)? _____

B.   Which proposes to make payments to the Company for property or services during the current fiscal year in excess of 5% of the Company's consolidated gross revenues for its last full fiscal year or the other entities consolidated gross revenues for its last full fiscal year? _____

C.   To which the Company was indebted at the end of the Company's last full fiscal year in an aggregate amount in excess of 5% of the Company's total consolidated assets at the end of the last fiscal year (in calculating indebtedness, debt securities which have been publicly offered, admitted to trading on a national securities exchange, or quoted on the automated quotation system of a registered securities association may be excluded)? _____

D.   To which the Company has made payments for property or services during such entity's last fiscal year in excess of 5% of the Company's consolidated gross revenues for its last full fiscal year or the other entities consolidated gross revenues for its last full fiscal year? _____

E.   To which the Company proposes to make payments for property or services during such entity's current fiscal year in excess of 5% of the Company's consolidated gross revenues for its last full fiscal year or the other entities consolidated gross revenues for its last full fiscal year? _____

6.   If you are a director, do you have any other relationships with the Company other than those described above? Answer: _____

IV.   SECURITIES OWNERSHIP

1.   A.   Please state the amount of equity securities of the Company of which you are the Beneficial Owner (if none, please so state in each case). It is assumed that such securities have not been pledged or otherwise deposited as collateral and are not the subject matter of any voting trust or other similar agreement or of any contract providing for the sale of other disposition of such securities. If any such arrangement exists, please give the details thereof. In addition, please identify the type of plan (i.e. employee stock ownership plans known as "ESOPs" or 401(k) plans with Company equity securities as an investment), if any, from which beneficial ownership of the equity securities arises.

Amount Beneficially Owned	No. of Shares Owned
Total Shares owned beneficially by you	_____
Of such shares:	
Shares as to which you have sole voting power	_____
Shares as to which you have shared voting power	_____
Shares as to which you have sole investment power	_____
Shares as to which you have shared investment power	_____

B.   Do you wish to disclaim Beneficial Ownership of any of the shares reported in response to 1(A) above? Answer: _____

If the answer is "Yes," please furnish the following information with respect to the person or persons who should be shown as the Beneficial Owner(s) of the shares in question.

Name of Actual Beneficial Owner	Relationship of Such Person to You	Number of Shares Beneficially Owned

You may want to consult with your attorney to decide whether to disclaim since a disclaimer may be important with regards to the securities laws and also without a disclaimer your reporting of such shares might be construed as an admission of ownership by you for other purposes.

2.   Please state whether you are aware of any change in control of the Company since the beginning of the Company's last fiscal year, or of any arrangements which could result in such a change of control at a subsequent date. If so, please describe:

_____

_____

3.   Are you aware of any Person, or any group consisting of two or more Persons acting as a partnership or syndicate (or otherwise in concert) for the purpose of acquiring, holding, voting, or disposing of stock, which has Beneficial Ownership of more than five percent (5%) of the outstanding stock of the Company? If so, please give the name(s) and address(es) of such Person(s) and a brief description of any agreement among them: _____

_____

_____

_____

V.   COMPENSATION

The Company is required to disclose all plan and non-plan compensation awarded to, earned by, or paid to certain executive officers and directors any Person for all services rendered in all capacities to the Company and its subsidiaries for each of the Company's last three completed fiscal years. The term plan includes, but is not limited to the following: any plan, contract, authorization or arrangement, whether or not set forth in any formal documents. The following questions are intended to provide the information necessary to comply with this required disclosure.

1.   Please state the dollar value amounts of and the basis upon which you received cash or non-cash salary, bonuses, fees, commission, or other compensation (other than Options, Appreciation Rights or reimbursement of out-of-pocket expenses actually incurred on behalf of the Company) from the Company or any other Person during each of the Company's last three fiscal years for services rendered in any capacity to the Company. For stock or any other form of non-cash compensation, please provide the fair market value at the time the compensation is awarded, earned or paid. Include any compensation that has been set aside or Accrued on your behalf by the Company or has been deferred at your election pursuant to a 401(k) plan or otherwise, during such period:_____

2.   Please describe any remuneration received or Accrued by you in any capacity from the Company during each of the Company's last three fiscal years in the form of (i) securities or other property (other than Company Stock Options or Stock Appreciation Rights) transferred or purchased for an acquisition price below fair market value, unless such discounts are available generally; (ii) the payment of or reimbursement for health insurance premiums (excluding Company wide group insurance plans) or payments pursuant to a medical reimbursement plan; (iii) the payment of or reimbursement for premiums for life insurance for the benefit of yourself and any interest that you are to receive in any cash surrender value under such life insurance policy; and (iv) reimbursement for the payment of taxes. If necessary, provide the information on a separate sheet and attach it to this Questionnaire: _____

_____
_____
_____
_____

3.   Certain personal benefits to directors and Executive Officers (commonly referred to as "fringe benefits" or "perquisites") must be valued and included in the total remuneration disclosed in offering materials. The following questions are designed to assist us in complying with this requirement:

   A.   During each of the Company's last three fiscal years:

   (1) Did you or any member of your family use any property or assets of the Company (e.g., Company cars or club memberships paid for by the Company) for personal (i.e., non business related) purposes? Answer: _____

   (2) Did the Company pay or reimburse you or any member of your family for any personal expenses (e.g., personal purchases made with Company credit cards or included in non-itemized expense accounts)? Answer: _____

   (3) Did employees on the professional staff of the Company (e.g., legal or accounting personnel) provide you or any member of your family with personal, financial, accounting, legal, or other professional services? Answer: _____

   (4) Did any supplier, customer, or other party with whom the Company or any subsidiary does or intends to do business (including banks, attorneys, and accountants) provide you or any member of your family with any benefits (e.g., product discounts, free or reduced rate services or low interest loans) because of any compensation (whether oral or written, express or implied) by the Company for doing so? The term "compensation" should be taken in its broadest sense, and would include such things as an express or implied promise by the Company to continue doing business or to do increased business with the party which provided the benefit: _____

_____
_____
_____
_____
_____

(5) Did you or any member of your family receive any other type of personal benefit directly or indirectly from the Company for purposes unrelated to job performance? Answer: _____

If you answered "Yes" to any of the foregoing questions, please give the details on a separate sheet and attach it to this Questionnaire.

4. Please provide the following information regarding Options and Appreciation Rights which you were granted or which you exercised during the last fiscal year. If necessary, provide the information on a separate sheet and attach it to this Questionnaire:

A. With respect to options granted during the last fiscal year:

(1) the number of options granted: _____

_____

(2) the per unit exercise price of each option: _____

_____

(3) indicate whether the exercise prices of any of the options were adjusted in connection with an option re-pricing transaction: _____

_____

(4) the market value of the securities on the date of each grant: _____

_____

(5) the expiration date of each option: _____

(6) indicate whether any instruments were granted in tandem with the options, (information on Appreciation Rights should be provided in paragraph C): _____

_____

B. With respect to the exercise or realization during the last fiscal year of options:

(1) state the net value of securities (market value less any exercise price) or cash realized during the last fiscal year: _____

(2) the number of shares received upon exercise of each option: _____

_____

C. With respect to plans pursuant to which appreciation rights were granted:

(1) the number of rights granted: _____

_____

(2) indicate whether the exercise prices of any of the rights were adjusted in connection with an right re-pricing transaction: _____

_____

(3) the base price of each right: _____

_____

(4) the market value of the securities on the date of each grant: _____

_____

_____

_____

(5) the expiration date of each right: _____

_____

D. With respect to the exercise or realization during the last fiscal year of appreciation rights:

(1) state the net value of securities (market value less any exercise price) or cash realized: _____

_____

(2) the number of securities with respect to which the rights were exercised: ___

_____

_____

E. The total number of unexercised options and appreciation rights held at the end of the last completed fiscal year: _____

_____

F. The total number of unexercised options and appreciation rights held at the end of the last completed fiscal year which have an exercise or base price which is less than the fair market value of the underlying security: _____

_____

5.   Please describe any amounts contributed, paid or Accrued for your account by the Company with respect to any pension, retirement or deferred compensation plan, annuity, or similar arrangement, during each of the Company's last three fiscal years:

_____

_____

6.   Please describe any amounts contributed, paid or Accrued for your account by the Company with respect to any incentive or compensation plan or arrangement, during each of the Company's last three fiscal years: _____

_____

7.   Please state the number of shares, units or other rights awarded under any long term incentive plan (meaning any plan providing compensation intended to serve as incentive for performance to occur over a period longer than one fiscal year) during each of the Company's last three fiscal years and include, if applicable (if necessary, provide the information on a separate sheet and attach it to this Questionnaire): _____

_____

_____

A. The dollar value of any award of equity securities: _____

_____

B. The sum of the number of options granted, with or without tandem Appreciation Rights and the number of free standing Appreciation Rights: _____

_____

C. Please state the dollar value of all payouts pursuant to long-term incentive plans: _____

_____

D. The number and value of the aggregate equity security holdings at the end of the last completed fiscal year: _____

_____

E. Whether dividends will be paid on the equity securities reported above: ____

_____

F. Has the exercise price of any of the Options or Appreciation Rights been adjusted or amended? Answer: _____

_____

G. Has any specified performance, target, goal, or condition been waived with regards to any of the payouts received from an award? Answer: _____

_____

8. Please state the amounts of and the basis upon which any interest or earnings on any equity securities, Options, Appreciation Rights, deferred compensation or, long-term incentive plan compensation were paid to you, earned, Accrued on your behalf, or deferred at your election during each of the Company's last three fiscal years. Note: long-term incentive plan means any plan providing compensation intended to serve as incentive for performance to occur over a period longer than one fiscal year. (Please provide the interest rate at which interest was earned if applicable): _____

_____

9. Please describe any remuneration paid to you by a third party under an arrangement between such third party and the Company: _____

_____

10. Please describe any remuneration payments proposed to be made to you in the future, directly or indirectly, by the Company pursuant to any ongoing plan or arrangement (information need not be furnished with respect to any group life, health, hospitalization or medical reimbursement plans which do not discriminate in scope, terms or operation in favor of executive officers and directors of the Company and which are available generally to all salaried employees): _____

_____

11. With regard to services as a director, please provide the following:
A. A description of any standard arrangement, include the remuneration received, under which you are compensated for any services provided as a director. Remuneration received for committee participation or special assignments should also be provided: _____

_____

_____

B. A description of any remuneration received by you which is in addition to or is in lieu of that specified by the Company's standard arrangement, including any type of consulting arrangement: _____

_____

12. Please indicate whether you served as a member of the Company's compensation committee during the last fiscal year, or if the Company has no compensation committee, whether you participated in deliberations of the Company's Board of Directors concerning compensation of Executive Officers during the last fiscal year:

    A. Were you an officer or employee of a subsidiary of the Company? Answer:

    B. Did you serve on the compensation committee or the Board of Directors or were you an executive officer of another entity or subsidiary of the Company? If so, provide the name of the entity or subsidiary and the position: _____

13. Please describe any remuneration paid, payable, or accrued on your behalf pursuant to any compensatory plan or arrangement, if such remuneration will result from your resignation, retirement, or any other termination of your employment with the Company, or from a change in control of the Company, or a change in your responsibilities following a change in control of the Company: _____

VI. INDEBTEDNESS TO THE COMPANY

1. If you or any of your Associates were indebted to the Company at any time during the Company's last fiscal year in an amount exceeding $60,000, please specify (a) the largest aggregate amount of indebtedness outstanding at any time during the period, (b) the nature of the indebtedness and of the transaction in which it was incurred, (c) the amount thereof outstanding as of the latest practicable date, and (d) the rate of interest paid or charged thereon. If the answer is none, please so state:

VII. LEGAL PROCEEDINGS

1. If you are a director or an Executive Officer of the Company, have any of the following events occurred during the past five (5) years. If so, describe the circumstances below:

    A. Was a petition under any federal or state bankruptcy or insolvency law filed by or against, or a receiver, fiscal agent or similar officer appointed by a court for the business or property of, (i) yourself, (ii) any partnership in which you were a general partner at or within two years before such event, or (iii) any corporation or business association of which you were an Executive Officer at or within two years before such event? Answer: _____

    B. Were you convicted in a criminal proceeding, or are you the named subject of a criminal proceeding which is presently pending? Omit traffic violations and other minor offenses: _____

    C. Were you the subject of any court order, judgment or decree, not subsequently reversed, suspended, or vacated, which permanently or temporarily enjoined you from any of the following activities:

(1) Acting as a futures commission merchant, introducing broker, commodity trading advisor, commodity pool operator, floor broker, leverage transaction merchant, any other person regulated by the Commodity Futures Trading Commission, or an associated person of any of the foregoing, or as an investment advisor, underwriter, broker, or dealer in securities, or as an affiliated person, director, or employee of any investment company, bank, savings and loan association or insurance company, or engaging in or continuing any conduct or practice in connection with such activities? _____

(2) Engaging in any type of business? _____

(3) Engaging in any activity in connection with the purchase or sale of any security or commodity, or in connection with any violation of federal or state securities laws or federal commodities laws? Answer: _____

D.   Were you the subject of any order, judgment, or decree, not subsequently reversed, suspended, or vacated, of any federal or state authority barring, suspending, or otherwise limiting for more than sixty (60) days your right to engage in any of the activities described above or for your right to be associated with Persons in any of such activities? Answer: _____

E.   Were you found by a court in a civil action or by the Securities and Exchange Commission to have violated any federal or state securities laws where such judgment has not subsequently been reversed, suspended or vacated? Answer: _____

F.   Were you found by a court of competent jurisdiction in a civil action or by the Commodity Futures Trading Commission to have violated any federal commodities law, and the judgment in such civil action or finding by the Commodity Futures Trading Commission has not been subsequently reversed, suspended or vacated? _____

G.   Were you named in or are you currently named in, any formal administrative proceeding initiated by any Federal or State administrative agency having jurisdiction over you on any business of which you were an Executive officer, director, Affiliate or Principal Shareholder? _____

If you answered "Yes" to any of the foregoing questions, please give details of the circumstances on a separate sheet and attach it to this Questionnaire.

2.   Are you or, to your knowledge, any of your Affiliates or any other director or officer of the Company or any of their Affiliates a party in any litigation to which the Company is also a party or by which any of them may be bound or to which any of them or their properties may be subject? If so, please explain. Answer: _____

---

3.   Do you know of any pending legal proceedings in which either you or any Associate of yours is a party adverse to the Company, or in which either you or any Associate has an interest adverse to the Company? Answer: _____

If your answer is "Yes," please give the details on a separate sheet and attach it to this Questionnaire.

I consent to the disclosure of the foregoing information in the Disclosure Documents as may be required in the Company's discretion.

Present relationships) to and positions) by title with the Company: _____

Additional proposed relationships) to and positions) by title with the Company: _____

_____

I understand that the information that I am furnishing to you herein will be used by the Company in the preparation of a Private Placement Memorandum which may be used by the Company in connection with the offer and sale of its securities. I will advise the Company as to any events relating to the items in this Questionnaire which occur between now and the time the Company completes its contemplated transaction.

Signature: _____

Print Name: _____

Date: _____

APPENDIX
DEFINITIONS

(1) "Executive Officer" means the president, secretary, treasurer, any vice president in charge of a principal business function (such as sales, administration, or finance), and any other person who performs similar policy making functions for the Company.
(2) You are the "Beneficial Owner" of a security, as defined in Rule 13d 3 under the Exchange Act, if you, directly or indirectly, through any contract, arrangement, understanding, relationship, or otherwise have or share: (1) voting power which includes the power to vote, or to direct the voting of, such security, or (2) investment power which includes the power to dispose, or to direct the disposition, of such security. You also are the beneficial owner of a security if you directly or indirectly realize economic benefits of a type commonly associated with the ownership of such security, including but not limited to the receipt or right to receive income from the security or receive or control the disposition of proceeds in a liquidation. You also are the beneficial owner of a security if you, directly or indirectly, create or use a trust, proxy, power of attorney, pooling arrangement or any other contract, arrangement, or device with the purpose or effect of divesting yourself of beneficial ownership of a security or preventing the vesting of such beneficial ownership. Additionally, you are deemed to be the beneficial owner of a security if you have the right to acquire beneficial ownership of such security at any time within sixty (60) days including but not limited to any right to acquire (a) through the exercise of any option, warrant or right, (b) through the conversion of a security, or (c) pursuant to the power to revoke a trust, discretionary account, or similar arrangement.
The above definition is very broad and even though you may not actually have or share voting or investment power with respect to securities owned by persons in your family or living in your home, you may wish to include such shares in your beneficial ownership disclosure, out of an abundance of caution, and then disclaim beneficial ownership of such securities. If you do disclaim, please furnish the information described in Question 4(b).
(3) "Affiliate" means a person who directly, or through one or more intermediaries, controls, is controlled by, or is under common control with another person. An Affiliate of a person includes members of this family and trusts for his or their benefit.

(4) "Principal Shareholder" when used with respect to any entity, means any person who owns of record or beneficially owns more than 5 percent of the outstanding capital stock or other equity of the entity.

(5) "Material" or "Materially," with respect to any subject, refers to the kind of information an average, prudent investor would require or desire in order to be reasonably informed before purchasing, selling, or voting shares of stock or other equity securities.

(6) "Person" means an individual as well as any corporation, association, trust, unincorporated organization or other entity.

(7) Remuneration is "Accrued" if there is a reasonable certainty that it will be distributed or unconditionally vested in the future.

(8) "Options" includes all options, warrants or rights, other than those issued to security holders as such on a pro rata basis.

(9) The term "Appreciation Right" means a right representing a share of the Company or another person under which right the holder may in the future realize compensation measurable by reference to the future market price of such share and payable in cash, securities or other property where a change in the market value of the share is properly taken into account in the expensing of such compensation for financial reporting purposes for the fiscal year in which the change in market value occurs. Thus, this definition may include interests in certain plans, such as some phantom stock plans, which are not denominated as stock appreciation right plans.

(10) The term "Associate," as defined in Rule 12b 2 under the Exchange Act means (a) any corporation or organization (other than the Company or any of its subsidiaries) of which you are an officer or partner or are, directly or indirectly, the beneficial owner of ten percent or more of any class of equity securities, (b) any trust or other estate in which you have a beneficial interest or as to which you serve as trustee or in a similar capacity, and (c) your spouse, or any relative of yours or relative of your spouse living in your home or who is a director or officer of the Company or of its subsidiaries. Please identify your associate referred to in your answer and indicate your relationship.

Form 10 C: Subscription Agreement

SUBSCRIPTION AGREEMENT

COMMON STOCK

Subscriber: _____

Residence Address: _____

_____

Telephone Number: _____

Email Address: _____

Subscription Dollar Amount: _____

GENERAL INSTRUCTIONS

IF, AFTER YOU HAVE CAREFULLY REVIEWED THE COMMON STOCK PRI-VATE PLACEMENT MEMORANDUM OF **** CORPORATION (THE "COMPANY") DATED _____, 20___ (THE "PRIVATE PLACEMENT MEMORAN-DUM"), AND ALL OTHER MATERIALS PROVIDED TO YOU BY THE COMPANY, YOU WISH TO SUBSCRIBE TO PURCHASE SHARES OF THE COMPANY'S COM-MON STOCK (THE "SHARES"), PLEASE FOLLOW CAREFULLY THE INSTRUC-TIONS BELOW.

THE INFORMATION REQUESTED IN THE SUBSCRIPTION AGREEMENT IS REQUIRED IN CONNECTION WITH THE COMPANY'S INTENDED RELIANCE UPON CERTAIN EXEMPTIONS FROM THE REGISTRATION AND QUALIFICATION REQUIREMENTS OF FEDERAL AND STATE SECURITIES LAWS. SUCH INFOR-MATION IS CONFIDENTIAL AND WILL NOT BE REVIEWED BY ANYONE OTHER THAN THE COMPANY AND ITS ADVISORS.

ALL SUBSCRIBERS:

Carefully read this Subscription Agreement. Sections I, II, III, and VI contain under-standings as to certain matters, subscriber representations and warranties, and reg-istration information that pertain to all subscribers. Section IV requests information regarding the financial condition and experience of prospective investors who are individuals and should be completed only by individual subscribers. Section V requests information regarding the financial condition and experience of prospective investors that are entities and should be completed only by entity subscribers.

Generally, each subscriber must fill out and sign a copy of the Subscription Agree-ment. However, in the case of joint subscribers, where such subscribers are husband and wife or are relatives and have the same principal residence, only the subscriber primarily responsible for evaluating the investment and making the decision to invest must complete Section IV of this Agreement. In the case of joint subscribers who are not husband and wife or are not relatives or do not have the same principal resi-dence, each joint subscriber must complete his own Subscription Agreement. Joint subscribers must take title to the Shares jointly and shall supply instructions to the Company as to the form of ownership desired in Section VI.

The Company will be relying on the representations and warranties you make and on the information you supply. Subscribers may be required to furnish additional information to enable the Company to determine whether each subscriber is a qualified investor.

When used herein, the terms "I," "you," "your," and "the undersigned" shall mean the Prospective Investor executing this Agreement below.

I.   IMPORTANT NOTICES CONCERNING THE OFFERING

The offering by the Company of the Shares (the "Offering") is intended to raise a total of _____ Dollars ($___). There is no minimum funding level, and funds accepted by the Company will be used immediately for the purposes described in the Private Placement Memorandum.

THE SHARES HAVE NOT BEEN REGISTERED UNDER THE SECURITIES ACT OF 1933, AS AMENDED (THE "SECURITIES ACT"), OR ANY STATE "BLUE SKY" OR SECURITIES LAWS. THE SHARES CANNOT BE SOLD, TRANSFERRED, ASSIGNED OR OTHERWISE DISPOSED OF EXCEPT IN COMPLIANCE WITH APPLICABLE FEDERAL AND STATE SECURITIES LAWS AND WILL NOT BE TRANSFERRED OF RECORD EXCEPT IN COMPLIANCE WITH SAID LAWS. THESE SECURITIES HAVE NOT BEEN APPROVED OR DISAPPROVED BY THE SECURITIES AND EXCHANGE COMMISSION OR BY ANY STATE SECURITIES COMMISSION OR REGULATORY AUTHORITY, NOR HAVE ANY OF THE FOREGOING AUTHORITIES PASSED UPON OR ENDORSED THE MERITS OF THIS OFFERING. ANY REPRESENTATION TO THE CONTRARY IS UNLAWFUL.

THIS OFFERING INVOLVES CERTAIN MATERIAL RISKS AND AN INVESTMENT IN THE COMPANY COULD RESULT IN THE LOSS OF YOUR ENTIRE INVESTMENT.

IN MAKING AN INVESTMENT DECISION INVESTORS MUST RELY ON THEIR OWN EXAMINATION OF THE ISSUER AND THE TERMS OF THE OFFERING, INCLUDING THE MERITS AND RISKS INVOLVED. THERE CURRENTLY IS NO TRADING MARKET FOR THE SECURITIES OF THE COMPANY, AND NONE IS EXPECTED TO DEVELOP FOLLOWING THIS OFFERING.

PROSPECTIVE INVESTORS MUST BE ABLE TO BEAR THE ECONOMIC RISK OF THE INVESTMENT FOR AN INDEFINITE PERIOD OF TIME, BECAUSE THE SECURITIES CANNOT BE SOLD OR TRANSFERRED EXCEPT AS PERMITTED BY THE SECURITIES ACT, AND APPLICABLE PROVISIONS OF STATE SECURITIES LAWS. IF, AS A RESULT OF SOME CHANGE OF CIRCUMSTANCES ARISING FROM AN EVENT NOT NOW IN CONTEMPLATION, OR FOR ANY OTHER REASON, AN INVESTOR WISHES TO TRANSFER HIS OR HER SECURITIES, SUCH INVESTOR MAY FIND NO MARKET FOR THOSE SECURITIES.

PRIOR TO THE ISSUANCE OF ANY SECURITIES, PROSPECTIVE INVESTORS SHALL BE GIVEN THE OPPORTUNITY TO ASK QUESTIONS AND RECEIVE ANSWERS CONCERNING ANY ASPECT OF THE INVESTMENT, AND TO OBTAIN ANY ADDITIONAL INFORMATION, TO THE EXTENT THE COMPANY POSSESSES SUCH INFORMATION OR CAN ACQUIRE IT WITHOUT UNREASONABLE EFFORT OR EXPENSE, NECESSARY TO MAKE AN INFORMED INVESTMENT DECISION AND TO VERIFY THE ACCURACY OF THE INFORMATION CONTAINED IN THE PRIVATE PLACEMENT MEMORANDUM OR IN ANY OTHER MATERIAL PROVIDED TO THE PROSPECTIVE INVESTOR BY THE COMPANY.

PROSPECTIVE INVESTORS ARE NOT TO CONSTRUE THE CONTENTS OF THIS SUBSCRIPTION AGREEMENT AS LEGAL, TAX OR INVESTMENT ADVICE. EACH INVESTOR SHOULD CONSULT HIS OWN LEGAL COUNSEL, ACCOUNTANT OR BUSINESS ADVISOR AS TO LEGAL, TAX AND RELATED MATTERS CONCERNING HIS POSSIBLE INVESTMENT IN THE SHARES. THE DELIVERY OF THIS SUBSCRIPTION AGREEMENT AT ANY TIME DOES NOT IMPLY THE INFORMATION CONTAINED HEREIN OR IN THE PRIVATE PLACEMENT MEMORANDUM, OR OTHER DOCUMENTS PREPARED BY THE COMPANY IS CORRECT AS OF ANY TIME SUBSEQUENT TO THE DATES THEREOF.

II. AGREEMENTS AND UNDERSTANDINGS

The undersigned agrees and understands as follows:

A. Except as may be provided under state securities laws, this Subscription Agreement is irrevocable; provided, however, that the execution and delivery of this Subscription Agreement will not constitute an agreement between the Company and the undersigned until this Subscription Agreement is accepted by the Company and will be interpreted in conjunction with the Private Placement Memorandum. I understand that the Company may request any other information, whether or not specifically called for in this Subscription Agreement, it deems desirable in evaluating this subscription. Furthermore, I understand that the Company has the right to reject this subscription with or without cause, for any or no reason.

B. The undersigned will make such representations and warranties and furnish such additional information as to investment experience and financial position as the Company may reasonably request, and if there should be any material change in the information set forth herein prior to the closing of the sale of Shares to me, the undersigned will immediately furnish such revised or corrected information to the Company.

C. The undersigned understands that in the event that this Subscription Agreement is not accepted for whatever reason, the subscription funds will be returned to the undersigned without interest or escrow fee.

D. The undersigned recognizes that in accepting this subscription to purchase Shares, the Company will rely on the accuracy and completeness of the statements, representations and warranties of the undersigned set forth herein. The undersigned agrees to defend, to indemnify and to hold harmless the Company, and each of its officers, directors, and agents from and against any and all loss, damage, liability or expense, including reasonable attorneys' fees and costs, which they or any of them may incur or become liable for by reason of, or in any way connected with, any misrepresentation or omission of relevant information, whether negligent or intentional, made by the undersigned in this Subscription Agreement, or arising out of any sale or distribution to the undersigned of the Shares in violation of the Securities Act, or any other applicable securities or "Blue Sky" laws.

III. REPRESENTATIONS AND WARRANTIES

The undersigned represents and warrants to the Company that:

A. The undersigned has received and reviewed the Private Placement Memorandum and the attachments thereto, is familiar with the terms and provisions thereof, and has been given full access to information appropriate to a determination of whether to invest in the Company.

B. The undersigned has further had an opportunity to meet with principals of the Company and discuss issues relevant to a determination of whether to invest in the Shares.

C. The undersigned has full legal capacity to enter into this Subscription Agreement.

D. The undersigned has carefully reviewed the merits and risks of, and other considerations relating to, an investment in the Company.

E. The undersigned has read and understood the notices set forth in Section I of this Subscription Agreement and understands that the transfer of the Shares is subject to various restrictions; that, as the Shares have not been registered under the Securities Act, or under the securities laws of any state, the Shares cannot be sold unless they are registered under said Act and qualified under said state laws or are exempt from registration or qualification thereunder; that the Company will not record the sale or other transfer of any Shares without compliance with said securities laws; and that the undersigned must bear the economic risk of ownership of Shares for an indefinite period of time. The undersigned shall not sell, assign, transfer or otherwise dispose of all or any part of my Shares or interests therein except in compliance with applicable federal and state securities laws.

F. The undersigned understands that an investment in the Company is not liquid. The undersigned has adequate means of providing for current needs and personal contingencies and has no need for liquidity in this investment.

G. Except for the Private Placement Memorandum, and any other information that my advisors or the undersigned may have requested and received directly from the Company, neither my advisors nor the undersigned have been furnished any other offering material or literature upon which the undersigned has relied in connection with the determination of whether or not to purchase Shares.

H. The undersigned has had an opportunity to review all the pertinent facts, to ask questions, and to obtain any additional information, to the extent possessed or obtainable without unreasonable effort and expense, regarding the Company, its key employees, its business, the offering of the Shares, the risks of investment in the Company and any other matters relating to any of the above or anything set forth in the Private Placement Memorandum, and any additional information necessary to verify the accuracy of any representation or information set forth therein. The Company has supplied all material requested, and has given complete and satisfactory answers to all inquiries, if any, that my advisors and I have put to it concerning the matters listed above.

I. All financial and other data that the undersigned has supplied in this Subscription Agreement is true, accurate, and complete and fairly reflects the current financial condition and investment experience of the undersigned to the best of my knowledge and belief.

J. The undersigned has been advised to consult with an attorney regarding legal matters concerning an investment in the Company and regarding tax and other financial consequences of investing in the Company. The undersigned understands that the information provided by the Company in connection with the offering of the Shares does not constitute legal, investment, tax or other advice.

K. The undersigned is acquiring the Shares for his own account, as principal, for investment and not with a view to or for sale in connection with any distribution of such Shares or any interest therein.

L. The undersigned understands and acknowledges that the Private Placement Memorandum contains certain statements of anticipated or expected results and certain projected financial information, all of which constitute "forward-looking statements" within the meaning of the Private Securities Litigation Reform Act. Such forward-looking statements are subject to various risks and uncertainties. The undersigned understands and further acknowledges that those forward-looking statements depend on certain assumptions about the Company, its market, the competition it faces, and its revenue model, and the undersigned acknowledges that those assumptions may prove to be inaccurate. As a result, the projected financial information and related information may not prove to be accurate statements of the actual financial results or the financial condition of the Company. The undersigned has had an opportunity to discuss such projected financial information, and their underlying assumptions, with the Company's management.

M. The undersigned has a prior personal or business relationship with one or more of the officers or directors of the Company, OR by reason of the undersigned's business or financial experience, the undersigned has the capacity to protect his own interests in connection with the purchase of the Shares.

IV. FINANCIAL CONDITION AND EXPERIENCE OF INDIVIDUAL SUBSCRIBERS

The undersigned further represents and warrants to the Company, as follows:

The undersigned [is] [is not] an "accredited investor" as defined in Rule 501 of Regulation D promulgated under the Securities Act. My qualification is based on the following (each "accredited investor" must initial Item 1 and/or Item 2, as appropriate):

_____ 1. The undersigned had an individual income (exclusive of the income of his spouse) in excess of $200,000 for each of the two most recent years, or joint income with his spouse in excess of $300,000 in each of those years, and reasonably expects the same income level for the current year; or

_____ 2. As of the date of this Subscription Agreement, the undersigned (either individually or with his spouse) has a net worth in excess of $1,000,000, exclusive of his primary residence.

OR

_____ 3. The undersigned is not an "accredited investor" (initial, if appropriate).

V. AUTHORITY AND FINANCIAL CONDITION OF ENTITY SUBSCRIBERS

The requested financial information should be furnished only with respect to the entity subscriber, and not with respect to any of the owners of the beneficial interests therein, except as indicated.

If the subscriber is a grantor trust (i.e. a trust that is amendable and revocable by the grantor at any time) please complete this Section V with respect to the trust and its assets alone and complete Section IV with respect to the grantor, including the assets held in the trust.

A. Entity Representations and Warranties

The undersigned represents and warrants to the Company as follows:

(1) The undersigned has been duly formed and is validly existing and in good standing under the laws of the state in which it was founded, with full power and authority to enter into the transactions contemplated by this Subscription Agreement.

(2) The execution of this Agreement has been duly and validly authorized, and, when delivered on behalf of the undersigned, will constitute a valid, binding, and enforceable agreement and obligation of the undersigned.

(3) The undersigned has not been formed, reformed, or recapitalized for the specific purpose of purchasing the Shares.

(4) The undersigned acknowledges that of all representations, warranties, agreements, and notices set forth in Sections I through III and V apply to the undersigned and acknowledges having read and understood them. Where appropriate in the context, the words "I," "me," and "his" have been read to mean "the undersigned" or "its."

B. Financial Position and Experience

Type of Entity: _____

Date of Organization: _____

State of Organization: _____

Number of Equity Owners (partners, beneficiaries, etc.): _____

If one or more of these equity owners owns individually or collectively more than fifty percent (50%) of the equity interest of the subscriber and is (are) also purchasing Shares, please identify such equity owner(s):

_____

_____

Indicate whether the Subscriber is any of the following types of entity (check any applicable category):

(i) _____ A bank or savings and loan institution, whether acting in its individual or fiduciary capacity.

(ii) _____ An insurance company.

(iii) _____ An investment company registered under the Investment Company Act of 1940.

(iv) _____ A business development company as defined in the Investment Company Act of 1940.

(v) _____ A private business development company as defined in the Investment Advisors Act of 1940.

(vi) _____ A Small Business Investment Company licensed by the U.S. Small Business Administration.

(vii) _____ An employee benefit plan within the meaning of Title I of the Employment Retirement Income Security Act of 1974 (ERISA), if the investment decision with respect to this investment is made by a plan fiduciary which is either a bank, savings and loan association, insurance company, or registered investment advisor, or if the employee benefit plan has total assets in excess of $5,000,000.

(viii) _____ An employee benefit plan established and maintained by a state or state agency, if the plan has total assets in excess of $5,000,000.

(ix) _____ Any tax exempt organization as defined in Section 501(c)(3) of the Internal Revenue Code, corporation, Massachusetts or similar business trust or partnership not formed for specific purpose of acquiring the securities offered, with total assets in excess of $5,000,000.

(x) _____ An entity of which the owners are (1) institutional investors described in the foregoing subparagraphs (i)-(ix), (2) "Individuals" who meet certain suitability standards, or (3) or a combination of both. For purposes of this paragraph, "Individuals" shall mean an individual: (A) who has a net worth individually, or jointly with his or her spouse, of more than $1,000,000; or (B) who has had individual annual gross income from all sources in excess of $200,000, or joint income with a spouse in excess of $300,000, in each of the two most recent years and a reasonable expectation of reaching the same income level in the current year; or (C) is an Officer or Director of the Company; or (D) is a broker or dealer registered pursuant to Section 15 of the Securities Exchange Act of 1934; or (E) in most cases, may reasonably be deemed by the Company to have such knowledge and experience in financial and business matters that he or she is capable of evaluating the merits and risks of the prospective investment.

(xi) _____ A trust with total assets in excess of $5,000,000, not formed for the specific purpose of acquiring the securities, whose purchase is directed by a person with knowledge and experience in financial matters, capable of evaluating the merits and risks of the prospective investment.

The net worth of the undersigned, as set forth in greater detail on the financial statements submitted herewith (if the Company so requests) is:

$ _____

The undersigned's principal activities are:

_____

_____

C. Investment Evaluation

Please certify the truth of the following statement by initialing where indicated:

The individuals authorizing this investment on behalf of Subscriber have such knowledge and experience in financial and business matters so as to be capable of evaluating the merits and risks of an investment in the Company.

_____ (Initials)

VI. ALL SUBSCRIBERS

A. Title. The subscriber, or joint subscribers, wish(es) to take title to the Shares as follows:

_____ Individual, as a Single Person

_____ Individual, Subject to Community Property Rights of Spouse

_____ Individual, as Separate Property

_____ Husband and Wife, as Community Property

_____ As Tenants-In-Common

_____ As Joint Tenants with Rights of Survivorship

_____ Other (e.g., corporation, partnership, trustee or custodian), please specify: _____

The exact spelling of the name(s) to be on the title:

_____

_____

_____

B. Legend. The Subscriber acknowledges that a legend to the following effect will appear upon the Shares:

THE SECURITIES REPRESENTED BY THIS INSTRUMENT HAVE NOT BEEN REGISTERED UNDER THE FEDERAL SECURITIES ACT OF 1933, AS AMENDED, OR REGISTERED OR QUALIFIED UNDER THE SECURITIES LAW OF ANY STATE AND MAY NOT BE SOLD OR OTHERWISE TRANSFERRED UNLESS (1) THERE IS AN EFFECTIVE REGISTRATION STATEMENT FOR THE SECURITIES UNDER THE ACT AND ANY APPLICABLE STATE SECURITIES LAW, (2) SUCH TRANSFER IS MADE IN COMPLIANCE WITH RULE 144 UNDER THE ACT AND PURSUANT

TO REGISTRATION OR QUALIFICATION UNDER ANY APPLICABLE STATE SECU-
RITIES LAW OR EXEMPTION THEREFROM, OR (3) THERE IS AN OPINION OF
COUNSEL SATISFACTORY TO THE CORPORATION THAT SUCH REGISTRATION
IS NOT REQUIRED AS TO SAID TRANSFER, SALE OR OFFER.

The Subscriber agrees promptly to deliver the certificate representing Subscriber's Shares to the Company if and when the Company, in its discretion, decides
to recall such certificate and reissue the same bearing a new or different legend or
legends reflecting appropriately any requirements of the exemptions from the state
and federal securities laws pursuant to which Shares have been sold to Subscriber.

IN WITNESS WHEREOF, the undersigned have executed this Subscription Agreement as of the date indicated below.

INDIVIDUAL SUBSCRIBERS:

Dated: _____

Signature: _____

Print Name: _____

If the subscriber has indicated that he will take title to the Shares as a joint tenant, tenant in common, or as community property, the co-owner or joint subscriber
must sign here:

Signature: _____

Print Name: _____

ENTITY SUBSCRIBERS:

Dated: _____

Name of Entity: _____

Signature: _____

Print Name: _____

Print Title: _____

Form 10 D: Blue-Sky Law Requirements and Rule 506 of Regulation D

Blue Sky Filing Requirements of all 50 States for offerings
under Rule 506 of Regulation D

1. Alabama
   a. Authority: Policy Statement ¶ 7,570
   b. Filing Requirements:
      Form D (manually signed)
      Form U-2 (name Alabama Secretary of State for service of process)
      Copy of the offering documents
      Notice to be filed upon termination of offering
   c. Fee: $250 made payable to the "Alabama Securities Commission"
   d. Address: Alabama Securities Commission
                770 Washington Street
                Suite 570
                Montgomery, AL 36130-4700
                (Overnight mail zip code 36104)
   e. Phone: 334-242-2984
   f. Fax: 334-242-0240
   g. Website: http://asc.alabama.gov
2. Alaska
   a. Authority: Sec. 45.55.075 (¶ 8,121 A); Reg. Sec. 3AAC 08.506 (¶ 8,449C);
See also ¶ 8,464
   b. Filing Requirements:
      Form D
      Form U-2
   c. Fee: $600 (valid for one year); $1,100 (if an automatic extension of one year is
desired by the issuer at the time the notice is filed) made payable to "Department of
Commerce of the State of Alaska"
   d. Renewal: To renew a notice, the issuer must submit items (i) - (ii) above as if
the issuer were making an initial filing.
   e. Note: A notice filing is valid for one year or two years if the issuer paid for an
automatic extension at the time of the initial filing.
   f. Address: Alaska Dept. of Community & Economic Development
                Division of Banking, Securities & Corporations
                State Office Building, 9th Floor
                150 Third Street
                Juneau, AK 99801
                Mailing Address: P.O. Box 110807
                Juneau, AK 99811-0807
   g. Phone: 907-465-2521
   h. Fax: 907-465-2549
3. Arizona
   a. Authority: Sec. 44-1843.02(C) (¶ 9,135); Sec. 44-1861E (1861 E (¶ 9,151)
   b. Filing Requirements:
      Form D
   c. Fee: $250 made payable to "Arizona Corporation Commission"

    d. Address: Arizona Corporation Commission
                 Securities Division
                 1300 West Washington, Third Floor
                 Phoenix, AZ 85007
    e. Phone: 602-542-4242
    f. Fax: 602-594-7470
    g. Website: http://www.azcc.gov/Divisions/securities

4. Arkansas
    a. Authority: Sec. 23-42-509(c) (¶ 10,169); Rule 509.01(B) (¶ 10,509)
    b. Filing Requirements:
        Form D (and any subsequent amendments) (manually signed)
        Form U-2
    c. Fee: 1/10 of 1% of maximum aggregate offering price sold in Arkansas (minimum of $100 and maximum of $500) made payable to "Arkansas Securities Department"
    d. Address: Arkansas Securities Department
                 Heritage West Building - Room 300
                 201 East Markham
                 Little Rock, AR 72201-1692
    e. Phone: 501-324-9260
    f. Fax: 501-324-9268
    g. Website: http://www.securities.arkansas.gov

5. California
    a. Authority: Sec. 25102.1(d) (¶ 11,133A); Sec. 25608.1(c) (¶ 11,339A); Release No. 103-C (¶ 12,638)
    b. Filing Requirements:
        Form D
        Form U-2
    c. Fee: $300 made payable to "Department of Corporations"
    d. Note: Cover letter must state that the filing is made pursuant to Rule 506 and Section 18(b)(4)(D) of the Securities Act of 1933 and if a Consent to Service of Process is not included in the filing, a statement that the issuer is a California corporation or already has a Consent to Service of Process on file.
    e. Address: California Dept. of Corporation
                 Securities Regulation Division
                 1515 K Street, Suite 200
                 Sacramento, CA 95814-4052
    f. Phone: 916-445-7205
    g. Fax: 916-322-8864

6. Colorado
    a. Authority: Sec. 11-51-308(1)(p) (¶ 13,112); Reg. Sec. 51-3.7 (¶ 13,551); See also ¶ 13,579
    b. Filing Requirements:
        Form D
    c. Fee: $75 made payable to the "Colorado State Treasurer"
    d. Address: Colorado Division of Securities
                 1560 Broadway, Suite 900
                 Denver, CO 80202
    e. Phone: 303-894-2320
    f. Fax: 303-861-2126
    g. Website: http://www.dora.state.co.us/securities/

7. Connecticut
   a. Authority: Sec. 36b-21(e) (¶ 14,120); Sec. 36b-33 (¶ 14,133)
   b. Filing Requirements:
      Form D (manually signed)
      Form U-2
      Sales Agent/Broker-Dealer Questionnaire
   c. Fee: $150 payable to "Treasurer of State of Connecticut"
   d. Address: Connecticut Dept. of Banking
               Division of Securities
               260 Constitution Plaza
               Hartford, CT 06103-1800
   e. Phone: 860-240-8230 or 1-800-831-7225
   f. Fax: 860-240-8295
   g. Website: http://www.ct.gov/dob
8. Delaware
   a. Authority: Sec. 7309A(b) (¶ 15,109A); Sec. 7302(17) (¶ 15,102); Sec. 406 (¶ 15,506)
   b. Filing Requirements:
      Form D (manually signed)
      Form U-2
   c. Fee: No Fee
   d. Address: Delaware Dept. of Justice
               Division of Securities
               Carvel State Office Building
               820 N. French Street, 5th Floor
               Wilmington, DE 19801
   e. Phone: 302-577-8424
   f. Fax: 302-577-6987
   g. Website: http://www.investorresourcecenter.org
9. Florida
   a. Authority: Sec. 517.061(11) (¶ 17,106); Rule 3E-500.005 (¶ 17,445)
   b. Requirements of "Limited Offering" Exemption: No more than 35 purchasers in Florida in any consecutive 12 month period (Note: Sec. 517.061(11)(b) lists types of purchasers that are excluded from the calculation of the number of purchasers, including accredited investors)
      (i)   No general solicitation or general advertising
      (ii) Each purchaser must be provided with full and fair disclosure of all material information prior to the sale (pursuant to Rule 3E-500.005)
      (iii) No person who is defined as a "dealer" may be paid a commission or compensation for the sale
      (iv) Purchaser may void the sale within 3 days after tender of consideration if sales are made to 5 or more persons in Florida
   c. Disclosure Requirements: Prior to the sale of any security in the State of Florida, the issuer must provide one of the following to each investor:
      (i)   (A) access to all material books and records of the issuer, (B) access to all material contracts and documents relating to the proposed transaction, and (C) an opportunity to question the appropriate executive officers or partners of the issuer
      (ii) Offering Documents which include the following information: (A) material risks of the offering, (B) legend in the offering documents stating that the securities have not been registered with the state of Florida and stating that the purchaser may void the sale within 3 days after the sale pursuant to Sec. 517.061(11)(a)(5), (C) use of

proceeds from the offering, (D) unaudited balance sheet and statement of profit and loss as of a date not earlier than the end of the issuer's last fiscal year (Note: Rule 3E-500.005(5)(b) (1 17,445) provides a more detailed list of the information required to be included in the offering documents)

    d. Timing: Provided to purchaser prior to sale

    e. Miscellaneous: Issuer may make notice filing under NSMIA, but still must register as a "dealer" under Sec. 517.12. The issuer would be the applicant, but the application would also require information about the partners, officers and directors of the issuer and any person directly or indirectly controlling the issuer and would require these natural persons to successfully pass examinations. Therefore, an issuer should instead use the limited offering exemption outlined above.

    f. Address: Financial Services Commission
                  Office of Financial Regulation
                  200 East Gaines Street
                  Tallahassee, FL 32399-0372

    g. Phone: 850-410-9748
    h. Fax: 850-410-9431
    i. Website: http://www.flofr.com/Securities/index.htm

10. Georgia

    a. Authority: Sec. 10-5-9(16) (0118,109); Sec. 10-5-5(g)(2)(1 18,105)

    b. Filing Requirements:
    Form D
    Form U-2

    c. Fee: $250 payable to "Georgia Secretary of State"

    d. Note: The commissioner shall issue to the issuer a certificate stating compliance or noncompliance with the filing requirements

    e. Renewal: If any sale is made more than 12 months after the date of the commissioner's certificate, a $100 renewal fee must be paid. The issuer must repeat this process every 12 months the offer is "open" in the State of Georgia

    f. Address: Office of the Secretary of State
                  Division of Securities and Business Regulation
                  Two Martin Luther King, Jr. Drive SE
                  802 West Tower
                  Atlanta, GA 30334

    g. Phone: 404-656-3920
    h. Fax: 404-657-8410
    i. Website: http://www.sos.state.ga.us/securities/

11. Hawaii

    a. Authority: Sec. 485-4.5(b) (1120,104A)

    b. Filing Requirements:
    Form D (manually signed)
    Form U-2

    c. Fee: $200 payable to "Commissioner of Securities of State of Hawaii"

    d. Address: Dept. of Commerce and Consumer Affairs
                  335 Merchant Street, Room 203
                  Honolulu, HI 96813
                  Mailing Address: P.O. Box 40
                  Honolulu, HI 96810

    e. Phone: 808-586-2744
    f. Fax: 808-586-2733

12. Idaho
   a. Authority: Sec. 30-1433A(2) (¶ 21,133A); Sec. 30-1437(b) (¶ 21,137);
Administrative Order ¶ 21,562
   b. Filing Requirements:
      Form D
      Form U-2
   c. Fee: $50 made payable to "Department of Finance of State of Idaho"
   d. Address: Dept. of Finance
              800 Park Boulevard, Suite 200
              Boise, ID 83712
              Mailing Address: P.O. Box 83720
              Boise, ID 83720-0031
   e. Phone: 208-332-8004
   f. Fax: 208-332-8099
   g. Website: http://finance.idaho.gov
13. Illinois
   a. Authority: Sec. 130.293(a)(1) (¶ 22, 635A)
   b. Filing Requirements:
      Form D (manually signed)
   c. Fee: $100 payable to "Secretary of State of Illinois"
   d. Address: Illinois Office of the Secretary of State
              Securities Department
              Jefferson Terrace
              Suite 300 A
              300 West Jefferson Street
              Springfield, IL 62702
   e. Phone: 217-782-2256 or 800-628-7937
   f. Fax: 217-782-8876
   g. Website: http://www.cyberdriveillinois.com/departments/securities/home.html
14. Indiana
   a. Authority: Sec. 23-2-1-6.1(b) (¶ 24,106A); Administrative Order ¶ 24,692
   b. Filing Requirements:
      Form D
   c. Fee: No fee
   d. Address: Indiana Office of the Secretary of State
              Securities Division
              302 West Washington, E-111
              Indianapolis, IN 46204
   e. Phone: 317-232-6681
   f. Fax: 317-233-3675
   g. Website: http://www.in.gov/sos/securities/
15. Iowa
   a. Authority: Sec. 191-50.14 (502) (¶ 25,414)
   b. Filing Requirements:
      Form D (manually signed)
      Form U-2
   c. Fee: $100 made payable to "Iowa Securities Bureau"
   d. Address: Iowa Insurance Division
              Securities Bureau
              340 Maple Street
              Des Moines, IA 50319-0066

    e. Phone: 515-281-4441
    f. Fax: 515-281-3059
    g. Website: http://www.iid.state.ia.us/
16. Kansas
    a. Authority: Sec. 17-1270a(b) (¶ 26,123a); Sec. 17-1259(b)(3) (¶ 26,111)
Administrative Order ¶ 26,590
    b. Filing Requirements:
        Form D (manually signed)
    c. Fee: $100 made payable to the "Kansas Securities Commissioner"
    d. Address: Office of the Kansas Securities Commissioner
                  618 South Kansas Ave.
                  2nd Floor
                  Topeka, KS 66603-3804
    e. Phone: 785-296-3307
    f. Fax: 785-296-6872
    g. Website: http://www.securities.state.ks.us
17. Kentucky
    a. Authority: Sec. 292.327 (¶ 27,103A)
    b. Filing Requirements:
        Form D (manually signed)
        Form U-2
    c. Fee: $250 made payable to "Kentucky State Treasurer"
    d. Address: Kentucky Dept. of Financial Institutions
                  Division of Securities
                  1025 Capital Center Drive, Suite 200
                  Frankfort, KY 40601
    e. Phone: 502-573-3390 or 800-223-2579
    f. Fax: 502-573-2182
    g. Website: http://www.kfi.ky.gov
18. Louisiana
    a. Authority: Sec. 709(15) (¶ 28,1309); Sec. 703 (¶ 28,513)
    b. Filing Requirements:
        Form D (manually signed)
        Form U-2 (appoint Louisiana Commissioner of Securities)
        Form U-2A (revised to relate to LLC)
    c. Timing: Must file no later than 15 days after the receipt of consideration from
an investor in Louisiana
    d. Fee: $300 made payable to "Commissioner of Securities, State of Louisiana"
    e. Note: Cover letter should include an undertaking that the issuer will furnish to
the Commissioner, upon written request, the information furnished by the issuer to
the offerees
    f. Address: Securities Commission
                  8660 United Plaza Boulevard, Second Floor
                  Baton Rouge, LA 70809-7024
    g. Phone: 225-925-4512
    h. Fax: 225-925-4548
    i. Website: http://www.ofi.state.la.us
19. Maine
    a. Authority: Sec. 10502 2R (¶ 29,072); Sec. 10505 2 (¶ 29075)
    b. Filing Requirements:
        Form D (manually signed)

Form U-2
c. Fee: $300 made payable to "Securities Administrator, State of Maine"
d. Address: Dept. of Professional and Financial Regulation
Securities Division
121 State House Station
Augusta, ME 04333-0121
e. Phone: 207-624-8551
f. Fax: 207-624-8590
g. Website: http://www.investors.maine.gov

20. Maryland
a. Authority: Sec. 11-503.1 (c) (¶ 30,153A); Rule .09 (¶ 30,539); Sec. 11-506(b) (¶ 30,156)
b. Filing Requirements:
Form D (manually signed)
Form U-2
c. Fee: $100 made payable to "Maryland Office of Attorney General"
d. Note: Cover letter should include the date of the first sale in Maryland, the name and CRD number, if any, of at least one broker-dealer or issuer agent that will effect transactions in the securities in Maryland
e. Address: Office of the Attorney General
Division of Securities
200 St. Paul Place
Baltimore, MD 21202-2020
f. Phone: 410-576-6360
g. Fax: 410-576-6532
h. Website: http://www.oag.state.md.us/securities

21. Massachusetts
a. Authority: Sec. 14.402(B)(13)(i) (¶ 31,472); Statement of Policy ¶ 31,637
b. Filing Requirements:
Form D (manually signed)
Form U-2
Form U-2A Corporate Resolution, if applicable
c. Fee: $250 for aggregate offerings of not more than $2,000,000, $500 for aggregate offerings of between $2,000,001 and $7,500,000 and $750 for aggregate offerings of more than $7,500,001 made payable to "Commonwealth of Massachusetts"
d. Address: Secretary of the Commonwealth
Securities Division
One Ashburton Place, Room 1701
Boston, MA 02108
e. Phone: 617-727-3548
f. Fax: 617-248-0177
g. Website: http://www.sec.state.ma.us/sct

22. Michigan
a. Authority: MCL 451.2302(4) (¶ 32,132)
b. Filing Requirements:
Form D (manually signed)
c. Fee: $100 made payable to "State of Michigan"
d. Note: Cover letter should include an undertaking that the issuer will furnish to the state securities administrator, upon written request, the information furnished by the issuer to the offerees.

e. Address: Dept. of Energy, Labor, and Economic Growth
              Office of Financial and Insurance Regulation
              Division of Securities
              Ottawa Building, 2nd floor
              611 W. Ottawa St.
              Lansing, MI 48933
              Overnight Address: 7150 Harris Drive
              Lansing, MI 48909
              Mailing Address: P.O. Box 30220
              Lansing, MI 48909-7720
f. Phone: 517-241-6350
g. Fax: 517-335-4978
h. Website: http://www.michigan.gov/ofis

23. Minnesota
    a. Authority: Sec. 80A.46; Sec. 80A.45
    b. Filing Requirements:
        Form D (manually signed)
        Form U-2
    c. Fee: $50 made payable to "Minnesota Secretary Treasurer"
    d. Address: Department of Commerce
                 85 East Seventh Place, Suite 500
                 St. Paul, MN 55101-2198
    e. Phone: 651-296-4026
    f. Fax: 651-296-4328
    g. Website: http://www.state.mn.us/

24. Mississippi
    a. Authority: Sec. 75-71-408(2) (¶ 34,169A); Rule 235 (¶ 34,435)
    b. Filing Requirements:
        Form D (manually signed)
        Form U-2 (manually signed)
    c. Fee: $300 payable to "Mississippi Secretary of State"
    d. Address: Office of the Secretary of State
                 Securities Enforcement and Regulation
                 700 North Street, Suite 601
                 Jackson, MS 39202
                 Mailing Address: P.O. Box 136
                 Jackson, MS 39205-0136
    e. Phone: 601-359-6371
    f. Fax: 601-359-2663
    g. Website: http://www.sos.ms.gov/securities_and_charities_securities.aspx

25. Missouri
    a. Authority: Sec. 409.307(b) (¶ 35,112A)
    b. Filing Requirements:
        Form D (manually signed)
        Form U-2
    c. Fee: $100 made payable to "Director of Revenue, State of Missouri"
    d. Address: Missouri Office of the Secretary of State
                 Securities Division
                 600 West Main St.
                 P.O. Box 1276
                 Jefferson City, MO 65101-1276
    e. Phone: 573-751-4136

f. Fax: 573-526-3124
g. Website: http://www.sos.mo.gov/securities
26. Montana
   a. Authority: Sec. 30-10-211(2) (¶ 36,117A); Sec. 30-10-209(a),(b),(c) (¶ 36,116); Sec. 6.10.147 (¶36,489)
   b. Filing Requirements:
      Form D (manually signed)
      Form U-2
   c. Fee: $200 for the first $100,000 offering amount in Montana, plus 1/10 of 1% of any offering amount over $100,000 (maximum fee is $1,000) made payable to "Montana State Auditor, Securities Commissioner"
   d. Note:
      Each succeeding year, a notice of filing may be renewed prior to its termination date for an additional year upon consent of the commissioner and payment of a renewal fee of 1/10 of 1% if the aggregate offering price for the securities offered in Montana. The fee may not be less than $200 or more than $1,000.
      If excess sales are made and no amendment is filed to cover such excess sales prior to the expiration date of the notice issuers must pay a specified penalty for those sales. Notice of the excess securities is effective retroactively to the date of the existing notice. The penalty for failure to file an amendment shall be three times the amount calculated for a renewal fee in (i).
   e. Address: Office of the State Auditor
               Securities Department
               840 Helena Ave.
               Helena, MT 59601
               Mailing Address: P.O. Box 4009
               Helena, MT 59604-4009
   f. Phone: 406-444-2040
   g. Fax: 406-444-5558
   h. Website: http:/sao.mt.gov/securities/index.asp
27. Nebraska
   a. Authority: Sec. 8-1108.2(2) (¶ 37,109A); Ch. 20 (¶ 37,420(003))
   b. Filing Requirements:
      Form D (manually signed)
      Form U-2
   c. Fee: $200 made payable to "Nebraska Department of Banking and Finance"
   d. Note: The paragraphs cited appear to be in conflict regarding when the notice needs to be filed. ¶ 37,109A(2) requires filing within 15 days of the first sale in the state and ¶ 37,420(003) requires filing within 30 days of the first sale in the state.The Nebraska Department of Banking & Finance indicated that they are aware of the discrepancy and that believe the statutory time period of 15 days within the first sale to control, but they would still accept filings within 30 days of the first sale.
   e. Address: Dept. of Banking & Finance
               Securities Bureau
               Commerce Court
               1230 "O" Street, Suite 400
               Lincoln, NE 68508
               Mailing Address: P.O. Box 95006
               Lincoln, NE 68509-5006
   f. Phone: 402-471-3445
   g. Website: http://www.ndbf.ne.gov

28. Nevada
   a. Authority: Sec. 90.532 (¶ 38,479)
   b. Filing Requirements:
       Form D (manually signed)
   c. Fee: $150 made payable to "Nevada Secretary of State"
   d. Renewal: Need to renew on an annual basis. Need to file another Form D and pay another $150 fee.
   e. Address: Office of the Secretary of State
                 Securities Division
                 555 E. Washington Ave., 5th Floor
                 Suite 5200
                 Las Vegas, NV 89101
   f. Phone: 702-486-2440
   g. Fax: 702-486-2452
   h. Website: http://nvsos.gov/securities
29. New Hampshire
   a. Authority: Sec. 421-B: 11, I-a(e) (¶ 39,171); Sec. 421-B: 31, I(h), (I I (¶ 39,194) [Atg-Se 703.01(¶ 39,482E)]
   b. Filing Requirements:
       Form D (manually signed)
       Form U-2
       The name of any registered broker-dealer who will effect transactions in New Hampshire
   c. Fee: $500 made payable to "State of New Hampshire"
   d. Note: Issuer needs to complete an Issuer Agent Registration. It must file a form U-4 with New Hampshire and a fee of $130. All documents including the U-4 must be filed within 15 days after the first sale of securities in Vermont.
   e. Renewal: $500 made payable to "State of New Hampshire" on or before the initial effective date
   f. Address: Department of State
                 Bureau of Securities Regulation
                 107 N. Main Street
                 State House, Room 204
                 Concord, NH 03301-4989
                 Mailing Address: State House, Room 204
                 Concord, NH 03301-4989
   g. Phone: 603-271-1463
   h. Fax: 603-271-7933
   i. Website: http://www.sos.nh.gov/securities
30. New Jersey
   a. Authority: Sec. 49: 3-60.1(b) (¶ 40,125A); Amended Policy Statement ¶ 40,691 O)
   b. Filing Requirements:
       Form D (manually signed)
       Form U-2 (manually signed)
   c. Fee: $250 payable to "New Jersey Bureau of Securities"
   d. Address: Department of Law and Public Safety
                 Bureau of Securities
                 Mailing Address: P.O. Box 47029
                 Newark, NJ 07101
                 Newark, NJ 07101
                 153 Halsey Street, 6th Floor
                 Newark, NJ 07102

    e. Phone: 973-504-3600
    f. Fax: 973-504-3601
    g. Website: http://www.njsecurities.gov
31. New Mexico
    a. Authority: Sec. 58-13B-24, Q (¶ 41,179); Rule 12 NMAC 11.4.11.2 (¶ 41,592)
    b. Filing Requirements:
    Form D (manually signed)
    Form U-2
    c. Fee: $350 made payable to "New Mexico Securities Division"
    d. Address: Regulation & Licensing Dept.
              Securities Division
              Toney Anaya Building
              2550 Cerrillos Road, Third Floor
              Santa Fe, NM 87505-7605
    e. Phone: 505-827-7140
    f. Fax: 505-984-0617
    g. Website: http://www.rld.state.nm.us/securities/index.html
32. New York
    a. Authority: Sec. 359-e (¶ 42,128); Sec. 359-f(2)(d) (¶ 42,131); Form 99, Notification Filing Pursuant to NSMIA (¶ 42,587)
    b. Filing Requirements:
    New York State Department of Law—Bureau of Investor Protection and Securities
    Form 99 (one manually signed, one copy)
    Form D (one copy)
    Form U-2 (one copy)
    Copy of offering documents as defined in Form 99
    c. Fee: $300 for aggregate offerings of $500,000 or less and $1,200
for aggregate offerings of more than $500,000 (effective for 4 years) made payable to
"New York State Department of Law"
    d. Timing: Must be filed and approved before any offer or sale
    e. Address: Office of Attorney General
              Bureau of Investor Protection and Securities
              120 Broadway, 23rd Floor
              New York, NY 10271
    f. Phone: 212-416-8222
    g. Fax: 212-416-8816
    h. Website: http://www.oag.state.ny.us/bureaus/investor_protection/about.html
    i. New York State Department of State Division of Corporations
        Form U-2 (one manually signed) with Certificate of Designation backer/cover
sheet.
        Fee: $35 made payable to "New York State Department of State"
    j. Address: New York State Department of State
              Division of Corporations
              One Commerce Plaza
              99 Washington Ave.
              Albany, NY 12231
    k. Bureau of Miscellaneous Records
        State Notice and Further State Notice
        Fee: $150 made payable to "New York State Department of State"
    l. Address: New York State Department of State
              Bureau of Miscellaneous Records
              One Commerce Plaza

99 Washington Ave.
Albany, NY 12231

m. Note: The New York State Department of Law will send a notification letter upon approval of the Form 99.

n. Filing Date: Once approved, the effective filing date is the day that the New York State Department of Law received the Form 99.

o. New Offering: If within the 4 year period, only need to file a Further State Notice. Do not need to file new Form 99 nor wait for notification letter to begin new offering of securities.

p. Renewal: If want to extend current offering or initiate a new offering after the expiration of the year period, only need to file a new Form 99 and wait for receipt of a new notification letter.

33. North Carolina
   a. Authority: Sec. 78A-31(b) (¶ 43,138); Rule .1211 (¶ 43,421)
   b. Filing Requirements:
      Form U-2
   c. Fee: $75 made payable to "North Carolina Secretary of State-Securities Division"
   d. Address: Department of the Secretary of State
      Securities Division
      2 S. Salisbury Street
      Raleigh, NC 27601-2903
      Mailing Address: P.O. Box 29622
      Raleigh, NC 27626-0622
   e. Phone: 919-733-3924
   f. Fax: 919-821-0818
   g. Website: http://www.secretary.state.nc.us/sec/

34. North Dakota
   a. Authority: Sec. 10-04-08.4(2) (¶ 44,113A)
   b. Filing Requirements:
      Form D (manually signed)
      Form U-2
   c. Fee: $100 made payable "Securities Commissioner of the State of North Dakota"
   d. Note: Filings are valid for only 12 months and after such time period has expired, the issuer must re-file all of the required documents and fee
   e. Address: North Dakota Securities Department
      State Capitol Building, 5th Floor
      600 East Boulevard Ave., Department 414
      Bismarck, ND 58505-0510
   f. Phone: 701-328-2910
   g. Fax: 701-328-2946
   h. Website: http://www.ndsecurities.com

35. Ohio
   a. Authority: Interpretive Opinion ¶ 45,737; §1707.03(X) (¶ 45,103(X)); Rule 1301: 6 3 03(F) (¶ 45,523)
   b. Filing Requirements:
      Form D (manually signed)
      Form U-2
   c. Fee: $100 made payable to "Ohio Division of Securities"

d. Note: Any commission, discount, or other remuneration for sales of securities in Ohio may be paid or given only to dealers or salespersons licensed under this chapter.

d. Note: Interpretive Opinion notes that NSMIA has no real effect on Ohio's Blue Sky laws because § 1707.03(Q) and Rule 1301: 6-3-03(B) already permit notice filing for "covered securities" as defined under § 18(b)(4)(D) of the Act.

e. Address: Ohio Department of Commerce
Division of Securities
77 South High Street, 22nd Floor
Columbus, OH 43215-6131

f. Phone: 614-644-7381

g. Fax: 614-466-3316

h. Website: http://www.com.ohio.gov/secu/

36. Oklahoma

a. Authority: Sec. 401(b)(10)(B) (¶ 46,151); Sec. 660: 10-11-50(b) (¶ 46,523); Sec. 412(12) (¶ 46,162)

b. Filing Requirements:
Form D (manually signed)
Form U-2
Form U-2A

c. Fee: $250 made payable to "Oklahoma Securities Commission"

d. Timing: Must be filed within 15 days of issuer's receipt of a subscription agreement from an investor.

e. Note: Cover letter should include (i) an undertaking that the issuer will furnish to the Administrator, upon written request, the information furnished by the issuer to the offerees, and (ii) the basic structure of the offering.

f. Address: Department of Securities
The First National Center
120 N. Robinson, Suite 860
Oklahoma City, OK 73102

g. Phone: 405-280-7700

h. Fax: 405-280-7742

i. Website: http://www.securities.ok.gov

37. Oregon

a. Authority: Sec. 59.049(3) (¶ 47,105AA); Rule 441-49-1021 (¶ 47,556N); Rule 441-49-1051 (¶ 47,556Q); Interim Statement of Policy ¶ 47,673

b. Filing Requirements:
Form D (manually signed)

c. Fee: $1 per $1,000 of the aggregate price of the securities that will be offered in Oregon on the first $100,000 or fraction of this amount, $0.50 per $1,000 on the next $200,000 or fraction of this amount and $25 per $100,000 for each additional $100,000 or fraction thereof, with minimum and maximum fees of $25 and $500, respectively, made payable to "State of Oregon."

d. Renewal: Issuers can renew the notice by submitting the same form, documents and fee before the anniversary date of the initial filing or previous renewal date. The renewal is good for 1 year.

e. Address: Dept. of Consumer & Business Services
Div. of Finance and Corporate Securities
350 Winter Street, N. E., Suite 410
Salem, OR 97310-3881

f. Phone: 503-378-4140

g. Fax: 503-947-7862

h. Website: http://www.dfcs.oregon.gov

38. Pennsylvania

 a. Authority: Sec. 211(b) (¶ 48,120A); Sec. 602(b.1)(vii) (¶ 98,162)

 b. Filing Requirements:

   Form D (manually signed)

 c. Fee: $500 made payable to "Commonwealth of Pennsylvania"

 d. Address: Securities Commission

         Eastgate Office Building

         1010 N. Seventh Street, 2nd Floor

         Harrisburg, PA 17102-1410

 e. Phone: 717-787-8061

 f. Fax: 717-783-5122

 g. Website: http://www.psc.state.pa.us/

39. Rhode Island

 a. Authority: Sec. 7-11-307(b) (¶ 50,122A)

 b. Filing Requirements:

   Form D

   Form U-2 (Appoint Director of Business Regulation of Rhode Island as agent for service of process)

 c. Fee: $300 made payable to "Department of Business Regulation Securities Division"

 d. Address: Dept. of Business Regulation

         Securities Division

         1511 Pontiac Avenue, John O. Pastore Complex

         Building 69-1

         Cranston, RI 02920

 e. Phone: 401-462-9527

 f. Fax: 401-462-9645

 g. Website: http://www.dbr.state.ri.us/

40. South Carolina

 a. Authority: Sec. 35-1-1100(b) (¶ 51,195A); Order 99001 (¶ 51,502)

 b. Filing Requirements:

   Form D (manually signed)

   Form U-2

 c. Fee: $300 made payable to "Attorney General of South Carolina"

 d. Address: Office of the S.C. Attorney General

         Securities Division

         Rembert C. Dennis Office Building

         1000 Assembly Street, Suite 501

         Columbia, SC 29201

         Mailing Address: P.O. Box 11549

         Columbia, SC 29211-1549

 e. Phone: 803-734-9916

 f. Fax: 803-734-3677

 g. Website: http://www.scattorneygeneral.org/securities/index.html

41. South Dakota

 a. Authority: Sec. 4731 A-307(b) (¶ 52,327)

 b. Filing Requirements:

   Form D

   Form U-2

    c. Fee: $200 made payable to "Division of Securities"
    d. Address: Division of Securities
               445 East Capitol Ave.
               Pierre, SD 57501
    e. Phone: 605-773-4823
    f. Fax: 605-773-5953
    g. Website: http://www.state.sd.us/drr2/reg/securities/

42. Tennessee
    a. Authority: Sec. 48-2-125 (¶ 54,179); Rule 0780-4-4-.12 (¶ 54,415B)
    b. Filing Requirements:
    Form D (manually signed)
    Form U-2
    (iii) Copy of issuer's prospectus
    c. Fee: 500 made payable to "Tennessee Department of Commerce and Insurance"
    d. Note: Cover letter should state date of first sale in Tennessee.
    e. Address: Dept. of Commerce and Insurance
               Division of Securities
               Davy Crockett Tower, Suite 680
               500 James Robertson Parkway
               Nashville, TN 37243-0575
    f. Phone: 615-741-2947
    g. Fax: 615-532-8375
    h. Website: http://www.tennessee.gov/commerce/securities

43. Texas
    a. Authority: Sec. 109.13(k) (¶ 55,563); Sec. 114.4(b)(1) (¶ 55,590S)
    b. Filing Requirements:
    Form D (manually signed)
    Form U-2
    c. Fee: 1/10 of 1% of the aggregate amount of securities described as being offered for sale, but in no event more than $500 made payable to "State Securities Board"
    d. Address: Texas State Securities Board
               208 East 10th, Street 5th Floor
               Austin, TX 78701
               Mailing Address: P.O. Box 13167
               Austin, TX 78711-3167
    e. Phone: 512-305-8300
    f. Fax: 512-305-8310
    g. Website: http://www.ssb.state.tx.us

44. Utah
    a. Authority: Sec. 61-1-15.5(2) (¶ 57,146A); R164-15-2 (¶ 57,415N); (¶ 57,171)
    b. Filing Requirements:
    Form D (manually signed)
    Form U-2
    c. Fee: $60 made payable to "Division of Securities"
    d. Address: Utah Department of Commerce
               Division of Securities
               160 East 300 South, 2nd Floor
               Salt Lake City, UT 84111
               Mailing Address: P.O. Box 146760

Salt Lake City, UT 84114-6760
  e. Phone: 801-530-6600
  f. Fax: 801-530-6980
  g. Website: http://www.securities.state.ut.us

45. Vermont
  a. Authority: Sec. 4209a(b),(d) (¶ 58,109a); Policy Statement No. 97-4-S (¶ 58,447) Sec. 4202a(9),(15) (¶ 58,102); Sec. 4213 (¶ 58,113); Sec. 4217 (¶ 58,116)
  b. Filing Requirements:
    Form D (manually signed)
    Form U-2
  c. Fee: $1 for each $1,000 of the aggregate amount of the offering, with minimum and maximum fees of $400 and $1,250 made payable to "Treasurer of State of Vermont"
  d. Note: Issuer needs to complete an Issuer Agent Registration. It must file a form U-4 with Vermont and pay a $45 fee. All documents including the U-4 must be filed within 15 days after the first sale of securities in Vermont.
  e. Renewal: Need to re-file all documents and pay fee every 12 months
  f. Address: Vermont Dept. of Banking, Insurance and Securities
    Securities Division
    89 Main Street, 3rd Floor
    Montpelier, VT 05620-3101
  g. Phone: 802-828-3420
  h. Fax: 802-828-2896
  i. Website: http://www.bishca.state.vt.us/securitiesdiv/securindex.htm

46. Virginia
  a. Authority: Rule 21 VAC 5-40-120 (¶ 60,440H)
  b. Filing Requirements:
    Form D (manually signed)
    Form U-2
  c. Fee: $250 made payable to "Treasurer of Virginia"
  d. Address: State Corporation Commission
    Division of Securities and Retail Franchising
    1300 E. Main St., 9th Floor
    Richmond, VA 23219
    Mailing Address: P.O. Box 1197
    Richmond, VA 23218
  e. Phone: 804-371-9051
  f. Fax: 804-371-9911
  g. Website: http://www.scc.virginia.gov/srf

47. Washington
  a. Authority: Sec. 21.20.327(2) (¶ 61,134A); WAC 460-44A-503(1)(a)(i), (a)(ii),(b),(c) (¶ 61,754); WAC 460-44A-506 (¶ 61,757)
  b. Filing Requirements:
    Form D (manually signed)
    Form U-2
  c. Fee: $300 made payable to "Washington State Treasurer"
  d. Address: Dept. of Financial Institutions
    Securities Division
    150 Israel Road SW

Tumwater, WA 98501
Mailing Address: P.O. Box 9033
Olympia, WA 98507-9033
  e. Phone: 360-902-8760
  f. Fax: 360-902-0524
  g. Website: http://www.dfi.wa.gov/sd

48. West Virginia
  a. Authority: Sec. 32-3-304a(c) (¶ 63,124A); Sec. 15.06 (¶ 63,496)
  b. Filing Requirements:
      Form D (manually signed)
      Form U-2
  c. Fee: $125 made payable to "State Auditor"
  d. Note: Cover letter should include (A) an undertaking by the issuer to promptly provide the Commissioner, upon written request, the information furnished to the offerees by the issuer, and (B) notification if commissions are being paid to any broker-dealer registered with West Virginia.
Must notify Commissioner no later than 30 days after the termination of the offering.
  e. Address: West Virginia State Auditor's Office
                   Securities Commission
                   Building 1, Room W-100
                   Charleston, WV 25305
  f. Phone: 304-558-2257
  g. Fax: 304-558-4211
  h. Website: http://www.wvsao.gov/securitiescommission

49. Wisconsin
  a. Authority: 551.29(2) (¶ 64,119); DFI-Sec. 2.04(2) (¶ 64,514)
  b. Filing Requirements:
      Form D (manually signed)
  c. Fee: $200 made payable to "Office of Commissioner of Securities"
  d. Address: Wisconsin Department of Financial Institutions
                   Securities Division
                   345 W. Washington Ave., 4th Floor
                   Madison, WI 53703
                   Mailing Address: P.O. Box 1768
                   Madison, WI 53701-1768
  e. Phone: 608-266-1064
  f. Fax: 608-264-7979
  g. Website: http://www.wdfi.org/fi/

50. Wyoming
  a. Authority: Sec. 17-4-132(b) (¶ 66,132); Sec.2 (¶ 66,457)
  b. Filing Requirements:
      Form D (manually signed)
      Form U-2
  c. Fee: $200 made payable to "Secretary of State"
  d. Address: Wyoming Secretary of State
                   Compliance Division, Securities Regulation
                   State Capitol Bldg., Room 109
                   200 W. 24th Street
                   Cheyenne, WY 82002-0020

e. Phone: 307-777-7370
f. Fax: 307-777-7640
g. Website: http://soswy.state.wy.us/compliance/secregistration.aspx

51. Washington DC
   a. Authority: CCH
   b. Filing Requirements:
       Form D (manually signed)
       Form U-2
   c. Fee: $250 made payable to "DC Treasurer"
   d. Address: Department of Insurance and Securities Regulation
                  810 First Street, N.E., Suite 701
                  Washington, DC 20002
   e. Phone: 202-442-7800
   f. Fax: 202-535-1196
   g. Website: http://www.disr.dc.gov

CHAPTER 11

Seed Financing and Angel Investors

11.1 Where Can a New Business Find Seed Financing?

Traditionally, "seed" level financing refers to a company's very first round of financing and is typically less than $1 million. "Early" financing rounds follow and are typically between $1 million and $5 million. "Growth" financing (a typical venture capital investment) is usually completed in rounds of $5 million to $20 million. A classic progression of development and funding is as follows:

- Seed: Funding for proof of concept, often funded by the entrepreneur, friends, and family;
- Development: Funding for product development and marketing, often funded by Angels (defined below);
- First Round/Series A: Funding to expand sales and establish commercial manufacturing, often funded by Angels and venture capitalists;
- Second Round/Series B: Growth capital from venture capitalists for companies producing revenue but not yet profitable;
- Third Round/Mezzanine: Funding from venture capitalists to fuel further growth for newly profitable companies; and
- Fourth Round/Bridge: Venture capital funding for the exit process.

However, the traditional lines between stages of development and rounds of financing have become more blurred as the costs of starting a business come down, through technology and development tools, and new approaches to investment take hold, such as highly organized Angel networks and exchanges for privately-held securities.

Many start-up enterprises need initial or "seed" financing before they have tested their concept with a strategic partner, launched a website or the beta version of a new software application, or assembled a complete management team. The founders may have overextended their personal resources and need to turn to others for additional start-up funding.

511

The best and most likely sources of investment funds at the very beginning of a company's life are usually family members and close friends—the "friends and family" of a start-up team who fund the seed round. These are the people who know the founders and believe in them—and are likely to invest a small sum in their endeavors, whatever the business plan may say and despite the large risks. However, anyone investing in an early stage business should have some investment experience. An investor needs to understand that he or she is investing in an untested business, in a private company with no track record and no revenues—and that there are significant risks involved in investing in any enterprise at this stage.

An "Angel" investor is typically a high net worth investor who meets the requirements of an "Accredited Investor" and is seeking investments in early stage companies. As investors, angels are preferable over investors without such qualifications, for several reasons. First, the angel is more likely to have contacts with other sources of financing or strategic relationships. Second, investors who are not accredited may later claim they did not receive the required written disclosure materials, that they did not fully understand the risks, and/or that they have a right to their money back (a "rescission"). Prospective investors may decline to invest if there are too many unsophisticated investors with equity in the company.

11.2 How Is a Small Business Valued for Purposes of Seed Round Financing?

A company may have a pretty good idea of how much money it needs in a seed round of financing, and it may be able to raise it from a group of a few close friends and family. But how does a company determine how much stock it should issue to them in exchange for their investment? And at what price? If the valuation is too high, investors will not receive a fair percentage of the company; but if it is too low, investors will receive an unfairly high percentage of the company. The pricing of the seed round will also influence stock option pricing and may affect pricing (or valuation) in later rounds.

Fair market value is defined as the price at which property will change hands between a willing buyer and a willing seller, neither party being under compulsion to buy or sell and both having reasonable knowledge of relevant facts. In other words, fair market value can be described in terms of a hypothetical, arms-length purchase price for cash between two parties who are not forced to participate in the transaction (as opposed to liquidation value), and who possess information relevant to negotiating a reasonable price on or before the date of the transaction. Where there is a public market for a security, of course, market forces determine fair market value. For privately held companies, there are three other recognized methods for valuing noncash property:

- Cost analysis (net asset value) approach
- Income analysis approach
- Market analysis approach

All three approaches are incorporated within the eight-point guidelines of Rev. Rul. 59-60, which originally was promulgated by the IRS to assist taxpayers in determining the fair market value of closely held companies or blocks of securities for estate and gift tax purposes, and has become the standard within the business valuation industry.

The best approach for an early stage company is to obtain guidelines for the valuation by comparison to similar companies, industry standards, and the company's financial projections.

Some seed investors may seek preferred stock. Most venture capitalists (VCs) don't participate in seed round financing; but when they do, they demand preferred stock with certain rights, preferences, and privileges. Examples include preferential dividend rights, information rights, possibly special voting rights, and preferential "liquidation rights"—the provisions that allow for a premium return to the preferred stock investors upon an early stage merger or sale of the company or similar "liquidation" transaction. Many Angels also want preferred stock when they invest in start-up companies. But companies typically prefer to delay the establishment of preferred stock with a complex assortment of designations until a later, more substantial financing round.

Sometimes a company can delay resolving the issue of valuation and the creation of a complex set of preferred stock provisions by issuing to seed round investors a convertible promissory note or a convertible debenture, rather than shares of stock. The note (or debenture) can be convertible into common or preferred stock at a later date, such as the closing of a subsequent round of financing, at a price determined in accordance with the later offering.

11.3 What Is an "Angel" Investor?

As a company gets into initial fund-raising efforts, it may find that it either needs, or prefers, to raise money from "Angel" investors. An Angel is generally a wealthy individual who invests in his or her individual capacity, typically in amounts of $100,000 or less for each investment. Angel investors often form groups, such as the Band of Angels in Silicon Valley and the Common Angels in the Boston area, and Keiretsu Forum, for purposes of screening suitable investments. Angel groups provide companies an opportunity to reach a number of prospective investors in a relatively efficient manner, but the financing terms of such groups have become more and more onerous, to the extent they may not be any more favorable than a traditional venture capital transaction.

11.4 What Do Angel Investors Typically Expect for Their Investment?

Angels will typically expect preferred stock. Sometimes, however, they will invest in convertible debt.

11.5 Is Preferred Stock Better Than
a Convertible Debenture?

Preferred stock is a widely accepted security for early stage financings. Relative to convertible notes, however, it has certain shortcomings.

One shortcoming is that issuing preferred stock to angel investors requires that a valuation be determined at a time when evaluation may not be favorably established by the company (e.g., pre-revenue). The company and the Angels may not be entirely comfortable with placing a valuation on the company at such a stage, for fear that it will turn out to be substantially different from the valuation established in the next round of financing, which is often with professional investors (i.e., venture capitalists).

Another drawback of preferred stock is that once a series of preferred stock has been issued, the company typically needs the consent of the preferred stockholders to approve future issuances of preferred stock, such as the issuance of stock to VCs. This can result in problems where prior investors disagree with the subsequent valuation or subsequent investors demand preferences that are superior to prior investors' rights.

11.6 What Is Preferred Stock?

Preferred stock gives the holder certain rights, preferences, and privileges relative to the holders of common stock and other series of preferred stock. The preferences associated with preferred stock purchased by angels are, with an increasingly sophisticated angel investor base, very similar to what VCs require, and they are likely to include at least the following provisions.

1. Liquidation Preference.

A liquidation preference gives the holder of the stock the right to receive a preferential distribution, typically equal to the original purchase price, upon liquidation or dissolution of the company before distributions are made to other stockholders. Once the preferred stockholders have gotten their original investment back, the common stockholders typically get whatever is remaining. The liquidation preference usually includes declared or accrued but unpaid dividends.

2. Dividends.

Some preferred stock may also have a dividend associated with it, which may be a fixed percentage return on the original purchase price for the stock every year—much the way interest works on a loan. This dividend may be cumulative (if it is not paid in one year, it will continue to build until it is eventually paid) or noncumulative (the dividend does not carry over from one year to the next if not declared by the company), and it may be automatic (the company must declare it every year or at some other predetermined time such as upon or before selling the company) or discretionary (the dividend is payable only if and when declared by the company's board of directors). This dividend may either capitalize (any unpaid amount is added to the total original purchase price against which the dividend rate is applied) or not. In the event of a liquidation or dissolution, preferred stockholders may also be entitled to get any dividends they are owed before the common stockholders are entitled to anything.

3. Conversion.

Preferred stock is typically convertible into common stock. Usually the conversion ratio at the time the preferred stock is issued is one to one—that is, the preferred stockholder may convert each share of preferred stock into one share of common stock at any time. There are normally provisions to adjust the conversion ratio in the event of a stock dividend, reorganization, or a subsequent sale of stock at a price below the price paid by the preferred stockholders, among others.

4. Anti-Dilution.

The conversion ratio is a key concept for understanding the mechanics of anti-dilution protection. The number of shares into which each share of preferred stock may be converted may change, upon the sale of stock at below the price per share paid by the preferred stockholder, into a number of shares equal to the original purchase price per share of the preferred stock divided by the "conversion price": The calculation of the conversion price depends on the nature of the anti-dilution protection.

The most favorable kind of anti-dilution protection for a preferred stockholder is called "full ratchet" protection. In full ratchet protection, the conversion price equals the most recent price per share of common stock sold by the company. To take a simple example, assume there were 300 shares of common stock held by the founders on January 1 and that the company sold 100 shares of preferred stock to investors at $1.00 per share on that date, convertible 1:1 into 100 shares of common stock, or 25 percent of all common stock. Then assume that 100 shares of common stock were subsequently sold at $0.50 per share, the new conversion ratio would be $1.00/$.50, or 2, and the preferred stock would then be convertible into 200 shares of common stock, which on an as if converted basis would equal 33 percent of all common stock. Typically full ratchet anti-dilution protection is applied without regard to how many shares of stock are subsequently sold at the lower price. In the above example, if just one share of common stock were sold at $0.50, the result would have been much more favorable to the preferred stockholder, who would still have the benefit of the 2:1 conversion ratio, which would mean that the preferred stockholder would then own stock convertible into 200 out of a total of 501 shares of common stock, or nearly 40 percent of the common stock. Full ratchet is no longer considered the customary form of anti-dilution protection.

A type of anti-dilution protection more favorable to the company, "weighted average" protection, has become the standard. Weighted average protection gives effect to the dilutive effect that the subsequent issuance has, and typically results in a much less dramatic change in the conversion ratio. To take a simple example, assume there were 300 shares of common stock held by the founders on January 1 and that the company sold 100 shares of preferred stock to investors at $1.00 per share on that date, convertible 1:1 into 100 shares of common stock, or 25 percent of all common stock. Then assume that 100 shares of common stock were subsequently sold at $0.50 per share; the new conversion ratio would be $1.00/[(300 + 100)/(300 + 200)]$, or 1.2, and the preferred stock would then be convertible into 120 shares of common stock, which on an as if converted basis would equal 24 percent of all common stock.

Often times preferred stockholders have one of two options upon the sale of the company in the form of an asset sale or a stock merger. The preferred stockholder may either opt to treat such sale or merger as a liquidation, and get the liquidation preference back before the distribution of the proceeds to any of the common stockholders, or the preferred stockholder may convert to common stock before the sale and be entitled to receive what the common stockholders are getting. A preferred stockholder has to decide which of these two options makes the most economic sense. Occasionally a preferred stockholder will be entitled to both the liquidation preference and the consideration that common stockholders are entitled to. This is sometimes referred to as "participating preferred," and more disparagingly as the "double dip": Most of the time, preferred stock is nonparticipating. To the extent preferred stock participates, there is typically a point at which the return is high enough—that is, 5 ×—that the participating feature essentially falls away.

11.7 What Are the Basic Terms of a Convertible Debenture?

Early stage companies often issue notes that convert into whatever form of equity the company issues in a subsequent offering, presumably to VCs. The single most attractive benefit of this practice is that the valuation of the company can be deferred until the VCs, who are professional investors, make their investment. The tax consequences of an issuance of convertible debt may be more complicated than those associated with preferred stock financings, and they should be considered carefully by the company and the investors.

The basic terms of a convertible note (or "debenture") offering are described in the following subsections.

1. Debt.

The security sold in a convertible debt offering is a promissory note that converts into common or preferred stock at some future time, either automatically or at the option of the holder.

2. Convertible into Equity.

The intent of the company and investors is usually that the stock into which the note will convert will be whatever is negotiated between the company and the VCs in the first venture financing—typically Series A preferred stock. The debt often converts at some discount—usually in the 15 to 30 percent range. Companies occasionally try to come up with complicated discount matrixes where the discount may vary as a function of the VC valuation (i.e., the higher the valuation, the steeper the discount in order to align the interests of the note holders and the company) and of the time elapsed from the sale of the convertible note until the closing of the VC round. This approach is based on the theory that a longer interval justifies a steeper discount, because the venture must have been much riskier at the earlier time. These complicated structures can be difficult to explain, confusing to investors, and should probably be avoided. Convertible debt financings seem to work best when they are kept clean and simple.

3. Contingency Provisions.

In the event that there is no subsequent VC financing within a certain period of time, the notes may convert (usually automatically, but sometimes at the option of either the company or the investors) into a predefined class of preferred stock, at a predetermined pre-money valuation. This type of default conversion allows the company to remove the debt from its books.

11.8 Sample Documents and Checklists.

This section includes the following forms:

- Term Sheet—Series A (Form 11 A)
- Term Sheet—Series B (Form 11 B)
- Term Sheet—Convertible Debenture (Form 11 C)
- Placement Agent Agreement (Form 11 D)
- Warrant for Placement Agent Agreement (Form 11 E)
- Convertible Debenture (Form 11 F)
- Purchase Agreement—Series A (Form 11 G)
- Convertible Note Subscription Agreement with Form of Convertible Note (Form 11 H)

Form 11 A: Term Sheet—Series A

Note: The following sample term sheets are provided to illustrate how widely term sheets vary. The first term sheet is very simple—probably too simple, in fact. The second term sheet (Form 11 B) is pretty detailed and is a typical investment banker term sheet. Your client's term sheet should outline the rights, benefits, restrictions, and so forth of the equity being offered; it should also provide valuation and capital structure information.

**** Inc.
Term Sheet

$1,000,000

Series A Preferred Stock

The following is an outline of the proposed terms and conditions of the offering:

A. 1,00,000 shares of Series A Preferred Stock to be offered to Accredited Investors at $1.00 per share.

B. The Series A Preferred will represent 25% of the company.

C. The rights and privileges of the Series A Preferred Stock are summarized as follows:

- **The rights and privileges of the Series A Preferred Stock are summarized as follows:**
- **The same voting rights as Common Stock.**
- **A liquidation preference of $1.00 per share.**
- **Convertible into Common Stock at any time at the option of the holder on a share-for-share basis.**

D. 3,000,000 shares of Common Stock have been issued or reserved for founders.

E. The total number of shares outstanding following $1,000,000 investment: 4,000,000.

Prospective investors must review and complete a Subscription Agreement and comply with the payment provisions contained therein to make an investment in the company.

Form 11 B: Term Sheet—Series B

CONFIDENTIAL TERM SHEET
[Date]

**** INC.
SERIES B CONVERTIBLE PREFERRED STOCK OFFERING

Issuer: ****, Inc. (the "Company"). All terms below are post a 2:1 stock split that has been approved by the Board of Directors of the Company.

Offering: Series B Convertible Preferred Stock (the "Series B Preferred").

Offering Size: The Company will issue Series B Preferred generating gross proceeds of no less than $_____ and no more than $_____. Once the Company has received $_____ into the escrow account pursuant to executed subscription agreements, the Escrow Agent may release such funds to the Company. Thereafter, funds may be released directly to the Company for immediate use without escrow.

Price per Share: Each share of Series B Preferred will be sold for $_____ per share (the "Purchase Price").

Shares Issued: The Company will issue no fewer than _____ shares of Series B Preferred, and no more than _____ shares, in the Offering.

Existing Capitalization: The Company's current capitalization, assuming the consummation of the 2:1 stock split approved by the board of directors of the Company but prior to the issuance of the Series B Preferred, is as follows:

Common Shares outstanding: _____

Series A Preferred outstanding (1): _____

Warrants to purchase common: _____

    TOTAL (2): _____

(1) Each share of Series A Preferred is convertible into one share of common stock.

(2) Total excludes stock options issued to management and employees of the Company. The Company has reserved _____ shares of common stock for issuance under its Stock Option/Stock Issuance plan, and has issued _____ options under such plan. It is also expected that the number of shares reserved for employee stock options will be increased to support continued growth of the Company's staff.

Implied Pre-Money Valuation:	$_____, excluding the employee option pool.
Ranking:	The Series B Preferred will be pari passu in liquidation preference with the Company's Series A Convertible Preferred Stock (the "Series A Preferred"), and will rank senior to the Company's common stock.
Dividends:	The holders of Series B Preferred shall be entitled to participate pro rata in any dividends paid on the Common Stock on an as-converted basis.
Conversion:	The holders of the Series B Preferred shall have the right to convert the Series B Preferred, at any time, into shares of Common Stock. The initial conversion rate shall be 1:1, subject to adjustment as provided below.
Automatic Conversion:	The Series B Preferred shall be automatically converted into Common Stock, at the then-applicable conversion price, (i) in the event that the holders of at least a majority of the outstanding Series B Preferred consent to such conversion or (ii) upon the closing of an underwritten public offering of shares of Common Stock of the Company at a per share price of not less than $10.00 per share (as adjusted for stock splits, dividends, etc.) generating gross proceeds of not less than $25 million (before deduction of underwriters' commissions and expenses) (a "Qualified IPO").
Anti-Dilution Provisions:	The conversion price of the Series B Preferred will be subject to: (1) a weighted average adjustment to reduce dilution in the event that the Company issues additional equity securities (other than shares issued to employee as incentive compensation) at a purchase price less than the then-applicable conversion price; (2) a 100% adjustment in the event that the Company issues any Series B Preferred, or any financing substantially similar to the A-2 Preferred if less than the maximum gross proceeds of Series B Preferred is issued, at a price lower than the Purchase Price. The conversion price will also be subject to proportional adjustment for stock splits, stock dividends, recapitalizations, etc., or if the Company's stock split is not consummated before the Series B Preferred is issued.
Voting:	The Series B Preferred will vote on an as-converted basis on all matters brought before the common shareholders of the Company.
Protective Provisions:	As long as any shares of Series B Preferred remain outstanding, consent of the holders of at least a majority of the Series B Preferred shall be required for any action that (i) alters or changes the rights, preferences or privileges of the Series B Preferred vis a vis those of any other class of capital stock, (ii) results in any merger, other corporate reorganization, sale of control, or any transaction in which all or

substantially all of the assets of the Company are sold at a price lower than the post-money valuation, or (iii) amends or waives any provision of the Company's Articles of Incorporation or Bylaws relative to the Series B Preferred.

Information Rights: So long as an Investor continues to hold shares of Series B Preferred or Common Stock issued upon conversion of the Series B Preferred, the Company shall deliver to the Investor audited annual and unaudited quarterly financial statements. Each Investor shall also be entitled to standard inspection and visitation rights. These provisions shall terminate upon a Qualified IPO.

Registration Rights: Demand Rights: If Investors holding more than 50% of the outstanding shares of Series B Preferred, including Common Stock issued on conversion of Series B Preferred ("Registrable Securities"), request that the Company file a Registration Statement, the Company will use its best efforts to cause such shares to be registered; provided, however, that the Company shall not be obligated to effect any such registration prior to 180 days after a Qualified IPO. The Company shall have the right to delay such registration under certain circumstances for one period not in excess of one hundred twenty (120) days in any twelve (12) month period.

The Company shall not be obligated to effect more than one (1) registration under these demand right provisions.

Company Registration: The Investors shall be entitled to "piggy-back" registration rights on all registrations of the Company or on any demand registrations of any other investor subject to the right, however, of the Company and its underwriters to reduce the number of shares proposed to be registered pro rata in view of market conditions. If the Investors are so limited, however, no party other than the Company or the Investor, if any, invoking the demand registration shall have superior rights to sell shares in such registration.

S-3 Rights: Investors shall be entitled to unlimited demand registrations on Form S-3 (if available to the Company) so long as such registered offerings are not less than $500,000.

Expenses: The Company shall bear the registration expenses (exclusive of underwriting discounts and commissions) of all such demands, piggy-backs, and S-3 registrations (including the expense of one special counsel of the selling shareholders not to exceed $20,000 per offering).

Lock-Up Provision: Each Investor agrees that it will not sell its shares for a specified period (not to exceed 180 days) following the effective date of the Company's initial public offering; provided that all officers, directors, and other 1% shareholders are similarly bound.

<u>Sales under Rule 144</u>. The Company shall not be obligated to register the Registrable Securities if the Investors requesting such registration could sell their shares under Rule 144 within 90 days of the time of making such request.

Right to Participate in Future Offerings: Investors shall have the right in the event the Company proposes to offer equity securities to any person (other than to employees or securities issued pursuant to acquisitions or to a strategic investor) to purchase their pro rata portion of such securities. Any securities not subscribed for by an eligible Investor may be reallocated among the other eligible Investors, and, if not purchased by an eligible Investor, may be sold to the other investors. Such participation right will terminate upon a Qualified IPO, and will not include the equity securities offered in such Qualified IPO.

Right of Transfer: Each Investor shall have the right to transfer shares of its Series B Preferred to entities affiliated with such Investor, provided that all rights and obligations of both the Company and the Investor shall inure to the transferees.

Distribution: The Series B Preferred will be offered by the Company directly to accredited investors only, in one or more offerings exempt from registration under the Securities Act.

Company Counsel: [Name and contact information.]

Form 11 C: Term Sheet—Convertible Debenture

****, Inc.
8.5% CONVERTIBLE DEBENTURES
Term Sheet
[Date]

- Maximum Offering - $500,000

- 3 Years to Maturity

- Simple Interest at the Rate of 8.5%

- Principal and Interest Convertible in Whole or in Part into Common Stock

- Conversion Price is 80% of the Offering Price in the Next Round of Financing

- Warrants to Purchase Shares:

    a) if holder converts to stock, warrants to purchase additional shares at $0.10 per share, with number of warrants equal to 1/3 of the dollar amount of the debenture ($30,000 debenture = 10,000 warrants); or

    b) if holder does not convert, warrants to purchase shares at price set in next round of financing, or $3.00 per share if no financing has occurred, with number of warrants equal to 1/5 of the dollar amount of the debenture ($30,000 debenture = 6,000 warrants).

- Next Round of Financing to Raise a Minimum of $1,000,000

- Conversion Price to be Adjusted for Cash or Stock Dividends or Reorganization

- Debenture to be Subordinated to all Other Indebtedness of the Company

Form 11 D: Placement Agent Agreement

****, Inc.
[series and class of stock] Stock
$__.00 per Share

PLACEMENT AGENT AGREEMENT

[Date]

[Name and]
[Address of Placement Agent]

Dear Sirs:

****, Inc. is a _____ corporation (the "Company"), engaged in the business of _____. The Company has determined to raise funds through a private placement offering of its equity securities to qualified investors (the "Offering") in order to provide financing for its expansion and ongoing operations.

The Company proposes to offer and sell up to _____ shares of _____ Stock (the "Shares") to selected accredited investors. The Offering is described in the Company's Confidential Private Placement Memorandum, dated as of the ___ day of _____, 20___ (as the same may be amended or supplemented, the "Memorandum"), copies of which have been delivered to you. It is intended that the offer and sale of the Shares will be made in a manner so as to comply with exemptions from registration available under the Private Placement Exemptions, as such term is defined herein. Certain terms used in this Agreement are defined in Section 0.

Subject to the terms and conditions and on the basis of the representations and warranties contained herein, the Company and you hereby confirm their and your respective agreements as follows:

1. Appointment as Placement Agent; Compensation; Closing.

(a) Authorization of Placement Agent. The Company hereby appoints you the exclusive agent of the Company (the "Placement Agent") during the Selling Period (and any Extended Selling Period) to offer and sell the Shares on the terms and subject to the conditions set forth in this Agreement and in the Memorandum; and you accept such appointment to offer and sell the Shares during the Selling Period. You have agreed to offer the first _____ Shares on a "best efforts—all or none" basis and the remaining _____ Shares on a "best efforts" basis.

(b) Compensation. As compensation for your services as Placement Agent hereunder, the Company agrees to pay to you a placement fee (the "Placement Fee") in the amount of ten percent (10.0%) of the offering price of the Shares sold. You shall also be paid a nonaccountable expense reimbursement ("Expense Reimbursement") equal to one percent (1.0%) of the offering price of the Shares sold. In addition, you shall be issued warrants (the "Placement Agent's Warrants") to purchase ten percent

(10.0%) of the number of Shares sold in the Offering at an exercise price equal to the Offering Price per Share. The Placement Agent's Warrants shall be exercisable at any time until five (5) years after the date of final closing of the Offering and containing registration rights substantially the same as those applicable to the Shares. The form of Placement Agent's Warrant is set forth in *Exhibit A* attached hereto and made a part hereof. The Placement Fee and Expense Reimbursement will be due and payable to you at the Initial Closing and at each Subsequent Closing referred to in Section 0 hereof. It is understood that for the purposes hereof, no Shares shall be considered to have been sold by you until the purchaser thereof shall be accepted by the Company. You have also agreed that only for Share sales made to certain "family and friends" as specifically detailed in *Exhibit B* you shall receive a Placement Fee of 5% and warrants to purchase 5% of those Shares sold to "family and friends."

The compensation payable under this Section 0 shall be paid by the Company to you with respect to any offering of equity securities that is closed during the term of this Agreement or in the eighteen (18) month period following any termination of this Agreement; provided, however, that the Company shall not be obligated to pay Placement Agent pursuant to this Section 0 after any termination of this Agreement if such termination is initiated by Placement Agent; and provided further, that in no event shall the Company be obligated to pay Placement Agent pursuant to this Section 0 with respect to any Offering that closes more than three (3) years after the execution of this Agreement.

(c) Selling Period and Number of Shares Offered. The Company is attempting to sell up to a total of _____ Shares at a purchase price of _____ per Share (the "Offering Price"), for a maximum offering amount of $_____. The Offering is intended to run from the date hereof until _____, 20__ (the "Closing Date"; the period from the date of this Agreement until the Closing date to be referred to as the "Selling Period"), unless extended to a date not later than _____, 20___ (the "Extended Selling Period"), upon at least five (5) days written notice to you. If acceptable subscriptions to purchase at least _____ Shares (the "Minimum Offering Amount") are not received by the Closing Date, the Selling Period shall terminate. If acceptable subscriptions to purchase at least the Minimum Offering Amount are received by Closing Date, an initial closing shall be held as provided in Section 0.

(d) Closing. All funds received from purchasers or prospective purchasers of Shares shall be made payable to the order of _____ Escrow Company, for the benefit of _____, and shall be deposited in an escrow account established at _____Escrow Company, located at _____, described in *Exhibit C* and not released to the Company until the date of the closing of the sale of the Shares and unless and until the conditions set forth in Section 0 shall have been satisfied, and you deliver to us a written confirmation to such effect (the "Initial Closing"). Provided acceptable subscriptions are received for at least the Minimum Offering Amount, the Initial Closing shall be held at your offices no later than five (5) business days after the request of either you or the Company to close on the Shares subscribed for to as of that date, or on such other date and at such other place as the parties hereto may agree. If shares aggregating less than the Minimum Offering Amount are purchased by the Closing Date, you shall have until the end of the Selling Period, including any extension, if any, to sell the remaining unsold Shares (the "Unsold Shares"). All funds received from purchasers or prospective purchasers of the Unsold Shares shall be deposited in the escrow account established pursuant to Section 0 hereof and not released to the Company unless and until the conditions set forth in Section 0 shall have been satisfied at a closing for the Unsold Shares (the "Subsequent Closings"). After the Initial Closing, the Company may request a Subsequent Closing each time acceptable subscriptions for at least ten percent (10%) of the Unsold Shares have been received. Subsequent Closings shall be held at your offices no later than on the fifth (5th) business day following each such request by the Company after the end of the Selling Period, or on such other dates and at such other places as the parties hereto may agree. (As used herein, the term "Closing" will refer to both the Initial Closing and the Subsequent Closings, unless the context otherwise requires.)

2. Representations and Warranties of the Company.

The Company represents, warrants and agrees with you that as of the date hereof and as of the date of each Closing:

(a) Regulation D Exemption. The offer, offer for sale, and sale of the Shares have not been and will not be registered with the Securities and Exchange Commission (the "Commission"). The Shares will be offered, offered for sale and sold pursuant to the exemption from the registration requirements of Section 5 of the Securities Act provided by Section 4(2) and Regulation D thereof ("Regulation D"). Assuming the offer, offer for sale and sale of the Shares is in compliance with the terms of the Memorandum, the compliance by you with the Securities Act's requirements of broker-dealers participating in a private placement offering, and subject to the performance of your obligations hereunder, the Company will have complied with Section 4(2) and Regulation D of the Securities Act and with all state securities laws and regulations applicable to them in connection with the offering and sale of the Shares.

(b) Memorandum. The Company will have prepared and delivered to you the Memorandum describing the Offering and the Shares. A Subscription Agreement delivered with the Memorandum will contain the information required to be delivered to offerees to establish an exemption under Section 4(2) or Regulation D of the Securities Act and will conform to the requirements of the Securities Act. The Memorandum, when prepared and at the Closing Date, will not contain an untrue statement of any material fact or omit to state a material fact necessary in order to make the statements therein, in light of the circumstances under which they were made, not misleading.

(c) No Defaults. The Company is not in default in the performance of any obligation, agreement or condition contained in any debenture, note or other evidence of indebtedness or any indenture or loan agreement of the Company, other than as set forth in the Memorandum. The execution and delivery of this Agreement and the consummation of the transactions herein contemplated, and compliance with the terms of this Agreement will not conflict with or result in a breach of any of the terms, conditions or provisions of, or constitute a default under, the articles of incorporation or bylaws of the Company, or any note, indenture, mortgage, deed of trust, or other agreement or instrument to which the Company is a party or by which it or any of its property is bound, or any existing law, order, rule, regulation, writ, injunction, or decree or any government, governmental instrumentality, agency or body, arbitrator, tribunal or court, domestic or foreign, having jurisdiction over the Company or its property. The consent, approval, authorization, or order of any court or governmental instrumentality, agency or body is not required for the consummation of the transactions herein contemplated except such as may be required under the Securities Act or under the securities laws of any state or jurisdiction.

(d) Organization and Standing. The Company is duly organized, validly existing and qualified in all jurisdictions in which it conducts business, and has all requisite authority to own its property and conduct its business as described in the Memorandum.

(e) Shares Authorized. Subject to the performance of your obligations hereunder, the Shares, upon the payment therefor and issuance thereof, will conform to all statements in relation thereto contained in the Memorandum, will have the rights set forth in the Company's charter documents and will be duly and validly authorized and issued, fully paid and non-assessable, except as set forth in Memorandum, and will subject the holders thereof to no liability as such holders except as set forth in the Memorandum; and the Company, upon such issuance, will have an authorized and issued capitalization as set forth in the Memorandum.

(f) Investment Company. The Company will not be an "investment company" as such term is defined in the Investment Company Act of 1940, as amended, or the General Rules and Regulations thereunder.

(g) Further Information. The Company shall provide to you and each offeree, and their representatives, if any, such information, documents, and instruments as the Company believes is reasonably requested.

(h) Prior/Concurrent Sales. The Company or any of its predecessors or affiliates:

(i) Have not offered, offered to sell, or sold any of the Shares or interest in the Company or any other securities, the offer, offer to sell, or sale of which would be "integrated" under the standards of existing published rules and regulations under the Securities Act with the offer, offer to sell or sale of the Shares proposed to be made by you pursuant hereto.

(ii) Shall not offer, offer to sell, or sell any Shares or interest in the Company or other securities to the extent such offer, offer to sell, or sale, renders unavailable the exemptions from registration and qualification requirements of applicable federal and state securities laws relied upon with respect to the offering and sale of the Shares contemplated by this Agreement.

(i) No Additional Liabilities. Since the respective dates as of which information is given in the Memorandum, the Company has not, nor during the period of the Offering will it have, incurred any material liabilities or obligations contingent or otherwise on behalf of the Company, except in the ordinary course of business, and there has not been, and during the period of the Offering there will not have been, any material adverse change in the condition of the Company, financial or otherwise.

(j) Finder. No person has acted as a finder in connection with the transactions contemplated herein, and the Company will indemnify the Placement Agent with respect to any claim for finder's fees in connection herewith. The Company further represents that it has no management or financial consulting or advisory agreement with anyone except as set forth in the Memorandum. The Company additionally represents that no officer, director, or 5% or greater shareholder of the Company is, directly or indirectly, associated with a FINRA member broker-dealer, other than such persons as the Company has advised the Placement Agent in writing are so associated.

3. Representations and Warranties of Placement Agent.

You hereby represent and warrant that as of the date hereof and as of the date of each Closing:

(a) Authority. You have the authority to enter into and perform this Agreement; the execution and delivery of this Agreement by you has been duly and validly authorized by all necessary corporate action; and when executed and delivered, this

Agreement will be your valid and binding obligation enforceable in accordance with its terms.

(b) Registered Broker-Dealer. You are (i) registered as a broker-dealer under the Securities Exchange Act of 1934, as amended (the "Exchange Act"), and no proceeding has been initiated to revoke such registration, (ii) registered as a broker-dealer under the securities or blue sky laws of each jurisdiction in which you offer the Shares, except where such registration is not required or where the failure to so register would not reasonably be expected to materially and adversely affect your ability to perform your obligations hereunder, and (iii) a member in good standing of FINRA.

(c) Ability to Act as Agent. There is not now pending or, to the knowledge of the Placement Agent, threatened against the Placement Agent any action or proceeding of which the Placement Agent has been advised, either in any court of competent jurisdiction, before FINRA, the Securities and Exchange Commission or any state securities commission concerning the Placement Agent's activities as a broker or dealer, nor has the Placement Agent been named as a "cause" in any action or proceeding, any of which may be expected to have a material adverse effect upon the Placement Agent's ability to act as agent to the Company as contemplated herein.

4. Covenants of the Company.

(a) Securities Compliance. The Company will in good faith use its best efforts to conduct the offering of the Shares in a manner intended to comply with the Private Placement Exemptions and Rule 506 of Regulation D, in particular. Subject to the provisions hereof, the Company will make available to you, at its own expense, such number of copies of the Memorandum and any Selling Material as you may reasonably request. In addition, for a period of six months after the Closing, the Company will not take any action if the result of such action would be the disqualification of the sale of the Shares under any Private Placement Exemption, except with your permission.

(b) Cooperation on Securities Matters. The Company will cooperate with you and your counsel in registering or qualifying the Shares for offering and sale or in exempting the Shares from registration or qualification under the securities laws of such jurisdictions as you may reasonably request, and which the Company shall approve, provided that such approval shall not be unreasonably withheld, and will furnish all such information and documents as may be reasonably necessary for such purpose. The Company undertakes as directed in writing by you or your counsel to file all reports required to be filed subsequent to the completion of the Offering and otherwise to continue to comply with the securities law of each jurisdiction in which the Company has sold or has offered to sell Shares, except that the Company shall not for any purpose be required to execute a general consent to service of process or to qualify to do business as a foreign corporation in any jurisdiction wherein it is not so qualified.

(c) Blue Sky Memorandum. As a condition of Closing, the Company will qualify the Shares, or such part thereof as requested by the Placement Agent, for offer and sale and will take whatever action necessary in connection with filing or maintaining any appropriate exemption from such qualification or registration under the applicable laws of such states as may be selected by the Placement Agent and agreed to by the Company, and continue such qualifications and exemption in effect so long as required for the purposes of the offer and sale of the Shares. The Company will cause a Blue Sky Memorandum to be prepared by counsel to the Company to be delivered to the Placement Agent on the date of this Agreement and the dates of any Subsequent

Closings. The Blue Sky Memorandum shall set forth those states or jurisdictions wherein the Shares have been registered or otherwise qualified for sale or shall specify the exemption from registration that may be relied on for the offer and sale of the Shares. The Blue Sky Memorandum will be amended promptly as necessary. The Company agrees that the Placement Agent and Selected Dealers, if any, may rely on the Blue Sky Memorandum in connection with the offer and sale of the Shares.

(d) Notification of Changes. The Company will promptly advise the Placement Agent, and will confirm such advice in writing, upon the happening of any event which, in the judgment of the Company, makes any material statement in the Memorandum untrue or which requires the making of any changes in the Memorandum in order to make the statements therein not misleading, and upon the refusal of any state securities administrator or similar official to qualify, or the suspension of the qualification of the Shares for offering or sale in any jurisdiction where the Shares are not exempt from qualification or registration, or of the institution of any proceedings for the suspension of any exemption or for any other purposes. The Company will use every reasonable effort to prevent any such refusal to qualify or any such suspension and to obtain as soon as possible the lifting of any such order, the reversal of any such refusal, and the termination of any such suspension.

(e) Supplements to Memorandum and Selling Material. The Company will comply with all requirements imposed upon it by the rules and regulations of the Securities and Exchange Commission, and by all applicable state securities laws and regulations, to permit the continuance of offers and sales of the Shares, in accordance with the provisions hereof and of the Memorandum. If during the Offering any event occurs or any event known to the Company relating to or affecting the Company shall occur as a result of which the Memorandum as then amended or supplemented would include an untrue statement of a material fact, or omits to state any material fact necessary to make the statements therein, in light of the circumstances under which they were made, not misleading, or if it is necessary at any time after the Offering Date to amend or supplement the Memorandum to comply with the Securities Act, following notice to the Placement Agent as described in Section 0, the Company will prepare such further amendment to the Memorandum or supplemental or amended Memorandum or Memoranda as may be required and furnish and deliver to the Placement Agent, all at the cost of the Company, a reasonable number of copies of the supplemental or amended Memorandum which as so amended or supplemented will not contain any untrue statement of a material fact or omit to state any material fact necessary in order to make the Memorandum not misleading in the light of the circumstances existing at the time it is delivered.

(f) Furnishing of Information. The Company stands ready to furnish to you and to any offeree (and his purchaser representative, if any) any information, including, without limitation, the information in the Memorandum, reasonably necessary for the offeree to make an informed investment decision.

(g) Application of Proceeds. The Company will apply the net proceeds from the offering received by it in the manner set forth under the "Use of Proceeds" section in the Memorandum.

(h) Placement Agent's Warrants. As of the Closing Date, the Company shall have reserved for issuance a number of shares of its Common Stock sufficient for issuance upon exercise of the Placement Agent's Warrants.

5. Covenants of Placement Agent.

(a) Securities Compliance. You will in good faith use your commercially reasonable best efforts to conduct the offering of Shares in a manner intended to comply with the Private Placement Exemptions and Rule 506 of Regulation D in particular. Specifically, you agree that:

You will not knowingly engage in any form of General Solicitation in connection with the offering of the Shares. You will not offer any Shares to any person unless, immediately prior to making such offer, you reasonably believe that (i) such person, either alone or with a purchaser representative, has such knowledge and experience in financial and business matters that he is capable of evaluating the risks and merits of such investment; and (ii) such person meets such other investor suitability standards as are specified in the Memorandum. You shall make no offers other than through your registered representative(s) licensed in the jurisdiction in which such offer is made, except where such licensing is not required or where the failure to be so licensed would not reasonably be expected to materially and adversely effect your ability to perform your obligations hereunder. You shall maintain a record of all offers and the jurisdictions in which made and will maintain information obtained by you as to the suitability of subscribers. You will forward the completed originals of all subscription documents and a copy of the record of offers to the Company or its counsel for review. You shall make offers and sales only in those jurisdictions in which you have been advised by the Company that offers and sales may be made.

(b) Notice of Facts Affecting Memorandum. In the event that you learn of any circumstances or facts which you believe would make the Memorandum or any Selling Material inaccurate or misleading as to any material facts, you will promptly bring such circumstances or facts to the attention of the Company.

(c) Your Offers. Neither you nor any officer or other person employed by you will provide any information or make any representations to the offerees of the Shares, other than such information and representations as are either contained in the Memorandum or are not otherwise inconsistent with information set forth in the Memorandum and such information and representations are otherwise true and accurate in all material respects.

(d) Exchange Act Obligations. You shall:

(i) take all actions necessary to fulfill your duties as described in Rule 15c2-4 under the Exchange Act, as applicable, which duties relate to the transmission or maintenance of funds received from potential participants; and

(ii) notify the Company if, prior to any Closing, cleared funds have not been received into the escrow account established pursuant to Section 0 hereof sufficient to satisfy the amount being closed upon.

6. Conditions to Closing.

The right of the Company to obtain the amounts received by you, as agent, from the purchasers of the Shares shall be subject to the satisfaction at the time of any Closing of each of the following conditions:

(a) You shall have received a certificate or certificates of the Company directed to you and dated the date of the Closing to the effect that:

(i) Each of the representations and warranties of the Company contained in this Agreement is true and correct as of that date;

(ii) Each of the covenants and agreements of the Company contained in this Agreement has been fully performed to the extent that performance of any such covenant and agreement is required on or prior to that date; and

(iii) Without having made special investigation, and based upon the information provided to it by subscribers in the Offering, the Company believes that each person to whom an offer or sale was made, at the time of said offer or sale, met the investor suitability standards set forth in the Memorandum.

(b) You shall have delivered to the Company a certificate or certificates directed to it dated the date of the Closing to the effect that:

(i) Each of your representations and warranties contained in this Agreement is true and correct as of that date;

(ii) Each of your covenants and agreements contained in this Agreement has been duly performed to the extent that performance of any such covenant or agreement is required on or prior to that date;

(iii) Based upon the information provided to you by subscribers in the Offering, you reasonably believe that each person to whom an offer or sale was made, at the time of said offer or sale, met the investor suitability standards set forth in the Memorandum; and

(iv) There shall have been executed and timely filed with the Securities and Exchange Commission a Notice of Sales on Form D (or such form as shall be adopted from time to time as a successor to Form D), in form and substance reasonably satisfactory to your counsel.

(c) All proceedings and documents in connection with the transactions contemplated by the Memorandum and this Agreement shall be reasonably satisfactory in form and substance to you and your counsel, and you and your counsel shall have received all such certificates and other documents in connection with such transactions as you or they may reasonably request, including, but not limited to, any certificates which your counsel may reasonably request in order to render opinions and memoranda to you or any third persons.

(d) The Company shall have received the required approval of the Offering by any and all approving or governing agency.

7. Indemnification and Contribution.

(a) Indemnification by the Company. The Company agrees to indemnify and hold harmless you, your officers, directors, employees and agents and each person, if any, who controls any of such persons within the meaning of the Applicable Securities Laws (an "Indemnified Party" for purposes of this Section 0) against any losses, claims, damages or liabilities, joint or several, to which any Indemnified Party may become subject, under the Applicable Securities Laws or otherwise, insofar as such losses, claims, damages or liabilities (or actions in respect thereof) arise out of or are based upon (i) a breach by the Company of any of its representations, warranties, covenants or agreements in this Agreement, (ii) any untrue statement or alleged untrue statement of any material fact contained in the Memorandum or in any Selling Material, or any amendment or supplement thereto, (iii) any omission or alleged omission to state therein a material fact required to be stated therein by Section 0 hereof or necessary in order to make the statements contained therein not misleading in the light of the circumstances under which they were made, except that the Company shall not indemnify any Indemnified Party for any untrue statement or alleged untrue statement of fact provided by such Indemnified Party in writing and specifically intended for use in the Memorandum or any Selling Material or any omission or alleged omission to state in such written materials a material fact required to be stated therein or necessary in order to make the statements contained therein not misleading; and to reimburse any Indemnified Party for any legal or other expenses reasonably incurred by any Indemnified Party in connection with investigating or defending against any such loss, claim, damage, liability or action; provided, however, that the Company shall not be required to indemnify any Indemnified Party for any payment made to any claimant in settlement of any suit or claim unless such settlement is approved by the Company, which approval shall not unreasonably be withheld. This indemnity agreement shall remain in full force and effect notwithstanding any investigation made by you or on behalf of you, shall survive consummation of the sale of the Shares hereunder and any termination of this Agreement, and shall be in addition to any other liability which the Company may now or hereafter have.

(b) Indemnification by You. You agree to indemnify and hold harmless the Company and its officers, directors, employees and agents and each person, if any, who controls any of them within the meaning of the Applicable Securities Laws (an "Indemnified Party" for purposes of this Section 0) against any losses, claims, damages or liabilities to which the Indemnified Party may become subject, under the Applicable Securities Laws or otherwise, insofar as such losses, claims, damages or liabilities (or actions in respect thereof) arise out of or are based upon (i) any untrue statement or alleged untrue statement of any material fact made by you to any offeree or purchaser of any of the Shares (other than any statement which is based upon information contained in the Memorandum or in any selling Material, or any amendment for supplement thereto), (ii) any omission or alleged omission by you to state to any offeree or purchaser of any of the Shares a material fact necessary in order to make the statements made to such offeree or purchaser not misleading in light of the circumstances under which they were made (other than any material fact omitted from the Memorandum or any Selling Material, or any amendment or supplement thereto), (iii) the failure or alleged failure of you to make offers and sales of the Shares in compliance with the Applicable Securities Laws, or (iv) the material breach by you of any of your representations, warranties, covenants or agreements hereunder; and to reimburse the Indemnified Party for any legal or other expenses reasonably incurred by the Indemnified Party in connection with investigating or defending against any such loss, claim, damage, liability or action; provided, however, that you shall not be required to indemnify the Indemnified Party for any payment made to any claimant in settlement of any suit or claim unless such settlement is approved by you, which approval shall not be unreasonably withheld; and provided further that you shall not be liable under this Section 0 for any losses, claims, damages or liabilities arising out of any act or failure to act on the part of any Indemnified Party but shall be liable only with respect to your own acts or failures to act. This indemnity agreement shall remain in full force and effect notwithstanding any investigation made by the Company, or on its behalf, shall survive consummation of the sale of the Shares hereunder and any termination of this Agreement, and shall be in addition to any other liability which you may now or hereafter have.

(c) Notice and Defense. No indemnifying Party under Section 0 or 0 shall be liable under the indemnity agreements contained in those sections unless the Indemnified Party shall have notified such indemnifying party in writing promptly after the summons or other first legal process giving information of the nature of the claim shall have been served upon the Indemnified Party, but failure to notify an indemnifying party of any such claim shall not relieve it from any liability which it may have to the Indemnified Party against whom action is brought otherwise than on account of its indemnity agreement contained in Sections 0 and 0. In case any action is brought against any Indemnified Party upon any such claim, and it notifies the indemnifying party of the commencement thereof as aforesaid, the indemnifying party shall be entitled to participate at its own expense in the defense, or, if it so elects, in accordance with arrangements satisfactory to any other indemnified party and any other indemnified parties who are defendants in such action; and after notice from the indemnifying party to such Indemnified Party of its election to so assume the defense thereof and the retaining of such counsel by the indemnifying party, the indemnifying party shall not be liable to such Indemnified Party for any legal or other expenses subsequently incurred by such Indemnified Party in connection with the defense thereof, other than the reasonable costs of investigation.

(d) Contribution. If the right to indemnification provided for in Sections 0 and 0 would by its terms be available to a party or parties hereunder, but is held to be unavailable for any reason other than because of the terms of such indemnification provision, then, in that case, the Company and you shall contribute to the aggregate of such losses, claims, damages and liabilities as are contemplated in those sections to which the Company and you may be subject (including, but not limited to, any investigation, legal and other expenses incurred in connection with, and any amount paid in settlement of, any claim, action, suit or proceeding, but after deducting any contribution received by the Company from persons other than you or persons who control you (within the meaning of Applicable Securities Laws), such as persons who control the Company within the meaning of Applicable Securities Laws, who may also be liable for contribution). In such event you are responsible for, and shall contribute an amount equal to the percentage of such losses, claims, damages or liabilities equal to the percentage commission which you receive as compensation for sale of the Shares as provided in Section 0 hereof; the Company is responsible for, and shall contribute, the balance thereof. Any person who controls a party entitled to receive contribution hereunder shall have the same joint and several right with such other party to receive such contribution. However, the right of contribution described in the preceding sentences is subject to the following limitations:

(i) in no case shall you or the persons who control you (within the meaning of Applicable Securities Laws) be required to contribute any amount in excess of the aggregate sale price of the Shares; and

(ii) no person guilty of fraudulent misrepresentation (within the meaning of Section 11(f) of the Securities Act) shall be entitled to contribution from any person who was not guilty of such fraudulent misrepresentation.

The parties agree that they will not assert the unavailability of the indemnification provisions of Sections 0 through 0 hereof, other than because of the terms of such provisions, so as to bring this contribution provision into operation. Any party entitled to contribution will, promptly after receipt of notice of commencement of any action, suit or proceeding against such party in respect of which a claim for contribution may be made against another party or parties, notify such other party or parties. Failure to so notify such other party or parties shall not relieve such other party or parties from any other obligation it or they may have hereunder or otherwise. If such other party or parties are so notified, such other party or parties shall be entitled to contribution of its or their election to assume its or their own defense, and after notice from such party or parties to such other party or parties of its election to assume its or their own defense and the retaining of counsel by such party or parties, the electing party shall not be liable for any legal or other expenses of litigation subsequently incurred by the party entitled to contribution in connection with the defense thereof, other than the reasonable cost of investigation. No party shall be required to contribute with respect to any action or claim settled without its consent, which consent shall not unreasonably be withheld.

8. Future Services.

If the Company closes an acquisition, partnership, joint venture, financing, sale, or similar transaction (a "Transaction") for which Placement Agent has the right to receive compensation pursuant to this Agreement, Placement Agent shall have the right to serve as the Company's exclusive placement agent with respect to future financings. Notwithstanding the foregoing:

(a) Placement Agent's rights pursuant to this Section shall expire thirty-six (36) months after the closing of the Transaction giving rise to such rights;

(b) Placement Agent shall not have the right to participate in an initial public offering ("IPO") of stock or other public offering of securities;

(c) if the Company is seeking to raise more than $25 million in a private financing Transaction, the Company may request that Placement Agent agree to execute such assignment in combination with another placement agent or investment banking firm; provided that such other placement agent or investment banking firm is reasonably acceptable to Placement Agent and that Placement Agent shall earn at least 50% of the placement fees paid by the Company for such assignment; and

(d) the terms and conditions under which Placement Agent is retained to perform such future services shall be consistent with those under which Placement Agent offers such services to other clients.

9. Termination and Expenses.

(a) Termination at Expiration of Selling Period. This Agreement shall terminate at the Closing Date if acceptable subscriptions for at least the Minimum Offering Amount have not been received by such time unless otherwise agreed.

(b) Failure to Comply with Agreement. This Agreement may be terminated by either party hereto by notice to the other party in the event that such party shall have failed or been unable to comply with any of the terms, conditions or provisions of this Agreement required by the Company or the Placement Agent to be performed, complied with or fulfilled by it within the respective times herein provided for, unless compliance therewith or performance or satisfaction thereof shall have been expressly waived by the non-defaulting party in writing.

(c) Government Restrictions. This Agreement may be terminated by either party by notice to the other party at any time if, in the judgment of either party, payment for and delivery of the Shares are rendered impracticable or inadvisable because:

(i) additional material governmental restrictions not in force and effect on the date hereof shall have been imposed upon the offer and sale of equity securities; or

(ii) a war or other national calamity shall have occurred; or

(iii) the condition of any matter affecting the Company or any other circumstance is such that it would be undesirable, impracticable or inadvisable in the judgment of the Placement Agent to proceed with this Agreement or with the sale of the Shares.

(d) Liability on Termination. Any termination of this Agreement pursuant to this Section 0 shall be without liability of any character (including, but not limited to, loss of anticipated profits or consequential damages on the part of any party thereto); except that the Company and the Placement Agent shall be obligated to pay, respectively, all losses, claims, damages or liabilities, joint or several, under Section 0 in the case of the Company, Section 0 in the case of the Placement Agent and Section 0 as to all parties.

(e) Survival of Representations, Warranties, Covenants, and Agreements. The representations, warranties, covenants, and agreements contained in this Agreement shall survive the sale of the Shares hereunder and, to the extent applicable, shall survive any termination of this Agreement.

(f) Selling Expenses. In addition to the Placement Fee and the Expense Reimbursement to be paid to the Placement Agent, all expenses incident to the performance of or compliance with this Agreement shall be paid by the Company, including, without limitation, all filing fees, professional fees, and other expenses of compliance with Federal, state and other securities laws; printing expenses; messenger, telephone, and delivery expenses; fees and disbursements of counsel for the Company; fees and disbursements of counsel for the Placement Agent and any fees and disbursements of independent certified public accountants retained by the Company; fees and expenses of other Persons retained by the Company; and the Company's internal expenses (including, without limitation, and all salaries and expenses of its officers and employees performing legal or accounting duties).

10. Definitions.

As used herein, the following terms have the following respective meanings:

Applicable Securities Laws: The Securities Act, the Securities Exchange Act, and any applicable state securities or blue sky laws or regulations.

Exchange Act: The Securities Act of 1934, as amended.

General Solicitation: General Solicitation includes any advertisement, article, notice, or other communication published in a newspaper, magazine or similar publication, or broadcast over television or radio, any seminar or meeting for potential investors, or any letter, circular or notice sent to potential investors and any other form of general solicitation or general advertising within the meaning or Rule 502(c) if Regulation D.

FINRA: The Financial Industry Regulatory Authority.

Private Placement Exemptions: Sections 3(b), 4(2), and 4(6) of the Securities Act and/or Regulation D promulgated pursuant thereunder, and equivalent exemptions from registration under applicable state securities laws.

Securities Act: The Securities Act of 1933, as amended.

Selling Material: This shall mean any written material prepared by or under the direction of the Company for use in connection with the offering and sale of the Shares.

Certain other terms used herein are defined elsewhere in this Agreement.

11. Miscellaneous.

(a) Notices. Every notice or other communication required or contemplated by this Agreement by either party shall be delivered either by (i) personal delivery, (ii) postage prepaid return receipt requested certified mail (airmail if available), or overnight delivery, or (iii) fax addressed to the party for whom intended at the address written below or at such other address as the intended recipient previously shall have designated in writing to the other party.

If to the Company:

_____

_____

_____

Attn: _____

Fax: _____

with a copy to:

_____

_____

Attn: _____

Fax: _____

If to Placement Agent:

_____

_____

_____

Attn: _____

Fax: _____

with a copy to:

_____

_____

Attn: _____

Fax: _____

(b) Successors and Assigns. This Agreement is made solely for the benefit of you and the Company (and, to the extent provided in Section 0, the controlling persons of each referred to therein), and their respective successors and assigns, and no other person shall acquire or have any right under or by virtue of this Agreement. The term "successors and assigns" as used herein shall not include any purchaser, as such, of any of the Shares. This Agreement shall be governed by and construed and enforced in accordance with the laws of California, and may be executed in several counterparts, each of which shall be deemed to be an original, but all of which together shall constitute one and the same instrument. If any provision of this Agreement is held to be illegal, invalid or unenforceable under applicable law, that provision will be deemed ineffective to the extent of such illegality, invalidity or unenforceabilty, without invalidating or otherwise affecting the remainder of this Agreement. Captions and heading used herein are solely for convenience of reference and shall not be deemed to affect the meaning or interpretation of any provision of this Agreement.

(c) Authority. The undersigned are duly authorized by the Company and the Placement Agent, respectively, to enter into this Agreement on behalf of such entities.

(d) Amendment. This Agreement may only be amended by an agreement in writing signed by all of the parties hereto.

(e) Counterparts. This Agreement may be executed in one or more counterparts, and each counterpart shall constitute an original instrument, but all such separate counterparts shall constitute only one and the same instrument.

If the foregoing correctly sets forth the understanding between us, please so indicate by signing in the space provided and return to us a counterpart hereof so signed by you, whereupon this letter shall become and evidence a binding agreement between us.

Very truly yours,

THE COMPANY
**** Inc.

By: _____

Name, title: _____

The foregoing Placement Agent Agreement is hereby accepted and agreed to as of the date first above written.

PLACEMENT AGENT
**** LLC

By: _____

Name, title: _____

EXHIBIT A: WARRANT

EXHIBIT B: FAMILY AND FRIENDS

EXHIBIT C: ESCROW DEPOSIT INSTRUCTIONS

EXHIBIT D: INDEMNIFICATION AND CO-SALE AGREEMENT

(Attached)

Form 11 E: Warrant for Placement Agent Agreement

EXHIBIT A

THE SECURITIES REPRESENTED BY THIS CERTIFICATE HAVE BEEN ACQUIRED FOR INVESTMENT AND HAVE NOT BEEN REGISTERED UNDER THE SECURITIES ACT OF 1933, AS AMENDED (THE "SECURITIES ACT") OR ANY STATE SECURITIES LAWS. SUCH SECURITIES MAY NOT BE SOLD OR TRANSFERRED IN THE ABSENCE OF SUCH REGISTRATION OR AN EXEMPTION THEREFROM UNDER THE SECURITIES ACT AND ANY APPLICABLE STATE SECURITIES LAWS.

WARRANT TO PURCHASE SHARES
OF THE COMMON STOCK OF
**** *Inc.*
(Void after [*EXPIRATION DATE*])

This certifies that _____ or its assigns (each individually, the "Holder") for value received, shall be entitled to purchase from ****, Inc., a _____ corporation (the "Company"), having its principal place of business at _____ _____, a maximum of _____ fully paid and nonassessable shares of the Company's Common Stock ("Common Stock") for cash at a price equal to $_____ per share (the "Exercise Price") at any time, or from time to time, up to and including 5:00 p.m. (local time) on the tenth (10th) anniversary from the date of this Warrant (the "Expiration Date"), upon the surrender to the Company at its principal place of business (or at such other location as the Company may advise the Holder in writing) of this Warrant properly endorsed, a Form of Subscription in substantially the form attached hereto duly filled in and signed and, if applicable, upon payment in cash or by check of the aggregate Exercise Price for the number of shares for which this Warrant is being exercised determined in accordance with the provisions hereof. The Exercise Price and the number of shares of Common Stock purchasable hereunder are subject to adjustment as provided in Section 0 of this Warrant.

This Warrant is subject to the following terms and conditions:

1. Exercise; Issuance of Certificates; Payment for Shares.

(a) General. This Warrant is exercisable at the option of the holder of record hereof at any time or from time to time, up to the Expiration Date for all or any part of the shares of Common Stock (but not for a fraction of a share) which may be purchased hereunder. The Company agrees that the shares of Common Stock purchased under this Warrant shall be and are deemed to be issued to the Holder hereof as the record owner of such shares as of the close of business on the date on which this Warrant shall have been surrendered, properly endorsed, the completed, executed Subscription Form delivered and payment made for such shares. Certificates for the shares of Common Stock so purchased, together with any other securities or property to which the Holder is entitled upon such exercise, shall be delivered to the Holder by the Company at the Company's expense within a reasonable time after the rights represented by this Warrant have been so exercised, and in any event, within fifteen (15) days of such exercise. In case of a purchase of less than all the shares which may be purchased under this Warrant, the Company shall cancel this Warrant and execute and deliver a new Warrant or Warrants of like tenor for the balance of the shares purchasable under the Warrant surrendered upon such purchase to the Holder hereof within a reasonable time. Each stock certificate so delivered shall be in such denominations of Common Stock as may be requested by the Holder hereof and shall be registered in the name designated by such Holder.

(b) Net Issue Exercise. Notwithstanding any provisions herein to the contrary, if the fair market value of one share of the Company's Common Stock is greater than the Exercise Price (at the date of calculation as set forth below), in lieu of exercising this Warrant for cash, the Holder may elect to receive shares equal to the value (as determined below) of this Warrant (or the portion thereof being canceled) by surrender of this Warrant at the principal office of the Company together with the properly endorsed Form of Subscription and notice of such election in which event the Company shall issue to the Holder a number of shares of Common Stock computed using the following formula:

$$X = \frac{Y(A - B)}{A}$$

Where X = the number of shares of Common Stock to be issued to the Holder, Y = the number of shares of Common Stock purchasable under the Warrant or, if only a portion of the Warrant is being exercised, the portion of the Warrant being canceled (at the date of such calculation), A = the fair market value of one share of the Company's Common Stock (at the date of such calculation), and B = Exercise Price (as adjusted to the date of such calculation).

For purposes of the above calculation, the fair market value of one share of Common Stock shall be determined by the Company's Board of Directors in good faith; provided, however, that where there is a public market for the Company's Common Stock, the fair market value per share shall be the average of the closing prices of the Company's Common Stock quoted on the Nasdaq National Market (or similar system) or on any exchange on which the Common Stock is listed, whichever is applicable, over the five (5) day period ending one (1) day before the day the current fair market value is being determined.

2. Shares to be Fully Paid; Reservation of Shares.

The Company covenants and agrees that all shares of Common Stock which may be issued upon the exercise of the rights represented by this Warrant will, upon issuance, be duly authorized, validly issued, fully paid and nonassessable and free from all preemptive rights of any shareholder and free of all taxes, liens and charges with respect to the issue thereof. The Company further covenants and agrees that, during the period within which the rights represented by this Warrant may be exercised, the Company will at all times have authorized and reserved, for the purpose of issue or transfer upon exercise of the subscription rights evidenced by this Warrant, a sufficient number of shares of authorized but unissued Common Stock, or other securities and property, when and as required to provide for the exercise of the rights represented by this Warrant. The Company will take all such action as may be necessary to assure that such shares of Common Stock may be issued as provided herein without violation of any applicable law or regulation, or of any requirements of any domestic securities exchange upon which the Common Stock may be listed; provided, however, that the Company shall not be required to effect a registration under Federal or State securities laws with respect to such exercise. The Company will not take any action which would result in any adjustment of the Exercise Price (as set forth in Section 0 hereof) if the total number of shares of Common Stock issuable after such action upon exercise of all outstanding warrants, together with all shares of Common Stock then outstanding and all shares of Common Stock then issuable upon exercise of all options and upon the conversion of all convertible securities then outstanding, would exceed the total number of shares of Common Stock then authorized by the Company's Articles/Certificate of Incorporation (the "Company Charter").

3. Adjustment of Exercise Price and Number of Shares.

The Exercise Price and the number of shares purchasable upon the exercise of this Warrant shall be subject to adjustment from time to time upon the occurrence of certain events described in this Section 0. Upon each adjustment of the Exercise Price, the Holder of this Warrant shall thereafter be entitled to purchase, at the Exercise Price resulting from such adjustment, the number of shares obtained by multiplying the Exercise Price in effect immediately prior to such adjustment by the number of shares purchasable pursuant hereto immediately prior to such adjustment, and dividing the product thereof by the Exercise Price resulting from such adjustment.

(a) Subdivision or Combination of Stock. In case the Company shall at any time subdivide its outstanding shares of Common Stock into a greater number of shares, the Exercise Price in effect immediately prior to such subdivision shall be proportionately reduced, and conversely, in case the outstanding shares of Common Stock of the Company shall be combined into a smaller number of shares, the Exercise Price in effect immediately prior to such combination shall be proportionately increased.

(b) Dividends in Common Stock, Other Stock, Property, Reclassification. If at any time or from time to time the Holders of Common Stock (or any shares of stock or other securities at the time receivable upon the exercise of this Warrant) shall have received or become entitled to receive, without payment therefor, Common Stock or any shares of stock or other securities which are at any time directly or indirectly convertible into or exchangeable for Common Stock, or any rights or options to subscribe for, purchase or otherwise acquire any of the foregoing by way of dividend or other distribution, any cash paid or payable otherwise than as a cash dividend, or Common Stock or additional stock or other securities or property (including cash) by way of spinoff, split-up, reclassification, combination of shares or similar corporate rearrangement, (other than shares of Common Stock issued as a stock split or adjustments in respect of which shall be covered by the terms of Section 0 above), then and in each such case, the Holder hereof shall, upon the exercise of this Warrant, be entitled to receive, in addition to the number of shares of Common Stock receivable thereupon, and without payment of any additional consideration therefor, the amount of stock and other securities and property which such Holder would hold on the date of such exercise had he been the holder of record of such Common Stock as of the date on which holders of Common Stock received or became entitled to receive such shares or all other additional stock and other securities and property.

(c) Reorganization, Reclassification, Consolidation, Merger or Sale. If any recapitalization, reclassification or reorganization of the capital stock of the Company, or any consolidation or merger of the Company with another corporation, or the sale of all or substantially all of its assets or other transaction shall be effected in such a way that holders of Common Stock shall be entitled to receive stock, securities, or other assets or property (an "Organic Change"), then, as a condition of such Organic Change, lawful and adequate provisions shall be made by the Company whereby the Holder hereof shall thereafter have the right to purchase and receive (in lieu of the shares of the Common Stock of the Company immediately theretofore purchasable and receivable upon the exercise of the rights represented by this Warrant) such shares of stock, securities or other assets or property as may be issued or payable with respect to or in exchange for a number of outstanding shares of such Common Stock equal to the number of shares of such stock immediately theretofore purchasable and receivable upon the exercise of the rights represented by this Warrant. In the event of any Organic Change, appropriate provision shall be made by the Company with respect to the rights and interests of the Holder of this Warrant to the end that the provisions hereof (including, without limitation, provisions for adjustments of the Exercise Price and of the number of shares purchasable and receivable upon the exercise of this Warrant) shall thereafter be applicable, in relation to any shares of stock, securities or assets thereafter deliverable upon the exercise hereof. The Company will not effect any such consolidation, merger or sale unless, prior to the consummation thereof, the successor corporation (if other than the Company) resulting from such consolidation or the corporation purchasing such assets shall assume by written instrument reasonably satisfactory in form and substance to the Holders executed and mailed or delivered to the registered Holder hereof at the last address of such Holder appearing on the books of the Company, the obligation to deliver to such Holder such shares of stock, securities or assets as, in accordance with the foregoing provisions, such Holder may be entitled to purchase.

(d) Certain Events. If any change in the outstanding Common Stock of the Company or any other event occurs as to which the other provisions of this Section 0 are not strictly applicable or if strictly applicable would not fairly protect the purchase rights of the Holder of the Warrant in accordance with such provisions, then the Board of Directors of the Company shall make an adjustment in the number and class of shares available under the Warrant, the Exercise Price or the application of such provisions, so as to protect such purchase rights as aforesaid. The adjustment shall be such as will give the Holder of the Warrant upon exercise for the same aggregate Exercise Price the total number, class and kind of shares as he would have owned had the Warrant been exercised prior to the event and had he continued to hold such shares until after the event requiring adjustment.

(e) Notices of Change. Immediately upon any adjustment in the number or class of shares subject to this Warrant and of the Exercise Price, the Company shall give written notice thereof to the Holder, setting forth in reasonable detail and certifying the calculation of such adjustment. The Company shall give written notice to the Holder at least 10 business days prior to the date on which the Company closes its books or takes a record for determining rights to receive any dividends or distributions. The Company shall also give written notice to the Holder at least 30 business days prior to the date on which an Organic Change shall take place.

(f) Issue Tax. The issuance of certificates for shares of Common Stock upon the exercise of the Warrant shall be made without charge to the Holder of the Warrant for any issue tax (other than any applicable income taxes) in respect thereof; provided, however, that the Company shall not be required to pay any tax which may be payable in respect of any transfer involved in the issuance and delivery of any certificate in a name other than that of the then Holder of the Warrant being exercised.

4. Closing of Books.

The Company will at no time close its transfer books against the transfer of any warrant or of any shares of Common Stock issued or issuable upon the exercise of any warrant in any manner which interferes with the timely exercise of this Warrant.

5. No Voting or Dividend Rights; Limitation of Liability.

Nothing contained in this Warrant shall be construed as conferring upon the Holder hereof the right to vote or to consent or to receive notice as a shareholder of the Company or any other matters or any rights whatsoever as a shareholder of the Company. No dividends or interest shall be payable or accrued in respect of this Warrant or the interest represented hereby or the shares purchasable hereunder until, and only to the extent that, this Warrant shall have been exercised. No provisions hereof, in the absence of affirmative action by the holder to purchase shares of Common Stock, and no mere enumeration herein of the rights or privileges of the holder hereof, shall give rise to any liability of such Holder for the Exercise Price or as a shareholder of the Company, whether such liability is asserted by the Company or by its creditors.

6. Warrants Transferable.

Subject to compliance with applicable federal and state securities laws, this Warrant and all rights hereunder are transferable, in whole or in part, without charge to the holder hereof (except for transfer taxes), upon surrender of this Warrant properly endorsed. Each taker and holder of this Warrant, by taking or holding the same, consents and agrees that this Warrant, when endorsed in blank, shall be deemed negotiable, and that the holder hereof, when this Warrant shall have been so endorsed, may be treated by the Company, at the Company's option, and all other persons dealing with this Warrant as the absolute owner hereof for any purpose and as the person entitled to exercise the rights represented by this Warrant, or to the transfer hereof on the books of the Company any notice to the contrary notwithstanding; but until such transfer on such books, the Company may treat the registered owner hereof as the owner for all purposes.

7. Rights and Obligations Survive Exercise of Warrant.

The rights and obligations of the Company, of the holder of this Warrant and of the holder of shares of Common Stock issued upon exercise of this Warrant, shall survive the exercise of this Warrant.

8. Further Representations, Warranties, and Covenants of the Company.

(a) Articles and Bylaws. The Company has made available to Holder true, complete, and correct copies of the Company Charter and Bylaws, as amended, through the date hereof.

(b) Due Authority. The execution and delivery by the Company of this Warrant and the performance of all obligations of the Company hereunder, including the issuance to Holder of the right to acquire the shares of Common Stock, have been duly authorized by all necessary corporate action on the part of the Company, and the Warrant is not inconsistent with the Company Charter or Bylaws and constitutes a legal, valid and binding agreement of the Company, enforceable in accordance with its terms.

(c) Consents and Approvals. No consent or approval of, giving of notice to, registration with, or taking of any other action in respect of any state, federal or other governmental authority or agency is required with respect to the execution, delivery and performance by the Company of its obligations under this Warrant, except for any filing required by applicable federal and state securities laws, which filing will be effective by the time required thereby.

(d) Issued Securities. All issued and outstanding shares of capital stock of the Company have been duly authorized and validly issued and are fully paid and nonassessable. All outstanding shares of capital stock were issued in full compliance with all federal and state securities laws.

(e) Exempt Transaction. Subject to the accuracy of the Holder's representations in Section 0 hereof, the issuance of the Common Stock upon exercise of this Warrant will constitute a transaction exempt from (i) the registration requirements of Section 5 of the Securities Act of 1933, as amended (the "Securities Act"), in reliance upon Section 4(2) thereof, and (ii) the qualification requirements of the applicable state securities laws.

(f) Compliance with Rule 144. At the written request of the Holder, who proposes to sell Common Stock issuable upon the exercise of the Warrant in compliance with Rule 144 promulgated by the Securities and Exchange Commission, the Company shall furnish to the Holder, within thirty (30) days after receipt of such request, a written statement confirming the Company's compliance with the filing requirements of the Securities and Exchange Commission as set forth in such Rule, as such Rule may be amended from time to time.

9. Representations and Covenants of the Holder.

This Warrant has been entered into by the Company in reliance upon the following representations and covenants of the Holder:

(a) Investment Purpose. The Warrant or the Common Stock issuable upon exercise of the Warrant will be acquired for investment and not with a view to the sale or distribution of any part thereof, and the Holder has no present intention of selling or engaging in any public distribution of the same except pursuant to a registration or exemption.

(b) Private Issue. The Holder understands (i) that the Warrant and the Common Stock issuable upon exercise of this Warrant are not registered under the Securities Act or qualified under applicable state securities laws on the ground that the issuance contemplated by this Warrant will be exempt from the registration and qualifications requirements thereof, and (ii) that the Company's reliance on such exemption is predicated on the representations set forth in this Section 9.

(c) Disposition of Holders Rights. In no event will the Holder make a disposition of the Warrant or the Common Stock issuable upon exercise of the Warrant unless and until (i) it shall have notified the Company of the proposed disposition, and (ii) if requested by the Company, it shall have furnished the Company with an opinion of counsel (which counsel may either be inside or outside counsel to the Holder) satisfactory to the Company and its counsel to the effect that (A) appropriate action necessary for compliance with the Securities Act has been taken, or (B) an exemption from the registration requirements of the Securities Act is available. Notwithstanding the foregoing, the restrictions imposed upon the transferability of any of its rights to acquire Common Stock or Common Stock issuable on the exercise of such rights do not apply to transfers from the beneficial owner of any of the aforementioned securities to its nominee or from such nominee to its beneficial owner, and shall terminate as to any particular share of Common Stock when (1) such security shall have been effectively registered under the Securities Act and sold by the holder thereof in accordance with such registration or (2) such security shall have been sold without registration in compliance with Rule 144 under the Securities Act, or (3) a letter shall have been issued to the Holder at its request by the staff of the Securities and Exchange Commission or a ruling shall have been issued to the Holder at its request by such Commission stating that no action shall be recommended by such staff or taken by such Commission, as the case may be, if such security is transferred without registration under the Securities Act in accordance with the conditions set forth in such letter or ruling and such letter or ruling specifies that no subsequent restrictions on transfer are required. Whenever the restrictions imposed hereunder shall terminate, as hereinabove provided, the Holder or holder of a share of Common Stock then outstanding as to which such restrictions have terminated shall be entitled to receive from the Company, without expense to such holder, one or more new certificates for the Warrant or for such shares of Common Stock not bearing any restrictive legend.

(d) Financial Risk. The Holder has such knowledge and experience in financial and business matters as to be capable of evaluating the merits and risks of its investment, and has the ability to bear the economic risks of its investment.

(e) Risk of No Registration. The Holder understands that if the Company does not register with the Securities and Exchange Commission pursuant to Section 12 of the Securities Act, or file reports pursuant to Section 15(d), of the Securities Exchange Act of 1934 (the "Exchange Act"), or if a registration statement covering the securities under the Securities Act is not in effect when it desires to sell (i) the Warrant, or (ii) the Common Stock issuable upon exercise of the Warrant, it may be required to hold such securities for an indefinite period. The Holder also understands that any sale of the Warrant or the Common Stock issuable upon exercise of the Warrant which might be made by it in reliance upon Rule 144 under the Securities Act may be made only in accordance with the terms and conditions of that Rule.

(f) Accredited Investor. Holder is an "accredited investor" within the meaning of Rule 501 of Regulation D under the Securities Act, as presently in effect.

10. Modification and Waiver.

This Warrant and any provision hereof may be changed, waived, discharged, or terminated only by an instrument in writing signed by the party against which enforcement of the same is sought.

11. Notices.

Any notice, request, or other document required or permitted to be given or delivered to the holder hereof or the Company shall be delivered or shall be sent by certified mail, postage prepaid, to each such holder at its address as shown on the books of the Company or to the Company at the address indicated therefor in the first paragraph of this Warrant or such other address as either may from time to time provide to the other.

12. Binding Effect on Successors.

This Warrant shall be binding upon any corporation succeeding the Company by merger, consolidation or acquisition of all or substantially all of the Company's assets. All of the obligations of the Company relating to the Common Stock issuable upon the exercise of this Warrant shall survive the exercise and termination of this Warrant. All of the covenants and agreements of the Company shall inure to the benefit of the successors and assigns of the holder hereof.

13. Descriptive Headings and Governing Law.

The description headings of the several sections and paragraphs of this Warrant are inserted for convenience only and do not constitute a part of this Warrant. This Warrant shall be construed and enforced in accordance with, and the rights of the parties shall be governed by, the laws of the State of _____.

14. Lost Warrants.

The Company represents and warrants to the Holder hereof that upon receipt of evidence reasonably satisfactory to the Company of the loss, theft, destruction, or mutilation of this Warrant and, in the case of any such loss, theft, or destruction, upon receipt of an indemnity reasonably satisfactory to the Company, or in the case of any such mutilation upon surrender and cancellation of such Warrant, the Company, at its expense, will make and deliver a new Warrant, of like tenor, in lieu of the lost, stolen, destroyed, or mutilated Warrant.

15. Fractional Shares.

No fractional shares shall be issued upon exercise of this Warrant. The Company shall, in lieu of issuing any fractional share, pay the holder entitled to such fraction a sum in cash equal to such fraction multiplied by the then effective Exercise Price.

In Witness Whereof, the Company has caused this Warrant to be duly executed by its officers, thereunto duly authorized this ___ day of _____, 20__.

****, Inc.

By: _____

Name, title: _____

ATTEST:

_____, Secretary

APPENDIX A: SUBSCRIPTION FORM

Date: _____, 20___
[Company Name]
[Address]
Attn: President

Dear Sir:

The undersigned hereby elects to exercise the warrant issued to it by ****, Inc. (the "Company") and dated as of the _____ day of _____, 20___ (the "Warrant") and to purchase _____ shares of the Common Stock of the Company (the "Shares") at a purchase price of _____ Dollars ($_____) per Share for an aggregate purchase price of _____ Dollars ($_____) (the "Exercise Price").

The undersigned hereby elects to convert _____ percent (____%) of the value of the Warrant pursuant to the provisions of Section 0 of the Warrant.

Pursuant to the terms of the Warrant the undersigned has delivered the Exercise Price herewith in full in cash or by certified check or wire transfer.

Very truly yours,

_____

By: _____

Name, title: _____

Form 11 F: Convertible Debenture

8.5% CONVERTIBLE DEBENTURE

[City], [State]   **[Date]**

FOR VALUE RECEIVED, ****, Inc., a _____ corporation, (the "Company") hereby promises to pay, on or before _____, 20___ (the "Maturity Date"), to _____, or order ("Holder") at _____, the principal amount of $ _____ and to pay simple interest on the unpaid principal amount from date hereof at the rate of nine and one-half percent (9.5%) per annum until payment in full of the principal amount hereof.

This Debenture shall be subject to the following terms and conditions:

1. <u>Conversion.</u>

(a) The registered holder of this Debenture, at his, her or its option, at any time within thirty days of the closing of the Company's next round of financing, may convert the principal amount and any interest of this Debenture then remaining outstanding in whole or in part, into that number of shares of the Common Stock (par value $0.001) of the Company as the principal amount and any interest of the Debenture so converted is a multiple of the applicable conversion price as hereinafter determined pursuant to this paragraph 1, and upon the terms and subject to the conditions hereinafter specified in this paragraph 1, upon the surrender to the Company at its principal office of the Debenture to be converted. If the Debenture shall be converted in part, the Company shall, at its option and without charge to the holder, either (i) execute and deliver to the registered holder a Debenture for the balance of the principal amount hereof not so converted or (ii) make note hereon of the portion of the principal amount and any interest converted.

(b) The conversion price (herein called "the basic conversion price") shall be that price which is equal to eighty percent (80%) of the offering price in the Company's next round of financing. For the purposes of this paragraph 1, the Company's next round of financing shall be defined as any offering in which the Company raises $_____. This Debenture cannot be converted unless and until the Company has completed its next round of financing. The basic conversion price is subject to adjustment from time to time as hereinafter provided.

(c) In case at any time or from time to time after the date hereof, the holders of the Company's Common Stock shall have received, or (on or after the record date fixed for determination of stockholders eligible to receive) shall have become entitled to receive, without payment therefor: (i) other or additional Common Stock or other securities or property (other than cash) by way of dividend; or (ii) any cash paid or payable (including, without limitation, by way of dividend), except out of earned surplus of the Company; or (iii) other or additional (or less) stock or other securities or property (including cash) by way of spin-off, split-up, reclassification, recapitalization, combination of shares or similar corporate rearrangement; then, and in each such case, the registered holder of this Debenture, upon the exercise of his, her, or its conversion privilege, shall be entitled to receive the amount of Common Stock and other securities, and property (including cash in the cases referred to in subdivisions (c)(ii) and (d)(iii) above) which such holder would receive on the date of such exercise if on the date hereof he, she, or it had been the holder of record of the number of shares of Common Stock into which this Debenture may be converted, and had thereafter, during the period from the date hereof to and including the date of such exercise, retained such shares and such other or additional (or less) stock and other securities and property (including cash in the case referred to in subdivisions (c)(ii) and (d)(iii) hereinabove) receivable by him, her, or it during such period, giving effect to all adjustments called for during such period by this paragraph.

(d) In case the company after the date hereof shall (i) effect a reorganization, (ii) consolidate with or merge with any other person, or (iii) transfer all or substantially all of its properties or assets to any other person under any plan or arrangement contemplating the dissolution of the Company within twenty-four (24) months from the date of such transfer, then, in each case, the registered holder of this Debenture, upon exercise of his, her, or its conversion privilege at any time after the consummation of such reorganization, consolidation or merger or the effective date of such dissolution, as the case may be, shall be entitled to receive, in lieu of the Common Stock issuable upon such exercise prior to such consummation or such effective date, the stock and other securities and property to which such holder would have been entitled upon such consummation or in connection with such dissolution, as the case may be, if such registered holder had so exercised his, her, or its conversion privilege immediately prior thereto, subject to further adjustment as provided in this paragraph. Upon any reorganization, consolidation, merger, or transfer (and any dissolution following any transfer pursuant to this paragraph), this Debenture, and the conversion privileges appertaining thereto, shall continue in full force and effect and the terms thereof shall be applicable to the shares of stock and other securities and property receivable upon exercise of such conversion privilege after consummation of such reorganization, consolidation, merger, transfer or dissolution, as the case may be, and shall be binding upon the issuer of any such stock or other securities including, in the case of any such transfer, the person acquiring all or substantially all of the properties or assets of the Company, whether or not such person shall have expressly assumed the terms of this Debenture.

2. <u>Subordination</u>. The indebtedness evidenced by this Debenture is subordinated and junior in right of payment to all other indebtedness of the Company, whether created prior or subsequent to the date of this Debenture. Other indebtedness shall include principal of, and premium, if any, and interest on indebtedness (secured or unsecured) incurred, assumed, or guaranteed by the Company for money borrowed or of any nature whatsoever. Upon any receivership, insolvency, bankruptcy, assignment for the benefit of creditors, reorganization, dissolution, liquidation, or other marshaling of the assets of the Company, no amount shall be paid by the Company of the principal of, or interest on, this Debenture unless and until all other indebtedness shall have been paid in full, together with all interest thereon and all other amounts that may be payable in connection therewith. In the event of any default in the payment of principal of or interest on any other indebtedness, and during its continuance, no amount shall be paid by the Company with respect to the principal or interest on this Debenture.

3. <u>Warranties</u>. The Company warrants and covenants that:

(a) The Company is a corporation duly organized and existing under the laws of the State of _____; and

(b) All corporate actions on the part of the Company and its directors necessary for the authorization, execution and delivery of the Debenture have been duly taken.

4. <u>Default</u>. The following shall be deemed to be events of default hereunder:

(a) Nonpayment when due of any principal or interest on the Debenture at maturity;

(b) Any affirmative act of insolvency by the Company, or filing by the Company of any petition or action under any bankruptcy, reorganization, or insolvency law, or any other law or laws for the relief of debtors; and

(c) The filing against the Company of any involuntary petition under any bankruptcy statute, or an appointment of any receiver or trustee to take possession of the properties of the Company, unless such petition or appointment is set aside or withdrawn or ceases to be in effect within sixty (60) days from the date of such filing or appointment.

5. <u>Company's Right of Repayment</u>. Subject to Holder's right of conversion pursuant to Section 1 hereof, the Company shall have the right to make pre-payment of all principal due on this Debenture, and all interest accrued thereon (a "call"), at any time during the term of this Debenture upon sixty (60) days' notice to Holder.

6. <u>Warrant, Registration Rights</u>.

(a) In the event this Debenture is held until the Maturity Date, the holder shall receive, in addition to repayment of principal and interest due thereon, a warrant to purchase shares of the Company's Common Stock at a price equal to the offering price in the most recently completed offering by the Company of its equity securities in which it raised $_____ or more, or in the event no such offering has been completed, at the price of $_____ per share. The number of shares the holder shall be entitled to purchase under the warrant shall be one-fifth (1/5) of the principal amount of this Debenture. For example, if the principal amount of this Debenture was one hundred thousand dollars ($100,000), the number of shares the holder would be entitled to purchase under the warrant would be twenty thousand (20,000) shares. The warrant shall expire three (3) years from the date of issue, or thirty (30) days after the Company concludes an underwritten initial public offering, whichever is earlier.

(b) In the event this Debenture is converted prior to the Maturity Date, the holder shall receive, in addition to the shares issuable to holder upon conversion, a warrant to purchase shares of the Company's Common Stock at the price of $_____ per share. The number of shares the holder shall be entitled to purchase under the warrant shall be one-third (1/3) of the principal amount of this Debenture. For example, if the principal amount of this Debenture was one hundred thousand dollars ($100,000), the number of shares the holder would be entitled to purchase under the warrant would be thirty-three thousand, three hundred thirty-three (33,333) shares. The warrant shall expire three (3) years from the date of issue, or thirty (30) days after the Company concludes an underwritten initial public offering, whichever is earlier.

(c) Registration Rights: (i) If at any time the Company shall of its own volition register any securities under the Act, the Company will give the registered holder(s) of the Debenture at least thirty (30) days prior written notice thereof and, upon such registered holder(s)' request, include in such registration, at the cost and expense of the Company, such shares issuable upon the exercise of the warrant(s) described herein in the amount so requested; provided, however, that the Company's underwriters do not object to the inclusion of such securities in the registration statement; (ii) In the event the Company's underwriters object to the inclusion of such securities in the registration statement, the Company shall complete a separate registration of such securities within ninety (90) days of the closing of the registration undertaken of its own volition at its own cost and expense, and will maintain such registration statement current for a period of nine (9) months subsequent to its effective date; (iii) The

Company agrees to use its best efforts, at its expense, to register or qualify the securities covered by such registration statement under such other securities or blue sky laws of such jurisdiction as the registered holder of the debenture(s) shall reasonably request; (iv) In connection with any registration statement to be filed on behalf of the Company, the primary responsibility for preparing and filing such registration statement shall be that of the Company, but the registered holder(s) of the Debenture shall furnish such information to the Company, in writing, as it may reasonably request to assist in the preparation of such registration statement; (v) If the offering to which the proposed registration statement relates is to be on an underwritten basis, and the registered holder(s) of the Debenture shall not consent to have such registered holder(s)' shares of stock distributed upon the same terms and conditions as those applicable to the other person(s) (including the corporation) whose securities are being included in such registration statement, then the registered holder(s) of the Debenture will not, without the written consent of the Company, commence the distribution of any shares of stock of the Company held by such registered holder(s) until ninety (90) days after the effective date of such registration statement.

7. Acceleration.

(a) If any one or more of the events of default described in paragraph 4 hereof shall occur, the registered holder(s) of the Debenture, by notice in writing to the Company, may declare the principal of and all accrued interest on all Debentures then outstanding immediately due and payable without further notice or demand; provided, however, that at any time within fifteen (15) days after such declaration the same may be rescinded and such event of default may be waived by the registered holder(s) of the Debenture by written notice from them to the Company.

(b) Upon any such acceleration of the maturity of the Debenture, the Company will, within thirty (30) days thereof, pay to the registered holder(s) of the Debenture the entire principal balance unpaid on such Debenture, together with accrued interest thereon to the date of such payment. If the Company shall fail to make payment to the registered holder(s) of the Debenture as provided above, the registered holder(s) of the Debenture shall be entitled and empowered to take such measures as may be appropriate to enforce the Company's obligations under the Debenture, by judicial proceedings or otherwise. In the event suit shall be brought to enforce payment of this Debenture, the Company promises to pay reasonable attorneys' fees to be fixed by the court.

8. Transferability.

(a) This Debenture is transferable only by the registered holder hereof in person or by his, her, or its attorney duly authorized in writing on a register maintained by the Company, upon the surrender of this Debenture, duly endorsed without recourse, and the Company shall not be required to make any transfer unless and until it receives this Debenture duly and properly endorsed without recourse by the registered holder hereof or by his, her, or its attorney duly authorized in writing. Upon the surrender of this Debenture for transfer of registration hereof, the Company shall issue a new Debenture in place hereof, and shall cause such Debenture to be delivered to the transferee. The Company may treat the registered holder hereof as the absolute owner hereof for the purpose of receiving payment of, or on account of, principal hereof and interest due hereon, for the purpose of effecting the conversion of this Debenture into shares of Common Stock of the Company, and for all other purposes, and may require guarantee of authenticity of signatures with respect to endorsements.

(b) By the acceptance of this Debenture, the initial payee of this Debenture represents and warrants that he, she or it is purchasing this Debenture for investment for his, her, or its own account and with no present intention of dividing such participation with others, or reselling or otherwise distributing the same. He, she, or it understands and acknowledges that the Company has advised him, her, or it that said Debenture has not been registered under the Securities Act of 1933, as amended, nor qualified under the securities laws of any other state on the grounds that this transaction is exempt from such registration and qualification requirements, and that the Company's reliance on such exemption is predicated in part on his, her, or its representation and warranty herein set forth.

(c) By the acceptance of this Debenture, the holder hereof agrees that the transfer of this Debenture and the transfer of any shares of Common Stock of the Company into which this Debenture may be converted shall be subject to the restriction that no such transfer hereof or thereof shall be effected until either (i) the holder hereof or of said shares has obtained either an opinion of counsel satisfactory to the Company and its counsel to the effect that the proposed transfer will not result in a violation of the Securities Act of 1933, as then amended; or (ii) a registration statement with respect to this Debenture and/or the shares of Common Stock of the Company into which this Debenture may be converted shall then be effective in current form under the Securities Act of 1933, as then amended. This provision shall be binding upon all subsequent transferees of this Debenture and/or the shares of Common Stock into which this Debenture may be converted.

9. <u>Notices</u>. Any communication or notices hereunder may be delivered or mailed to the offices of the company at:

****, Inc.

_____

_____

Attn: _____

and to the registered holder hereof at his address set forth below, or to such other addresses as either the Company or such registered holder may designate by notice in writing to the other from time to time.

10. <u>Interpretation</u>. The validity, interpretation and performance of this Debenture shall be construed under and controlled by the laws of the State of _____, without regard to its choice-of-law principles.

11. <u>Legend</u>.

THIS CONVERTIBLE DEBENTURE HAS NOT BEEN REGISTERED UNDER THE FEDERAL SECURITIES ACT OF 1933, AS AMENDED ("THE ACT") OR ANY STATE SECURITIES LAW. THE DEBENTURE HAS BEEN ACQUIRED FOR INVESTMENT AND NEITHER SAID DEBENTURE NOR ANY INTEREST THEREIN MAY BE TRANSFERRED, SOLD OR OFFERED FOR SALE UNLESS (1) THERE IS AN EFFECTIVE REGISTRATION STATEMENT FOR THE DEBENTURE AS A SECURITY UNDER THE ACT AND QUALIFICATION UNDER ANY APPLICABLE STATE SECURITIES LAW, (2) SUCH TRANSFER IS MADE IN COMPLIANCE WITH RULE 144 UNDER THE ACT AND PURSUANT TO QUALIFICATION UNDER ANY APPLICABLE STATE SECURITIES LAW OR EXEMPTION THEREFROM, OR (3) THERE IS AN OPINION OF COUNSEL SATISFACTORY TO THE CORPORA-

TION THAT SUCH REGISTRATION AND QUALIFICATION ARE NOT REQUIRED AS TO SAID TRANSFER, SALE OR OFFER.

IN WITNESS WHEREOF, the Company has caused this Debenture to be duly executed by its officers thereunto duly authorized, of the day and year first above written.

****, Inc.

By: _____

_____, President

HOLDER(S):

_____
[Signature]

_____
[Name]

_____
[Address]

_____

_____

_____
[Signature]

_____
[Name]

_____
[Address]

_____

_____

Form 11 G: Purchase Agreement—Series A

Note: The following is a typical angel investor Series A purchase agreement.

PURCHASE AGREEMENT
SERIES A PREFERRED

This Purchase Agreement for Series A Preferred Stock (this "**Agreement**") is made and entered into as of this __ day of _____, 20__ (the "**Effective Date**") by and between ****, Inc., a [California] corporation (the "**Company**"), and _____, individuals residing in the State of [California] (*jointly,* the "**Purchaser**").

WHEREAS, Purchaser desires to purchase from the Company, and the Company desires to sell to Purchaser shares of the Company's Series A Preferred Stock upon the terms and conditions of this Agreement;

NOW, THEREFORE, in consideration of the mutual covenants contained herein, and for other good and valuable consideration, the receipt and sufficiency of which are hereby acknowledged, the parties hereby agree as follows:

1. **Purchase of Preferred Shares.** On the Effective Date and subject to the terms and conditions of this Agreement, Purchaser hereby purchases from the Company, and Company hereby sells to Purchaser, an aggregate of _____ shares of the Company's Series A Preferred Stock (the "**Preferred Shares**"). The consideration paid by Purchaser for the Preferred Shares issued by the Company shall be $_____ per share, or an aggregate of $_____ (the "Purchase Price"). As used in this Agreement, the term "Preferred Shares" refers to the Preferred Shares purchased under this Agreement and includes all securities received (i) in replacement of the Preferred Shares, (ii) as a result of stock dividends or stock splits with respect to the Preferred Shares, and (iii) in replacement of the Preferred Shares in a merger, recapitalization, reorganization or similar corporate transaction.

2. **Closing.**

(a) **Deliveries by Purchaser.** Purchaser hereby delivers to the Company the following documents: (i) a duly executed copy of this Agreement; (ii) a blank Stock Power and Assignment Separate from Stock Certificate in the form of **Exhibit "A"** (the "**Stock Powers**"); (iii) a duly executed copy of the Accredited Investor Qualification Form in the form of **Exhibit "B"** attached hereto; and (iv) a check made out to the Company in the amount of the Purchase Price.

(b) **Deliveries by the Company.** Upon its receipt of all of the documents to be executed and delivered by Purchaser to the Company under this **Paragraph 2,** the Company will: (i) issue a duly executed stock certificate evidencing the Preferred Shares in the name of Purchaser, registered in Purchaser's name in accordance with **Paragraph 15,** with such certificate to be placed in escrow as provided in **Paragraph 9** until expiration or termination of the Company's Right of First Refusal described in **Paragraph 7** or redemption of all of the Preferred Shares; (ii) immediately file the Amended and Restated Articles of Incorporation of the Company attached hereto as **Exhibit "C"** with the California Secretary of State; and (iii) deliver a duly executed copy of the Indemnification and Co-Sale Agreement attached hereto as **Exhibit "D."**

3. **Rights of a Preferred Shareholder.**

(a) Subject to the terms and conditions of this Agreement and as more particularly described in the Amended and Restated Articles of Incorporation of the

Company attached hereto as **Exhibit "C,"** Purchaser shall have all of the rights, preferences, privileges and restrictions of a holder of shares of Series A Preferred Stock of the Company with respect to the Preferred Shares from and after the Effective Date of this Agreement until such time as Purchaser disposes of the Preferred Shares or the Company and/or its assignee(s) exercises the Right of First Refusal. The rights, preferences, privileges and restrictions of the Preferred Shares described in **Exhibit "C"** as the Amended and Restated Articles of Incorporation of the Company shall be filed with the California Secretary of State on the Effective Date of this Agreement.

(b) Upon the exercise of the Right of First Refusal, or the redemption of all of Purchaser's Preferred Shares, Purchaser will have no further rights as a holder of the Preferred Shares so purchased or redeemed, except the right to receive payment for the Preferred Shares in accordance with the provisions of this Agreement or the Amended and Restated Articles of Incorporation of the Company.

4. **Representations and Warranties of Purchaser.** Purchaser warrants and represents to the Company that:

(a) **Purchase for Own Account for Investment.** Purchaser is purchasing the Preferred Shares for Purchaser's own account for investment purposes only and not with a view to, or for sale in connection with, a distribution of the Preferred Shares within the meaning of the Securities Act of 1933, as amended (the "**1933 Act**"). Purchaser has no present intention of selling or otherwise disposing of all or any portion of the Preferred Shares and no one other than Purchaser has any beneficial ownership of any of the Preferred Shares.

(b) **Access to Information.** Purchaser has had access to all information regarding the Company and its present and prospective business, assets, liabilities and financial condition that Purchaser reasonably considers important in making the decision to purchase the Preferred Shares, and Purchaser has had ample opportunity to ask questions of the Company's representatives concerning such matters and this investment.

(c) **Understanding of Risks.** Purchaser is an investor of the Company and is fully aware of: (i) the highly speculative nature of the investment in the Preferred Shares; (ii) the financial hazards involved; (iii) the lack of liquidity of the Preferred Shares and the restrictions on transferability of the Preferred Shares (e.g., that Purchaser may not be able to sell or dispose of the Preferred Shares or use them as collateral for loans); (iv) the qualifications and backgrounds of the management of the Company; and (v) the tax consequences of investment in the Preferred Shares.

(d) **Purchaser's Qualifications.** Either: (i) Purchaser has a preexisting personal or business relationship with the Company and/or certain of its shareholders and/or officers and/or directors of a nature and duration sufficient to make Purchaser aware of the character, business acumen and general business and financial circumstances of the Company and/or such shareholders and/or officers and/or directors; or (ii) by reason of Purchaser's business or financial experience, Purchaser is capable of evaluating the merits and risks of this investment, has the ability to protect Purchaser's own interests in this transaction and is financially capable of bearing a total loss of this investment. Pursuant to the attached Accredited Investor Qualification Form attached hereto as **Exhibit "B,"** Purchaser has provided sufficient information to the Company to determine that Purchaser has met the qualifications as an "Accredited Investor" as defined by the Securities Act and is a "suitable investor" under the California Corporate Securities Law of 1968, as amended (the "**Securities Law**").

(e) **No General Solicitation.** At no time was Purchaser presented with or solicited by any publicly issued or circulated newspaper, mail, radio, television or other form of general advertising or solicitation in connection with the offer, sale and purchase of the Preferred Shares.

(f) **Compliance with Securities Laws.** Purchaser understands and acknowledges that, in reliance upon the representations and warranties made by Purchaser herein, the Preferred Shares are not being registered with the Securities and Exchange Commission ("**SEC**") under the Securities Act or being qualified under the Securities Law, but instead are being issued under an exemption or exemptions from the registration and qualification requirements, including Section 4(2) of the Securities Act and the provisions of Regulation D promulgated thereunder and Section 25102(f) of the Securities Law, which impose certain restrictions on Purchaser's ability to transfer the Preferred Shares.

(g) **Restrictions on Transfer.** Purchaser understands that Purchaser may not transfer any of the Preferred Shares unless such Preferred Shares are registered under the 1933 Act and qualified under the Securities Law or unless, in the opinion of counsel to the Company, exemptions from such registration and qualification requirements are available. Purchaser understands that only the Company may file a registration statement with the SEC or the California Commissioner of Corporations and that the Company is under no obligation to do so with respect to the Preferred Shares. Purchaser has also been advised that exemptions from registration and qualification may not be available or may not permit Purchaser to transfer all or any of the Preferred Shares in the amounts or at the times proposed by Purchaser.

(h) **Rule 144.** In addition, Purchaser has been advised that SEC Rule 144 promulgated under the Securities Act, which permits certain limited sales of unregistered securities, is not presently available with respect to the Preferred Shares because under Rule 144, the Company must be a reporting company and the sale of the Preferred Shares must be made through a broker-dealer. Rule 144 will almost assuredly not become available because the Company will not become a reporting company under the Security Act. However, see **Paragraph 4(g)** above, regarding the opinion of counsel to the Company in connection with the applicable exemption to a transfer of Preferred Shares by a shareholder under the Securities Laws and Security Act.

5. **Representations and Warranties of the Company.** The Company warrants and represents to Purchaser that:

(a) **Corporate Status.** The Company is duly organized, validly existing, and in good standing under the laws of [California].

(b) **Corporate Authority.** This Agreement has been duly and validly authorized, executed and delivered by the Company, and constitutes the valid and binding obligation of the Company enforceable against the Company in accordance with the terms hereof, except to the extent that such enforcement may be limited by bankruptcy, insolvency or similar laws now or hereafter in effect relating to creditors' rights and remedies generally.

(c) **Capitalization.** Immediately prior to the Effective Date, the authorized capital stock of the Company consisted of _____ shares of common stock, of which _____ shares are issued and outstanding. The Company has reserved _____ shares of its common stock to be granted to employees, consultants and directors pursuant to the Company's stock option plan. The Company's outstanding shares have been duly authorized and are validly issued, and are fully paid and nonassessable. Except as set forth herein, there are no options, warrants or other rights to purchase any of the Company's authorized and unissued capital stock. The Amended and Restated Articles of Incorporation attached hereto as **Exhibit "C"** have been duly and validly authorized, executed and delivered by the Company's Board of Directors and shareholders holding the requisite number of shares and will be filed with the California Secretary of State on the Effective Date. Upon filing of the Amended and Restated Articles of Incorporation with the California Secretary of State, the authorized capital stock of the Company shall consist of two classes of shares to be designated respectively "Preferred" and "Common" with no par value. The total number of Preferred shares authorized shall be _____, of which _____ shares shall be designated Series A Preferred Stock, and the total number of Common shares authorized shall be _____.

(d) **Offering.** Provided that the representations and warranties made by Purchaser herein are complete, true and accurate, then the issuance and sale of the Preferred Shares pursuant to this Agreement are exempt from registration under the 1933 Act and the Securities Law.

6. **Compliance with Securities Laws.** THE SALE OF THE SECURITIES THAT ARE THE SUBJECT OF THIS AGREEMENT, IF NOT YET QUALIFIED WITH THE STATE COMMISSIONER OF CORPORATIONS AND NOT EXEMPT FROM SUCH QUALIFICATION, ARE SUBJECT TO SUCH QUALIFICATION, AND THE ISSUANCE OF SUCH SECURITIES, AND THE RECEIPT OF ANY PART OF THE CONSIDERATION THEREFOR PRIOR TO SUCH QUALIFICATION IS UNLAWFUL UNLESS THE SALE IS EXEMPT (PURSUANT TO PARAGRAPH 4(f) HEREIN, IT IS INTENDED THAT THE SALE OF SUCH SECURITIES BE EXEMPT UNDER SECTION _____ OF THE SECURITIES LAW). THE RIGHTS OF THE PARTIES TO THIS AGREEMENT ARE EXPRESSLY CONDITIONED UPON SUCH QUALIFICATION BEING OBTAINED OR AN EXEMPTION BEING AVAILABLE.

7. **Right of First Refusal.** Before any Preferred Shares held by Purchaser or any transferee of such Preferred Shares (sometimes referred to herein as the "**Holder**") may be sold or otherwise transferred (including without limitation a transfer by gift or operation of law), the Company and/or its assignee(s) will have a right of first refusal to purchase the Preferred Shares to be sold or transferred (the "**Offered Shares**") on the terms and conditions set forth in this **Paragraph 7** (the "**Right of First Refusal**").

(a) **Notice of Proposed Transfer.** The Holder of the Offered Shares will deliver to the Company a written notice (the "**Notice**") stating: (i) the Holder's bona fide intention to sell or otherwise transfer the Offered Shares; (ii) the name and address of each proposed purchaser or other transferee (the "**Proposed Transferee**"); (iii) the number of Offered Shares to be transferred to each Proposed Transferee; (iv) the bona fide cash price or other consideration for which the Holder proposes to transfer the Offered Shares (the "**Offered Price**"); and (v) that the Holder acknowledges this Notice is an offer to sell the Offered Shares to the Company and/or its assignee(s) pursuant to the Company's Right of First Refusal at the Offered Price as provided for in this Agreement.

(b) **Exercise of Right of First Refusal.** At any time within thirty (30) days after the date of the Notice, the Company and/or its assignee(s) may, by giving written notice to the Holder, elect to purchase all (or, with the consent of the Holder, less than all) the Offered Shares proposed to be transferred to any one or more of the Proposed Transferees named in the Notice, at the purchase price determined in accordance with **Paragraph 7(c)** below.

(c) **Purchase Price.** The purchase price for the Offered Shares purchased under this **Paragraph 7** will be the Offered Price, provided that if the Offered Price consists of no legal consideration (as, for example, in the case of a transfer by gift), the purchase price will be the fair market value of the Offered Shares as determined in good faith by the Company's Board of Directors. If the Offered Price includes consideration other than cash, then the value of the non-cash consideration, as determined in good faith by the Company's Board of Directors, will conclusively be deemed to be the cash equivalent value of such non-cash consideration.

(d) **Payment.** Payment of the purchase price for the Offered Shares will be payable, at the option of the Company and/or its assignee(s) (as applicable), by check or by cancellation of all or a portion of any outstanding indebtedness owed by the Holder to the Company (or to such assignee, in the case of a purchase of Offered Shares by such assignee) or by any combination thereof. The purchase price will be paid without interest within sixty (60) days after the Company's receipt of the Notice, or, at the option of the Company and/or its assignee(s), in the manner and at the time(s) set forth in the Notice.

(e) **Holder's Right to Transfer.** If Holder has not consented to the purchase of less than all of the Offered Shares proposed in the Notice to be transferred to a given Proposed Transferee by the Company and/or its assignee(s) as provided in this **Paragraph 7,** then the Holder may sell or otherwise transfer all such Offered Shares to each Proposed Transferee at the Offered Price or at a higher price (and if Holder consented to the purchase of less than all the Offered Shares proposed in the Notice to be transferred to a given Proposed Transferee by the Company and/or its assignee(s) as provided in this **Paragraph 7(e),** then the Holder may sell or otherwise transfer any remaining Offered Shares to each Proposed Transferee at the Offered Price or at a higher price), provided that (i) such sale or other transfer is consummated within one hundred twenty (120) days after the date of the Notice, (ii) any such sale or other transfer is effected in compliance with all applicable securities laws, and (iii) each Proposed Transferee agrees in writing that the provisions of this **Paragraph 7(e)** will continue to apply to the Offered Shares in the hands of such Proposed Transferee. If the Offered Shares described in the Notice are not transferred to each Proposed Transferee within such one hundred twenty (120) day period, then a new Notice must be given to the Company, pursuant to which the Company will again be offered the Right of First Refusal before any Preferred Shares held by the Holder may be sold or otherwise transferred.

(f) **Exempt Transfers.** Notwithstanding anything to the contrary in this **Paragraph 7,** the following transfers of Preferred Shares will be exempt from the Right of First Refusal: (i) the transfer of any or all of the Preferred Shares during Purchaser's lifetime by gift or on Purchaser's death by will or intestacy to Purchaser's "Immediate Family" (as defined below) or to a trust or other entity for the benefit of Purchaser or Purchaser's Immediate Family, provided that each transferee or other recipient agrees in a writing satisfactory to the Company that the provisions of this **Paragraph 7(f)** will continue to apply to the transferred Preferred Shares in the hands of such transferee or other recipient; (ii) any transfer of Preferred Shares made pursuant to a statutory merger or statutory consolidation of the Company with or into another corporation or corporations (except that the Right of First Refusal will continue to apply thereafter to such Preferred Shares, in which case the surviving corporation of such merger or consolidation shall succeed to the rights of the Company under this **Paragraph 7** unless (i) the common stock of the surviving corporation is registered under the Securities Exchange Act of 1934, as amended; or (ii) the agreement of merger or consolidation expressly otherwise provides); or (iii) any transfer of Preferred Shares pursuant to the winding up and dissolution of the Company. As used herein, the term "**Immediate Family**" will mean Purchaser's spouse, the lineal descendant or antecedent, father, mother, brother or sister, child, adopted child or grandchild or adopted grandchild of Purchaser or Purchaser's spouse, or the spouse of any child, adopted child, grandchild or adopted grandchild of Purchaser or Purchaser's spouse or Spousal Equivalent, as defined herein. As used herein, a person is deemed to be a "**Spousal Equivalent**" provided the following circumstances are true: (i) irrespective of whether or not the Purchaser and the Spousal Equivalent are the same sex, they are the sole spousal equivalent of the other for the last twelve (12) months, (ii) they intend to remain so indefinitely, (iii) neither are married to anyone else, (iv) both are at least 18 years of age and mentally competent to consent to contract, (v) they are not related by blood to a degree of closeness that which would prohibit legal marriage in the state in which they legally reside, (vi) they are jointly responsible for each other's common welfare and financial obligations, and (vii) they have resided together in the same residence for the last twelve (12) months and intend to do so indefinitely.

    (g) **Termination of Right of First Refusal.** The Right of First Refusal will terminate as to all Preferred Shares on the effective date of the first sale of common stock of the Company to the general public pursuant to a registration statement filed with and declared effective by the SEC under the 1933 Act (other than a registration statement relating solely to the issuance of Common Stock pursuant to a business combination or an employee incentive or benefit plan).

    8. **Encumbrances on Shares.** Purchaser may grant a lien or security interest in, or pledge, hypothecate or encumber Preferred Shares only if each party to whom such lien or security interest is granted, or to whom such pledge, hypothecation or other encumbrance is made, agrees in a writing satisfactory to the Company that: (i) such lien, security interest, pledge, hypothecation or encumbrance will not apply to such Preferred Shares after they are acquired by the Company and/or its assignees under **Paragraph 7;** and (ii) the provisions of this **Paragraph 8** will continue to apply to such Preferred Shares in the hands of such party and any transferee of such party.

    9. **Escrow.** As security for Purchaser's faithful performance of this Agreement, Purchaser agrees that the stock certificate(s) evidencing the Preferred Shares shall be delivered, together with the Stock Powers executed by Purchaser, to the Secretary of the Company or other designee of the Company (the "**Escrow Holder**"), who is hereby appointed to hold such certificate(s) and Stock Powers in escrow and to take all such actions and to effectuate all such transfers and/or releases of such Preferred Shares as are in accordance with the terms of this Agreement. Escrow Holder will act solely for the Company as its agent and not as a fiduciary. Purchaser and the Company agree that Escrow Holder will not be liable to any party to this Agreement (or to any other party) for any actions or omissions unless Escrow Holder is grossly negligent or intentionally fraudulent in carrying out the duties of Escrow Holder under this Agreement. Escrow Holder may rely upon any letter, notice or other document executed with any signature purported to be genuine and may rely on the advice of counsel and obey any order of any court with respect to the transactions contemplated by this Agreement. The certificate representing the Preferred Shares will be released from escrow upon termination of the Company's Right of First Refusal.

    10. **Tax Consequences. PURCHASER UNDERSTANDS THAT PURCHASER MAY SUFFER ADVERSE TAX CONSEQUENCES AS A RESULT OF PUR-**

CHASER'S PURCHASE, OWNERSHIP, OR DISPOSITION OF THE PREFERRED SHARES. PURCHASER REPRESENTS (i) THAT PURCHASER HAS OR WILL SEEK TAX ADVICE IN CONNECTION WITH THE PURCHASE, OWNERSHIP OR DISPOSITION OF THE PREFERRED SHARES AND (ii) THAT PURCHASER IS NOT RELYING ON THE COMPANY OR ITS AGENTS FOR ANY TAX ADVICE.

11. **Restrictive Legends and Stop-Transfer Orders.**

(a) **Legends.** Purchaser understands and agrees that the Company will place the legends set forth below or similar legends on any stock certificate(s) evidencing the Preferred Shares, together with any other legends that may be required by state or federal securities laws, the Company's Articles of Incorporation or Bylaws, any other agreement between Purchaser and the Company or any agreement between Purchaser and any third party:

THE SECURITIES REPRESENTED BY THIS INSTRUMENT HAVE NOT BEEN REGISTERED UNDER THE FEDERAL SECURITIES ACT OF 1933, AS AMENDED, OR REGISTERED OR QUALIFIED UNDER THE SECURITIES LAW OF ANY STATE AND MAY NOT BE SOLD OR OTHERWISE TRANSFERRED UNLESS (1) THERE IS AN EFFECTIVE REGISTRATION STATEMENT FOR THE SECURITIES UNDER THE ACT AND ANY APPLICABLE STATE SECURITIES LAW, (2) SUCH TRANSFER IS MADE IN COMPLIANCE WITH RULE 144 UNDER THE ACT AND PURSUANT TO REGISTRATION OR QUALIFICATION UNDER ANY APPLICABLE STATE SECURITIES LAW OR EXEMPTION THEREFROM, OR (3) THERE IS AN OPINION OF COUNSEL SATISFACTORY TO THE COMPANY THAT SUCH REGISTRATION IS NOT REQUIRED AS TO SAID TRANSFER, SALE OR OFFER.

THE TRANSFER, SALE, ASSIGNMENT, HYPOTHECATION, ENCUMBRANCE OR ALIENATION OF THE SHARES REPRESENTED BY THIS CERTIFICATE IS RESTRICTED BY A RESTRICTED STOCK PURCHASE AGREEMENT DATED _____, 20___. A COPY OF THIS AGREEMENT IS AVAILABLE FOR INSPECTION DURING NORMAL BUSINESS HOURS AT THE PRINCIPAL OFFICE OF THE CORPORATION. ALL OF THE TERMS AND PROVISIONS OF THE RESTRICTED STOCK PURCHASE AGREEMENT ARE HEREBY INCORPORATED BY REFERENCE AND MADE A PART OF THIS CERTIFICATE.

(b) **Stop-Transfer Instructions.** Purchaser agrees that, to ensure compliance with the restrictions imposed by this Agreement, the Company may issue appropriate "stop-transfer" instructions to its transfer agent, if any, and if the Company transfers its own securities, it may make appropriate notations to the same effect in its own records.

(c) **Refusal to Transfer.** The Company will not be required (i) to transfer on its books any shares that have been sold or otherwise transferred in violation of any of the provisions of this Agreement or (ii) to treat as owner of such shares, or to accord the right to vote or pay dividends, to any purported purchaser or other transferee to whom such shares have been so transferred.

12. **Market Standoff Agreement.** Purchaser agrees in connection with any registration of the Company's securities under the Securities Act that, upon the request of the Company or the underwriters managing any registered public offering of the Company's securities, Purchaser will not sell or otherwise dispose of any of the

securities without the prior written consent of the Company or such underwriters, as the case may be, for such period of time (not to exceed one hundred eighty (180) days) after the effective date of such registration requested by such managing underwriters and subject to all restrictions as the Company or the managing underwriters may specify for shareholders generally, provided the shares held by the officers of the Company are similarly restricted. Purchaser further agrees to enter into any agreement reasonably required by the underwriters to implement the foregoing.

13. **Co-Sale Agreement.** The majority shareholder of the Company has agreed not to sell his stock to a third party without first providing the holders of Preferred Shares the opportunity to sell their stock on the same terms and conditions pro rata based on the stock owned by the majority shareholder and the Preferred Shareholders. The Company hereby agrees it will not transfer on its books any shares owned by such majority shareholder of the Company, or treat as owner of such shares any purported purchaser or other transferee, which are sold or otherwise transferred in violation of Purchaser's co-sale rights as set forth in the Indemnification and Co-Sale Agreement attached hereto as **Exhibit "D":**

14. **Information Rights.**

(a) **Books to be Maintained by the Company.** The Company will maintain true books and records of account in which full and correct entries will be made of all its business transactions pursuant to a system of accounting established and administered in accordance with generally accepted accounting principles consistently applied, and will set aside on its books all such proper accruals and reserves as shall be required under generally accepted accounting principles consistently applied.

(b) **Annual Financial Statements.** As soon as practicable after the end of each fiscal year of the Company, and in any event within one hundred twenty (120) days thereafter, the Company will furnish Purchaser a balance sheet of the Company, as at the end of such fiscal year, and a statement of income and a statement of cash flows of the Company, for such year, and setting forth in each case in comparative form the figures for the previous fiscal year, all in reasonable detail.

(c) **Quarterly Financial Statements.** The Company will furnish Purchaser, as soon as practicable after the end of the first, second and third quarterly accounting periods in each fiscal year of the Company, and in any event within forty-five (45) days thereafter, a balance sheet of the Company as of the end of each such quarterly period, and a statement of income and a statement of cash flows of the Company for such period and for the current fiscal year to date.

(d) **Budget; Operating Plan; Monthly Financial Statements.** The Company will furnish Purchaser: (i) at least thirty (30) days prior to the beginning of each fiscal year a preliminary annual budget and operating plans for such fiscal year and within sixty (60) days after the start of each fiscal year the final annual budget and operating plan and (ii) as soon as practicable after the end of each month, and in any event within twenty (20) days thereafter, a balance sheet of the Company as of the end of each such month, and a statement of income and a statement of cash flows of the Company for such month and for the current fiscal year to date, including a comparison to plan figures for such period.

(e) **Inspection Rights.** Purchaser shall have the right to visit and inspect the offices of the Company or any of its subsidiaries, and to discuss the affairs, finances and accounts of the Company or any of its subsidiaries with its officers, and to review such information as is reasonably requested all at such reasonable times and as often as may be reasonably requested.

15. **Indemnification.** Purchaser shall be entitled to the protections set forth in the Indemnification and Co-Sale Agreement attached hereto as **Exhibit "D,"** which shall be delivered at closing in accordance with **Paragraph 2.**

16. **Compliance with Laws and Regulations.** The issuance and transfer of the Preferred Shares will be subject to and conditioned upon compliance by the Company and Purchaser with all applicable state and federal laws and regulations and with all applicable requirements of any stock exchange or automated quotation system on which the Company's Preferred Shares may be listed or quoted at the time of such issuance or transfer.

17. **General Provisions.**

(a) **Assignments; Successors and Assigns.** The Company may assign any of its rights and obligations under this Agreement, including its rights to repurchase the Preferred Shares under the Right of First Refusal. Any assignment of rights and obligations by any other party to this Agreement requires the Company's prior written consent. This Agreement, and the rights and obligations of the parties hereunder, will be binding upon and inure to the benefit of their respective successors, assigns, heirs, executors, administrators and legal representatives.

(b) **Governing Law.** This Agreement will be governed by and construed in accordance with the laws of the State of [California], without giving effect to that body of laws pertaining to conflict of laws.

(c) **Notices.** Any and all notices required or permitted to be given to a party pursuant to the provisions of this Agreement will be in writing and will be effective and deemed to provide such party sufficient notice under this Agreement on the earliest of the following: (i) at the time of personal delivery, if delivery is in person; (ii) at the time of transmission by facsimile, addressed to the other party at its facsimile number specified herein (or hereafter modified by subsequent notice to the parties hereto), with confirmation of receipt made by both telephone and printed confirmation sheet verifying successful transmission of the facsimile; (iii) one (1) business day after deposit with an express overnight courier for United States deliveries, or two (2) business days after such deposit for deliveries outside of the United States; or (iv) three (3) business days after deposit in the United States mail by certified mail (return receipt requested) for United States deliveries.

All notices for delivery outside the United States will be sent by facsimile or by express courier. All notices not delivered personally or by facsimile will be sent with postage and/or other charges prepaid and properly addressed to the party to be notified at the address or facsimile number set forth below the signature lines of this Agreement or at such other address or facsimile number as such other party may designate by one of the indicated means of notice herein to the other party hereto. Notices by facsimile shall be machine verified as received.

(d) **Further Assurances.** The parties agree to execute such further documents and instruments and to take such further actions as may be reasonably necessary to carry out the purposes and intent of this Agreement.

(e) **Titles and Headings.** The titles, captions and headings of this Agreement are included for ease of reference only and will be disregarded in interpreting or construing this Agreement. Unless otherwise specifically stated, all references herein to "paragraphs" and "exhibits" will mean "paragraphs" and "exhibits" to this Agreement.

(f) **Counterparts.** This Agreement may be executed in any number of counterparts, including facsimile signatures, each of which when so executed and delivered will be deemed an original, and all of which together shall constitute one and the same agreement.

(g) **Severability.** If any provision of this Agreement is determined by any court or arbitrator of competent jurisdiction to be invalid, illegal or unenforceable in any respect, such provision will be enforced to the maximum extent possible given the intent of the parties hereto. If such clause or provision cannot be so enforced, such provision shall be stricken from this Agreement and the remainder of this Agreement shall be enforced as if such invalid, illegal or unenforceable clause or provision had (to the extent not enforceable) never been contained in this Agreement.

(h) **Amendment and Waivers.** This Agreement may be amended only by a written agreement executed by each of the parties hereto. No amendment of or waiver of, or modification of any obligation under this Agreement will be enforceable unless set forth in a writing signed by the party against which enforcement is sought. Any amendment effected in accordance with this Paragraph will be binding upon all parties hereto and each of their respective successors and assigns. No delay or failure to require performance of any provision of this Agreement shall constitute a waiver of that provision as to that or any other instance. No waiver granted under this Agreement as to any one provision herein shall constitute a subsequent waiver of such provision or of any other provision herein, nor shall it constitute the waiver of any performance other than the actual performance specifically waived.

(i) **Entire Agreement.** This Agreement and the documents referred to herein constitute the entire agreement and understanding of the parties with respect to the subject matter of this Agreement, and supersedes all prior understandings and agreements, whether oral or written, between or among the parties hereto with respect to the specific subject matter hereof.

(j) **Attorney Fees.** In any action, proceeding, or arbitration arising out of this Agreement, the prevailing party, by judgment or settlement, in that action or proceeding shall be entitled to recover reasonable attorney fees, expert witness fees, and court costs as may be fixed by the court, jury, or arbitration panel.

(k) **No Third Party Beneficiaries.** This Agreement is made only for the benefit of the parties hereto and is not intended to give any other person or entity any rights or remedies hereunder.

(l) **No Drafting Party.** The parties agree that each party has reviewed and provided input into this Agreement and that any rule of construction to the effect that ambiguities are to be resolved against the drafting party shall not apply to any interpretation of this Agreement.

(m) **Legal Review.** Each party acknowledges and represents that, in executing this Agreement, he/she/it has had the opportunity to seek advice as to his/her/its legal rights from legal counsel and that it has read and understood all of the terms and provisions of this Agreement.

18. **Title to Preferred Shares.** The exact spelling of the name(s) under which Purchaser will take title to the Preferred Shares is:

_____.

Purchaser desires to take title to the Preferred Shares as follows:
[ ] Individual, as separate property
[ ] Husband and wife, as community property
[ ] Joint Tenants
[ ] Tenants in Common
[ ] Other (Corporation, single person, trust, etc., please indicate) _____
Purchaser's social security number or tax payer identification number is:

_____

IN WITNESS WHEREOF, the parties hereto have executed this Agreement as of the Effective Date.

The Company:

**** INCORPORATED

[Address] _____

By: _____, President

Purchaser:

[Address] _____

By: _____, [Name]

EXHIBIT A: STOCK POWER AND ASSIGNMENT SEPARATE FROM CERTIFICATE

FOR VALUE RECEIVED and pursuant to that certain Restricted Stock Purchase Agreement for Series A Preferred Stock dated _____ _____, 20___, the ("**Agreement**"), by and between the undersigned ("**Purchaser**") and ****** INCORPORATED,** a [California] corporation (the "**Company**"), the undersigned hereby sells, assigns and transfers unto _____, _____ shares of the Company's [Series A Preferred Stock] (the "**Shares**"), standing in the undersigned's name on the books of the Company represented by Certificate No(s). _____ delivered herewith, and does hereby irrevocably constitute and appoint the Secretary of the Company as the undersigned's attorney-in-fact, with full power of substitution, to transfer said Preferred Shares on the books of the Company. THIS ASSIGNMENT MAY ONLY BE USED AS AUTHORIZED BY THE AGREEMENT AND ANY EXHIBITS THERETO.

Dated:_____

PURCHASER:
By: _____

Instructions to Purchaser: Please do not fill in any blanks other than the signature line. The purpose of this Stock Power and Assignment is to enable the Company and/or its assignee(s) to acquire the Preferred Shares upon exercise of its "Right of First Refusal" set forth in the Agreement without requiring additional signatures on the part of the Purchaser.

EXHIBIT B: ACCREDITED INVESTOR QUALIFICATION FORM

In order for the sale of the Preferred Shares to meet the exemption requirements pursuant to Section 25102(f) of the Securities Law, the undersigned Purchaser warrants and represents that Purchaser (INITIAL THE APPROPRIATE SPACES BELOW):

(1) _____ (initial) has a preexisting personal or business relationship with the Company or any of its partners, officers, directors, controlling person, or managers, more fully described as follows (describe):

(2) _____ (initial) by reason of investor's business or financial experience or the business or financial experience of investor's professional advisers who are unaffiliated with and who are not compensated by the Company or any affiliate or selling agent of the Company, directly or indirectly, could reasonably assumed to have the capacity to protect investor's own interests in connection with this transaction.

Accredited Investor. Purchaser warrants and represents that Purchaser is an accredited investor, as defined in the Securities Act of 1933 and rules promulgated thereby, because Purchaser has (INITIAL THE APPROPRIATE SPACES BELOW):

(1) _____ (initial) A net worth alone or a joint net worth with my spouse in excess of $1,000,000 excluding the value of my primary residence at the time of this investment;

(2) _____ (initial) An annual income (not including income of my spouse) (i) in excess of $200,000 per year for the last two years or joint income with my spouse in excess of $300,000 in each of those years and (ii) has a reasonable expectation of reaching the same income level in the current year;

(3) _____ (initial) A bank as defined in Section 3(a)(2) of the Securities Act, or any savings and loan association or other institution as defined in Section 3(a)(5)(A) of the Securities Act whether acting in its individual or fiduciary capacity; any broker or dealer registered pursuant to Section 15 of the Securities Exchange Act of 1934; any insurance company as defined in Section 2(13) of the Securities Act; an investment company registered under the Investment Company Act of 1940 or a business development company as defined in Section 2(a)(48) of the Investment Company Act; a small business investment company licensed by the U.S. Small Business Administration under Section 301(c) or (d) of the Small Business Investment Act of 1958; any plan established and maintained by a state, its political subdivisions, or any agency or instrumentality of a state or its political subdivisions, for the benefit of its employees, if such a plan has total assets in excess of $5,000,000; or an employee benefit plan within the meaning of Title I of the Employee Retirement Income Security Act of 1974, if the investment decision is made by a plan fiduciary, as defined in Section 3(21) of the Employee Retirement Income Security Act of 1974, which is either a bank, insurance company, or registered investment adviser, or if the employee benefit plan has total assets in excess of $5,000,000 or, if a self-directed plan, with investment decisions made solely by persons that are accredited investors;

(4) _____ (initial) A private business development company as defined in Section 202(a)(22) of the Investment Advisers Act of 1940;

(5) _____ (initial) A corporation, partnership or an organization described in Section 501(c)(3) of the Internal Revenue Code of 1986, as amended, corporation,

Massachusetts or similar business trust, or partnership, not formed for the specific purpose of acquiring the securities offered, and with total assets in excess of $5,000,000;

(6) _____ (initial) A director, executive officer, or general partner of the Company of the securities being offered or sold, or any director, executive officer, or general partner of a general partner of the Company;

(7) _____ (initial) An entity in which all of the equity owners meet the requirements of at least one of the above subparagraphs;

(8) _____ (initial) A trust with total assets in excess of $5,000,000, not formed for the purpose of acquiring the Securities, whose purchase is directed by a sophisticated person;

(9) _____ (initial) Investor has relied on the advice of the following Purchaser Representative in evaluating the merits and risks of this investment:

_____   _____
(Name)   (Relationship)

The above-named professional advisor and Investor together have such knowledge and experience in financial and business matters that they have the capacity to protect Investor's interests in this investment.

Investor hereby acknowledges that: (i) the Purchaser Representative is Investor's "Purchaser Representative" as defined in Regulation D promulgated by the Securities and Exchange Commission under the Securities Act of 1933, as amended; (ii) in evaluating Investor's investment, as contemplated hereby, Investor has relied upon the advice of the Purchaser Representative as to the merits of the investment in general and the suitability of investment for Investor in particular; and (iii) the Purchaser Representative has confirmed to Investor in writing (a copy of which instrument is attached to this Purchase Agreement) of any past, present or future material relationship, actual or contemplated, between the Purchaser Representative and the Company.

EXECUTED this __ day of _____, 20___, at San Francisco, California.

_____
    Signature of Investor

**EXHIBIT C: AMENDED AND RESTATED
ARTICLES OF INCORPORATION OF
**** INCORPORATED**

EXHIBIT D: INDEMNIFICATION
AND CO-SALE AGREEMENT

Form 11 H: Convertible Note Subscription Agreement with Form of Convertible Note

****, Inc.
CONVERTIBLE NOTE
SUBSCRIPTION AGREEMENT

This document is to be read and responded to in its entirety. (Please Type or Print in Ink)

Purchaser Full Name: _____

Residence Address: _____

_____

Mailing Address (if different): _____

_____

Telephone Number: _____

Co-Purchaser (if any)

Full Name: _____

Residence Address: _____

_____

Mailing Address (if different): _____

_____

Telephone Number: _____

Purchase Amount: $_____

The exact spelling of the name(s) to be on the Convertible Notes:

_____

_____

GENERAL INSTRUCTIONS FOR PURCHASERS

IF, AFTER YOU HAVE CAREFULLY REVIEWED THIS CONVERTIBLE NOTE SUBSCRIPTION AGREEMENT, INCLUDING THE FORM OF CONVERTIBLE NOTE ATTACHED HERETO AS AN EXHIBIT AND ALL OTHER MATERIALS PROVIDED TO YOU BY ****, INC. (THE "COMPANY") IN CONNECTION WITH THE OFFER AND SALE OF ITS CONVERTIBLE NOTES (THE "OFFERING MATERIALS"), YOU WISH TO INVEST IN THE CONVERTIBLE NOTES OF THE COMPANY (THE "NOTES"), PLEASE FOLLOW CAREFULLY THE INSTRUCTIONS BELOW.

THE INFORMATION REQUESTED IN THIS AGREEMENT IS REQUIRED IN CONNECTION WITH THE COMPANY'S INTENDED RELIANCE UPON CERTAIN EXEMPTIONS FROM THE REGISTRATION AND QUALIFICATION REQUIRE-MENTS OF FEDERAL AND STATE SECURITIES LAWS. AGREEMENTS THAT ARE MISSING REQUESTED INFORMATION AND/OR SIGNATURES CANNOT AND

WILL NOT BE ACCEPTED UNLESS AND UNTIL SUCH INFORMATION AND/OR SIGNATURES ARE PROVIDED. SUCH INFORMATION IS CONFIDENTIAL AND WILL NOT BE REVIEWED BY ANYONE OTHER THAN THE COMPANY AND ITS ADVISORS.

ALL PURCHASERS:

Carefully read this Convertible Note Subscription Agreement (the "**Agreement**'). Sections I–IV contain certain important notices, understandings as to certain matters, purchaser representations and warranties, and registration information. These sections pertain to ALL PURCHASERS. Section V requests information regarding the financial condition and experience of prospective investors that are entities ("**Entity Purchasers**", together with Purchasers who are individuals, "**Purchasers**") and should be completed only by Entity Purchasers.

One copy of this Agreement must be filled out completely and signed by each Purchaser. All parties involved in reviewing and evaluating this Agreement will be relying on the representations and warranties you make and on the information you supply. Any Purchaser may be required to furnish additional information to enable the Company to determine whether the Purchaser is a qualified investor.

JOINT PURCHASERS:

In the case of joint Purchasers, where such Purchasers are husband and wife or relatives and have the same principal residence, only the Purchaser primarily responsible for evaluating the investment and making the decision to invest must complete Section IV of this Agreement. In the case of joint Purchasers who are not husband and wife or relatives or do not have the same principal residence, each joint Purchasers must complete an Agreement. Joint Purchasers must take title to the Notes jointly and shall supply instructions to the Company as to the form of ownership desired.

ENTITY PURCHASERS:

The Company may request that each Entity Purchaser submit with its completed Agreement the form of certificate corresponding to its form of organization together with a copy of its most recent financial statements. The Company reserves the right to require, at its sole discretion, an opinion of legal counsel from any Entity Purchaser.

When used herein, the terms "I", "you", "your," and "the undersigned" shall mean the Purchaser executing this Agreement below.

I.   IMPORTANT NOTICES CONCERNING THE OFFERING

The minimum investment in this offering is $_____. However, the Company, in its sole discretion, may accept subscriptions in smaller amounts. There is no minimum offering amount, so funds will become immediately available to the company upon its acceptance of subscriptions. The maximum offering amount is $_____. Subscription funds will be used for administrative, sales, marketing, and general operating expenses in accordance with the business plan and budget included in the Offering Materials.

THE NOTES HAVE NOT BEEN REGISTERED UNDER THE SECURITIES ACT OF 1933, AS AMENDED (THE "**SECURITIES ACT**"), OR ANY STATE "**BLUE SKY**"

OR SECURITIES LAWS. THE NOTES CANNOT BE SOLD, TRANSFERRED, ASSIGNED, OR OTHERWISE DISPOSED OF EXCEPT IN COMPLIANCE WITH APPLICABLE FEDERAL AND STATE SECURITIES LAWS AND WILL NOT BE TRANSFERRED OF RECORD EXCEPT IN COMPLIANCE WITH SAID LAWS. THESE SECURITIES HAVE NOT BEEN APPROVED OR DISAPPROVED BY THE SECURITIES AND EXCHANGE COMMISSION OR BY ANY STATE SECURITIES COMMISSION OR REGULATORY AUTHORITY, NOR HAVE ANY OF THE FORE-GOING AUTHORITIES PASSED UPON OR ENDORSED THE MERITS OF THIS OFFERING. ANY REPRESENTATION TO THE CONTRARY IS UNLAWFUL.

THIS OFFERING INVOLVES CERTAIN MATERIAL RISKS. PLEASE SEE THE "**RISK FACTORS**" DISCUSSION BELOW IN DETAIL FOR SOME OF THE FAC-TORS THAT SHOULD BE CONSIDERED BY PURCHASERS BEFORE INVESTING IN THE NOTES. HOWEVER, THERE MAY BE SUBSTANTIAL, MATERIAL RISKS TO AN INVESTMENT IN THE NOTES WHICH ARE NOT EXPLICITLY DISCUSSED IN THIS AGREEMENT OR IN THE OFFERING MATERIALS.

IN MAKING AN INVESTMENT DECISION INVESTORS MUST RELY ON THEIR OWN EXAMINATION OF THE ISSUER AND THE TERMS OF THE OFFERING, INCLUDING THE MERITS AND RISKS INVOLVED. THERE CURRENTLY IS NO TRADING MARKET FOR THE SECURITIES OF THE COMPANY, AND NONE IS EXPECTED TO DEVELOP FOLLOWING THIS OFFERING.

PURCHASERS MUST BE ABLE TO BEAR THE ECONOMIC RISK OF THE INVESTMENT FOR AN INDEFINITE PERIOD OF TIME, BECAUSE THE SECURI-TIES CANNOT BE SOLD OR TRANSFERRED EXCEPT AS PERMITTED BY THE SECURITIES ACT AND APPLICABLE PROVISIONS OF STATE SECURITIES LAWS. IF, AS A RESULT OF SOME CHANGE OF CIRCUMSTANCES ARISING FROM AN EVENT NOT NOW IN CONTEMPLATION, OR FOR ANY OTHER REA-SON, AN INVESTOR WISHES TO TRANSFER HIS OR HER SECURITIES, SUCH INVESTOR MAY FIND NO MARKET FOR THOSE SECURITIES.

PRIOR TO THE ISSUANCE OF ANY SECURITIES, PURCHASERS SHALL BE GIVEN THE OPPORTUNITY TO ASK QUESTIONS AND RECEIVE ANSWERS CONCERNING ANY ASPECT OF THE INVESTMENT, AND TO OBTAIN ANY ADDI-TIONAL INFORMATION, TO THE EXTENT THE COMPANY POSSESSES SUCH INFORMATION OR CAN ACQUIRE IT WITHOUT UNREASONABLE EFFORT OR EXPENSE, NECESSARY TO VERIFY THE ACCURACY OF THE INFORMATION CONTAINED IN THE OFFERING MATERIALS OR IN ANY OTHER MATERIAL PRO-VIDED TO THE PURCHASER BY THE COMPANY.

PURCHASERS ARE NOT TO CONSTRUE THE CONTENTS OF THIS AGREE-MENT OR THE OFFERING MATERIALS AS LEGAL, TAX, OR INVESTMENT ADVICE. EACH INVESTOR SHOULD CONSULT HIS OWN LEGAL COUNSEL, ACCOUNTANT, OR BUSINESS ADVISOR AS TO LEGAL, TAX, AND RELATED MATTERS CONCERNING HIS POSSIBLE INVESTMENT IN THE SECURITIES OFFERED HEREBY. THE DELIVERY OF THIS AGREEMENT AT ANY TIME DOES NOT IMPLY THE INFORMATION CONTAINED HEREIN OR IN THE OFFERING MATERIALS IS CORRECT AS OF ANY TIME SUBSEQUENT TO THE DATE HEREOF.

RISK FACTORS

Investors should carefully consider the risks of investment before deciding whether to subscribe for the Notes. The risks described below are just a few of the risks we actually face. Additional risks not set forth herein or not presently known to us or that we currently believe are immaterial may also impair our business operations and financial results. If any of these risks actually occur, our business, financial condition, or results of operations could be adversely affected, and you could lose all or part of your investment. In evaluating us, our business, and any investment in our business, readers should carefully consider all of the possible risks of investment, including the following factors.

We have a limited operating history on which to judge future prospects and results of operations.

The Company is currently an early stage company with a limited operating history upon which to base its projections and forecasts. The Offering Materials may contain "forward-looking statements" within the meaning of the Private Securities Litigation Reform Act of 1995. These statements can be identified by introductory words such as "expects," "plans," "intends," "believes," "will," "estimates," "forecasts," "projects," or words of similar meaning, and by the fact that they do not relate strictly to historical or current facts. Forward-looking statements frequently are used in discussing potential product sales, distribution channels, product development activities, and similar operating matters. Many factors may cause actual results to differ from forward-looking statements, including inaccurate assumptions and a broad variety of risks and uncertainties, some of which are known and others of which are not. No forward-looking statement is a guarantee of future results or events, and one should avoid placing undue reliance on such statements. The Company claims the protection of the safe harbor for forward-looking statements that is contained in the Private Securities Litigation Reform Act.

The securities being offered are subject to certain restrictions on transfer.

The Notes being offered have restrictions and limited transferability. There is currently no public trading market for the Notes and no guarantee can be given that one will develop. The Notes have not been registered under the Securities Act or under any state securities laws. The Notes are being offered and sold pursuant to exemptions from applicable federal and state registration requirements, allowing for transactions, which do not involve a "public offering." The Company is under no obligation to provide for registration of the securities in the future. Any subsequent sales by investors of the Notes or the securities into which they may convert may only be permissible if an exemption from the applicable federal and state registration provisions is available at the time of the proposed sale. The Company cannot guarantee to any investor that such an exemption will be available. The Company is not presently subject to the periodic reporting requirements of Sections 13 or 15(d) of the Securities Exchange Act of 1934 and may or may not choose to make available to the public, in the foreseeable future, information with respect to the Company's affairs sufficient to permit the use of Rule 144 under the 1933 Act as a means of disposing of an investment in the Company. Consequently, holders of the Notes may not be able to liquidate their investment in the event of an emergency.

We are dependent upon our ability to raise capital.

We are dependent on the proceeds of this Offering and at least one more financing in order to implement our business plan. In the event we are unable to raise the projected amount of financing, we may not be able to generate enough cash flow from operations to satisfy our financial obligations, including repayment of Notes that are not converted into Common or Series A Preferred Stock of the Company. There can be no assurance that we will be able to raise sufficient funds in this offering or in an additional financing on a timely basis, on acceptable terms, or at all.

The Notes may not be first in line for repayment in the event of a liquidation.

The terms of the Notes require that Note holders execute such documentation as the Company may request to subordinate repayment of the Notes to any credit facility provided to the Company by a commercial bank, provided no default has occurred under the Note. Therefore, if the Notes are subordinated to bank debt, they will not be first in line for repayment in the event the Company is liquidated.

Investors will have little control over the direction of the Company.

Our existing shareholders have substantial influence over the Company, and their interests may not be aligned with the interests of Note holders or future shareholders. Our management team has substantial or complete influence over our business, including decisions regarding significant corporate actions. Purchasers in this offering will not be able to take a direct role in the management of the Company, such that the success of the Company is contingent on the judgment and expertise of its executive officers. Management reserves the right to formulate the Company's capitalization, Board composition, and financial strategy on an "as needed" basis. Persons who are not willing to rely upon the skills and expertise of the Management of the Company should not invest in the Notes.

Investors will experience dilution of their investment.

Investors purchasing Notes in this offering will sustain an immediate and substantial dilution of their investment on a profits, but not capital, basis upon conversion of the Notes. Moreover, investors can expect to be further diluted should the Company engage in subsequent rounds of financing in the future.

We are unlikely to make distributions.

There can be no guarantee that we will achieve our corporate goals and be in a position to pay any cash or non-cash distributions to our shareholders. Even if and when we achieve profitable operations, it is unlikely that we will pay distributions in the foreseeable future.

The conversion price is arbitrary.

The optional conversion price of the Notes being offered herein has been arbitrarily determined and bears no relationship to assets, book value, earnings, or other established criteria of value. In determining the optional conversion price, such factors as the limited financial resources of the Company, the nature of the Company's assets, estimates of the business potential of the Company, the amount of equity and voting control desired to be retained by the Company's existing shareholders upon conversion of the Notes, the amount of dilution to investors, and the general conditions of the securities market, were considered. The automatic conversion price will be determined by the terms of the Company's Series A Preferred Stock financing, which have yet to be established and are dependent upon our ability to complete a Series A Preferred Stock financing.

AGREEMENTS AND UNDERSTANDINGS

I agree and understand as follows:

A.   Except as may be provided under state securities laws, this Agreement is irrevocable; provided, however, that the execution and delivery of this Agreement will not constitute an agreement between the Company and me until this Agreement is accepted by the Company. I understand that the Company may request any other information, whether or not specifically called for in this Agreement, that it deems desirable in evaluating my investment. Furthermore, I understand that the Company has the right to reject my investment with or without cause, for any or no reason.

B.   Although I realize that the Company will make a good faith effort to sell the Notes without undue delay, I understand that some time may pass after my execution and submission of this Agreement before any decision to accept or reject my investment is made. I understand that a delay in deciding whether to accept or reject my investment, even if such delay involves not including my investment in a given closing or in any closing, can in no way be interpreted as limiting the discretion of the Company to accept or reject my investment.

C.   I will make such representations and warranties and furnish such additional information as to my investment experience and financial position as the Company may reasonably request, and if there should be any material change in the information set forth herein prior to the closing of the sale of Notes to me, I will immediately furnish such revised or corrected information to the Company.

D.   I understand that in the event that my Agreement is not accepted for whatever reason, my investment funds will be returned to me without interest or escrow fee.

E.   I recognize that in accepting my purchase of Notes, the Company will rely on the accuracy and completeness of my statements, representations, and warranties set forth herein. I hereby agree to defend, to indemnify, and to hold harmless the Company and each of its officers, directors, principals, or agents from and against any and all loss, damage, liability, or expense, including reasonable attorneys' fees and costs, which they or any of them may incur or become liable for by reason of, or in any way connected with, any misrepresentation or omission of relevant information, whether negligent or intentional, made by me in this Agreement, any breach of my warranties or my failure to perform any of my covenants or agreements set forth in this Agreement, or arising out of any sale or distribution by me of any Notes or the securities into which they may be converted in violation of the Securities Act, or any other applicable securities or "Blue Sky" laws.

F.   Legend. I acknowledge that a legend to the following effect will appear upon the Notes:

THIS CONVERTIBLE NOTE (THE "*NOTE*") HAS NOT BEEN REGISTERED UNDER THE FEDERAL SECURITIES ACT OF 1933, AS AMENDED ("*THE ACT*") OR ANY STATE SECURITIES LAW. THE NOTE HAS BEEN ACQUIRED FOR INVESTMENT AND NEITHER SAID NOTE NOR ANY INTEREST THEREIN MAY BE TRANSFERRED, SOLD, OR OFFERED FOR SALE UNLESS (1) THERE IS AN EFFECTIVE REGISTRATION STATEMENT FOR THE NOTE AS A SECURITY UNDER THE ACT AND QUALIFICATION UNDER ANY APPLICABLE STATE SECURITIES LAW, (2) SUCH TRANSFER IS MADE IN COMPLIANCE WITH RULE 144 UNDER THE ACT AND PURSUANT TO QUALIFICATION UNDER ANY APPLICABLE STATE SECURITIES LAW OR EXEMPTION THEREFROM, OR (3) THERE IS AN OPINION OF COUNSEL SATISFACTORY TO THE COMPANY THAT SUCH REGISTRATION AND QUALIFICATION ARE NOT REQUIRED AS TO SAID TRANSFER, SALE OR OFFER. ADDITIONAL RESRICTIONS MAY APPLY.

I agree promptly to deliver the Note to the Company if and when the Company, in its discretion, decides to recall such Note and reissue the same bearing a new or different legend or legends reflecting appropriately any requirements of the exemptions from the state and federal securities laws pursuant to which Notes have been sold to me.

REPRESENTATIONS AND WARRANTIES

I represent and warrant to the Company that:

A.   I have received and reviewed the Offering Materials and have been given full access to information appropriate to my determination of whether to invest in the Company, and I am familiar with the terms and provisions thereof. I have also reviewed the risk factors set forth in the Offering Materials, which should be considered when determining whether to invest in the Notes.

B.   I understand that following this offering, the Company will likely attempt to raise additional funds in a subsequent offering.

C.   I have further had an opportunity to meet with principals of the Company and discuss issues relevant to my determination of whether to invest in the Notes.

D.   I have full legal capacity to enter into this Agreement and, if not an individual, have duly authorized the execution of this Agreement in accordance with my constitutive documents.

E.   I have carefully reviewed the merits and risks of, and other considerations relating to, investment in the Company.

F.   I have read and understood the notices set forth in Section I and I understand that the transfer of the Notes is subject to various restrictions; that, as the Notes have not been registered under the Securities Act, or under the securities laws of any state, the Notes cannot be sold unless they are registered under said Act and qualified under said state laws or are exempt from registration or qualification thereunder; that the Company will not record the sale or other transfer of any Notes without compliance with said securities laws; and that I must bear the economic risk of ownership of Notes and any securities into which they may convert for an indefinite period of time. I shall not sell, assign, transfer or otherwise dispose of all or any part of my Notes or my interests therein except in compliance with applicable federal and state securities laws.

G.   I understand that my investment in the Company is not liquid. I have adequate means of providing for my current needs and personal contingencies and I have no need for liquidity in this investment.

H.   Except for the Offering Materials and any other information that my advisors or I may have requested and received directly from the Company, neither my advisors nor I have been furnished any other offering material or literature upon which I have relied in connection with my determination of whether or not to purchase Notes.

I.   I have been advised that I and my advisors, if any, would have an opportunity to review all the pertinent facts, to ask questions, and to obtain any additional information, to the extent possessed or obtainable without unreasonable effort and expense, regarding the Company, its key employees, its business, the offering of the Notes, the risks of investment in the Company, and any other matters relating to any of the above or anything set forth in the Offering Materials, and any additional information necessary to verify the accuracy of any representation or information set forth in the Offering Materials. The Company has supplied all material requested, if any, and has given complete and satisfactory answers to all inquiries, if any, that my advisors and I have put to it concerning the matters listed above.

J.   All financial and other data that I have supplied in this Agreement is true, accurate, and complete and fairly reflects my financial condition and investment experience to the best of my knowledge and belief.

K.   I have been advised to consult with my own attorney regarding legal matters concerning an investment in the Company and regarding tax and other financial consequences of investing in the Company. I understand that the information provided to me by the Company in connection with my purchase of the Notes does not constitute legal, investment, tax or other advice.

L.   I am acquiring the Notes for my own account, as principal, for investment and not with a view to or for sale in connection with any distribution of such Notes or any interest therein or in any securities into which the Notes may convert.

M.   I understand and acknowledge that the Offering Materials contain certain statements of anticipated or expected financial results and certain projected financial statement information, including internally-prepared projected revenues, projected cash flow statements, and projected balance sheets for the Company, all of which constitute "forward-looking statements" within the meaning of the Private Securities Litigation Reform Act. Such forward-looking statements are subject to various risks and uncertainties. I understand and further acknowledge that those forward-looking statements depend on certain assumptions about the Company, its market, the competition it faces, and its revenue model, and I acknowledge that those assumptions may prove to be inaccurate and, as a result, the projected financial statement information and related information may not prove to be accurate statements of the actual financial results or the financial condition of the Company. I have had an opportunity to discuss those projected financial statements, and the assumptions underlying such projected financial statements, with the Company's management.

FINANCIAL CONDITION AND EXPERIENCE OF ALL PURCHASERS:

I further represent and warrant to the Company, as follows:

A.   I am an "accredited investor" as defined in Rule 501 of Regulation D promulgated under the Securities Act. My qualification is based on the following (each "accredited investor" must initial the appropriate item or items):

_____ 1. I had an individual income (exclusive of the income of my spouse) in excess of $200,000 for each of the two most recent years, or joint income with my spouse in excess of $300,000 in each of those years, and reasonably expect the same income level for the current year; or

_____ 2. As of the date of this Agreement, I (either individually or with my spouse) have a net worth in excess of $1,000,000 (excluding the value of my residence); or

I am:

_____ 3. A bank or savings and loan institution, whether acting in its individual or fiduciary capacity;

_____ 4. An insurance company;

_____ 5. An investment company registered under the Investment Company Act of 1940;

_____ 6. A business development company as defined in the Investment Company Act of 1940;

_____ 7. A private business development company as defined in the Investment Advisors Act of 1940;

_____ 8. A Small Business Investment Company licensed by the U.S. Small Business Administration;

_____ 9. An employee benefit plan within the meaning of Title I of the Employment Retirement Income Security Act of 1974 (ERISA), if the investment decision with respect to this investment is made by a plan fiduciary which is either a bank, savings and loan association, insurance company, or registered investment advisor, or if the employee benefit plan has total assets in excess of $5,000,000;

_____ 10. An employee benefit plan established and maintained by a state or state agency, if the plan has total assets in excess of $5,000,000;

_____ 11. Any tax exempt organization as defined in Section 501(c)(3) of the Internal Revenue Code, corporation, Massachusetts or similar business trust, or partnership not formed for specific purpose of acquiring the securities offered, with total assets in excess of $5,000,000;

_____ 12. An entity of which the owners are (a) institutional investors described in the foregoing subparagraphs (1)–(12), (b) "Individuals" who meet certain suitability standards,[1] or (c) or a combination of both;

_____ 13. A trust with total assets in excess of $5,000,000, not formed for the specific purpose of acquiring the securities, whose purchase is directed by a person with knowledge and experience in financial matters, capable of evaluating the merits and risks of the prospective investment.

B.   I am not an "accredited investor" (initial, if appropriate).

AUTHORITY AND FINANCIAL CONDITION OF ENTITY PURCHASERS:

THE REQUESTED FINANCIAL INFORMATION SHOULD BE FURNISHED ONLY WITH RESPECT TO THE ENTITY PURCHASERS, AND NOT WITH RESPECT TO ANY OF THE OWNERS OF THE BENEFICIAL INTERESTS THEREIN, EXCEPT AS INDICATED.

GRANTOR TRUST PURCHASERS: IF THE PURCHASER IS A GRANTOR TRUST, THAT IS, A TRUST AMENDABLE AND REVOCABLE BY THE GRANTOR AT ANY TIME, PLEASE COMPLETE THIS SECTION V WITH RESPECT TO THE TRUST AND ITS ASSETS ALONE. PLEASE ALSO COMPLETE SECTION IV WITH RESPECT TO THE GRANTOR INCLUDING THE ASSETS HELD IN THE TRUST.

A.   REPRESENTATIONS AND WARRANTIES

The Entity Purchaser represents and warrants to the Company as follows:

(1) The Entity Purchaser has been duly formed and is validly existing in good standing under the laws of the state in which it was founded with full power and authority to enter into the transactions contemplated by this Agreement.

---

1. For purposes of paragraph (13) above, "Individuals" shall mean natural persons, each of whom: (i) has a net worth individually, or jointly with his or her spouse, of more than $1,000,000; or (ii) has had individual annual gross income from all sources in excess of $200,000, or joint income with a spouse in excess of $300,000, in each of the two most recent years and a reasonable expectation of reaching the same income level in the current year; or (iii) is an Officer or Director of the Company; or (iv) is a broker or dealer registered pursuant to Section 15 of the Securities Exchange Act of 1934; or (v) in most cases, may reasonably be deemed by the Company to have such knowledge and experience in financial and business matters that he or she is capable of evaluating the merits and risks of the prospective investment.

(2) The execution of this Agreement has been duly and validly authorized, and, when delivered on behalf of the undersigned, will constitute a valid, binding and enforceable agreement and obligation of the Entity Purchaser.

(3) The Entity Purchaser has not been formed, reformed, or recapitalized for the specific purpose of purchasing Notes.

(4) The Entity Purchaser acknowledges that all representations, warranties, agreements and notices set forth in Sections I–IV apply to the Entity Purchaser and acknowledges having read and understood them. Where appropriate in the context, the words "I" and "me" have been read to mean the Entity Purchaser.

B.   FINANCIAL POSITION AND EXPERIENCE

Type of entity: _____

Date of Organization: _____

State of Organization: _____

Number of equity owners (partners, beneficiaries, etc.): _____

If one or more of these equity owners owns individually or collectively more than fifty percent (50%) of the equity interest of the Purchaser and is (are) also purchasing Notes, please identify such equity owner(s):

_____

The net worth of the Entity Purchaser, as set forth in greater detail on the financial statements submitted herewith (if the Company so requests) is:

$_____

The Entity Purchaser's principal activities are:

_____

_____

_____

C.   INVESTMENT EVALUATION

Please certify the truth of the following statement by initialing where indicated:

The individuals authorizing this investment on behalf of Purchaser have such knowledge and experience in financial and business matters so as to be capable of evaluating the merits and risks of an investment in the Company.

_____ (Initials)

IN WITNESS WHEREOF, the undersigned has executed this Agreement as of the date indicated below.

INDIVIDUAL PURCHASERS:

Dated: _____, 20__

Title. I/we wish(es) to take title to the Notes as follows:

_____   Individual, as a Single Person
_____   Individual, Subject to Community Property Rights of Spouse
_____   Individual, as Separate Property
_____   Husband and Wife, as Community Property

_____   As Tenants-In-Common
_____   As Joint Tenants with Rights of Survivorship
_____   Other (e.g., trustee or custodian)

_____

_____
(Print Name Here)

IF THE PURCHASER HAS INDICATED THAT HE OR SHE WILL HOLD THE NOTES AS A JOINT TENANTS, AS A TENANT IN COMMON, OR AS COMMUNITY PROPERTY, THE CO-OWNER OR JOINT PURCHASER MUST SIGN HERE:

_____

_____
(Print Name Here)

ENTITY PURCHASERS:

Dated: _____, 20__

_____
(Name of Entity)

By: _____

_____
(Print Name Here)

Its: _____
(Print Capacity Here)

By: _____

_____
(Print Name Here)

Its: _____
(Print Capacity Here)

Accepted as of _____, 20__

****, Inc.

By_____

_____, President, President

Exhibit A

SERIES A CONVERTIBLE NOTE

THIS CONVERTIBLE NOTE (THE "*NOTE*") HAS NOT BEEN REGISTERED UNDER THE FEDERAL SECURITIES ACT OF 1933, AS AMENDED ("*THE ACT*") OR ANY STATE SECURITIES LAW. THE NOTE HAS BEEN ACQUIRED FOR INVESTMENT AND NEITHER SAID NOTE NOR ANY INTEREST THEREIN MAY BE TRANSFERRED, SOLD, OR OFFERED FOR SALE UNLESS (1) THERE IS AN EFFECTIVE REGISTRATION STATEMENT FOR THE NOTE AS A SECURITY UNDER THE ACT AND QUALIFICATION UNDER ANY APPLICABLE STATE SECURITIES LAW, (2) SUCH TRANSFER IS MADE IN COMPLIANCE WITH RULE 144 UNDER THE ACT AND PURSUANT TO QUALIFICATION UNDER ANY APPLICABLE STATE SECURITIES LAW OR EXEMPTION THEREFROM, OR (3) THERE IS AN OPINION OF COUNSEL SATISFACTORY TO THE COMPANY THAT SUCH REGISTRATION AND QUALIFICATION ARE NOT REQUIRED AS TO SAID TRANSFER, SALE OR OFFER. ADDITIONAL RESRICTIONS MAY APPLY.

****, INC.

CONVERTIBLE NOTE NO. ____

_____ [Date]

FOR VALUE RECEIVED, ****, Inc., a [California] corporation, (the "**Company**") hereby promises to pay, on or before _____, 20__ (the "**Maturity Date**"), to _____ [note holder], or order ("**Holder**"), at _____ _____ [note holder address], the principal amount of _____ Dollars ($_____) (the unpaid principal amount together with accrued and unpaid interest thereon calculated in accordance with Section 2 hereof the "**Amount Outstanding**").

WHEREAS, this Convertible Note (the "**Note**") is being issued in connection with that certain Convertible Note Subscription Agreement between the Company and Holder of even date herewith (the "**Subscription Agreement**");

NOW THEREFORE, this Note shall be subject to the terms of the Subscription Agreement and the following terms and conditions:

1. Maturity; Prepayment; Conversion.
   (a) Maturity. The Amount Outstanding shall be paid in full on the Maturity Date or on such other date as the Amount Outstanding may be declared due and payable following an Event of Default.

(b) Prepayment. Subject to Holder's conversion rights, the Company may pre-pay this Note upon written notice to Holder without penalty or fee. Any amounts paid shall be applied (i) first, to the accrued but unpaid interest, and (ii) second, to the principal amount then outstanding. Any amounts repaid or prepaid may not be reborrowed.

(c) Conversion.

(i) Optional Conversion Into Common Stock at Any Time. The Holder may, at its sole option at any time, cause the conversion of all of the outstanding principal under this Note, and all accrued but unpaid interest under the Note, into Common Stock of the Company at a price equal to $____ per share, subject to adjustment as set forth in subdivision (v).

(ii) Automatic Conversion. The Amount Outstanding shall automatically con-vert at the closing of a Trade Sale (as defined below) or, if earlier, the clos-ing of the Company's Next Round of Financing (as defined below). The Amount Outstanding will not be converted unless and until the Company has completed a Trade Sale, its Next Round of Financing, or Holder elects to convert this Note under the terms set forth in subdivision (i) or (vi) hereof.

(iii) Trade Sale Conversion. The Amount Outstanding shall convert into shares of the Company's Common Stock upon the closing of a Trade Sale. The conversion price (herein called "the basic conversion price") shall be that price which results in the Holder receiving a return (in cash or equiva-lent value in listed securities of the acquirer) equal to one and a half ($1\frac{1}{2}$) times the face value of the Note. For the avoidance of doubt, Holder cannot be compelled to accept illiquid securities of an acquirer in connection with a Trade Sale. For the purposes of this Note, "**Trade Sale**" shall mean a trans-action, or series of related transactions, which results in the Company's shareholders immediately prior to such transaction(s) holding less than 50% of the voting power of the surviving, continuing or purchasing entity, or the sale of all or substantially all of the Company's assets.

(iv) Next Round of Financing Conversion. The Amount Outstanding shall convert into the same class of stock as is purchased and sold in the Next Round of Financing and shall be subject to the same terms and conditions. The conversion price (herein called "the basic conversion price") shall be that price which is equal to the lower of eighty percent (80%) of the pur-chase price in the Company's Next Round of Financing and $____ per share (subject to adjustment as set forth in subdivision (v)). For the pur-poses of this Note, the Company's "**Next Round of Financing**" shall be defined as any offering in which the Company raises at least $_____ through the sale of shares of its stock.

(v) Adjustment to Conversion Price. In case at any time or from time to time after the date hereof, the holders of the Company's Common Stock shall have received, or shall have become entitled to receive, without payment therefor: (a) other or additional Common Stock or other securities or prop-erty (other than cash) by way of dividend; or (b) any cash paid or payable by way of dividend or otherwise, except out of earned surplus of the Company; or (c) other or additional (or less) stock or other securities or property (including cash) by way of spin-off, split-up, reclassification, recapitalization, combination of shares or similar corporate rearrangement; then, and in each such case, the Holder, upon conversion hereof, shall be entitled to receive the amount of securities and property which such Holder would have received if on the date hereof it had been the holder of record of the number of shares of Common Stock issuable upon conversion this Note and/or conversion of the preferred stock into which this Note may be converted, and had thereafter, during the period from the date hereof to and including the date of such exercise, retained such shares and such other or additional (or less) stock and other securities and property receivable by it during such period, giving effect to all adjustments called for during such period by this paragraph.

(vi) Holder's Right to Convert. At such time as the Company gives Holder notice of its intention to prepay the Note, the Holder shall have ten (10) days within which to give the Company notice of exercise of its right to convert the Note into shares of the Company's Common Stock at a price equal to $____ per share, subject to adjustment as set forth in subdivision (v).

(vii) Additional Documentation. Conversion of the Note pursuant to subdivision (iv) is contingent upon Holder's execution of a counterpart signature page to the shareholder, voting, and similar documentation executed in connection with the Next Round of Financing, in addition to such other documentation as the Company may reasonably request.

2. Interest. Interest on the outstanding principal amount shall accrue at a rate per annum equal to eight percent (8%). Such interest shall be computed on the basis of a year of three hundred sixty-five (365) days for the actual number of days elapsed (including the first day but excluding the last day) and shall be compounded annually. No payments of principal or interest shall be due prior to Maturity.

3. Default. A material breach of the terms of this Note by Company, including the payment of principal and interest on Maturity, shall constitute a default hereunder (an "Event of Default"). Upon the occurrence and during the continuance of any Event of Default and in every such event, the Holder, upon notice to the Company, may declare all or any portion of the Amount Outstanding immediately due and payable.

4. Presentment. The Company hereby waives any right to presentment, protest or notice of dishonor and protest of this Note and any other notice. No single or partial exercise of any power under this Note shall preclude any other or further exercise of such power or exercise of any other power. No delay or omission on the part of the Holder in exercising any right under this Note shall operate as a waiver of such right or any other right hereunder.

5. Subordination to Bank Loan. Upon request by the Company, and provided that no default shall have occurred under this Note, the Holder agrees to enter into a mutually-acceptable and commercially reasonable subordination agreement with a commercial bank subordinating the Company's obligations under this Note to up to the lesser of (a) the principal amount of the indebtedness to such bank, or (b) the Amount Outstanding under this Note. If the Company is unable because of Holder's mental or physical incapacity or for any other reason to secure Holder's signature to sign a subordination agreement, then Holder hereby irrevocably designates and appoints the Company and its duly authorized officers and agents as its agent and attorney in fact, to act for and in Holder's behalf and stead to execute any such subordination agreement and to do all other lawfully permitted acts to secure bank financing on behalf of the Company with the same legal force and effect as if executed by Holder.

6.   Miscellaneous.

(a) Governing Law. This Note shall be governed by and construed under the laws of the State of [California] applied to contracts between residents of said State and executed and wholly performed in said State. The Company and the Holder agree that any dispute regarding the interpretation or validity of, or otherwise arising out of, this Note may be brought in any court of competent jurisdiction in [the City and County of San Francisco, California], and each party hereby agrees to submit to the personal jurisdiction and venue of such courts and not to seek the transfer of any case or proceeding out of such courts.

(b) Successors and Assigns. This Note shall be binding on, and shall inure to the benefit of, the Company, the Holder and each of their successors and assigns.

(c) Severability. If one or more provisions of this Note are held to be unenforceable under applicable law, such provision shall be excluded from this Note and the balance of this Note shall be interpreted as if such provision was so excluded and shall be enforceable in accordance with its terms.

(d) Modification. Any term of this Note may be amended and the observance of any term of this Note may be waived (either generally or in a particular instance and either retroactively or prospectively), only with the written consent of the Company and the Holder.

(e) Notices. Except as otherwise expressly provided herein, any notice required or permitted hereunder shall be given in writing and it or any certificates or other documents delivered hereunder shall be deemed effectively given or delivered (as the case may be) upon personal delivery (professional courier permissible), by facsimile (with written confirmation of receipt), when mailed by registered or certified United States mail, three (3) business days after deposit in the United States mail. Such notice may be personally delivered or sent to the following address or fax number:

   (i) if to the Holder, to the address first set forth above Attention: _____, or by facsimile to: _____, or to such other address or fax number which Holder shall have given notice pursuant hereto to the Company, or

   (ii) if to the Company, to ****, Inc., at _____, Attn: _____, President, or by facsimile to: _____, or to such other address or fax number of which the Company shall have given notice pursuant hereto.

(f) Number and Gender. Whenever used herein, the singular number shall include the plural and the plural the singular, and the use of any gender shall be applicable to all genders.

(g) Counterparts. This Note may be executed in two or more counterparts, each of which shall be deemed an original, but all of which together shall constitute one and the same instrument.

(h) Titles and Subtitles. The titles and subtitles used in this Note are used for convenience only and are not to be considered in construing or interpreting this Note.

(i) Attorneys Fees. If any action at law or in equity is necessary to enforce or interpret the terms of this Note the prevailing party shall be entitled to reasonable attorneys fees, costs and disbursements in addition to any other relief to which such party may be entitled.

(j) Investment Purpose. By the acceptance of this Note, the initial payee of this Note represents and warrants that it is purchasing this Note for investment for its own account and with no present intention of dividing such participation with others, or reselling or otherwise distributing the same. Such initial payee understands and acknowledges that the Company has advised it that this Note has not been registered under the Securities Act of 1933, as amended, nor qualified under the securities laws of any other state on the grounds that this transaction is exempt from such registration and qualification requirements, and that the Company's reliance on such exemption is predicated in part on his, her, or its representation and warranty herein set forth.

(k) Restriction on Transfer. By the acceptance of this Note, Holder agrees that the transfer of this Note and the transfer of any shares of stock of the Company into which this Note may be converted shall be subject to the restriction that no such transfer hereof or thereof shall be effected until either (i) the holder hereof or of said shares has obtained either an opinion of counsel satisfactory to the Company and its counsel to the effect that the proposed transfer will not result in a violation of the Securities Act of 1933, as then amended; or (ii) a registration statement with respect to this Note and/or the shares of stock of the Company into which this Note may be converted shall then be effective under the Securities Act of 1933, as then amended. This provision shall be binding upon all subsequent transferees of this Note and/or the shares of stock into which this Note may be converted.

The undersigned has executed this Convertible Note as of the date first set forth above.

Company: ****, INC., a [California] corporation

By: _____

_____, President

Accepted and agreed:

Holder: _____

By: _____

_____

[Name and title of signatory]

CHAPTER 12

Venture Capital

12.1 Is Your Client Ready to Talk with Venture Capitalists?

Your client has a dynamite business concept, a written business plan, and a top-notch management team; but are they ready to talk with venture capital (VC) firms? If a relatively small additional investment will enable your client to reach a significant milestone, such as revenue (which many VCs require before they will invest anyway), it's probably too soon. The VCs probably wouldn't be interested; but if they were, your client would be beat up on valuation. The discussion of business plans and executive summaries in Chapter 3 provides details on what VCs typically look for in an investment.

By way of background, the term "venture capital" refers to a type of private equity capital funded primarily with institutional funding, usually through a limited partnership. Professional investors typically manage the funds through a firm that acts as the general partner of the limited partnership fund. Venture capitalists are usually actively engaged with companies to help them grow and get to an exit, which can provide significant additional value. VCs typically see hundreds of proposals for every investment. One investment made for every 100–400 proposals reviewed is not unusual.

VCs are looking to invest in the following:

- Deals with exceptional high growth potential, innovations with the potential to revolutionize existing industries or give birth to new ones;
- Teams with proven track records;
- Proven business models in proven markets;
- Businesses in industries in which the VC team has expertise and/or can add value; and
- Business plans with the likelihood of an exit in 3–7 years (with some exceptions, of course).

Companies funded with venture capital include FedEx, Starbucks, Google, Microsoft, eBay, Genentech, Intel, and Apple.

The process for obtaining VC financing is as follows:

- Complete any necessary corporate clean-up;
- Get the meeting(s);
- Negotiate a Term Sheet;
- Respond to due diligence;
- Complete definitive documentation; and
- Close (funding).

1. Common Mistakes Companies Make in Approaching VCs.

- They attempt VC financing too early in their development.
- They approach VCs that already have an investment in the space.
- They approach VCs with a plan that does not address the VC's preferred target markets.
- The management team leader cannot communicate well or actively listen.

Careful selection of the VCs to be approached, based on existing knowledge about the VCs and/or research, can help your clients avoid most of these common mistakes. The following terms may be helpful in matching a company's stage of development to a VC's stated interests. They are set forth in the order of start-up to the turning point for profitability (there are, of course, later stages on the company's way to its sunset stage):

- Proof of concept
- Reduction to practice/prototype
- Pre-product testing
- Alpha testing (in-house)
- Beta testing (with end users)
- Pre-commercial product sales (e.g., sales to beta customers)
- Scale-up and production; design and manufacturing
- Commercial product launch and sales

In some cases, it may be worthwhile for the management team leader to undergo specific training and preparation before making VC investor presentations. A company's chances can be dashed rather quickly if the management team makes a poor impression.

2. Help Make Sure Your Client Can Pass the Due Diligence Test.

Once a VC firm is interested in a company, it will typically issue a nonbinding term sheet. And once the term sheet has been accepted, the VC will conduct due diligence and negotiate definitive documentation of the investment. Venture capitalist due diligence typically covers review of the following:

- Management
- Board of directors and shareholders
- Business and market opportunity
- Technology and intellectual property
- Business plan
- Operations
- Financial projections and underlying assumptions
- Financial and statutory records
- Key contracts and agreements, including employment agreements

12.2 How Is a Typical Venture Capital Deal Structured?

With few exceptions, venture capital deals are structured as follows:

- One or more venture capital funds organized as limited partnerships (the Investors) invests in.... . .
- A Delaware corporation (the portfolio company) in which the.... . .
- Founders and key employees hold Common Stock (and options to acquire Common Stock through an option pool); and
- The Investors hold Preferred Stock with specific rights, preferences, and privileges, which are outlined in a term sheet and detailed in definitive documentation.

1. Only C Corps Need Apply.

If your client is structured as a limited liability company, or other form of entity that is not a corporation, VCs are almost certainly going to require that the entity be converted to a C corporation. VCs consider limited liability companies much more complicated and costly as investment vehicles. Typically, a company's assets are contributed to a newly formed Delaware C corporation and the investors then invest in the C Corp.

The basic terms of a typical venture capital financing are very similar to the angel financing terms outlined in Chapter 11. However, certain additional terms that you might not see in an angel financing are likely to be included in a typical VC term sheet. They are described in the following subsections.

2. Protective Provisions.

VCs will uniformly require the right to approve certain corporate transactions. These typically include the sale of all or substantially all of the assets of the company, a merger, liquidation or dissolution, changes to the company charter or bylaws, and certain other fundamental actions; these terms are set forth in the company's articles or certificate of incorporation.

3. Board of Directors.

VCs will typically require the right to place one or more persons on the board of directors of the company. After the first round of VC financing, a common board of directors structure is to have a total of five directors, with two members elected by the holders of common stock (the founders), two to three members elected by the holders of the Series A preferred stock (the VCs), with the possibility that a fifth director is chosen by the first four directors.

4. Dividends and Liquidation Preferences.

The Series A preferred stock will often accrue a cumulative dividend in lieu of a specified liquidation preference. The dividend is typically a stated percentage, such as 10 percent per annum, in preference to any dividend on the common stock, which Series A is payable upon a liquidation or redemption. Accrued and unpaid Series A dividends would be canceled upon conversion of the Series A preferred to common. The payment of a dividend on the company's common stock typically requires prior approval of the Series A investors, through protective provisions in the company's articles or certificate of incorporation. To the extent there are dividends or distributions paid on the common stock, the holders of the Series A preferred stock are typically entitled to participate with the common on an as-converted basis.

The reasoning behind allowing preferred investors to participate in any dividends paid to the common stockholders is that large dividends could be paid to the common investors if the company is very successful; but if the Series A did not participate in that dividend, and things went badly for the company after that, the Series A could end up not receiving its full liquidation preference (i.e., original purchase price plus accrued but unpaid dividends).

An alternative to cumulative dividends is a stated liquidation preference.

5. Redemption Rights.

VCs will often seek to have a right to sell the Series A preferred stock back to the company at an agreed-upon price under certain circumstances (a "redemption right"). This gives them the opportunity to get their money back out, plus some nominal return, after a certain period of time if the company does not appear to be headed toward a significant liquidity event. This right of redemption often does not kick in until four or five years after the closing of the financing.

Instead of giving the Series A investors the right to appoint a majority of the board if the company cannot honor a redemption obligation, VCs may require provisions that provide two thirds of the Series A investors have the right to force a sale of the company. The Series A investors would not be able to force a sale in any other context.

Also, at redemption, the company is often required to pay the Series A investors the greater of (i) fair market value or (ii) original purchase price plus accrued but unpaid dividends.

6. Registration Rights.

The right to include securities in a registration statement filed by the company in connection with a public offering ("registration rights") is absolutely the norm in venture capital financings. VCs are likely to require a comprehensive set of registration rights, including the right to initiate what is called a demand registration after a certain period of time has elapsed since the closing of the Series A financing—usually three years, or six months post-IPO (initial public offering). Even if the company thinks it will never go public, it will likely have to include registration rights in its VC financing documentation. However, drafting a registration rights agreement is very simple and will not incur much cost, and it isn't usually much of an issue unless the registration rights give investors the power to force the company to go public.

7. Rights of First Refusal.

VCs will negotiate for the right to purchase shares that are issued in the future by the company ("rights of first refusal"). These rights will at minimum give the VCs the ability to preserve their pro rata share of the stock of the company on an as-converted, fully diluted basis and may allow them to purchase all of the stock issued in a future financing. Presumably as a result of the run-up in the price of stocks that have gone public in the recent past, certain VC deals now extend this right to participate to include the company's IPO.

8. Anti-Dilution Protection.

VC deals typically include some form of anti-dilution protection. The shares of Series A preferred stock usually will be subject to weighted average anti-dilution protection for issuances of any securities, at a price per share less than the purchase price per share for the Series A preferred, with exceptions for (i) securities issuable upon conversion of any of the Series A preferred, or as a dividend or distribution on the Series A preferred; (ii) securities issued upon the conversion of any debenture, warrant, option, or other convertible security outstanding at the time the Series A shares are issued; (iii) common stock issuable upon a stock split, stock dividend, or any subdivision of shares of common; and (iv) shares of common stock (or options to purchase such shares of common) issued or issuable to employees or directors of, or consultants to, the company pursuant to any plan approved by the company's board of directors.

In some cases, preferred stock investors agree to lose anti-dilution protection in the event they do not buy their pro rata share of a future financing (a "pay-to-play" provision). Although this feature is not common in deals where a single VC is completing the round, it is useful in deals in which several VCs participate to help ensure that all of the VCs in the group support future rounds of financing. In any case, if a future financing is done at a higher per share price and a Series A investor does not participate, the Series A investor will get diluted. On the other hand, if the company does a future financing at a lower price, and a Series A investor with anti-dilution protection chooses not to participate, the Series A investor will get additional shares (to reduce or eliminate the dilutive effect of the issuance of shares at a lower price) according the formula provided, in the absence of a pay-to-play provision.

9. Conditions to Closing.

Typical conditions precedent to the closing of a venture capital financing include

- Completion of due diligence to the investor's satisfaction;
- Agreement on a final business plan and financial projections acceptable to the investor;
- Receipt of all required investment approvals of the investor and the company;
- Execution of an investor rights agreement, preferred stock purchase agreement, voting rights agreement, and any other documentation required by the investor to give effect to the terms set forth in the nonbinding term sheet;
- Execution of employment agreements between the company, key executives, and key employees identified during due diligence;
- Provision of acceptable representations and warranties by the company and key executives;
- Execution of confidentiality and invention assignment agreements and satisfactory licenses and/or assignments of intellectual property necessary for the operation of the company; and
- Organization as a Delaware C corporation.

Definitive documentation is typically comprised of the following:

- Preferred Stock Purchase Agreement;
- Amended and Restated Certificate of Incorporation;
- Indemnification Agreement;
- Investors' Rights Agreement;
- Management Rights Letter;
- Right of First Refusal and Co-Sale Agreement;
- Voting Agreement; and
- Legal Opinion of Company Counsel.

Examples of most of the foregoing can be found online at the National Venture Capital Association website at www.nvca.org.

12.3 How Is a Business Valued for Purposes of Venture Capital Financing?

VCs place a pre-money valuation on the company, which is the negotiated value of the company before their investment. The VCs then specify how much they are willing to invest; this number, when added to the pre-money valuation, yields the post-money valuation. By way of illustration, if a company's pre-money valuation is set at $10 million, and VCs invest $3 million on that valuation, the post-money valuation is $13 million and the VCs will expect a 23 percent stake in the company, on an as if converted, fully diluted basis (including the entire employee pool specified in the term sheet). Companies should be prepared to suggest an appropriate valuation when speaking with VCs, but they should also be prepared for the fact that the VCs will have their own sense of what the company is worth. Discussions may break down completely if these initial estimations of value are leagues apart.

Many companies find it useful to put together a spreadsheet that, based on certain assumptions, projects founders' ownership through several rounds of financing. Such a budget can be a helpful tool for thinking about the dilutive impact that financings will have on the founders' equity. Founders who retain between 15 and 20 percent of a company at the time of an IPO have done extremely well.

12.4 What Is the Employee Pool?

The "employee pool" is group of shares reserved for issuance to key employees, typically at the time of, or immediately following, a Series A preferred investment, through the adoption of an incentive stock option (ISO) plan. A typical employee pool ranges from 10 to 25 percent of the fully diluted capital stock of the company, even though no awards may have been made at the time of the closing. The more key hires the VCs perceive will be necessary to fill out the management team, the larger the required employee pool. Standard vesting requirements for employee options are 25 percent after 12 months, with the remainder vesting monthly over the next 36 months. Very few first-time founders fully understand the implications of the size of the employee pool in a VC financing transaction. In one sense, it is advisable to authorize a large pool from the beginning, to avoid or at least delay the future annoyance of having to amend the stock option plan or adopt a new one; but since the employee pool is typically treated as issued and outstanding in determining the number of shares to be issued to VC investors, founders are much better off trying to keep the required employee pool very small since it will minimize the immediate dilution of their ownership interest. Stock option grants typically require the approval of the board of directors, so the board controls the number of options actually granted within the overall number authorized by the plan.

12.5 Sample Documents and Checklists.

The National Venture Capital Association publishes sample venture capital forms on its website at http://www.nvca.org. This section includes the following forms:

- Investor Scorecard (Form 12 A)
- Term Sheet for Venture Capital Investment—Series A (Form 12 B)
- Preferred Stock Provisions for Venture Capital Investment (Form 12 C)
- Stock Purchase Agreement (Form 12 D)
- Shareholders Agreement (Form 12 E)
- Investor Rights Agreement (Form 12 F)

Form 12 A: Investor Scorecard

Rank each of the following categories 1 (problematic) to 20 (excellent):

Quality and Experience of the Management Team
      1. Are they A/B/C players?
      2. Experience and track record?
      3. Is the team complete?
      4. Stability and longevity?   _____

Market Opportunity
      5. What is the opportunity/plan?
      6. Barriers to entry?
      7. Competition level?   _____

Quality and Stage of the Product or Solution
      8. Defensible IP?
      9. Does the product exist?
      10. Product road map?
      11. Time to market?   _____

Quality and Stage of the Business Model
      12. Revenue/scalability?
      13. Viable?
      14. Complete/focused?   _____

Potential Return on Investment
      15. Deal terms (especially valuation)?
      16. Potential upside/market size?
      17. Momentum?   _____

      Total Score (out of 100):   _____
      90-100 = A
      80-90 = B
      70-80 = C
      60-70 = D
      59 or lower = F

Form 12 B: Term Sheet for Venture Capital Investment—Series A

Note: Venture capitalists are expected to bring more to the table than just money. VCs typically participate on the board of directors and may even get involved at an operational level, giving a company the benefit of their connections and knowledge within certain industries. A company with a perfect scorecard doesn't need—and a VC is not likely to be able to create value by providing—these other forms of support. However, there are usually one or more categories where a company needs improvement (but if there are too many, the company simply won't make the grade and will be passed over by investors).

MEMORANDUM OF TERMS FOR PRIVATE PLACEMENT OF SERIES A CONVERTIBLE PREFERRED STOCK OF **** INC.

This memorandum summarizes the principal terms of a Series A Convertible Preferred Stock financing of **** Inc.

General

Issuer:	**** Inc., a _____ corporation (the "Company").
Amount of Financing:	Up to $_____, of which **** Fund, Inc. (the "Fund") may take up to $_____.
Securities to be Issued:	Shares of Series A Convertible Preferred Stock, par value $.001 (the "Series A Preferred Stock" or the "Preferred Stock") to be purchased by the Investors (as defined below). Assuming a funding of the entire $_____, the Series A Preferred Stock will represent ____% of the post-closing Common Stock as determined on a fully diluted basis (assuming the authorization of employee stock options for up to **[15%]** of the Company's capitalization).
Investors:	The Fund and other investors acceptable to the Fund (the "Investors").
Purchase Price:	$_____ per share (the "Base Amount").
Post-Financing Valuation:	$_____
Closing Date:	_____, 20__, or as soon thereafter as practicable.
Use of Proceeds:	To be used for general working capital purposes.
Conditions to Closing:	(a) Satisfactory due diligence; and (b) Agreement to final terms and conditions.
Conversion of Loan:	The existing _____ loan will be converted into Common Stock at closing.

Dividends:

No dividends will accrue or be payable on any class of the Company's securities. In the event the Board of Directors of the Company (the "Board") declares a dividend that is approved by the holders of at least 51% of the Series A Preferred Stock, the Common Stock and the Preferred Stock shall participate *pro rata* (on a fully diluted basis) in any such dividend.

Liquidation Preference:

In the event of any liquidation or winding up of the Company, the holders of the Series A Preferred Stock shall be entitled to receive **[twice]** the Base Amount for each share of Series A Preferred Stock (the "Liquidation Amount"), in preference to the holders of any other equity securities of the Company. A merger, consolidation, reorganization or sale of all or substantially all of the Company's assets shall be deemed a liquidation unless otherwise agreed by the holders of at least 51% of the Series A Preferred Stock.

Redemption:

Mandatory redemption by the Company of Series A Preferred Stock at the option of the holder of any Series A Preferred Stock, shall occur upon any (a) sale, merger or consolidation of, or other business combination transaction involving, the Company following which any person or entity (including any "group") beneficially owns or controls (by contract or otherwise) a majority of (i) the capital stock of the Company generally entitled to vote in the election of directors or (ii) the equity interests of the Company; or (b) the sale or disposition of all or substantially all of the Company's direct or indirect assets; or (c) the fifth anniversary of the Closing Date. In the event of a redemption pursuant to clause (a) or (b) above, the Company must immediately redeem all of the Series A Preferred Stock then subject to redemption at the Liquidation Amount. In the event of a redemption pursuant to clause (c) above, the Company may make such redemption in three equal annual installments. Any redemption amount not paid when due will, to the extent permitted by applicable law, be converted into a note obligation of the Company and shall accrue at a default interest rate.

Conversion:

(a) Optional Conversion. The holders of the Series A Preferred Stock shall have the right to convert the Series A Preferred Stock at any time into shares of Common Stock. The initial conversion price shall be the original purchase price for the Series A Preferred Stock, subject to adjustment as provided in the Anti-dilution Protection provisions below (at any time, the "Conversion Price"). The conversion rate applicable to the Series A Preferred Stock shall be determined by dividing the Base Amount of the Series A Preferred Stock by the Conversion Price.

(b) Automatic Conversion. The Series A Preferred Stock shall be automatically converted into Common Stock, at the then-applicable conversion rate, (i) immediately prior to the closing of an underwritten public offering of shares of the Common Stock of the Company at a per-share price of not less than the Liquidation Amount and for aggregate offering proceeds (net of underwriting discounts, commissions and expenses) of not less than $20,000,000 (a "Qualified Initial Public Offering" or "QIPO"), or (ii) upon the request by the holders of at least **[51%]** of the Series A Preferred Stock.

Anti-Dilution Protection: In the event that the Company issues (a) additional shares of Common Stock or (b) additional shares of capital stock (or instruments convertible into or exchangeable for capital stock) without consideration or for a consideration per share of less than the Base Amount (other than (i) the issuance of options for up to 15% of the Company's post-closing Common Stock on a fully diluted basis for shares of Common Stock to employees, directors and consultants (the "Authorized Option Pool") of the Company pursuant to an employee incentive stock option plan approved by the Board, (ii) the issuance of Common Stock upon conversion of Preferred Stock or (iii) dividends or distributions on the Preferred Stock), then, and in such event, the Conversion Price for the Series A Preferred Stock shall be lowered to a price based on a base weighted average anti-dilution formula.

Pay-to-Play Feature: If a holder of Series A Preferred Stock fails to participate in any future Qualified Financing (as defined below) on a *pro rata* basis (according to its total equity ownership immediately after such financing, assuming all stockholders subject to this provision participate), then such holder shall lose its anti-dilution protection for that Qualified Financing on all Series A Preferred Stock that it then owns. If such holder participates in such future Qualified Financing but not to the full extent of its *pro rata* share, then it shall lose such rights only on that stock equal to the percentage of its *pro rata* contribution that it failed to contribute. A "Qualified Financing" is that portion of any financing by the Company that the Board and the holders of at least a majority of the Preferred Stock determine must be purchased *pro rata* among the stockholders of the Company subject to this provision. Such determination will be made regardless of whether the price is higher or lower than any series of Preferred Stock of the Company.

Voting Rights: Each share of Series A Preferred Stock shall carry a number of votes equal to the number of shares of Common Stock then issuable upon its conversion. The Preferred Stock shall vote together with the Common Stock and not as a separate class, except as specifically provided herein, in the final documents or as otherwise required by law.

Protective Provisions: Consent of the holders of at least 51% of the outstanding Series A Preferred Stock shall be required for any action that (i) declares or pays any dividends on Common Stock or any other Company security junior in liquidation or dividend preference to the Series A Preferred Stock; (ii) repurchases Preferred Stock or Common Stock (except for repurchases pursuant to Board-approved employee stock purchase plans or redemption contemplated herein); (iii) makes any loans or advances to employees, except in the ordinary course of business as part of travel advances or salary; (iv) makes guarantees except in the ordinary course of business; (v) merges, consolidates, sells or disposes of all or substantially all of the properties or assets of the Company unless the Company is the surviving or acquiring corporation; (vi) mortgages or pledges, or creates a security interest in, or permits any subsidiary to mortgage, pledge or create a security interest in, all or substantially all of the property of the Company or such subsidiary, unless unanimously approved by the Board; (vii) owns, or permits any subsidiary to own, any stock or other securities of any subsidiary or other corporation, partnership or entity unless it is wholly owned by the Company; (viii) repurchases any shares of any employee or stockholder that would cause the Investors not to qualify their stock under Section 1202 of the Internal Revenue Code (the "IRC"); (ix) alters or changes the rights, preferences or privileges of the Series A Preferred Stock; (x) increases or decreases the authorized number of shares of Series A Preferred Stock; (xi) creates (by reclassification or otherwise) any new class or series of securities having rights, preferences or privileges senior to or on a parity with the Series A Preferred Stock; (xii) results in a material change in the Company's line(s) of business; (xiii) results in the Company acquiring the stock, assets or business of any other entity in any transaction with an aggregate value (and/or cost to the Company) in excess of $1,000,000; (xiv) amends the Company's Articles of Incorporation or Bylaws; (xv) results in the Company's or any subsidiary's incurring indebtedness in excess of **[$500,000]** (excluding trade payables incurred in the ordinary course of business); (xvi) results in the Company's or any subsidiary's incurring capital expenditures in any twelve-month period in excess of **[$500,000];** (xvii) authorizes any annual budget(s); or (xviii) materially increases the compensation of any senior management personnel.

Representations, Warranties, and Indemnities:

Standard Company and subsidiary representations and warranties, including financial information through the closing of the transaction. Company and subsidiary indemnifications as are customary for transactions of this type.

Registration Rights:

(a) Registrable Securities. Common Stock and/or Common Stock equivalents issued to Investors ("Registrable Securities").

(b) Demand Rights. Beginning the earlier of the third anniversary of the closing date, and six months after a QIPO, two demand registrations upon initiation by holders of at least 25% of the Registrable Securities. In either demand registration, at least 15% of Registrable Securities requesting registration must be sold.

(c) <u>Piggyback Rights</u>. Unlimited piggyback registration rights, subject to *pro rata* cutback, after cutback of all securities of the Company held by persons not contractually entitled to registration, at the underwriter's discretion. Terminates as to an Investor upon availability of Rule 144(k).

(d) <u>S-3 Rights</u>. Unlimited S-3 registrations of at least $250,000 each, limited to two per each twelve-month period.

(e) <u>Expenses</u>. Expenses paid by the Company (other than underwriting discounts and commissions and special counsel for selling stockholders).

(f) <u>Lock-Up Provision</u>. Upon request by the underwriter, the holders of Registrable Securities shall not transfer any shares beginning upon the date of the QIPO and continuing for such a period thereafter as determined by the Board upon advice of underwriters; provided that such period will not exceed 180 days; **[and, provided further, that each officer, director and key employee of the Company's voting securities shall agree to execute a similar agreement]**.

(g) <u>Transfer</u>. Registration rights will be freely transferable.

Preemptive Rights: The Investors shall have a *pro rata* right, based upon their percentage ownership of Common Stock and common stock equivalents of the Company, to participate in future equity financings of the Company subject to the following exclusions: (i) Common Stock issued out of the Authorized Option Pool, (ii) Common Stock issued upon conversion or exercise of shares of convertible or exercisable securities and (iii) Common Stock sold in connection with a QIPO. Each holder of Series A Preferred Stock may assign this right to affiliated venture capital funds or partners of such funds.

Drag-Along Right: The Board, with the consent of the holders of at least 51% of the Series A Preferred Stock, will have the right to require all holders of Common Stock and Common Stock equivalents to sell their shares to a third party purchaser in a liquidation transaction approved by the Board and such holders of Series A Preferred Stock.

Co-Sale Right: Certain key managers (the "Key Management") will agree not to sell stock to a third party without first providing the holders of Series A Preferred Stock the opportunity to sell their stock on the same terms and conditions *pro rata* based on all stock owned by Key Management and such holders.

Right of First Refusal: Each holder of Series A Preferred Stock will, subject to the following sentence, have a right of first refusal to acquire (on a *pro rata* basis) any such stock as is proposed to be transferred or sold by any holder of Common Stock who is a non-institutional investor (other than to Permitted Transferees). The right of first refusal shall be subject to the Company's prior right to purchase all the shares proposed to be transferred or sold. Restrictions shall terminate upon a QIPO. As used herein, "Permitted Transferees" shall include certain family members, trusts, affiliates, partners, and stockholders and such other specified persons as are agreed upon by the Company and the Investors.

Search Committee:
The Board shall establish a "Search Committee" consisting of _____ and two directors designated by the Investors. The Search Committee shall retain a consultant to locate qualified candidates for the position of CEO and President of the Company. A simple majority of the members of the Search Committee will recommend a candidate to the Board. The candidate must be acceptable to a simple majority of the Board and the Search Committee.

Board of Directors:
The Board will consist of seven people, as follows: the newly appointed CEO and President as one director, two directors designated by existing management (as Chairman of the Board and as a director), two outside independent directors acceptable to the Investors (and _____ being expressly acceptable), and two Investor directors, which shall include at least one such director designated by the Fund. To the extent the Fund chooses to resign as a director, it will have customary board observation and information rights.

Information Rights:
The Company will furnish to each Investor standard information including annual and quarterly information, financials and certificates of compliance with provisions of the Purchase Agreement, and monthly financials, management reports, budgets and summaries of financial plans.

Closing Conditions:
Customary closing conditions, including completion of legal and financial due diligence to the satisfaction of the Investors.

Section 1202 Covenant:
The Company will represent that the Investors are purchasing stock that will qualify under Section 1202 of the IRC if the stock is held by the Investor for five years. The Company will also covenant not to take any action, including the repurchase of stock from an employee or stockholder, that would disqualify the Investor stock under Section 1202.

Fees and Expenses:
The Company will pay the fees and expenses of legal counsel to the Fund, _____ . Such legal fees shall not exceed $30,000.

Certain Other Terms and Conditions

Employee Options:
Grants of options or sale of Common Stock to employees will be pursuant to an Incentive Stock Option Plan or Stock Purchase Plan administered and approved by the Board.

Vesting under any such plans shall provide that no options or stock shall vest until completion of at least one year's employment with the Company, and shall vest in equal monthly amounts over a minimum of four years.

Proprietary Information: All employees will enter into proprietary Agreements: information agreements containing provisions satisfactory to the Investors with respect to confidentiality, corporate ownership of inventions and innovations during employment, and non-solicitation of employees and customers during and for one year after employment. Certain key managers will execute non-competition agreements.

Life Insurance: The Company will obtain term life insurance on key employees at the discretion of the Board, provided that the Company can obtain such insurance at normally prevailing rates for persons in good health.

Indemnification Agreements: The officers and directors will have standard indemnification agreements acceptable to the Investors.

Directed Share Agreement: The Company will enter into a Directed Share Agreement with the Investors, pursuant to which the Company shall agree to request that its underwriter in an initial public offering designate 10% of the Common Stock of the Company to be sold in the initial public offering for sale to the Investors who hold shares of Series A Preferred Stock (or Common Stock as a result of the conversion of Series A Preferred Stock) on a *pro rata* basis.

Governing Law: _____ .

Documentation: Main transaction documents to be drafted by _____, counsel to the Fund.

No Commitment: Nothing in this Memorandum of Terms, or any actions occurring after there is an agreement on this Memorandum of Terms, will be construed as a commitment by any Investor to proceed with any stage of the financing contemplated hereby until a definitive Purchase Agreement shall be executed.

Form 12 C: Preferred Stock Provisions for Venture Capital Investment

**AMENDED AND RESTATED
CERTIFICATE OF INCORPORATION OF
**** INC.**

**** Inc., a corporation organized and existing under the laws of the State of [Delaware], hereby certifies as follows:

1. The name of this corporation is **** Inc. (the "*Corporation*").

2. The date of filing of the Corporation's original Certificate of Incorporation with the Secretary of State of the State of [Delaware] was _____, 20__ (the "*Certificate of Incorporation*").

3. Pursuant to Sections 242 and 245 of the General Corporation Law of the State of Delaware, this Amended and Restated Certificate of Incorporation restates, integrates and further amends the provisions of the Certificate of Incorporation.

4. This Amended and Restated Certificate of Incorporation has been duly adopted in accordance with Sections 242 and 245 of the General Corporation Law of the State of [Delaware] and the stockholders of the Corporation have given their written consent hereto in accordance with Section 228 of the General Corporation Law of the State of [Delaware].

5. The Certificate of Incorporation of this Corporation is hereby amended and restated in its entirety to read as follows:

ARTICLE I

The name of the corporation is **** Inc. (hereinafter, the "*Corporation*").

ARTICLE II

The address of the registered office of the Corporation in the State of [Delaware] is located at _____ _____, [Delaware] _____, in the County of _____. The name of its registered agent at that address is _____.

ARTICLE III

The nature of the business or purposes of the Corporation is to engage in any lawful act or activity for which a corporation may be organized under the General Corporation Law of the State of [Delaware].

ARTICLE IV

This Corporation is authorized to issue two classes of shares, designated "Series A Convertible Preferred Stock" and "Common Stock." The total number of shares that this Corporation shall have authority to issue is _____, of which _____ shares shall be Common Stock, $0.001 par value per share, and _____ shares shall be Series A Convertible Preferred Stock, $0.001 par value per share (the "Series A Preferred Stock").

Series A Preferred Stock

A statement of the rights, preferences, privileges and restrictions granted to or imposed on the Series A Preferred Stock and the holders thereof is as follows:

Section 1. Dividends.

(a) In the event that the Board of Directors of the Corporation (the "*Board*"), shall declare a dividend with respect to the Common Stock of the Corporation, the holders of Series A Preferred Stock shall be entitled to receive, when and as declared by the Board, out of any assets of the Corporation legally available therefor, dividends which shall be distributed among all holders of Series A Preferred Stock in proportion to the number of shares of Common Stock that would be held by each such holder if all shares of Series A Preferred Stock were converted into Common Stock at the then effective Conversion Price (as defined in Section 4 hereof). No dividend or distribution shall be declared or paid on any shares of Common Stock unless at the same time an equivalent dividend or distribution is declared or paid on all outstanding shares of Series A Preferred Stock.

(b) In the event that the Corporation shall have declared but unpaid dividends outstanding immediately prior to, and in the event of, a conversion of Series A Preferred Stock (as provided in Section 4 hereof), the Corporation shall, at the option of each holder of Series A Preferred Stock, pay in cash to each holder of Series A Preferred Stock subject to conversion the full amount of any such dividends, or allow such dividends to be converted into Common Stock in accordance with, and pursuant to the terms specified in, Section 4 hereof.

Section 2. Liquidation.

(a) In the event of any liquidation, dissolution or winding up of the Corporation, whether voluntary or involuntary, distributions to the stockholders of the Corporation shall be made in the following manner:

(i) *Series A Preferred Stock Preference:* The holders of Series A Preferred Stock shall be entitled to receive, subject to the holders of Series A Preferred Stock's right to convert their shares of Series A Preferred Stock pursuant to Section 4, prior and in preference to any distribution of any of the assets or surplus funds of the Corporation available for distribution to the holders of Common Stock by reason of their ownership thereof, the amount of $0.___ per share of Series A Preferred Stock held by such holder (as adjusted for any stock splits, stock dividend, recapitalizations or the like with respect to such shares), plus, with respect to each share of Series A Preferred Stock, all declared but unpaid dividends in respect of each such share of Series A Preferred Stock then held by them. If, upon the occurrence of such event, the assets and funds thus distributed among the holders of the Series A Preferred Stock shall be insufficient to permit the payment to such holders of the full preferential amount, then the entire assets and funds of the Corporation legally available for distribution shall be distributed ratably among the holders of the Series A Preferred Stock in proportion to the preferential amount each such holder is otherwise entitled to receive.

(ii) After payment has been made to the holders of the Series A Preferred Stock of the full amounts to which they shall be entitled as provided in Section 2(a)(i) hereof, the entire remaining assets and funds of the Corporation legally available for distribution, if any, shall be distributed ratably among the holders of the Common Stock in proportion to the number of shares of Common Stock held by each such holder.

(b) Unless otherwise determined by the holders of shares of Series A Preferred Stock who hold shares of Series A Preferred Stock representing at least __% of the issued and outstanding shares of Series A Preferred Stock, for purposes of this Section 2, a liquidation, dissolution or winding up of the Corporation shall be deemed to be occasioned by, or to include, (i) the acquisition of the Corporation by another entity by means of any transaction or series of related transactions (including, without limitation, any reorganization, merger or consolidation, but excluding any merger effected exclusively for the purpose of changing the domicile of the Corporation); or (ii) a sale of all or substantially all of the assets of the Corporation, <u>unless</u>, in each case, the Corporation's stockholders of record as constituted immediately prior to such acquisition or sale will, immediately after such acquisition or sale (by virtue of securities issued as consideration for the Corporation's acquisition or sale or otherwise) hold at least 50% of the voting power of the surviving or acquiring entity in approximately the same relative percentages after such acquisition or sale as before such acquisition or sale.

(c) For purposes of this Section 2, the amount of assets and surplus funds of the Corporation available for distribution upon a liquidation, dissolution or winding up of the Corporation shall be determined as follows:

(i) insofar as it consists of cash, it shall be computed at the aggregate amount of cash held by this Corporation at the time of the liquidation, dissolution or winding up, excluding amounts paid or payable for accrued interest; and

(ii) insofar as it consists of property other than cash, it shall be computed at the fair market value thereof at the time of the liquidation, dissolution or winding up, as determined in good faith by the Board.

Section 3. <u>Voting.</u>

(a) <u>General.</u> The holders of each share of Series A Preferred Stock shall have the right to one vote for each share of Common Stock into which such Series A Preferred Stock could then be converted, and with respect to such vote, such holder shall have full voting rights and powers equal to the voting right and powers of the holders of Common Stock, and shall be entitled, notwithstanding any provision hereof, to notice of any stockholders meeting in accordance with the Bylaws of the Corporation, and shall be entitled to vote, together with the holders of Common Stock, with respect to election of directors and any question or matter upon which holders of Common Stock have the right to vote.

(b) <u>Amendment to Certificate of Incorporation.</u> The consent of the holders of shares of Series A Preferred Stock holding at least ___% of the issued and outstanding shares of Series A Preferred Stock, voting separately as a class, shall be required in connection with any amendment or waiver of any provision of the Corporation's By-laws or this Amended and Restated Certificate of Incorporation or any other event, if such event affects, alters or changes the rights, preferences, privileges and restrictions of the Series A Preferred Stock.

Section 4. <u>Conversion.</u> The holders of the Series A Preferred Stock shall have the following conversion rights and obligations (the "*Conversion Rights*"):

(a) <u>Right to Convert Preferred Stock.</u> Subject to Section 4(b) hereof, each share of Series A Preferred Stock shall be convertible at the option of the holder thereof at any time after the date of issuance of such share at the office of the Corporation or any transfer agent for the Series A Preferred Stock, into such number of fully paid and nonassessable shares of Common Stock as is determined by dividing the Purchase

Price by the Conversion Price, determined as hereinafter provided, in effect at the time of conversion. The Purchase Price and the initial Conversion Price with respect to each share of Series A Preferred Stock shall be $0.___. The Conversion Price with respect to the Series A Preferred Stock shall be subject to adjustment as hereinafter provided.

(b) <u>Automatic Conversion</u>. Each share of Series A Preferred Stock shall automatically be converted into shares of Common Stock as provided in this Section 4 upon the earlier of (a) the closing of a firm commitment underwritten public offering pursuant to an effective registration statement under the Securities Act of 1933, as amended (the "*Securities Act*"), covering the offer and sale of Common Stock to the public at an aggregate offering price of no less than $_____ per share (appropriately adjusted for stock dividends, stock splits, combinations, subdivisions, or other similar recapitalizations and events) and which results in net cash proceeds to the Corporation of at least $_____ (a "*Qualified Public Offering*") or (b) the affirmative vote of the holders of at least ___% of the issued and outstanding shares of Series A Preferred Stock.

(c) <u>Mechanics of Conversion</u>. No fractional shares of Common Stock shall be issued upon conversion of the Series A Preferred Stock. In lieu of any fractional shares to which the holder would otherwise be entitled, the Corporation shall pay to such holder cash equal to such fraction multiplied by the then applicable Conversion Price with respect to such fractional share.

(i) Subject to clause (ii) below, before any holder of Series A Preferred Stock shall be entitled to convert the same into full shares of Common Stock, such holder shall surrender the certificate or certificates therefor, duly endorsed, at the office of the Corporation or any transfer agent for the Series A Preferred Stock, and shall give written notice to the Corporation at such office that the holder elects to convert the same. Such notice shall also state whether the holder elects, pursuant to Section 1 hereof, to receive in cash any declared but unpaid dividends on the Series A Preferred Stock proposed to be converted, or to convert such dividends into shares of Common Stock at their fair market value as determined by the Board. The Corporation shall, as soon as practicable thereafter, issue and deliver at such office to such holder of Series A Preferred Stock (1) a certificate or certificates for the number of shares of Common Stock to which such holder shall be entitled as aforesaid, (2) a check payable to such holder in the amount of any cash amounts payable as a result of the conversion of any shares of Series A Preferred Stock into fractional shares of Common Stock, and, if such holder elects not to convert unpaid dividends into Common Stock, all declared and unpaid dividends on such holder's converted Series A Preferred Stock and, (3) if less than all of the shares of the Series A Preferred Stock represented by such certificate are converted into Common Stock, a certificate representing the shares of Series A Preferred Stock not converted into Common Stock. In the event of any conversion at the election of a holder of Series A Preferred Stock, such conversion shall be deemed to have been made immediately prior to the close of business on the date of such surrender of the shares of Series A Preferred Stock to be converted, and the person or persons entitled to receive the shares of Common Stock issuable upon such conversion shall be treated for all purposes as the record holder or holders of such shares of Common Stock on such date.

(ii) If the conversion is in connection with an underwritten public offering of securities registered pursuant to the Securities Act, the conversion shall be conditioned upon the closing with the underwriter of the sale of securities pursuant to such offering, in which event the person(s) entitled to receive the Common Stock issuable upon such conversion of the Series A Preferred Stock shall not be deemed to have converted such Series A Preferred Stock until immediately prior to the closing of such sale of securities. Notice of such conversion shall be given by the Corporation by mail, postage pre-paid, to the holders of the Series A Preferred Stock at their addresses shown in the Corporation's records, within a reasonable time after the closing date of the sale of such securities. Promptly after the closing date of the sale of such securities as specified in such notice, each holder of Series A Preferred Stock shall surrender the certificate or certificates representing such holder's shares of Series A Preferred Stock for the number of shares of Common Stock to which such holder is entitled, at the office of the Corporation or any transfer agent for the applicable series of Series A Preferred Stock. Upon surrendering such shares each holder of Series A Preferred Stock shall deliver a notice to the Corporation which shall state whether the holder elects, pursuant to Section 1 hereof, to receive in cash any declared but unpaid dividends on the Series A Preferred Stock to be converted, or to convert such dividends into shares of Common Stock at their fair market value as determined in good faith by the Board. The Corporation shall, as soon as practicable thereafter, issue and deliver at such office to such holder of Series A Preferred Stock (1) a certificate or certificates for the number of shares of Common Stock to which such holder shall be entitled as aforesaid, and (2) a check payable to the holder in the amount of any cash amounts payable as a result of the conversion of any shares of Series A Preferred Stock into fractional shares of Common Stock, and, if such holder elects not to convert unpaid dividends into Common Stock, all declared or accrued and unpaid dividends on such holder's converted Series A Preferred Stock. Notwithstanding that any certificate representing the Series A Preferred Stock to be converted shall not have been surrendered, each holder of such Series A Preferred Stock shall thereafter be treated for all purposes as the record holder of the number of shares of Common Stock issuable to such holder upon such conversion, assuming that such holder had elected to convert all declared or accrued but unpaid dividends on its Series A Preferred Stock into Common Stock.

(d) Adjustment of Conversion Price. The Conversion Price shall be subject to adjustment as follows:

(i) Adjustments for Subdivision, Combinations, or Consolidations of Common Stock. In the event the outstanding shares of Common Stock shall be subdivided or increased (by stock split, stock dividend, recapitalization, or otherwise) into a greater number of shares of Common Stock, and no equivalent subdivision or increase is made with respect to the Series A Preferred Stock, the respective Conversion Price then in effect for each series of Series A Preferred Stock shall, concurrently with the effectiveness of such subdivision or increase, be proportionately decreased. In the event the outstanding shares of Common Stock shall be combined or consolidated, by reclassification or otherwise, into a lesser number of shares of Common Stock, the respective Conversion Price then in effect for each series of Series A Preferred Stock shall, concurrently with the effectiveness of such combination or consolidation, be proportionately increased.

(ii) Adjustments for Other Dividends and Distributions. In the event the Corporation at any time or from time to time makes or fixes a record date for the determination of holders of Common Stock entitled to receive a dividend or other distribution payable in securities of the Corporation, and no equivalent dividend or other distribution is declared or made to the Series A Preferred Stock, then and in each such event provision shall be made so that the holders of Series A Preferred Stock shall receive, concurrently therewith, the amount of such securities which they would have received had their Series A Preferred Stock been converted into Common Stock on the date of such event.

(iii) <u>Adjustments for Reclassification, Exchange, and Substitution</u>. In the event the Common Stock issuable upon conversion of the Series A Preferred Stock shall be changed into the same or a different number of shares of any other class or classes of stock, whether by capital reorganization, reclassification, or otherwise (other than a subdivision or combination of shares provided for above), and no equivalent capital reorganization, reclassification, or other change is made with respect to the Series A Preferred Stock, the Conversion Price then in effect for the Series A Preferred Stock shall, concurrently with the effectiveness of such reorganization or reclassification, be proportionately adjusted such that the Series A Preferred Stock shall be convertible into, in lieu of the number of shares of Common Stock which the holders thereof would otherwise have been entitled to receive, a number of shares of such other class or classes of stock equivalent to the number of shares of Common Stock that would have been subject to receipt by the holders thereof upon conversion of the Series A Preferred Stock immediately before such change.

(e) <u>Adjustments to Conversion Price for Certain Dilutive Issues</u>. The Conversion Price of each of the Series A Preferred Stock shall be subject to adjustment as follows:

(i) <u>Special Definitions</u>. For purposes of this Section 4(e), the following definitions shall apply:

(1) "*Options*" shall mean rights, options, or warrants to subscribe for, purchase, or otherwise acquire either Common Stock or Convertible Securities.

(2) "*Original Issue Date*" shall mean with respect to a share of Series A Preferred Stock the date on which such share was issued.

(3) "*Convertible Securities*" shall mean any evidence of indebtedness, shares (other than Common Stock) or other securities convertible into or exchangeable for Common Stock.

(4) "*Additional Shares of Common*" shall mean all shares of Common Stock issued (or, pursuant to Section 4(e)(iii), deemed to be issued) by the Corporation on or after the Original Issue Date, other than shares of Common Stock issued or issuable at any time:

(A) upon conversion of the Series A Preferred Stock authorized herein;

(B) to employees, officers, directors, and consultants of the Corporation pursuant to any one or more employee stock incentive plans or agreements approved by the Board in an aggregate amount, net of repurchases and cancellations, of not more than ____ shares (appropriately adjusted for stock dividends, stock splits, combinations, subdivisions, or other similar recapitalizations and events), unless a greater number is approved by the written agreement of the holders of at least ___% of the issued and outstanding shares of Series A Preferred Stock; or

(C) pursuant to any event for which adjustment is made pursuant to this Section 4 (other than this Section 4(e)).

(ii) <u>No Adjustment of Conversion Price</u>. No adjustment in the Conversion Price shall be made in respect of the issuance of Additional Shares of Common unless the consideration per share for an Additional Shares of Common issued or deemed to be issued by the Corporation is less than the respective Conversion Price of the Series A Preferred Stock in effect on the date of, and immediately prior to, such issue.

(iii) <u>Deemed Issuance of Additional Shares of Common</u>. In the event the Corporation at any time or from time to time after the Original Issue Date shall issue any Options or Convertible Securities or shall fix a record date for the determination of holders of any class of securities entitled to receive any such Options or Convertible Securities, then the maximum number of shares (as set forth in the instrument relating thereto without regard to any provisions contained therein for a subsequent adjustment of such number) of Common Stock issuable upon the exercise of such Options or, in the case of Convertible Securities and options therefor, the conversion or exchange of such Convertible Securities, shall be deemed to be Additional Shares of Common issued as of the time of such issue, or in the case such a record date shall have been fixed, as of the close of business on such record date; *provided* that Additional Shares of Common shall not be deemed to have been issued unless the consideration per share (determined pursuant to Section 4(e)(v) hereof) of such Additional Shares of Common would be less than the Conversion Price in effect on the date of and immediately prior to such issue, or such record date, as the case may be; and *provided further* that in any such case in which Additional Shares of Common are deemed to be issued:

(1) except as provided in clause (B) below, no further adjustment in the Conversion Price shall be made upon the subsequent issue of Convertible Securities or shares of Common Stock upon the exercise of such Options or conversion or exchange of such Convertible Securities;

(2) if such Options or Convertible Securities by their terms provide, with the passage of time or otherwise, for any increase in the consideration payable to the Corporation, or decrease in the number of shares of Common Stock issuable, upon the exercise, conversion or exchange thereof, the Conversion Price computed upon the original issue thereof (or upon the occurrence of a record date with respect thereto), and any subsequent adjustments based thereon, shall, upon any such increase or decrease becoming effective, be recomputed to reflect such increase or decrease insofar as it affects such Options or the rights of conversion or exchange under such Convertible Securities;

(3) upon the expiration of any such Options or any rights of conversion or exchange under such Convertible Securities which shall not have been exercised, the Conversion Price computed upon the original issue thereof (or upon the occurrence of a record date with respect thereto), and any subsequent adjustments based thereon, shall, upon such expiration, be recomputed as if:

(A) in the case of Convertible Securities or Options for Common Stock, the only Additional Shares of Common issued were shares of Common Stock, if any, actually issued upon the exercise of such Options or the conversion or exchange of such Convertible Securities and the consideration received therefor was the consideration actually received by the Corporation for the issue of all such Options, whether or not exercised, plus the consideration actually received by the Corporation upon such exercise, or for the issue of all such Convertible Securities which were actually converted or exchanged, plus the additional consideration, if any, actually received by the Corporation upon such conversion or exchange; and

(B) in the case of Options for Convertible Securities, only the Convertible Securities, if any, actually issued upon the exercise thereof were issued at the time of issue of such Options, and the consideration received by the Corporation for the Additional Shares of Common deemed to have been then issued was the consideration actually received by the Corporation for the issue of all such Options, whether or not exercised, plus the consideration deemed to have been received by the Corporation upon the issue of the Convertible Securities with respect to which such Options were actually exercised;

(4) no readjustment pursuant to clause (B) or (C) above shall have the effect of increasing the Conversion Price to an amount which exceeds the lower of (i) the Conversion Price on the original adjustment date or (ii) the Conversion Price

that would have resulted from any issuance of Additional Shares of Common between the original adjustment date and such readjustment date; and

(5)   in the case of any Options which expire by their terms not more than 30 days after the date of issue thereof, no adjustment of the Conversion Price shall be made until the expiration or exercise of all such Options, whereupon such adjustments shall be made in the same manner provided in clause (C) above.

(iv) Adjustment of Conversion Price upon Issuance of Additional Shares of Common. In the event the Corporation shall issue Additional Shares of Common after the Original Issue Date (including Additional Shares of Common deemed to be issued pursuant to Section 4(e)(iii)) without consideration or at a price per share or "Net Consideration Per Share" (as defined below) less than the Conversion Price then in effect immediately prior to such issue, then and in such event, the Conversion Price shall be reduced, concurrently with such issue, to a price (calculated to the nearest cent) determined as follows:

(1)   if such issuance or sale is consummated on or prior to _____, 20___, then and in such event, the Conversion Price shall be reduced, concurrently with such issuance, to a price equal to the Net Consideration Per Share received by the Corporation in such issuance or sale; and

(2)   if such issuance or sale is consummated after _____, 20___, then and in such event, the Conversion Price shall be lowered so as to be equal to an amount determined by multiplying the Conversion Price by the following fraction:

$$\frac{N_0 + N_1}{N_0 + N_2}$$

Where:

N_0 = the number of shares of Common Stock outstanding immediately prior to the issuance of such Additional Shares of Common, Convertible Securities, or Options (calculated on a fully-diluted basis assuming the exercise or conversion of all then exercisable or convertible options, warrants, purchase rights, and convertible securities).

N_1 = the number of shares of Common Stock which the aggregate consideration, if any, (including the Net Consideration Per Share with respect to the issuance of Additional Shares of Common) received or receivable by the Corporation for the total number of such Additional Shares of Common so issued or deemed to be issued would purchase at the Conversion Price in effect immediately prior to such issuance.

N_2 = the number of such Additional Shares of Common so issued or deemed to be issued.

(3)   The provisions of this Section 4(e)(iv) may be waived as to all shares of Series A Preferred Stock in any instance (without the necessity of convening any meeting of stockholders of the Corporation) upon the written agreement of the holders of at least ___% of the issued and outstanding shares of Series A Preferred Stock.

(v) Determination of Consideration. For purposes of this Section 4(e), the "Net Consideration Per Share" which shall be receivable by the Corporation for the issuance of any Additional Shares of Common shall be computed as follows:

(1)   Cash and Property: Such consideration shall:

(A)   insofar as it consists of cash, be computed at the net amount of cash received by the Corporation excluding expenses, discounts and commissions payable by the Corporation in connection with such issuance or sale and amounts paid or payable for accrued interest;

(B) insofar as it consists of property other than cash, be computed at the fair value thereof at the time of such issue, as determined in good faith by the Board net of expenses as set forth in clause (A) above; and

(C) in the event Additional Shares of Common are issued together with other shares or securities or other assets of the Corporation for consideration which covers both, be the proportion of such consideration so received, computed as provided in clauses (A) and (B) above, as determined in good faith by the Board.

(2) <u>Options and Convertible Securities</u>. The consideration per share received by the Corporation for Additional Shares of Common deemed to have been issued pursuant to Section 4(e)(iii), relating to Options and Convertible Securities, shall be determined by dividing:

(A) the total amount, if any, received or receivable by the Corporation as consideration for the issue of such Options or Convertible Securities, plus the minimum aggregate amount of additional consideration (as set forth in the instruments relating thereto, without regard to any provision contained therein for a subsequent adjustment of such consideration) payable to the Corporation upon the exercise of such Options or the conversion or exchange of such Convertible Securities, or in the case of Options for Convertible Securities, the exercise of such options for Convertible Securities and the conversion or exchange of such Convertible Securities, by

(B) the maximum number of shares of Common Stock (as set forth in the instruments relating thereto, without regard to any provision contained therein for a subsequent adjustment of such number) issuable upon the exercise of such Options or the conversion or exchange of such Convertible Securities or, in the case of Option for Convertible Securities, the exercise of such options for Convertible Securities and the conversion or exchange of such Convertible Securities.

(3) <u>Stock Dividends</u>. Any Additional Shares of Common deemed to have been issued relating to stock dividends shall be deemed to have been issued for no consideration.

(f) <u>No Impairment</u>. This Corporation will not, by amendment of its Amended and Restated Certificate of Incorporation or through any reorganization, transfer of assets, consolidation, merger, dissolution, issuance, or sale of securities or any other voluntary action, avoid or seek to avoid the observance or performance of any of the terms to be observed or performed hereunder by this Corporation but will at all times in good faith assist in the carrying out of all the provisions of this Section 4 and in the taking of all such action as may be necessary or appropriate in order to protect the Conversion Rights of the holders of the Series A Preferred Stock against impairment.

(g) <u>Reservation of Common Issuable upon Conversion</u>. The Corporation shall at all times reserve and keep available out of its authorized but unissued shares of Common Stock solely for the purpose of effecting the conversion of the shares of the Series A Preferred Stock such number of its shares of Common Stock as shall from time to time be sufficient to effect the conversion of all outstanding shares of Series A Preferred Stock; and if at any time the number of authorized but unissued shares of Common Stock shall not be sufficient to effect the conversion of all then outstanding shares of the Series A Preferred Stock, in addition to such other remedies as shall be available to the holder of such Series A Preferred Stock, the Corporation will take such corporate action as may, in the option of its counsel, be necessary to increase its authorized but unissued shares of Common Stock to such number of shares as shall be sufficient for such purposes, including, without limitation, engaging in reasonable efforts to obtain the necessary stockholder approval of any necessary amendment to this Amended and Restated Certificate of Incorporation.

(h) <u>Certificate as to Adjustments</u>. Upon the occurrence of each adjustment or readjustment of the Conversion Price pursuant to this Section 4, the Corporation at its expense shall promptly compute such adjustment or readjustment in accordance with the terms hereof and furnish to each holder of Series A Preferred Stock a certificate setting forth such adjustment or readjustment and showing in detail the facts upon which such adjustment or readjustment is based. The Corporation shall, upon the written request at any time of any holder of Series A Preferred Stock, furnish or cause to be furnished to such holder a like certificate setting forth (i) all such adjustments and readjustments since the Original Issue Date, (ii) the Conversion Price at the time in effect and (iii) the number of shares of Common Stock and the amount, if any, of other property which at the time would be received upon the conversion of the Series A Preferred Stock.

Section 5.   <u>No Reissuance of Series A Preferred Stock</u>. No shares of Series A Preferred Stock acquired by the Corporation by reason of purchase, conversion or otherwise shall be reissued.

Section 6.   <u>Redemption</u>.

(a) Commencing at any time after five years from the Original Issue Date, upon receipt by the Corporation, from time to time, of the written request from the holders of shares of Series A Preferred Stock representing at least ____% of the issued and outstanding shares of Series A Preferred Stock that all or any portion of such holders' shares be redeemed, the Corporation shall, to the extent it may lawfully do so, redeem, on a pro rata basis among the holders of the Series A Preferred Stock:

(i) one-third of the then outstanding shares of Series A Preferred Stock to be redeemed as soon as practicable but in no event later than thirty (30) days after receipt of such a request (the "First Redemption Date");

(ii) one-third of the then outstanding shares of Series A Preferred Stock to be redeemed upon the first anniversary of the First Redemption Date (the "Second Redemption Date");

(iii) all of the then remaining shares of Series A Preferred Stock to be redeemed upon the second anniversary of the First Redemption Date (the "Third Redemption Date," and together with the First Redemption Date and the Second Redemption Date, the "Redemption Date").

(b) The Corporation shall redeem the Series A Preferred Stock by paying in cash therefor a price per share of $____ (as adjusted for any stock dividends, combinations or splits with respect to such shares) plus all accrued by unpaid dividends on each such share (the "Redemption Price").

(c) At least 15 but no more than 30 days prior to each Redemption Date, written notice shall be mailed, first class postage prepaid, to each holder of record (at the close of business on the business day next preceding the day on which notice is given) of the Series A Preferred Stock to be redeemed, at the address last shown on the records of the Corporation for such holder, notifying such holder of the redemption to be effected, specifying the number of shares to be redeemed from such holder, the Redemption Date, the Redemption Price, the place at which payment may be obtained and calling upon such holder to surrender to the Corporation, in the manner and at the place designated, his, her or its certificate or certificates representing the shares to be redeemed (the "*Redemption Notice*"). Except as provided in subsection 6(c) on or after the Redemption Date, each holder of Series A Preferred

Stock to be redeemed shall surrender to the Corporation the certificate or certificates representing such shares, in the manner and at the place designated in the Redemption Notice, and thereupon the Redemption Price of such shares shall be payable to the order of the person whose name appears on such certificate or certificates as the owner thereof and each surrendered certificate shall be cancelled. In the event less than all the shares represented by any such certificate are redeemed, a new certificate shall be issued representing the unredeemed shares.

(d) From and after the Redemption Date, unless there shall have been a default in payment of the Redemption Price, all rights of the holders of shares of Series A Preferred Stock designated for redemption in the Redemption Notice as holders of Series A Preferred Stock (except the right to receive the Redemption Price without interest upon surrender of their certificate or certificates) shall cease with respect to such shares, and such shares shall not thereafter be transferred on the books of the Corporation or be deemed to be outstanding for any purpose whatsoever. Subject to the rights of series of Series A Preferred Stock which may from time to time come into existence, if the funds of the Corporation legally available for redemption of shares of Series A Preferred Stock on any Redemption Date are insufficient to redeem the total number of shares of Series A Preferred Stock to be redeemed on such date, those funds which are legally available will be used to redeem the maximum possible number of such shares ratably among the holders of such shares to be redeemed based upon their holdings of Series A Preferred Stock. The shares of Series A Preferred Stock not redeemed shall remain outstanding and entitled to all the rights and preferences provided herein. At any time thereafter when additional funds of the Corporation are legally available for the redemption of shares of Series A Preferred Stock, such funds will immediately be used to redeem the balance of the shares which the Corporation has become obliged to redeem on any Redemption Date but which it has not redeemed.

Section 7. Protective Provisions.

(a) The consent of the holders of shares of Series A Preferred Stock representing at least ___% of the issued and outstanding shares of Series A Preferred Stock shall be required in connection with:

(i) any sale, conveyance, assignment, or other disposition of, or liquidation or encumbrance of all or any material portion of the Corporation's assets, property or business;

(ii) any merger into or consolidation with any other corporation (other than a wholly-owned subsidiary) or any transaction or series of related transactions which will result in the holders of the outstanding voting equity securities of the Corporation immediately prior to such transaction or series of related transactions holding fewer than 50% of the voting equity securities of the surviving entity immediately following such transaction in approximately the same relative percentages after such transaction as before such transaction;

(iii) entering into any transaction with an officer, senior manager, or director of the Corporation or a member of his or her immediate family or an entity owned or controlled by such officer, director, senior manager or family member;

(iv) any increase or decrease in the number of authorized shares of capital stock of the Corporation;

(v) the authorization or issuance of, or undertaking of an obligation to authorize or issue, any equity security or any security convertible into or exercisable for any equity security, except for shares of Common Stock issued or issuable at any time:

(1) upon conversion of the Series A Preferred Stock authorized herein;

(2)   to employees, officers, directors, and consultants of the Corporation pursuant to any one or more employee stock incentive plans or agreements approved by the Board, including the approval of the director designated by S.R. One, Limited; or

(3)   which are sold in a Qualified Public Offering.

(vi) the reclassification, authorization, or designation of any security of the Corporation that is senior to or on parity with the Series A Preferred Stock with respect to dividends, liquidation rights, redemption rights or voting rights;

Section 8.   <u>Right of First Offer</u>. The holders of Series A Preferred Stock are hereby expressly granted first offer rights to subscribe to any additional issue of capital stock of the Corporation or other security convertible into such capital stock, all as set forth in the Investor Rights Agreement, dated _____, 20__, among the Corporation and the holders of Series A Preferred Stock, as may be amended from time to time.

ARTICLE V
<u>Common Stock</u>

Section 1.   <u>Priority</u>. All preferences, voting powers, relative, participating, optional, or other special rights and privileges, and qualifications, limitations, or restrictions of the Common Stock are expressly made subject to and subordinate to those that may be fixed with respect to the Preferred Stock to the extent provided for herein.

Section 2.   <u>Dividend Rights</u>. Subject to the prior rights of holders of all classes of stock at the time outstanding having prior rights as to dividends, the holders of the Common Stock shall be entitled to receive, when and as declared by the Board, out of any assets of the Corporation legally available therefor, such dividends as may be declared from time to time by the Board; *provided, however,* that no dividend or distribution shall be declared or paid on any shares of Common Stock, other than a dividend payable in shares of Common Stock (and subject to Section 4(d)), unless at the same time an equivalent dividend or distribution is declared or paid on all outstanding shares of Series A Preferred Stock.

Section 3.   <u>Liquidation Rights</u>. Upon the liquidation, dissolution, or winding up of the Corporation, the assets of the Corporation shall be distributed as provided in Article IV, Section 2 hereof.

Section 4.   <u>Redemption</u>. The Common Stock is not redeemable.

Section 5.   <u>Voting Rights</u>. The holder of each share of Common Stock shall have the right to one vote, and shall be entitled to notice of any stockholders' meeting in accordance with the Bylaws of the Corporation, and shall be entitled to vote upon such matters and in such manner as may be provided by law.

ARTICLE VI
The Corporation is to have perpetual existence.

ARTICLE VII
Elections of directors need not be by written ballot unless a stockholder demands election by written ballot at the meeting and before voting begins or unless the Bylaws of the Corporation provide otherwise.

ARTICLE VIII

In furtherance and not in limitation of the powers conferred by statute, the Board is expressly authorized to make, alter, amend, or repeal the Bylaws of the Corporation.

ARTICLE IX

(a) To the fullest extent permitted by the Delaware General Corporation Law as the same exists or as may hereafter be amended, a director of the Corporation shall not be personally liable to the Corporation or its stockholders for monetary damages for breach of fiduciary duty as a director.

(b) The Corporation shall indemnify to the fullest extent permitted by law any person made or threatened to be made a party to an action or proceeding, whether criminal, civil, administrative or investigative, by reason of the fact that he, his testator or intestate is or was a director, officer or employee of the Corporation or any predecessor of the Corporation or serves or served at any other enterprise as a director, officer or employee at the request of the Corporation or any predecessor to the Corporation.

(c) Neither any amendment nor repeal of this Article IX, nor the adoption of any provision of this Corporation's Amended and Restated Certificate of Incorporation inconsistent with this Article IX, shall eliminate or reduce the effect of this Article IX, in respect of any matter occurring, or any action or proceeding accruing or arising or that, but for this Article IX, would accrue or arise, prior to such amendment, repeal or adoption of an inconsistent provision.

ARTICLE X

Meetings of the stockholders may be held within or without the State of Delaware, as the Bylaws may provide. The books of the Corporation may be kept (subject to any provision contained in the statutes) outside of the State of Delaware at such place or places as may be designated from time to time by the Board or in the Bylaws of the Corporation.

* * * * *

IN WITNESS WHEREOF, the Corporation has caused this Amended and Restated Certificate of Incorporation to be duly executed this ___ day of _____, 20___.

**** INC.

By: _____

Title: _____

Form 12 D: Stock Purchase Agreement

STOCK PURCHASE AGREEMENT

THIS STOCK PURCHASE AGREEMENT (this "Agreement") is entered into as of _____, 20___ by and among **** Inc., a [Delaware] corporation (the "Company"), _____ Capital, L.P. ("Capital") and _____ Venture Fund, L.P. ("Venture Fund") (Capital and Venture Fund are hereinafter sometimes individually referred to as a "Purchaser" and collectively referred to as "Purchasers").

NOW, THEREFORE, in consideration of the respective representations, warranties, covenants, and agreements set forth herein, the parties hereto, intending to be legally bound hereby, agree as follows:

ARTICLE I
AUTHORIZATION AND ISSUANCE OF THE PREFERRED SHARES

1.1 Authorization of Series A Convertible Preferred Stock. The Company has duly authorized the issuance and sale to the Purchasers of an aggregate of _____ shares (the "Series A Preferred Shares") of the Company's Series A Convertible Preferred Stock, $____ par value per share (the "Series A Preferred Stock"). The designations, rights, preferences and other terms and conditions relating to the Series A Preferred Stock shall be as set forth on Exhibit A. [Note: Amended and Restated Certificate or Articles of Incorporation, or Certificate of Preferred Stock Designations, to be attached as Exhibit A and filed with the applicable Secretary of State.]

1.2 Issuance of the Series A Preferred Shares. Subject to the terms and conditions set forth herein, at the Closing (as defined in Section 1.4 hereof), the Company shall issue and sell to each Purchaser, and each Purchaser shall purchase from the Company, that number of Series A Preferred Shares set forth opposite the name of such Purchaser under the heading "Number of Series A Preferred Shares to be Purchased" on Schedule 1, at the aggregate purchase price set forth opposite the name of such Purchaser under the heading "Aggregate Purchase Price" on Schedule 1.

1.3 The Conversion Shares. The Company has authorized and has reserved, and covenants to continue to reserve, a sufficient number of its previously authorized, but unissued, shares of Common Stock, par value $_____ per share ("Common Stock"), to satisfy the rights of conversion of the holders of the Series A Preferred Stock (the "Conversion Shares").

1.4 Closing. The closing shall take place in person or by fax at the offices of _____, located at _____, San Francisco, California _____, at 10:00 a.m., on _____, 20___, or at such other location, date, and time as may be agreed upon between the Purchasers and the Company (such closing being called the "Closing" and such date and time being called the "Closing Date"). At the Closing, the Company shall issue and deliver to each Purchaser a stock certificate or certificates in definitive form, registered in the name of such Purchaser, representing the Series A Preferred Shares being purchased by such Purchaser at the Closing. As payment in full for the Series A Preferred Shares being purchased by each Purchaser under this Agreement, and against delivery of the stock certificate or certificates therefor, on the Closing Date each Purchaser shall deliver to the Company the amount of such Purchaser's Aggregate Purchase Price, by (i) [certified] check, (ii) wire transfer of same day funds, (iii) delivery to the Company for cancellation of promissory notes issued by the Company, or (iv) any combination of such methods of payment.

1.5 [Optional:] Sale of Issuance of Additional Series A Preferred Shares. Subject to the terms and conditions of this Agreement, until _____, 20___, the Company shall have the right to issue and sell to certain additional investors (the "Additional Purchasers"), up to an aggregate of _____ Series A Preferred Shares (the "Additional Securities"), each at a price of $_____ for an aggregate purchase price of $_____.

1.6 [Optional:] Additional Closings. The purchase and sale of the Additional Securities shall take place at such time(s) and place(s) as the Company and the Additional Purchasers purchasing a majority of the Additional Securities mutually agree upon orally or in writing (each of such time and place is designated as an "Additional Closing"). The issuance, sale and delivery of any Additional Securities to an Additional Purchaser shall be subject to and conditioned upon each such Additional Purchaser becoming a party to this Agreement, the Rights Agreements (as hereinafter defined), the Shareholders Agreement (as hereinafter defined) and the Voting Agreement (as hereinafter defined) on the terms set forth herein and therein, and executing a counterpart signature page to each of this Agreement, the Rights Agreement, the Shareholders Agreement and the Voting Agreement. The Purchasers shall have no obligation to purchase any of the Additional Securities. In connection with the sale of any Additional Securities to any Additional Purchaser, each Purchaser hereby waives any preemptive rights to purchase shares from the Company that may arise pursuant to the Rights Agreement.

ARTICLE II
REPRESENTATIONS AND WARRANTIES OF THE COMPANY

[Generally the Company will attempt to limit each representation and warranty by provisions such as materiality and knowledge qualifiers and the Purchasers will attempt to broaden each representation and warranty to the extent possible.]

The Company represents and warrants to each of the Purchasers the matters set forth in this Article II as of the Closing Date:

2.1 Organization, Standing, and Qualification. The Company is a corporation duly organized, validly existing and in good standing under the laws of the Commonwealth of Pennsylvania, and has all requisite corporate power and authority to own or lease and operate its properties, to carry on its business as currently conducted and as now proposed to be conducted, and to carry out the transactions contemplated hereby. The Company is duly qualified to do business as a foreign corporation in _____, and there is no other jurisdiction in which the conduct of its business or its ownership, leasing or operating of property requires such qualification. The Company has no subsidiaries. The Company has made available to the Purchasers true, correct and complete copies of its Articles of Incorporation and its Bylaws, in each case as amended and as in effect on the date hereof (the "Amended Articles of Incorporation" and the "Bylaws," respectively), and has previously made available to the Purchasers the Company's complete corporate minute and stock books, which include all actions of the Company's Board of Directors and shareholders, whether by meeting or by written consent in lieu of a meeting.

2.2 Power and Authority. The Company has the power and authority to make, deliver and perform this Agreement and the transactions contemplated hereby. The execution, delivery and performance of this Agreement, the Investors Rights Agreement of even date herewith in the form attached hereto as Exhibit B (the "Rights

Agreement"), the Shareholders Agreement of even date herewith in the form attached hereto as Exhibit C (the "Shareholders Agreement") and the Voting Agreement of even date herewith in the form attached hereto as Exhibit D (the "Voting Agreement") have been duly authorized by all necessary corporate actions. In addition, the issuance, sale and delivery of the Series A Preferred Shares and the Conversion Shares, in accordance with the terms of this Agreement, have been duly authorized by all requisite corporate action of the Company. When issued, sold and delivered in accordance with this Agreement, the Series A Preferred Shares issued hereunder and the Conversion Shares issuable upon conversion of the Series A Preferred Shares, will be validly issued and outstanding, fully paid for, nonassessable, and will not be subject to preemptive or any other similar rights of the shareholders of the Company or others.

2.3 Authorization of Agreements, etc. The execution and delivery by the Company of this Agreement, the Rights Agreement, the Shareholders Agreement, and the Voting Agreement (together, the "Transaction Agreements"), the performance by the Company of its obligations hereunder and thereunder, the issuance, sale, and delivery of the Series A Preferred Shares and the issuance and delivery of the Conversion Shares will not violate any provision of law, any order of any court or other agency of government, the Amended Articles of Incorporation, the Bylaws or any provision of any indenture, agreement or other instrument to which the Company or any of its properties or assets is bound, or conflict with, result in a breach of or constitute with due notice or lapse of time or both a default under, any such indenture, agreement, or other instrument, or result in the creation or imposition of any lien, charge, restriction, claim, or encumbrance of any nature whatsoever upon any of the properties or assets of the Company. No provision of any of the Transaction Agreements violates, conflicts with, results in a breach of or constitutes with due notice or lapse of time or both a default under, any indenture, agreement or other instrument to which the Company is bound or by which the assets of the Company are bound regardless, in each such case, of whether any such violation, conflict, breach or default relates to the Company or, to the Company's best knowledge, to another party to any such indenture, agreement or other instrument. Except for the filing with the Secretary of State of Pennsylvania of the Amended Articles of Incorporation and except for applicable federal and state securities filings relating to the execution and delivery of this Agreement, no consent, approval or authorization of, or declaration, filing or registration with, any governmental or regulatory authority or other party is required to be made or obtained by the Company in connection with the execution and delivery of the Transaction Agreements by the Company, or the performance by the Company of its obligations hereunder, thereunder or under the Amended Articles of Incorporation.

2.4 Validity. This Agreement has been duly executed and delivered by the Company and constitutes the legal, valid and binding obligation of the Company, enforceable in accordance with its terms. The Rights Agreement, the Shareholders Agreement and the Voting Agreement, when executed and delivered in accordance with this Agreement, will constitute the legal, valid and binding obligations of the Company, enforceable in accordance with their respective terms.

2.5 Capitalization; Ownership of Other Entities.

(a) The authorized capital stock of the Company immediately after the Closing shall consist of: (i) _____ shares of Preferred Stock (the "Preferred Stock"), of which _____ shares have been designated Series A Preferred Stock; and (ii) _____ shares of Common Stock. Immediately prior to the Closing, _____ shares of Common Stock will be validly issued and outstanding, fully paid and nonassessable and no shares of Preferred Stock will have been issued. In addition, _____ shares of Common Stock are reserved for issuance under the Company's _____

Stock Option Plan (the "Plan"). The shareholders of record and holders of subscriptions, warrants, options, convertible securities and other rights, contingent or other, including those holding awards under the Plan to purchase or otherwise acquire equity securities of the Company, and the number of shares of Common Stock and the number of such subscriptions, warrants, options, convertible securities, and other such rights held by each or issuable to each, are as set forth in the attached Schedule 2.5. The designations, powers, preferences, rights, qualifications, limitations and restrictions in respect of each class and series of authorized capital stock of the Company are as set forth in the Amended Articles of Incorporation, and all such designations, powers, preferences, rights, qualifications, limitations and restrictions are valid, binding and enforceable and in accordance with all applicable laws. Except as set forth in Schedule 2.5: (i) no person owns of record or is known to the Company to own beneficially any shares of Common Stock or Preferred Stock, or any securities or instruments convertible into Common Stock or Preferred Stock; (ii) no subscription, warrant, option, convertible security, or other right, contingent or other, to purchase or otherwise acquire equity securities of the Company from the Company is authorized or outstanding; (iii) no options, shares, or other rights have been granted or issued under the Plan; and (iv) there is no commitment by the Company to issue shares, subscriptions, warrants, options, convertible securities or other such rights or to distribute to holders of any of its equity securities any evidence of indebtedness or asset. Except as provided for in the Amended Articles of Incorporation or as set forth in Schedule 2.5, the Company has no obligation, contingent or other, to purchase, redeem or otherwise acquire any of its equity securities or any interest therein or to pay any dividend or make any other distribution in respect thereof. Except as set forth in Schedule 2.5, there are no voting trusts or agreements, shareholders agreements, pledge agreements, buy-sell agreements, rights of first refusal, preemptive rights or proxies relating to any securities of the Company, whether or not the Company is a party thereto. All of the outstanding securities of the Company were issued in compliance with all applicable federal and state securities laws.

(b) The Company does not: (i) own of record or beneficially, directly or indirectly, (A) any shares of capital stock or securities convertible into capital stock of any other corporation or (B) any participating interest in any partnership, limited liability company, joint venture, or other non-corporate business enterprise; or (ii) control, directly or indirectly, any other entity.

2.6 No Defaults. The Company is not in default: (a) under (i) the Amended Articles of Incorporation or Bylaws, or (ii) any material written, oral or implied contract, agreement, lease or other commitment to which the Company is a party and, to the best knowledge of the Company, the other party to such contract, agreement, lease or other commitment is not in default thereunder; or (b) with respect to any order, writ, injunction or decree of any court or any federal, state, municipal, or other domestic or foreign governmental department, commission, board, bureau, agency or instrumentality which, in the aggregate, would have a Material Adverse Effect on the Company's business, financial condition, results of operations or prospects.

2.7 Financial Reports.

(a) The books of account, ledgers, order books, records, and documents of the Company accurately and completely reflect all information relating to the business of the Company, the location and collection of its assets, and the nature of all transactions giving rise to the obligations or accounts receivable of the Company in accordance with generally accepted accounting principles in the United States, consistently applied ("GAAP"). The Company has delivered to each Purchaser the following financial statements (the "Financial Reports") which are attached hereto as Exhibit G:

(i) income statements, statements of operating income, and statements of cash flows of the Company: _____ and;

(ii) balance sheets of the Company as of _____ and _____, respectively.

(b) The Financial Reports: (i) are correct and complete and in accordance with the books and records of the Company, (ii) fairly present the financial condition, assets and liabilities of the Company as at its respective dates and the results of its operations and cash flows for the periods covered thereby, and (iii) have been prepared in accordance with GAAP.

(c) All of the accounts receivable reflected on the balance sheets comprising part of the Financial Reports were generated from bona fide transactions by the Company in the ordinary course of business consistent with past practice and, except for reserves and appropriate trade provisions reflected in the Financial Reports (which reserves are reasonable and adequate), constitute valid, undisputed claims of the Company in the amounts reflected therein, are collectible in the ordinary course of its business, and are not subject to valid defenses, or claims of set-off or counterclaims.

(d) The Company's inventory and work in process is in good condition, not obsolete, and saleable at standard cost without material variance. The Company is reasonably satisfied with the products produced by and services performed by outside vendors and suppliers.

(e) The Company has no liability or obligation of any nature, whether due or to become due, matured or unmatured, absolute, contingent or otherwise, including liabilities for or in respect of federal, state and local taxes and any interest, or penalties relating thereto, except to the extent fully reflected as a liability on the balance sheet as of _____, 20___.

(f) Since _____, 20___, the Company has conducted its business only in the ordinary course and has not:

(i) suffered any material adverse change in its operations, condition (financial or otherwise), assets, properties, liabilities, earnings, or prospects;

(ii) increased, or experienced any change in any assumptions underlying or methods of calculating, any bad debt, contingency, or other reserves;

(iii) paid, discharged, or satisfied any claims, liabilities, or obligations (absolute, accrued, contingent, or otherwise) other than the payment, discharge, or satisfaction in the ordinary course of business of liabilities and obligations reflected or reserved against in the balance sheet dated _____ included in the Financial Reports or incurred in the ordinary course of business since _____, 20___;

(iv) permitted or allowed any of its assets to be subjected to any mortgage, pledge, lien, security interest, encumbrance, restriction, or charge of any kind;

(v) written down the value of any inventory or written off as uncollectible any notes or accounts receivable other than in the ordinary course of business that would have a Material Adverse Effect on its financial conditions, results of operations or prospects;

(vi) canceled any debts or waived any claims or rights of substantial value;

(vii) sold, transferred, or otherwise disposed of any of its properties or assets including but not limited to any Intellectual Property Right (as such term is defined in Section 2.10), except in the ordinary course of business;

(viii) granted any increase in the compensation of employees (including any such increase pursuant to any bonus, pension, profit sharing, or other plan or commitment) or any increase in the compensation payable or to become payable to any employee, and no such increase is customary on a periodic basis or required by agreement or understanding; or experienced any material loss of personnel of the Company, material change in the terms and conditions of the employment of the Company's key personnel, or any labor trouble involving the Company;

(ix) made any capital expenditure or commitment for additions to its property, equipment, or intangible capital assets other than in the ordinary course of business;

(x) made any change in any method of accounting or accounting practice or failed to maintain its books, accounts and records in the ordinary course of business;

(xi) failed to maintain any properties or equipment in good operating condition and repair;

(xii) failed to maintain in full force and effect all existing policies of insurance at least at such levels as were in effect prior to such date or canceled any such insurance or taken or failed to take any action that would enable the insurers under such policies to avoid liability for claims arising out of occurrences prior to the Closing;

(xiii) entered into any transaction or made or entered into any material contract or commitment, or terminated or amended any material contract or commitment, except in the ordinary course of business, and not in excess of current requirements;

(xiv) taken any action or experienced any development that has had or that is reasonably likely to have a Material Adverse Effect on its business organization or its current relationships with its employees, suppliers, distributors, advertisers, subscribers, or others having business relationships with it;

(xv) declared, paid, or set aside for payment any dividend or other distribution in respect of its capital stock or redeemed, purchased, or otherwise acquired, directly or indirectly, any shares of its capital stock or other securities; or

(xvi) agreed in writing to take or otherwise taken any corporate action with respect to any of the matters described in this Section 2.7.

2.8 Litigation. Except as set forth in Schedule 2.8, there is no: (i) litigation, action, suit, claim, proceeding, or investigation pending or, to the best of the Company's knowledge, threatened against or affecting the Company, or any of its properties or assets, at law or in equity, or before or by any federal, state, municipal or other governmental department, commission, board, bureau, agency or instrumentality, domestic or foreign; or (ii) governmental inquiry pending or, to the best of the Company's knowledge, threatened against or affecting the Company, including without limitation any inquiry as to the qualification of the Company to hold or receive any license or permit, and, to the best of the Company's knowledge, there is no basis for any of the foregoing. The Company has not received any opinion or memorandum or legal advice from legal counsel to the effect that it is exposed, from a legal standpoint, to any liability that may be material to its business, prospects, financial condition, operations, property or affairs, or which might call into question the validity of this Agreement or any of the securities to be issued hereunder or any action taken or to be taken pursuant hereto or thereto. The Company is not in default with respect to any order, writ, injunction or decree, known to or served upon the Company, of any court or of any federal, state, municipal or other governmental department, commission, board, bureau, agency or instrumentality, domestic or foreign. Except as set forth in Schedule 2.8, there is no action or suit by the Company pending or threatened against others.

2.9 Compliance. The Company has complied with all federal, state, local and foreign laws, ordinances, rules, regulations and orders applicable to it or to its business, operations, properties, assets, products and services and the Company has obtained all necessary permits, licenses, and other authorizations required to conduct its business with such exceptions that do not have a Material Adverse Effect on the Company's business, financial condition, results of operations, or prospects. Such licenses and permits are in full force and effect and no violations have been recorded in respect of any such licenses or permits, no proceeding is pending or, to the knowledge of the Company, threatened to revoke or limit any thereof, and no notice of non-compliance, assessment, or material change has been received by the Company. There is no existing law, ordinance, rule, regulation or order, whether federal, state, local, or foreign, that would prohibit or restrict the Company from, or otherwise have a Material Adverse Effect on the Company in, conducting its business in any jurisdiction in which it is conducting business.

2.10 Intellectual Property Rights. The Company owns or has a valid right to use the Intellectual Property Rights (as defined below) being used to conduct its business as now operated and as now proposed to be operated (a complete list of licenses and registrations of such Intellectual Property Rights is attached to Schedule 2.10 hereto). The conduct of the Company's business as now operated and as now proposed to be operated does not and will not, to the Company's best knowledge, conflict with or infringe upon the Intellectual Property Rights of others. Except as otherwise set forth on Schedule 2.10, no claim is pending or, to the best of the Company's knowledge, threatened against the Company or its officers, employees and consultants to the effect that any such Intellectual Property Right owned or licensed by the Company, or which the Company otherwise has the right to use, is invalid or unenforceable by the Company. Except pursuant to the terms of any licenses specified on Schedule 2.10, the Company has no obligation to compensate any Person for the use of any such Intellectual Property Rights and the Company has not granted any Person any license or other right to use any of the Intellectual Property Rights of the Company, whether requiring payment of royalties or not. The Company has taken all reasonable measures to protect and preserve the security, confidentiality and value of its Intellectual Property Rights, including its trade secrets and other confidential information. All employees and consultants of the Company involved in the design, review, evaluation or development of products or Intellectual Property Rights have executed a nondisclosure and assignment of inventions agreement. For purposes of this Agreement, "Intellectual Property Rights" shall mean all forms of intellectual property rights and protections that may be obtained including, without limitation, all right, title and interest in and to all foreign, federal, state and common law rights relating to: (i) patents, patent rights and all filed, pending or potential applications for patents or patent rights, including any reissue, reexamination, division, continuation or continuation-in-part applications now or hereafter filed; (ii) trade secret rights and equivalent rights; (iii) copyrights, mask works and other literary property and authors' rights, whether or not protected by copyright or as a mask work; and (iv) trademarks, trade names, service marks, symbols, logos, brand names and other proprietary indicia.

2.11 Business Plan. All factual information contained in the Business Plan of the Company dated _____, 20___ (the "Business Plan") was prepared by management and was, when given, and is on the Closing Date, true, complete and accurate in all material respects and not misleading. Without prejudice to the generality of the foregoing, the financial forecasts contained in the Business Plan have been diligently prepared and such assumptions upon which they are based have been carefully considered and are honestly believed to be reasonable, having regard to the information available and to the market conditions prevailing at the time of their preparation by management.

2.12 Title to Properties.

(a) The Company owns, or has a valid leasehold interest in, or valid license for, all assets necessary for the conduct of its business as currently conducted. All tangible assets of the Company are in a good state of maintenance and repair and adequate for use in the Company's business to the extent of its current operations. The Company owns no real property. The Company enjoys peaceful and undisturbed possession under all leases under which it is operating, and all such leases are valid and subsisting in full force and effect without any default of the Company thereunder and, to the best of the Company's knowledge, without any default thereunder of any other party thereto. No event has occurred and is continuing which, with due notice or lapse of time or both, would constitute a default or event of default by the Company under any such lease or agreement or, to the best of the Company's knowledge, by any other party thereto. The Company's possession of such property has not been disturbed and no claim has been asserted against the Company that is adverse to its rights in such leasehold interests.

(b) The Company has good and marketable title to its properties and assets reflected on the Financial Reports or acquired by it since the date of the Financial Reports other than properties and assets disposed of in the ordinary course of business since the date of the Financial Reports, and all such properties and assets are free and clear of mortgages, pledges, security interests, liens, charges, claims, restrictions and other encumbrances, except for liens for current taxes not yet due and payable and minor imperfections of title, if any, not material in nature or amount and not materially detracting from the value or impairing the use of the property subject thereto or impairing the operations or proposed operations of the Company.

2.13 Taxes.

(a) The term "taxes" as used herein means all federal, state, local, foreign and other net income, gross income, gross receipts, sales, use, ad valorem, transfer, franchise, profits, license, lease, service, service use, withholding, payroll, employment, excise, severance, stamp, occupation, premium, property, windfall profits, customs duties, or other taxes, fees, assessments or other charges of any kind whatever, together with any interest and any penalties, additions to tax or additional amounts with respect thereto, and the term "tax" means any one of the foregoing taxes. The term "returns" as used herein, means all returns, declarations, reports, statements and other documents required to be filed in respect of taxes, and "return" means any one of the foregoing returns. The term "Code" means the Internal Revenue Code of 1986, as amended. All citations to the Code, or to the Treasury Regulations promulgated thereunder, shall include any amendments or any substitute or successor provisions thereto.

(b) The Company and its subsidiaries have filed all returns required to be filed in accordance with applicable laws with the appropriate governmental agencies in all jurisdictions in which such returns are required to be filed. The Company and its subsidiaries have paid all taxes required to have been paid by the Company and its subsidiaries and adequate reserves have been established for all taxes accrued but not yet payable. No issues have been raised and are currently pending by any taxing authority in connection with any of the returns or taxes. No waivers of statutes of limitation with respect to any of the returns have been given by or requested from the Company or its subsidiaries. All deficiencies asserted or assessments made as a result of any examinations have been fully paid, or are fully reflected as a liability in the Financial Reports as being contested and an adequate reserve therefor has been established and is fully reflected in the Financial Reports. There are no liens for taxes other than for current taxes not yet due and payable upon the assets of the Company or its subsidiaries. All elections with respect to taxes affecting the Company or its subsidiaries as of the date hereof are set forth in the Financial Reports or are annexed hereto. After the date hereof, no election with respect to taxes will be made without the written consent of the Purchasers. The Company and its subsidiaries have not agreed to make, nor is it required to make, any adjustment under Section 481(a) of the Code by reason of a change in accounting method or otherwise. The Company and its subsidiaries are not a party to any agreement, contract, arrangement, or plan that has resulted or would result, separately or in the aggregate, in the payment of any "excess parachute payments" within the meaning of Section 280G of the Code. The Company and its subsidiaries does not have and has not had a permanent establishment in any foreign country as defined in any applicable tax treaty or convention between the United States of America and such foreign country. The Company and its subsidiaries have satisfied all federal, state, local and foreign withholding tax requirements, including but not limited to income, social security, and employment tax.

(c) Neither the Company nor any of its shareholders has ever filed: (a) an election pursuant to Section 1362 of the Code that the Company be taxed as an S corporation; or (b) a consent pursuant to Section 341(f) of the Code relating to collapsible corporations.

2.14 Insurance. The Company carries insurance covering its properties and businesses customary for the type and scope of its properties and businesses, but in any event in the amounts sufficient to prevent the Company from becoming a co-insurer.

2.15 Other Agreements. Except as set forth in Schedule 2.15, the Company is not a party to or otherwise bound by any written, oral, or implied agreement, contract, instrument, lease, commitment, or other restriction that individually or in the aggregate could have a Material Adverse Effect on the business, prospects, financial condition, operations, property or affairs of the Company. [Alternatively: describe the specific types of contracts to be disclosed.] The Company and, to the best of the Company's knowledge, each other party thereto, have in all material respects performed all the obligations required to be performed by them to date, have received no notice of default and are not in material default with due notice or lapse of time or both under any lease, agreement or contract now in effect to which the Company is a party or by which it or its property may be bound. The Company has no present expectation or intention of not fully performing all its obligations under each such lease, contract or other agreement, and the Company has no knowledge of any breach or anticipated breach by the other party to any contract or commitment to which the Company is a party. The Company is in full compliance with all of the terms and provisions of the Amended Articles of Incorporation and Bylaws.

2.16 Loans and Advances. Except as set forth in Schedule 2.16, the Company does not have any outstanding loans or advances to any Person and is not obligated to make any such loans or advances, except, in each case, for advances to employees of the Company in respect of reimbursable business expenses anticipated to be incurred by them in connection with their performance of services for the Company.

2.17 Assumptions and Guaranties of Indebtedness. The Company has not assumed, guaranteed, endorsed or otherwise become directly or contingently liable on any indebtedness of any other person including, without limitation, liability by way of agreement, contingent or otherwise, to purchase, to provide funds for payment, to supply funds to or otherwise invest in the debtor, or otherwise to assure the creditor against loss.

2.18 Governmental Approvals. No registration or filing with, or consent or approval of or other action by, any federal, state or other governmental agency or instrumentality is or will be necessary for the valid execution, delivery and performance by the

Company of the Transaction Agreements, the issuance, sale, and delivery of the Series A Preferred Shares or, upon conversion of the Series A Preferred Shares, the issuance and delivery of the Conversion Shares, other than: (i) filings pursuant to state securities laws and Regulation D under the Securities Act of 1933, as amended (the "Securities Act"), all of which filings have been made, or shall be timely made, by the Company in connection with the sale of the Series A Preferred Shares and the issuance of the Conversion Shares; and (ii) with respect to the Rights Agreement, the registration of the shares covered thereby with the Securities and Exchange Commission and filings pursuant to state securities laws.

2.19 Disclosure. The Company has fully provided each Purchaser with all the information that such Purchaser has requested and all information that the Company believes is reasonably necessary to enable such Purchaser to make its decision to purchase the Series A Preferred Shares. Neither this Agreement, including all Schedules and Exhibits hereto, nor any other Transaction Agreement, nor any other written statements or certificates made or delivered herewith or therewith, contains any untrue statement of a material fact or omits to state a fact necessary to make the statements contained herein or therein not misleading. There is no fact within the knowledge of the Company or any of the Company's officers that has not been disclosed herein or in writing by them to the Purchasers and that has a Material Adverse Effect, or in the future in their opinion may, insofar as they can now foresee, could have a Material Adverse Effect on the business, properties, assets or condition, financial or otherwise, of the Company. Other than as stated in the Schedule 2.19, without limiting the foregoing, the Company has no knowledge or belief that there exists, or there is pending or planned, any patent, invention, device, application or principle or any statute, rule, law, regulation, standard or condition that would have a Material Adverse Effect on the condition, financial or otherwise, or the operations or prospects of the Company.

2.20 Offering Exemption. Subject to the accuracy of the representations and warranties of the Purchasers set forth under Article III of this Agreement, the offering and sale of the Series A Preferred Shares is exempt from registration under the Securities Act pursuant to Section 4(2) thereof, and under applicable state securities and "blue sky" laws.

2.21 Brokers. No broker, investment banker, finder, financial advisor, or other Person is entitled to any broker's, finder's, financial advisor's or other similar fee or commission in connection with the transactions contemplated by this Agreement based on arrangements made by or on behalf of the Company.

2.22 Officers.

(a) Set forth in Schedule 2.22 is a list of the names of the officers and key employees of the Company (collectively, the "Key Employees") together with the title or job classification of each such person and the total compensation anticipated to be paid to each such person by the Company in 20___. Except as set forth on Schedule 2.22, none of such persons has an employment agreement or understanding, whether oral or written, with the Company, which is not terminable on notice by the Company without cost or other liability to the Company.

(b) No officer, employee or consultant of the Company is now in violation of any term of any employment contract, patent disclosure agreement, proprietary information agreement, noncompetition agreement, nonsolicitation agreement, confidentiality agreement or any other similar contract or agreement or any restrictive covenant relating to the right of any such officer, employee or consultant to be employed or engaged by the Company because of the nature of the business conducted or to be conducted by the Company or relating to the use of trade secrets or proprietary information of others, and the continued employment or engagement of the Company's officers, employees or consultants does not subject the Company or any of the Purchasers to any liability with respect to any of the foregoing matters.

(c) No officer or Key Employee of the Company, whose termination, either individually or in the aggregate, could have an adverse effect on the Company, has terminated his or her employment, or, to the Company's knowledge, has any present intention of terminating his or her employment with the Company or has any health problems that could adversely affect his or her ability to continue performing his or her duties for the Company.

2.23 Employees. Each of the executive officers and Key Employees has executed an Employee Non-Disclosure and Developments Agreement in the form attached hereto as Exhibit E, and all such agreements are in full force and effect. The Company has complied with all applicable laws relating to the employment of labor, including provisions relating to wages, hours, equal opportunity, collective bargaining and the payment of Social Security and other taxes, and with the Employee Retirement Income Security Act of 1974, as amended ("ERISA"). To the best knowledge of the Company, relations with the employees of the Company are good, and the Company has no reason to believe that any labor difficulties will arise in the foreseeable future. There is no charge or complaint pending or, to the best of the Company's knowledge, threatened against the Company before the Equal Employment Opportunity Commission or the Department of Labor or any state or local agency of similar jurisdiction. No employees of the Company are represented by any labor union and there is no collective bargaining agreement in effect with respect to such employees. During the past three years, to the knowledge of the Company, no labor union has engaged in any organizing activities with respect to the Company's employees. The Company is not in default with respect to any obligation to any of its employees. The Company is not aware that any of its employees or independent contractors is obligated under any contract (including licenses, covenants or commitments of any nature) or other agreement, or subject to any judgment, decree or order of any court or administrative agency, that would interfere with the use of such employee's or independent contractor's best efforts to promote the interest of the Company or that would conflict with the Company's business as now conducted. Neither the execution or delivery of this Agreement, nor the carrying on of the Company's business by the employees and independent contractors of the Company, nor the conduct of the Company's business as now conducted will conflict with or result in a breach of the terms, conditions, or provisions of, or constitute a default under, any contract, covenant or instrument under which any such employee or independent contractor is now obligated and of which the Company is aware.

2.24 Transactions with Affiliates. Except as set forth in Schedule 2.24, no director, officer, employee or shareholder of the Company or member of the family of any such person, or any corporation, partnership, trust or other entity in which any such person or any member of the family of any such person, has a substantial interest or is an officer, director, trustee, partner or holder of more than 5% of the outstanding capital stock thereof, is a party to any transaction with the Company, including any loan, debt or contract, agreement or other arrangement providing for the employment of, furnishing of services by, rental of real or personal property from or otherwise requiring payments to, any such person or firm, or has a pecuniary interest in any supplier or customer of the Company or in any other business enterprise with which the Company conducts business.

2.25 U.S. Real Property Holding Corporation. The Company is not now and has never been a "United States real property holding corporation," as defined in Section

897(c) (2) of the Code and Section 1.897-2(b) of the regulations promulgated by the Internal Revenue Service.

2.26 Employees; Benefit Plans. The Company is not a party to any collective bargaining agreement and is not a party to any pending or threatened labor dispute. Except as set forth in Schedule 2.26, there is no employee of the Company whose employment is not terminable at will. The Company's only employee benefit plans are listed on Schedule 2.26 (the "Employee Benefit Plans"). With respect to the Employee Benefit Plans: (a) the Company is, and always has been, in compliance in all material respects with the applicable provisions of ERISA and the Code and the regulations promulgated thereunder; (b) there has been no violation of ERISA's fiduciary obligations nor have there been any prohibited transactions; (c) there does not exist any liability for any federal, state or local taxes nor does any Employee Benefit Plan have any unfunded liability; and (d) all reports required to be filed with all governmental entities have been so filed. [Expand this representation and warranty as necessary under the circumstances.]

2.27 Stock Option Plan. The Company has authorized the Plan and the issuance and sale of up to _____ shares of Common Stock under the Plan. As of the date hereof, no options, shares, or other rights have been granted or issued under the Plan.

2.28 Environmental Matters. To the knowledge of the Company, (i) there is no environmental litigation or other environmental proceeding pending or threatened by any governmental regulatory authority or others with respect to the business of the Company, (ii) no state of facts exists as to environmental matters or Hazardous Substances (as defined below) that involves the reasonable likelihood of a material capital expenditure by the Company or that may otherwise have a Material Adverse Effect, and (iii) no Hazardous Substances have been used, treated, stored or disposed of, or otherwise deposited, in or on the properties owned or leased by the Company in violation of any applicable environmental laws. As used herein, "Hazardous Substances" means any substance, waste, contaminant, pollutant or material that has been determined by any governmental authority to be capable of posing a risk of injury to health, safety, property or the environment. [Expand this representation and warranty as necessary under the circumstances.]

2.29 Registration Rights. Except as provided in the Rights Agreement, the Company is not presently under any obligation, and has not granted any rights, to register (as defined in the Rights Agreement) any of the Company's presently outstanding securities or any of its securities that may hereafter be issued.

2.30 Investment Company. The Company is not an "investment company" as such term is defined in the Investment Company Act of 1940, as amended, and will not be an investment company under such Act after giving effect to the use of proceeds from the purchase of the Series A Preferred Shares.

2.31 Securities Laws. Subject to the accuracy of each Purchaser's representations under Article III, the offer, sale and issuance of the shares of Series A Preferred Stock under this Agreement and the Common Stock issuable upon conversion thereunder, respectively, in each case without registration, will not violate the Securities Act of 1933, as amended (the "Securities Act"), or any applicable state securities or "blue sky" laws.

2.32 Investment Banking; Brokerage. There are no claims for investment banking fees, brokerage commissions, finder's fees or similar compensation (exclusive of professional fees to lawyers and accountants) in connection with the Transaction Agreements based on any arrangement or agreement made by or on behalf of the Company or any affiliate.

2.33 Small Business Concern. [Insert if appropriate.] The Company with its "affiliates" (as that term is defined in Section 121.401 of Title 13 of the Code of Federal Regulations) is a "small business concern" within the meaning of the Small Business Act and Section 121.802 of said Regulations. The information pertaining to the Company set forth in Small Business Administration Forms 480, 652 and 1031 is accurate and complete.

2.34 Qualified Small Business Stock. [Insert if appropriate.] The Series A Preferred Shares constitute "qualified small business stock" as defined in Section 1202(c) of the Code.

ARTICLE III
REPRESENTATIONS AND WARRANTIES OF THE PURCHASERS

3.1 Authorization. Each of the Purchasers has all requisite power and authority to execute and deliver the Transaction Agreements and to carry out their provisions. The execution and delivery of the Transaction Agreements and the performance by each of the Purchasers of its obligations hereunder and thereunder, have been duly authorized by each of the Purchasers. The Transaction Agreements have been duly executed and delivered by each of the Purchasers and are valid and binding obligations of each Investor, enforceable against it in accordance with their terms.

3.2 Investment Representations. Each of the Purchasers, severally and not jointly, represents to the Company that:

(a) It is purchasing the Series A Preferred Shares for its own account for investment only and not with a view to or for sale in connection with the distribution thereof except for sales contemplated by the Rights Agreement or the Shareholders Agreement.

(b) It has such knowledge and experience in financial and business matters that it is capable of evaluating the merits and risks of the investment contemplated by this Agreement and making an informed investment decision with respect thereto. Investor must bear the economic risk of this investment indefinitely unless the Series A Preferred Shares or the Conversion Shares are registered pursuant to the Securities Act, or an exemption from registration is available.

(c) It is an "Accredited Investor" as such term is defined in Rule 501 under the Securities Act.

(d) It has had the opportunity to ask questions and receive answers concerning the terms and conditions of the offering of securities purchased hereunder, as well as the opportunity to obtain additional information necessary to verify the accuracy of information furnished in connection with such offering that the Company possesses or can acquire without unreasonable effort or expense; provided, however, the Purchaser has relied upon the representations and warranties of the Company set forth in this Agreement, as modified in the Disclosure Schedules thereto, and this Article III shall not be interpreted to limit that reliance.

(e) It understands that neither the Series A Preferred Shares nor the Conversion Shares registered under the Securities Act or any state securities laws, and may not be transferred unless subsequently registered thereunder or pursuant to an exemption from registration, and that a legend indicating such restrictions will be placed on the certificates representing such shares. The Purchaser understands that the Company has no present intention of registering any shares of its Series A Preferred Shares or its Common Stock. The Purchaser also understands that there is no assurance that any exemption from registration under the Securities Act will be available and that, even if available, such exemption may not allow the Purchaser to transfer all or any portion of the Series A Preferred Shares or the Conversion Shares under the circumstances, in the amounts or at the times Purchaser might propose.

(f)   The Purchaser acknowledges and agrees that Series A Preferred Shares and the Conversion Shares must be held indefinitely unless they are subsequently registered under the Securities Act or an exemption from such registration is available. The Purchaser has been advised or is aware of the provisions of Rule 144 promulgated under the Securities Act as in effect from time to time, which permits limited resale of shares purchased in a private placement subject to the satisfaction of certain conditions, including, among other things: the availability of certain current public information about the Company, the resale occurring following the required holding period under Rule 144 and the number of shares being sold during any three-month period not exceeding specified limitations.

(g)   If the Purchaser is an individual, then the Purchaser resides in the state or province identified in the address of the Purchaser set forth on Schedule 1; if the Purchaser is a partnership, corporation, limited liability company or other entity, then the office or offices of the Purchaser in which its investment decision was made is located at the address or addresses of the Purchaser set forth on Schedule 1.

(h)   There are no claims for investment banking fees, brokerage commissions, finder's fees or similar compensation (other than professional fees to lawyers, accountants and other consultants) in connection with the transactions contemplated by the Transaction Agreements based on any arrangement or agreement made by or on behalf of the Purchaser.

(i)   The Purchaser has all necessary power and authority to execute and deliver this Agreement and each of the Transaction Agreements. Upon their execution and delivery, each Transaction Agreement will be valid and binding upon the Purchaser, enforceable in accordance with its terms, except (i) as limited by applicable bankruptcy, insolvency, reorganization, moratorium or other laws of general application affecting enforcement of creditors' rights, (ii) general principles of equity that restrict the availability of equitable remedies, and (iii) to the extent that the enforceability of the indemnification provisions of the Rights Agreement may be limited by applicable laws.

(j)   The Purchaser acknowledges and agrees that the Conversion Shares are subject to restrictions on transfer as set forth in the Shareholders Agreement and the Rights Agreement.

ARTICLE IV
CONDITIONS TO THE OBLIGATIONS OF THE PURCHASERS

The obligation of each Purchaser to purchase and pay for the Series A Preferred Shares being purchased by it on the Closing Date is, at its option, subject to the satisfaction, on or before the Closing Date, of the following conditions:

[Modify as appropriate for additional closings.]

4.1 Opinion of Company's Counsel. The Purchasers shall have received from _____, counsel for the Company, an opinion dated the Closing Date as to the matters set forth in Exhibit F.

4.2 Representations and Warranties to Be True and Correct. The representations and warranties contained in Article II shall be true, complete and correct on and as of the Closing Date with the same effect as though such representations and warranties had been made on and as of such date, and the President and the Chief Financial Officer of the Company shall have certified to the Purchasers in writing to such effect.

4.3 Performance. The Company shall have performed and complied with all agreements contained herein required to be performed or complied with by it prior to or at the Closing Date, and the President and the Chief Financial Officer of the Company shall have certified to the Purchasers in writing to such effect and to the further effect that all of the conditions set forth in this Article IV have been satisfied.

4.4 Due Diligence. The Purchasers shall have completed their due diligence investigation of the Company and shall be satisfied in their sole discretion in all respects with the findings thereof.

4.5 Proceedings to Be Satisfactory. All corporate and other proceedings to be taken by the Company in connection with the transactions contemplated hereby and all documents incident thereto shall be reasonably satisfactory in form and substance to the Purchasers and their counsel, and the Purchasers and their counsel shall have received all such counterpart originals or certified or other copies of such documents as they reasonably may request.

4.6 Purchase by the Purchasers. Each Purchaser shall have purchased and paid for the Series A Preferred Shares being purchased by it on the Closing Date, and the Aggregate Purchase Price paid by all of the Purchasers for the Series A Preferred Shares being purchased by them on the Closing Date shall be $_____.

4.7 Articles of Incorporation. The Articles of Incorporation shall be amended to include the provisions of the Series A Preferred Stock as set forth in Exhibit A.

4.8 Supporting Documents. The Purchasers and their counsel shall have received copies of the following documents:

(i)   (A) the Amended Articles of Incorporation, certified as of a recent date by the Secretary of State of _____; (B) a certificate of the Secretary of State of _____ dated as of a recent date as to the due incorporation and good standing of the Company, the payment of all taxes by the Company and listing all documents of the Company on file with said Secretary; and (C) a certificate of the Secretary of the State of _____ as to the good standing of the Company with the State of _____.

(ii) a certificate of the Secretary or an Assistant Secretary of the Company dated the Closing Date and certifying: (A) that attached thereto is a true and complete copy of the Bylaws of the Company as in effect on the date of such certification; (B) that attached thereto is a true and complete copy of all resolutions adopted by the Board of Directors or the shareholders of the Company authorizing the execution, delivery and performance of the Transaction Agreements, the issuance, sale and delivery of the Series A Preferred Shares and the reservation, issuance and delivery of the Conversion Shares and that all such resolutions are in full force and effect and are all the resolutions adopted in connection with the transactions contemplated by the Transaction Agreements; (C) that the Amended Articles of Incorporation has not been amended since the date of the last amendment referred to in the certificate delivered pursuant to clause (i)(B) above; and (D) to the incumbency and specimen signature of each officer of the Company executing the Transaction Agreements or any of the stock certificates representing the Series A Preferred Shares and any certificate or instrument furnished pursuant hereto and a certification by another officer of the Company as to the incumbency and signature of the officer signing the certificate referred to in this clause (ii); and

(iii) such additional supporting documents and other information with respect to the operations and affairs of the Company as the Purchasers or their counsel reasonably may request.

4.9 Rights Agreement. The Company shall have executed and delivered the Rights Agreement.

4.10 Shareholders Agreement; Voting Agreement. The Shareholders Agreement and the Voting Agreement shall have been executed and delivered by the Company and the shareholders listed therein.

4.11 Employee Agreements. Each of the executive officers, Key Employees and other employees shall have entered into Employee Non-Disclosure and Developments Agreements with the Company in the form attached as Exhibit E, and copies thereof shall have been delivered to counsel for the Purchasers.

4.12 Consents. The Company shall have obtained the written consents of all parties necessary for the execution and delivery by the Company of the Transaction Agreements, all of which written consents shall be reasonably satisfactory in form, scope and substance to the Investors.

4.13 Stock Option Plan. The Company shall have amended to the Stock Option Plan with _____ shares of Common Stock authorized and reserved for issuance under such Option Plan.

4.14 No Material Adverse Change. Since _____, there shall have been no material adverse change in the Company's business or financial condition.

4.15 Expenses. The Company shall have paid the expenses of the Purchasers as set forth in Section 7.1 hereof.

4.16 Board of Directors. _____ and _____ shall have been elected directors of the Company.

4.17 Preemptive Rights; Termination of Shareholder Agreements. All shareholders of the Company having any preemptive, first refusal or other rights with respect to the issuance of the Series A Preferred Shares or Conversion Shares shall have irrevocably waived the same in writing. All shareholder agreements, voting agreements, registration rights agreements and similar agreements relating to the capital stock of the Company shall have been terminated by all parties to such agreements. [Consider whether other agreements must be terminated.]

4.18 Other Waivers and Consents. The Company shall have obtained all other necessary waivers or consents to the execution of this Agreement and the related agreements.

All such documents shall be reasonably satisfactory in form and substance to the Purchasers and their counsel.

ARTICLE V
INDEMNIFICATION
[Optional provision.]

5.1 Indemnification.

(a) In addition to all rights and remedies available to the Purchasers at law or in equity, the Company shall indemnify, defend, and hold harmless each of the Purchasers and any parent, subsidiary, associate, affiliate, partner, shareholder, director, officer, employee, or agent of each such Purchaser, and each subsequent holder of Series A Preferred Stock and their respective affiliates, shareholders, officers, directors, employees, agents, representatives, successors, and permitted assigns (all of the foregoing are collectively referred to as the "Indemnified Parties") from and against and pay on behalf of or reimburse such party as and when incurred all losses, including, without limitation, diminutions in value, liabilities, demands, claims, actions or causes of action, costs, damages, judgments, debts, settlements, assessments, deficiencies, taxes, penalties, fines, or expenses, whether or not arising out of any claims by or on behalf of any third party, including interest, penalties, reasonable attorneys' fees and expenses, and all reasonable amounts paid in investigation, defense or settlement of any of the foregoing (collectively, "Losses") which any such party may suffer, sustain or become subject to, as a result of, in connection with, or relating to or by virtue of:

(i) any material misrepresentations or material breach of warranty on the part of the Company under Article II;

(ii) any material misrepresentation in or material omission from any of the representations or warranties contained in any certificate, document or instrument or the Schedules delivered to the Purchasers by or on behalf of the Company in connection herewith;

(iii) any material nonfulfillment or breach of any covenant or agreement on the part of the Company under this Agreement or under any certificate, document, or instrument delivered in connection therewith; or

(iv) any action, demand, proceeding, investigation, or claim by any third party, including, without limitation, governmental agencies against or affecting the Company or its affiliates or subsidiaries which, if successful, would give rise to or evidence the existence of or relate to a material breach of (A) any of the representations or warranties at the time made or (B) covenants of the Company.

(b) Notwithstanding the foregoing, and subject to the following sentence, upon judicial determination which is final and no longer appealable, that the act or omission giving rise to the indemnification hereinabove provided resulted primarily out of or was based primarily upon the Indemnified Party's gross negligence, fraud or willful misconduct, the Company shall not be responsible for any Losses sought to be indemnified in connection herewith, and the Company shall be entitled to recover from the Indemnified Party all amounts previously paid in full or partial satisfaction of such indemnity, together with all costs and expenses of the Company reasonably incurred in effecting such recovery, if any.

(c) All indemnification rights hereunder shall survive the execution and delivery of this Agreement and the consummation of the transactions contemplated hereunder indefinitely, regardless of any investigation, inquiry or examination made for or on behalf of, or any knowledge of, any of the Purchasers and/or any of the other Indemnified Parties or the acceptance by the Purchasers of any certificate or opinion.

5.2 Contribution. If for any reason the indemnity provided for in Section 5.1 is unavailable to any Indemnified Party or is insufficient to hold each such Indemnified Party harmless from all such Losses arising with respect to the transactions contemplated hereunder, then the Company and the Indemnified Party shall each contribute to the amount paid or payable by such Loss in such proportion as is appropriate to reflect not only the relative benefits received by the Company on the one hand, and such Indemnified Party on the other, but also the relative fault of the Company on the one hand, and the Indemnified Party on the other, as well as any relevant equitable considerations. In addition, the Company agrees to reimburse any Indemnified Party upon demand for all reasonable expenses, including legal counsel fees, incurred by such Indemnified Party or any such other person in connection with investigating, preparing or defending any such action or claim. The indemnity, contribution and expense reimbursement obligations that the Company has under this Section 5.1 shall be in addition to any liability that the Company may otherwise have. The Company further agrees that the indemnification and reimbursement commitments set forth in this Agreement shall apply whether or not the Indemnified Party is a formal party to any such lawsuits, claims or other proceedings.

5.3 Payment. Any indemnification or contribution of any Purchasers or any other Indemnified Party by the Company pursuant to Section 5.1 shall be effected by wire transfer of immediately available funds from the Company to an account designated by such Purchaser or such other Indemnified Party within 15 days after the determination thereof.

ARTICLE VI
SBIC PROVISIONS

[Insert only if a Purchaser is a SBIC]

The Company acknowledges that Capital is a small business investment company licensed by the United States Small Business Administration (the "SBA"), and makes the following representations, warranties and covenants:

6.1 Small Business Concern. The Company, taken together with its "affiliates" (as that term is defined in 13 C.F.R. 121.401), is a "Small Business Concern" within the meaning of 15 U.S.C. 662(5), that is Section 103(5) of the Small Business Investment Company Act of 1958, as amended (the "SBIC Act"), and the regulations thereunder, including 13 C.F.R. 107, and meets the applicable size eligibility criteria set forth in 13 C.F.R. 121.301 (c)(1) or the industry standard covering the industry in which the Company is primarily engaged as set forth in 13 C.F.R. 121.301(c)(2), and is not engaged in any activities for which a small business investment company is prohibited from providing funds by the SBIC Act and the regulations thereunder, including 13 C.F.R. 107.

6.2 Informational Covenant.

(a) The Company will furnish or cause to be furnished to Capital information required by the SBA concerning the economic impact of Capital's investment, including but not limited to, information concerning taxes paid and number of employees. At the Closing, the Company will deliver to Capital SBA Form 480 (Size Status Declaration) and SBA Form 652 (Assurance of Compliance) which have been completed and executed by the Company and SBA Form 1031 (Portfolio Financing Report), Part A of which has been completed by the Company.

(b) The Company will also furnish or cause to be furnished to Capital such other information regarding the business, affairs and condition of the Company as Capital may from time to time reasonably request for purposes of its compliance with the SBIC Act or at the request of the SBA. The Company will permit Capital and examiners of the SBA to inspect the books and any of the properties or assets of the Company and its subsidiaries and to discuss the Company's business with senior management employees at such reasonable times as Capital may from time to time request.

6.3 Use of Proceeds. The Company will deliver within 90 days of the Closing to Capital a written report, certified as correct by the Company's Chief Financial Officer verifying the purposes and amounts for which proceeds from the Series A Preferred Shares have been disbursed, and, if the proceeds have not been fully disbursed within that 90-day period, an additional report also so certified, delivered not later than the end of each succeeding 90-day period, verifying the purposes and amounts for which proceeds have been disbursed. The Company will supply to Capital such additional information and documents as Capital reasonably requests with respect to the use of proceeds, and will permit Capital, or its designee, to have access to any and all Company records and information and personnel as Capital deems necessary to verify how proceeds have been or are being used, and to assure that the proceeds have been used for the purposes specified.

6.4 Activities and Proceeds.

(a) The Company will not engage in any activities or use directly or indirectly the proceeds from the Series A Preferred Shares for any purpose for which a small business investment company is prohibited from providing funds by the SBIC Act and the regulations promulgated thereunder, including 13 C.F.R. 107. The Company will use the proceeds of the Capital investment for domestic working capital purposes.

(b) Without obtaining the prior written approval of Capital, which will not be unreasonably withheld, the Company will not change within one year of the Closing the Company's business activity to a business activity prohibited by Section 6.4(a) hereof (such change of business activity being referred to as an "Activity Event of Default"). Upon the occurrence of an Activity Event of Default which is not cured within 30 days after Capital gives the Company written notice specifying such default (the "Default Notice"), the Company and Capital shall meet and in good faith attempt to agree upon a plan pursuant to which Capital is able to sell its Series A Preferred Shares to the Company or a third party, and the Company will use its best efforts to assist Capital in selling its Series A Preferred Shares. If the Company and Capital are unable to agree within 60 days of the Default Notice upon a mutually satisfactory plan for Capital to sell its Series A Preferred Shares, then at Capital's request, the Company shall repurchase Capital's Series A Preferred Shares, together with declared, but unpaid, dividends, at the earliest time following the date of the Default Notice by at least 90 days at which time the Company may repurchase such stock at the fair market value of such Series A Preferred Shares, determined in accordance with an appraisal conducted by an independent appraiser mutually selected by the Company and Capital, who is knowledgeable in the industry and market place in which the Company operates and in accordance with applicable law and the Company's agreements with its lenders and investors other than the holders of Series A Preferred Shares.

ARTICLE VII
MISCELLANEOUS

7.1 Expenses. Irrespective of any approvals necessary to consummate the transactions contemplated hereby from the Board of Directors of the Company or from the Company's shareholders, the Company shall pay all reasonable costs, expenses and disbursements incurred by the Purchasers, in connection with the negotiation, preparation, execution, delivery, and performance of the Transaction Agreements, and all transactions contemplated herein or therein, including, without limitation, their consulting, accounting and attorneys' fees and expenses incurred in investigating the business and affairs of the Company (including, without limitation, travel expenses) up to $35,000.

7.2 Survival of Agreements. All covenants, agreements, representations and warranties made herein or in any other agreement, or any certificate or instrument delivered to the Purchasers pursuant to or in connection with this Agreement, shall survive the Closing, and all statements contained in any certificate or other instrument delivered by the Company hereunder or thereunder or in connection herewith or therewith shall be deemed to constitute representations and warranties made by the Company.

7.3 Remedies. [Optional provision; remedies can vary.] In case any one or more of the representations, warranties, covenants or agreements set forth in this Agreement shall have been breached by any party hereto, the party or parties entitled to the benefit of such representations, warranties, covenants or agreements may proceed to protect and enforce their rights either under the Indemnification provisions of this Agreement or by suit in equity and/or action at law, including, but not limited to, an action for damages as a result of any such breach and/or an action for specific performance of any such covenant or agreement contained in this Agreement. In addition to, and not to the exclusion of, any other remedy, in the event of a breach by the Company which is not cured by the later to occur of 15 days after receipt by the Company of notice of such breach or 30 days after the occurrence of such breach, the Purchasers shall have the right to require the Company and the Company shall redeem their Series A Preferred Shares pursuant to Section _____ of the Amended

Articles of Incorporation. The rights, powers and remedies of the parties under this Agreement are cumulative and not exclusive of any other right, power or remedy which such parties may have under any other agreement or law. No single or partial assertion or exercise of any right, power or remedy of a party hereunder shall preclude any other or further assertion or exercise thereof.

7.4 Brokerage. The Company or the Purchasers, as applicable, will indemnify and hold harmless the Purchasers or the Company, as applicable, against and in respect of any claim for brokerage or other commissions relative to this Agreement or to the transactions contemplated hereby, based in any way on agreements, arrangements or understandings made or claimed to have been made with any third party.

7.5 Parties in Interest. All representations, covenants, and agreements contained in this Agreement by or on behalf of any of the parties hereto shall bind and inure to the benefit of the respective successors and assigns of the parties hereto whether so expressed or not. Without limiting the generality of the foregoing, all representations, covenants, and agreements benefiting the Purchasers shall inure to the benefit of any and all subsequent holders from time to time of Series A Preferred Shares or Conversion Shares. The parties hereto understand and agree that each of Capital and Venture Fund is a limited partnership formed under the laws of the State of _____ or _____, as applicable, and that the limited partners of such limited partnership will not be liable for any liabilities of such Purchaser, nor will they be required to perform any of the obligations of such Purchaser pursuant to this Agreement and that neither the Company, nor the shareholders or officers of the Company, will seek to enforce such liabilities and/or obligations or otherwise seek relief with respect thereto against such limited partners.

7.6 Notices. All notices, requests, consents, and other communications hereunder shall be in writing and shall be delivered in person or sent by overnight delivery or by certified or registered mail, return receipt requested, or by confirmed telecopy addressed as follows:

(a) if to the Company, at **** Inc., at _____, [San Jose, California] _____, fax: _____, Attention: _____, President, with a copy to _____, Esquire, at _____, [San Francisco, California]] _____, fax: _____;

(b) if to any Purchaser, at the address of such Purchaser set forth in Schedule 1, with a copy to _____, Esquire, at _____ _____, [Palo Alto, California] _____, fax: _____;

or, in any such case, at such other address or addresses as shall have been furnished in writing by such party to the others.

All notices, consents, or other communications required or permitted to be given under this Agreement shall be deemed to have been duly given (i) when delivered personally, (ii) three business days after being mailed by first class mail, postage prepaid, or (iii) one business day after being sent by a reputable overnight delivery service, postage or delivery charges prepaid, to the parties at their respective addresses stated on the signature page of this Agreement. Notices may also be given by telecopier and shall be effective on the date transmitted if confirmed within 24 hours thereafter by a signed original sent in the manner provided in the preceding sentence.

7.7 Governing Law. This Agreement shall be governed by and construed in accordance with the laws of the state of Delaware notwithstanding any conflicts-of-law doctrines of such state or any other jurisdiction to the contrary. EACH OF THE

PARTIES HEREBY WAIVES ANY RIGHT IT MAY HAVE TO TRIAL BY JURY IN ANY LITIGATION DIRECTLY OR INDIRECTLY ARISING OUT OF THIS AGREEMENT OR ANY OF THE TRANSACTION AGREEMENTS.

7.8 Entire Agreement. This Agreement, including the Schedules and Exhibits hereto, together with the other writings referred to herein or delivered pursuant hereto which form a part hereof, constitutes the sole and entire agreement of the parties with respect to the subject matter hereof, including without limitation the letter of intent dated _____, 20___ between the Company and _____ with respect to the transactions contemplated herein. All Schedules and Exhibits hereto are hereby incorporated herein by reference.

7.9 Counterparts. This Agreement may be executed in two or more counterparts, each of which shall be deemed an original, but all of which together shall constitute one and the same instrument.

7.10 Amendments, Waivers, and Consents. For the purposes of this Agreement and all agreements executed pursuant hereto, no course of dealing between the Company and the Purchasers and no delay on the part of any party hereto in exercising any rights hereunder or thereunder shall operate as a waiver of the rights hereof or thereof. Any term of this Agreement may be amended or waived only with the written consent of the Company and the holders of at least _____% of the shares of Common Stock issued or issuable upon conversion of the Series A Preferred Shares purchased hereunder voting as a single class. Any amendment or waiver effected in accordance with this Section 7.10 shall be binding upon the Investors and each transferee of the Series A Preferred Shares (or the Common Stock issuable upon conversion thereof). No provision hereof may be waived except by a written instrument signed by the party so waiving such provision. No supplement or modification of this Agreement shall be binding unless in writing and approved and executed by the requisite parties in accordance with this Section 7.10. Any amendment or waiver effected in accordance with this Section 7.10 shall be binding upon each holder of Series A Preferred Shares purchased under this Agreement at the time outstanding and each future holder of all such Series A Preferred Shares or such converted securities of the Company.

7.11 Severability. The invalidity or unenforceability of any term, phrase, clause, paragraph, restriction, covenant, agreement, or other provision hereof shall in no way affect the validity or enforceability of any other provision, or any part thereof, but this Agreement shall be construed as if such invalid or unenforceable term, phrase, clause, paragraph, restriction, covenant, agreement or other provision had never been contained herein unless the deletion of such term, phrase, clause, paragraph, restriction, covenant, agreement, or other provision would result in such a material change as to cause the covenants and agreements contained herein to be unreasonable or would materially and adversely frustrate the objectives of the parties as expressed in this Agreement.

7.12 Titles and Subtitles. The titles and subtitles used in this Agreement are for convenience only and are not to be considered in construing or interpreting any term or provision of this Agreement.

7.13 Certain Defined Term. As used in this Agreement, the following term shall have the following meaning, such meaning to be equally applicable to both the singular and plural forms of the term defined:

"Material Adverse Effect" shall mean any material adverse effect on the operations, condition (financial or other), assets, liabilities, earnings or prospects of the Company or on the transactions contemplated hereby.

"Person" shall mean an individual, corporation, trust, partnership, joint venture, unincorporated organization, government agency or any agency or political subdivision thereof, or other entity.

7.14 Publicity. The Company shall be entitled to issue a press release or other public statement upon the Closing, subject to the prior written approval of the Purchasers, which approval shall not be unreasonably withheld.

IN WITNESS WHEREOF, the Company and the Purchasers have executed this Agreement as of the day and year first above written.

**** INC.

By: _____

Name and Title: _____

PURCHASERS:

**** CAPITAL, L.P.

By: **** Partners, L.P., its general partner

By: _____ ****, Inc.,its general partner

By: _____

Name and Title: _____

**** VENTURE FUND, L.P.

By: **** Partners, L.P., its general partner

By: _____

Name and Title: _____

SCHEDULE 1
List of Purchasers and Number of Shares Purchased

Name and Address of Purchaser	Number of Series A Preferred Shares to Be Purchased	Aggregate Purchase Price

Schedule 2.5
Capitalization, Ownership of Other Entities

Schedule 2.8
Litigation

Schedule 2.10
Intellectual Property Rights

Schedule 2.15
Other Agreements

Schedule 2.16
Loans and Advances

Schedule 2.19
Disclosure

Schedule 2.22
Officers

Schedule 2.24
Transactions with Affiliates

Schedule 2.26
Employee Benefit Plans

Exhibits:
A   **Amended and Restated Certificate of Incorporation**
B   **Investors Rights Agreement**
C   **Shareholder Agreement**
D   **Voting Agreement**
E   **Employee Non-Disclosure and Developments Agreement**
F   **Opinion of Company's Counsel**
G   **Financial Statements**

Form 12 E: Shareholders Agreement

SHAREHOLDERS AGREEMENT

SHAREHOLDERS AGREEMENT entered into as of _____, 20___, by and among **** Inc. a [Delaware] corporation (the "Company"), the investors listed on Schedule A hereto (the "Investors") and the holders of Common Stock listed on Schedule B hereto (the "Common Shareholders"). (The Investors and the Common Shareholders, together with any other person or entity that shall hereafter become a shareholder of the Company, as long as they are shareholders of the Company, are collectively referred to herein as the "Shareholders" or individually a "Shareholder.")

Recitals:

The parties have determined that it is in the best interests of the Company and the Shareholders to provide for: (a) restricting the future disposition of the Company's Common Stock, par value $_____ per share (the "Common Stock"); (b) the election of directors; and (c) various other matters set forth herein.

NOW, THEREFORE, in consideration of the agreements and mutual covenants set forth herein, the parties hereto, intending to be legally bound hereby, agree as follows:

SECTION 1
TRANSFERABILITY OF SHARES

Section 1.1 Restrictions on Transferability. A Common Shareholder shall not sell, give, transfer, assign, bequeath, pledge, encumber or otherwise dispose of, whether voluntarily or involuntarily, by operation of law or otherwise, (collectively "transfer") any legal or beneficial interest in any securities of the Company owned by such Common Shareholder, whether now owned or hereafter acquired ("Shares"), or any option or right to acquire any Shares or any other interest in any Shares, unless all of the following conditions that are applicable have first been satisfied:

(a) **Compliance with Section 2.** Except in the case of a Permitted Transfer (as defined in Section 1.2 hereof), the Common Shareholder shall have complied with Section 2 of this Agreement. The Company shall not record in its books or otherwise recognize any purported or intended transfer of any Shares, whether by operation of law or otherwise, that is not made in accordance with the terms of this Agreement, and any such transfer shall be null, void and of no effect. In such event, the purported transferor shall remain the beneficial and record owner of the Shares subject to the invalid transfer. The Company shall be protected in relying on the record of shareholders maintained by it or on its behalf for all purposes, notwithstanding any notice of any purported transfer to the contrary.

(b) **Opinion of Counsel.** The transferor shall have delivered to the Company an opinion of counsel, satisfactory in form and substance to counsel to the Company, stating that the transfer may be effected without registration under applicable federal and state securities laws; provided, however, that the requirement of an opinion of counsel may be waived by the Company in its sole discretion; and

(c) Joinder to This Agreement. The transferee shall have agreed to become a party to this Agreement by executing and delivering to the Company a written joinder to this Agreement, as provided in Section 5.1 hereof.

Section 1.2 Permitted Transfers. Notwithstanding the other provisions of this Agreement, and as long as the conditions of Section 1.1 of this Agreement are satisfied, transfers of Shares by a Common Shareholder shall be permitted ("Permitted Transfers") in each of the following circumstances:

(a) Family Transfers. Transfers by a Common Shareholder to his or her spouse, parents, siblings, issue of his siblings, children or grandchildren or trusts solely for the benefit of any one or more of the foregoing;

(b) Transfers to Other Common Shareholders. Transfers from one Common Shareholder to another, if approved by the Company's Board of Directors;

(c) Transfers by Deceased Shareholders. Transfers from the estate of a deceased Common Shareholder to any spouse or member of the immediate family of the decedent or any trust for the benefit of any one or more of the foregoing.

(d) Transfers to Affiliates. Transfers by any Common Shareholder to an 'affiliate' (as that term is defined in Rule 405 of the Securities Act of 1933) of the Shareholder.

SECTION 2
STOCK RESTRICTION PROVISIONS

Section 2.1 Rights of First Refusal.

(a) Offer to Purchase; Notice to Company. If at any time any Common Shareholder (the "Selling Shareholder") wishes to sell any Shares or any right or interest therein beneficially owned by such Common Shareholder (the "Offered Shares"), such Common Shareholder shall first obtain a bona fide written offer (an "Offer") from a third party (the "Proposed Transferee") to purchase the Offered Shares for a fixed cash price. The Selling Shareholder who wishes to accept the Offer shall transmit a written notice ("Notice of Sale") to the Company and each other Shareholder stating the Selling Shareholder's intention to do so. A Notice of Sale shall set forth the name and address of the Proposed Transferee, the number of Offered Shares proposed to be sold, the total number of shares owned by the Selling Shareholder, the price, the terms and conditions of the Offer and shall have attached thereto a copy of the Offer. The Offer shall further state that the Company may acquire, in accordance with the provisions of this Agreement, all or any portion of the Offered Shares for the price and upon the other terms and conditions, including deferred payment (if applicable) of the proposed sale to the Proposed Transferee set forth therein. A "Proposed Transferee," as used herein, shall mean the prospective record owner or owners of the Offered Shares and all other persons and entities proposed to have a beneficial interest in the Offered Shares.

(b) Exercise of Purchase Right by the Company. Transmittal of the Offer to the Company by the Selling Shareholder shall constitute an offer by the Selling Shareholder to sell the Offered Shares to the Company at the price and upon the terms set forth in the Offer. For a period of 30 days after the submission of the Offer to the Company, the Company shall have the option (the "Right of First Refusal Option"), exercisable by written notice to the Selling Shareholder, to accept the Selling Shareholder's offer as to all or any part of the Offered Shares. The exercise or non-exercise by the Company of its rights pursuant to this Section 2.1 shall be without prejudice to its rights under this Section 2 with respect to any future sales of Offered Shares.

(c) Notice to Investors. In the event that the Company does not exercise its Right of First Refusal Option with respect to any or all of the Offered Shares in accordance with Section 2.1(b) hereof, the Selling Shareholder, upon notice from the Company of the Company's decision not to accept the Selling Shareholder's Offer as to any or all of the Offered Shares or upon expiration of the 30 day option period referred to in Section 2.1(b) hereof if the Company fails to give such notice, shall be deemed to have offered in writing to sell the remaining Offered Shares to the Investors at the price and upon the terms set forth in the Offer (the "Right of Second Refusal Option"). The Company, within five days after the earlier to occur of its decision not to purchase all of the Offered Shares or the expiration of the option period, shall deliver to the Investors copies of the Offer and the notice of the Company's decision stating therein the number of Offered Shares the Company will purchase, if any, and the number of Offered Shares available to be purchased by the Investors.

(d) Exercise of Purchase Right by Investors. Transmittal of the Offer to the Investors by the Selling Shareholder shall constitute an offer by the Selling Shareholder to sell the Offered Shares to the Investor at the price and upon the terms set forth in the Offer (the "Right of Second Refusal"). For a period of 30 days after such Offer by the Selling Shareholder to the Investors, the Investors shall have the option, exercisable by written notice to the Selling Shareholder with a copy to the Company and to each of the other Investors, to accept the Selling Shareholder's Offer as to all or a portion of the Selling Shareholder's remaining Offered Shares. Each Investor who exercises the Right of Second Refusal Option shall agree, by doing so, to purchase that proportionate part of the Selling Shareholder's remaining Offered Shares which the number of Shares owned by such Investor bears to the total number of Shares owned by all Investors or in such other proportion as the Investor shall decide.

In the event that one or more of the Investors does not exercise its Right of Second Refusal Option in accordance with Section 2.1(d) hereof, the Investors who exercised their options pursuant to Section 2.1(d) hereof shall have a further option for a period of five additional days after the expiration of the 20-day period set forth in Section 2.1(d) hereof to accept the Selling Shareholder's Offer as to the Selling Shareholder's then remaining Offered Shares (the "Additional Right of Second Refusal Option"). Each such Investor who exercises this further option shall agree, by doing so, to purchase that proportionate part of the Selling Shareholder's then remaining Shares, which the number of Shares owned by such Investor bears to the total number of Shares owned by all of the Investors exercising their option pursuant to this Section 2.1(d) or in such other proportions as such Investors may agree among themselves. The exercise or non-exercise by an Investor of its rights pursuant to this Section 2.1 shall be without prejudice to its rights under this Section 2 with respect to any future sales of Offered Shares.

(e) Sale of Offered Shares to Proposed Transferee. If, at the end of the option periods described in Sections 2.1(b) and (d) hereof, options have not been exercised by the Company and/or the Investors to purchase all of the Selling Shareholder's Offered Shares, the Selling Shareholder shall be free, subject to the co-sale provisions of Section 3 hereof, for a period of 45 days thereafter to sell any or all of the Offered Shares as to which options have not been exercised (the "Remaining Shares") to the Proposed Transferee at the price and upon the terms and conditions set forth in the Offer. If the Remaining Shares are not so sold within such 45-day transfer period, the Selling Shareholder shall not be permitted to sell such shares without again complying with this Section 2.

Section 2.2 Right of Participation in Sales.

(a) Co-Sale Right. Within five days after the end of the option periods described in Sections 2.1 hereof, if there are any Remaining Shares available for sale to the Proposed Transferee, the Selling Shareholder shall submit a written notice (the "Co-Sale Notice") to the Investors disclosing the number of Remaining Shares proposed to be sold and the total number of Shares owned by the Selling Shareholder, including those, if any, designated for sale to the Company and the Investors pursuant to Section 2.1 hereof. Upon receipt of a Co-Sale Notice from the Selling Shareholder, each Investor shall have the right to sell to the Proposed Transferee, at the same price per share and on the same terms and conditions set forth in the Offer, such number of Shares held by such Investor equal to the Remaining Shares multiplied by a fraction, the numerator of which is the aggregate number of Shares held by such Investor and the denominator of which is the sum of: (i) all Shares held by such Selling Shareholder (excluding those Shares, if any, designated for sale to the Company and the Investors pursuant to Section 2.1 hereof); and (ii) all of the Shares held by the Investors participating in such sale.

(b) Notice of Intent to Participate. If an Investor wishes to participate in any sale under Section 2.2(a) hereof, such Investor shall notify the Selling Shareholder in writing of such intention as soon as practicable after such Investor's receipt of the Co-Sale Notice made pursuant to Section 2.2(a) hereof, and in any event within 10 days after the date such Co-Sale Notice has been delivered.

(c) Sale to Proposed Transferee. The Selling Shareholder and each participating Investor shall sell to the Proposed Transferee all, or, at the option of the Proposed Transferee, any part, of the Shares proposed to be sold by them at not less than the price and upon other terms and conditions, if any, not more favorable to the Proposed Transferee than those in the Co-Sale Notice provided by the Selling Shareholder under Section 2.2(a) hereof; provided, however, that any purchase of less than all of such shares by the Proposed Transferee shall be made from the Selling Shareholder and each participating Investor pro rata based upon the relative amount of the Shares that the Selling Shareholder and each such participating Investor is otherwise entitled to sell pursuant to Section 2.2(a) hereof.

Section 2.3 Purchase Price and Terms; Closings.

(a) Purchase Price. Any closing for the purchase of Shares by the Company or by an Investor pursuant to the provisions of Section 2 hereof shall be made within 30 days after the date of exercise of the last option exercised. The purchase price per Share and the terms of payment shall be the price per Share contained in the Offer. Every closing for the purchase and sale of Shares shall, unless otherwise agreed to by all of the purchasers and sellers, be held at the principal office of the Company during regular business hours.

(b) Closing. At any closing pursuant to Section 2 hereof, the stock certificate or certificates representing the Shares being sold shall be delivered by the seller to the purchaser or purchasers, duly endorsed for transfer or with executed stock powers attached, with any necessary documentary and transfer tax stamps affixed by the seller, free and clear of all liens, claims and encumbrances except for the terms of this Agreement, against payment to the respective seller of the purchase price therefor.

Section 2.4 Drag-Along Rights.

(a) Drag-Along Right of Investors. If at any time Investors holding shares of Series A Convertible Preferred Stock representing at least ____% of the issued and outstanding shares of Series A Preferred Stock (the "Drag-Along Investors") receive an offer from a Proposed Transferee to purchase all of the capital stock of the Company, then the Drag-Along Investors shall have the right to elect to cause the other Shareholders (the "Other Shareholders") to sell, and such Other Shareholders shall be obligated to sell to the Proposed Transferee, at the same price per share and other terms and conditions as involved in such sale by the Drag-Along Investors to such Proposed Transferee, all of the shares of capital stock of the Company owned by such Drag-Along Investors.

(b) Notice of Intent to Participate. If the Drag-Along Investors elect to exercise their rights pursuant to this Section 2.4, they shall deliver a notice to the Other Shareholders describing the terms of the transaction and all documents required to be executed by the Other Shareholders in order to consummate such transaction. At least five days prior to the proposed closing date, the Other Shareholders shall deliver to the Drag-Along Investors all documents previously furnished to the Other Shareholders for execution in connection with such transaction, together with the certificates for their Shares, duly endorsed in blank for transfer to the Proposed Transferee.

(c) Sale to Proposed Transferee. The Drag-Along Investors shall have 60 days from the date of the notice set forth in Section 2.4(b) hereof to consummate the transaction. Promptly after the consummation of the transaction, the Drag-Along Investors shall notify the Other Shareholders and furnish to them evidence of such sale, including the time of sale and the terms thereof, as the Other Shareholders may reasonably request. The Drag-Along Investors shall also cause to be remitted to the Other Shareholders the proceeds of such sale attributable to the sale of the Other Shareholders' Shares not later than the third business day following such sale. If any such transaction is not consummated prior to the expiration of the 60-day period, the Drag-Along Investors may not, without the consent of the Other Shareholders, thereafter consummate such transaction and shall return to the Other Shareholders all documents previously delivered to the Drag-Along Investors in connection with such transaction.

SECTION 3
ELECTION OF DIRECTORS

Section 3.1 Board of Directors; Voting of Shares; Observer Rights. In each election of directors of the Company (whether at a meeting of shareholders or by written consent in lieu of a meeting), each Shareholder shall vote or cause to be voted all Shares presently owned or hereafter acquired by such Shareholder or over which such Shareholder has voting control in favor of the following actions:

(a) Series A Directors. To cause and maintain the election to the Board of Directors two individuals nominated by the Investors (the "Series A Directors"); one Series A Director shall be nominated by _____ and one Series A Director shall be nominated by _____; the Series A Directors shall initially be _____ and _____.

(b) Management Directors. To cause and maintain the election to the Board of Directors of two individuals (the "Management Directors") nominated by a majority of the Common Shareholders, and reasonably acceptable by the prior written consent of _____; one of the Management Directors shall initially be _____.

(c) Independent Directors. To cause and maintain the election to the Board of Directors of one individual nominated by a majority of the Common Shareholders, and reasonably acceptable by the prior written consent of _____ (the "Independent Director").

The Company shall cause the nomination for election to the Board of Directors of the individuals set forth above.

Section 3.2 Committees. The Company and the Common Shareholders shall cause the Board of Directors to nominate and appoint to each committee of the Board of Directors a Series A Director and the Independent Director, and cause each such committee to have no more than three members.

Section 3.3 Vacancies and Removal. Each of the directors designated in Section 3.1 shall be elected at any annual or special meeting of shareholders (or by written consent in lieu of a meeting of shareholders) and shall serve until his or her successor is elected and qualified or until his or her earlier resignation or removal. Each of the Series A Directors may be removed during their respective terms of office, without cause, by and only by the written consent of the holders of at least a majority of the shares of Series A Convertible Preferred Stock entitled to designate such Series A Director pursuant to Section 3.1(a); the Founding Directors may be removed during each such director's term of office, without cause, by and only by the written consent of the holders Common Stock holding at least a majority of the issued and outstanding Common Stock; the Independent Director may be removed during his or her term of office without cause, by and only by the written consent of (i) the holders of Common Stock holding at least a majority of the issued and outstanding Common Stock and (ii) _____.

Pending any vote or written consent of holders of capital stock provided for in this paragraph, any vacancy in the office of a Series A Director shall be filled as set forth in Section 3.1(a) above; any vacancy in an office of a Management Director shall be filled by the vote of the holders of Common Stock holding at least a majority of the issued and outstanding Common Stock; any vacancy in the office of the Independent Director shall be filled by the vote of holders of Common Stock holding at least a majority of the issued and outstanding Common Stock, and who shall be reasonably acceptable by the prior written consent of _____.

Section 3.4 Observer Right. The Company agrees that as long as _____ owns at least **[50%]** of the shares purchased by _____ pursuant to the Purchase Agreement, it will provide _____ prior notice of each meeting of the Company's Board of Directors and afford _____ the right to have one of its authorized representatives, who shall be reasonably acceptable to the Board of Directors, present at each meeting of the Board of Directors in a non-voting observer capacity (the "_____ Observer"). _____ agrees that the _____ Observer will maintain the confidentiality of all information learned or obtained by him at any meeting of the Board of Directors that is proprietary or confidential and will act in a fiduciary manner (as fully as if he were a director) with respect to all information so learned or obtained. No _____ Observer shall have any right to vote at any meeting of the Board of Directors, and, if the Board of Directors of the Company, in the exercise of its fiduciary obligations, should determine that any _____ Observer should not be present at any meeting or portion thereof, or should not receive any information provided to the Board of Directors, each Observer shall abide by such determination of the Board of Directors.

Section 3.5 Change in Number of Directors. Without the consent of the Series A Directors, the Company shall not increase the size of the Board of Directors to greater than five directors, and the Shareholders will not vote for any amendment or change to the Amended Articles of Incorporation or Bylaws providing for the election of greater than five directors, or any other amendment or change which is inconsistent with the terms of this Agreement.

Section 3.6 Action by the Company. If the Company shall elect to acquire Shares under this Agreement, the Shareholders shall cause the Company to take all action necessary to complete settlement and to satisfy the obligations of the Company. If, at the time the Company is required to make payment on account of the purchase price for Shares, it would be precluded from doing so under law because it does not have legally available funds from which to make such purchase, all legally available funds shall be paid on account of such purchase price and the Shareholders shall use their respective best efforts to cause the Company to take all action required to permit the remaining portion of such purchase price to be paid as promptly as practicable thereafter.

SECTION 4
CONFIDENTIALITY

Section 4.1 Confidentiality. From and after the date hereof, each Shareholder agrees to maintain the confidentiality of, and not use for any purpose unrelated to the business of the Company, all information that it receives from or about the Company, other than information that (a) is or becomes generally available to the public other than as a result of a disclosure by such Shareholder, (b) is already in such Shareholder's possession, provided that such information is not subject to another confidentiality agreement with, or other legal or fiduciary obligations of secrecy or confidentiality to, the Company, or (c) becomes available to such Shareholder on a non-confidential basis from a person unrelated to the Company who is under no obligation of confidentiality to the Company. Notwithstanding the foregoing, the Company acknowledges and agrees that each Shareholder is permitted to disclose such confidential information to its limited partners, if any, and business associates and such disclosure shall not be deemed a violation of this Section 4.

SECTION 5
MISCELLANEOUS

Section 5.1 Subsequent Shareholders. Each person who after the date hereof shall purchase, be issued or otherwise receive shares of the Company's capital stock, or shall be granted any options or other rights to purchase shares of the Company's capital stock, shall, as a condition to such purchase, issuance, receipt or grant, become a party to this Agreement by signing a written joinder to this Agreement or such separate agreement as shall be acceptable to the Company, and each such person shall thereafter be a "Common Shareholder" or an "Investor" (as the case may be) for purposes of this Agreement, and Schedule I to this Agreement shall thereafter be deemed to be amended, without any further action on the part of the Company or any Shareholder, to include the name of such additional Shareholder. Furthermore, any shares of the Company's capital stock hereafter issued, or issuable pursuant to any options or other rights, shall thereafter become subject to this Agreement and shall be deemed "Shares" for purposes of this Agreement, including additional shares issued or issuable to any person who is already a Shareholder at that time, and such additional shares shall be reflected on Schedule I to this Agreement.

Section 5.2 Legend on Certificates. All certificates representing Shares now or hereafter issued shall be marked with the following legend in addition to any other legends that the Company may deem appropriate to reflect restrictions imposed by applicable federal and state securities laws:

THE TRANSFER AND SALE OF THIS CERTIFICATE AND THE SHARES IT REPRESENTS IS RESTRICTED AND MAY NOT BE ACCOMPLISHED

EXCEPT IN ACCORDANCE WITH THE AMENDED AND RESTATED SHAREHOLDERS AGREEMENT DATED AS OF _____, 20___, AND ANY AMENDMENTS THERETO, AMONG **, INC. AND ITS SHARE-HOLDERS, A COPY OF WHICH MAY BE INSPECTED AT THE PRINCIPAL OFFICE OF THE COMPANY.**

Section 5.3 Notices. All notices, requests, instructions, consents, and other communications to be given pursuant to this Agreement shall be in writing and shall be deemed delivered (i) on the same day if delivered in person or by same-day courier, (ii) on the next business day if delivered by overnight mail or overnight courier, or (iii) on the fifth calendar day (excluding Sundays) if delivered by certified or registered mail, postage prepaid, to the party for whom intended to the following addresses:

If to the Company:

_____

_____

_____

Attention: _____

If to any Shareholder: addressed to such Shareholder at the address set forth on <u>Schedule A or B</u> or at such other address or to the attention of such other person as the recipient party shall have specified by prior written notice to the sending party.

Section 5.4 Headings. The Section and paragraph headings of this Agreement are for convenience only; they form no part of this Agreement and shall not affect its interpretation.

Section 5.5 Governing Law. This Agreement shall be governed by and construed in accordance with the laws of the State of _____.

Section 5.6 Counterparts. This Agreement may be executed in any number of counterparts, each of which shall be deemed to be an original as against any party whose signature appears thereon, and all of which shall together constitute one and the same instrument. This Agreement shall become binding when one or more counterparts hereof, individually or taken together, shall bear the signature of the Company and all the Shareholders.

Section 5.7 Equitable Relief. The parties acknowledge that the Shares are unique, and that any violation of this Agreement cannot be compensated for in damages alone. Therefore, in addition to all of the other remedies that may be available under applicable law, any party hereto shall have the right to equitable relief, including without limitation, the right to enforce specifically the terms of this Agreement by obtaining injunctive relief against any violation or nonperformance hereof.

Section 5.8 Assignment. None of the parties to this Agreement shall assign, transfer, pledge or otherwise encumber or dispose of any of such party's respective rights and obligations or both under this Agreement, except as otherwise expressly permitted herein. Subject to the foregoing, this Agreement shall be binding upon and inure to the benefit of the respective parties hereto, and their personal representatives, estates, successors and assigns, including any transferee of the Shares subject to this Agreement.

Section 5.9 Severability. Whenever possible, each provision of this Agreement shall be interpreted in such manner as to be effective and valid under applicable law, but if any provision of this Agreement is held to be invalid, illegal or unenforceable in any respect under any applicable law or rule in any jurisdiction, such invalidity, illegality or unenforceability shall not affect any other provision or any other jurisdiction, but this Agreement shall be reformed, construed, and enforced in such jurisdiction as if such invalid, illegal or unenforceable provision had never been contained herein.

Section 5.10 Supersedes Other Agreements. This Agreement constitutes the entire agreement of the parties with respect to the subject matter hereof. If this Agreement shall conflict in any respect with all or any portion of any other agreement or instrument to which any party hereto is a party, the provisions of this Agreement shall supersede such conflicting agreement or instrument or portion thereof. Upon execution of this Agreement by the Common Shareholders in accordance with Section ____ of the Prior Agreement, the Prior Agreement is hereby expressly terminated in its entirety.

Section 5.11 Amendments and Waivers. This Agreement may be amended, or any provision hereof may be waived, provided that such amendment or waiver is set forth in writing executed by the Company and (a) holders of Common Stock holding at least a majority of the issued and outstanding Common Stock and (b) holders of Series A Preferred Stock holding at least ____% of the issued and outstanding Series A Convertible Preferred Stock. No course of dealing between or among any persons having any interest in this Agreement will be deemed effective to modify, amend or discharge any part of this Agreement or any rights or obligations of any person under or by reason of this Agreement.

Section 5.12 Termination. This Agreement shall terminate automatically upon the effectiveness of a registration statement covering any of the Company's equity securities to be sold in an underwritten public offering and filed by the Company pursuant to the Securities Act of 1933, as amended, except insofar as rights or obligations have accrued thereunder prior to such effectiveness. All of the provisions of this Agreement shall terminate upon the written agreement of the holders of all of the Shares.

IN WITNESS WHEREOF, the parties hereto have executed and delivered this Agreement as of the date first above written.

By: _____

Name and Title: _____

INVESTORS:

_____ CAPITAL, L.P.

By: _____ Partners, L.P.,
its general partner
By: _____

Name and Title: _____

_____ VENTURE FUND, L.P.

By: _____ Management
Corp., its general partner

By: _____

Name and Title: _____

COMMON SHAREHOLDERS:

_____

_____

_____

Form 12 F: Investor Rights Agreement

**** INC.
INVESTOR RIGHTS AGREEMENT

THIS INVESTOR RIGHTS AGREEMENT is made as of _____, 20___, among **** Inc., a Delaware corporation (the "Company"), and the purchasers of the Company's Series A Preferred Stock listed on **Exhibit A** hereto (the "Investors").

BACKGROUND

Concurrently with the execution of this Agreement, the Company will sell to the Investors and the Investors will purchase from the Company shares of the Company's Series A Preferred Stock (the "Preferred Stock") pursuant to the Series A Convertible Preferred Stock Purchase Agreement (the "Purchase Agreement"), dated as of _____, 20___. As a condition to the Investors' entering into the Purchase Agreement, the Company has agreed to enter into this Agreement in order to provide the Investors with (i) certain rights to register shares of the Company's Common Stock issuable upon conversion of the Preferred Stock held by the Investors, (ii) certain rights to receive or inspect information pertaining to the Company, and (iii) a preemptive right with respect to certain issuances by the Company of its securities. The Company desires to facilitate the sale and purchase of shares of the Series A Preferred Stock pursuant to the Purchase Agreement, by agreeing to the terms and conditions set forth below.

SECTION 1
REGISTRATION RIGHTS

The Company and the Investors each covenant and agree as follows:

1.1 Definitions.

The terms "register," "registered," and "registration" refer to a registration effected by preparing and filing a registration statement or similar document in compliance with the Securities Act of 1933, as amended (the "Securities Act"), and the declaration or ordering of effectiveness of such registration statement or document;

The term "Registrable Securities" means (i) the shares of Common Stock issuable or issued upon conversion of the Preferred Stock (whether now outstanding or issued after the date of this Agreement) and any shares received or issued in respect of such shares (including upon exercise of preemptive rights, rights of first refusal, and the like) and any other shares of Common Stock of the Company issued as (or issuable upon the conversion or exercise of any warrant, right or other security which is issued as) a dividend or other distribution with respect to, or in exchange for or in replacement of, such shares. Notwithstanding the foregoing, Registrable Securities shall cease to be a Registrable Security when (a) a registration statement covering such Registrable Security has been declared effective by the SEC and it has been disposed of pursuant to such effective registration statement or (b) such Registrable Security may be sold pursuant to Rule 144 (or any successor or comparable provision) without volume restriction;

The number of shares of "Registrable Securities then outstanding" shall be determined by the number of shares of Common Stock outstanding which are, and the number of shares of Common Stock issuable pursuant to then exercisable or convertible securities which are, Registrable Securities;

The term "Holder" means any person owning or having the right to acquire Registrable Securities or any assignee thereof in accordance with Section 1.12 of this Agreement;

The term "Form S-3" means such form under the Securities Act as in effect on the date hereof or any successor form under the Securities Act;

The term "SEC" means the Securities and Exchange Commission; and

The term "Qualified IPO" means the initial firm commitment underwritten public offering by the Company of shares of its Common Stock pursuant to a registration statement under the Securities Act, the public offering price of which is not less than $_____ per share (appropriately adjusted for stock dividends, stock splits, combinations, subdivisions, or other similar recapitalizations and events) and which results in aggregate cash proceeds to the Company of $_____ (net of underwriting discounts and commissions).

1.2 <u>Request for Registration.</u>

(a) If, at any time after the earlier to occur of (i) _____, 20__, or (ii) six months following a Qualified IPO, the Company shall receive a written request from the Holders of at least __% of the Registrable Securities then outstanding that the Company file a registration statement under the Securities Act covering the registration of Registrable Securities where the anticipated aggregate offering price, net of underwriting discounts and commissions, of Registrable Securities to be sold is at least $_____, then the Company shall, within 10 days of the receipt thereof, give written notice of such request to all Holders and shall, subject to the limitations of subsection 1.2(b), use its best efforts to effect as soon as practicable, and in any event within 60 days of the receipt of such request, the registration under the Securities Act of all Registrable Securities which the Holders request to be registered within 20 days of the mailing of such notice by the Company in accordance with Section 3.4.

(b) If the Holders initiating the registration request hereunder ("Initiating Holders") intend to distribute the Registrable Securities covered by their request by means of an underwriting, they shall so advise the Company as a part of their request made pursuant to this Section 1.2 and the Company shall include such information in the written notice referred to in subsection 1.2(a). The underwriter will be selected by a majority in interest of the Initiating Holders and shall be reasonably acceptable to the Company. In such event, the right of any Holder to include his Registrable Securities in such registration shall be conditioned upon such Holder's participation in such underwriting and the inclusion of such Holder's Registrable Securities in the underwriting (unless otherwise mutually agreed by a majority in interest of the Initiating Holders and such Holder) to the extent provided herein. All Holders proposing to distribute their securities through such underwriting shall (together with the Company as provided in subsection 1.5(e)) enter into an underwriting agreement in customary form with the underwriter or underwriters selected for such underwriting. Notwithstanding any other provision of this Section 1.2, if the underwriter advises the Initiating Holders in writing that marketing factors require a limitation of the number of shares to be underwritten, then the Initiating Holders shall so advise all Holders of Registrable Securities which would otherwise be underwritten pursuant hereto, and the number of shares of Registrable Securities that may be included in the underwriting shall be allocated among all Holders thereof, including the Initiating Holders, in proportion (as nearly as practicable) to the amount of Registrable Securities of the

Company owned by each Holder; *provided, however,* that the number of shares of Registrable Securities to be included in such underwriting shall not be reduced unless all other securities are first entirely excluded from the underwriting.

(c) Notwithstanding the foregoing, if the Company shall furnish to Holders requesting a registration statement pursuant to this Section 1.2, a certificate signed by the President of the Company stating that in the good faith judgment of the Board of Directors of the Company, it would be seriously detrimental to the Company and its stockholders for such registration statement to be effective at such time, the Company shall have the right to defer such filing for a period of not more than 120 days after receipt of the request of the Initiating Holders; *provided, however,* that the Company may not utilize this right more than once in any twelve-month period.

(d) In addition, the Company shall not be obligated to effect, or to take any action to effect, any registration pursuant to this Section 1.2:

(i) After the Company has effected two registrations pursuant to this Section 1.2 and such registrations have been declared or ordered effective and maintained effective for at least 120 days (or less if the distribution contemplated in the registration statement has been completed); or

(ii) During the period ending (A) 180 days after the effective date of a registration subject to Section 1.3 hereof or (B) 90 days after the effective date of any other registration statement pertaining to Common Stock of the Company, or such shorter periods if such shorter periods are acceptable to the underwriters of such offering.

1.3 Company Registration.

If (but without any obligation to do so) the Company proposes to register (including for this purpose a registration effected by the Company for stockholders other than the Holders) any of its stock under the Securities Act in connection with the public offering of such securities solely for cash (other than a registration statement on Form S-4 or S-8 or any successor forms thereto or any registration statement filed in connection with an exchange offer of securities solely to the Company's existing security holders), the Company shall, at such time, promptly give each Holder written notice of such registration. Upon the written request of each Holder given within 20 days after mailing of such notice by the Company in accordance with Section 3.4, the Company shall, subject to the provisions of Section 1.8, cause to be registered under the Securities Act all of the Registrable Securities that each such Holder has requested to be registered.

1.4 Form S-3 Registration.

(a) If the Company shall receive a written request from any Holder or Holders that the Company file a registration on Form S-3 (or any successor form thereto) for a public offering of Registrable Securities, the Company will:

(i) promptly give written notice of the proposed registration to all other Holders; and

(ii) as soon as practicable, effect such registration and all such qualifications and compliances as may be so requested and as would permit or facilitate the sale and distribution of all or such portion of such Holders' Registrable Securities as are specified in such request, together with all or such portion of the Registrable Securities of any other Holder or Holders joining in such request as are specified in a written request given within 15 days after receipt of such written notice from the Company; *provided, however,* that the Company shall not be obligated to effect any such registration, qualification or compliance, pursuant to this Section 1.4: (A) if Form S-3 is not available for such offering by the Holders; (B) if the Holders, together with the holders of any other securities of the Company entitled to inclusion in such registration, propose to sell Registrable Securities and such other securities (if any) at an aggregate price to the public (net of any underwriters' discounts or commissions) of less than $1,000,000; or (C) if the Company shall furnish to the Holders a certificate signed by the President of the Company stating that in the good faith judgment of the Board of Directors of the Company, it would be seriously detrimental to the Company and its stockholders for such Form S-3 Registration to be effected at such time, in which event the Company shall have the right to defer the filing of the Form S-3 registration statement for a period of not more than 120 days after receipt of the request of the Holder or Holders under this Section 1.4; *provided, however,* that the Company shall not utilize this right more than once in any twelve month period.

Subject to the foregoing, the Company shall file a registration statement covering the Registrable Securities and other securities so requested to be registered as soon as practicable after receipt of the request or requests of the Holders. Registrations effected pursuant to this Section 1.4 shall not be counted as demands for registration or registrations effected pursuant to Sections 1.2 or 1.3, respectively.

1.5 Obligations of the Company.

Whenever required under this Section 1 to effect the registration of any Registrable Securities, the Company shall, as expeditiously as reasonably possible:

(a) prepare and file with the SEC a registration statement with respect to such Registrable Securities and use its best efforts to cause such registration statement to become effective and keep such registration statement effective for at least 120 days (or less if the distribution contemplated in the registration statement has been completed);

(b) prepare and file with the SEC such amendments and supplements to such registration statement and the prospectus used in connection with such registration statement as may be necessary to comply with the provisions of the Securities Act with respect to the disposition of all securities covered by such registration statement;

(c) furnish without charge to each Holder, at least three business days prior to the pertinent sale or sales by such Holder, such numbers of copies of a prospectus, including a preliminary prospectus, in conformity with the requirements of the Securities Act, and such other documents as they may reasonably request in order to facilitate the disposition of Registrable Securities owned by them;

(d) use its best efforts to register and qualify the securities covered by such registration statement under such other securities or Blue Sky laws of such jurisdictions as shall be reasonably requested by the Holders; *provided* that the Company shall not be required in connection therewith or as a condition thereto to qualify to do business or to file a general consent to service of process in any such states or jurisdictions;

(e) in the event of any underwritten public offering, enter into and perform its obligations under an underwriting agreement, in usual and customary form, with the managing underwriter of such offering. Each Holder participating in such underwriting shall also enter into and perform its obligations under such an agreement;

(f) immediately notify each Holder of Registrable Securities covered by such registration statement, at any time when a prospectus relating thereto is required to be delivered under the Securities Act, upon learning of the happening of any event as a result of which the prospectus included in such registration statement, as then in effect, includes an untrue statement of a material fact or omits to state a material fact required to be stated therein or necessary to make the statements therein not misleading in the light of the circumstances then existing and, at the request of the Holders, the Company shall prepare a supplement or amendment to such prospectus so that, as thereafter delivered to the purchasers of such Registrable Securities, such prospectus shall not contain an untrue statement of a material fact or omit to state any fact necessary to make the statements therein not misleading in the light of the circumstances then existing;

(g) cause all such Registrable Securities registered pursuant hereunder to be listed on each securities exchange on which similar securities issued by the Company are then listed, or on the NASD automated quotation system if similar securities issued by the Company are then listed on the NASD automated quotation system, and if such similar securities are designated as Nasdaq "national market system securities" within the meaning of Rule 11Aa2-1 of the Securities and Exchange Commission, to cause the Registered Securities to be so designated;

(h) make available for inspection by the Holders, any underwriter participating in any disposition pursuant to such registration statement and any attorney, accountant or other agent retained by the Holders or such underwriter, all financial and other records, pertinent corporate documents and properties of the Company, and cause the Company's officers, directors, employees and independent accountants to supply all information in each case as may reasonably be requested by the Holders or such underwriter, attorney, accountant or agent in connection with such registration statement, subject to such reasonable confidentiality requirements as may be requested the Company;

(i) provide a transfer agent and registrar for all Registrable Securities registered pursuant hereunder and a CUSIP number for all such Registrable Securities, in each case not later than the effective date of such registration.

(j) otherwise use its reasonable efforts to comply with all applicable rules and regulations of the SEC, and make available to its security holders, as soon as reasonably practicable, an earnings statement covering the period of at least twelve months beginning with the first day of the Company's first full calendar quarter after the effective date of the registration statement, which earnings statement shall satisfy the provisions of Section 11(a) of the Securities Act and Rule 158 thereunder;

(k) permit a Holder, if such Holder reasonably believes it might be deemed to be an underwriter or a controlling person of the Company, to participate in the preparation of such registration or comparable statement;

(l) in the event of the issuance of any stop order suspending the effectiveness of a registration statement, or of any order suspending or preventing the use of any related prospectus or suspending the qualification of any common stock included in such registration statement for sale in any jurisdiction, the Company shall use its reasonable efforts promptly to obtain the withdrawal of such order;

(m) make available its senior management to participate in any "road shows" scheduled in connection with the offering of any Registrable Securities pursuant to such registration, with all reasonable out-of-pocket costs and expenses incurred by the Company in connection with such attendance and participation to be paid by the Company; and

(n) furnish to the underwriters, if such securities are being sold through underwriters, at the request of such underwriters, on the date that such Registrable Securities are delivered to the underwriters for sale in connection with a registration pursuant to this Agreement, (i) an opinion, dated such date, of the counsel representing the Company for the purposes of such registration, in form and substance as is customarily given to underwriters in an underwritten public offering, addressed to the underwriters, and (ii) a comfort letter dated such date, from the independent certified public accountants of the Company, in form and substance as is customarily given by independent certified public accountants to underwriters in an underwritten public offering, addressed solely to the underwriters, which letter specifies the parties entitled to rely thereon.

1.6 Furnishing Information.

It shall be a condition precedent to the obligations of the Company to take any action pursuant to Section 1.2, 1.3 or 1.4 that the selling Holders shall furnish to the Company such information regarding themselves, the Registrable Securities held by them and the intended method of distribution of such securities and such other information as shall be required to effect the registration of their Registrable Securities.

1.7 Expenses of Registration.

(a) Demand Registration. All expenses other than underwriting discounts and commissions incurred in connection with registrations, filings or qualifications pursuant to Section 1.2, including (without limitation) all registration, filing and qualification fees, printers' and accounting fees, fees and disbursements of counsel for the Company, and the reasonable out-of-pocket fees and disbursements of one counsel for the selling Holders selected by them shall be borne by the Company.

(b) Company Registration. All expenses other than underwriting discounts and commissions incurred in connection with registrations, filings or qualifications pursuant to Section 1.3, including (without limitation) all registration, filing, and qualification fees, printers' and accounting fees, fees and disbursements of counsel for the Company, and the reasonable out-of-pocket fees and disbursements of one counsel for the selling Holders selected by them shall be borne by the Company.

(c) Registration on Form S-3. All expenses incurred in connection with registrations, filings or qualifications pursuant to Section 1.4, including (without limitation) all registration, filing, and qualification fees, printers' and accounting fees, fees and disbursements of one counsel for the selling Holders selected by them, and the reasonable fees and disbursements of counsel for the Company, and any underwriting discounts or commissions associated with Registrable Securities, shall be borne pro rata by the Holder or Holders participating in the Form S-3 Registration.

1.8 Underwriting Requirements.

In connection with any offering involving an underwriting of shares of the Company's capital stock, the Company shall not be required under Section 1.3 to include any of the Holders' securities in such underwriting unless they accept the terms of the underwriting as agreed upon between the Company and the underwriters selected by it (or by other persons entitled to select the underwriters), and then only in such quantity as the underwriters determine in their sole discretion will not jeopardize the success of the offering by the Company. If the total amount of securities, including Registrable Securities, requested by stockholders to be included in such offering exceeds the amount of securities sold other than by the Company that the underwriters determine in their sole discretion is compatible with the success of the offering, then the Company shall be required to include in the offering only that number of such securities, including Registrable Securities, which the underwriters determine in their sole discretion will not jeopardize the success of the offering (the securities so included to be apportioned pro rata among the selling stockholders according to the total amount of securities entitled to be included therein owned by each selling stockholder or in such other proportions as shall mutually be agreed to by such selling stockholders), *provided, however,* that the number of shares of Registrable Securities to be included in any such underwriting held by an Investor shall not be reduced unless all junior securities are first entirely excluded from the underwriting. The foregoing notwithstanding, except in connection with a Qualified IPO, no such reduction shall reduce the amount of securities of the selling Holders included in the registration below twenty-five percent (25%) of the total amount of securities included in such registration.

1.9 Delay of Registration.
No Holder shall have any right to obtain or seek an injunction restraining or otherwise delaying any such registration as the result of any controversy that might arise with respect to the interpretation or implementation of this Section 1.

1.10 Indemnification.
(a) The Company will indemnify each Holder, each of its officers, directors and partners, stockholders, employees, agents (including such Holder's legal counsel and independent accountants), and each person controlling such Holder within the meaning of Section 15 of the Securities Act, with respect to which registration, qualification or compliance has been effected pursuant to this Agreement, and each underwriter, if any, and each person who controls any underwriter within the meaning of Section 15 of the Securities Act, against all expenses, claims, losses, damages and liabilities (or actions in respect thereof, including any of the foregoing incurred in settlement of any litigation, arising out of or based on (i) any untrue statement (or alleged untrue statement) of a material fact contained in any registration statement, prospectus, offering circular or other document, or any amendment or supplement thereto, incident to any such registration, qualification or compliance, or based on any omission (or alleged omission) to state therein a material fact required to be stated therein or necessary to make the statements therein, in light of the circumstances in which they were made, not misleading, (ii) any violation by the Company of any rule or regulation promulgated under the Securities Act applicable to the Company and relating to action or inaction required of the Company in connection with any such registration, qualification or compliance and will reimburse each such Holder, each of its officers, directors and partners, stockholders, employees, agents and such Holder's legal counsel and independent accountants, and each person controlling such Holder, each such underwriter and each person who controls any such underwriter, for any legal and any other expenses reasonably incurred in connection with investigating, preparing or defending any such claim, loss, damage, liability or action; *provided* that the Company will not be liable in any such case to the extent that any such claim, loss, damage, liability or expense arises out of or is based on (i) any untrue statement or omission or alleged untrue statement or omission, made in reliance upon and in conformity with written information furnished to the Company by an instrument duly executed by such Holder or underwriter and stated to be specifically for use therein, or (ii) the failure of such Holder to effectively cause the prospectus delivery requirement of the Securities Act to be satisfied provided that the Company has complied with its obligations under Section 1.5(c) of this Agreement.

(b) Each Holder will, severally and not jointly, if Registrable Securities held by such Holder are included in the securities as to which such registration, qualification or compliance is being effected, indemnify the Company, each of its directors and officers, stockholders, employees and agents (including its legal counsel and independent accountants), each underwriter, if any, of the Company's securities covered by such a registration statement, each person who controls the Company or such underwriter within the meaning of Section 15 of the Securities Act, and each other such Holder, each of its officers and directors and each person controlling such Holder within the meaning of Section 15 of the Securities Act, against all claims, losses, damages and liabilities (or actions in respect thereof), including any of the foregoing incurred in settlement of any litigation, arising out of or based on (i) any untrue statement (or alleged untrue statement) of a material fact contained in any such registration statement, prospectus, offering circular or other document, or any omission (or alleged omission) to state therein a material fact required to be stated therein or necessary to make the statements therein not misleading, in each case to the extent, but only to the extent, that such untrue statement (or alleged untrue statement) or omission (or alleged omission) is made in such registration statement, prospectus, offering circular or other document in reliance upon and in conformity with written information furnished to the Company by an instrument duly executed by such Holder and stated to be specifically for use therein, (ii) any violation by the Company of any rule or regulation promulgated under the Securities Act applicable to the Company and relating to action or inaction required of the Company in connection with any such registration, qualification or compliance, in each case to the extent, but only to the extent, that such violation occurred solely as a result of the use, in such registration statement, prospectus, offering circular or other document of written information furnished to the Company by an instrument duly executed by such Holder and stated to be specifically for use therein, or (iii) provided that the Company has complied with its obligations under Section 1.5(c) of this Agreement, any failure to effectively cause the prospectus delivery requirement of the Securities Act to be satisfied; and each Holder will reimburse the Company, such Holders, such directors, officers, stockholders, employees and agents (including its legal counsel and independent accountants), underwriters or control persons for any legal or any other expenses reasonably incurred in connection with investigating or defending any such claim, loss, damage, liability or action for which such Holder is obligated to provide indemnification pursuant to clauses (i), (ii), or (iii); *provided, however,* that the obligations of such Holders hereunder shall be limited to an amount equal to the gross proceeds before expenses and commissions to each such Holder of Registrable Securities sold as contemplated herein.

(c) Each party entitled to indemnification under this Section 1.10 (the "Indemnified Party") shall give notice to the party required to provide indemnification (the "Indemnifying Party") promptly after such Indemnified Party has knowledge of any claim as to which indemnity may be sought, and shall permit the Indemnifying Party to assume the defense of any such claim or any litigation resulting therefrom; *provided* that counsel for the Indemnifying Party, who shall conduct the defense of such claim or litigation, shall be approved by the Indemnified Party (whose approval shall not be unreasonably withheld), and the Indemnified Party may participate in such defense at such party's expense; and *provided further* that the failure of any Indemnified Party to give notice as provided herein shall not relieve the Indemnifying Party of its obligations under this Agreement, except to the extent, but only to the extent, that the Indemnifying Party's ability to defend against such claim or litigation is materially adversely affected as a result of such failure to give notice. No Indemnifying Party, in the defense of any such claim or litigation, shall, except with the consent of each Indemnified Party, consent to entry of any judgment or enter into any settlement which does not include as an unconditional term thereof the giving by the claimant or plaintiff to such Indemnified Party of a release from all liability in respect to such claim or litigation.

(d) If the indemnification provided for in paragraphs (a) and (b) of this Section 1.10 is unavailable or insufficient to hold harmless an Indemnified Party under such paragraphs in respect of any losses, claims, damages or liabilities or actions in respect thereof referred to therein, then each Indemnifying Party shall in lieu of indemnifying such Indemnified Party contribute to the amount paid or payable by such Indemnified Party as a result of such losses, claims, damages, liabilities or actions in such proportion as appropriate to reflect the relative fault of the Company, on the one hand, and the Holders of Registrable Securities, on the other, in connection with the statements or omissions which resulted in such losses, claims, damages, liabilities or actions as well as any other relevant equitable considerations, including the failure to give any notice under paragraph (c) of this Section 1.10. The relative fault shall be determined by reference to, among other things, whether the untrue or alleged untrue statement of a material fact relates to information supplied by the Company, on the one hand, or the Holders of Registrable Securities, on the other hand, and to the parties' relative intent, knowledge, access to information and opportunity to correct or prevent such statement or omission. The Company and the Holders of Registrable Securities agree that it would not be just and equitable if contributions pursuant to this paragraph were determined by pro rata allocation (even if all of the Holders of Registrable Securities were treated as one entity for such purpose) or by any other method of allocation that did not take account of the equitable considerations referred to above in this paragraph. The amount paid or payable by an Indemnified Party as a result of the losses, claims, damages, liabilities or action in respect thereof, referred to above in this paragraph, shall be deemed to include any legal or other expenses reasonably incurred by such Indemnified Party in connection with investigating or defending any such action or claim. Notwithstanding the provisions of this paragraph, the Holders of Registrable Securities shall not be required to contribute any amount in excess of the amount of the total price at which the Common Stock sold by each of them was offered to the public. No person guilty of fraudulent misrepresentations (within the meaning of Section 11(f) of the Securities Act), shall be entitled to contribution from any person who is not guilty of such fraudulent misrepresentation.

(e) The indemnification of underwriters provided for in this Section 1.10 shall be on such other terms and conditions as are at the time customary and reasonably required by such underwriters. In that event the indemnification of the Holders of Registrable Securities in such underwriting shall at the sellers' request be modified to conform to such terms and conditions.

1.11 Reports Under Securities Exchange Act of 1934.

With a view to making available to the Holders the benefits of Rule 144 promulgated under the Securities Act and any other rule or regulation of the SEC that may at any time permit a Holder to sell securities of the Company to the public without registration or pursuant to a registration on Form S-3, the Company agrees to:

(a) make and keep public information available, as those terms are understood and defined in SEC Rule 144, at all times after 90 days after the effective date of the first registration statement filed by the Company for the offering of its securities to the general public so long as the Company remains subject to the periodic reporting requirements under Sections 13 or 15(d) of the Exchange Act;

(b) take such action, including the voluntary registration of its Common Stock under Section 12 of the Exchange Act, as is necessary to enable the Holders to utilize Form S-3 for the sale of their Registrable Securities, such action to be taken as soon as practicable after the end of the fiscal year in which the first registration statement filed by the Company for the offering of its securities to the general public is declared effective;

(c) file with the SEC in a timely manner all reports and other documents required of the Company under the Securities Act and the Exchange Act; and

(d) furnish to any Holder, so long as the Holder owns any Registrable Securities, forthwith upon request (i) a written statement by the Company that it has complied with the reporting requirements of SEC Rule 144 (at any time after 90 days after the effective date of the first registration statement filed by the Company), the Securities Act and the Exchange Act (at any time after it has become subject to such reporting requirements), or that it qualifies as a registrant whose securities may be resold pursuant to Form S-3 (at any time after it so qualifies), (ii) a copy of the most recent annual or quarterly report of the Company and such other reports and documents so filed by the Company, and (iii) such other information as may be reasonably requested in availing any Holder of any rule or regulation of the SEC which permits the selling of any such securities without registration or pursuant to such form.

1.12 Assignment of Registration Rights. The rights to cause the Company to register Registrable Securities under Sections 1.2, 1.3 and 1.4 may be assigned by a Holder to a transferee or assignee of such Registrable Securities with respect to the Registrable Securities being assigned or transferred; *provided* that (a) such transfer may otherwise be effected in accordance with applicable securities laws and restrictions on transfer agreed upon by the Holder and the Company (including those set forth in the Purchase Agreement), (b) notice of such assignment is given to the Company within a reasonable time after such assignment with the name and address of such assignee and the securities with respect to which such registration rights are being assigned, (c) such transferee or assignee is (i) a wholly-owned subsidiary or constituent partner, retired partner, member, retired member or shareholder of such Holder, or (ii) an 'affiliate' (as that term is defined in Rule 405 promulgated by the Commission under the Securities Act of 1933) of the Holder, including, without limitation, where a Holder is a limited partnership, an affiliated limited partnership managed by the same management company or managing general partner of such Holder or an entity which controls, is controlled by, or is under common control with, such management company or managing general partner, or (iii) a beneficiary of the Holder, where such Holder is a trust or (iv) acquires from such Holder or Holders at least 100,000 Registrable Securities (as appropriately adjusted for stock splits and the like) in a simultaneous transaction or transactions and (d) such transferee or assignee agrees to be bound by all provisions of this Agreement by executing a counterpart signature page hereto (which shall not be deemed an amendment hereto).

1.13 Limitations on Subsequent Registration Rights. From and after the date of this Agreement, the Company shall not, without the prior written consent of the Holders of a majority of the outstanding Registrable Securities, enter into any agreement with any holder or prospective holder of any securities of the Company that would grant such holder registration rights pari passu or senior to those granted to the Holders hereof.

1.14 Market-Standoff Agreement.
(a) Market-Standoff Period; Agreement. Upon any contemplated registration by the Company of shares of its Common Stock in an underwritten public offering, each Holder agrees not to sell, make any short sale of, loan, grant any option for the purchase of, or otherwise dispose of any securities of the Company (other than those

included in the registration) without the prior written consent such underwriters for such period of time (not to exceed 180 days) from the effective date of such registration and to execute an agreement reflecting the foregoing if requested by the underwriters at such time.

(b) Limitations. The obligations described in Section 1.14(a) shall apply only if all officers and directors of the Company, all one-percent security holders, and all other persons with registration rights (whether or not pursuant to this Agreement) enter into similar agreements, and shall not apply to a registration relating solely to employee benefit plans, or to a registration relating solely to a transaction pursuant to Rule 145 under the Securities Act.

(c) Stop-Transfer Instructions. In order to enforce the foregoing covenants, the Company may impose stop-transfer instructions with respect to the securities of each Holder (and the securities of every other person subject to the restrictions in Section 1.14(a)).

(d) Transferees Bound. Each Holder agrees that it will not transfer securities of the Company unless each transferee agrees in writing to be bound by all of the provisions of this Section 1.14.

SECTION 2
COVENANTS OF THE COMPANY

2.1 Delivery of Financial Statements. The Company shall deliver to each Holder who holds at least 25% of the Preferred Stock originally purchased by such Holder:

(a) as soon as practicable, but in any event within 90 days after the end of each fiscal year of the Company, an income statement for such fiscal year, a balance sheet of the Company and statement of stockholder's equity as of the end of such year, and a statement of cash flows for such year, such year-end financial reports to be in reasonable detail, on a consolidated basis, prepared in accordance with generally accepted accounting principles ("GAAP"), and audited and certified by an independent public accounting firm of nationally recognized standing selected by the Company;

(b) as soon as practicable, but in any event within 30 days after the end of each of the first three (3) quarters of each fiscal year of the Company, an unaudited profit or loss statement, a statement of cash flows for such fiscal quarter and an unaudited balance sheet as of the end of such fiscal quarter, on a consolidated basis. In addition, these reports will be presented in a comparative format, *provided, however* that delivery of comparative reports shall not begin until after the Company has hired a chief financial officer;

(c) within 30 days of the end of each month, an unaudited income statement and a statement of cash flows and balance sheet for and as of the end of such month, in reasonable detail (the "Monthly Report"), *provided, however* that delivery of Monthly Reports shall not begin until after the Company has hired a chief financial officer;

(d) as soon as practicable, but in any event 30 days prior to the end of each fiscal year, a budget and business plan for the next fiscal year, prepared on a monthly basis, an updated list of all stockholders of the Company that includes the name of each stockholder and the number and class of shares held by each stockholder, and, as soon as prepared, any other budgets or revised budgets prepared by the Company; and

(e) with respect to the financial statements called for in subsections (b) and (c) of this Section 2.1, an instrument executed by the Chief Financial Officer or President of the Company and certifying that such financials were prepared in accordance with GAAP consistently applied with prior practice for earlier periods (with the exception of footnotes that may be required by GAAP) and fairly present the financial condition of the Company and its results of operation for the period specified, subject to year-end audit adjustment; *provided* that the foregoing shall not restrict the right of the Company to change its accounting principles consistent with GAAP, if the Board of Directors determines that it is in the best interest of the Company to do so.

2.2 <u>Inspection</u>. The Company shall permit each Holder who holds at least 25% of the Preferred Stock originally purchased by such Holder to visit and inspect the Company's properties, to examine its books of account and records and to discuss the Company's affairs, finances and accounts with its officers, all upon prearrangement and at such reasonable times as may be requested by such Holder.

2.3 <u>Preemptive Right</u>. Subject to the terms and conditions specified in this Section 2.3, the Company hereby grants to each Holder a preemptive right with respect to future sales by the Company of its Shares (as hereinafter defined). A Holder who chooses to exercise the preemptive right may designate as purchasers under such right itself or its partners or affiliates in such proportions as it deems appropriate.

Each time the Company proposes to offer any shares of, or securities convertible into or exercisable for any shares of, any class of its capital stock ("Shares"), the Company shall first make an offering of such Shares to each Holder in accordance with the following provisions:

(a) The Company shall deliver a notice by certified mail ("Notice") to the Holders stating (i) its bona fide intention to offer such Shares, (ii) the number of such Shares to be offered, and (iii) the price and terms, if any, upon which it proposes to offer such Shares.

(b) Within 15 calendar days after delivery of the Notice, the Holder may elect to purchase or obtain, at the price and on the terms specified in the Notice, up to that portion of such Shares which equals the proportion that the number of shares of Common Stock issuable upon conversion and exercise of all convertible or exercisable securities then held by such Holder bears to the total number of shares of Common Stock then outstanding (assuming full conversion and exercise of all convertible or exercisable securities). The Company shall promptly, in writing, inform each Holder that purchases all the Shares available to it (each, a "Fully-Exercising Investor") of any other Holder's failure to do likewise. During the 10-day period commencing after receipt of such information, each Fully-Exercising Investor shall be entitled to purchase up to that portion of the Shares for which Holders were entitled to subscribe but which were not subscribed for by the Holders that is equal to the proportion that the number of Shares of Common Stock issuable upon conversion and exercise of all convertible or exercisable securities then held by such Fully-Exercising Investor bears to the total number of Shares of Common Stock owned by other Fully Exercising Investors (assuming full conversion and exercise of all convertible or exercisable securities).

(c) The Company may, during the 45-day period following the expiration of the period provided in subsection 2.3(b) hereof, offer the remaining unsubscribed portion of the Shares to any person or persons at a price not less than, and upon terms no more favorable to the offeree than those specified in the Notice. If the Company does not enter into an agreement for the sale of the Shares within such period, or if such agreement is not consummated within 60 days of the execution thereof, the right provided hereunder shall be deemed to be revived and such Shares shall not be offered unless first reoffered to the Holders in accordance herewith.

(d) The term "Shares" shall not include Shares of Common Stock issued or other securities issuable at any time (i) upon conversion of Preferred Stock, (ii) to employees, officers, directors and consultants of the Company pursuant to any one or more employee stock incentive plans or agreements approved by the Board of Directors, including the approval of the director designated by _____; or (iii) in connection with any merger or other acquisition, license agreement, lease, debt financing, joint venture, strategic alliance or other similar transaction approved by the Board of Directors, including the director designated by _____ pursuant to the Amended and Restated Stockholders Agreement dated as of the date hereof, among the Company and the holders of the Company's capital stock, the primary purpose of which is not an equity financing.

2.4 Director/Officer Insurance. The Company shall use its best efforts to keep in full force and effect directors and officers insurance in the minimum amount of $_____ on each of its directors and officers if such coverage is available at commercially reasonable rates.

2.5 Stock Option Plan. The Company shall set the number of Shares of Common Stock reserved for issuance under its stock option plan at _____ Shares of the Company's Common Stock. The Company shall subject all options and rights to purchase Common Stock of the Company granted after the date hereof (the "Options") to the following terms and conditions, unless otherwise granted by the board of directors: (a) no Option shall vest in less than four years; (b) no Option shall have a term of more than ten years; and (c) if the Option is granted to an employee of the Company, it will contain a right of first refusal and a repurchase right in favor of the Company upon termination of employment. For purposes of this section, the term "vest" shall mean either (i) such options becoming exercisable or (ii) such stock being no longer subject to a right of repurchase by the Company.

2.6 License Agreement. The Company shall obtain the prior consent of the Investors before the Company enters into a license agreement with _____.

2.7 Key Man Life Insurance. The Company shall use its best efforts to obtain and keep in full force and effect key man life insurance policies covering its key officers for a 5-year term in the amount of $_____ per person payable to the Company.

SECTION 3
MISCELLANEOUS

3.1 Entire Agreement. This Agreement and the other documents delivered pursuant hereto constitute the full and entire understanding and agreement among the parties with regard to the subjects hereof and thereof.

3.2 Successors and Assigns. The terms and conditions of this Agreement shall inure to the benefit of and be binding upon the respective successors and assigns of the parties. The Company shall not permit the transfer of any Registrable Securities on its books or issue a new certificate representing any Registrable Securities unless and until the person to whom such security is to be transferred shall have executed a counterpart signature page hereto, pursuant to which such person becomes a party to this Agreement and agrees to be bound by all the provisions hereof as if such person were a Holder. Nothing in this Agreement, express or implied, is intended to confer upon any party other than the parties hereto or their respective successors and assigns any rights, remedies, obligations, or liabilities under or by reason of this Agreement, except as expressly provided in this Agreement.

3.3 **Amendments and Waivers.** Any term hereof may be amended or waived only with the written consent of the Company and the holders of __% of the outstanding shares of Series A Preferred Stock (on an as converted basis). Any amendment or waiver effected in accordance with this Section 3.3 shall be binding upon the Company, the Investors, and each of their respective successors and assigns.

3.4 **Notices.** All notices and other communications required or permitted hereunder to the Company and the Investors shall be in writing and be deemed to have been duly given on the day after the date telecopied or two days after deposit with FedEx or UPS or other guaranteed overnight delivery service for overnight delivery (three days, in case of international delivery), addressed (a) if to a Holder, to the address set forth below such Holder's name on **Exhibit A,** or such other address as each Holder shall have furnished to the Company in writing, or (b) if to the Company, at _____, fax: _____ and addressed to the attention of the Corporate Secretary, or such other address as the Company shall have furnished to the Shareholders in writing.

3.5 **Severability.** If for any reason any provision of this Agreement shall be determined to be invalid or inoperative, the validity and effect of the other provisions hereof shall not be affected thereby; *provided* that no such severability shall be effective if it causes a material detriment to any party.

3.6 **Applicable Law.** This Agreement shall be governed by and construed in accordance with the laws of the State of _____ applicable to contracts among residents of that state entered into and to be performed entirely within the state.

3.7 **Counterparts.** This Agreement may be executed in any number of counterparts, each of which may be executed by fewer than all of the parties, each of which shall be enforceable against the parties actually executing such parts, and all of which together shall constitute one instrument.

3.8 **Titles and Subtitles.** The titles and subtitles used in this Agreement are used for convenience only and are not to be considered in construing or interpreting this Agreement.

3.9 **Authority.** Each party represents and warrants that such party has full power to execute, deliver and perform this Agreement, which has been duly executed and delivered by and evidences the valid and binding obligation of such party enforceable in accordance with terms.

3.10 **Specific Performance.** The parties hereto agree that any violation or threatened violation of this Agreement will cause irreparable injury to the parties thus entitling the party against whom a breach occurred or was threatened to obtain injunctive relief, in addition to all legal remedies.

3.11 <u>Aggregation of Stock</u>. All shares of the Preferred Stock held or acquired by affiliated entities or persons shall be aggregated together for the purpose of determining the availability of any rights under this Agreement.

IN WITNESS WHEREOF, the parties hereto have caused this Investor Rights Agreement to be executed as of the date first written above.

THE COMPANY
**** INC.

By: _____

Name and Title: _____

INVESTORS

_____

By: _____

Name and Title: _____

CHAPTER 13

Hiring Employees

13.1 When Is an Independent Contractor Really an Employee?

Unfortunately, the law on exactly when someone is an employee on the one hand, or an independent contractor on the other, is quite vague. The Internal Revenue Service will, at least in some cases, give you a ruling on the issue. It has a form (Form SS-8) that can be used for this purpose. The form lists twelve criteria the IRS uses to decide the employee/contractor issue:

1. The right to control the activities of the person. As the general rule suggests, the most important factor used by courts and the government to judge whether someone is an employee or an independent contractor is this right to control. We are talking about the right to control the how, not the end result. Also, remember it is the right to control—not actual control.

2. Who supplies the tools?

3. Who supplies the place where the work will be done? (If the person is going to work on your property on a regular and continuing basis, you will have an uphill battle proving that the person is an independent contractor and not an employee—but it is possible.)

4. What costs are borne by the worker? Does the worker bear any risk of bad checks; must the worker pay state licensing fees; does the worker buy his or her own supplies?

5. Can the worker profit from his or her own managerial skills? Can the worker make a "profit" over and above the value of his or her time, or will the total income be limited to a relatively fixed amount?

6. What special skills are provided? The more skill the worker has, the better your chances of calling him or her an independent contractor.

7. As the relationship long term or short term? Long-term relationships tend to look like an employer/employee relationships; short-term ones look like independent contractor relationships.

8. Is the service ancillary to your business? For example, having your office building cleaned is ancillary to your business. On the other hand, routine typing in an office would not be ancillary.
9. How are the payments structured? Fixed pay for certain times (hourly, weekly, etc.) tend to look like employer/employee relationships. Pay for the job tends to look like an independent contractor arrangement.
10. Do your fringe benefits apply to the person? If you elect to give the person some or all of your fringe benefits, it may be very difficult for you to call the person an independent contractor.
11. How do the parties treat the transaction? This is not determinative—even if both parties agree that the relationship is an independent contractor one, the IRS can say differently. However, this criterion is a factor.
12. What is the custom in the trade or industry? Painters, plumbers, carpenters, public stenographers, doctors, lawyers, accountants, and so on are traditionally treated as independent contractors by the people for whom they perform services. Thus, your arguments for these kinds of people are much stronger than if you are talking about some other type of work.

There is also a lot of litigation on this issue, and practically every Congress for the past several sessions has debated whether the law should be clarified or the powers of the Internal Revenue Service curtailed or expanded to recharacterize independent contractors as employees.

Under state law, specific circumstances may dictate whether your client is hiring an independent contractor versus an employee. Check the website for the employment or labor department in the state where you are hiring for additional guidance in this regard.

13.2 What Are Some of the Most Common Hiring Mistakes?

One of the most common hiring mistakes companies make is automatically hiring a full-time employee every time they determine they need help. There are a variety of options when bringing on additional help, and the full-time regular employee option isn't always the company's best bet. Other alternatives include the following:

- Part-time employees
- Seasonal or other temporary employees
- Consultants
- Outsourcing
- Expanding the responsibilities of current staff

Another common hiring mistake is failing to do sufficient diligence on an applicant before making an offer. When companies are growing quickly, they sometimes fall into a "just get me a warm body" mentality and fail to conduct adequate interviews, reference checks, and other basic hiring diligence before bringing a new person on board. These rash hiring decisions frequently lead to unpleasant surprises. However, clients can also err on the other end of the extreme, and should be cautioned about the potential misuse of background checks and credit reports in connection with employment decisions.

Employee background checks are governed by both federal and state law and have gotten a lot of attention and undergone changes in recent years. Check applicable laws if your client plans to conduct background checks in connection with the hiring process, including laws specific to credit reporting, if a credit report is included. Rules can vary depending on whether background checks are conducted in-house or by an outside agency. For example, the federal Fair Credit Reporting Act (FCRA) (15 U.S.C. §§ 1681 *et seq.*) excludes in-house background checks, while the California Investigative Consumer Reporting Agencies Act (ICRAA) (CA Civil Code § 1786 *et seq.*) and, where a credit report is included, the California Consumer Credit Reporting Agencies Act (CCRAA) (CA Civil Code § 1785 *et seq.*) cover employers who conduct background checks in-house.

In general, a California employer must provide notice and obtain an employee's prior consent to conduct a background check and the employer must provide the employee with a copy of the results of the background check. Best practices call for the observance of the following procedures in connection with California employees (please adapt to your state and/or check for changes in the law):

A.   If an employer intends to conduct an in-house background check, the employer must:

- Give the employee notice on a separate document that a background check may be required;
- Obtain the employee's permission (unless the employer suspects the employee of wrongdoing or misconduct, in which case permission is not required and the employee is not entitled to prior notice of a background check to be conducted in-house);
- Get the employee's specific permission if medical information is requested;
- Give a specific notice if the employee's neighbors, friends, or associates will be interviewed about the employee's "character, general reputation, personal characteristics, or mode of living."

B.   If the employer conducts background checks in-house, the job application form or a related document should include a box for the employee to check indicating that the employee (or applicant) wants a copy of public records obtained in the investigation.

C.   If an outside agency will be used to perform the background check, the employer must also give the employee notice that:

- States the purpose of the report;
- Gives the name, address, and telephone number of the screening company;

- Includes a summary of the employee's rights to see and copy any report about such employee; and
- Includes a box to check if the employee wants a copy of the report.

D.   If the employee wants a copy of the report, it should be sent within three business days of the date the employer receives it. The report may come from the employer or from the screening company.

E.   Finally, the employer must give the employee a "pre-adverse action notice" along with a copy of the background report before an adverse action is taken, such as termination of employment, as well as a "post-adverse action notice," telling the employee how to dispute any inaccurate or incomplete information in the report. There is a Federal Trade Commission publication called "Using Consumer Reports: What Employers Need to Know," available at http://business .ftc.gov/documents/bus08-using-consumer-reports-what-employers-need-know, that may prove useful.

F.   The CCRAA also gives employees certain rights when a credit report is requested as part of an employment background check. Some examples:

- The employee's written permission is required for a credit check;
- The credit report cannot include any information about the employee that would violate equal employment opportunity laws, such as age, marital status, race, color, or religion;
- The employee can elect to get a copy of the credit report; and
- There are penalties for noncompliance by users of reports as well as agencies that issue the reports.

It may be worthwhile to suggest that your client use an outside agency for background checks, as an agency may be able to guide them through the process and guarantee compliance with applicable laws on a more cost effective basis.

Most hiring mistakes can be attributed to a company's failure to approach hiring the way a successful entrepreneur approaches business in general—with a plan. Hiring decisions should be made in accordance with a strategic plan that identifies and defines critical personnel needs, timing, available resources, and takes applicable laws into account.

13.3 Should a Small Business Have a Payroll Service?

Once it has employees, the company will be required to withhold federal income tax and social security tax from taxable wages paid to its employees. Funds withheld must be deposited in certain depositories accompanied by a Federal Tax Deposit Form 8109. An Employer's Quarterly Federal Tax Return (IRS Form 941) must then be filed before the end of the month following each calendar quarter. Any officer or other person charged with the withholding of taxes may become personally liable fora 100 percent penalty if he or she fails to file the appropriate forms or fails to pay the withheld funds to the Internal Revenue Service.

The company will also be required to withhold state income tax from its employees' taxable wages. In California, for example, within 15 days after becoming subject to the personal income tax withholding requirements, the employer must register with the Department of Employment Development. A booklet entitled "Employer's Tax Guide for the Withholding, Payment and Reporting of California Income Tax" may be obtained from this department and is available online.

With hiring comes a range of human resource issues, including payroll administration, health insurance, 401k plans, and other benefits. There are companies that allow companies to outsource these functions, and through the aggregation of client-employee bases, offer the small company the ability to acquire benefits at group discounts, making it easier for a small business to compete for talent.

13.4 Are Companies Required to Pay Unemployment Tax?

Once a company has employees, it will have to pay unemployment taxes. A federal form called the Unemployment Tax Return (IRS Form 940) must be filed, and any balance due must be paid on or before January 31 each year. Details may be found in IRS Circular E, the "Employer's Tax Guide." Registration with your state's unemployment agency may also be required. Companies will also be required to carry workers' compensation insurance or provide an undertaking to self-insure in accordance with the requirements in each state where they have employees.

13.5 Should a Small Business Use Offer Letters?

Offers of employment are typically extended to new hires using simple offer letters. These letters serve to outline the key terms of the offer, including the position of employment, the base pay, the options package, and the benefits. The company may also attach a form of employee agreement and/or a proprietary information and inventions agreement that each new hire must sign as a condition precedent to becoming an employee.

13.6 Should a Small Business Have Formal Employment Agreements?

Employment agreements are often used for the benefit of the company, not the employee. In addition to setting forth the employee's wage, term of employment, and benefits information, an employment agreement typically has four basic provisions for the company's protection: (i) a confidentiality agreement whereby the employee agrees not to misappropriate the confidential information of the company during or after the period of employment; (ii) an assignment of rights provision, whereby the employee agrees to assign any and all rights in any work product resulting from or related to the employee's services, to the company; (iii) a non-solicitation provision whereby the employee agrees not to solicit the employees or customers of the company for a period of time (usually one year) after the termination of employment; and (iv) a non-compete provision whereby the employee agrees not to compete with the company for a period of time (again, usually one year) after the termination of the employee's employment. It is important to note that these provisions may be subject to statutory or case law limitations in your state, such as in California, where covenants not to compete are generally prohibited by statute (see California Business and Professions Code, Section 16600). Alternatively, the company may wish to have all prospective hires sign a separate proprietary information and inventions agreement, with similar protective provisions.

An employment agreement may also provide additional protection for the employee, including severance, acceleration of vesting upon termination, and other similar provisions, in the case of senior management people who have significant negotiation leverage coming into the company. As with all legal documents relating to your company, make sure your agreements come from a knowledgeable source, such as your legal counsel.

13.7 What Should a Small Business Know About Terminating an Employment Relationship?

When a client is preparing to let an employee go, there are some steps they should take to help avoid unnecessary liability. First, the employee's offer letter, employment agreement, employee handbook, and any correspondence with the client company should be reviewed to determine the terms of employment. Assuming there is nothing in the documentation to alter the employment-at-will relationship, check the state law where the employee is employed to determine the notice requirements. There are few other areas where small business clients often get in trouble in the employment law area:

(a) Lack of written policies so that employees are left to the interpretation of informal correspondence, discussions with other employees, or observance of other employee behavior to determine what is "company policy" regarding vacation, benefits, work hours, etc;

(b) Mischaracterizing employees as "exempt"; and

(c) Lack of time cards, sign-in logs, or time sheets of employee hours so that employees can claim uncompensated overtime and holiday pay.

Also, if an employee is disabled, is in poor health, or has family members with such conditions, problems can arise if the termination is related to absences due to the disability, health issues, or the need to care for a seriously ill family member, as such absences may be protected under the law as family or medical leave. In California for example, employees who are absent for family or medical leave reasons should be given the EDD pamphlet Paid Family Leave (http://www.edd.ca.gov/pdf_pub_ctr/de2511.pdf). Of course, disabled employees are entitled to reasonable accommodation the Americans with Disabilities Act. See www.ada.gov for details.

Assuming disability and/or family leave are not at issue, your client should assemble the relevant documentation for termination, including the employee's personnel file, employment-related correspondence, and disciplinary notices, and prepare to provide the following at the time of termination:

1. Written notice of termination, with a request for the return of all company property and details for the same;
2. Final paycheck through the date of termination, including all accrued, unpaid vacation;
3. State unemployment insurance information such as the California EDD's pamphlet *For Your Benefit, California Program for the Unemployed* (http://www.edd.ca.gov/pdf_pub_ctr/de2320.pdf);
4. All required federal and state notices relating to health care and health insurance such as the federal Continuation of Health Coverage—COBRA—notices, online at www.dol.gov/dol/topic/health-plans/cobra .htm and the California HIPP notice, available online at www.dhcs .ca.gov/formsandpubs/forms/Documents/CobraEnglish.pdf; and
5. Copies of any policies or contract provisions under which the employee will have continuing obligations, such as confidentiality, non-solicitation, and invention assignment agreements.

If not already posted, it is also advisable to have your client post all currently required labor and employment law information prior to a termination. Posters containing both federal and state law requirements are available from private services and state chambers of commerce. The required information is also available online directly from the U.S. Department of Labor and state employment agencies, but it can be time consuming to accumulate all of the required components and your client will have to check often for changes.

In the case of an employee with an employment agreement for a specific term, the agreement must be analyzed in light of the circumstances leading to termination to determine the appropriate grounds for termination and the amount due to the employee upon termination.

Clients should be cautioned about deducting anything, other than regular employment taxes, from an employee's final paycheck. When an employee has misappropriated funds, damaged company property, or taken more vacation than they earned, the client will be tempted to take an offset. However, labor and employment laws are typically very protective of the employee. Often such deductions would have to be authorized in writing by the employee in advance and/or the company would have to be able to prove that the damage or loss was the result of the employee's dishonesty, willfulness, or gross negligence. If it is later determined that the employee was not guilty or the amounts were incorrect, the employee can often recover the amount wrongfully deducted plus penalties. A safer route may be to have your client pursue the former employee separately for damages, if the damages warrant it and the employee has the means to pay.

13.8 Sample Documents and Checklists.

This section includes the following forms:

- Employment Application with Background Check (Form 13 A)
- Employment Offer Letter (Form 13 B)
- Confidential Information and Invention Assignment Agreement (Form 13 C)
- Employment Agreement (Form 13 D)
- Executive Employment Agreement (Form 13 E)
- Sales Representative Agreement (Form 13 F)
- Severance Agreement (Form 13 G)

Form 13 A: Employment Application with Background Check

PRELIMINARY APPLICATION FOR EMPLOYMENT
AND BACKGROUND CHECK AUTHORIZATION

Applicant Name (include all names used):

_____

_____

Date of Birth (MO/DY/YEAR):

_____

Place of Birth:

_____

Social Security Number:

_____

CRD Number, if applicable:

_____

Residential Address(es) for last two years including county:

_____

_____

_____

    The undersigned hereby certifies that the foregoing information is true and correct and hereby authorizes ****, LLC, a licensed broker-dealer and National Association of Securities Dealers member firm ("Company"), as well as any investigative agency retained by it, to investigate and obtain information about the undersigned's background in connection with this application to become associated with Company. Such background investigation may include: criminal background search; civil litigation search; credit report; driving record; worker's compensation claim history; address verification; Social Security Number verification; and professional licensing history.

    The undersigned hereby authorizes any company, governmental agency, court, law enforcement agency or person contacted by Company, or any investigative agency retained by it, to furnish to Company, directly or indirectly, copies of all documents, records or information in their custody or control.

The undersigned acknowledges having the right to make a written request within a reasonable period of time for a complete and accurate disclosure of additional information concerning the nature and scope of the investigation. The undersigned hereby releases Company, as well as any agents acting on its behalf, from any and all claims, losses and liability arising from the above.

_____

Date   Applicant Signature

Form 13 B: Employment Offer Letter

****, INC.
[Address]

[Date]

[Offeree Name]
[Offeree Address]

    RE: Employment with ****, Inc.

Dear Ms. _____:

    ****, Inc. (the "Company") is pleased to offer you a full-time position as an at-will employee of the Company on the terms and conditions set forth herein. Subject to the approval of the Board of Directors, you will hold the position of Chief Financial Officer of the Company and will have all of the duties normally attendant to such a position. We would like for you to begin work with the Company immediately.

    Your initial rate of compensation will be _____ Dollars ($_____) per year, paid bi-monthly in accordance with the Company's regular payroll procedures. Further, subject to the approval of the Board of Directors, you will receive an Incentive Stock Option Grant for _____ Thousand (_____) shares of the Company's Common Stock, representing _____ percent (___%) of the Company's currently issued and outstanding stock on a fully-diluted basis.

    Upon completion of _____ (___) months of service with the Company, you will be eligible to participate in all benefits established for executive officers of the Company.

    Your employment pursuant to this offer is contingent upon you executing the enclosed At-Will Employment, Confidential Information and Invention Assignment Agreement, and upon you providing the Company with the legally-required proof of your identity and authorization to work in the United States.

    Your employment with the Company, should you accept this offer, will not be for any specific term and may be terminated by you or by the Company at any time, with or without cause and with or without notice as more fully described in the At-Will Employment, Confidential Information And Invention Assignment Agreement. Any contrary representations or agreements which may have been made to you are superseded by this offer.

    As an employee of the Company, you will be required to comply with all Company policies and procedures. In particular, you will be required to familiarize yourself with and to comply with the Company's policy prohibiting unlawful harassment and discrimination and the policy prohibiting the use of, or being under the influence of, drugs or alcohol while at work, except as prescribed by a physician. Violations of these policies may lead to immediate termination of employment.

    If you accept this offer of employment, you agree that during your employment and for 12 months after you leave the Company, you will not solicit or encourage, directly or indirectly, any employee or consultant of the Company to leave the Company, to reduce his or her duties or time commitment to the Company, or to perform work for any other person or entity, as set forth more fully in the At-Will Employment, Confidential Information And Invention Assignment Agreement.

695

If you wish to accept this offer, please sign below and return the fully executed letter to us, along with the executed At-Will Employment, Confidential Information and Invention Assignment Agreement. You should keep a copy of this letter and the At-Will Employment, Confidential Information and Invention Assignment Agreement for your records.

We are looking forward to having you join ****, Inc. If you have any questions, please call me at _____ [Telephone number].

Very truly,
****, Inc.

By: _____
President

I have read and accept this employment offer.

Dated: _____

_____
[Offeree]

Form 13 C: Confidential Information and Invention Assignment Agreement

AT-WILL EMPLOYMENT, CONFIDENTIAL INFORMATION AND INVENTION ASSIGNMENT AGREEMENT

As a condition of my employment with ****, Inc., its subsidiaries, affiliates, successors, or assigns (together the "Company"), and in consideration of my employment with the Company and my receipt of the compensation now and hereafter paid to me by the Company, I agree to the following:

1. <u>At-Will Employment</u>. I understand and acknowledge that my employment with the Company is for an unspecified duration and constitutes "at-will" employment, unless otherwise specifically set forth in writing. I acknowledge that this employment relationship may be terminated at any time, with or without good cause or for any or no cause, at the option either of the Company or myself, with or without notice, except as otherwise specifically set forth in writing.

2. <u>Confidential Information</u>.

(a) <u>Company Information</u>. I agree at all times during the term of my employment and thereafter, to hold in strictest confidence, and not to use, except for the benefit of the Company, or to disclose to any person, firm or corporation without written authorization of the Board of Directors of the Company, any Confidential Information of the Company. I understand that "Confidential Information" means any Company proprietary information, technical data, trade secrets or know-how, including, but not limited to, research, product plans, products, services, customer lists and customers (including, but not limited to, customers of the Company on whom I called or with whom I became acquainted during the term of my employment), markets, software, developments, inventions, processes, formulas, technology, designs, drawings, engineering, hardware configuration information, marketing, finances, or other business information disclosed to me by the Company either directly or indirectly in writing, orally or by drawings or observation of parts or equipment. I further understand that Confidential Information does not include any of the foregoing items which have become publicly known and made generally available through no wrongful act of mine or of others who were under confidentiality obligations as to the item or items involved.

(b) <u>Former Employer Information</u>. I agree that I will not, during my employment with the Company, improperly use or disclose any proprietary information or trade secrets of any former or concurrent employer or other person or entity and that I will not bring onto the premises of the Company any unpublished document or proprietary information belonging to any such employer, person or entity unless consented to in writing by such employer, person or entity.

(c) <u>Third-Party Information</u>. I recognize that the Company has received and in the future will receive from third parties their confidential or proprietary information subject to a duty on the Company's part to maintain the confidentiality of such information and to use it only for certain limited purposes. I agree to hold all such confidential or proprietary information in the strictest confidence and not to disclose it to any person, firm or corporation or to use it except as necessary in carrying out my work for the Company consistent with the Company's agreement with such third party.

3. Inventions.

(a) Inventions Retained and Licensed. I have attached hereto, as Exhibit A, a list describing all inventions, original works of authorship, developments, improvements, and trade secrets which were made by me prior to my employment with the Company (collectively referred to as "Prior Inventions"), which belong to me, which relate to the Company's proposed business, products or research and development, and which are not assigned to the Company hereunder; or, if no such list is attached, I represent that there are no such Prior Inventions. If in the course of my employment with the Company, I incorporate into a Company product, process or machine a Prior Invention owned by me or in which I have an interest, the Company is hereby granted and shall have a nonexclusive, royalty-free, irrevocable, perpetual, worldwide license to make, have made, modify, use and sell such Prior Invention as part of or in connection with such product, process or machine.

(b) Assignment of Inventions. I agree that I will promptly make full written disclosure to the Company, will hold in trust for the sole right and benefit of the Company, and hereby assign to the Company, or its designee, all my right, title, and interest in and to any and all inventions, original works of authorship, developments, concepts, improvements or trade secrets, whether or not patentable or subject to registration under copyright or similar laws, which I may solely or jointly conceive or develop or reduce to practice, or cause to be conceived or developed or reduced to practice, during the period of time I am in the employ of the Company (collectively referred to as "Inventions"), except as provided in Section 3(f) below. I further acknowledge that all original works of authorship which are made by me (solely or jointly with others) within the scope of and during the period of my employment with the Company and which are subject to copyright protection are "works made for hire," as that term is defined in the United States Copyright Act.

(c) Inventions Assigned to the United States. I agree to assign to the United States government all my right, title, and interest in and to any and all Inventions whenever such full title is required to be in the United States by a contract between the Company and the United States or any of its agencies.

(d) Maintenance of Records. I agree to keep and maintain adequate and current written records of all Inventions made by me (solely or jointly with others) during the term of my employment with the Company. The records will be in the form of notes, sketches, drawings, and any other format that may be specified by the Company. The records will be available to and remain the sole property of the Company at all times.

(e) Patent and Copyright Registrations. I agree to assist the Company, or its designee, at the Company's expense, in every proper way to secure the Company's rights in the Inventions and any copyrights, patents, mask work rights or other intellectual property rights relating thereto in any and all countries, including the disclosure to the Company of all pertinent information and data with respect thereto, the execution of all applications, specifications, oaths, assignments and all other instruments which the Company shall deem necessary in order to apply for and obtain such rights and in order to assign and convey to the Company, its successors, assigns and nominees the sole and exclusive rights, title and interest in and to such Inventions, and any copyrights, patents, mask work rights or other intellectual property rights relating thereto. I further agree that my obligation to execute or cause to be executed, when it is in my power to do so, any such instrument or papers shall continue after the termination of this Agreement. If the Company is unable because of my mental or physical incapacity or for any other reason to secure my signature to apply for or to pursue any application for any United States or foreign patents or copyright registrations covering Inventions or original works of authorship assigned to the Company as above, then I hereby irrevocably designate and appoint the Company and its duly authorized officers and agents as my agent and attorney in fact, to act for and in my behalf and stead to execute and file any such applications and to do all other lawfully permitted acts to further the prosecution and issuance of letters patent or copyright registrations thereon with the same legal force and effect as if executed by me.

(f) <u>Exception to Assignments</u>. I understand that the provisions of this Agreement requiring assignment of Inventions to the Company do not apply to any Invention which qualifies fully under the provisions of California Labor Code Section 2870 (attached hereto as Exhibit B). I will advise the Company promptly in writing of any inventions that I believe meet the criteria in California Labor Code Section 2870 and not otherwise disclosed on Exhibit A.

4. <u>Conflicting Employment</u>. I agree that, during the term of my employment with the Company, I will not engage in any other employment, occupation, consulting or other business activity directly related to the business in which the Company is now involved or becomes involved during the term of my employment, nor will I engage in any other activities that conflict with my obligations to the Company.

5. <u>Returning Company Documents</u>. I agree that, at the time of leaving the employ of the Company, I will deliver to the Company (and will not keep in my possession, recreate or deliver to anyone else) any and all devices, records, data, notes, reports, proposals, lists, correspondence, specifications, drawings, blueprints, sketches, materials, equipment, other documents or property, or reproductions of any aforementioned items developed by me pursuant to my employment with the Company or otherwise belonging to the Company, its successors or assigns. In the event of the termination of my employment, I agree to sign and deliver the "Termination Certification" attached hereto as Exhibit C.

6. <u>Notification to New Employer</u>. In the event that I leave the employ of the Company, I hereby grant consent to notification by the Company to my new employer about my rights and obligations under this Agreement.

7. <u>Non-Solicitation of Employees</u>. I agree that for a period of twelve (12) months immediately following the termination of my relationship with the Company for any reason, whether with or without cause, I shall not either directly or indirectly solicit, induce, recruit or encourage any of the Company's employees or consultants to leave their employment, or take away such employees or consultants, or attempt to solicit, induce, recruit, encourage or take away employees or consultants of the Company, either for myself or for any other person or entity.

8. <u>Conflict of Interest Guidelines</u>. I agree to diligently adhere to the Conflict of Interest Guidelines attached as Exhibit D hereto.

9. <u>Representations</u>. I agree to execute any proper oath or verify any proper document required to carry out the terms of this Agreement. I represent that my performance of all the terms of this Agreement will not breach any agreement to keep in confidence proprietary information acquired by me in confidence or in trust prior to my employment by the Company. I have not entered into, and I agree I will not enter into, any oral or written agreement in conflict herewith.

10. <u>Arbitration and Equitable Relief</u>.

(a) <u>Arbitration</u>. I hereby irrevocably and knowingly waive to the fullest extent permitted by law any right to a trial by jury in any action or proceeding arising out of this Agreement. I agree that any such action or proceeding shall be tried before a court and not a jury. In the event this waiver of a trial by jury is deemed invalid, I hereby agree that any action or claim arising out of any dispute in connection with this agreement, any rights, remedies, obligations, or duties hereunder, or the performance or enforcement hereof or thereof shall be determined by judicial reference.

(b) <u>Equitable Remedies.</u> I agree that it would be impossible or inadequate to measure and calculate the Company's damages from any breach of the covenants set forth in Sections 2, 3, and 5 herein. Accordingly, I agree that if I breach any of such Sections, the Company will have available, in addition to any other right or remedy available, the right to obtain an injunction from a court of competent jurisdiction restraining such breach or threatened breach and to specific performance of any such provision of this Agreement. I further agree that no bond or other security shall be required in obtaining such equitable relief and I hereby consent to the issuance of such injunction and to the ordering of specific performance.

11. <u>General Provisions.</u>

(a) <u>Governing Law; Consent to Personal Jurisdiction.</u> This Agreement will be governed by the laws of the State of _____. I hereby expressly consent to the personal jurisdiction of the state and federal courts located in the State of _____ for any lawsuit filed there against me by the Company arising from or relating to this Agreement.

(b) <u>Entire Agreement.</u> This Agreement sets forth the entire agreement and understanding between the Company and me relating to the subject matter hereof and merges all prior discussions between us. No modification of or amendment to this Agreement, nor any waiver of any rights under this Agreement, will be effective unless in writing signed by the party to be charged. Any subsequent change or changes in my duties, salary or compensation will not affect the validity or scope of this Agreement.

(c) <u>Severability.</u> If one or more of the provisions in this Agreement are deemed void by law, then the remaining provisions will continue in full force and effect.

(d) <u>Successors and Assigns.</u> This Agreement will be binding upon my heirs, executors, administrators and other legal representatives and will be for the benefit of the Company, its successors, and its assigns.

Date: _____

_____
Signature

_____
Name of Employee (typed or printed)

_____
Witness

EXHIBIT A

LIST OF PRIOR INVENTIONS
AND ORIGINAL WORKS OF AUTHORSHIP

Give title, date, and identifying number or brief description for each:

_____

_____

_____

_____

_____

_____

_____

_____ No inventions or improvements
_____ Additional sheets attached

Signature of Employee: _____

Print Name of Employee: _____

Date: _____

EXHIBIT B

CALIFORNIA LABOR CODE
SECTION 2870 EMPLOYMENT AGREEMENTS;
ASSIGNMENT OF RIGHTS

"(a) Any provision in an employment agreement which provides that an employee shall assign, or offer to assign, any of his or her rights in an invention to his or her employer shall not apply to an invention that the employee developed entirely on his or her own time without using the employer's equipment, supplies, facilities, or trade secret information except for those inventions that either:

(1) Relate at the time of conception or reduction to practice of the invention to the employer's business, or actual or demonstrably anticipated research or development of the employer.

(2) Result from any work performed by the employee for the employer.

(b) To the extent a provision in an employment agreement purports to require an employee to assign an invention otherwise excluded from being required to be assigned under subdivision (a), the provision is against the public policy of this state and is unenforceable."

EXHIBIT C
TERMINATION CERTIFICATION

This is to certify that I do not have in my possession, nor have I failed to return, any devices, records, data, notes, reports, proposals, lists, correspondence, specifications, drawings, blueprints, sketches, materials, equipment, other documents or property, or reproductions of any aforementioned items belonging to ****, Inc., its subsidiaries, affiliates, successors, or assigns (together, the "Company").

I further certify that I have complied with all the terms of the Company's Confidential Information and Invention Assignment Agreement signed by me, including the reporting of any inventions and original works of authorship (as defined therein), conceived or made by me (solely or jointly with others) covered by that agreement.

I further agree that, in compliance with the Confidential Information and Invention Assignment Agreement, I will preserve as confidential all trade secrets, confidential knowledge, data, or other proprietary information relating to products, processes, know-how, designs, formulas, developmental, or experimental work, computer programs, data bases, other original works of authorship, customer lists, business plans, financial information, or other subject matter pertaining to any business of the Company or any of its employees, clients, consultants, or licensees.

I further agree that for twelve (12) months from this date, I will not hire any employees of the Company and I will not solicit, induce, recruit, or encourage any of the Company's employees to leave their employment.

Date:_____

_____
(Employee's Signature)
_____
(Type/Print Employee's Name)

705

EXHIBIT D

CONFLICT OF INTEREST GUIDELINES

It is the policy of ****, Inc., its subsidiaries, affiliates, successors, or assigns (together the "Company") to conduct its affairs in strict compliance with the letter and spirit of the law and to adhere to the highest principles of business ethics. Accordingly, all officers, employees and independent contractors must avoid activities which are in conflict, or give the appearance of being in conflict, with these principles and with the interests of the Company. The following are potentially compromising situations which must be avoided. Any exceptions must be reported to the President and written approval for continuation must be obtained.

1. Revealing confidential information to outsiders or misusing confidential information. (Unauthorized divulging of information is a violation of this policy whether or not for personal gain and whether or not harm to the Company is intended. The Confidential Information and Invention Assignment Agreement elaborates on this principle and is a binding agreement.)

2. Accepting or offering substantial gifts, excessive entertainment, favors, or payments which may be deemed to constitute undue influence or otherwise be improper or embarrassing to the Company.

3. Participating in civic or professional organizations that might involve divulging confidential information of the Company.

4. Initiating or approving personnel actions affecting reward or punishment of employees or applicants where there is a family relationship or is or appears to be a personal or social involvement.

5. Initiating or approving any form of personal or social harassment of employees.

6. Investing or holding outside directorships in suppliers, customers, or competing companies, including financial speculation, where such investment or directorship might influence in any manner a decision or course of action of the Company.

7. Borrowing from or lending to employees, customers, or suppliers.

8. Acquiring real estate or other property of interest to the Company.

9. Improperly using or disclosing to the Company any proprietary information or trade secrets of any former or concurrent employer or other person or entity with whom obligations of confidentiality exist.

10. Unlawfully discussing prices, costs, customers, sales, or markets with competing companies or their employees.

11. Making any unlawful agreements with distributors with respect to prices.

12. Improperly using or authorizing the use of any inventions which are the subject of patent claims of any other person or entity.

13. Engaging in any conduct which is not in the best interests of the Company.

Each officer, employee, and independent contractor must take every necessary action to ensure compliance with these guidelines and to bring problem areas to the attention of higher management for review. Violations of this conflict of interest policy may result in immediate discharge.

Form 13 D: Employment Agreement

EMPLOYMENT AGREEMENT

THIS EMPLOYMENT AGREEMENT (this "Agreement") is made and entered into effective as of this _____ day of _____, 20___, by and between ****, LLC, a [California] limited liability company (hereinafter the "Company"), and _____ (hereinafter "Employee").

RECITAL

The Company desires to hire Employee as a _____ of the Company; and Employee desires to accept such employment, on the terms and subject to the conditions set forth herein.

AGREEMENT

NOW, THEREFORE, in consideration of the mutual agreements, covenants, representations, and warranties contained in this Agreement, the parties hereto hereby agree as follows:

1. Employment Duties.
    a. General. The Company hereby agrees to employ Employee, and Employee hereby agrees to accept employment with the Company, on the terms and conditions hereinafter set forth.
    b. Company's Duties. The Company shall allow Employee to, and Employee shall, perform responsibilities normally incident to his position as _____ of the Company, commensurate with his background, education, experience, and professional standing.
    c. Employee's Duties. Employee shall devote his full productive time, attention, energy, and skill to the business of the Company during the employment term set forth below, and shall not become engaged to render similar services on behalf of any other entity while employed hereunder, without the Company's consent. Employee shall report directly to the Company's _____.
2. Term. This Agreement shall commence as of _____, 20___ and shall continue for a period of one (1) year, unless sooner terminated under the terms of this Agreement.
3. Compensation. Employee shall be compensated as follows:
    a. Salary. Employee shall receive a fixed annual salary of _____ Dollars ($_____).
    b. Payment. Employee's salary shall be payable on a semi-monthly basis.
    c. Vacation. Employee shall accrue paid vacation at the rate of _____ (__) days for each twelve (12) months of employment. Employee shall be compensated at his usual rate of compensation during any such vacation. Employee shall be entitled to eight (8) paid holidays during each twelve (12) months of employment.
    d. Benefits. During the employment term, Employee and his dependents shall be entitled to participate in any group plans or programs maintained by the Company for any employees relating to group health, disability, life insurance, and other related benefits as in effect from time to time.

4.   Confidentiality and Competitive Activities. Employee agrees that during the employment term he is in a position of special trust and confidence and has access to confidential and proprietary information about the Company's business and plans. Employee agrees that, during the term of this Agreement, he will not directly or indirectly, either as an employee, employer, consultant, agent, principal, partner, stockholder, corporate officer, director, or in any similar individual or representative capacity, engage or participate in any business that is in competition, in any manner whatsoever, with the Company. Notwithstanding anything in the foregoing to the contrary, Employee shall be allowed to invest as a shareholder in publicly traded companies.

5.   Trade Secrets.

a.   Special Techniques. It is hereby agreed that the Company has developed or acquired certain products, technology, unique or special methods, trade secrets, special written marketing plans and special customer arrangements, client lists, and other proprietary rights and confidential information and shall during the employment term continue to develop, compile and acquire said items (all hereinafter collectively referred to as the "Company's Property"). It is expected that Employee will gain knowledge of and utilize the Company's Property during the course and scope of his employment with the Company, and will be in a position of trust with respect to the Company's Property.

b.   Company's Property. It is hereby stipulated and agreed that the Company's Property shall remain the Company's sole property. In the event that Employee's employment is terminated, for whatever reason, Employee agrees not to copy, make known, disclose or use, any of the Company's Property without the Company's prior written consent which shall not be unreasonably withheld. In such event, Employee further agrees not to endeavor or attempt in any way to interfere with or induce a breach of any prior proprietary contractual relationship that the Company may have with any employee, customer, contractor, supplier, representative, or distributor. Employee agrees upon termination of employment to deliver to the Company all confidential papers, documents, records, lists, and notes (whether prepared by Employee or others) comprising or containing the Company's Property. Employee recognizes that violation of covenants and agreements contained in this Section 5 may result in irreparable injury to the Company which would not be fully compensable by way of money damages.

c.   Non-Solicitation. Employee hereby agrees that he will not directly or indirectly, during the term of this Agreement and for one (1) year thereafter, solicit for employment any current or future employee of the Company for employment in any other business.

6.   Termination.

a.   General. The Company may terminate this Agreement without cause at anytime by giving Employee thirty (30) days' prior written notice. Employee may voluntarily terminate his employment hereunder upon thirty (30) days' advance written notice to the Company. Upon termination with or without cause, Employee shall be entitled to maintain his pro rata portion of any bonus he has earned during his employment hereunder less a discount based upon his tenure as an employee of the Company as follows:

Employment Tenure at Company	Discount on Bonus
0–12 months	25%
13–24 months	20%
25–36 months	15%
37 or more months	10%

The Company may pay the above earned pro-rata portion of any bonus in kind as the securities comprising such bonus are available for transfer to Employee.

b.   Termination for Cause. The Company may immediately terminate Employee's employment at any time for cause. Termination for cause shall be effective from the receipt of written notice thereof to Employee specifying the grounds for termination and all relevant facts. Cause shall be deemed to include: (i) neglect of his duties or a violation of any of the provisions of this Agreement, which continues after written notice and a reasonable opportunity (not to exceed thirty (30) days) in which to cure; (ii) fraud, embezzlement, defalcation, or conviction of any felonious offense; or (iii) intentionally imparting confidential information relating to the Company or its business to competitors or to other third parties other than in the course of carrying out his duties hereunder. The Company's exercise of its rights to terminate with cause shall be without prejudice to any other remedy it may be entitled at law, in equity, or under this Agreement.

c.   Termination Upon Death or Disability. This Agreement shall automatically terminate upon Employee's death. In addition, if any disability or incapacity of Employee to perform his duties as the result of any injury, sickness, or physical, mental, or emotional condition continues for a period of one hundred twenty days (120) out of any one hundred eighty (180) consecutive days, the Company may terminate Employee's employment upon written notice. Payment of salary to Employee during any sick leave shall only be to the extent that Employee has accrued sick leave or vacation days. Employee shall accrue sick leave at the same rate generally available to the Company's employees.

7.   Corporate Opportunities.

a.   Duty to Notify. In the event that Employee, during the employment term, shall become aware of any business opportunity related to the Company's business, Employee shall promptly notify the Company's managers of such opportunity. Employee shall not appropriate for himself or for any other person other than the Company, or any affiliate of the Company, any such opportunity unless, as to any particular opportunity, the Company fails to take appropriate action within sixty (60) days. Employee's duty to notify the Company and to refrain from appropriating all such opportunities for sixty (60) days shall neither be limited by, nor shall such duty limit, the application of the general law of California, relating to the fiduciary duties of an agent or employee.

b.   Failure to Notify. In the event that Employee fails to notify the Company of, or so appropriates, any such opportunity without the express written consent of the Company, Employee shall be deemed to have violated the provisions of this Section notwithstanding the following:

i) The capacity in which Employee shall have acquired such opportunity; or
ii) The probable success in the Company's hands of such opportunity.

8.   Miscellaneous.

a.   Entire Agreement. This Agreement constitutes the entire agreement and understanding between the parties with respect to the subject matters herein, and supersedes and replaces any prior agreements and understandings, whether oral or written between them with respect to such matters. The provisions of this Agreement may be waived, altered, amended or repealed in whole or in part only upon the written consent of both parties to this Agreement.

b.   Title and Subtitles. The titles of the Sections and subsections of this Agreement and any exhibits are for the convenience of reference only and are not to be considered in construing this Agreement.

c. No Implied Waivers. The failure of either party at any time to require performance by the other party of any provision hereof shall not affect in any way the right to require such performance at any time thereafter, nor shall the waiver by either party of a breach of any provision hereof be taken or held to be a waiver of any subsequent breach of the same provision or any other provision.

d. Personal Services. It is understood that the services to be performed by Employee hereunder are personal in nature and the obligations to perform such services and the conditions and covenants of this Agreement cannot be assigned by Employee. Subject to the foregoing, and except as otherwise provided herein, this Agreement shall inure to the benefit of and bind the successors and assigns of the Company.

e. Severability. If for any reason any provision of this Agreement shall be determined to be invalid or inoperative, the validity and effect of the other provisions hereof shall not be affected thereby, provided that no such severability shall be effective if it causes a material detriment to any party.

f. Applicable Law. This Agreement shall be governed by and construed in accordance with the laws of the State of California, applicable to contracts between California residents entered into and to be performed entirely within the State of California.

g. Notices. All notices, requests, demands, instructions, or other communications required or permitted to be given under this Agreement shall be in writing and shall be deemed to have been duly given upon delivery, if delivered personally, or if given by prepaid telegram, or mailed first-class, postage prepaid, registered, or certified mail, return receipt requested, shall be deemed to have been given seventy-two (72) hours after such delivery, if addressed to the other party at the addresses as set forth on the signature page below. Either party hereto may change the address to which such communications are to be directed by giving written notice to the other party hereto of such change in the manner above provided.

h. Merger, Transfer of Assets, or Dissolution of the Company. This Agreement shall not be terminated by any dissolution of the Company resulting from either merger or consolidation in which the Company is not the consolidated or surviving Company or a transfer of all or substantially all of the assets of the Company. In such event, the rights, benefits and obligations herein shall automatically be assigned to the surviving or resulting Company or to the transferee of the assets.

IN WITNESS WHEREOF, the parties have executed this Agreement as of the date first written above.

****, LLC   EMPLOYEE

By: _____   By: _____

_____, Manager   _____

(Print Name)   (Print Name)

_____   _____

_____   _____

(Print Address)   (Print Address)

Form 13 E: Executive Employment Agreement

EXECUTIVE EMPLOYMENT AGREEMENT

This Executive Employment Agreement is made as of this ___ day of _____, 20___ (the "Effective Date"), by and between ****, Inc, a [Delaware] corporation (the "Company"), and _____ ("Executive"), an individual residing in the State of _____.

WHEREAS the Company is engaged in the business of _____ _____; and

WHEREAS the Company wishes to retain the services of Executive and Executive is willing to accept employment by the Company, on the terms and subject to the conditions set forth in this Agreement;

NOW, THEREFORE, in consideration of the promises and covenants contained herein, the parties hereby agree as follows:

1. DUTIES AND POSITION. During the term of this Agreement, Executive agrees to be employed by and to serve the Company as its _____, reporting directly to _____. The Company agrees to employ and retain Executive in such capacity and Executive accepts and agrees to such employment, subject to the general supervision, advice and direction of the Company's Board of Directors. The Company reserves the right to reassign and or redefine the scope of the Executive's duties and responsibilities as the business of the Company dictates. Executive shall devote full-time attention to the performance of such duties as are customarily performed by an executive in a similar position. Executive's reasonable attention to personal investments and other business matters of her immediate family shall not be deemed to be a violation of this Agreement.

2. TERMS OF EMPLOYMENT.

2.1 <u>Definitions</u>. For purposes of this Agreement, the following terms shall have the following meanings:

(a) "Termination For Cause" shall mean termination by the Company of Executive's employment by the Company for reasons of Executive's conviction of a felony involving moral turpitude, persistent dishonesty or fraud, persistent willful breaches of the material terms of this Agreement, or habitual neglect of the duties which she is required to perform hereunder.

(b) "Termination Other Than For Cause" shall mean termination by the Company of Executive's employment by the Company (other than a Termination For Cause).

(c) "Voluntary Termination" shall mean termination of Executive's employment with the Company by action of Executive (other than termination by reason of Executive's disability or death as described in Sections 2.6 and 2.7).

2.2 <u>Term of Employment</u>. The term of Executive's employment pursuant to this Agreement is deemed to have commenced on the Effective Date. The Company agrees to continue Executive's employment, and Executive agrees to remain employed by the Company, from the Effective Date until _____[Date] (the "Term").

2.3 <u>Place of Performance</u>. Executive shall be based at the executive offices of the Company located in the City of _____, in the State of _____, or such other location as the Company may determine, although it is anticipated that

Executive will perform some of her work away from the Company's offices. In no case will Executive be required or expected to move her principal residence from _____ [geographic area].

2.4 <u>Termination for Cause</u>. Termination for Cause may be effected by the Company at any time during the Term of this Agreement and shall be effected by notice to Executive. Upon Termination for Cause, Executive immediately shall be paid any accrued salary, any bonus compensation to the extent earned, any vested deferred compensation (other than pension plan or profit sharing plan benefits which will be paid in accordance with the applicable plan), any benefits under any plan of the Company in which Executive is a participant to the full extent of Executive's rights under any such plan, any accrued vacation pay and any appropriate business expenses incurred by Executive in connection with her duties hereunder, all to the date of termination, but Executive shall not be paid any other compensation or reimbursement of any kind, including without limitation, severance compensation.

2.5 <u>Termination Other Than for Cause</u>. Notwithstanding anything else in this Agreement, the Company may effect a Termination Other Than for Cause at any time during the Term of this Agreement upon giving notice to Executive of such termination. Upon any Termination Other Than for Cause, Executive shall be paid any accrued salary, any bonus compensation to the extent earned, any deferred compensation (other than pension plan or profit sharing plan benefits which will be paid in accordance with the applicable plan), any benefits under any plan of the Company in which Executive is a participant to the full extent of Executive's rights under any such plan, any accrued vacation pay and any appropriate business expenses incurred by Executive in connection with her duties hereunder, all to the date of termination, and any severance compensation provided in Section 4, but no other compensation or reimbursement of any kind.

2.6 <u>Termination by Reason of Disability</u>. If, during the Term, Executive is determined by an examining physician to have failed to perform her duties under this Agreement on account of illness or physical or mental incapacity, and such illness or incapacity continues for a consecutive period of more than four (4) months, or an aggregate of more than six (6) months in a twelve (12) month period, the Company shall have the right to terminate Executive's employment hereunder by notice to Executive and payment to the Executive of any accrued salary, any bonus compensation to the extent earned, any vested deferred compensation (other than pension plan or profit sharing plan benefits which will be paid in accordance with the applicable plan), any benefits under any plan of the Company in which Executive is a participant to the full extent of Executive's rights under any such plan, any accrued vacation pay and any appropriate business expenses incurred by Executive in connection with her duties hereunder, all to the date of termination, and any severance compensation provided in Section 4, but no other compensation or reimbursement of any kind.

2.7 <u>Death</u>. In the event of Executive's death during the Term, Executive's employment shall be deemed to terminate as of the last day of the month during which her death occurs and the Company shall pay to her estate any accrued salary, any bonus compensation to the extent earned, any vested deferred compensation (other than pension plan or profit sharing plan benefits which will be paid in accordance with the applicable plan), any benefits under any plan of the Company in which Executive is a participant to the full extent of Executive's rights under any such plan, any accrued vacation pay and any appropriate business expenses incurred by Executive in connection with her duties hereunder, all to the date of termination, and any severance compensation provided in Section 4, but no other compensation or reimbursement of any kind.

2.8 <u>Voluntary Termination.</u> Executive may effect a Voluntary Termination of this Agreement at any time during the Term of this Agreement upon sixty (60) days notice to the Company. In the event of a Voluntary Termination, the Company immediately shall pay any accrued salary, any bonus compensation to the extent earned, any vested deferred compensation (other than pension plan or profit sharing plan benefits which will be paid in accordance with the applicable plan), any benefits under any plan of the Company in which Executive is a participant to the full extent of Executive's rights under any such plan, any accrued vacation pay and any appropriate business expenses incurred by Executive in connection with her duties hereunder, all to the date of termination, but no other compensation or reimbursement of any kind, including without limitation, severance compensation.

3. SALARY, BENEFITS, AND BONUS COMPENSATION.

3.1 <u>Salary.</u> As payment for the services to be rendered by Executive as provided in Section 1 and subject to the terms and conditions of Section 2, the Company agrees to pay to Executive an annual salary of _____ dollars ($_____) during the Term hereof (the "Base Salary"), payable semi-monthly. Executive's salary shall be reviewed by the Company' Board of Directors annually and Executive shall be eligible for such increases in salary and benefits as may be determined by the Company's Board of Directors in its discretion. In no event shall Executive's salary be reduced below the Base Salary except with Executive's express written consent which may be withheld in the exercise of Executive's sole discretion.

3.2 <u>Bonuses.</u> Executive shall be eligible to receive bonuses in amounts related to the Company's revenues and/or the accomplishment of certain milestones by Executive, as may be determined by the Company's Board of Directors in its discretion.

3.3 <u>Additional Benefits and Compensation.</u> During the Term of this Agreement, Executive shall be entitled to the following additional benefits:

3.3.1 <u>Employee Benefits.</u> Executive shall be eligible to participate in all benefit plans generally available to employees who are managers of the Company, including health, dental, and life insurance. In the event the Company does not immediately make such benefits plans generally available, the Company will reimburse Executive for the cost to maintain her healthcare coverage.

3.3.2 <u>Expense Allowance.</u> The Company shall reimburse Executive for any reasonable travel, education, entertainment, or other expense incurred in furtherance of the Company's business and submitted to the Company for reimbursement with appropriate documentation. All expenses shall be reimbursed semi-monthly, together with salary.

3.3.3 <u>Stock Participation.</u> Executive shall be granted, as of the Effective Date, incentive stock options for _____ shares of the Company's Common Stock at the then current price per share, as determined by the Company's Board of Directors, subject to the terms and conditions of the Company's Incentive Stock Option Plan. Ownership of these options will vest as to twenty-five percent (25%) twelve (12) months from the Effective Date and as to the remainder in thirty-six (36) equal monthly increments thereafter. Executive shall be eligible for subsequent incentive stock option grants on an annual basis, as determined by the Company's Board of Directors in its discretion.

4. SEVERANCE COMPENSATION.

In the event Executive's employment by the Company is terminated for any reason other than Termination For Cause or Executive's Voluntary Termination, Executive or her estate shall be paid as severance compensation an amount equal to _____ months' salary, at her then current salary rate, in addition to and not in lieu of other benefits to which Executive may be entitled as set forth elsewhere in this Agreement.

5. VACATION. Initially, Executive shall accrue vacation on a monthly basis (at the rate of 1.25 days per month). Executive shall thereby be entitled to three (3) weeks of paid vacation for each year of employment. Beginning with her third (3rd) year of employment, Executive shall accrue vacation on a monthly basis (at the rate of 1.66 days per month) and shall thereby be entitled to four (4) weeks of paid vacation for each year of employment thereafter. Executive is ineligible to accrue vacation benefits while Executive is absent without pay including, but not limited to unpaid leaves of absence. The purpose of paid vacation is to provide time for recreation and relaxation. The Company encourages all of its employees to take accrued vacation each year. Accordingly, the maximum vacation time Executive will be permitted to accrue is thirty (30) days. Once this cap on the accrual of vacation has been reached, no additional vacation will accrue until Executive has reduced the balance of her unused vacation time accrued to less than thirty (30) days. Thereafter, vacation will accrue on a prospective basis as long as Executive's total accrual remains under the cap. The Company reserves the right to compensate Executive for earned, unused vacation time at any time in its sole discretion.

6. SICK LEAVE/PERSONAL BUSINESS. Executive shall accrue sick/personal business leave on a monthly basis (at the rate of .417 days per month). Executive shall thereby be entitled to five (5) days of paid sick/personal business leave for each year of employment, after Executive's first six (6) months of employment. The maximum sick/personal business leave Executive will be permitted to accrue is five (5) days. Once this cap on the accrual of sick/personal business leave has been reached, no additional sick/personal business leave will accrue until Executive has reduced the balance of her unused sick/personal business leave accrued to less than five (5) days. Thereafter, sick/personal business leave will accrue on a prospective basis as long as Executive's total accrual remains under the cap. Executive will not be paid for accrued but unused sick/personal business leave. If Executive is unable to work for more than five (5) days because of sickness, personal business, or total disability, Executive's accrued unused vacation time may be applied to such absence.

7. HOLIDAYS. Executive shall be entitled to take holidays off with pay during each calendar year consistent with the holiday schedule applicable to management employees of the Company.

8. COMPLIANCE WITH EMPLOYER'S RULES. Executive shall execute the Confidential Information and Invention Assignment Agreement attached hereto as Appendix 1 and will be expected to abide by all other Company rules and regulations. Executive may be required to sign an acknowledgment that she has read and understood such rules and regulations as set forth in a handbook distributed by the Company to all its employees. It is hereby understood that the Company's policies, procedures, rules, and regulations may be amended or changed at any time by the Company.

9. RETURN OF PROPERTY. Upon termination of this Agreement, Executive shall deliver all property (including files, keys, records, notes, lists, data, formulas, and equipment) that is in the Executive's possession or under the Executive's control which is the Company's property or related to the Company's business.

10. NOTICES. All notices required or permitted under this Agreement shall be in writing and shall be deemed delivered when delivered in person or deposited in the United States mail, postage paid, addressed as follows:

If to the Company: ****, Inc.

_____

_____

Fax: _____

Attn: _____

With a copy to (such copy not constituting notice):

_____, Esq.

_____

_____

Fax: _____

If to Executive: _____

Fax: _____

Attn: _____

Either party may change its or her address for notice from time to time by providing written notice in the manner set forth above.

11. JURY TRIAL WAIVER. The parties hereby irrevocably and knowingly waive to the fullest extent permitted by law any right to a trial by jury in any action or proceeding arising out of this Agreement. The parties agree that any such action or proceeding shall be tried before a court and not a jury. In the event the parties' waiver of a trial by jury is deemed invalid, the parties hereby agree that any action or claim arising out of any dispute in connection with this agreement, any rights, remedies, obligations, or duties hereunder, or the performance or enforcement hereof or thereof shall be determined by judicial reference.

12. EQUITABLE REMEDIES. Executive agrees that it would be impossible or inadequate to measure and calculate the Company's damages from any breach of the covenants set forth in Sections 8 and 9 herein. Accordingly, Executive agrees that if she breaches any of such Sections, the Company will have available, in addition to any other right or remedy available, the right to obtain an injunction from a court of competent jurisdiction restraining such breach or threatened breach and to specific performance of any such provision of this Agreement. Executive further agrees that no bond or other security shall be required in obtaining such equitable relief and hereby consents to the issuance of such injunction and to the ordering of specific performance.

13. CONSENT TO PERSONAL JURISDICTION. Executive hereby expressly consents to the personal jurisdiction of the state and federal courts located in [California] for any lawsuit filed there against her by the Company arising from or relating to this Agreement.

14. ATTORNEYS FEES. In the event litigation shall be instituted to enforce any provision of this Agreement, the prevailing party in such litigation shall be entitled to recover reasonable attorneys' fees and expenses incurred in such litigation, including on appeal, in addition to any other recovery to which such party may be legally entitled.

15. ENTIRE AGREEMENT. The terms set forth in this Agreement represent the entire understanding and agreement between the parties regarding compensation, employment, status and position.

16. SUCCESSORS AND ASSIGNS. This Agreement will be binding upon Executives heirs, executors, administrators, and other legal representatives and will be for the benefit of the Company, its successors, and its assigns.

17. AMENDMENT. No modification of or amendment to this Agreement, nor any waiver of any rights under this Agreement, will be effective unless in writing signed by the party to be charged. No oral statement to Executive may alter the terms of this Agreement. Any subsequent change or changes in Executive's duties, salary, or compensation will not affect the validity or scope of this Agreement.

18. SEVERABILITY. If any provision(s) of this Agreement shall be held to be invalid or unenforceable for any reason, the remaining provisions shall continue to be valid and enforceable. If a court finds that any provision of this Agreement is invalid or unenforceable, but that by limiting such provision it would become valid or enforceable, then such provision shall be deemed to be written, construed, and enforced as so limited.

19. NO WAIVER OF CONTRACTUAL RIGHT. The failure of either party to enforce any provision of this Agreement shall not be construed as a waiver or limitation of that party's right subsequently to enforce and compel strict compliance with every provision of this Agreement.

20. APPLICABLE LAW. This Agreement shall be governed by and constructed in accordance with laws of the State of California.

IN WITNESS WHEREOF, the parties have executed this agreement as of the date first above written.

The Company:
****, Inc.

By: _____
    [Name], [Title]

Executive:

_____
    [Name]

APPENDIX 1
CONFIDENTIAL INFORMATION AND
INVENTION ASSIGNMENT AGREEMENT

Form 13 F: Sales Representative Agreement

SALES REPRESENTATIVE AGREEMENT

THIS SALES REPRESENTATIVE AGREEMENT (this "Agreement") is made as of the ___ day of _____, 20___ (the "Effective Date"), by and between ****, Inc. a _____ corporation having its primary office at _____, ("Manufacturer") and _____, LLC a _____ limited liability company having its primary office at _____, ("Representative").

    1. **APPOINTMENT AND ACCEPTANCE.** Manufacturer hereby appoints Representative as its exclusive representative to sell Products (as defined in Section 3) to customers based in the Territory (as defined in Section 2). Representative accepts the appointment and agrees to sell and promote the sale of Manufacturer's Products in the Territory.

    2. **TERRITORY.** The Territory shall consist of the State of _____.

    3. **PRODUCTS AND SERVICES.** The Products shall consist of: All of Manufacturer's standard and custom Industrial Safety and Controls products as of the date of this Agreement, and any new standard or custom products that may be added to Manufacturer's Industrial Safety and Controls product line during the Term (as hereinafter defined) of this Agreement. The Products specifically do not include any of Manufacturer's _____ products, whether currently existing or developed in the future. Representative shall not, during the Term of this Agreement, sell, market, distribute, promote, or represent, whether directly or indirectly, in the Territory any products competitive with the Products.

    4. **COMMISSION.**

        (a) Manufacturer shall pay Representative a commission for services performed ("Normal Commission"), which shall be equal to ten percent (10%) of the "net invoice price" of all Products shipped into the Territory on all customer orders, regardless of whether the orders are transmitted to Manufacturer by Representative or received directly by Manufacturer from the customer. "Net invoice price" shall mean the total price at which an order is invoiced to the customer including any increase or decrease in the total amount of the order, but excluding shipping and insurance costs, sales, use or excise taxes, tariffs, duties, and export fees. In any case in which a price negotiation with the customer must occur to obtain an order from the customer, the percentage discount given to the customer off of Manufacturer's published price (or normal price) shall affect the percentage discount off Representative's Normal Commission as follows:

        (i) Customers may be offered up to and including a 10% discount from Manufacturer's published price without any reduction in Normal Commission.

        (ii) If Representative sells any Product at a price that is more than 10% below Manufacturer's published price, the Normal Commission for such Product shall be reduced by an amount equal to (A) the total percentage discount, less (B) 10%. For example, if Representative sells a Product at a 12% discount off of Manufacturer's published price, the Normal Commission for such Product shall be equal to 8% (i.e., 10% Normal Commission - (12% total discount − 10%)).

        (b) Manufacturer shall solicit and consider Representative's input in regard to any possible customer discount in which Representative's commission shall be affected before any quote or offer is made to the customer; however, all decisions regarding customer discounts shall be made by Manufacturer in its sole discretion.

(c) If Manufacturer uses distributors to resell Products in the Territory in accordance with this Agreement, Representative shall be compensated for Product sold by such distributors based upon monthly reports by Manufacturer. Manufacturer shall pay Representative 70% of Normal Commission (on the "net invoice price" invoiced to the distributor) on all Product sales by a distributor in any single year, up to the average of the Product sales by such distributor in the prior two (2) years. For all sales by a distributor in a given year in excess of the distributor's average Product sales during the prior two (2) years, Manufacturer shall pay Representative 100% of Normal Commission. For example, if the average annual Product sales by a distributor during the prior two (2) years were $5,000 per year, Representative would receive 70% of Normal Commission for all Product sales by such distributor in any year, up to $5,000 in Product sales. For any Products sales in excess of $5,000 in the same year, Representative would be paid 100% of Normal Commission.

5. COMPUTATION AND PAYMENT OF COMMISSION. Representative's commission is earned when an order is accepted by Manufacturer. "Order" shall mean any agreement to purchase Manufacturer's Products that requires shipment into the Territory, or that is subject to a "split commission" as defined below, and includes but is not limited to all follow-on orders for Products and all portions of any blanket order or requirements order that includes Products, regardless of when such portions are released or required. Commissions are due and payable on or before the 15th day of the month immediately following the month in which customer is invoiced. At the time of payment of commissions to Representative, Manufacturer shall send Representative a current commission statement listing all invoices on which commissions are being paid, and listing all unpaid commissions due Representative from any prior payment periods. Manufacturer shall deduct from any sums due Representative an amount equal to commissions paid or credited on sales of Products for which Manufacturer authorized a return or credit against the original invoice or for any part of an invoice if not paid within 120 days by the customer for any reason. If sums are received on any delinquent or previously classified "Uncollectible" sale, Manufacturer shall pay Representative a portion of such sums based upon the percentage commission applicable at the time of the original sale.

6. SPLIT COMMISSIONS. In the event that an order originates in the territory of one representative but is shipped into the territory of another representative, Manufacturer shall split the commission due using the following as a guide:

(a) One-third of the total commission shall be paid to the representative in the territory into which the shipment is made;

(b) One-third of the total commission shall be paid to the representative in the territory in which the purchase order is issued; and

(c) One-third of the total commission shall be paid to the representative in the territory in which the Product is designed or specified.

If Manufacturer does not have a representative in any one or more of the territories outlined in (a), (b), or (c) above, the total commission on any split order shall be shared equally between the remaining representatives.

7. ACCEPTANCE OF ORDERS; REPORTING; QUOTES. All orders are subject to acceptance or rejection by an authorized officer of Manufacturer at its main order entry office and to the approval of Manufacturer's credit department. Manufacturer shall advise Representative of any order rejected within five (5) days of rejection. Manufacturer shall be responsible for all credit risks and collections. If Manufacturer notifies a customer of its acceptance or rejection of an order, a copy of any written notification shall be transmitted to Representative. At least once every month, Manufacturer shall supply Representative with copies of all orders received, copies of all order acknowledgments, and copies of all correspondence relating to Product orders in the Territory, and Manufacturer shall send a tabulation at least every month of all invoices with purchase order numbers, quantity, price and commission due for Products sold in the Territory. Copies of quotations and related correspondence made by Manufacturer to customers in the Territory shall be faxed or mailed to Representative at the time the quotation is made. If Representative is authorized by Manufacturer in writing to generate quotes to customers, copies of each quotation shall be faxed or mailed to Manufacturer at the time the quotation is made.

8. TERMS OF SALE. All Product sales shall be at prices and upon written terms established by Manufacturer, and it shall have the right, from time to time, to establish, change, alter or amend prices and other terms and conditions of sale. Representative shall not accept orders in Manufacturer's name or make price quotations or delivery promises without Manufacturer's prior written approval.

9. REPRESENTATIVE RELATIONSHIP; CONDUCT OF BUSINESS; INDEMNITY.

(a) Representative shall promote the sale of and solicit orders for Products in the Territory and shall conduct all its business in its own name and in such a manner as it may see fit, pay all its own expenses including, without limitation, all commissions, salaries, bonuses, and expenses of employees and salespersons, and any and all taxes properly and lawfully associated with doing business as an independent contractor in the Territory. Representative is not an employee of Manufacturer for any purpose whatsoever, but is an independent contractor with limited authority. Representative shall have sole control of the manner and means of performing under this Agreement and shall be solely responsible for the acts of its employees and agents. Nothing in this Agreement shall be construed to constitute Representative as a partner, joint venturer, employee or general agent of Manufacturer, nor shall either party have any authority to bind the other in any respect.

(b) Representative shall abide by Manufacturer's terms and conditions pertaining to the sale of Products and shall communicate same to customers.

(c) Each party hereto (an "Indemnifying Party") shall indemnify the other party and hold it harmless from and against all liabilities, losses, costs, expenses, and damages, including court costs and reasonable attorneys' fees, incurred by such other party as a result of the Indemnifying Party's breach of any of its obligations, representations, or warranties contained in this Agreement.

(d) Manufacturer shall furnish Representative, at no expense to Representative, samples, catalogs, literature, demonstration equipment, and any other material necessary for the proper promotion and solicitation of orders for Products in the Territory. If for any reason Representative takes possession of Manufacturer's Products, reasonable use and care of the Products shall be exercised by Representative while they are in its possession, but the risk of loss or damage to the Products is to be covered by Manufacturer's insurance at Manufacturer's cost. Any literature which is not used or samples, demonstration equipment or other items belonging to Manufacturer shall be returned by Representative to Manufacturer at its request upon reasonable notice.

10. NON-SOLICITATION. Neither Manufacturer nor Representative shall, during the Term of this Agreement and for one (1) year after the expiration or termination of this Agreement for any reason, hire, employ, solicit for employment or contract with in any manner, any salespersons, employees or other individuals that were under contract or employed by the other party during the Term, unless otherwise agreed to by both Manufacturer and Representative in writing.

11. TERM AND TERMINATION.

(a) The initial term of this Agreement (the "Initial Term") shall commence on the Effective Date and shall continue for a period of one (1) year thereafter. Following the Initial Term, this Agreement shall automatically renew for successive one (1) year periods (each, a "Renewal Term"), unless either party provides the other with at least sixty (60) days prior written notice of its intent to terminate this Agreement at the end of the then-current Initial Term or Renewal Term. The Initial Term and any Renewal Terms are referred to herein collectively as the "Term."

(b) During the period of time from the date any notice of termination is given until the effective date of termination ("Notice Period"), both parties shall continue to fulfill their obligations under this Agreement. During the Notice Period, Manufacturer shall have the right to interview, evaluate, select, and train a replacement representative for the Territory. During the Notice Period, Representative shall have the right to interview, evaluate, select, and become trained by a replacement manufacturer.

(c) This Agreement may be terminated by either party upon a breach of any term or condition of this Agreement by the other party; *provided,* that the non-breaching party shall first give written notice to the breaching party, setting forth in reasonable detail the reason for such termination, and the non-breaching party shall then have fifteen (15) days in which to cure such breach to the other party's reasonable satisfaction.

(d) Following the Initial Term, either party may terminate this Agreement at any time any for any reason (with or without cause), upon at least sixty (60) days' prior written notice to the other party.

(e) Either party may terminate this Agreement upon thirty (30) days' written notice if the other party files or has filed against it a petition in bankruptcy (which is not dismissed within thirty (30) days after it is filed).

12. RIGHTS UPON TERMINATION. Upon the expiration or termination of this Agreement for any reason:

(a) Representative shall be paid commissions on all Product orders calling for shipment into the Territory which are dated or communicated to Manufacturer prior to the effective date of expiration or termination, or during any added period authorized by this Agreement as set forth below, regardless of when such orders are shipped or fulfilled.

(b) Representative shall be paid commissions on all Product orders dated or communicated to Manufacturer after the effective date of expiration or termination and during the added period described below, regardless of when such orders are shipped or fulfilled, as follows:

Length of time Agreement has been in effect	Added period for orders transmitted after effective date of expiration or termination
Less than two years	0
Two to four years	30 days added.
More than four, up to five years	60 days added.
Five or more, up to six years	90 days added.
More than six years	120 days added.

(c) Representative shall be paid its share of any split commissions to which it is entitled under Section 6 of this Agreement.

(d) Manufacturer shall continue to furnish Representative copies of orders and invoices and other documentation on all customer business in the Territory on which Representative has earned or is to be paid a commission under this Agreement until the date of the final commission payment to Representative.

(e) Both parties have the right to audit (and shall retain such right for a period of six (6) months after the effective date of termination of this Agreement) all documentation related to this Agreement. Any such audit shall be scheduled on a date and at a place to be mutually agreed upon by the parties, but not greater than thirty (30) days after written request, allowing the other party or its duly appointed representative to audit documents of the other party, to be limited to documents relating to Products sold, shipments, invoices, customer purchase orders, customer communications, customer payments, quotes, and commission on sales in the Territory.

13. PROPRIETARY RIGHTS; CONFIDENTIALITY.

(a) During the Term of this Agreement, Representative shall have the limited right to, and agrees that it shall, use Manufacturer's name and any applicable trademark, trade name and copyright of Manufacturer in any and all advertising and promotional material which it uses with respect to Products.

(b) Representative acknowledges and agrees that Manufacturer is the sole owner of Manufacturer's name and any trademark, trade name, patent, and copyright of Manufacturer; that Representative, by virtue of its use of Manufacturer's name and any trademark, trade name, patent, or copyright as permitted by the provisions of this Agreement, shall not acquire any ownership or registration rights therein; and that, upon the expiration or termination of this Agreement for any reason whatsoever, the right of Representative to use Manufacturer's name or any trademark, trade name, copyright, or patent of Manufacturer shall thereupon cease.

(c) Representative acknowledges that the information, observations, and data obtained by Representative in connection with the relationship contemplated by this Agreement and concerning the business or affairs of Manufacturer and its businesses and Products that are not generally available to the public ("Confidential Information") are the property of Manufacturer. Representative shall not disclose to any unauthorized person or use for its own account any Confidential Information without the prior written consent of Manufacturer unless, and in such case only to the extent that, such matters become generally known to and available for use by the public other than as a result of Representative's acts or omissions. In the event of a breach or threatened breach of this Section 13, Manufacturer may, in addition to other rights and remedies existing in its favor, apply to any court of competent jurisdiction for specific performance and/or injunctive or other relief in order to enforce, or prevent any violation of, the provisions hereof (without posting a bond or other security). Notwithstanding anything herein to the contrary, the provisions of this Section 13 shall survive and continue in full force and effect in accordance with their terms notwithstanding any termination or expiration of this Agreement.

14. ENTIRE AGREEMENT; MODIFICATION.
This Agreement contains the entire understanding of the parties with respect to the subject matter hereof, shall supersede any other oral or written agreements relating to such subject matter, and shall be binding upon the parties' respective successors and permitted assigns. It may not be modified in any way without the written consent of both parties.

15. SURVIVABILITY OF AGREEMENT.
If any provision of this Agreement is held to be invalid or unenforceable, such provision shall be considered deleted from this Agreement and shall not invalidate the remaining provisions of this Agreement.

16. GOVERNING LAW. This Agreement shall in all respects be governed by and construed in accordance with the laws of the State of _____, U.S.A., as if entirely performed therein, and regardless of conflict of laws principles.

17. WAIVER. The failure of either party to enforce, at any time or for any period of time, any provision of this Agreement shall not be construed as a waiver of such provision or of the right of such party thereafter to enforce such provision.

18. ASSIGNMENT. This Agreement shall be binding upon and shall inure to the benefit of Manufacturer and Representative and their successors and assigns; *provided*, however, that no assignment, whether voluntary or by operation of law, or delegation of performance, shall be made by Representative or any of its rights or obligations without the prior written consent of Manufacturer.

19. NOTICES. Unless otherwise agreed in writing, all notices, requests and other communications pursuant to this Agreement shall be addressed as follows:

If to Manufacturer: _____

Attention: _____

If to Representative: _____

Attention: _____

Any notice or other communication under this Agreement shall be deemed to be sufficiently given if made in writing addressed as above provided and delivered (i) by hand against receipt, (ii) by first class registered or certified mail, or (iii) nationally recognized overnight delivery service. Notice shall be deemed to have been given (i) at the time of receipt if hand delivered, (ii) at the expiration of five (5) business days after the date on which a notice by registered or certified mail has been posted, or (iii) on the first business day after delivery to a nationally recognized overnight delivery service.

20. HEADINGS. The headings and subheadings of this Agreement are provided for reference purposes only and are not part of this Agreement.

21. COUNTERPARTS. This Agreement may be executed in one or more counterparts, each of which shall be deemed to be an original, but all of which shall be considered one and the same instrument.

IN WITNESS WHEREOF, the parties hereto have caused this Agreement to be executed by their respective officers thereunto duly authorized as of the date first above written.

_____

Name: _____ Title: _____

_____

Name: _____ Title: _____

Form 13 G: Severance Agreement

Note: The following is a severance agreement for an employee of a company that had been issued stock in exchange for a promissory note and subject to the possibility of repurchase by the company. The agreement contains waiver language specific to California law that can be used for any state without the statutory references, or the statutory references can be replaced with citation to the appropriate laws in the state in which the agreement is made. The possibility that a founder may not always remain with the company is a good reason to put owner agreements in place and to make founders' shares subject to vesting or subject to repurchase.

SEVERANCE AGREEMENT

This Severance Agreement (the "Agreement") is entered into as of _____, 20___ by and between ****, INC., a _____ corporation (the "Company") and _____, an individual residing in the State of California ("Founder").

WHEREAS, pursuant to that certain Founder Stock Purchase Agreement entered between Founder and the Company as of the ___ day of _____, 20___ (the "Stock Purchase Agreement"), Founder purchased _____ shares of the Common Stock of the Company (the "Shares"), subject to a right of repurchase by the Company in the event of the termination of Founder's employment by the Company; and

WHEREAS, the Company terminated Founder' employment as of the _____ day of _____, 20___; and

WHEREAS, the Company's right to repurchase the Shares lapsed according to the vesting schedule provided in the Stock Purchase Agreement such that, as of the date of termination of Founder's employment by the Company, Founder had vested in, and the right of repurchase had lapsed with regard to, _____ shares of the Company's Common Stock (the "Vested Shares"), while _____ shares remain subject to the right of repurchase (the "Unvested Shares"); and

WHEREAS, the Company wishes to exercise its right of repurchase as to the Unvested Shares at a price per share of $_____, for a total price of $_____ (the "Repurchase Price"); and

WHEREAS, as consideration for his purchase of the Shares, Founder (1) gave to the Company a Promissory Note (the "Note"), payable on or before the _____ day of _____, 20___, in the amount of $_____, and (2) transferred to the Company certain technology owned by Founder and valued at $_____, as evidenced by a Technology Transfer Agreement executed concurrently with the Stock Purchase Agreement; and

WHEREAS, as of the date hereof, the date for repayment of the Note has passed without any payment from Founder to the Company, and the entire principal balance of $_____, plus interest, is now due,

NOW THEREFORE, Founder and the Company agree as follows:
1. <u>Repurchase of Unvested Shares</u>.
The Company hereby exercises its right to repurchase the Unvested Shares, and shall pay the Repurchase Price in accordance with Section 2 below. The Company's

records shall be revised to reflect the ownership by Founder of only the Vested Shares, and in recognition of the further consideration provided by Founder under Section 2 hereof, a share certificate shall be prepared and delivered to Founder representing the Vested Shares.

2.   Repurchase Price; Forgiveness of Debt.

(a) As payment by the Company of the Repurchase Price, the parties agree to cancel $_____ of the principal and accumulated interest due on the Note.

(b) In consideration of the general release by Founder under Section 3 of any and all claims he may have against the Company, and as a severance payment in connection with the termination of Founder, the Company further agrees to forgive Founder the remaining balance on the Note, in the principal amount of $_____, plus all interest accrued to the date hereof. The Note shall therefore be deemed fully cancelled, and the Company shall make no further claim for payment under it.

3.   Release; Waiver of [California Civil Code Section 1542].

(a) Founder hereby releases any and all claims he may have and agrees to hold the Company harmless in connection with, or in regard to, the Note, the Shares, or Founder' employment by the Company, including but not limited to any claims for unpaid salary, accrued but unpaid bonuses, vacation pay or benefits of any kind.

(b) Founder acknowledges that he may not now know fully the number or magnitude of any claims he may have against the Company, and that he may suffer some further loss or damage in some way connected with the subject matter of this Agreement, but which is unknown or unanticipated at this time. Yet Founder has taken these risks and possibilities into account and accepts that, nevertheless, this Agreement covers all claims which, although unknown at the time of the execution of this Agreement, may be discovered later. Founder understands and assumes these risks and expressly waives the provisions of [California Civil Code § 1542, which states:

A GENERAL RELEASE DOES NOT EXTEND TO CLAIMS WHICH THE CREDITOR DOES NOT KNOW OR SUSPECT TO EXIST IN HIS FAVOR AT THE TIME OF EXECUTING THE RELEASE, WHICH IF KNOWN BY HIM MUST HAVE MATERIALLY AFFECTED HIS SETTLEMENT WITH THE DEBTOR.]

Founder expressly waives any right to assert hereafter that any claim was excluded from this Agreement through ignorance, oversight, or error.

4.   Market Stand-Off.

Founder acknowledges that the market stand-off provisions regarding the Shares, described in the Stock Purchase Agreement, shall remain in effect as to the Vested Shares.

5.   Entire Agreement; No Oral Modification.

This Agreement supersedes all previous agreements between the parties, contains the whole of the Agreement between the parties, and may not be modified except in writing signed by both parties.

6.   Governing Law.

This Agreement shall be governed by and construed in accordance with the laws of the State of California.

7.   Counterparts.

This Agreement may be executed in two or more counterparts, each of which shall be deemed an original, but all of which shall constitute one agreement.

In Witness Whereof, the parties hereto have executed this Agreement as of the date first set forth above.

Company ****, Inc.   Founder

_____   _____

By: _____   _____

    _____, President   _____

                                                 [Print Name]

CHAPTER 14

Providing Equity Incentives
to Employees

14.1 Should Your Client Offer Employees
Ownership in the Company?

When a company is very closely held, there are a couple of items it should consider in connection with the issuance of stock to new shareholders. These items are described in this section.

1. Administrative Headaches.

The company will be required to give notice of shareholder meetings and consents to all shareholders (even where one shareholder owns a majority of the outstanding stock). Corporations are typically required to have at least one shareholder meeting annually for the election of directors and other business requiring shareholder approval (e.g., under Calif. Corp. Code, Section 600). Alternatively, shareholder actions can usually be taken by written consent. However, unless all of the shareholders are solicited in writing for their consent, the company may be required to give advance notice to all shareholders of the action approved by written consent before such action takes effect (e.g., under Calif. Corp. Code, Section 603).

2. Shareholder Agreements.

The company and its shareholders may wish to consider entering into a shareholder agreement to provide rights of first refusal to the company and remaining shareholders in the event of a proposed sale or transfer of the issued shares and to provide for buyout provisions in the event of a shareholder's death, bankruptcy, or other defined events. The obvious benefits of this type of agreement are that it gives the company the opportunity to maintain control over its ownership and provides some liquidity to the shareholders. A sample Shareholder Agreement is included in Chapter 9 (see Form 9 B).

3. Section 409A Rules on Deferred Compensation.

Much has been written on the enactment of Internal Revenue Code Section 409A and the significant challenges it creates for private companies wishing to award incentive stock options to employees, because of the possibility that such options may be deemed to have been issued with an exercise price below the fair market value at the time of grant. That is, they may be deemed to have been "discounted stock options," which constitute "deferred compensation" and have adverse tax consequences to the holder and impose a tax withholding obligation on the company. To avoid these results, it must be demonstrated that "fair market value" was determined in good faith at the time of issuance, using a "reasonable valuation" method. Three specified valuation methods will create a presumption of reasonableness in the determination of fair market value, and it is advisable that companies adopt one of these and consistently apply it, thereby putting the burden on the IRS to prove that both (i) the company's stock option prices were below fair market value, and (ii) the company's application of the presumptive method was "grossly unreasonable." The three methods can generally be described as:

- Independent appraisal;
- Illiquid start-up; and
- Binding formula.

Each of these methods will be presumed reasonable if consistently used for all of an employer's equity-based compensation arrangements. The valuation resulting from any of these presumptive methods will be considered to be fair market value and may only be rebutted by the Internal Revenue Service if the company's application of the method is found to be "grossly unreasonable."

1. **Independent Appraisal.** A valuation performed by a qualified independent appraiser using traditional appraisal methodologies, such as those applicable to an appraisal for an employee stock ownership plan (ESOP).
2. **Illiquid Start-Up.** A special presumption is provided for "illiquid stock of a start-up corporation." A start-up corporation is a corporation with no publicly traded stock that has conducted business for less than 10 years. A valuation of illiquid start-up stock will be considered reasonable if five requirements are satisfied:

(i) The valuation is evidenced by a written report;
(ii) The valuation takes into account the General Valuation Factors described below;
(iii) The valuation is performed by a person with significant knowledge and experience or training in performing similar valuations;
(iv) The stock being valued is not subject to any put or call right, other than the company's right of first refusal or right to repurchase stock of an employee (or other service provider) upon termination of service; and

(v) The company does not reasonably anticipate an IPO, sale, or change in control of the company within 12 months following the equity grant to which the valuation applies.

The General Valuation Factors specified in the regulations are:

(a) The value of tangible and intangible assets of the company;
(b) The present value of future cash flows;
(c) The public trading price or private sale price of comparable companies;
(d) Control premiums and discounts for lack of marketability;
(e) Whether the method is used for other purposes; and
(f) Whether all available information is taken into account in determining value.

Even if a valuation applies these factors, it will not be considered reasonable if it is more than 12 months old. In addition, significant events occurring before the 12-month anniversary will require the valuation to be updated. Examples of such events include the possibility of (or plans for) a future investment in the company by an outside investor, an initial public offering or sale of the company, resolution of material litigation, or the issuance of a patent.

3. **Binding Formula.** A valuation based on a formula used in a shareholder buy-sell agreement or similar binding agreement will be presumed reasonable if the formula price is used for all non-compensatory purposes requiring the valuation of the company's stock, such as regulatory filings, loan covenants, and sales of stock to third parties. This method will not be available if the stock may be transferred other than through operation of the buy-sell or similar arrangement to which the formula price applies.

Additional details available on the Internal Revenue Service website at http://www.irs.gov.

14.2 What Kinds of Equity Incentives Are Used by Companies?

There are two basic types of equity incentives used by start-up companies—stock options and restricted stock. Stock options come in two forms—incentive stock options and nonqualified stock options. These basic forms of incentives differ primarily in tax consequences to the recipient.

14.3 What Are Stock Options?

A stock option is a contract between the company and the recipient that gives the recipient, usually an employee, the right to pay a certain exercise price per share specified in the option grant agreement, and in exchange therefore to receive a certain number of shares of common stock. This right to "exercise" the option applies only to that portion of the stock subject to the option that has vested, and the underlying stock typically vests over a period of time—usually three or four years, in equal monthly or quarterly installments.

The two types of stock options most commonly used by emerging companies to incentivize employees, directors and consultants are incentive stock options (ISOs) and non-statutory stock options (NSOs, or nonqualified stock options). Section 14.8 provides a suggested form of stock option plan (Form 14 A) and related option grant and agreement contracts (Form 14 B), which is a plan designed to allow a company to grant both types of options, ISOs, and NSOs.

Many provisions regarding option grants are prescribed by statute in the U.S. Internal Revenue Code (the "Code").

The following is a summary of some important provisions regarding options and some tax consequences of exercising options. Please note that the company should seek tax advice in connection with any incentive plan, as should its employees. This summary covers only major issues; it does not address all the tax rules, and it should be noted that an individual's tax situation may differ greatly from the norm. Nor does this summary address state or foreign tax consequences, which also may be significant. Finally, this summary assumes optionees will pay cash to the company to exercise their options. Other rules apply if optionees may pay the exercise price in stock.

Many companies adopt stock option plans as part of their compensation packages because they recognize that maintaining a talented and diligent workforce is one of the principal requirements to being a strong competitor. Stock option plans allow employees and other valued individuals a way to acquire stock ownership in the corporation.

In designing a stock option program, a company needs to consider carefully how much stock it is willing to make available, who will be eligible to receive stock options, and how much the workforce is expected to expand. A common error is granting too many stock options too soon. In such cases, the company may be unable to grant options to employees in the future.

In most cases, a combination of ISO and NSO options is the best way to provide incentives for all valued contributors to a company. The company should consider its present and anticipated future needs carefully when adopting a plan. Counsel should help the company design a stock option plan that will meet its specific objectives.

14.4 What Are Incentive Stock Options or ISOs?

Incentive stock options (ISOs) are a common type of equity currency used by start-up companies.

1. Beneficial Tax Treatment for Option Holders.

The Code defines an ISO as "an option granted to an individual for any reason connected with his employment by a corporation, if granted by the employer corporation, or its parent or subsidiary corporation, to purchase stock of any of such corporations" (Code Section 422(b)). Thus, ISOs may be granted only to employees of the corporation. Note that the Code does not specify full-time employees, so any person who receives W-2 income should be eligible to receive an ISO.

Options may qualify as ISOs and thereby receive favorable tax treatment under the Code if they meet a strict set of eligibility requirements. Options that do not meet these requirements, either at the time of grant or before their exercise, are deemed NSOs (Code Section 421(b)).

ISOs are not treated as ordinary income taxable in the year of the grant, as are NSOs and outright stock issuances (Code Sections 63, 64; see also Code Section 83(a)). When an option is granted pursuant to an ISO plan, no income tax is assessed against the grantee in the year of the ISO grant or at the time he or she exercises the option and receives shares of stock in the corporation (Code Section 421(a)). Assuming the employee holds the stock purchased for the requisite holding period, generally one year, any gain from the sale will be taxed as long-term capital gain rather than as ordinary income. Long-term capital gain is preferable to ordinary income for purposes of federal income tax because the former is subject to the favorable maximum rate of 20 percent, whereas ordinary tax rates can be much higher (Code Sections 1, 1221, 1231). Note, however, that if the employee sells his or her stock within one year of the exercise of the ISO or within two years of the option grant, the gain will be treated as ordinary income to the employee.

2. Tax Effect on Corporation.

The corporation will be unable to deduct any amount for the grant of an option pursuant to an ISO plan (Code Section 421(a)). However, in the event that the grantee of an ISO fails to meet the holding period requirements discussed below, the corporation will be able to take a deduction in the year of exercise of the option equivalent to the income realized by the grantee (Code Section 421(b)). Otherwise, there is no deduction allowed with respect to the "spread" between the exercise price and the fair market value at the time of exercise.

3. Alternative Minimum Tax Considerations.

When an ISO is exercised, its holder may be required to pay alternative minimum tax (AMT) resulting from any difference between the exercise price of the option and the fair market value of the stock at the time of exercise. AMT liability can be substantial and can, in some cases, create an incentive for option holders to exercise options as soon as possible.

You should note as well that, based on AMT considerations, some option holders may prefer to exercise their options before they are fully vested. Form 14 A will permit a company to establish mechanisms to permit a so-called pre-vesting exercise, if desired.

4. Requirements for Treatment as ISO.

The requirements for a stock option grant to receive ISO treatment can be grouped into three categories: terms of grant, "disqualifying dispositions," and ceiling on exercise.

- **Terms of Grant.** There are several statutory guidelines specified in Code Section 422(b) that must be followed when granting ISOs:

  (a) The option must be granted pursuant to a plan that provides for the aggregate number of shares issuable under the plan and specifies which employees are eligible to receive them;

  (b) The plan must be approved by the stockholders of the granting corporation within twelve months before or after the date such plan is adopted;

  (c) The option must be granted within ten years from the date the plan was either adopted or approved by the stockholders, whichever is earlier;

  (d) The terms of the option must state that the option is not exercisable beyond ten years from the date the option is granted;

  (e) The price of the option cannot be less than the fair market value of the stock at the time the option is granted;

  (f) The terms of the option must prohibit the transfer of the option by the employee, other than by will or the laws of descent and distribution, and must state that it is exercisable only by the employee during his or her lifetime; and

  (g) At the time of the grant of the option, if the employee possesses stock that accounts for 10 percent or more of the total combined voting power of all classes of stock of the corporation, its parent, or its subsidiary, then the exercise price of the option must be at least 110 percent of the fair market value of the stock.

- **Disqualifying Disposition—Holding Period Requirement.** Stock received on exercise of an ISO will receive favorable ISO tax treatment as long as the stock has been held until the later of either (i) the date two years after the grant of the ISO or (ii) the date one year after exercise of the ISO.

  Stock otherwise qualifying for ISO treatment will lose its status as ISO stock if the holder breaches the holding period requirement (Code Section 421(b)). In other words, if a grantee transfers shares of stock received pursuant to exercise of an ISO within either two years of the grant, or one year after the stock was purchased on exercise of the ISO, he or she has effected a disqualifying disposition of the stock, which precludes favorable tax treatment for stock acquired pursuant to an ISO. Instead, the amount realized by the employee from the disqualifying disposition will be taxed as ordinary income in the year it occurred. The corporation may take a corresponding deduction in the year the employee makes the disqualifying disposition (Code Section 421(b)).

  Conversely, if all requirements for a qualifying ISO are met and the grantee makes no disqualifying disposition, there will be no tax liability to the grantee until he or she sells the stock. Again, any gain realized by the grantee upon the disposition of the stock will be taxed at the more favorable long-term capital gains rate, and there will be no deduction for the employer corporation.

- **Ceiling on Exercise.** There is a $100,000 per year limitation per employee on ISO treatment of stock received on exercise of options (Code § 422(d)). When options become or are exercisable during a given tax year, only the first $100,000 worth of stock received on exercise of options may be treated as ISO stock for tax purposes. The excess over $100,000 will be treated as stock received on exercise of NSOs. The rule is applied to multiple option grants by disqualifying them in the order that they were granted. The fair market value of the stock is determined as of the time the option was granted, and options do not become disqualified solely by reason of the appreciation in value of the underlying stock after the option is granted (Code § 422(c)).

  For example, if an employee holds options to buy 50,000 shares of stock at $5.00 per share, and if the entire option is exercisable during the current year, then only 20,000 shares qualify for ISO treatment. The remaining 30,000 shares will be treated as NSO stock, even if the option holder exercises the option or a portion thereof in a subsequent year. It does not matter when the option actually is exercised, only when and to what extent it is exercisable.

14.5 What Is a Nonqualified Stock Option?

Nonqualified stock options (or NSOs) are often used when ISOs are unavailable, such as when the grantee is not an employee.

1. Definition and Typical Provisions.

Non-statutory stock options do not receive the favorable tax treatment of ISOs. NSOs are still highly useful, however, for attracting and keeping talented individuals because they do not have to meet specific Code requirements. NSOs have no statutorily defined holding period, term guidelines, or ceilings on exercise; and they may be granted to nonemployee individuals valuable to the corporation, such as outside directors and consultants.

Because the Code does not specify a holding period or other guidelines that the corporation and grantee must follow, it is possible for a grantee to exercise the option and then sell the underlying shares immediately. This would, however, run contrary to the guiding principle behind stock option plans: to encourage employees and other valued contributors to the corporation to align their interests with those of the corporation by turning such people into shareholders. Thus, NSO plans often contain repurchase provisions designed to encourage the employee to stay with the employer (or continue providing services to the corporation) for a number of years or lose some of the upside in the stock.

A common practice is to include a repurchase provision in NSO grants to persons (directors and consultants) whose positions involve service to the corporation over a term of several years. The repurchase provision gives the corporation the right, after exercise of the NSOs, to buy back some or all of the shares purchased pursuant to the NSO. Such repurchase rights generally lapse over time so long as the optionee continues in the employment of, or providing services to, the corporation. Another common type of repurchase right is one permitting the corporation to repurchase all shares on the employee's or service provider's termination of employment or termination of a service provider contract. In either case, once the repurchase right has lapsed, the optionee may freely transfer his or her rights in the stock (Code Section 83(c)).

2. Tax Consequences of NSOs.

- **Ordinary Income.** The grantee of an NSO may be taxed at the time of grant and upon exercise of the option. At the time of grant, the grantee will have ordinary income based on the value of the option. If the option exercise price is at or close to the fair market value of the underlying stock at the time of the option grant, the option will not be considered to have value. However, if the exercise price is a substantial discount from the stock's fair market value at the time of grant, the option will have an independent value, taxable to the grantee and deductible by the corporation. The amount of income will depend upon the amount of the discount from the stock's fair market value at the time of the grant, as well as upon the various restrictions that may apply to the stock received upon exercise (e.g., repurchase rights as discussed above). Generally, lawyers encourage companies to issue NSOs with exercise prices equal to fair market value on the date of grant.

  The grantee of an NSO will be taxed again at the time of exercise of the NSO, in the event that the stock has appreciated between the time of the NSO grant and the time of exercise, or under any circumstance where the exercise price is less than fair market value at the time the option is exercised. The taxable income is included in the grantee's gross income and is subject to federal taxation in the year that the grantee acquires the stock (i.e., in the year of exercise). Taxable income is calculated by subtracting the exercise price from the fair market value of the stock at the time the stock was purchased (Code Section 83(a)).

- **Deferral of Tax and Section 83(b).** When stock is acquired subject to vesting provisions such as repurchase rights in the corporation if the employee leaves, the tax otherwise payable upon exercise of an NSO is deferred until the repurchase rights lapse. In a corporation whose stock is expected to appreciate rapidly, this deferral of tax would result in a greatly increased tax due at the time the restriction lapses. The reason is that the taxable income is calculated as the difference between the exercise price and the stock's fair market value at the time the restriction lapses. Under these circumstances, the employee may exercise an election to be taxed at the time he or she acquires the stock as provided in Code Section 83(b), hence it is called an "83(b) election." If the employee makes an 83(b) election, the taxable income realized at the time the stock is acquired is the last income event until the employee sells the stock. Thus, the employee holding stock for the applicable long-term capital gain holding period would convert any appreciation occurring after exercise and up to the time the restriction lapses from ordinary income to long-term capital gain. Option holders must file Section 83(b) elections with the Internal Revue Service within thirty days of the date the option holder has notified the corporation in writing that he or she is exercising options. Failure to take advantage of the Section 83(b) election is a common mistake among shareholders in emerging companies.

14.6 How Much Equity Should Be Granted to an Early Executive Hire?

Clients often ask counsel to comment on an appropriate percentage ownership for an executive hire, and you may serve your client well to volunteer such information to help ensure they are able to hire talented executives without giving up too much of the company. While there are ranges that can be helpful as points of reference, the amount of equity that a person can command as a condition of employment is a very fact-specific question that depends on how much risk the prospective employee is being asked to take, as well as on the individual's background. In determining the level of risk, relevant considerations include whether the company has been venture funded, whether the prospective employee is being asked to forgo salary in exchange for equity, how far along the company is in validating its product, service, or technology (i.e., are there any customers or partners lined up?), and whether the management team is largely in place.

As is always the case in a hiring situation, the individual's credentials, and the resultant supply and demand forces for such individual's services, are major factors in determining appropriate compensation. In addition, the nature of the company and its hiring needs weigh heavily in the equation, because a technology company may pay more in equity for a technology officer than for a marketing person, whereas a consumer products company may be the other way around. Finally, the size of the upside opportunity is also relevant; the higher the potential for the company, the less the company may ultimately be able to get away with paying the individual in equity.

While these and other factors make it difficult to generalize about equity participation levels, there are certain ranges that are recognized as "market": CEO, 6 to 10 percent; VP Technology, 3 to 6 percent; VP Marketing, 1 to 3 percent; VP Business Development, 1 to 3 percent; and VP Finance and Operations, 0.5 to 2 percent. These numbers are determined as of the closing of the first VC round and are not subject to dilution by the grant of options out of the employee pool (i.e., if there is a 20 percent employee pool, a chief technology officer (CTO) receiving 5 percent would be granted options or receive restricted stock for 25 percent of the shares in the employee pool).

If offers are being extended to prospective hires before VC funding but after the founders are established, the company might offer one of these key persons an amount that after the first round, assuming for this purpose a certain level of dilution (i.e., 50 percent), would bring the person into the appropriate range. For example, the VP Business Development might be offered 6 percent before the first round, which would result in 3 percent after the first round. This practice brings up a matter that should be pointed out to your client, which is that whatever percentage the new hire starts off with, it will be diluted over time and should not be expressed in a way that could give rise to an argument that the new hire's ownership has antidilution protection.

14.7 How Should Stock Be Valued for Purposes of Equity Incentives?

As briefly discussed above, with the enactment of Internal Revenue Code Section 409A, privately held companies face new challenges in connection with the pricing of stock options. Stock options that are awarded with an exercise price that is below the fair market value of the underlying stock as of the grant date are considered discounted stock options and constitute deferred compensation under the new rules, typically resulting in adverse tax consequences to the option holder and responsibility for tax withholding for the company that issues them. Companies issuing stock options should take care to adopt one of the presumptively reasonable valuation methods described above in Section 14.1 to value the underlying stock and set the exercise price of its stock options accordingly. Once a valuation method is adopted, it should be consistently applied to all options pricing determinations.

Fair market value is generally defined as the price at which a willing buyer sells to a willing seller, neither party being under compulsion to buy or sell, and both having reasonable knowledge of relevant facts (a hypothetical, arms-length purchase price for cash between two parties with equal information under ordinary circumstances). Of course, if there is a public market for a security, trading prices determine fair market value. For privately held companies, three other methods for valuing noncash property are

- Cost analysis (net asset value) approach
- Income analysis approach
- Market analysis approach

All three of these approaches are incorporated within the eight-point guidelines of Rev. Rul. 59-60. This rule originally was promulgated by the IRS to assist taxpayers in determining the fair market value of closely held companies or blocks of securities for estate and gift tax purposes, and it has become the standard within the business valuation industry.

14.8 Do Securities Laws Apply?

The issuance of stock options is governed by state and federal securities laws, regardless of whether a company is publicly, or privately, held. The Securities Act of 1933, as amended, prohibits the offer or sale of any security unless it is registered with the Securities and Exchange Commission or is exempt from registration requirements. State securities laws ("Blue Sky Laws") apply in each state in which option grantees reside.

The issuance of options to employees and service providers located in the U.S. is exempt from the registration requirements of the Securities Act pursuant to Rule 701 under the Securities Act (available to issuers that are not subject to the reporting requirements of Section 13 or 15(d) of the Securities Exchange Act of 1934, i.e., non-public issuers), provided such issuance is made pursuant to a written stock purchase plan or stock option plan established by the issuer, its parents, majority-owned subsidiaries of the issuer, or majority-owned subsidiaries of the parents. The rule requires that such plans be established for the benefit of employees, directors, officers, or consultants and advisors, who must be natural persons who provide services to the issuer, its parents, majority-owned subsidiaries of the issuer, or majority-owned subsidiaries of the parents, at the time of the offer or sale. The maximum aggregate value of the shares being offered or sold in a 12-month period under Rule 701 is the greatest of $1,000,000, or 15% of the total assets of the issuer, or 15% of the outstanding amount of the class of securities being offered and sold in reliance on Rule 701. Sales of securities underlying options are counted as sales as of the date of the option grant, and such options are valued at the exercise price. Issuers are required to provide "adequate" disclosure to grantees to satisfy the antifraud provisions of the U.S. federal securities laws (at a minimum, such disclosure should include the company's financial statements and a copy of the Plan).

State securities laws also typically provide exemptions for the issuance of options to employees, but many have limitations and notice filing requirements. Additional Blue Sky Law requirements may require:

1. That the Plan receive shareholder approval within 12 months of adoption;
2. Provision for disclosure of financial statements to securities holders at least annually;
3. Purchase price of at least 85% of fair value at the time of grant, except in the case of a 10% or more shareholder whose purchase price must be at least 100% of fair value;
4. Non-transferability;

5. Adjustment in the case of stock split, stock dividend, etc.;

6. Plan termination date not more than 10 years from adoption; and

7. Standard voting rights.

14.9 Sample Documents and Checklists.

This section includes the following forms:

- Stock Option Plan (Form 14 A)
- Stock Option Grant and Stock Option Agreement (Form 14 B)

Form 14 A: Stock Option Plan

[****], INC.
20___ STOCK OPTION PLAN

1. Purposes of the Plan. The purposes of this Stock Option and Stock Issuance Plan are to attract and retain the best available personnel for positions of substantial responsibility, to provide additional incentive to Employees, Directors and Consultants and to promote the success of the Company's business. Options granted under the Plan may be Incentive Stock Options or Nonstatutory Stock Options, as determined by the Administrator at the time of grant. Stock Purchase Rights may also be granted under the Plan.

2. Definitions. As used herein, the following definitions shall apply:

(a) "Administrator" means the Board or any of its Committees as shall be administering the Plan in accordance with Section 4 hereof.

(b) "Applicable Laws" means the requirements relating to the administration of stock option plans under U.S. state corporate laws, U.S. federal and state securities laws, the Code, any stock exchange or quotation system on which the Common Stock is listed or quoted and the applicable laws of any other country or jurisdiction where Options or Stock Purchase Rights are granted under the Plan.

(c) "Board" means the Board of Directors of the Company.

(d) "Code" means the Internal Revenue Code of 1986, as amended.

(e) "Committee" means a committee of Directors appointed by the Board in accordance with Section 4 hereof.

(f) "Common Stock" means the Common Stock of the Company.

(g) "Company" means [****], Inc., a [Delaware] corporation.

(h) "Consultant" means any person who is engaged by the Company or any Parent or Subsidiary to render consulting or advisory services to such entity.

(i) "Director" means a member of the Board of Directors of the Company.

(j) "Disability" means total and permanent disability as defined in Section 22(e)(3) of the Code.

(k) "Employee" means any person, including Officers and Directors, employed by the Company or any Parent or Subsidiary of the Company. A Service Provider shall not cease to be an Employee in the case of (i) any leave of absence approved by the Company or (ii) transfers between locations of the Company or between the Company, its Parent, any Subsidiary, or any successor. For purposes of Incentive Stock Options, no such leave may exceed ninety (90) days, unless reemployment upon expiration of such leave is guaranteed by statute or contract. If reemployment upon expiration of a leave of absence approved by the Company is not so guaranteed, on the 181st day of such leave any Incentive Stock Option held by the Optionee shall cease to be treated as an Incentive Stock Option and shall be treated for tax purposes as a Nonstatutory Stock Option. Neither service as a Director nor payment of a director's fee by the Company shall be sufficient to constitute "employment" by the Company.

(l) "Exchange Act" means the Securities Exchange Act of 1934, as amended.

(m) "Fair Market Value" means, as of any date, the value of Common Stock determined as follows:

(i) If the Common Stock is listed on any established stock exchange or a national market system, including without limitation the Nasdaq National Market or The Nasdaq SmallCap Market of The Nasdaq Stock Market, its Fair Market Value

741

shall be the closing sales price for such stock (or the closing bid, if no sales were reported) as quoted on such exchange or system for the last market trading day prior to the time of determination, as reported in The Wall Street Journal or such other source as the Administrator deems reliable;

(ii) If the Common Stock is regularly quoted by a recognized securities dealer but selling prices are not reported, its Fair Market Value shall be the mean between the high bid and low asked prices for the Common Stock on the last market trading day prior to the day of determination; or

(iii) In the absence of an established market for the Common Stock, the Fair Market Value thereof shall be determined in good faith by the Administrator.

(n) "Incentive Stock Option" means an Option intended to qualify as an incentive stock option within the meaning of Section 422 of the Code.

(o) "Nonstatutory Stock Option" means an Option not intended to qualify as an Incentive Stock Option.

(p) "Officer" means a person who is an officer of the Company within the meaning of Section 16 of the Exchange Act and the rules and regulations promulgated thereunder.

(q) "Option" means a stock option granted pursuant to the Plan.

(r) "Option Agreement" means a written or electronic agreement between the Company and an Optionee evidencing the terms and conditions of an individual Option grant. The Option Agreement is subject to the terms and conditions of the Plan.

(s) "Option Exchange Program" means a program whereby outstanding Options are exchanged for Options with a lower exercise price.

(t) "Optioned Stock" means the Common Stock subject to an Option or a Stock Purchase Right.

(u) "Optionee" means the holder of an outstanding Option or Stock Purchase Right granted under the Plan.

(v) "Parent" means a "parent corporation," whether now or hereafter existing, as defined in Section 424(e) of the Code.

(w) "Plan" means this 20___ Stock Option Plan.

(x) "Restricted Stock" means shares of Common Stock acquired pursuant to a grant of a Stock Purchase Right under Section 11 below.

(y) "Service Provider" means an Employee, Director, or Consultant.

(z) "Share" means a share of the Common Stock, as adjusted in accordance with Section 12 below.

(aa)"Stock Purchase Right" means a right to purchase Common Stock pursuant to Section 11 below.

(bb)"Subsidiary" means a "subsidiary corporation," whether now or hereafter existing, as defined in Section 424(f) of the Code.

3.   Stock Subject to the Plan. Subject to the provisions of Section 12 of the Plan, the maximum aggregate number of Shares which may be subject to option and sold under the Plan is _____ Shares. The Shares may be authorized but unissued, or reacquired Common Stock.

If an Option or Stock Purchase Right expires or becomes unexercisable without having been exercised in full, or is surrendered pursuant to an Option Exchange Program, the unpurchased Shares which were subject thereto shall become available for future grant or sale under the Plan (unless the Plan has terminated). However, Shares that have actually been issued under the Plan, upon exercise of either an Option or Stock Purchase Right, shall not be returned to the Plan and shall not become available for future distribution under the Plan, except that if Shares of Restricted Stock are repurchased by the Company at their original purchase price, such Shares shall become available for future grant under the Plan.

4. Administration of the Plan.

(a) Administrator. The Plan shall be administered by the Board or a Committee appointed by the Board, which Committee shall be constituted to comply with Applicable Laws.

(b) Powers of the Administrator. Subject to the provisions of the Plan and, in the case of a Committee, the specific duties delegated by the Board to such Committee, and subject to the approval of any relevant authorities, the Administrator shall have the authority in its discretion:

(i) To determine the Fair Market Value;

(ii) To select the Service Providers to whom Options and Stock Purchase Rights may from time to time be granted hereunder;

(iii) To determine the number of Shares to be covered by each such award granted hereunder;

(iv) To approve forms of agreement for use under the Plan;

(v) To determine the terms and conditions, of any Option or Stock Purchase Right granted hereunder. Such terms and conditions include, but are not limited to, the exercise price, the time or times when Options or Stock Purchase Rights may be exercised (which may be based on performance criteria), any vesting acceleration or waiver of forfeiture restrictions, and any restriction or limitation regarding any Option or Stock Purchase Right or the Common Stock relating thereto, based in each case on such factors as the Administrator, in its sole discretion, shall determine;

(vi) To determine whether and under what circumstances an Option may be settled in cash under subsection 9(e) instead of Common Stock;

(vii) To reduce the exercise price of any Option to the then current Fair Market Value if the Fair Market Value of the Common Stock covered by such Option has declined since the date the Option was granted;

(viii) To initiate an Option Exchange Program;

(ix) To prescribe, amend, and rescind rules and regulations relating to the Plan, including rules and regulations relating to sub-plans established for the purpose of qualifying for preferred tax treatment under foreign tax laws;

(x) To allow Optionees to satisfy withholding tax obligations by electing to have the Company withhold from the Shares to be issued upon exercise of an Option or Stock Purchase Right that number of Shares having a Fair Market Value equal to the amount required to be withheld. The Fair Market Value of the Shares to be withheld shall be determined on the date that the amount of tax to be withheld is to be determined. All elections by Optionees to have Shares withheld for this purpose shall be made in such form and under such conditions as the Administrator may deem necessary or advisable; and

(xi) To construe and interpret the terms of the Plan and awards granted pursuant to the Plan.

(c) Effect of Administrator's Decision. All decisions, determinations, and interpretations of the Administrator shall be final and binding on all Optionees.

5. Eligibility.

(a) Nonstatutory Stock Options and Stock Purchase Rights may be granted to Service Providers. Incentive Stock Options may be granted only to Employees.

(b) Each Option shall be designated in the Option Agreement as either an Incentive Stock Option or a Nonstatutory Stock Option. However, notwithstanding such designation, to the extent that the aggregate Fair Market Value of the Shares with respect to which Incentive Stock Options are exercisable for the first time by the Optionee during any calendar year (under all plans of the Company and any Parent or Subsidiary) exceeds One Hundred Thousand Dollars ($100,000), such Options shall be treated as Nonstatutory Stock Options. For purposes of this Section 5(b), Incentive Stock Options shall be taken into account in the order in which they were granted. The Fair Market Value of the Shares shall be determined as of the time the Option with respect to such Shares is granted.

(c) Neither the Plan nor any Option or Stock Purchase Right shall confer upon any Optionee any right with respect to continuing the Optionee's relationship as a Service Provider with the Company, nor shall it interfere in any way with his or her right or the Company's right to terminate such relationship at any time, with or without cause.

6.   Term of Plan. The Plan shall become effective upon its adoption by the Board. It shall continue in effect for a term of ten (10) years unless sooner terminated under Section 14 of the Plan.

7.   Term of Option. The term of each Option shall be stated in the Option Agreement; provided, however, that the term shall be no more than ten (10) years from the date of grant thereof. In the case of an Incentive Stock Option granted to an Optionee who, at the time the Option is granted, owns stock representing more than ten percent (10%) of the voting power of all classes of stock of the Company or any Parent or Subsidiary, the term of the Option shall be five (5) years from the date of grant or such shorter term as may be provided in the Option Agreement.

8.   Option Exercise Price and Consideration.

(a) The per share exercise price for the Shares to be issued upon exercise of an Option shall be such price as is determined by the Administrator, but shall be subject to the following:

(i) In the case of an Incentive Stock Option:

(A) Granted to an Employee who, at the time of grant of such Option, owns stock representing more than ten percent (10%) of the voting power of all classes of stock of the Company or any Parent or Subsidiary, the exercise price shall be no less than 110% of the Fair Market Value per Share on the date of grant.

(B) Granted to any other Employee, the per Share exercise price shall be no less than 100% of the Fair Market Value per Share on the date of grant.

(ii) In the case of a Nonstatutory Stock Option:

(A) Granted to a Service Provider who, at the time of grant of such Option, owns stock representing more than ten percent (10%) of the voting power of all classes of stock of the Company or any Parent or Subsidiary, the exercise price shall be no less than 110% of the Fair Market Value per Share on the date of grant.

(B) Granted to any other Service Provider, the per Share exercise price shall be no less than 85% of the Fair Market Value per Share on the date of grant.

(iii) Notwithstanding the foregoing, Options may be granted with a per Share exercise price other than as required above pursuant to a merger or other corporate transaction.

(b) The consideration to be paid for the Shares to be issued upon exercise of an Option, including the method of payment, shall be determined by the Administrator (and, in the case of an Incentive Stock Option, shall be determined at the time of grant). Such consideration may consist of (1) cash, (2) check, (3) promissory note, (4) other Shares which (x) in the case of Shares acquired upon exercise of an Option, have been owned by the Optionee for more than six months on the date of surrender, and (y) have a Fair Market Value on the date of surrender equal to the aggregate exercise price of the Shares as to which such Option shall be exercised, (5) consideration received by the Company under a cashless exercise program implemented by the Company in connection with the Plan, or (6) any combination of the foregoing methods of payment. In making its determination as to the type of consideration to accept, the Administrator shall consider if acceptance of such consideration may be reasonably expected to benefit the Company.

9.   Exercise of Option.

(a) Procedure for Exercise; Rights as a Shareholder. Any Option granted hereunder shall be exercisable according to the terms hereof at such times and under such conditions as determined by the Administrator and set forth in the Option Agreement. Except in the case of Options granted to Officers, Directors, and Consultants, Options shall become exercisable at a rate of no less than 20% per year over five (5) years from the date the Options are granted. Unless the Administrator provides otherwise, vesting of Options granted hereunder to Officers and Directors shall be tolled during any unpaid leave of absence. An Option may not be exercised for a fraction of a Share.

An Option shall be deemed exercised when the Company receives: (i) written or electronic notice of exercise (in accordance with the Option Agreement) from the person entitled to exercise the Option, and (ii) full payment for the Shares with respect to which the Option is exercised. Full payment may consist of any consideration and method of payment authorized by the Administrator and permitted by the Option Agreement and the Plan. Shares issued upon exercise of an Option shall be issued in the name of the Optionee or, if requested by the Optionee, in the name of the Optionee and his or her spouse. Until the Shares are issued (as evidenced by the appropriate entry on the books of the Company or of a duly authorized transfer agent of the Company), no right to vote or receive dividends or any other rights as a shareholder shall exist with respect to the Shares, notwithstanding the exercise of the Option. The Company shall issue (or cause to be issued) such Shares promptly after the Option is exercised. No adjustment will be made for a dividend or other right for which the record date is prior to the date the Shares are issued, except as provided in Section 12 of the Plan.

Exercise of an Option in any manner shall result in a decrease in the number of Shares thereafter available, both for purposes of the Plan and for sale under the Option, by the number of Shares as to which the Option is exercised.

(b) Termination of Relationship as a Service Provider. If an Optionee ceases to be a Service Provider, such Optionee may exercise his or her Option within such period of time as is specified in the Option Agreement (of at least thirty (30) days) to the extent that the Option is vested on the date of termination (but in no event later than the expiration of the term of the Option as set forth in the Option Agreement). In the absence of a specified time in the Option Agreement, the Option shall remain exercisable for three (3) months following the Optionee's termination. If, on the date of termination, the Optionee is not vested as to his or her entire Option, the Shares covered by the unvested portion of the Option shall revert to the Plan. If, after termination, the Optionee does not exercise his or her Option within the time specified by the Administrator, the Option shall terminate, and the Shares covered by such Option shall revert to the Plan.

(c) Disability of Optionee. If an Optionee ceases to be a Service Provider as a result of the Optionee's Disability, the Optionee may exercise his or her Option within such period of time as is specified in the Option Agreement (of at least six (6) months) to the extent the Option is vested on the date of termination (but in no event later than the expiration of the term of such Option as set forth in the Option Agreement). In the absence of a specified time in the Option Agreement, the Option shall remain exercisable for twelve (12) months following the Optionee's termination. If, on the date of termination, the Optionee is not vested as to his or her entire Option, the Shares covered by the unvested portion of the Option shall revert to the Plan. If, after termination, the Optionee does not exercise his or her Option within the time speci-fied herein, the Option shall terminate, and the Shares covered by such Option shall revert to the Plan.

(d) Death of Optionee. If an Optionee dies while a Service Provider, the Option may be exercised within such period of time as is specified in the Option Agreement (of at least six (6) months) to the extent that the Option is vested on the date of death (but in no event later than the expiration of the term of such Option as set forth in the Option Agreement) by the Optionee's estate or by a person who acquires the right to exercise the Option by bequest or inheritance. In the absence of a specified time in the Option Agreement, the Option shall remain exercisable for twelve (12) months following the Optionee's termination. If, at the time of death, the Optionee is not vested as to the entire Option, the Shares covered by the unvested portion of the Option shall immediately revert to the Plan. If the Option is not so exercised within the time specified herein, the Option shall terminate, and the Shares covered by such Option shall revert to the Plan.

(e) Buyout Provisions. The Administrator may at any time offer to buy out for a payment in cash or Shares, an Option previously granted, based on such terms and conditions as the Administrator shall establish and communicate to the Optionee at the time that such offer is made.

10. Non-Transferability of Options and Stock Purchase Rights. The Options and Stock Purchase Rights may not be sold, pledged, assigned, hypothecated, trans-ferred, or disposed of in any manner other than by will or by the laws of descent or distribution and may be exercised, during the lifetime of the Optionee, only by the Optionee.

11. Stock Purchase Rights.

(a) Rights to Purchase. Stock Purchase Rights may be issued either alone, in addition to, or in tandem with other awards granted under the Plan and/or cash awards made outside of the Plan. After the Administrator determines that it will offer Stock Purchase Rights under the Plan, it shall advise the offeree in writing or elec-tronically of the terms, conditions and restrictions related to the offer, including the number of Shares that such person shall be entitled to purchase, the price to be paid, and the time within which such person must accept such offer. The terms of the offer shall comply in all respects with Section 260.140.42 of Title 10 of the California Code of Regulations. The offer shall be accepted by execution of a Restricted Stock purchase agreement in the form determined by the Administrator.

(b) Repurchase Option. Unless the Administrator determines otherwise, the Restricted Stock purchase agreement shall grant the Company a repurchase option exercisable upon the voluntary or involuntary termination of the purchaser's service with the Company for any reason (including death or disability). The purchase price for Shares repurchased pursuant to the Restricted Stock purchase agreement shall be the original price paid by the purchaser and may be paid by cancellation of any indebtedness of the purchaser to the Company. The repurchase option shall lapse at such rate as the Administrator may determine. Except with respect to Shares pur-chased by Officers, Directors and Consultants, the repurchase option shall in no case lapse at a rate of less than 20% per year over five (5) years from the date of purchase.

(c) Other Provisions. The Restricted Stock purchase agreement shall contain such other terms, provisions and conditions not inconsistent with the Plan as may be determined by the Administrator in its sole discretion.

(d) Rights as a Shareholder. Once the Stock Purchase Right is exercised, the purchaser shall have rights equivalent to those of a shareholder and shall be a shareholder when his or her purchase is entered upon the records of the duly authorized transfer agent of the Company. No adjustment shall be made for a dividend or other right for which the record date is prior to the date the Stock Purchase Right is exercised, except as provided in Section 12 of the Plan.

12. Adjustments Upon Changes in Capitalization, Merger, or Asset Sale.

(a) Changes in Capitalization. Subject to any required action by the shareholders of the Company, the number of shares of Common Stock covered by each outstanding Option or Stock Purchase Right, and the number of shares of Common Stock which have been authorized for issuance under the Plan but as to which no Options or Stock Purchase Rights have yet been granted or which have been returned to the Plan upon cancellation or expiration of an Option or Stock Purchase Right, as well as the price per share of Common Stock covered by each such outstanding Option or Stock Purchase Right, shall be proportionately adjusted for any increase or decrease in the number of issued shares of Common Stock resulting from a stock split, reverse stock split, stock dividend, combination or reclassification of the Common Stock, or any other increase or decrease in the number of issued shares of Common Stock effected without receipt of consideration by the Company. The conversion of any convertible securities of the Company shall not be deemed to have been "effected without receipt of consideration." Such adjustment shall be made by the Board, whose determination in that respect shall be final, binding and conclusive. Except as expressly provided herein, no issuance by the Company of shares of stock of any class, or securities convertible into shares of stock of any class, shall affect, and no adjustment by reason thereof shall be made with respect to, the number or price of shares of Common Stock subject to an Option or Stock Purchase Right.

(b) Dissolution or Liquidation. In the event of the proposed dissolution or liquidation of the Company, the Administrator shall notify each Optionee as soon as practicable prior to the effective date of such proposed transaction. The Administrator in its discretion may provide for an Optionee to have the right to exercise his or her Option or Stock Purchase Right until fifteen (15) days prior to such transaction as to all of the Optioned Stock covered thereby, including Shares as to which the Option or Stock Purchase Right would not otherwise be exercisable. In addition, the Administrator may provide that any Company repurchase option applicable to any Shares purchased upon exercise of an Option or Stock Purchase Right shall lapse as to all such Shares, provided the proposed dissolution or liquidation takes place at the time and in the manner contemplated. To the extent it has not been previously exercised, an Option or Stock Purchase Right will terminate immediately prior to the consummation of such proposed action.

(c) Merger or Asset Sale. In the event of a merger of the Company with or into another corporation, or the sale of substantially all of the assets of the Company, each outstanding Option and Stock Purchase Right shall be assumed or an equivalent option or right substituted by the successor corporation or a Parent or Subsidiary of the successor corporation. In the event that the successor corporation refuses to assume or substitute for the Option or Stock Purchase Right, the Optionee shall fully vest in and have the right to exercise the Option or Stock Purchase Right as to all of the Optioned Stock, including Shares as to which it would not otherwise be vested or exercisable. If an Option or Stock Purchase Right becomes fully vested and exercisable in lieu of assumption or substitution in the event of a merger or sale of assets, the Administrator shall notify the Optionee in writing or electronically that the Option or Stock Purchase Right shall be fully exercisable for a period of fifteen (15) days from the date of such notice, and the Option or Stock Purchase Right shall terminate upon the expiration of such period. For the purposes of this paragraph, the Option or

Stock Purchase Right shall be considered assumed if, following the merger or sale of assets, the option or right confers the right to purchase or receive, for each Share of Optioned Stock subject to the Option or Stock Purchase Right immediately prior to the merger or sale of assets, the consideration (whether stock, cash, or other securities or property) received in the merger or sale of assets by holders of Common Stock for each Share held on the effective date of the transaction (and if holders were offered a choice of consideration, the type of consideration chosen by the holders of a majority of the outstanding Shares); provided, however, that if such consideration received in the merger or sale of assets is not solely common stock of the successor corporation or its Parent, the Administrator may, with the consent of the successor corporation, provide for the consideration to be received upon the exercise of the Option or Stock Purchase Right, for each Share of Optioned Stock subject to the Option or Stock Purchase Right, to be solely common stock of the successor corporation or its Parent equal in fair market value to the per share consideration received by holders of Common Stock in the merger or sale of assets.

13. Time of Granting Options and Stock Purchase Rights. The date of grant of an Option or Stock Purchase Right shall, for all purposes, be the date on which the Administrator makes the determination granting such Option or Stock Purchase Right, or such other date as is determined by the Administrator. Notice of the determination shall be given to each Service Provider to whom an Option or Stock Purchase Right is so granted within a reasonable time after the date of such grant.

14. Amendment and Termination of the Plan.

(a) Amendment and Termination. The Board may at any time amend, alter, suspend, or terminate the Plan.

(b) Shareholder Approval. The Board shall obtain shareholder approval of any Plan amendment to the extent necessary and desirable to comply with Applicable Laws.

(c) Effect of Amendment or Termination. No amendment, alteration, suspension, or termination of the Plan shall impair the rights of any Optionee, unless mutually agreed otherwise between the Optionee and the Administrator, which agreement must be in writing and signed by the Optionee and the Company. Termination of the Plan shall not affect the Administrator's ability to exercise the powers granted to it hereunder with respect to Options granted under the Plan prior to the date of such termination.

15. Conditions Upon Issuance of Shares.

(a) Legal Compliance. Shares shall not be issued pursuant to the exercise of an Option unless the exercise of such Option and the issuance and delivery of such Shares shall comply with Applicable Laws and shall be further subject to the approval of counsel for the Company with respect to such compliance.

(b) Investment Representations. As a condition to the exercise of an Option, the Administrator may require the person exercising such Option to represent and warrant at the time of any such exercise that the Shares are being purchased only for investment and without any present intention to sell or distribute such Shares if, in the opinion of counsel for the Company, such a representation is required.

16. Inability to Obtain Authority. The inability of the Company to obtain authority from any regulatory body having jurisdiction, which authority is deemed by the Company's counsel to be necessary to the lawful issuance and sale of any Shares hereunder, shall relieve the Company of any liability in respect of the failure to issue or sell such Shares as to which such requisite authority shall not have been obtained.

17. Reservation of Shares. The Company, during the term of this Plan, shall at all times reserve and keep available such number of Shares as shall be sufficient to satisfy the requirements of the Plan.

18. Shareholder Approval. The Plan shall be subject to approval by the shareholders of the Company within twelve (12) months after the date the Plan is adopted. Such shareholder approval shall be obtained in the degree and manner required under Applicable Laws.

19. Information to Optionees and Purchasers. The Company shall provide to each Optionee and to each individual who acquires Shares pursuant to the Plan, not less frequently than annually during the period such Optionee or purchaser has one or more Options or Stock Purchase Rights outstanding, and, in the case of an individual who acquires Shares pursuant to the Plan, during the period such individual owns such Shares, copies of annual financial statements. The Company shall not be required to provide such statements to key employees whose duties in connection with the Company assure their access to equivalent information.

Form 14 B: Stock Option Grant and Stock Option Agreement

[****], INC.
20___ STOCK OPTION PLAN
STOCK OPTION AGREEMENT

Unless otherwise defined herein, the terms defined in the Plan shall have the same defined meanings in this Stock Option Agreement.

I. NOTICE OF STOCK OPTION GRANT
[Optionee's Name and Address]
The undersigned Optionee has been granted an Option to purchase Common Stock of the Company, subject to the terms and conditions of the Plan and this Option Agreement, as follows:

Date of Grant   _____

Vesting Commencement Date   _____

Exercise Price per Share $_____

Total Number of Shares Granted   _____

Total Exercise Price $_____

Type of Option: _____ Incentive Stock Option

                                     _____ Nonstatutory Stock Option

Term/Expiration Date: _____

Vesting Schedule:

   This Option shall be exercisable, in whole or in part, according to the following vesting schedule: Twenty-five percent (25%) of the Shares subject to the Option shall vest twelve (12) months after the Vesting Commencement Date, and one-forty-eighth (1/48) of the Shares subject to the Option shall vest each month thereafter, subject to Optionee's continuing to be a Service Provider on such dates.

Termination Period:

   This Option shall be exercisable for three (3) months after Optionee ceases to be a Service Provider. Upon Optionee's death or Disability, this Option may be exercised for one (1) year after Optionee ceases to be a Service Provider. In no event may Optionee exercise this Option after the Term/Expiration Date as provided above.

II. AGREEMENT
   1. Grant of Option. The Plan Administrator of the Company hereby grants to the Optionee named in the Notice of Grant (the "Optionee"), an option (the "Option") to purchase the number of Shares set forth in the Notice of Grant, at the exercise price per Share set forth in the Notice of Grant (the "Exercise Price"), and subject to the terms and conditions of the Plan, which is incorporated herein by reference.

Subject to Section 14(c) of the Plan, in the event of a conflict between the terms and conditions of the Plan and this Option Agreement, the terms and conditions of the Plan shall prevail.

If designated in the Notice of Grant as an Incentive Stock Option ("ISO"), this Option is intended to qualify as an Incentive Stock Option as defined in Section 422 of the Code. Nevertheless, to the extent that it exceeds the One Hundred Thousand Dollars ($100,000) rule of Code Section 422(d), this Option shall be treated as a Nonstatutory Stock Option ("NSO").

2.   Exercise of Option.

(a) Right to Exercise. This Option shall be exercisable during its term in accordance with the Vesting Schedule set out in the Notice of Grant and with the applicable provisions of the Plan and this Option Agreement.

(b) Method of Exercise. This Option shall be exercisable by delivery of an exercise notice in the form attached as Exhibit A (the "Exercise Notice") which shall state the election to exercise the Option, the number of Shares with respect to which the Option is being exercised, and such other representations and agreements as may be required by the Company. The Exercise Notice shall be accompanied by payment of the aggregate Exercise Price as to all Exercised Shares. This Option shall be deemed to be exercised upon receipt by the Company of such fully executed Exercise Notice accompanied by the aggregate Exercise Price.

No Shares shall be issued pursuant to the exercise of an Option unless such issuance and such exercise complies with Applicable Laws. Assuming such compliance, for income tax purposes the Shares shall be considered transferred to the Optionee on the date on which the Option is exercised with respect to such Shares.

3.   Optionee's Representations. In the event the Shares have not been registered under the Securities Act of 1933, as amended, at the time this Option is exercised, the Optionee shall, if required by the Company, concurrently with the exercise of all or any portion of this Option, deliver to the Company his or her Investment Representation Statement in the form attached hereto as Exhibit B.

4.   Lock-Up Period. Optionee hereby agrees that, if so requested by the Company or any representative of the underwriters (the "Managing Underwriter") in connection with any registration of the offering of any securities of the Company under the Securities Act, Optionee shall not sell or otherwise transfer any Shares or other securities of the Company during the 180-day period (or such other period as may be requested in writing by the Managing Underwriter and agreed to in writing by the Company) (the "Market Standoff Period") following the effective date of a registration statement of the Company filed under the Securities Act. Such restriction shall apply only to the first registration statement of the Company to become effective under the Securities Act that includes securities to be sold on behalf of the Company to the public in an underwritten public offering under the Securities Act. The Company may impose stop-transfer instructions with respect to securities subject to the foregoing restrictions until the end of such Market Standoff Period.

5.   Method of Payment. Payment of the aggregate Exercise Price shall be by any of the following, or a combination thereof, at the election of the Optionee:

(a) cash or check;

(b) consideration received by the Company under a formal cashless exercise program adopted by the Company in connection with the Plan; or

(c) surrender of other Shares which, (i) in the case of Shares acquired upon exercise of an option, have been owned by the Optionee for more than six (6) months on the date of surrender, and (ii) have a Fair Market Value on the date of surrender equal to the aggregate Exercise Price of the Exercised Shares.

6. Restrictions on Exercise. This Option may not be exercised until such time as the Plan has been approved by the shareholders of the Company, or if the issuance of such Shares upon such exercise or the method of payment of consideration for such shares would constitute a violation of any Applicable Law.

7. Non-Transferability of Option. This Option may not be transferred in any manner otherwise than by will or by the laws of descent or distribution and may be exercised during the lifetime of Optionee only by Optionee. The terms of the Plan and this Option Agreement shall be binding upon the executors, administrators, heirs, successors and assigns of the Optionee.

8. Term of Option. This Option may be exercised only within the term set out in the Notice of Grant, and may be exercised during such term only in accordance with the Plan and the terms of this Option.

9. Tax Consequences. Set forth below is a brief summary as of the date of this Option of some of the federal tax consequences of exercise of this Option and disposition of the Shares. THIS SUMMARY IS NECESSARILY INCOMPLETE, AND THE TAX LAWS AND REGULATIONS ARE SUBJECT TO CHANGE. THE OPTIONEE SHOULD CONSULT A TAX ADVISER BEFORE EXERCISING THIS OPTION OR DISPOSING OF THE SHARES.

(a) Exercise of NSO. There may be a regular federal income tax liability upon the exercise of an NSO. The Optionee will be treated as having received compensation income (taxable at ordinary income tax rates) equal to the excess, if any, of the Fair Market Value of the Shares on the date of exercise over the Exercise Price. If Optionee is an Employee or a former Employee, the Company will be required to withhold from Optionee's compensation or collect from Optionee and pay to the applicable taxing authorities an amount in cash equal to a percentage of this compensation income at the time of exercise, and may refuse to honor the exercise and refuse to deliver Shares if such withholding amounts are not delivered at the time of exercise.

(b) Exercise of ISO. If this Option qualifies as an ISO, there will be no regular federal income tax liability upon the exercise of the Option, although the excess, if any, of the Fair Market Value of the Shares on the date of exercise over the Exercise Price will be treated as an adjustment to the alternative minimum tax for federal tax purposes and may subject the Optionee to the alternative minimum tax in the year of exercise.

(c) Disposition of Shares. In the case of an NSO, if Shares are held for at least one year, any gain realized on disposition of the Shares will be treated as long-term capital gain for federal income tax purposes. In the case of an ISO, if Shares transferred pursuant to the Option are held for at least one year after exercise and of at least two years after the Date of Grant, any gain realized on disposition of the Shares will also be treated as long-term capital gain for federal income tax purposes. If Shares purchased under an ISO are disposed of within one year after exercise or two years after the Date of Grant, any gain realized on such disposition will be treated as compensation income (taxable at ordinary income rates) to the extent of the difference between the Exercise Price and the lesser of (1) the Fair Market Value of the Shares on the date of exercise, or (2) the sale price of the Shares. Any additional gain will be taxed as capital gain, short-term or long-term depending on the period that the ISO Shares were held.

(d) Notice of Disqualifying Disposition of ISO Shares. If the Option granted to Optionee herein is an ISO, and if Optionee sells or otherwise disposes of any of the Shares acquired pursuant to the ISO on or before the later of (1) the date two years after the Date of Grant, or (2) the date one year after the date of exercise, the

Optionee shall immediately notify the Company in writing of such disposition. Optionee agrees that Optionee may be subject to income tax withholding by the Company on the compensation income recognized by the Optionee.

10. Entire Agreement; Governing Law. The Plan is incorporated herein by reference. The Plan and this Option Agreement constitute the entire agreement of the parties with respect to the subject matter hereof and supersede in their entirety all prior undertakings and agreements of the Company and Optionee with respect to the subject matter hereof, and may not be modified adversely to the Optionee's interest except by means of a writing signed by the Company and Optionee. This agreement is governed by the internal substantive laws but not the choice of law rules of [California].

11. No Guarantee of Continued Service. OPTIONEE ACKNOWLEDGES AND AGREES THAT THE VESTING OF SHARES PURSUANT TO THE VESTING SCHEDULE HEREOF IS EARNED ONLY BY CONTINUING AS A SERVICE PROVIDER AT THE WILL OF THE COMPANY (NOT THROUGH THE ACT OF BEING HIRED, BEING GRANTED THIS OPTION OR ACQUIRING SHARES HEREUNDER). OPTIONEE FURTHER ACKNOWLEDGES AND AGREES THAT THIS AGREEMENT, THE TRANSACTIONS CONTEMPLATED HEREUNDER AND THE VESTING SCHEDULE SET FORTH HEREIN DO NOT CONSTITUTE AN EXPRESS OR IMPLIED PROMISE OF CONTINUED ENGAGEMENT AS A SERVICE PROVIDER FOR THE VESTING PERIOD, FOR ANY PERIOD, OR AT ALL, AND SHALL NOT INTERFERE IN ANY WAY WITH OPTIONEE'S RIGHT OR THE COMPANY'S RIGHT TO TERMINATE OPTIONEE'S RELATIONSHIP AS A SERVICE PROVIDER AT ANY TIME, WITH OR WITHOUT CAUSE.

Optionee acknowledges receipt of a copy of the Plan and represents that he or she is familiar with the terms and provisions thereof, and hereby accepts this Option subject to all of the terms and provisions thereof. Optionee has reviewed the Plan and this Option in their entirety, has had an opportunity to obtain the advice of counsel prior to executing this Option and fully understands all provisions of the Option. Optionee hereby agrees to accept as binding, conclusive and final all decisions or interpretations of the Administrator upon any questions arising under the Plan or this Option. Optionee further agrees to notify the Company upon any change in the residence address indicated below.

Optionee   [****], Inc.

_____   By_____
[Optionee Name]   [Name, Title]

_____
[Optionee Address]

_____

EXHIBIT A

20___ STOCK OPTION PLAN EXERCISE NOTICE

[****], Inc.
[Address]

Attention: Chief Financial Officer

Ladies and Gentlemen:

1. Exercise of Option. Effective as of today, _____, 20__, the under-signed ("Optionee") hereby elects to exercise Optionee's option to purchase _____ shares of the Common Stock (the "Shares") of [****], Inc. (the "Company") under and pursuant to the 20___ Stock Option Plan (the "Plan") and the Stock Option Agreement dated _____, 20__ (the "Option Agreement").

2. Delivery of Payment. Purchaser herewith delivers to the Company the full purchase price of the Shares, as set forth in the Option Agreement.

3. Representations of Optionee. Optionee acknowledges that Optionee has received, read and understood the Plan and the Option Agreement and agrees to abide by and be bound by its terms and conditions.

4. Rights as Shareholder. Until the issuance of the Shares (as evidenced by the appropriate entry on the books of the Company or of a duly authorized transfer agent of the Company), no right to vote or receive dividends or any other rights as a shareholder shall exist with respect to the Optioned Stock, notwithstanding the exercise of the Option. The Shares shall be issued to the Optionee as soon as practicable after the Option is exercised. No adjustment shall be made for a dividend or other right for which the record date is prior to the date of issuance except as provided in Section 12 of the Plan.

5. Company's Right of First Refusal. Before any Shares held by Optionee or any transferee (either being sometimes referred to herein as the "Holder") may be sold or otherwise transferred (including transfer by gift or operation of law), the Company or its assignee(s) shall have a right of first refusal to purchase the Shares on the terms and conditions set forth in this Section (the "Right of First Refusal").

(a) Notice of Proposed Transfer. The Holder of the Shares shall deliver to the Company a written notice (the "Notice") stating: (i) the Holder's bona fide intention to sell or otherwise transfer such Shares; (ii) the name of each proposed purchaser or other transferee ("Proposed Transferee"); (iii) the number of Shares to be transferred to each Proposed Transferee; and (iv) the bona fide cash price or other consideration for which the Holder proposes to transfer the Shares (the "Offered Price"), and the Holder shall offer the Shares at the Offered Price to the Company or its assignee(s).

(b) Exercise of Right of First Refusal. At any time within thirty (30) days after receipt of the Notice, the Company and/or its assignee(s) may, by giving written notice to the Holder, elect to purchase all or any portion of the Shares proposed to be transferred to any one or more of the Proposed Transferees, at the purchase price determined in accordance with subsection (c) below.

(c) Purchase Price. The purchase price ("Purchase Price") for the Shares purchased by the Company or its assignee(s) under this Section shall be the Offered Price. If the Offered Price includes consideration other than cash, the cash equivalent value of the non-cash consideration shall be determined by the Board of Directors of the Company in good faith.

(d) Payment. Payment of the Purchase Price shall be made, at the option of the Company or its assignee(s), in cash (by check), by cancellation of all or a portion of any outstanding indebtedness of the Holder to the Company (or, in the case of repurchase by an assignee, to the assignee), or by any combination thereof within 30 days after receipt of the Notice or in the manner and at the times set forth in the Notice.

(e) Holder's Right to Transfer. If all of the Shares proposed in the Notice to be transferred to a given Proposed Transferee are not purchased by the Company and/or its assignee(s) as provided in this Section, then the Holder may sell or otherwise transfer such Shares to that Proposed Transferee at the Offered Price or at a higher price, provided that such sale or other transfer is consummated within 120 days after the date of the Notice, that any such sale or other transfer is effected in accordance with any applicable securities laws, and that the Proposed Transferee agrees in writing that the provisions of this Section shall continue to apply to the Shares in the hands of such Proposed Transferee. If the Shares described in the Notice are not transferred to the Proposed Transferee within such period, a new Notice shall be given to the Company, and the Company and/or its assignees shall again be offered the Right of First Refusal before any Shares held by the Holder may be sold or otherwise transferred.

(f) Exception for Certain Family Transfers. Anything to the contrary contained in this Section notwithstanding, the transfer of any or all of the Shares during the Optionee's lifetime or on the Optionee's death by will or intestacy to the Optionee's immediate family or a trust for the benefit of the Optionee's immediate family shall be exempt from the provisions of this Section. "Immediate Family" as used herein shall mean spouse, lineal descendant or antecedent, father, mother, brother, or sister. In such case, the transferee or other recipient shall receive and hold the Shares so transferred subject to the provisions of this Section, and there shall be no further transfer of such Shares except in accordance with the terms of this Section.

(g) Termination of Right of First Refusal. The Right of First Refusal shall terminate as to any Shares upon the first sale of Common Stock of the Company to the general public pursuant to a registration statement filed with and declared effective by the Securities and Exchange Commission under the Securities Act of 1933, as amended.

6.   Tax Consultation. Optionee understands that Optionee may suffer adverse tax consequences as a result of Optionee's purchase or disposition of the Shares. Optionee represents that Optionee has consulted with any tax consultants Optionee deems advisable in connection with the purchase or disposition of the Shares and that Optionee is not relying on the Company for any tax advice.

7.   Restrictive Legends and Stop-Transfer Orders.

(a) Legends. Optionee understands and agrees that the Company shall cause the legends set forth below or legends substantially equivalent thereto, to be placed upon any certificate(s) evidencing ownership of the Shares together with any other legends that may be required by the Company or by state or federal securities laws:

THE SECURITIES REPRESENTED HEREBY HAVE NOT BEEN REGISTERED UNDER THE SECURITIES ACT OF 1933 (THE "ACT") AND MAY NOT BE OFFERED, SOLD, OR OTHERWISE TRANSFERRED, PLEDGED, OR HYPOTHE-CATED UNLESS AND UNTIL REGISTERED UNDER THE ACT OR, IN THE OPIN-ION OF COMPANY COUNSEL SATISFACTORY TO THE ISSUER OF THESE SECURITIES, SUCH OFFER, SALE OR TRANSFER, PLEDGE, OR HYPOTHECA-TION IS IN COMPLIANCE THEREWITH.

THE SHARES REPRESENTED BY THIS CERTIFICATE ARE SUBJECT TO CERTAIN RESTRICTIONS ON TRANSFER AND A RIGHT OF FIRST REFUSAL HELD BY THE ISSUER OR ITS ASSIGNEE(S) AS SET FORTH IN THE EXERCISE NOTICE BETWEEN THE ISSUER AND THE ORIGINAL HOLDER OF THESE SHARES, A COPY OF WHICH MAY BE OBTAINED AT THE PRINCIPAL OFFICE OF THE ISSUER. SUCH TRANSFER RESTRICTIONS AND RIGHT OF FIRST REFUSAL ARE BINDING ON TRANSFEREES OF THESE SHARES.

(b) Stop-Transfer Notices. Optionee agrees that, in order to ensure compliance with the restrictions referred to herein, the Company may issue appropriate "stop transfer" instructions to its transfer agent, if any, and that, if the Company transfers its own securities, it may make appropriate notations to the same effect in its own records.

(c) Refusal to Transfer. The Company shall not be required (i) to transfer on its books any Shares that have been sold or otherwise transferred in violation of any of the provisions of this Exercise Notice or (ii) to treat as owner of such Shares or to accord the right to vote or pay dividends to any purchaser or other transferee to whom such Shares shall have been so transferred.

8. Successors and Assigns. The Company may assign any of its rights under this Exercise Notice to single or multiple assignees, and this Exercise Notice shall inure to the benefit of the successors and assigns of the Company. Subject to the restrictions on transfer herein set forth, this Exercise Notice shall be binding upon Optionee and his or her heirs, executors, administrators, successors and assigns.

9. Interpretation. Any dispute regarding the interpretation of this Exercise Notice shall be submitted by Optionee or by the Company forthwith to the Administrator which shall review such dispute at its next regular meeting. The resolution of such a dispute by the Administrator shall be final and binding on all parties.

10. Governing Law; Severability. This Exercise Notice is governed by the internal substantive laws but not the choice of law rules, of [California].

11. Entire Agreement. The Plan and Option Agreement are incorporated herein by reference. This Exercise Notice, the Plan, the Option Agreement, and the Investment Representation Statement constitute the entire agreement of the parties with respect to the subject matter hereof and supersede in their entirety all prior undertakings and agreements of the Company and Optionee with respect to the subject matter hereof, and may not be modified adversely to the Optionee's interest except by means of a writing signed by the Company and Optionee.

Submitted by: Accepted by:

Optionee   [****], Inc.

                                       By_____
_____
[Optionee Name]   [Name, Title]

_____
[Optionee Address]

_____

EXHIBIT B:

INVESTMENT REPRESENTATION STATEMENT

OPTIONEE: [Optionee's Name]
COMPANY: [****], INC.
SECURITY: Common Stock
AMOUNT:
DATE:

In connection with the purchase of the above-listed Securities, the undersigned Optionee represents to the Company the following:

(a) Optionee is aware of the Company's business affairs and financial condition and has acquired sufficient information about the Company to reach an informed and knowledgeable decision to acquire the Securities. Optionee is acquiring these Securities for investment for Optionee's own account only and not with a view to, or for resale in connection with, any "distribution" thereof within the meaning of the Securities Act of 1933, as amended (the "Securities Act").

(b) Optionee acknowledges and understands that the Securities constitute "restricted securities" under the Securities Act and have not been registered under the Securities Act in reliance upon a specific exemption therefrom, which exemption depends upon, among other things, the bona fide nature of Optionee's investment intent as expressed herein. In this connection, Optionee understands that, in the view of the Securities and Exchange Commission, the statutory basis for such exemption may be unavailable if Optionee's representation was predicated solely upon a present intention to hold these Securities for the minimum capital gains period specified under tax statutes, for a deferred sale, for or until an increase or decrease in the market price of the Securities, or for a period of one year or any other fixed period in the future. Optionee further understands that the Securities must be held indefinitely unless they are subsequently registered under the Securities Act or an exemption from such registration is available. Optionee further acknowledges and understands that the Company is under no obligation to register the Securities. Optionee understands that the certificate evidencing the Securities will be imprinted with a legend which prohibits the transfer of the Securities unless they are registered or such registration is not required in the opinion of counsel satisfactory to the Company, and any other legend required under applicable state securities laws.

(c) Optionee is familiar with the provisions of Rule 701 and Rule 144, each promulgated under the Securities Act, which, in substance, permit limited public resale of "restricted securities" acquired, directly or indirectly from the issuer thereof, in a non-public offering subject to the satisfaction of certain conditions. Rule 701 provides that if the issuer qualifies under Rule 701 at the time of the grant of the Option to the Optionee, the exercise will be exempt from registration under the Securities Act. In the event the Company becomes subject to the reporting requirements of Section 13 or 15(d) of the Securities Exchange Act of 1934, ninety (90) days thereafter (or such longer period as any market stand-off agreement may require) the Securities exempt under Rule 701 may be resold, subject to the satisfaction of certain of the conditions specified by Rule 144, including: (1) the resale being made through a broker in an unsolicited "broker's transaction" or in transactions directly with a market maker (as said term is defined under the Securities Exchange Act of 1934); and, in the case of an affiliate, (2) the availability of certain public information about the Company, (3) the amount of Securities being sold during any three month period not exceeding the limitations specified in Rule 144(e), and (4) the timely filing of a Form 144, if applicable.

In the event that the Company does not qualify under Rule 701 at the time of grant of the Option, then the Securities may be resold in certain limited circumstances subject to the provisions of Rule 144, which requires the resale to occur not less than one year after the later of the date the Securities were sold by the Company or the date the Securities were sold by an affiliate of the Company, within the meaning of Rule 144; and, in the case of acquisition of the Securities by an affiliate, or by a non-affiliate who subsequently holds the Securities less than two years, the satisfaction of the conditions set forth in sections (1), (2), (3), and (4) of the paragraph immediately above.

(d) Optionee further understands that in the event all of the applicable requirements of Rule 701 or 144 are not satisfied, registration under the Securities Act, compliance with Regulation A, or some other registration exemption will be required; and that, notwithstanding the fact that Rules 144 and 701 are not exclusive, the Staff of the Securities and Exchange Commission has expressed its opinion that persons proposing to sell private placement securities other than in a registered offering and otherwise than pursuant to Rules 144 or 701 will have a substantial burden of proof in establishing that an exemption from registration is available for such offers or sales, and that such persons and their respective brokers who participate in such transactions do so at their own risk. Optionee understands that no assurances can be given that any such other registration exemption will be available in such event.

Signature of Optionee:

_____

[Optionee Name]

_____

[Optionee Address]

_____

CHAPTER 15

Liquidity Events

15.1 What Type of Liquidity Event Might Your Client Experience?

Of course, not all small businesses are destined for, or even interested in, an initial public offering or acquisition by a publicly held company. However, every small business should engage in discussions and planning for the owners' exit. Succession planning can be very time consuming and complex—there are many factors to consider and document to implement the plan—but such planning can help ensure that a business continues after the founders move on and that they, or their families, get the benefit of the value they created.

15.2 How Can a Small Business Generate a Liquidity Event?

Consultants, business brokers, investment bankers, and underwriters can be invaluable in helping a company assess its prospects for a liquidity event and helping make such an event a reality. It's never too soon for a company to start talking with experts about its exit plan and to start putting the necessary elements in place. A company's venture capital (VC) investors, or angels or other advisors who are well connected in the company's industry, are often the source of a company's ultimate exit strategy, whether through an introduction to an acquiring company or an underwriter willing to take on the company's initial public offering (IPO).

15.3 How Can a Small Business Prepare for a Successful Liquidity Event?

When it comes time to negotiate with an investor or acquirer, your client is likely to receive a term sheet or memorandum of understanding with a disclaimer along the lines of the following:

> These terms do not constitute any form of binding contract and create no obligations or the basis of any claims against any party but rather are solely for the purpose of outlining the terms pursuant to which a definitive agreement may ultimately be entered into. The proposed transaction is in all respects contingent upon, and subject to, among other things, Buyer's completion of due diligence and satisfaction with the results thereof and the negotiation and execution of satisfactory documentation containing, among other things, mutually agreeable closing conditions, covenants, and representations and warranties.

Therefore, to close a deal after one has been identified, your client will have to stand up under scrutiny. There are a lot of things a company should be doing long before it engages in discussions for a liquidity event to be prepared to take and pass a "due diligence test."

Although the Sarbanes-Oxley Act of 2002 applies only to publicly held companies, privately held companies may wish to consider adopting certain sections of the act, such as the provisions that focus on internal control over financial reporting (i.e., Section 404 of the act), to help ensure they can be successfully merged, acquired, or advanced to an IPO.

15.4 Sample Documents and Checklists.

This section includes the following forms:

- Agreement to Engage Business Consultants (Form 15 A)
- Due Diligence Checklist (Form 15 B)
- Asset Purchase Agreement (Form 15 C)
- Escrow Agreement for Asset Purchase (Form 15 D)
- Bill of Sale and Assignment for Asset Purchase (Form 15 E)
- Assignment and Assumption Agreement for Asset Purchase (Form 15 F)
- License Agreement for Asset Purchase (Form 15 G)
- Bulk Sale Notice for Asset Purchase (Form 15 H)
- Time and Responsibility Schedule for IPO (Form 15 I)
- Closing Checklist for Merger Transaction (Form 15 J)
- Due Diligence Checklist for Opinion of Counsel (Form 15 K)
- Officers' Certificate (Form 15 L)

Form 15 A: Agreement to Engage Business Consultants

**AGREEMENT TO ENGAGE
BUSINESS CONSULTANTS**

On the basis of previous telephone conversations and meetings between ****, Inc. ("Company") and ****, Inc. ("Business Consultant") as well as other discussions, initial reports submitted by Company, and the representations that Company has made to Business Consultant describing Company and its affiliated companies (collectively, "Affiliates") and their principals, present and proposed business activities, operations, financial condition and capital structure, and various agreements and documents related thereto, Business Consultant hereby submits to Company a proposal for the terms pursuant to which Business Consultant would be willing to consult to Company and its Affiliates on various activities related to their respective businesses.

I. ENGAGEMENT

Company hereby engages and retains Business Consultant as a Business Consultant for and on behalf of Company and its Affiliates to perform the Services (as that term is hereinafter defined) and Business Consultant hereby accepts such appointment on the terms and subject to the conditions hereinafter set forth and agrees to use its best efforts in providing such Services.

II. INDEPENDENT CONTRACTOR

A. Business Consultant shall be, and in all respects be deemed to be, an independent contractor in the performance of its duties hereunder, any law of any jurisdiction to the contrary notwithstanding.

B. Business Consultant shall not, by reason of this Agreement or the performance of the Services, be or be deemed to be, an employee, agent, partner, co-venturer, or controlling person of Company, and Business Consultant shall have no power to enter into any agreement on behalf of or otherwise bind Company.

C. Business Consultant shall not have or be deemed to have, fiduciary obligations or duties to Company or its Affiliates and shall be free to pursue, conduct, and carry on for its own account (or for the account of others) such activities, employments, ventures, businesses, and other pursuits as Business Consultant in its sole and absolute discretion may elect; provided, however, Business Consultant agrees that for the Term of this Agreement and for a period of three (3) years thereafter it will not enter into an engagement agreement with any company that competes with Company in its business.

III. SERVICES

A. As Company's Business Consultant, Business Consultant agrees to provide the following consulting services (collectively the "Services"):

1. Advise Company in its negotiations with one or more individuals, firms, or entities (the "Candidate(s)") that may have an interest in pursuing a form of Business Combination with Company and/or its Affiliates. As used in this Agreement, the term "Business Combination" shall be deemed to

mean any form of initial public offering, merger, acquisition, joint venture, debt or equity financing, restructuring or refinancing arrangement, licensing agreement, product sales and/or marketing, distribution, combination and/or consolidation, etc. involving Company and/or any of its Affiliates and any other entity. The acceptance and consummation of any transaction with a Candidate(s) will be solely within Company's discretion and control.

2. Advise Company in preparing an updated version of its business plan and in formulating and implementing a strategic and effective marketing and product distribution plan.

3. Advise Company's management in corporate finance matters, including advice on the structure, nature, extent, and other parameters of any transaction involving a Candidate(s).

4. Assist Company in the conduct of corporate-related due diligence in connection with the Services to be rendered under this Agreement.

5. Advise Company's management in its negotiations with Candidates, including evaluating proposals from Candidate(s).

6. Assist Company in locating and engaging certain professionals, including additional corporate executives and members of its Board of Directors, as well as negotiating employment-related contracts.

7. Advise Company regarding company operations, staffing, strategy, and other issues related to building shareholder value as Company may reasonably request, consistent with the provisions of this Agreement.

8. Assist Company in its efforts to establish strategic relationships with individuals and entities of particular interest to it in connection with its continued business development.

B. Business Consultant shall devote such time and best effort to the affairs of Company as is reasonable and adequate to render the Services contemplated by this Agreement. Business Consultant is not responsible for the performance of any services that may be rendered hereunder without Company providing the necessary information in writing prior thereto, nor shall Business Consultant provide any services that constitute the rendering of any legal opinions or performance of work that is in the ordinary purview of a Certified Public Accountant. Business Consultant cannot guarantee results on behalf of Company, but shall pursue all reasonable avenues available to successfully provide the Services contemplated herein.

C. Company and Business Consultant hereby confirm their express written intent that Business Consultant shall only be required to devote such time to the performance of the Services as Business Consultant shall, in its sole discretion, deem necessary and proper to discharge its responsibilities under this Agreement.

D. In conjunction with the Services, Business Consultant agrees to:
1. Make itself available to the officers of Company at such mutually agreed upon places during normal business hours for reasonable periods of time, subject to reasonable advance notice and mutually convenient scheduling, for the purpose of advising Company and its Affiliates in the preparation of such reports, summaries, corporate and/or transaction profiles, due diligence packages and/or other material and documentation ("Documentation") as shall be necessary to present to other entities and individuals that could be of benefit to Company and its Affiliates.

2. Make itself available for telephone conferences with the principal, financial, sales, and/or operating officer(s) of Company during normal business hours.

IV. EXPENSES

It is expressly agreed and understood that Business Consultant's compensation as provided in this Agreement does not include normal and reasonable out-of-pocket expenses, which expenses shall be *pre-approved* by Company. The expenses shall be reimbursed by Company independent of any fees described in the section below titled "COMPENSATION."

A. "Normal and reasonable out-of-pocket expenses" shall include, but are not limited to: accounting, long distance communication, express mail, outside consultants, travel (including: airfare, hotel lodging and meals, transportation, etc.), and other costs involved in the execution of Business Consultant's Services under this Agreement.

B. Company acknowledges that it may be necessary to hire certain professionals on a temporary or contract basis to execute some of Business Consultant's recommendations/advice and Company agrees that it may be necessary to pay those individuals separately from this Agreement at agreed upon rates. The current market value of those services may range from $1,500 to $2,500 per day depending on the expertise needed. Company must pre-approve the engagement of any such professionals in writing. Provided Company has given its pre-approval, such fees are payable immediately upon the initial receipt of an invoice by Company.

C. It is also agreed that Company will pay all out-of-pocket expenses incurred in connection with the preparation and printing of any Company marketing or advertising materials, offering memorandums, business plans, or executive summaries, including any amendments thereto.

D. Company also agrees to pay its own and Business Consultant's legal expenses in connection with any registration of the Engagement Securities as provided in Section V below.

E. Business Consultant shall not incur any travel-related expense in excess of one thousand dollars ($1,000) without Company's *prior* written consent, which consent shall not unreasonably be withheld.

F. Company hereby agrees to compensate Business Consultant promptly upon receipt of an expense invoice from Business Consultant. Whenever feasible, Business Consultant will request advance payment of approved expenses. Expenses shall not be subject to any maximum allocation, and shall be fully reimbursed.

V. COMPENSATION

In consideration for the Services, Company agrees that Business Consultant or its assigns shall be entitled to compensation as follows:

A. Upon the execution of this Agreement, Business Consultant will receive a fee of _____ shares of Company's issued and outstanding equity securities (collectively, the "Engagement Securities"). A portion of the Engagement Securities shall be subject to cancellation in the event the Engagement Securities exceed ten percent (10%) of Company's issued and outstanding securities (including, without limitation, common and preferred stock, warrants, options, etc.) on a fully-diluted basis through Company raising up to and including $_____ of investment capital and/or Business Combinations since the date of this Agreement, which shall in no event be later than one (1) year from the date of this Agreement. It is contemplated by the parties that once Company has raised $_____ of investment capital, it will have a capital structure of approximately _____ shares issued and outstanding, including the Engagement Securities. In the event Company's capital structure is less than _____ shares issued and outstanding at such time as its capital raising is completed, which shall in no event be later than one (1) year from the date of this Agreement, a portion of the Engagement Securities shall be canceled such that the total issued to Business Consultant and/or its assigns is equal to 10% of Company's then issued and outstanding securities.

B. It is not anticipated that Company founders/principals will obtain royalty rights in connection with Company's technology/processes in the future. However, in the event any Company founders/principals do obtain such royalty rights, the parties agree that Business Consultant shall receive a royalty right on the same terms and conditions equal to ten percent (10%) of whatever is obtained by such principals.

C. Due to Company's current capital resources and status of its business development, Company and Business Consultant mutually agree that the aforementioned Engagement Securities are being issued to Business Consultant in lieu of cash and that the current value of such securities is deemed to be $_____.

D. Company's Board of Directors shall authorize the issuance of the Engagement Securities upon the signing of this Agreement, and shall have such securities delivered immediately to Business Consultant. However, in no event shall the Engagement Securities be delivered later than seven (7) days from the date of the signing of this Agreement.

E. Once issued, the Engagement Securities shall be deemed fully earned and shall have all the same rights and all the same dilutive or anti-dilutive provisions as the "Founder's Securities" held by the original shareholders.

F. Business Consultant shall have "Piggyback Registration Rights" to register the Engagement Securities as part of any registration filing by Company and/or its successors and assigns. Further, Company agrees to pay for all expenses incurred in connection with such filing, including legal fees, and Business Consultant agrees that it shall not be entitled to separate counsel in this regard.

G. Company shall pay to Business Consultant, in advance, a monthly fee of $_____ (the "Monthly Advisory Fees") provided, however, that Business Consultant agrees to accrue such Monthly Advisory Fee until the earlier of (i) a Business Combination involving Company being completed, including the first round of any debt or equity financing secured by Company, or (ii) the Agreement's valid termination, at which time all accrued and unpaid Monthly Advisory Fees will be due and payable. The Monthly Advisory Fees are due and payable on the 1st day of each month. If this Agreement is entered into after the 1st day of the month, a pro rata portion of the Monthly Advisory Fees shall be paid for the remaining days of the month in which the Agreement is executed.

H. The Monthly Advisory Fees are exclusive of the other compensation and reimbursable pre-approved expenses elsewhere provided in this Agreement.

Said Monthly Advisory Fees shall continue for twenty-four (24) months, or shall end upon proper termination of this Agreement according to the section below titled, "TERM AND TERMINATION."

VI. REPRESENTATIONS, WARRANTIES, AND COVENANTS

A. **Execution.** The execution, delivery, and performance of this Agreement, in the time and manner herein specified, will not conflict with, result in a breach of, or constitute a default under any existing agreement, indenture, or other instrument to which either Company or Business Consultant is a party or by which either entity may be bound or affected.

B. **Non-Circumvention.** Company hereby irrevocably agrees not to circumvent, avoid, bypass, or obviate, directly or indirectly, the intent of this Agreement, including avoiding payment of fees or other compensation to Business Consultant or its affiliates.

C. **Timely Updates.** During the term of this Agreement, Company shall keep Business Consultant up to date and apprised of all business, market, and legal developments related to Company and its operations and management.
   1. Accordingly, Company shall provide Business Consultant with copies of all amendments, revisions, and changes to its business and marketing plans, bylaws, articles of incorporation private placement memoranda, key contracts, employment, and consulting agreements and other operational agreements.
   2. Company shall promptly notify Business Consultant of the threat or filing of any suit, arbitration or administrative action, injunction, lien, claim or complaint and promptly forward a copy of all related documentation directly to Business Consultant or at Business Consultant's option to Business Consultant's counsel.
   3. Company shall promptly notify Business Consultant of all new contracts, agreements, joint ventures, or filing with any state, federal, or local administrative agency, including without limitation the SEC, NASD, or any state agency, and shall provide all related documents, including copies of the exact documents filed, to Business Consultant, including, without limitation, all annual reports, quarterly reports and notices of change of events, and registration statements filed with the SEC and any state agency, directly to Business Consultant.
   4. Company shall also provide directly to Business Consultant current financial statements, including balance sheets, income statements, cash flows, and all other documents provided or generated by Company in the normal course of its business and as requested by Business Consultant from time to time.
   5. Business Consultant shall keep all documents and information confidential as described in the section below titled, "CONFIDENTIAL DATA."

D. **Corporate Authority.** Both Company and Business Consultant have full legal authority to enter into this Agreement and to perform the same in the time and manner contemplated.

E. **Authorized Signatures.** The individuals whose signatures appear below are authorized to sign this Agreement on behalf of their respective corporations.

F. **Cooperation.** Company will cooperate with Business Consultant, and will promptly provide Business Consultant with all pertinent materials and requested information in order for Business Consultant to perform its Services pursuant to this Agreement.

G. **Properly Issued Shares.** When issued to Business Consultant, the Engagement Securities shall be duly and validly issued, fully paid, and non-assessable.

H. **Underwriter Fees.** Company acknowledges and understands that Business Consultant is neither a broker/dealer nor a Registered Investment Advisor and Company may be required to pay underwriting fees to an underwriter and/or funding entity in connection with any offerings, underwritings, or financings.

I. **Prompt Notification of Material Occurrences.** Until the proper termination of this engagement (as outlined in the section below titled, "Term & Termination"), Company will notify Business Consultant promptly of the occurrence of any event, which might materially affect the condition (financial or otherwise) or prospects of Company.

VII. <u>TERM AND TERMINATION</u>

A. In no event shall any termination be effective until the expiration of at least ninety (90) days after the signing of this Agreement.

B. This Agreement shall be effective upon its execution and shall remain in effect for a period of one (1) year unless otherwise terminated as provided in this Section VII.

C. Subsequent to the ninety (90) day period referenced in Section A above, Company shall have the right to terminate Business Consultant's engagement hereunder by furnishing Business Consultant with thirty (30) days advance written notice of such termination (i.e., Company may terminate the Agreement at the end of 90 days provided it has given notice to Business Consultant within 30 days preceding the end of such 90 day period).

D. Notwithstanding the foregoing, no termination of this Agreement by Company shall in any way affect Business Consultant's right to receive:
   1. reimbursement for billed, accrued, and/or unbilled disbursements and expenses which right the parties hereby agree and consent is absolute;
   2. its fees, securities, and/or warrants, including the Engagement Securities, which have been earned by Business Consultant through the effective date of termination; and
   3. Business Consultant's Monthly Advisory Fees through the effective date of termination, including all accrued Monthly Advisory Fees.

VIII. <u>CONFIDENTIAL DATA</u>

A. Except for its employees, agents, and independent contractors, Business Consultant shall not divulge to others, any trade secret or confidential information, knowledge, or data concerning or pertaining to the business and affairs of Company, obtained by Business Consultant as a result of its engagement hereunder, unless authorized, in writing, by Company.

B. Except for its employees, agents, and independent contractors, Company shall not divulge to others, any trade secret or confidential information, knowledge, or data concerning or pertaining to the business and affairs of Business Consultant, obtained by Company as a result of its engagement hereunder, unless authorized, in writing, by Business Consultant.

C. Business Consultant shall not be required in the performance of its duties to divulge to Company or any officer, director, agent or employee of Company,

any secret or confidential information, knowledge, or data concerning any other person, firm or entity (including, but not limited to, any such persons, firm or entity which may be a competitor or potential competitor of Company) which Business Consultant may have or be able to obtain otherwise than as a result of the relationship established by this Agreement.

IX. **OTHER MATERIAL TERMS AND CONDITIONS:**

A. **Indemnity.** Company agrees to indemnify Business Consultant, its officers, directors, employees, and authorized agents, from and against any loss, claim, liability, or cost arising out of any material misrepresentation or omission by Company in connection with this Agreement or the Services contemplated herein. A copy of Business Consultant's standard indemnification provisions (the "Indemnification Provisions") is attached to this Agreement as Exhibit "A" and is incorporated herein and made a part hereof. Company hereby indemnifies Business Consultant according with the provisions attached as Exhibit "A."

B. **Consequential Damages.** Except as expressly provided herein or in the case of intentional misconduct on Business Consultant's behalf, Business Consultant and its affiliates shall not, by reason of the termination of this Agreement or otherwise, be liable to Company or its Affiliates for any special, incidental, consequential, or punitive damages such as, but not limited to, expenditures, investments, or commitments made in connection with the efforts by Company to acquire another entity or sell all or a portion of its equity to another entity.

C. **Provisions.** Neither termination nor completion of this Agreement shall affect the confidentiality provisions of this Agreement, or the Indemnification Provisions that are incorporated herein, both of which shall remain operative and in full force and effect.

D. **Additional Instruments.** Each of the parties shall from time to time, at the request of others, execute, acknowledge, and deliver to the other party any and all further instruments that may be reasonably required to give full effect and force to the provisions of this Agreement.

E. **Entire Agreement.** Each of the parties hereby covenants that this Agreement is intended to and does contain and embody herein all of the understandings and Agreements, both written or oral, of the parties hereby with respect to the subject matter of this Agreement, and that there exists no oral agreement or understanding expressed or implied liability, whereby the absolute, final, and unconditional character and nature of this Agreement shall be in any way invalidated, empowered or affected. There are no representations, warranties, or covenants other than those set forth herein.

F. **Laws of the State of _____.** This Agreement shall be deemed to be made in, governed by, and interpreted under and construed in all respects in accordance with the laws of the State of _____, irrespective of the country or place of domicile or residence of either party. In the event of controversy arising out of the interpretation, construction, performance, or breach of this Agreement, the parties hereby agree and consent to the exclusive jurisdiction and venue of the District or County Court of _____ County, in the State of _____, or the United States District Court for _____, and further agree and consent that personal service or process in any such action or proceeding outside of the State of _____ and _____ County shall be tantamount to service in person within

_____ County, in the State of _____ and shall confer personal jurisdiction and venue upon either of said Courts.

G. **Assignments.** The benefits of this Agreement shall inure to the respective successors and assigns of the parties hereto and of the indemnified parties hereunder and their successors and assigns and representatives, and the obligations and liabilities assumed in this Agreement by the parties hereto shall be binding upon their respective successors and assigns; provided that the rights and obligations of Company under this Agreement may not be assigned or delegated without the prior written consent of Business Consultant, and any purported assignment without such consent shall be null and void. Notwithstanding the foregoing, Business Consultant may assign or delegate its obligations and rights under this Agreement upon thirty (30) days written notice, to another business consulting firm of its choice with the consent of Company, which consent may be withheld in Company's sole discretion.

H. **Originals.** This Agreement may be executed in any number of counterparts, each of which so executed shall be deemed an original and constitute one and the same Agreement. Facsimile copies with signatures shall be given the same legal effect as an original.

I. **Addresses of Parties.** Each party shall at all times keep the other informed of its principal place of business if different from that stated herein, and shall promptly notify the other of any change, giving the address of the new place of business or residence.

J. **Notices.** All notices that are required to be or may be sent pursuant to the provision of this Agreement shall be sent by certified mail, return receipt requested, or by overnight package delivery service to each of the parties at the address appearing herein, and shall count from the date of mailing or the validated air bill.

K. **Modification and Waiver.** A modification or waiver of any of the provisions of this Agreement shall be effective only if made in writing and executed with the same formality as this Agreement. The failure of any party to insist upon strict performance of any of the provisions of this Agreement shall not be construed as a waiver of any subsequent default of the same or similar nature or of any other nature.

L. **Injunctive Relief.** Solely by virtue of their respective execution of this Agreement and in consideration for the mutual covenants of each other, Company and Business Consultant hereby agree, consent, and acknowledge that in the event of (i) the failure by Company to pay the consideration to Business Consultant or in the event of a breach of any other material term, or (ii) Business Consultant's breach of the exclusivity provision contained in Section II.C. above, Business Consultant and Company, respectively, will be without adequate remedy-at-law and shall therefore, be entitled to immediately redress such breaches of this Agreement by temporary or permanent injunctive or mandatory relief obtained in an action or proceeding instituted in the District or County Court of _____ County, State of _____ or the United States District Court for _____ without the necessity of proving damages and without prejudice to any other remedies which Business Consultant may have at law or in equity. For the purposes of this Agreement, the parties hereby agree and consent that upon a breach of this Agreement as aforesaid, in addition to any other legal and/or equitable remedies the non-breaching party may present a conformed copy of this Agreement to the aforesaid courts and shall thereby be able to obtain a permanent injunction enforcing this Agreement or barring enjoining or otherwise prohibiting the breaching party from circumventing the express written intent of the parties as enumerated in this Agreement.

M. **Attorney's Fees.** If any arbitration, litigation, action, suit, or other proceeding is instituted to remedy, prevent, or obtain relief from a breach of this Agreement, in relation to a breach of this Agreement or pertaining to a declaration of rights under this Agreement, the prevailing party will recover all such party's attorneys' fees incurred in each and every such action, suit or other proceeding, including any and all appeals or petitions therefrom.

APPROVED AND AGREED as of this _____ **day of** _____, **20**___.

****, INC.   ****, INC.

_____   _____

_____   _____

Phone: _____   Phone: _____

Fax: _____   Fax: _____

By: By:
_____, President   _____, President

EXHIBIT A

INDEMNIFICATION PROVISIONS

****, Inc. ("Company") agrees to indemnify and hold harmless ****, Inc., its officers, employees, and authorized agents (collectively, "Business Consultant") against any and all losses, claims, damages, obligations, penalties, judgments, awards, liabilities, costs, expenses, and disbursements (incurred in any and all actions, suits, proceedings, and investigations in respect thereof and any and all legal and other costs, expenses and disbursements in giving testimony or furnishing documents in response to a subpoena or otherwise), including without limitation, the costs, expenses and disbursements, as and when incurred, of investigating, preparing or defending any such action, suit, proceeding, or investigation (whether or not in connection with any action in which Business Consultant is a party), directly or indirectly, caused by, relating to, based upon, arising out of, or in connection with any misrepresentation or omission by Company or otherwise relating to Business Consultant's acting as a consultant for Company (other than those caused by, relating to, based upon, arising out of, or in connection with Business Consultant's negligence or willful misconduct), under the Agreement dated as of the ___ day of _____, 20___, between Company and Business Consultant to which these indemnification provisions are attached and form a part (the "Agreement"). Such indemnification does not apply to acts performed by Business Consultant, which are in criminal in nature or a violation of law. Company also agrees that Business Consultant shall not have any liability (whether direct or indirect, in contract or tort, or otherwise) to Company, for, or in connection with, the engagement of Business Consultant under the Agreement, except to the extent that any such liability resulted primarily and directly from Business Consultant's negligence or willful misconduct.

These indemnification provisions shall be in addition to any liability which Company may otherwise have to Business Consultant or the persons indemnified below in this sentence and shall extend to the following: Business Consultant, its affiliated entities, partners, employees, legal counsel, agents and controlling persons (within the meaning of the federal securities laws), and the officers, directors, employees, legal counsel, agents, and controlling persons of any of them (collectively, the "Business Consultant Parties"). All references to Business Consultant in these indemnification provisions shall be understood to include any and all of the foregoing.

If any action, suit, proceeding, or investigation is commenced, as to which any of the Business Consultant Parties propose indemnification under the Agreement, they shall notify Company with reasonable promptness. Company shall retain counsel of its own choice; provided, however, that no conflict exists and such counsel is reasonably acceptable to the Business Consultant Parties, and Company shall pay fees, expenses, and disbursements of such counsel; and such counsel shall, to the extent consistent with its professional responsibilities, cooperate with Business Consultant and any counsel designated by Business Consultant. Company shall be liable for any settlement of any claim against the Business Consultant Parties made with Company's written consent, which consent shall not be unreasonably withheld. Company shall not, without the prior written consent of the party seeking indemnification, which shall not be unreasonably withheld, settle or compromise any claim, or permit a default or consent to the entry of any judgment in respect thereof, unless such settlement, compromise or consent includes, as an unconditional term thereof, the giving by the claimant to the party seeking indemnification of an unconditional release from all liability in respect of such claim.

In order to provide for just and equitable contribution, if a claim for indemnification pursuant to these indemnification provisions is made but it is found in a final judgment by a court of competent jurisdiction (not subject to further appeal) that such indemnification may not be enforced in such case, even though the express provisions hereof provide for indemnification in such case, then Company, on the one hand, and Business Consultant, on the other hand, shall contribute to the losses, claims, damages, obligations, penalties, judgments, awards, liabilities, costs, expenses, and disbursements to which the indemnified persons may be subject in accordance with the relative benefits received by Company, on the one hand, and Business Consultant, on the other hand, and also the relative fault of Company, on the one hand, and Business Consultant, on the other hand, in connection with the statements, acts or omissions which resulted in such losses, claims, damages, obligations, penalties, judgments, awards, liabilities, costs, expenses, or disbursements and the relevant equitable considerations shall also be considered. No person found liable for a fraudulent misrepresentation shall be entitled to contribution from any person who is not also found liable for such fraudulent misrepresentation.

Neither termination nor completion of the engagement of Business Consultant referred to above shall effect these indemnification provisions which shall then remain operative and in full force and effect.

Form 15 B: Due Diligence Checklist

DUE DILIGENCE CHECKLIST FOR ISSUER

1. GENERAL

Item	Description	Responsible	Date Due	Date Sent
1.1.	Name, address, phone, email for: Executives Directors Attorneys Accountants			

2. CORPORATE MATTERS

Item	Description	Responsible	Date Due	Date Sent
2.1.	Minute Book including Articles of Organization, Operating Agreement, minutes and corporate consents and stock transfers.			
2.2.	List of jurisdictions where the company has substantial contacts (either assets or business operations) and certificates of good standing (corporate and tax) from each state in which company does business.			
2.3.	List of subsidiaries and related entities.			
2.4.	Ownership structure names and addresses of shareholders and number of shares owned by each (or percentages).			
2.5.	Annual, securities or other reports filed with state or federal regulatory agencies.			

3. FINANCIAL MATTERS

Item	Description	Responsible	Date Due	Date Sent
3.1.	Financial Statements – past 3 years (audited if available, otherwise reviewed if available, otherwise compiled) if not otherwise provided in such financial statements, provide breakdown of revenues by line of business.			
3.2.	All federal, state, local and other (e.g. form 5500) tax returns for past 3 years.			
3.3.	Quarterly management reports and budgets for past 3 years.			

Item	Description	Responsible	Date Due	Date Sent
3.4.	Bank letters or agreements confirming all lines of credit, checking accounts, and compensating balance arrangements. Name and phone number and authorization to contact bank contact.			
3.5.	All agreements or documents related to or evidencing material borrowing (secured and unsecured), loan and credit agreements, agreements with factors, indentures, debentures, promissory notes, and all guarantees related thereto.			
3.6.	Comprise list of assets owned, leased and used by the company and their location. Depreciation schedule and the estimated fair market value of each.			
3.7.	States and countries in which the company is (or should be) qualified to do business or has offices.			
3.8.	List of inventory by product, quantity, carrying value, inventory method (e.g. FIFO etc.), and valuation policy.			
3.9.	List of inventory sold by item over the most recent fiscal and interim period.			
3.10.	List of any inventory write-offs taken within the last five years. Obsolescence policy.			
3.11.	Schedule of insurance policies (including workers compensation insurance) and pending or threatened claims.			
3.12.	Copies of lawyer and accounting firm contracts. Auditors letters to management and replies for the past 5 years.			
3.13.	Accounts receivable listing quality, aging, special cases, write-offs.			
3.14.	Description of any guarantees by the company of obligation of third parties (including related parties).			
3.15.	Material joint venture, operating or consulting agreements.			
3.16.	All third party secrecy, confidentiality, or non-complete agreements.			
3.17.	All installment sales agreements.			
3.18.	Internal software used (accounting, operating system etc.).			
3.19.	All correspondence to or from any other regulatory authority.			

4. EMPLOYMENT MATTERS

Item	Description	Responsible	Date Due	Date Sent
4.1.	Personal references for senior executives.			
4.2.	List of employees, their positions, salaries, and perquisites (i.e. company car, health club, bonuses).			
4.3.	Employment agreements, covenants not to complete, non-disclosure agreements, and other agreements with present or former employee.			
4.4.	Retirement plan documents including agreements, trust instruments, and plan summaries. Name and phone number and authorization to contact plan consultant.			
4.5.	Description of all employee fringe benefits including health insurance, disability plans, life insurance, and any other employee benefits. Determination letters received from IRS.			
4.6.	Agreements relating to any deferred compensation including any options granted or promised or severance pay arrangements.			
4.7.	Any arrangement with personnel who are not employees, including any independent contractor agreements, consulting agreements, independent sales representatives.			

5. LITIGATION/REGULATORY MATTERS

Item	Description	Responsible	Date Due	Date Sent
5.1.	All application, filings, reports, complaints, consent decrees, inquiries, and orders involving any regulatory or governmental agency, including Internal Revenue Service, state tax authority, state and federal environmental authorities OSHA, etc.			
5.2.	Identify all litigation, administrative proceedings or governmental investigations or inquiries pending or threatened against the company or affecting any of its assets, and copies of complaints and other pleadings in any such actions.			
5.3.	Copies of judgments, orders, consent decrees, settlement agreements, and any other agreements by which the company is bound requiring or prohibiting any future activities including final documents from all material litigation.			

Item	Description	Responsible	Date Due	Date Sent
5.4.	Copies of all federal, state, county, and other local permits and licenses of the company.			
5.5.	Documentation regarding the storage or shipment of hazardous waste substances or material or waste oil.			

6. SALES AND MARKETING

Item	Description	Responsible	Date Due	Date Sent
6.1.	List of the company's customers indicating products, services purchases, date, and value. Contact and phone number for top five customers.			
6.2.	List of competition, barriers to entry, and market share.			
6.3.	List of all other significant or supplier contracts, governmental contracts, and partnership or joint venture agreements involving the company.			
6.4.	Management projections for future revenues and expenses with assumptions used.			
6.5.	Provide three typical actual contracts.			
6.6.	Forms of dealership and/or license agreements, rental; maintenance agreements, warranties and guaranties provided to customers.			
6.7.	Agreements with distributors.			
6.8.	Copies of all marketing material.			
6.9.	Purchase orders backlog at end of the most recent fiscal year or quarter.			

7. INTELLECTUAL PROPERTY AND RELATED PARTY TRANSACTIONS

Item	Description	Responsible	Date Due	Date Sent
7.1.	Identify and provide evidence of patents, trademarks, trade names, and other proprietary rights and intellectual property owned by the company or used by the company in its business.			
7.2.	Describe all agreements or arrangements (i.e. maintenance, rental/lease or purchasing agreements) between the company and related persons or entities and all transactions between the company and such parties for the last three years.			

8. REAL ESTATE

Item	Description	Responsible	Date Due	Date Sent
8.1.	Complete list of all real property owned or leased by the company.			
8.2.	Copies of all leases.			

Form 15 C: Asset Purchase Agreement

ASSET PURCHASE AGREEMENT

(Software)

This Asset Purchase Agreement (the "Agreement") is entered into as of this __ day of _____, 20__, by and among **** LLC, a [California] limited liability company ("Seller"), ****** and ******, the only members and employees of Seller (each a "Founder"), and **** Corporation, a [Delaware] corporation ("Buyer").

In consideration of the premises and of the mutual agreements, representations, warranties and covenants hereinafter set forth, the parties hereto agree as follows:

1. <u>Transfer of Assets</u>. Seller hereby sells to Buyer, and Buyer hereby purchases and accepts from Seller at the Closing (as defined in Section 6 below), all of Seller's right, title, and interest in and to the tangible and intangible assets of the Seller listed in Schedule 1 (collectively, the "Assets"), free and clear of any liens or encumbrances, which assets include certain software products (as described in Schedule 1, the "Products").

2. <u>Liabilities</u>. Except as otherwise specifically set forth herein, Buyer is not assuming and shall not be liable for, and Seller shall retain and, as between Buyer and Seller, remain solely liable for and obligated to discharge, all of the debts, contracts, agreements, commitments, obligations, and other liabilities of any nature of Seller, whether known or unknown, accrued or not accrued, fixed or contingent, and arising out of or resulting from the operations of the Seller at any time before or after the date hereof, including any liabilities resulting from the sale of the Assets constituting a "bulk sale" under any state commercial code.

3. <u>Certain Tax Matters</u>. Seller shall be responsible for any sales or use, transfer, real property gains, excise or other similar taxes, whether imposed on Seller, any Founder or Buyer, resulting directly from the sale of Assets or otherwise as a consequence of the transactions, contemplated by this Agreement. Seller shall pay promptly discharge when due, and reimburse, indemnify, and hold harmless Buyer from the taxes described in the preceding sentence, including interest, penalties, and additions to tax in respect thereof. The products and all other Assets in connection or relating to the foregoing that are to be delivered to Buyer pursuant to this Agreement or any other agreement contemplated hereby, will be delivered via electronic transmission to Buyer's offices in California (or such other location as may be mutually agreed by the parties), and the parties acknowledge that no other form of delivery of such assets shall be required.

4. <u>Service and Support</u>. After the Closing, each Founder may continue to provide support to the licensees of the Products listed in Schedule 4 (the "Licensees") for up to nine (9) months after the Closing (the "Support Period"), subject to any employment and other obligations of each Founder to Buyer after the Closing.

5. <u>Purchase Price; Allocation</u>.

(a) The total purchase price for the Assets and all other rights obtained pursuant to this Agreement will be $_____ (the "Purchase Price"). Upon execution of this Agreement, the Purchase Price will be deposited in an escrow account (the "Escrow Account"), pursuant to the terms of an Escrow Agreement substantially in the form attached as Exhibit A hereto. The Escrow Agreement will call for release of the Purchase Price and all interest thereon to the Seller immediately after all conditions specified in Section 6 have been met. In any other event, all funds in the Escrow Account will be returned to Buyer.

(b) For purposes of complying with the requirements of Section 1060 of the Internal Revenue Code of 1986, as amended (the "Code"), the Purchase Price shall be allocated as provided in Schedule 5(b). Each party hereto agrees to prepare its federal and state income tax returns for all current and future tax reporting periods and file Form 8594 (and corresponding state forms) with respect to transfer of the Assets to Buyer contemplated under this Agreement in a manner consistent with such allocation. If any state or federal taxing authority challenges such allocation, the party receiving notice of such challenge shall give the other prompt written notice of such challenge, and the parties shall cooperate in good faith in responding to such challenge in order to preserve the effectiveness of the allocation.

6. Closing.

(a) The Closing shall take place as soon as practicable after the parties have complied with the notice requirements of the applicable bulk sales laws under the California Commercial Code ("CCC"); provided, that no creditors of the Seller make any claims which in Buyer's sole judgment have or could have a material adverse effect on the Assets. If any such claims are made, Buyer shall have the option to waive this condition and proceed with the Closing or to terminate this Agreement and take back all funds deposited in the Escrow Account.

(b) At the Closing:

(i) Seller shall deliver the Assets to Buyer, to the extent possible transmitting such Assets electronically to Buyer as directed by Buyer.

(ii) Buyer shall deliver the Purchase Price to Seller.

(iii) Seller shall deliver to Buyer a Bill of Sale and Assignment substantially in the form of Exhibit B, and Buyer shall deliver an Assignment and Assumption Agreement substantially in the form of Exhibit C, in which Seller assigns to Buyer all of Seller's (and each Founder's) right, title and interest in and to the Assets and Buyer assumes certain rights and obligations of Seller.

(iv) Seller and each Founder shall deliver to Buyer any assignments, and any required consents to assignment, of all Transferred Agreements (as listed in Schedule 1, the "Transferred Agreements") assigned to Buyer, duly executed by the appropriate parties having the authority to so assign or consent to assign, in form and substance as Buyer shall reasonably request. Buyer shall assume the perform-ance of all obligations arising under the Transferred Agreements assigned to Buyer after the Closing, as set forth in the Assignment and Assumption Agreement.

(v) Each party shall deliver a certificate of an officer of such party stating that the representations and warranties of such party contained in this Agreement are true and correct in all material respects as of the Closing date as if made on such date, and that all covenants of such party that are required to be complied with prior to or at the Closing have been complied with.

7. Post-Closing Matters. After the Closing, Seller and each Founder will exe-cute and deliver, upon the request of Buyer, all such other and further materials and documents and instruments of conveyance, transfer or assignment as may reason-ably be requested by Buyer to effect, record, or verify the transfer to, and vesting in Buyer, of Seller's right, title and interest in and to the Assets, free and clear of all Liens (as defined in Section 8(f)), in accordance with the terms of this Agreement.

8. Representation and Warranties of Seller. Seller and each Founder jointly and severally represent and warrant to Buyer as follows (except as forth in the Seller

Disclosure Schedule, a copy of which prior to the execution of this Agreement was provided to Buyer by the Sellers):

(a) <u>Organization</u>. Seller is a limited liability company duly formed and validly existing under the laws of California, and has full corporate power and authority and legal right to own and operate or lease the Assets and to carry on its business as presently conducted, to execute and deliver this Agreement and all of the other agreements and instruments to be executed and delivered by Seller pursuant hereto, and to consummate the transactions contemplated hereby and thereby. Seller is qualified to do business in California and is not required to be qualified in any other state or other jurisdiction. The Founders are the only persons that hold any membership or other interest in Seller.

(b) <u>Authority</u>. The execution and delivery of this Agreement (and all other agreements and instruments contemplated hereunder) by Seller and each Founder, the performance by the Seller and each Founder of its or their obligations hereunder and thereunder, and the consummation by Seller and each Founder of the transactions contemplated hereby and thereby have been duly authorized by all necessary action by the Board of Directors and members of Seller.

(c) <u>Execution and Binding Effect</u>. This Agreement has been duly and validly executed and delivered by Seller and each Founder and constitutes, and the other agreements and instruments to be executed and delivered by Seller and each Founder pursuant hereto, upon their execution and delivery by Seller and each Founder, will constitute (assuming, in each case, the due and valid authorization, execution and delivery thereof by Buyer), legal, valid, and binding agreements of Seller and each Founder, enforceable against the Seller and each Founder in accordance with their respective terms.

(d) <u>Consents and Approvals of Governmental Entities</u>. There is no requirement applicable to Seller or either Founder to make any filing, declaration, or registration with, or to obtain any permit, authorization, consent or approval of, any Governmental Entity as a condition to the lawful consummation by Seller or either Founder of the transactions contemplated by this Agreement and the other agreements and instruments to be executed and delivered by Seller or either Founder pursuant hereto or the consummation by Seller or either Founder of the transactions contemplated herein or therein.

(e) <u>No Violation</u>. Neither the execution, delivery, and performance of this Agreement and all of the other agreements and instruments to be executed and delivered pursuant hereto, nor the consummation of the transactions contemplated hereby or thereby, will, with or without the passage of time or the delivery of notice or both: (i) conflict with, violate or result in any breach of the terms, conditions or provisions of the articles, operating agreement or other organizational documents or agreements of Seller; (ii) conflict with or result in a violation or breach of, or constitute a default or require consent of any individual, corporation, partnership, trust or unincorporated organization or Governmental Entity ("Person") (or give rise to any right of termination, cancellation or acceleration) under, any of the terms, conditions or provisions of any notice, bond, mortgage, indenture, license, franchise permit, agreement, lease or other instrument or obligation to which Seller or either Founder is a party or by which Seller or either Founder, any of the properties or assets of the Seller or either Founder may be bound, where such conflict, violation, breach, default or consent would have a material adverse effect on the Assets; or (iii) violate any statute, ordinance or law or any rule, regulation, order, writ, injunction or decree of any Governmental Entity applicable to Seller or either Founder or by which any properties or assets of Seller or either Founder may be bound, where such violation would have a material adverse effect on the Assets.

(f) <u>Assets Generally</u>. Seller holds valid title to all of the Assets and has the complete and unrestricted power and the unqualified right to sell, assign and deliver the Assets to Buyer. Upon consummation of the transactions contemplated by this Agreement, Buyer will acquire valid title to the Assets free and clear of any mortgages, pledges, liens, security interests, encumbrances, charges, or other claims of third parties of any kind ("Liens"). No Person other than Seller has any right or interest in the Assets, including the right to grant interests in the Assets to third parties.

(g) <u>Infringement</u>. The Assets do not infringe any patent, trade name, trademark, copyright, trade secret, or any other intellectual property right of any Person, without the necessity of relying upon any license held by Seller to any such intellectual property right of any Person. There is no pending or threatened claim by Seller or either Founder against any Person for infringement, misuse, or misappropriation of any Assets. Neither Seller nor any Founder is obligated or under any liability whatsoever to make any payments by way of royalties, fees, or otherwise to any owner of, licensor of, or other claimant to, any patent, trademark, trade name, copyright, trade secret, or other intellectual property rights, with respect to the use thereof or in connection with the conduct of Seller's business or otherwise. All development relating to the Products was performed by the Founders, and each Founder has, pursuant to a legally binding agreement, assigned all of such Founders rights in all of the Assets to Seller.

(h) <u>Employees</u>. The Founders are and have been the only employees of or consultants to Seller. No Seller employee or consultant is obligated under any contract (including licenses, covenants, or commitments of any nature) or other agreement, or subject to any judgment, decree, or order of any court or administrative agency, that would conflict with their obligation to use their best efforts to promote the interests of Seller in the Assets. There are no written or oral contracts of employment between Seller and any employee of or consultant to Seller.

(i) <u>Taxes</u>. All sales and use taxes, real and personal property taxes, gross receipts taxes, documentary transfer taxes, employment taxes, withholding taxes, unemployment insurance contributions, and other taxes or governmental charges of any kind, however denominated, including any interest, penalties and additions to tax in respect thereto, for which Buyer could become liable as a result of acquiring the Assets or which could result in a lien on or charge against the Assets (collectively, "Taxes") have been or will be paid for all periods (or portions thereof) prior to the due dates thereof. Seller and any other person required to file returns or reports of Taxes have duly and timely filed (or will file prior to the Closing Date) all returns and reports of Taxes required to be filed prior to such date, and all such returns and reports are true, correct, and complete. There are no liens for Taxes on any of the Assets. There are no pending or, to the knowledge of Seller or either Founder, threatened proceedings with respect to Taxes, and there are no outstanding waivers or extensions of statutes of limitations with respect to assessments of Taxes. Neither Seller, nor either Founder, is a "foreign person" within the meaning of Section 1445(f)(3) of the Code.

(j) <u>Claims</u>. There are no claims, actions, suits, inquiries, proceedings, or investigations relating to Seller or the Assets which are currently pending or, to the best knowledge of Seller and each Founder, threatened, at law or in equity or before or by any Governmental Entity. There are no claims relating to any of the Assets containing allegations that the Assets are defective or in breach of any warranty, or were improperly designed or manufactured or improperly labeled.

(k) Defaults. Neither Seller nor either Founder is in (or has received notice of any) default under or with respect to any judgment, order, writ, injunction, or decree of any court or any Governmental Entity relating to (or that could affect) any of the Assets. There does not exist any default by the Seller or either Founder or, to the knowledge of Seller, by any other Person, or event that, with notice or lapse of time, or both, would constitute a default under any agreement (including, without limitation, any of the Transferred Agreements) entered into by the Seller or either Founder which could adversely affect the Assets.

(l) Full Disclosure. Neither Seller nor either Founder is aware of any facts pertaining to the Assets which could affect the Assets in a material adverse manner or which are likely in the future to affect the Assets in a material adverse manner. Neither this Agreement nor any other agreement, exhibit, schedule, or certificate being entered into or delivered pursuant hereto contains any untrue statement of a material fact or omits to state any material fact necessary in order to make the statements therein contained not misleading.

(m) Fair Consideration; No Fraudulent Conveyance. The sale of the Assets pursuant to this Agreement is made in exchange for fair and equivalent consideration, and neither Seller nor either Founder is now insolvent and neither Seller nor either Founder will be rendered insolvent by the sale, transfer and assignment of the Assets pursuant to the terms of this Agreement. Neither Seller nor either Founder is entering into this Agreement and the other agreements referenced in this Agreement with the intent to defraud, delay or hinder its creditors and the consummation of the transactions contemplated by this Agreement, and the other agreements referenced in this Agreement, will not have any such effect. The transactions contemplated in this Agreement or any agreements referenced in this Agreement will not constitute a fraudulent conveyance, or otherwise give rise to any right of any creditor of Seller or either Founder whatsoever to any of the Asserts in the hands of Buyer after the Closing.

9.   Representations and Warranties of Buyer. Buyer represents and warrants to Seller as follows:

(a) Organization. Buyer is a corporation duly formed and validly existing under the laws of Delaware, and has full corporate power and authority to execute and deliver this Agreement and all of the other agreements and instruments to be executed and delivered by Buyer pursuant hereto, and to consummate the transactions contemplated hereby and thereby.

(b) Authority. The execution and delivery of this Agreement (and all other agreements and instruments contemplated hereunder) by Buyer, the performance by Buyer of its obligations hereunder and thereunder, and the consummation by Buyer of the transactions contemplated hereby and thereby have been duly authorized by all necessary action by the Board of Directors of Buyer. No other act or proceeding on the part of Buyer or its members is necessary to approve the execution and delivery of this Agreement and such other agreements and instruments, the performance by Buyer of its obligations hereunder and thereunder and the consummation of the transactions contemplated hereby and thereby.

(c) Execution and Binding Effect. This Agreement has been duly and validly executed and delivered by Buyer and constitutes, and the other agreements and instruments to be executed and delivered by Buyer pursuant hereto, upon their execution and delivery by Buyer, will constitute (assuming, in each case, the due and valid authorization, execution and delivery thereof by Sellers), legal, valid, and binding agreements of Buyer, enforceable against Buyer in accordance with their respective terms.

(d) <u>Consent and Approvals</u>. There is no requirement applicable to Buyer to make any filing, declaration, or registration with, or to obtain any permit, authorization, consent or approval of, any Governmental Entity as a condition to the lawful consummation by Buyer of the transactions contemplated by this Agreement and the other agreements and instruments to be executed and delivered by Buyer pursuant hereto or the consummation of the transactions contemplated herein or therein.

(e) <u>No Violation</u>. Neither the execution, delivery, and performance of this Agreement and all of the other agreements and instruments to be executed and delivered pursuant hereto, nor the consummation of the transactions contemplated hereby or thereby, will, with or without the passage of time or the delivery of notice or both: (a) conflict with, violate or result in any breach of the terms, conditions or provisions of the articles or bylaws of Buyer; (b) conflict with or result in a violation or breach of, or constitute a default or require consent of any Person (or give rise to any right of termination, cancellation or acceleration) under, any of the terms, conditions or provisions of any notice, bond, mortgage, indenture, license, franchise, permit, agreement, lease, or other instrument or obligation to which Buyer is a party or by which Buyer or any of its properties or assets may be bound, where such conflict, violation, breach, default or consent would have a material adverse effect on the business or assets of Buyer; or (c) violate any statute, ordinance, or law or any rule, regulation, order, writ, injunction, or decree of any Governmental Entity applicable to Buyer or by which any of its properties or assets may be bound, where such violation would have a material adverse effect on the business or assets of Buyer.

10. <u>Covenants of Seller and Founders</u>.

(a) <u>Taxes</u>. Seller and each Founder shall, to the extent that failure to do so could adversely affect the Assets following Closing: (i) continue to file within the required time period for filing all returns and reports relating to Taxes required to be filed by Seller and each Founder, and such returns and reports shall be true, correct and complete; and (ii) be responsible for and pay when due any and all Taxes attributable to, levied or imposed upon the Assets for periods (or portions thereof) ending on or prior to the Closing.

(b) <u>Post-Closing Cooperation</u>. Seller and each Founder agrees that, if requested by Buyer, they will cooperate with Buyer in enforcing the terms of any agreements between Seller or either Founder and any third party involving the Assets, including without limitation terms relating to confidentiality and the protection of intellectual property rights. In the event that Buyer is unable to enforce its intellectual property rights against a third party as a result of a rule or law barring enforcement of such rights by a transferee of such rights, Seller and each Founder agree to reasonably cooperate with Buyer by assigning to Buyer such rights as may be required by Buyer to enforce its intellectual property rights in its own name. If such assignment still does not permit Buyer to enforce its intellectual property rights against the third party, Seller or either Founder, as the case may be, agrees to initiate proceedings against such third party, and Buyer shall be entitled to participate in such proceedings, all at Buyer's expense.

(c) <u>Public Announcements</u>. Seller and each Founder shall obtain the prior written consent of Buyer prior to disclosing the existence of this Agreement (including the exhibits and schedules hereto) and the transactions contemplated herein or any information related to the Assets.

(d) <u>No Distribution of Products</u>. Seller has removed and will keep removed from Seller's website (and all other websites and similarly accessible locations) the ability to download copies of the Products or any portion of the Products. During the support period, only the Licensees will be permitted to order object code versions of the Products from Seller via email, provided that Seller provides notice to Buyer of all such orders during each month within five days of the end of such month. All distribution agreements under which Seller has granted a right to resell or otherwise distribute the products, including a brief description of the termination provisions of each such agreement, are listed in Schedule 10(d). All such agreements have been terminated as of the date hereof or are terminable by Seller and notice of termination has been sent to each distributor.

(e) <u>Breach by Licensees</u>. In the event that any Licensee breaches the terms of its license agreement with Seller or otherwise misuses the intellectual property or other assets of Seller being transferred to Buyer pursuant to this Agreement, Seller shall use its best efforts to take appropriate legal action against such Licensee to enforce such rights. In addition, at Buyer's request, Seller shall assign its right to enforce such intellectual property and other rights to Buyer, and Buyer shall be entitled to enforce such rights directly or in Seller's name.

(f) From and after the date of this Agreement until the earlier of the Closing or the termination of this Agreement (the "No Shop Period") in accordance with its terms, neither Seller nor the Founders shall: (a) directly or indirectly solicit, initiate discussions, or engage in negotiations with any person (whether such negotiations are initiated by Seller, Founder or otherwise), or take any other action intended or designed to facilitate the efforts of any person, other than Buyer, relating to the possible acquisition of all or a material portion of the Assets (whether by way of merger, purchase of equity in Seller, purchase of assets, or otherwise, each of which shall be considered an "Acquisition"); or (b) enter into an agreement with any person, other than Buyer, providing for any of the above. If during the No-Shop Period, Seller and/or the Founders enter into any agreement, whether through a binding or nonbinding letter of intent, any definitive agreement or otherwise, with respect to an Acquisition, Seller and the Founders collectively agree to pay to Oracle by certified or cashier's check an amount equal to $_____ (the "Break-Up Fee"), within 5 days following receipt of an invoice from Buyer for such Break-Up Fee. Seller and Buyer agree that the Break-Up Fee shall not be deemed to be liquidated damages, and that the right to the payment of the Break-Up Fee shall be in addition to any other rights and remedies under contract, at law or at equity to which Buyer may be entitled.

11. <u>Indemnification</u>.

(a) <u>Survival of Representations and Warranties</u>. The representations and warranties of Seller and each Founder in Section 8 shall survive for a period one year after the Closing Date, except for claims for fraud, which shall survive indefinitely, and claims for Taxes, which shall survive until lapse of the applicable statute of limitations (including extensions thereof). No investigation, or knowledge acquired, by Buyer or on behalf of Buyer with respect to any breach of any representation or warranty made by the Sellers or any other matter shall affect Buyer's rights to indemnification pursuant to this Section 11.

(b) <u>Indemnification by the Seller</u>. Seller and each Founder shall jointly and severally indemnify and hold harmless Buyer, each direct and indirect subsidiary of Buyer and each of their officers, directors, employees, agents, successors, and assigns ("Buyer Indemnitees") for any and all liabilities, losses, damages, claims, costs, and expenses, interest, awards, judgments and penalties (including, without limitation, legal costs and expenses and interest on the amount of any loss from the date suffered or incurred by Buyer Indemnitee) (a "Loss") arising out of, resulting from or caused by: (i) any breach or the inaccuracy of any of the representations, warranties, covenants, or agreements in this Agreement made by Seller or either Founder, and (ii) all liabilities or obligations, including, without limitation, those relating to Taxes, (whether known or unknown, accrued or not accrued, fixed or contingent) of Seller and each Founder existing at Closing. The obligation of Seller and each Founder to indemnify Buyer under this Section 11(b) shall not be limited in time or amount; provided, that (except in the case of fraud by Seller or either Founder and claims for Taxes) the aggregate liability for claims made solely for breaches of representations and warranties under Section 11(b)(i) shall not exceed the Purchase Price, and the indemnification obligations relating to such claims shall terminate one (1) year from the date of this Agreement.

(c) <u>Indemnification by Buyer</u>. Buyer shall indemnify and hold harmless Seller and each Founder ("Seller Indemnitees") for any and all Losses arising out of or resulting from a liability or obligation, including, without limitation, those relating to Taxes, (whether known or unknown, accrued or not accrued, fixed and determined or contingent) of Buyer arising out of or resulting from the use or sale of the Assets by Buyer after the Closing Date, other than a liability or obligation for which any Buyer Indemnitee is entitled to indemnification from Seller or either Founder pursuant to the provisions of Section 11(b). Buyer's obligation to indemnify Seller and each Founder under this Section 11(c) shall not be limited in time or amount.

(d) <u>Indemnification Procedure</u>.

(i) Whenever any Loss shall be asserted against or incurred by a Buyer Indemnitee or Sellers Indemnitee (the "Indemnified Party"), the Indemnified Party shall give written notice thereof (a "Claim") to the Sellers (and the Founders) or Buyer, respectively (the "Indemnifying Party"). The Indemnified Party shall furnish to the Indemnifying Party in reasonable detail such information as the Indemnified Party may have with respect to the Claim (including in any case copies of any summons, complaint, or other pleading which may have been served on it and any written claim, demand, invoice, billing or other document evidencing or asserting the same). The failure to give such notice shall not relieve the Indemnifying Party of its indemnification obligations under this Agreement.

(ii) If the Claim is based on a claim of a person that is not a party to this Agreement, the Indemnifying Party shall, at its expense, undertake the defense of such Claim with attorneys of its own choosing reasonably satisfactory to the Indemnified Party. In the event the Indemnifying Party, within a reasonable time after receiving notice of a Claim from the Indemnified Party, fails to defend the Claim, the Indemnified Party may, at the Indemnifying Party's expense, undertake the defense of the Claim and may compromise or settle the Claim, all for the account of the Indemnifying Party. After notice from the Indemnifying Party to the Indemnified Party of its election to assume the defense of such Claim, the Indemnifying Party shall not be liable to the Indemnified Party under this Section 8.4 for any legal expenses subsequently incurred by the Indemnified Party in connection with the defense thereof, except for such expenses incurred in connection with cooperation with, or at the request of, the Indemnifying Party; provided, however, that the Indemnified Party shall have the right to employ counsel to represent it if, in the Indemnified Party's reasonable judgment, based upon the advice of counsel, it is advisable, in light of the separate interests of the Indemnified Party and the Indemnifying Party, for the Indemnified Party to be represented by separate counsel, and in that event the reasonable fees and expenses of such separate counsel shall be paid by the Indemnifying Party.

(iii) The Indemnifying Party shall not, except with the consent of the Indemnified Party, given in its sole discretion, consent to entry of any judgment or enter into any settlement.

12. <u>Certain Actions Upon Execution of this Agreement</u>.

(a) Each of the Founders shall have received offers of employment from Buyer reasonably satisfactory to each such Founder.

(b) Seller and Buyer shall have entered into a license agreement in the form attached hereto as Exhibit D, relating to certain software of Seller that is not otherwise included in the Assets being acquired by Buyer. Such license agreement shall terminate upon any termination of this Agreement.

13. <u>General Terms</u>.

(a) <u>Notices</u>. Every notice or other communication required or contemplated by this Agreement by either party shall be delivered to the other party at the address set forth on the signature page hereto by: (i) personal delivery; (ii) postage prepaid, return receipt requested, registered or certified mail; (iii) internationally recognized express courier, such as Federal Express, UPS, or DHL; or (iv) facsimile with a confirmation copy sent simultaneously. Notice not given in writing shall be effective only if acknowledged in writing by a duly authorized representative of the party to whom it was given.

(b) <u>Severability</u>. In the event any provision of this Agreement shall be determined to be invalid or unenforceable under applicable law, all other provisions of this Agreement shall continue in full force and effect unless such invalidity or unenforceability causes substantial deviation from the underlying intent of the parties expressed in this Agreement or unless the invalid or unenforceable provisions comprise an integral part of, or are inseparable from, the remainder of this Agreement. If this Agreement continues in full force and effect as provided above, the parties shall replace the invalid provision with a valid provision which corresponds as far as possible to the spirit and purpose of the invalid provision.

(c) <u>Amendments and Waivers</u>. No amendment, modification, termination, or waiver of any provision of this Agreement or consent to any departure by any party therefrom shall in any event be effective without the written concurrence of the other party hereto. Any waiver or consent shall be effective only in the specific instance and for the specific purpose for which it is given. No notice to or demand on any party in any case shall entitle any other party to any other or further notice or demand in similar or other circumstances.

(d) <u>Absence of Third-Party Beneficiaries</u>. No provisions of this Agreement, express or implied, are intended or shall be construed to confer upon or give to any Person other than the parties hereto, any rights, remedies or other benefits under or by reason of this Agreement unless specifically provided otherwise herein, and except as so provided, all provisions hereof shall be personal solely between the parties to this Agreement.

(e) <u>Governing Law</u>. The validity, construction, performance and enforceability of this Agreement shall be governed in all respects by the laws of the State of _____, without reference to the choice of law principles thereof.

(f) <u>Interpretation</u>. This Agreement, including any exhibits, addenda, schedules, and amendments, has been negotiated at arm's length and between persons sophisticated and knowledgeable in the matters dealt with in this Agreement. Each party has been represented by experienced and knowledgeable legal counsel. The provisions of this Agreement shall be interpreted in a reasonable manner to effect the purposes of the parties and this Agreement. The article and section headings contained in this Agreement are for reference purposes only and will not affect in any way the meaning or interpretation of this Agreement.

(g) <u>Entire Agreement</u>. The terms of this Agreement and the other writings referred to herein and delivered by the parties hereto are intended by the parties to be the final expression of their agreement with respect to the subject matter hereof and may not be contradicted by evidence of any prior or contemporaneous agreement. The parties further intend that this Agreement, together with the exhibits and schedules hereto, shall constitute the complete and exclusive statement of its terms. The parties acknowledge and agree that this Agreement and exhibits and schedules hereto constitute the agreements necessary to accomplish the transactions contemplated by this Agreement and are parts of an integrated arrangement between the parties with respect to the purchase and sale of the Assets.

(h) <u>Counterparts</u>. This Agreement may be executed simultaneously in multiple counterparts, each of which shall be deemed an original, but all of which taken together shall constitute one and the same instrument. Execution and delivery of this Agreement by exchange of facsimile copies bearing the facsimile signature of a party hereto shall constitute a valid and binding execution and delivery of this Agreement by such party. Such facsimile copies shall constitute enforceable original documents.

(i) <u>Expenses</u>. Each of the parties agrees to pay its own expenses in connection with the transactions contemplated by this Agreement, including, without limitation, legal, consulting, accounting and investment banking fees, whether or not such transactions are consummated.

This Asset Purchase Agreement has been duly executed and delivered by the authorized officers of Sellers and Buyer as of the date first above written.

**** LLC

By: _____

Name: _____

Title: _____

Founders:

_____

_____ [Name]

_____

_____ [Name]

**** CORPORATION

By: _____

Name: _____

Title: _____

Schedule 1
(Schedule of Assets)

Software Products (the "Products"). All of the software products of Seller, including without limitation, [Product A], [Product B], [Product C], and [Product C Agent System], including any and all source and object codes, binaries, supplements, modifications, updates, corrections, and enhancements to past and current versions of such products, shipping versions of such products, and versions of such products currently under development, and any and all English and foreign language versions and back-up and archival tapes from the Seller's storage facilities of past and current versions of such products, shipping versions of such products, and versions of such products currently under development; in each case for all markets:

a. [Product A version 1.1 (Published 1/20___)]:
    1. [Module 1]
    2. [Module 2]
    3. documentation files for [Product A]

b. [Product B version 2.02 (Published 6/20___)]:
    1. [Module 1]
    2. [Module 2]
    3. [Module 3]
    4. [Module 4]
    5. documentation files for [Product B]

c. [Product C version 2.02 (Published 1/20___)]:
    1. [Module 1]
    2. [Module 2]

d. [Product C version 3.01 (Published 6/20___)]:
    1. [Module 1]
    2. [Module 2]
    3. [Module 3]
    4. [Module 4]
    5. [Module 5]
    6. [Module 6]
    7. documentation files for [Product C]

e. [Product C Utility (Unpublished trade secret)]:
    1. [Module 1]
    2. documentation files for [Product C Utility]

Copyrights. Any and all copyrights in and to the Products. There are no copyright registrations.

Trademarks. All rights to the following trademarks which are registered with the U.S. Patent and Trademark Office: *******, and *******.

Engineering Information. Any and all design and code documentation, methodologies, processes, trade secrets, design information, product information, technology, formulae, routines, engineering specifications, technical manuals and data, drawings, inventions (exclusive of inventions covered by patents and patent applications), know how, techniques, engineering work papers, works-in-progress, and programmer's notes which are necessary to the development, manufacture, operation, maintenance or use of the Assets (collectively, "Engineering Information").

<u>Transferred Agreements</u>. All rights under the following agreements (the "Transferred Agreements") between Seller and the third parties named therein:

_____

_____

_____

_____

<u>Testing Materials</u>. Any and all Engineering Information relating specifically to testing and correcting defects in the Assets (including, without limitation, regression tests, test beds, test plans, software defect database, and historical defect data) and all other documents and materials which are necessary or helpful to maintain, enhance, and correct errors and to provide continued customer technical support (the "Documentation");

<u>Customer Support Materials</u>. Any and all customer support materials relating specifically to the Assets, including support training materials and support bulletins (including, without limitation, copies of any and all information on electronic bulletin boards) (the "Customer Support Materials").

<u>Tangible Assets</u>. The following tangible assets:

_____

_____

_____

_____

<u>Books and Records</u>. All books and records relating to the Assets, and lists of all licensees and vendors of the Assets.

<u>Tools</u>. The software design tools and scripts, modifications and additions to such tools which were used to compile, link or build the Assets, including without limitation, all software development tools used exclusively in or for the development or maintenance of the Assets. The Development Tools include the following tools, all of which are off-the-shelf and commercially or freely available:

_____

_____

_____

_____

Schedule 4
(Licensees of the Products)
All licensees of the Products are listed in the attached as Schedule 4.

Schedule 5(b)
(Purchase Price Allocation)

Schedule 10(d)
(Distribution Agreements)

_____

_____

_____

_____

Form 15 D: Escrow Agreement for Asset Purchase

Exhibit A
(Escrow Agreement)

ESCROW AGREEMENT

(Asset Purchase Agreement)

This Escrow Agreement is made as of this __ day of _____, 20___, by and among **** Corporation, a Delaware corporation ("Buyer"), _____ (the "Escrow Agent"), and **** LLC (the "Seller").

Background

This Agreement is entered into pursuant to Section 5(a) of the Asset Purchase Agreement dated as of the date hereof (the "Purchase Agreement") by and among Buyer, **** LLC, Seller, and _____ and _____ (each a "Founder" and together the "Founders"). The Purchase Agreement provides for the purchase by Buyer, and the sale by Seller of certain Assets of Seller in exchange for a cash payment by Buyer of $_____. Capitalized terms used herein and not defined herein shall have their defined meanings as set forth in the Purchase Agreement.

The parties hereto agree as follows.

1. <u>Delivery of Funds to Escrow</u>. Upon execution of the Purchase Agreement, Buyer shall, pursuant to the Purchase Agreement, set aside and deliver to the Escrow Agent $_____ (the "Escrow Dollars") which Escrow Dollars shall be invested by the Escrow Agent solely in accordance with Section 3 hereof. The Escrow Agent agrees to hold the Escrow Dollars in escrow (the "Escrow Fund") on behalf of the other parties hereto until such time as it is required to deliver them as herein provided.

2. <u>Distribution Events</u>. The Escrow Agent will distribute and deliver all or part of the Escrow Dollars at the Closing, subject to provisions of Section 6 of the Purchase Agreement; provided, that no Escrow Dollars shall be distributed to Seller or either Founder as long as any claims have been made by creditors against the Assets and such claims have not been satisfied or waived to the satisfaction of Buyer, or if such distribution would conflict with any bulk sales laws governing the transfer of the Assets.

3. <u>Investment of Escrow Dollars; Interest</u>. The Escrow Agent shall invest the Escrow Dollars solely in direct obligations of the United States Government, obligations the principal and interest of which are fully guaranteed by the United States Government, any daily or weekly withdrawal money market fund investing solely in such obligations or interest bearing, time or demand deposits fully insured by the Federal Deposit Insurance Corporation (collectively, "Permitted Investments"), or any combination of the foregoing. Any interest earned net of any fees directly related to making the above investments shall become Escrow Dollars and shall be paid to Seller in accordance with Section 2 hereof, or be returned to Buyer in any other event. The Escrow Agent agrees to hold such funds in trust and not to allow the Escrow Dollars to be subject to any claim or adverse interest of any parties other than the parties to this Agreement.

793

4. <u>Court Orders.</u> It is the agreement and intent of Buyer and Seller that Buyer's rights hereunder and the subjection of the Escrow Dollars to this Agreement shall be prior and superior to any interest of any present or future creditor of Seller in the Escrow Dollars.

5. <u>Escrow Agent's Protection.</u>

(a) In taking any action whatsoever hereunder, the Escrow Agent shall be protected in relying upon any notice, paper, or other document reasonably believed by it to be genuine, or upon any evidence reasonably believed by it to be sufficient. The Escrow Agent shall not be liable to Buyer, Seller or the Founders for any act performed or omitted to be performed by it in good faith and shall be liable only in case of its own bad faith or willful misconduct. In addition, the Escrow Agent may consult with legal counsel in connection with its duties hereunder and shall be fully protected in any act taken, suffered or permitted by it in good faith in accordance with the advice of counsel.

(b) The duties and responsibilities of the Escrow Agent shall be limited to those expressly set forth herein and it shall not be obligated to recognize any other agreement among the parties hereto.

(c) If the Escrow Agent becomes a party to any litigation or dispute by reason hereof, it is hereby authorized to deposit with the clerk of a court of competent jurisdiction any and all funds, securities, or other property held by it pursuant hereto and, thereupon, shall stand fully relieved and discharged of any further duties hereunder. Also, if the Escrow Agent is threatened to be made a party to litigation by reason hereof, it is hereby authorized to interplead all interested parties in any court of competent jurisdiction and to deposit with the clerk of such court any funds and all or any part of the securities or other properties held by it pursuant hereto and, thereupon, shall stand fully relieved and discharged of any further duties hereunder in respect of such deposit and the matters giving rise thereto.

6. <u>Termination.</u> This Agreement shall terminate upon the earlier to occur of (i) the termination of the Purchaser Agreement, (ii) distribution of all of the Escrow Dollars in accordance with the terms hereof, or (iii) upon the mutual written agreement of Buyer, Seller, and the Founders.

7. <u>Transfer of Interests.</u> Neither Seller, nor the Founders, shall pledge, transfer, or otherwise dispose of any Escrow Dollars, or any interest therein, prior to the distribution of such Escrow Dollars in accordance with this Agreement.

8. <u>Miscellaneous.</u>

(a) <u>Amendments and Waiver.</u> This Agreement may not be modified or amended except by instrument or instruments in writing signed by the party against whom enforcement of any such modification or amendment is sought. Any party hereto may, by an instrument in writing, waive compliance by the other parties with any term or provision of this Agreement on the part of such party to be performed or complied with. No action taken pursuant to the Agreement, including any investigation by or on behalf of any party, shall be deemed to constitute a waiver by the party taking such action of compliance with any representation, warranty, covenant or agreement contained or contemplated herein. The waiver by any party hereto of a breach of any term or provision of this Agreement shall not be construed as a waiver of any subsequent breach.

(b) <u>Notices.</u> All notices, requests, demands, or other communications which are required or may be given pursuant to the terms of this Agreement shall be given pursuant to the notice provisions of the Purchaser Agreement. Any notice to the Escrow Agent will be sent to:

_____, Attn: _____ (Fax: ###-###-####).

(c) <u>Entire Agreement</u>. This Agreement contains the entire agreement among the parties hereto and supersedes all prior and contemporaneous agreements, arrangements, negotiations, and understandings among the parties hereto, relating to the subject matter hereof. However, with respect to Buyer and Seller, in the event of any conflict between any of the terms of this Agreement and any of the terms of the Purchase Agreement, the terms of the Purchase Agreement shall govern. The parties hereto acknowledge that the Escrow Agent is not charged with any duties or responsibilities with respect to the Purchase Agreement. This Agreement will inure to the benefit of and be binding upon and enforceable against the parties and their successors and assigns, and, in the case of individual parties to this Agreement, their respective heirs.

(d) <u>Applicable Law</u>. This Agreement shall be governed by and construed and enforced in accordance with and subject to the laws of the State of _____, without regard to its principles governing conflicts of laws.

(e) <u>Counterparts</u>. This Agreement may be executed in counterparts, each of which shall be deemed an original, but all of which together shall constitute one and the same instrument. The parties hereto agree to submit to the jurisdiction of the state and federal courts located in _____ County, _____.

(f) <u>Further Documents</u>. Each party agrees to execute and deliver, at any time and from time to time, upon the reasonable request of another party, such further instruments or documents as may be necessary or appropriate to carry out the provisions contained herein, and to take such other action as another party may reasonably request to effectuate the purposes of this Agreement.

(g) <u>Reformation and Severability</u>. If any provision of this Agreement is declared invalid by any tribunal, then such provision shall be deemed automatically adjusted to the minimum extent necessary to conform to the requirements for validity as declared at such time and, as so adjusted, shall be deemed a provision of this Agreement as though originally included herein. In the event that the provision invalidated is of such a nature that it cannot be so adjusted, the provision shall be deemed deleted from this Agreement as though such provision had never been included herein. In either case, the remaining provisions of this Agreement shall remain in effect.

This Escrow Agreement has been duly executed and delivered by the authorized officers of Buyer and Seller, and by each of the Escrow Agent, and the Founders, as of the date first set forth above.

**** LLC

By: _____

Name:_____

Title: _____

FOUNDERS:

_____

_____ [Name]

_____

_____ [Name]

**** CORPORATION

By: _____

    Name: _____

    Title: _____

ESCROW AGENT

By: _____

    Name: _____

    Title: _____

Form 15 E: Bill of Sale and Assignment for Asset Purchase

Exhibit B
(Bill of Sale and Assignment Agreement)

BILL OF SALE AND ASSIGNMENT AGREEMENT

This Bill of Sale and Assignment Agreement is entered into as of this ____ day of _____, 20___, by and among **** LLC, a California limited liability company ("Seller"), _____ and _____, the only members and employees of Seller (each a "Founder"), and **** Corporation, a Delaware corporation ("Buyer"). Capitalized terms used but not defined herein shall have the respective meanings set forth in that certain Asset Purchase Agreement by and among the parties hereto of even date herewith (the "Asset Purchase Agreement").

BACKGROUND

Pursuant to the Asset Purchase Agreement, the Seller is selling, assigning, transferring, conveying, and delivering the Assets to Buyer. Buyer is not assuming, and Seller and the Founders are not assigning, transferring, conveying, or delivering any liabilities related to the Assets or any other liabilities.

The parties hereto agree as follows:

1. For good and lawful consideration paid to it by Buyer, the sufficiency of which is hereby acknowledged, Seller hereby sells, assigns, transfers, conveys, and delivers to Buyer, and its permitted successors and assigns forever, all of Seller's right, title, and interest in and to the Assets, to have and to hold, all of the Assets hereby sold, assigned, transferred, conveyed, and delivered to Buyer, its permitted successors and assigns, for its own use and benefit forever.

2. Seller hereby acknowledges receipt of the Escrow Dollars (as defined in, and in accordance with the provisions of the Escrow Agreement by and among the parties hereto and the Escrow Agent named therein of even date herewith); and Buyer hereby acknowledges receipt of the Assets by electronic transmission.

3. The sale, assignment, transfer, conveyance, and delivery of the Assets under this Bill of Sale and Assignment Agreement is subject to and in accordance with the provisions of the Asset Purchase Agreement.

4. Except as otherwise specifically set forth in the Asset Purchase Agreement or related documentation, Buyer is not assuming or agreeing to perform, pay or discharge any liabilities or obligations of Seller or either Founder, and it is expressly understood and agreed that all debts, liabilities, and obligations of Seller and each Founder not specifically assumed by Buyer shall remain the sole obligations of Seller and each Founder, and their joint or respective successors and assigns, and no person other than Seller and each Founder (and their joint or respective successors and assigns) shall have any rights under this Bill of Sale and Assignment Agreement or the Asset Purchase Agreement.

5. Seller shall, from time to time after the delivery of this Bill of Sale and Assignment Agreement, at Buyer's request and without further consideration, execute and

deliver such other instruments of conveyance and transfer, consents, bills of sale, assignments, releases, powers of attorney, and assurances presented by Buyer and reasonably necessary to more effectively transfer any of the Assets or to confirm the intent of Section 3.

6.   Any notice, request, or other document to be given hereunder shall be given to the other party in the manner specified by the Asset Purchase Agreement.

7.   This Bill of Sale and Assignment Agreement shall be governed by and construed in accordance with the laws of the State of _____ without giving effect to otherwise applicable principles of conflicts of law.

8.   This Bill of Sale and Assignment Agreement, being further documentation of the conveyances, assignments and transfers provided for, in and by the Asset Purchase Agreement, neither expands nor limits the rights, obligations, and warranties of the parties under the Asset Purchase Agreement.

9.   This Bill of Sale and Assignment Agreement may be executed in two or more counterparts, each of which shall be deemed to be an original, but all of which together shall constitute one and the same document.

The parties have caused this Bill of Sale and Assignment Agreement to be duly executed as of the day and year first above written.

**** LLC

By: _____

    Name: _____

    Title: _____
FOUNDERS:

_____

_____ [Name]

_____

_____ [Name]

**** CORPORATION

By: _____

    Name: _____

    Title: _____

Form 15 F: Assignment and Assumption Agreement for Asset Purchase

Exhibit C
(Assignment and Assumption Agreement)

ASSIGNMENT AND ASSUMPTION AGREEMENT

This Assignment and Assumption Agreement is made and entered into as of this ___ day of _____, 20___ by and among **** Corporation, a Delaware corporation ("Buyer"), and **** LLC a California limited liability company ("Seller").

WHEREAS, pursuant to that certain Asset Purchase Agreement by and among Buyer, Seller, and _____ and _____ (the "Founders"), of even date herewith (the "Asset Purchase Agreement"), Seller has agreed to sell to Buyer and Buyer has agreed to purchase from Seller, for the consideration and upon the terms and conditions set forth in the Asset Purchase Agreement, all of Seller's right, title and interest in and to the Assets as the same are described in the Asset Purchase Agreement (the "Acquired Assets"); and

WHEREAS, pursuant to the Asset Purchase Agreement, Buyer has agreed to assume certain obligations of Seller as partial consideration for the purchase of the Acquired Assets; and

WHEREAS, capitalized terms used but not otherwise defined herein shall have the meanings ascribed to such terms in the Asset Purchase Agreement.

NOW, THEREFORE, pursuant to the Asset Purchase Agreement and in consideration of the premises, and for good and valuable consideration, the receipt and sufficiency of which are hereby acknowledged, it is hereby agreed that:

1. <u>Buyer Undertaking</u>. Buyer hereby assumes and agrees timely to pay and perform the following liabilities of Seller to the extent the same exist on the date hereof (the "Assumed Liabilities"):

_____

_____

_____

Except as specifically stated herein or in the Asset Purchase Agreement, Buyer assumes no debt, liability or obligation of Seller.

2. <u>The Asset Purchase Agreement</u>. Nothing contained in this Agreement supersedes any of the obligations, agreements, covenants, or warranties of Seller or Buyer under the Asset Purchase Agreement (all of which survive the execution and delivery of this Agreement as provided and subject to the limitations set forth in the Asset Purchase Agreement), or shall be deemed to require Buyer to pay or discharge any Assumed Liability so long as Buyer shall in good faith contest or cause to be contested the amount or validity thereof. If any conflict exists between the terms of this Agreement and the Asset Purchase Agreement, then the terms of the Asset Purchase Agreement shall be controlling.

3. <u>Governing Law</u>. This Agreement shall be governed by and construed in accordance with the laws of the State of _____.

IN WITNESS WHEREOF, the parties hereto have caused this Agreement to be executed in their names as of the date first above written.

**** LLC

By: _____

       Name: _____

       Title: _____

**** CORPORATION

By: _____

       Name: _____

       Title: _____

Form 15 G: License Agreement for Asset Purchase

Exhibit D
(License Agreement)

LICENSE AGREEMENT

This License Agreement ("Agreement") is entered into by and between **** LLC ("Licensor"), a [California] corporation having its principal place of business at _____ _____, and **** Corporation, a [Delaware] corporation having its principal place of business at _____ _____ ("Licensee") as of this _____ day of _____, 20___. Licensor and Licensee will be referred to individually as "Party" or collectively as "Parties."

Licensor is the owner of certain software known as _____ (the "Software"). Licensee wishes to obtain a license to use the Software in its business, and Licensor is willing to grant such license on the terms and conditions set forth herein.

1. DEFINITIONS. Capitalized terms in this Agreement have the following meanings:

a) "Asset Purchase Agreement" means that certain Asset Purchase Agreement by and among Licensor, Licensee, and _____ and _____ (the "Founders"), of even date herewith (the "Asset Purchase Agreement").

b) "Update Software" means the executable code, in machine-executable form only, included by Licensor in its releases of the Software whether distributed on diskette, tape, CD-ROM, or other media from Licensor or from a third party, or downloaded from the Internet or other electronic networks.

c) "Documentation" means the documentation, instructions, and user's guides, including updates thereto, relating to the Software, whether in electronic or printed form, as provided to the Licensee by Licensor for purposes of this Agreement.

d) "Effective date" is the date upon which this Agreement has been executed by both the Parties as set forth above, or the date at which Licensor makes the Software available to Licensee, whichever is earlier.

e) "Primary User Data" is the identification and contact information for the Licensee's employee who will function as the primary interface with Licensor in the event such interface is required in order for Licensor to fulfill its support obligations under the terms of this Agreement. Licensee's designation of Primary User Data as defined herein is as follows:

Name: _____
Title: _____
Company: _____
Address: _____
Telephone: _____
E-mail address: _____

2. LICENSE GRANT.

2.1 <u>License Rights Granted in Software and Documentation</u>. Subject to receipt by Licensor of applicable license fees and Licensee's compliance with the other terms of this Agreement, Licensor grants to Licensee a nonexclusive and nontransferable right to:

a)   Install and use a serialized copy of the Software on a single server at Licensee's location;

b)   Use the Documentation internally in connection with Licensee's permitted use of the Software;

c)   Make a reasonable number of copies of the Software and any Update Software for normal backup and archival purposes only. All such authorized copies of the Software and Update Software must comply with Section 5.5 herein;

d)   Make copies of the Documentation for reasonable internal use. All such authorized copies of the Documentation must comply with Section 5.5 herein.

2.2 <u>License Restrictions on Features and Performance</u>. The features and performance of the Software are subject to the restrictions encoded therein.

2.3 <u>License Restrictions on the Licensee</u>. Licensee expressly agrees that it will not, nor will it allow others to, perform the following upon the Software except as normally allowed by law:

a)   Reverse assemble, de-compile, translate, or otherwise attempt to derive source code, the underlying ideas, algorithms, structure or organization from the Software, except and only to the extent that such activity is expressly permitted by applicable law notwithstanding this limitation. If the Software is located in the European Community, then, if Licensee has requested interface information from Licensor and Licensor has refused to make such information available, Licensee may engage in limited reverse engineering to the extent such reverse engineering is "indispensable in order to obtain the information necessary to achieve the interoperability with other independently created computer programs" (pursuant to Article VI of the European Community Computer Software Directive 91/205), provided that (i) these acts are performed by Licensee and (ii) these acts are confined to the parts of the Software which are necessary to achieve interoperability. The provisions of this Section shall not permit the information obtained through its application (x) to be used for goals other than to achieve the interoperability with the independently created computer program, (y) to be given to others, except that interface information necessary for the interoperability with the independently created computer program or (z) to be used for the development, production or marketing of a computer program substantially similar in its expression or for any other act which infringes copyright;

b)   Sublicense the Software to any third party;

c)   Create derivative works from the Software;

d)   Modify the Software or incorporate the Software into any other product;

e)   Disable or circumvent any licensing or control features of the Software;

f)   Transmit, install, or otherwise export or re-export the Software to any country into which import or transmission of such Software has been prohibited by the United States government.

Permitting or assisting a third party in committing the acts identified in 2.3(a) through (f) herein will constitute a material breach of this Agreement.

3.   TERM AND TERMINATION.

3.1 <u>Term</u>. The term of this Agreement will begin upon the Effective Date and will continue for the specified period (fixed or perpetual) as encoded in the Software, unless sooner terminated in accordance with Sections 3.2, 3.3, 3.4, or 3.5 below, or unless written notice of termination is given by Licensee.

3.2 <u>Termination in the Event of Licensee's Breach of this Agreement</u>. If Licensee breaches a material provision of this Agreement and does not cure such breach within thirty (30) days after written notice from Licensor, Licensor will have the right at its option to (a) preclude use of the Software by Licensee until such breach is cured; (b) terminate this Agreement, such that Licensee must cease all use of the Software; or (c) seek a combination of (a) and (b) and those remedies available at law or equity to the extent not limited by this Agreement. The election of options (a), (b), or (c) herein will not excuse the Licensee from any obligation arising prior to the date of termination. Licensor reserves the right to terminate the Agreement in the event Licensee has breached a material provision of the Agreement two or more times, regardless of whether Licensee has cured such breaches within the permitted time.

3.3 <u>Termination in the Event of Termination of Asset Purchase Agreement</u>. If the Asset Purchase Agreement is terminated, Licensor will have the right to terminate this Agreement, such that Licensee must cease all use of the Software and shall have those remedies available at law or equity to the extent not limited by this Agreement. The termination of this Agreement will not excuse the Licensee from any obligation arising prior to the date of termination.

3.4 <u>Termination in the Event of Unauthorized Use</u>. If Licensee uses the Software in an authorized manner, Licensor will have the right at its option to: (a) preclude use of the Software by Licensee until such time as Licensee converts or limits their use of the Software exclusively to an authorized use; or (b) terminate this Agreement, such that Licensee must cease all use of the Software. The election of options (a) or (b) herein will not excuse the Licensee from any obligation arising prior to the date of termination.

3.5 <u>Termination in the Event of Expired Term</u>. In the event the term of this Agreement is not perpetual as encoded in the Software, Licensor may terminate the Agreement at the conclusion of the Term.

3.6 <u>Consequences of Termination</u>. Upon termination of this Agreement for any reason, Licensee will cease use of the Software immediately. Licensee will return to Licensor all copies of the Software and the Documentation in its possession or control, and immediately destroy any copies of the Software and Documentation installed on any servers at its location. Licensee will provide to Licensor written notice of such destruction, signed by an officer of Licensee, within thirty (30) days of termination. Licensor will not be liable to the Licensee for damages of any sort as a result of terminating this Agreement in accordance with its terms, and termination of this Agreement will be without prejudice to any other right or remedy of either Party.

4.   LICENSE AND SUPPORT FEES AND SUPPORT OBLIGATIONS.

4.1 <u>License Fees and Support Fees</u>. License fees for the Software and the fees for Licensor's on-going support of the Software will be governed by the price structure set forth in Addendum A attached hereto and made a part hereof.

4.2 <u>Support of Software.</u> Subject to the conditions in 4.4 below, Licensor shall provide support to for Licensee's use of the Software for a period ending one (1) year after the Effective Date. During that period, Software support shall consist of assisting Licensee in problem determination and isolation, and in providing code patches, maintenance releases, and software refreshes on a good faith basis.

4.3 <u>Support in Subsequent Years</u>. Subject to the conditions in 4.4 below, Licensor's support of Licensee will continue as in 4.2 above for any yearly period in which payment for support for that period is both made by Licensee and accepted by Licensor. Licensor reserves the right not to extend support for any yearly period beyond the first yearly period described in 4.2 above.

4.4 <u>No Obligation of Support in Certain Circumstances</u>. Notwithstanding the support provisions of 4.2 and 4.3 and notwithstanding any payments made to Licensor for purposes of support of Licensee, Licensor shall not be obligated to provide support to Licensee in any of the following circumstances:

a)   If Licensee is in breach of a material provision of the Asset Purchase Agreement with Licensor.

b)   If Licensee is in breach of a material provision of this Agreement.

c)   If after the expiration of the first yearly period Licensor has not received payment for support of Licensee for the then current or any previous yearly period.

d)   If Licensee refuses to provide dial-in or network access to the Software on Licensee's server and where arrangements acceptable to Licensor for Licensor support in lieu of such access has not been arranged.

e)   If the Primary User Data is no longer current and Licensee is unable to provide updated Primary User Data.

f)   If Licensee refuses to upgrade the version of the Software in cases where, in an attempt to resolve Licensee's support request, Licensor has requested that Licensee upgrade the Software to some later version.

4.5 <u>Initial Installation Warranty</u>. Licensor warrants to Licensee that for a period of sixty (60) days from the date of delivery of the Software to Licensee that the Software will substantially perform in accordance with the Documentation. Licensee's sole and exclusive remedy in the event of insubstantial performance will be for Licensor to (a) modify or correct the Software or, if Licensor is unable to provide a reasonable work around for the error, (b) accept the return of the defective Software in Licensee's possession and refund Licensee's license fees. This warranty will not apply in cases where the deviations between the Software and the Documentation do not significantly affect operation, or to cases where the Software is modified by Licensee, or operated in any manner other than as authorized by Licensor, or otherwise improperly installed or used in any manner other than as authorized by this Agreement. The Software is warranted only to Licensee, and Licensee will not extend any warranties for or on behalf of Licensor to any third parties.

5.   INTELLECTUAL PROPERTY RIGHTS AND PROTECTIONS.

5.1 <u>Licensor as Sole Owner of the Software and Documentation</u>. Licensor is the sole owner of the Software and Documentation, and use by Licensee of the Software and Documentation does not require the acquisition of any further licenses by Licensor.

5.2 <u>Indemnification by Licensor</u>. Licensor agrees to defend and hold Licensee harmless from all settlements agreed to by Licensor, and all costs and direct damages awarded to a third party, to the extent they arise out of allegations that the Software, as delivered to Licensee: (a) infringes a third party's registered United States patent or copyright under the laws of a country signatory to the Berne Convention; or (b) misappropriates a third party's trade secret as that term is defined in the Uniform Trade Secrets Act. No such defense will be undertaken unless: (i) the patent, copyright, or trade secret was in existence as of the Effective Date; (ii) Licensee notifies Licensor within thirty (30) days of the date Licensee first becomes aware of a claim; (iii) Licensor has the sole control over settlement, compromise, negotiation, and defense of any such action; and (iv) Licensee gives Licensor all reasonably available information, assistance, and authority to enable Licensor to defend Licensee in the third party action. The foregoing obligation will not apply to any infringement claim arising from the Software if it has been modified by parties other than Licensor, or use of the Software in conjunction with other software, hardware, or products in a manner other than as authorized by Licensor.

5.3 <u>Remedies</u>. Should the use of the Software be found to constitute infringement of any third party's United States patent or copyright under the laws of a country signatory to the Berne Convention or misappropriation of a trade secret as that term is defined in the Uniform Trade Secrets Act and Licensee's rights under the

Agreement be enjoined, then Licensor's sole obligations, at Licensor's option, will be as follows: (a) obtain for Licensee the right to continue to use the Software; or (b) modify the Software so that it no longer infringes; or (c) replace the Software with other functionally equivalent software that does not infringe; or (d) if none of the foregoing is reasonably possible, request the return of the Software and Documentation, and upon its return, terminate the Agreement and refund the fees paid to Licensor by Licensee.

5.4 <u>Limitation of Liability and Disclaimer of Warranties for Matters of Intellectual Property</u>. THE FOREGOING STATES LICENSOR'S SOLE LIABILITY FOR INFRINGEMENT OF ANY THIRD PARTY'S INTELLECTUAL PROPERTY RIGHTS OF ANY KIND, INCLUDING MISAPPROPRIATION OF TRADE SECRETS, AND IS IN LIEU OF ANY OTHER WARRANTY AGAINST INFRINGEMENT OF ANY KIND, WHETHER EXPRESS, IMPLIED, OR STATUTORY. LICENSOR DISCLAIMS ALL SUCH WARRANTIES AND ANY REMEDY, STATUTORY OR OTHERWISE, NOT SPECIFICALLY SET FORTH IN THIS AGREEMENT. IN CASES OF WILLFULL OR GROSSLY NEGLIGENT MISCONDUCT WITH REGARD TO MATTERS OF INTELLECTUAL PROPERTY, THIS EXCLUSION WILL NOT APPLY IN THOSE JURISDICTIONS WHERE FOR SUCH WILLFULL OR GROSSLY NEGLIGENT MISCONDUCT THERE IS MANDATORY LIABILITY. IN NO CASE HOWEVERWILL LICENSOR'S TOTAL MONETARY OBLIGATION PURSUANT TO THIS SECTION EXCEED THE LICENSE FEES PAID TO LICENSOR BY LICENSEE.

5.5 <u>Proprietary Rights</u>. Licensee acknowledges that the Software licensed under this Agreement is protected by United States and worldwide copyrights. Except for the rights expressly granted to Licensee under this Agreement, title and ownership of all proprietary rights in the Software and Documentation, including any copyright, patent, trade secret, trademark, or other intellectual property rights, will at all times remain the property of Licensor. Licensee agrees not to remove or obliterate any copyright, trademark, legend, or proprietary rights notices of Licensor from the Software or Documentation. Licensee will reproduce any copyright, patent, legal, or other proprietary Licensor marking on any authorized copy of the Software or Documentation as referenced in Section 2.1 herein. The license in this Agreement is not a sale of the Software or Documentation, and title will at all times remain with Licensor.

5.6 <u>Licensee's Acquisition of Third-Party Licenses</u>. Licensee is solely responsible for obtaining any and all licenses from third parties that are lawfully required for use by Licensee of any third-party product in conjunction with the Software. Licensor disclaims any obligation to bring information about such required licenses to Licensee's attention and will not be responsible for Licensee's failure to acquire any third-party license.

5.7 <u>Indemnification by Licensee</u>. Licensee will defend, indemnify, and hold Licensor, as well as Licensor's officers, directors, representatives, employees, agents, and attorneys (each a "Licensor Person"), harmless from, and Licensor and Licensor Persons will have no liability for, any claims arising out of: (a) Licensee's installation of the Software on an platform other than a platform authorized by Licensor; (b) Licensee's use of the Software modified in any way, or merged with other hardware or software by Licensee other than as authorized by Licensor; (c) Licensee's use of the Software in combination with other programs or products other than as authorized by Licensor; (d) Licensee's use of the allegedly infringing Software after being notified thereof and after being informed of modifications that would avoid the alleged infringement; and (e) Licensee's use of the Software that is not strictly in accordance with the terms of this Agreement.

5.8 <u>Intellectual Property Compliance</u>. Licensor will have the right to inspect the Software at Licensee's premises as reasonably necessary to verify that Licensee's use of the Software complies with this Agreement. Licensor will provide Licensee with reasonable notice prior to any inspections. Licensor will bear the costs and expenses associated with the exercise of these rights, unless such inspection reveals that Licensee is not in compliance with this Agreement, in which case Licensee agrees to pay Licensor the reasonable costs of such inspection plus any additional license fees related to unauthorized use of the Software in the amount of the additional fees that would have been owning had such use been authorized.

5.9 If, notwithstanding any terms in this Agreement prohibiting or otherwise limiting reverse engineering, Licensee engages in reverse engineering, or if the laws of the country in which Licensee uses the Software allows reverse engineering of the Software, then Licensee agrees that the product of any such reverse engineering shall be deemed to be the proprietary confidential information of Licensor.

6.   <u>General Disclaimer of Warranties</u>. EXCEPT AS SET FORTH IN SECTION 4, THE SOFTWARE IS PROVIDED "AS IS" WITHOUT ANY EXPRESS, IMPLIED, OR STATUTORY WARRANTY OF ANY KIND. LICENSOR AND ITS SUPPLIERS DIS-CLAIM ALL WARRANTIES, INCLUDING WITHOUT LIMITATION ANY WARRAN-TIES OF MERCHANTABILITY OR FITNESS FOR A PARTICULAR PURPOSE, AND THE ENTIRE RISK OF THE QUALITY AND PERFORMANCE OF THE SOFTWARE IS WITH LICENSEE. IF LICENSEE RECEIVES ANY OTHER WARRANTIES REGARDING THE SOFTWARE, THOSE WARRANTIES DO NOT ORIGINATE FROM, AND ARE NOT BINDING ON LICENSOR. LICENSOR DOES NOT WAR-RANT OR ASSUME RESPONSIBILITY FOR THE ACCURACY OR COMPLETE-NESS OF ANY INFORMATION OR OTHER ITEMS CONTAINED WITHIN THE SOFTWARE OR DOCUMENTATION.

7.   <u>General Limitation of Liability</u>. INDEPENDENT OF ANY REMEDY LIMITA-TION HEREOF, AND REGARDLESS OF WHETHER THE PURPOSE OF SUCH REMEDY IS SERVED, IT IS AGREED THAT IN NO EVENT SHALL LICENSOR OR ITS OFFICERS, EMPLOYEES, DIRECTORS, SUBSIDIARIES, REPRESENTATIVES, AFFILIATES, AND AGENTS HAVE ANY LIABILITY OTHER THAN THOSE SPECI-FIED IN SECTION 5 HEREIN, WHATSOEVER, TO LICENSEE OR ANY OTHER THIRD PARTY, FOR ANY LOST PROFITS, LOST DATA, LOSS OF USE OR COSTS OF PROCUREMENT OF SUBSTITUTE GOODS OR SERVICES, OR FOR ANY INDIRECT, SPECIAL OR CONSEQUENTIAL DAMAGES ARISING OUT OF THIS AGREEMENT OR OUT OF THE USE OF OR INABILITY TO USE THE SOFTWARE, UNDER ANY CAUSE OF ACTION OR THEORY OF LIABILITY, AND IRRESPEC-TIVE OF WHETHER LICENSOR OR ITS OFFICERS, EMPLOYEES, DIRECTORS, SUBSIDIARIES, REPRESENTATIVES, AFFILIATES, AND AGENTS HAVE ADVANCE NOTICE OF THE POSSIBILITY OF SUCH DAMAGES. THESE LIMITATIONS SHALL APPLY NOTWITHSTANDING THE FAILURE OF THE ESSENTIAL PURPOSE OF ANY LIMITED REMEDY. IN CASES OF PRODUCT LIABILITY, THIS EXCLUSION WILL NOT APPLY IN THOSE JURISDICTIONS WHERE FOR AN APPLICABLE PRODUCT LIABILITY STATUTE OF THAT JURISDICTION THERE IS MANDATORY APPLICATION OF THAT PRODUCT LIABILITY STATUE. IN CASES OF WILLFULL OR GROSSLY NEGLIGENT MISCONDUCT, THIS EXCLUSION WILL NOT APPLY IN THOSE JURISDICTIONS WHERE FOR SUCH WILLFULL OR GROSSLY NEGLI-GENT MISCONDUCT THERE IS MANDATORY LIABILITY. IN ANY CASE, LICEN-SOR'S AND ITS OFFICERS', EMPLOYEES', DIRECTORS', SUBSIDIARIES', REP-RESENTATIVES', AFFILIATES', AND AGENTS' ENTIRE LIABILITY UNDER ANY

PROVISION OF THIS AGREEMENT SHALL NOT EXCEED THE AMOUNTS OF THE FEES PAID TO LICENSOR BY LICENSEE.

THE SOFTWARE IS NOT FAULT-TOLERANT AND IS NOT DESIGNED, INTENDED, OR AUTHORIZED FOR USE IN ANY MEDICAL, LIFE SAVING, OR LIFE SUSTAINING SYSTEMS, OR FOR ANY OTHER APPLICATION IN WHICH THE FAILURE OF THE SOFTWARE COULD CREATE A SITUATION WHERE PER-SONAL INJURY OR DEATH MAY OCCUR. Should Licensee or Licensee's direct or indirect customers use the Software for any such unintended or unauthorized use, Licensee shall indemnify and hold Licensor and its officers, employees, directors, subsidiaries, representatives, affiliates, and agents harmless against all claims, costs, damages, and expenses, and attorney fees and expenses arising out of, directly or indirectly, any claim of product liability, personal injury or death associated with such unintended or unauthorized use, even if such claim alleges that Licensor was negligent regarding the design or manufacture of the part.

8.   GENERAL PROVISIONS.

8.1 <u>Severability</u>. If any provision of this Agreement is held to be ineffective, unenforceable, or illegal for any reason, such decision will not affect the validity or enforceability of any or all of the remaining portions thereof.

8.2 <u>Non-Assignment</u>. Without Licensor's prior written consent, neither this Agreement nor any interest therein or part thereof will be transferable or assignable by the Licensee, by operation of law or otherwise.

8.3 <u>Governing Law and Venue</u>. This Agreement will be governed by, interpreted, and enforced in accordance with the laws of _____, without giving effect to con-flict of law principles. Any action arising out of any dispute between the Parties to this Agreement will be settled by arbitration in _____, in the State of _____, by submission by either Party to an arbitrator to be selected pursuant to the rules of the Judicial Arbitration and Mediation Center ("JAMS"). A decision on any dispute arbitrated pursuant to this Section 8.3 must be rendered not later than sixty (60) days following conclusion of the arbitration hearing. A written statement of decision will be issued, providing specific reasoning for the decision on each specific issue presented for decision. The decision will be binding upon the Parties. Judgment on an award rendered by the arbitrator(s) may be entered in any court having jurisdic-tion thereof. Each Party hereby submits itself to the jurisdiction of JAMS for purposes of any such action. The rights and obligations of the Parties to this contract will not be governed by the United Nations Convention on Contracts for the International Sale of Goods.

8.4 <u>Arbitration Fees and Costs</u>. In the event an action is brought before JAMS to enforce any provision of this Agreement or declare a breach of this Agreement, the prevailing party will be entitled to recover, in addition to any other amounts awarded, reasonable legal and other related costs and expenses, including attorneys' fees, incurred thereby.

8.5 <u>Injunction</u>. The Parties agree that a material breach of this Agreement will cause irreparable harm to the non-breaching Party and that a remedy at law would be inadequate. Therefore, in addition to any and all remedies available at law, the non-breaching Party will be entitled to seek injunctive relief against the breaching Party in the event of a threatened or actual violation of any or all provisions of this Agreement.

8.6 <u>Waiver</u>. No failure or delay on the part of either Party in the exercise of any power, right, or privilege hereunder will operate to deprive a Party from making the argument that there has been no waiver thereof, nor will any single or partial exercise of any such power, right, or privilege preclude any other or further exercise thereof, or of any other right, power, or privilege.

8.7 <u>Other Licenses</u>. Nothing contained in this Agreement will be construed as conferring by implication, estoppel, or otherwise upon either Party hereunder any license or other right except the licenses and rights expressly granted hereunder to a Party hereto.

8.8 <u>Language</u>. This Agreement is in the English language only, which language will be controlling in all respects, and all versions hereof in any other language will be for accommodation only and will not be binding upon the Parties hereto for any of its terms which are in conflict with the English language version of this Agreement. All communications and technical documentation to be furnished hereunder will be in the English language only.

8.9 <u>Notice</u>. Unless either Party notifies the other of a different address, any notice or other communication required or permitted hereunder will be sufficiently given if sent by certified or registered mail or courier, postage prepaid, return receipt requested, to the addresses set forth in the preamble of this Agreement to the attention of the Chief Executive Officer, or to such other address as may be designated by a Party by giving written notice to the other Party.

8.10 <u>Survival</u>. The provisions of Sections 1 (Definitions), 3 (Consequences of Termination), 5 et seq. (Intellectual Property Rights and Indemnification), 6 (Warranty), 7 (Limitation of Liability), 8.3 (Governing Law), 8.7 (Other Licenses), 8.10 (Survival), and 8.14 (Government Restricted Rights) will survive the termination of this Agreement.

8.11 <u>Force Majeure</u>. Neither Party will be responsible or liable to the other Party for failure or delay in the performance of any of its obligations under this Agreement for the time and to the extent such failure or delay is caused by riots; civil commotion; wars; hostilities between nations; governmental laws, orders, or regulations; embargoes; actions by any government or any agency thereof; acts of God; earthquakes; storms; fires; accidents; strikes; sabotages; explosions; or other similar or different contingencies beyond the reasonable control of the respective Parties hereto. If as a result of legislation or governmental action either Party or both Parties are precluded from receiving any benefit to which they are entitled hereunder, the Parties hereto will make best efforts to revise the terms of this Agreement so as to restore such Party or Parties to the same relative positions as previously obtained or contemplated hereunder.

8.12 <u>Construction of Agreement & Headings</u>. This Agreement has been agreed to by the respective Parties, and the Agreement language and any vagueness or indefiniteness of any Agreement term, will not be construed for or against any Party. The headings of the Agreement Sections are inserted for reference only and will have no effect on the interpretation of this Agreement.

8.13 <u>No Agency</u>. Nothing herein contained will be construed to constitute the Parties hereto as partners or joint venturers or the agent of another Party in any sense of those terms whatsoever. Neither Party assumes any liability of the other Party nor will have any authority to enter into any binding obligation on behalf of the other Party.

8.14 <u>Government Restricted Rights</u>.

a) If the Software and Documentation is acquired by or on behalf of a unit or agency of the United States Government or any state or local government in the United States, this provision applies. The Software and Documentation (i) was developed at private expense, and no part of it was developed with government funds;

(ii) is a trade secret of the Licensor for all purposes of the Freedom of Information Act; (iii) is "Commercial Computer Software" subject to limited utilization (Restricted Rights) as provided in the contract between the Licensor and the government entity; and (iv) in all respects is proprietary data belonging solely to the Licensor.

b) For units of the Department of Defense ("DOD"), the Software and Documentation is licensed only with "Restricted Rights" as that term is defined in the DOD Supplement to the Federal Acquisition Regulations ("DFARS") 252.227-7013(c) or any other successor clause, and use, duplication or disclosure is subject to restriction as set forth in the Rights in Technical Data and Computer Software clause at DFARS 252.227-7013, 252.227-7014 or 252.227-7015 or any other successor clause. The manufacturer is: **** LLC, whose address is _____ _____.

c) Except as specifically stated in the contract between Licensor and the government entity under which this copy was licensed, use of the Software shall be limited to use as Commercial Computer Software-Restricted Rights as set forth in Federal Acquisition Regulation 52.227-19 or any other successor clause. U.S. Government personnel using the Software, otherwise than under a DOD contract or GSA Schedule, are hereby on notice that use of the Software is subject to restrictions which are the same as, or similar to, those specified above.

8.15 <u>Entire Agreement</u>. This Agreement and its Exhibits contain the entire Agreement and understanding between the Parties with respect to the subject matter hereof and merges and supersedes all prior oral and written agreements, understandings, and representations. No addition or modification to this Agreement is valid unless made in writing and signed by both Parties hereto.

8.16 <u>No Modification</u>. Licensee represents and warrants that it has not modified the terms of this Agreement in any way and is signing the latest version of the Agreement provided by Licensor as of the date first set forth above.

LICENSOR   LICENSEE
**** LLC   **** Corporation

By: _____   By: _____
Name:_____   Name: _____
Title: _____   Title: _____

ADDENDUM A
Schedule of License and Support Fees

Form 15 H: Bulk Sale Notice for Asset Purchase

RECORDING REQUESTED BY
AND WHEN RECORDED MAIL TO:

_____

_____

_____

_____

_____

Space above this line for Recorder's Use

NOTICE TO CREDITORS OF BULK SALE
(California Commercial Code Secs. 6101 et. seq.)

Notice is hereby given to creditors of the within named transferor that a bulk sale is about to be made on personal property hereinafter described.

The name and business address of the transferor is:

**** LLC, a California limited liability company

_____

_____

The location in the State of California of the chief executive office or principal business office of the transferor is: the same as listed above.

Within the past three (3) years, so far as known to Buyer, **** LLC has used the following names at the following addresses:

**** LLC

_____

_____

**** Software

_____

_____

The name and business address of the transferee is: **** Corporation, _____
_____.

The property pertinent hereto is described in general as:

the software products of **** LLC including without limitation, any and all source and object codes, binaries, supplements, modifications, updates, corrections and enhancements to past and current versions of such products,

811

shipping versions of such products and versions of such products currently under development, together with the books and records, contracts, claims, goodwill, trade names and trademarks, testing and customer support materials, and other intangible property.

The said bulk transfer is intended to be consummated at the office of: _____ _____ on or after _____, 20___.

This bulk transfer is subject to California Uniform Commercial Code Section 6106.2.

The name and address of the person with whom claims may be filed is: _____ _____.

The last day for filing claims for debts of the transferor is _____, 20___, which is the business day before the scheduled consummation of the bulk sale specified above.

Dated: _____

                 **** CORPORATION

                 By:_____
                     Name_____
                     Title_____

Dated: _____

                 **** CORPORATION

                 By:_____
                     Name_____
                     Title_____

State of California   )
                        ss.
County of _____   )

On _____, 20___, before me, _____, a Notary Public, personally appeared _____ and _____, proved to me on the basis of satisfactory evidence, to be the person(s) whose name(s) is subscribed to the within instrument and acknowledged to me that they executed the same in their authorized capacity, and that by their signature(s) on the instrument the person(s), or the entity upon behalf of which the person(s) acted, executed the instrument.

WITNESS MY HAND AND OFFICIAL SEAL.

_____
Notary Public   (This area for official notary seal)

Form 15 I:·Time and Responsibility Schedule for IPO

Note: Although the documentation for an initial public offering (IPO) is beyond the scope of this guide, the following sample time and responsibility schedule for an IPO of common stock will give you a good idea of how the process works and allow you to prepare your client for the same.

**** Inc.

PRELIMINARY TIME AND RESPONSIBILITY SCHEDULE
FOR AN
INITIAL PUBLIC OFFERING OF COMMON STOCK[1]

CO	Company/ ****, Inc.	**AU**	Auditors
CC	Company Counsel	**TA**	Transfer Agent/Registrar
UW	Managing Underwriter	**SS**	Selling Stockholders
UC	Underwriter's Counsel	**SC**	Selling Stockholders' Counsel

Date	Activity	Participants
Several months before formal commencement of preparation of the Registration Statement	Explore alternative means of financing.	CO, CC
	Prepare business plan and information memorandum describing company for presentation to prospective Managing Underwriter(s).	CO, CC
	Select Managing Underwriter(s).	CO, CC
	Select additional company counsel.	CO, CC
During the month before formal commencement of preparation of the Registration Statement	Meetings between CO and CC concerning "corporate housekeeping." The following matters should be discussed: (a) Amendments to Articles or Certificate of Incorporation; (b) Amendments to Bylaws; (c) Restructuring of CO into a single corporation or a parent corporation with subsidiaries, as appropriate; (d) Readjustment of individual stockholders' holdings in the CO, if desired; (e) Employment agreements; (f) Creation of stock option, stock purchase and Other desired employee benefit plans;	CO, CC

---

[1]This timetable assumes a firm commitment underwriting which involves a secondary offering by selling stockholders. It is also assumes that the timing of the offering will be such that the filing and effectiveness of the Registration Statement will be accomplished without the need to supplement the financial information included in the original filing, which may cause the offering to be delayed.

Date	Activity	Participants
	(g) Revision of existing employee benefit plans to comply with securities law requirements; (h) Verification that all existing employee benefit plans comply with requirements of ERISA and other applicable laws; (i) Status after offering of stockholders' and voting trust agreements and other restrictions on voting and transfer of stock; (j) Need to renegotiate covenants in loan agreements which restrict, or limit use of proceeds of, a public offering; (k) "Shark repellents"; (l) The need for experts other than accountants, such as engineers; (m) Other corporate housekeeping matters and review of corporate records; (n) Potential Blue Sky and NASD concerns in relation to CO status and terms of offering.	
	Preliminary negotiation of terms of offering, including Letter of Intent or term sheet.	CO, CC, UW, UC
	Meeting between CO and AU concerning need for change in accounting procedures (e.g., instituting necessary procedures and controls to comply with requirements of Foreign Corrupt Practices Act and to produce reports required under the Securities Exchange Act of 1934, as amended (the "Exchange Act")) when Company is a public company and the preparation of financial statements for the offering.	CO, AU
Week 1	Organizational meeting, at which the following matters should be discussed: (a) Timetable; (b) Assignment of responsibilities for tasks; (c) Selection of Financial Printer, engraver and form of share certificates; (d) Selection of Transfer Agent and Registrar; (e) Appropriateness of certain "corporate housekeeping" matters (e.g., reincorporation, employment agreements, shark repellents and other matters referred to above) in light of marketing considerations; (f) Listing on a national securities exchange or quotation on NASDAQ; if stock is to be quoted on NASDAQ, whether stock will be quoted on the NASDAQ National Market System; (g) Discussion of financial statements required and of any special accounting problems; effect of recent acquisitions on historical financials; availability of interim financials, if necessary; Comfort Letter; (h) Discussion of any anticipated disclosure problems; (i) Discussion of anticipated NASD or Blue Sky problems;	CO, CC, UW, UC, AU

Date	Activity	Participants
	(j) Arrangements with Selling Stockholders and other stockholders who have registration rights; (k) Desirability of pre-filing conferences with the SEC, Blue Sky authorities or the FINRA; (l) Recapitalization of the CO (e.g. stock split or reverse stock split) that will be required prior to offering; (m) Discussion of any desired stockholder concessions, such as lock-up agreements or (Blue Sky) escrow agreements; (n) Establishment of future public announcement policy; CO Officers and Directors obtain clearance from CC and UC prior to further distribution of publicity relating to CO or to the proposed public offering; (o) Any other agenda items.	
	Commence preparation of Registration Statement in accordance with Preliminary Responsibility Checklist.	CO, CC, UW, UC
	Initial due diligence meetings at the company (1-2 days); due diligence with accountants and discussion of Comfort Letter.	All
	Commence legal due diligence review of material contracts, litigation, claims and contingent liabilities, past corporate action (minute books, stock records, harter, by-laws, etc.), financial statements, documentation with regard to outstanding securities, etc.	CO, UC, UW
	Draft Officers' and Directors' Questionnaires.	CO, CC
	Commence preparation of Underwriting Agreement, Agreement Among Underwriters, Underwriters' Questionnaire, Underwriters' Power of Attorney[2] and Preliminary Blue Sky Memorandum; consider international underwriting matters.	UC
	Commence preparation of Selling Stockholder's Power of Attorney (including Questionnaire) and Custody Agreement.	SC, CC
	Commence preparation of necessary financial statements.	CO, AU
	Draft Powers of Attorney for Registration Statement and amendments thereto, if needed.	CO, CC
	Select banknote company to print stock certificates; advise banknote company of schedule and arrange for printing of stock certificates, including appropriate quantities.	CO
	Select Financial Printer; Select Transfer Agent and Registrar; Distribute "blackout" letter.	CO, CC

---

[2] A separate Agreement Among Underwriters, Underwriters' Questionnaire, and Underwriters' Power of Attorney will not be required if a Master Agreement Among Underwriters is applicable to the offering.

Date	Activity	Participants
Week 2	Send Officers' and Directors' Questionnaires and Powers of Attorney, if any, to Officers, Directors and 10% stockholders of Company (sometimes delayed until initial draft of Registration Statement is available).	CO
	Mail letter to stockholders relating to participation in secondary offering.	CO, CC, SC
	Reserve preferred stock exchange trading symbol (if stock is to be listed on a national securities exchange); determine availability of preferred NASDAQ trading symbols (if stock is to be quoted on NASDAQ).	CO, CC, SC
	Continue preparation of Registration Statement and underwriting documents.	CO, CC, UW, UC
	Commence negotiations with lenders concerning necessary consents and revisions of covenants that would restrict offering or use of proceeds thereof.	CO, CC
Week 3	Commence drafting necessary "corporate cleanup" documents (e.g. charter and by-law amendments, employment agreements, stock option plans), documents necessary to effect recapitalization and Board resolutions necessary to authorize the public offering (including standard form Blue Sky resolutions).	CO, CC
	Circulate drafts of Registration Statement and Underwriting Agreement (generally 10-14 days following initial meeting).	CC, UC
	Meetings to discuss Registration Statement and Underwriting Agreement; continued due diligence.	CO, CC, UW, UC, AU
	Revise Registration Statement and Underwriting Agreement.	CO, CC, UW, UC
	Discuss Comfort Letter content and procedures.	UC, UW, AU
	Commence preparation of stock exchange listing application, if applicable.	CO, CC
	Review and approve proofs of stock certificates.	CO
	Circulate drafts of financial statements.[3]	AU
	Determine representative to act for SS at time of offering.	CO, SS, SC
	Obtain completed questionnaires and Powers of Attorney, if any, from Officers and Directors and 0% shareholders; furnish copies to UC.	CO

---

[3] The precise timing of release of the financial statements will vary, depending on the proximity of the commencement of preparation of the Registration Statement to the end of the fiscal quarter for which financial statements are to be included in the Registration Statement.

Date	Activity	Participants
	Complete Preliminary Blue Sky Memorandum and draft Underwriters' Questionnaire, Power of Attorney, and Invitation Letter and send to printer.	UC
	Initial discussions regarding proposed syndicate.	CO, UW
Week 4	Draft of Registration Statement to printer.	CC
	Draft of Underwriting Agreement to printer.	UC
	Meeting to discuss initial printed proof of Registration Statement (including draft financial statements) and Underwriting Agreement.	CO, CC, UW, UC, AU
	Commence compilation and preparation of exhibits to Registration Statement.	CO, CC
	Circulate revised proofs of Registration Statement and Underwriting Agreement (including draft to Board of Directors).	CC, UC
	Finalize financial statements.	CO, AU
	Finalize Underwriting Agreement.	CO, CC, UW, UC
	Complete and distribute printed proof of underwriting papers.	UC
Weeks 5-6	Meetings to discuss revised proofs of Registration Statement and proof of underwriting papers.	CO, CC, UW, UC, AU
	Finalize "corporate housekeeping" and recapitalization documents.	
	Send drafts of Registration Statement to stock exchange on which the CO wishes to list stock for confidential review of eligibility (required by the New York and American Stock Exchanges if listing intention language is to be included in the preliminary prospectus).	CO, CC
	UW to deliver to UC list of states in which shares are to be offered.	
	Meeting of Board of Directors to approve financing program and "corporate housekeeping" matters, including adoption of resolutions relating to: (a) Authorization of issue, sale and delivery of stock; (b) Approving form of Underwriting Agreement and authorizing execution and delivery thereof; (c) If necessary, appointing a special committee of the Board of Directors to establish the price of stock to the UW and the initial public offering price; (d) Approving Registration Statement and Prospectus and authorizing execution and filing of Registration Statement and all amendments thereto, including attorney-in-fact;	

Date	Activity	Participants
	e) Authorizing listing of stock on NASDAQ or a stock exchange; (f) Registration of the stock and other Blue Sky matters; (g) Appointing Transfer Agent and Registrar; (h) Approving all necessary "corporate housekeeping" matters; (i) Calling an annual meeting of stockholders, if desired; (j) Approving recapitalization; (k) Approving form of stock certificates.	
	Meeting (or written consent in lieu of meeting) of stockholders of the Company, at which resolutions are adopted approving recapitalization and all "corporate cleanup" matters that require shareholder approval.	CO, CC
	Send Selling Shareholders' Power of Attorney (including Questionnaire) and Custody Agreement to Selling Shareholders.	CO, CC
	File charter amendments necessary to effectuate recapitalization.	CO, CC
	Circulate draft of Comfort Letter.	AU
	Prepare Form 8-A for Exchange Act registration, if applicable.	CO, CC
	Discuss road show presentation and proposed syndicate list.	UW, CO
Week 8	Meeting to finalize Registration Statement.	CO, CC, UW, UC, AU
	Determine requirements for preliminary material and give Printer instructions together with labels for mailing of preliminary prospectuses to officer of underwriters' representatives.	UW
	Obtain signature pages and Powers of Attorney for registration Statement and amendments from Directors and Officers.	CO
	Prepare letters and obtain labels for mailing to underwriters, institutions, Dealers and financial publications.	UW
	Complete compilation and preparation of exhibits to Registration Statement.	CO, CC
	Receive Selling Shareholders' Power of Attorney (including Questionnaire) and Custody Agreement; furnish copies to CC and UC.	CO
	Prepare transmittal letter to SEC.	CC
	Prepare application for CUSIP number.	CO, CC
	Prepare application for NASDAQ or stock exchange listing.	CO, CC, UC

Date	Activity	Participants
	Prepare transmittal letter to FINRA.	UC
	Obtain certified or official bank checks for SEC registration fee and FINRA filing fee.	CO
	Send final changes in Registration Statement and Underwriting Agreement to printer; prepare filing packages for SEC, FINRA.	CO, CC, UC, AU
	Syndicate list finalized for invitation purposes.	UW
	Prepare draft of press release and "broad tape" release for initial filing of Registration Statement.	UW, CO
	Execute Registration Statement and Auditors' Consent.	CO, AU
Specific Target Date During Week 8	File Registration Statement (including filing fees, exhibits and request for confidential treatment, if any).	CC
	File Form 8-A with SEC in Washington and with stock exchange on which listing is sought, if applicable.	CC
	File Registration Statement and related materials with FINRA in Washington.	UC
	Release of press and "broad press" announcements.	CO, UW
	Proceed with Blue Sky qualifications, as designated by UW.	CO, UC
	Apply for CUSIP number for stock; send copy of Registration Statement to CUSIP Service Bureau.	CO, CC
	Apply for listing on NASDAQ of stock exchange; send copies of Registration Statement to NASDAQ or exchange.	CO, CC, UC
Week 9	Request estimated date on which SEC comments will be furnished.	CC
	Print preliminary prospectuses in quantity.	CO
	Begin preparation of road show presentation.	CO, UW
	Distribute internal marketing documents and finalize road show schedule.	UW
	Finalize Comfort Letter.	UW, AU, UC
	Mail to proposed underwriters Registration Statement, Preliminary Prospectus, Preliminary Blue Sky Memorandum, Questionnaire, underwriting papers and Power of Attorney with Managing Underwriter's Invitational Letter of Transmittal.[4]	UW

---

[4] If a Master Agreement Among Underwriters is applicable to the offering, the Managing Underwriter(s) will send telexes to parties to the Master Agreement inviting them to participate in the offering.

Date	Activity	Participants
Week 10	File documents (e.g., opinion of CC) and otherwise finalize arrangements with Transfer Agent and Registrar necessary for its initial appointment.	CO, CC
	Internal marketing meetings held with UW.	CO, UW
Week 11	Informational meetings held in selected European cities.	CO, UW
	Obtain CUSIP number for stock.	CO, CC
	Approve final proof of stock certificates and order sufficient quantities from banknote company to be available at closing.	CO
	Transfer Agent supplied with all required documents.	CC
	Order closing documents with long lead times.	CC
	Resolve outstanding issues with FINRA and Blue Sky administrators.	UC
	Resolve problems with NASDAQ or stock exchange on which stock will be listed.	CO, CC
	Annual meeting (or consent in lieu of meeting) of stockholders of the Company, re-electing directors, if desired, followed by meeting of Board of Directors of Company, re-election officers.	CO, CC
	Receive stock exchange or NASDAQ approval, or listing or quotation of stock.	CC
	Prepare supplemental information for filing with SEC, if requested.	CC, UC
Week 12	Informational meetings held in selected U.S. cities.	CO, UW
	Receive comments from SEC.[5]	
	Review SEC comments, if any, and changes in Registration Statement in response thereto; clear responses to comment letter and schedule for filing of amendment to, and effectiveness of, Registration Statement (and Form 8-A, if applicable) with SEC.	CO, CC, UW, UC, AU
	Reach agreement with SEC staff as to appropriate responses to SEC comments; proof pages incorporating comments, if any, formally cleared with SEC examiner.	CC, UC, CO
	Obtain FINRA clearance of underwriting arrangements and deliver notification thereof to SEC.	UW, UC

---

[5] All subsequent dates are determined with reference to the date that SEC comments are actually received by the parties. The date for receipt of the SEC's comment letter may vary but is usually between five and seven weeks after filing. Upon receipt of comments, this schedule will be revised, if necessary, to take into account the date of actual receipt of the SEC's comment letter. It is assumed that Rule 430A will be employed in connection with the effectiveness and pricing of the offering.

Date	Activity	Participants
	Prepare request for acceleration of effective date of Registration Statement (and Form 8-A, if applicable) and Registration Statement amendment transmittal letter.	CO, CC, UW, UC
	Obtain letter from exchange on which stock will be listed, joining in the Company's request for acceleration of effectiveness of Form 8-A.	CO, CC
	Distribute initial draft of Closing Memorandum.	UC
	Notify NASDAQ of expected effective date of Registration Statement no less than 72 hours prior to anticipated effectiveness.	CO, CC
	Send acceleration request of the Company to SEC at least two business days in advance of desired effective date together with letter of Management.	CC
	Underwriter(s) joining in such request and providing information concerning distribution of preliminary prospectuses.	
	File with SEC and with exchange on which stock will be listed letter requesting acceleration of effective date of Form 8-A, if applicable.	CC
	Determination of printing quantities of final prospectuses and label and mailing instructions.	UW
	Deadline for receiving completed Underwriters' Questionnaire and Underwriters' Powers of Attorney from syndicate members.[6]	UW
	Deliver draft Comfort Letter.	AU
	Final Underwriters' due diligence meeting if necessary, held with representatives of the underwriting group. CO officers, counsel, and auditors discuss the affairs of the CO and details of the offering.	All
	Execute Amendment to Registration Statement and Auditor's Consent.	CO, AU
Specific Target Date During Week 12	File amendment to Registration Statement with SEC in Washington.	CC
	File amendment to Registration Statement and related materials with FINRA in Washington.	UC
	File amendment to Registration Statement with NASDAQ or stock exchange.	CC
	Registration Statement declared effective by SEC.	
	Form 8-A declared effective, if applicable.	

---

[6] If a Master Agreement Among Underwriters is applicable to the offering, telexes will be received from parties to the Master Agreement (and other parties who are invited to participate in the offering) who wish to participate in the offering.

Date	Activity	Participants
	Managing Underwriter notified of effectiveness of Registration Statement and Form 8-A, if applicable.	CO, UW
	NASDAQ or stock exchange notified of effectiveness of Registration Statement and Form 8-A, if applicable.	CO
	Complete Blue Sky registration.	UC
	Informal agreement reached between Company and Managing Underwriter(s) as to final terms of the offering (the price to the Underwriters of the stock and the initial public offering price thereof, etc.).	CO, UW
	Meeting of Board of Directors (or special pricing committee of the Board of Directors) to establish the price of stock to Underwriters and the initial public offering price thereof, to approve final form of the prospectus and the Underwriting Agreement and ratify acts of officers in connection with the offering.	CO, CC
	Deliver "lock-up" agreements from persons requested by Managing Underwriters.	CO
	Deliver Comfort Letter.	AU
Specific Target Date During Week 12	Sign Agreement Among Underwriters.	UW
	Sign Underwriting Agreement.	CO, UW
	Prepare "tombstone."	UW, UC
	Give printer labels and mailing instructions for Final Prospectus.	UW
	Send final changes in Prospectus and Underwriting Agreement to printer.	CO, CC, UC
	Finalize Final Blue Sky Survey.	UC
	Advise Blue Sky commissions of final terms of offering where required and distribute Final Blue Sky Survey.	UC
	Release wires to Underwriters and Dealers and commence public sales of stock and advise Company.	UW
	Issue press release re effectiveness of Registration Statement and price of stock.	CO, UW
	Release "tombstone."	UW
	Begin market-making activities.	UW
	Sign Selected Dealers' Agreements.	UW
	Distribute revised draft of Closing Memorandum.	UC
	Commence preparation of legal opinions, certificates and other closing documents; order good standing certificates.	UC, CC, TA

Date	Activity	Participants
	Contact banknote company to arrange for printing in quantity of stock certificates.	CO
	Print Final Prospectus in quantity.	CO
Week 12 Day After Pricing	"Tombstone" appears.	UW
	Notify syndicate of closing date and give instructions are payment; determine how SS wish to receive funds.	UW, CO, SS
	File ten copies of Final Prospectus with SEC pursuant to Rule 424(b) under the Securities Act of 1933.	CC
	Deliver copy of Final Prospectus to FINRA.	UC
	Deliver copy of Final Prospectus to NASDAQ or stock exchange.	UC
	Deliver copies of Final Prospectus to Blue Sky authorities.	CC
4 Days Prior to Closing	Furnish CO and TA with names and denominations in which stock certificates are to be registered.	UW
	CC opinion and instructions for certificates to transfer agent.	CO, CC
Week 13	Preliminary closing (2:00 p.m., New York time, on the business day preceding the closing).	CO, CC, UC
	Stock certificates packaged for closing.	UW, TA
	Closing (10:00 a.m., New York time).	CO, CC, UW, UC, TA
	Mailing of copies of opinions of counsel, Officer's Certificate and Comfort Letter to members of the syndicate.	UW
3 Months and 10 Days After Effective Date	File initial Form SR with SEC in Washington re offering expenses and use of proceeds (final Form SR filed within ten days after the application of the offering proceeds).	CO, CC
90 Days After Effective Date	Earliest date (in normal case) on which to file Form S-8 to register stock issuable pursuant to employee benefit plans.	CO, CC
Within 45 Days of End of First Fiscal Quarter After Effective Date (unless it is the last quarter of the fiscal year)	File report on Form 10-Q with SEC.	CO, CC AU

Date	Activity	Participants
Within 90 Days of End of Fiscal Year After Effective Date	File report on Form 10-K.	CO, CC, AU
Within _____ Days of First Fiscal Quarter Ending 1 Year After Effective Date	Make earnings statements meeting the requirements of Section 11(a) of the Securities Act available generally to stockholders.	CO, AU
120 Days from End of Fiscal Year in which Registration Statement Effective	Last date on which to file Registration Statement with respect to common stock under the Exchange Act on Form 8-A, if stock not voluntarily registered previously under the Exchange Act.	CO, CC
Effective Date of Common Stock Registration Statement under Exchange Act	Due date of initial reports of beneficial ownership of equity securities under Section 16(a) of the Exchange Act on Form 3 by Officers, Directors and 10% stockholders of the Company; proxy solicitation rules now applicable with respect to common stock of CO.	CO, CC
Various Dates After Effective Date	Mailings to stockholders as represented in Prospectus.	CO, CC
	Provide Underwriters with copies of filings as agreed upon in Underwriting Agreement.	CO, CC

Form 15 J: Closing Checklist for Merger Transaction

Note: The following sample closing checklist is for a merger transaction in which a small, privately held company was acquired by a public company and merged into a subsidiary of the public company that was formed specifically for the purposes of the transaction. This checklist will give you a good idea of the process and the typical documentation required to complete the transaction and allow you to prepare your client for the same.

Acquisition and Merger of
**** Corporation into
Subsidiary of ****, Inc.
Closing Checklist
Scheduled Closing Date: _____, 20____

F&F	Attorneys for Public Company and Sub
Public Co	****, Inc. (Acquiring Company; Parent Company)
Sub	**** Acquisition Corporation (Surviving Entity; Subsidiary of Acquiring Company)
Private Co	**** Corporation (Disappearing Entity)
D&D	Attorneys for Private Company

Description	Responsible Party	Signatures Needed	Status	Received?
Corporate Proceedings				
Sub Board resolutions approving transaction	F&F			
Sub Stockholder resolutions approving transaction	F&F			
Private Co Board resolutions approving transaction	D&D			
Private Co Shareholder resolutions approving transaction	D&D			
Primary Agreements				
Merger Agreement	F&F			
Exhibits:				
A Agreement of Merger	F&F			
B-1 Private Co Rights Holders	D&D			

Description	Responsible Party	Signatures Needed	Status	Received?
Exhibits:				
B-2 Private Co Rights Notice	D&D			
C Form of Opinion of D&D	D&D			
D Employment Agreements	F&F			
Public Co Employee Invention Assignment and Confidentiality Agreements	F&F			
Schedules:				
A Private Co Disclosure Letter	D&D			
B Calculation of Earnout	F&F			
Pre-Closing Items				
Conversion of Private Co Debt	Private Co/D&D			
Termination of Private Co 401(k) Plan	Private Co			
Resolutions terminating the Plan	D&D			
Closing Documents				
Private Co Good Standing Certificates – California / Franchise Tax Board	D&D			
Officer's Certificate	D&D			
Amendment terminating the 401(k) Plan	D&D			
Noncompetition Agreements	Public Co			
Transfer of registration for domain names	Private Co			
Technology Assignment Agreement	F&F			
Invention Assignment Agreement	F&F			
Confirmatory Assignment and License Agreements	F&F			

Description	Responsible Party	Signatures Needed	Status	Received?
Cross Receipt	F&F	Private Co		
Option termination letters	D&D			
Exercise / Cancellation of Options	D& D Private Co			
Resignations / termination of Private Co employment agreements	Private Co			
Director resignations	Private Co			
Agreement to Convert and Release	D&D			

Form 15 K: Due Diligence Checklist for Opinion of Counsel

Note: As counsel to a company that is being acquired, you will likely be requested to give an opinion as to certain matters concerning your client. The following attorney due diligence checklist is an example of the types of due diligence you should conduct, and of how to document the same, in connection with such an opinion.

Preamble to be included in opinion:

We have acted as counsel to **** Corporation, a [California] corporation ("Private Co"), for the limited purpose of rendering certain opinions in connection with a merger transaction (the "Merger"), pursuant to that certain Agreement and Plan of Merger, dated as of _____, 20___, (the "Agreement") by and among Private Co, ****, Inc., a [Delaware] corporation ("Public Co"), **** Acquisition Corporation, a [California] corporation that is a wholly-owned subsidiary of Public Co ("Sub") and certain individuals whose names are on the signature page thereto (the "Representatives"). This opinion is rendered pursuant to Section 7.5 of the Agreement. Capitalized terms used but not defined herein shall have the meanings ascribed to them in the Agreement.

Matters upon which counsel is asked to opine:

A. Private Co (i) is a corporation duly organized, validly existing in good standing under the laws of the State of California and (ii) has the requisite corporate power and authority to enter into the Agreement and the other Transaction Documents, and to carry out and perform its obligations thereunder and to consummate all of the transactions contemplated thereby.

B. The execution, delivery, and performance of the Agreement and each of the other Transaction Documents and the transactions contemplated thereby have been duly and validly authorized by Private Co by all necessary corporate action on the party of Private Co's Board of Directors and shareholders and do not require any consent, approval, authorization, or other action by, or filing with or notification to, any third party, including but not limited to any governmental or regulatory authority, other than consents already obtained and post-Closing filings called for by the Agreement to record the assignment to Public Co of any Intellectual Property Rights that are currently the subject of any filing, application, registration or recordation with any governmental authority.

C. No authorization, decree, or order of any court, bankruptcy court, bankruptcy trustee, creditors' committee, receiver, governmental authority, or any other person is required in order to authorize or enable Private Co to (i) enter into the Agreement or any of the other Transaction Documents, or (ii) to carry out and perform Private Co's obligations under the Agreement and each of the Transaction Documents.

D. Neither the execution and delivery by Private Co of the Agreement or any of the other Transaction Documents, nor the consummation of the transactions provided for therein, will conflict with or violate the Articles of Incorporation or Bylaws of Private Co.

E. The Agreement and each of the Transaction Documents to which Private Co is a party are the legal, valid and binding obligations of Private Co enforceable against Private Co in accordance with their respective terms.

Due diligence to be completed:

_____ 1. Review California law to determine that proper formation procedures were followed for Private Co.

_____ 2. Review certified Articles of Incorporation of Private Co.

_____ 3. Review any Amendments to Articles of Incorporation of Private Co.

_____ 4. Review certified Bylaws of Private Co.

_____ 5. Review Resolutions of Board of Directors of Private Co ("Consent Action").

_____ 6. Obtain Certificate of Good Standing from the California Secretary of State and Tax Clearance from the California Franchise Tax Board for Private Co.

_____ 7. Obtain telephone confirmation of good standing as of the date just before delivering the opinion.

_____ 8. Review Certificate from Secretary of Private Co certifying that documents are true and correct.

_____ 9. Review applicable laws, statutes, ordinances, rules, and regulations to determine the corporate action required to authorize the execution and delivery of the Transaction Documents.

_____ 10. Review the Bylaws of Private Co to verify that all necessary corporate action by Private Co to authorize, execute, deliver and perform the Transaction Documents and transactions contemplated therein has been taken and to determine whether they in any way limited the legality, validity, binding nature or enforceability as to Private Co of the Transaction Documents.

_____ 11. Review Resolutions of Board of Directors of Private Co ("Consent Action") certified by Secretary of Private Co.

_____ 12. Review Resolutions of shareholders of Private Co certified by Secretary of Private Co.

_____ 13. Review Articles of Incorporation and Bylaws to verify that the Transaction Documents do not conflict therewith.

_____ 14. Obtain Certificate of Private Co, and Corporate Officers, ("Certificate") providing that:

Private Co and Officers are not aware of any facts or circumstances whereby the execution and delivery of the Transaction Documents would violate or conflict with any judgment, order, writ, injunction, or decree binding on Private Co or conflict with or violate any law, rule, regulation or ordinance applicable to Private Co.

_____ 15. Review the Articles of Incorporation and Bylaws of Private Co to verify that they do not conflict with the terms of any of the Transaction Documents.

_____ 16. Review each of the Transaction Documents and verify that they are enforceable in accordance with their terms, including identifying any potential affirmative defenses as to their enforceability to be identified in legal opinion; and contain the basic elements of a contract, as necessary.

_____ 17. Insert appropriate assumptions and exceptions in legal opinion.

Form 15 L: Officers' Certificate

OFFICERS' CERTIFICATE

The undersigned, duly elected, qualified, and acting officers (the "Officers") of **** CORPORATION, a corporation incorporated under and by virtue of the laws of the State of _____ ("Company"), do hereby certify:

    1. that the undersigned are not aware of any facts or circumstances whereby the execution and delivery of (i) the Agreement and Plan of Merger, dated _____, 20___, by and among Company, and ****, Inc., (the "Agreement"), and (ii) other documents executed in connection with the merger transaction contemplated therein (together with the Agreement, the "Transaction Documents") would violate or conflict with any judgment, order, writ, injunction, or decree binding on Company or conflict with or violate any law, rule, regulation, or ordinance; and

    2. that the undersigned are not aware of any facts or circumstances whereby the execution and delivery of the Transaction Documents would conflict with or violate or result in a breach of any of the provisions of, or constitute a default under, or result in the creation or imposition of a lien, charge or encumbrance upon any of the properties or assets of Company, pursuant to any agreement or instrument which Company is a party or by which any of its properties or assets is bound.

    IN WITNESS WHEREOF, the undersigned has hereunto set my hand as such Officer and affixed the corporate seal of said corporation on the _____ day of _____, 20___.

_____

Name and title: _____

_____

Name and title: _____

INDEX